A STRATEGY FOR RURAL CHANGE

A STRATEGY FOR RURAL CHANGE

By

Charles P. Loomis and J. Allan Beegle

Schenkman Publishing Company

Halsted Press Division
JOHN WILEY & SONS, INC.
New York — London — Sydney — Toronto

Copyright © 1975
Schenkman Publishing Company, Inc.
Cambridge, Mass. 02138

Distributed solely by Halsted Press, a Division of
John Wiley & Sons, Inc., New York.

Library of Congress Cataloging in Publication Data

Loomis, Charles Price, 1905-
    A strategy for rural change.

      1. Sociology, Rural.   2. United States—Rural conditions.
        I. Beegle, Joseph Allan,   II. Title.
          1918- joint author.
HT421.L564   309.1'173'4   74-22100
ISBN 0-470-544-80-5

PREFACE

Whether or not one is engaged in the initiation of social change, such social systems as schools, cooperatives, churches, friendship groups, families, and political parties play important roles in our daily lives. The professional, the housewife, the worker, and the farmer alike have responsibilities to organizations, to family, to community, and to country.

Most people are effective in their work and in their responsibilities as citizens to the degree that they come to have a realistic understanding of the social organizations around them: Parents are more effective when they understand the functioning of the family and related systems; teachers accomplish more when they understand the functioning of schools in relation to themselves, students, administrators, and the community; and students, whether they live in rural or in urban areas, whether they become professionals or housewives, have much to gain from the study of sociology.

For those who have professional responsibility for changing or improving life, this study should be especially useful. It deals with those aspects of society that are subject to change, as well as with those agencies and systems through which the change may be achieved. Consequently, it should be valuable to the teacher, the minister, the forester, the conservationist, the social worker, and all the others who, through the application of their professions, are attempting to improve life. All chapters that follow are concerned with conditions of social life and strategies for its improvement, but Chapter 14, the summary chapter, gives special attention to strategies and concepts for change.

In the preceding paragraphs, use has been made of concepts such as "groups," "organizations," and "social systems" without attempting to assign a special meaning to any of them. Other terms, such as "human groups" or "going concerns," might be utilized to examine the phenomena that we wish to consider. Our decision to use the idea of social system stems from our desire to concentrate on social interaction as considered in present-day social science. This permits us to omit many irrelevant considerations. Social system implies a functioning entity or whole, composed of interrelated parts or elements. These ideas are compatible not only with our wish to stress social change but also with analysis at a given instant in time. The earlier work, *Rural Social Systems,* now out of print but available in most libraries throughout the world, was written primarily for advanced students of rural society. The present volume is prepared for both undergraduate and graduate student use.

The authors wish to express their gratitude to those who have contributed in making the present volume possible. Among these are the teachers and associates, sociological theorists, and authors who have most influenced our thinking. An attempt to list all of these individuals would undoubtedly be inaccurate and incomplete—our debts are greater than we can acknowledge.

In the task of writing, rewriting, editing, and typing, we wish to express our appreciation to those who have made invaluable contributions. We are indebted to Zona Kemp Loomis and Louis Ploch for their work on Chapters 15 and 7, respectively. We are also grateful to Richard Rodefeld for numerous intellectual exchanges especially about trends in the family farm; to Philip Fulton for his editorial work; and to Maria Olivia Mejorado, who did much of the typing.

Again for the revision the authors wish to express their indebtedness to their families for their forbearance. The task of preparing a manuscript in a schedule that families already define as "overloaded" is explosive, even in this atomic and space age. For their families' stoicism, the authors are grateful.

Charles P. Loomis
University of Houston and
University of Texas School of Public Health

J. Allan Beegle
Michigan State University

Contents

LIST OF FIGURES

Chapter 2

Chapter 3

Chapter 4

Chapter 5

Chapter 6

Chapter 9

Chapter 12

Chapter 14

Chapter 6

Chapter 7

Chapter 8

Chapter 12

Chapter 13

Chapter 14

Social Systems and Social Change

An effective understanding of group life and of groups experiencing change would be difficult, if not impossible, without consideration of relevant social systems, the elements comprising them, and the important processes involved in change. This chapter is devoted to an attempt to isolate and explain those elements and processes believed to be essential to the understanding of groups.

WHAT IS A SOCIAL SYSTEM?

It is possible to conceive of social systems as existing on two different levels that, for our purposes, will not often require differentiation. In the first place, a social system may be considered a concrete interactive social structure, such as a labor union local, a family, a church congregation, or a Parent Teachers Association. The members of such organizations interact more with members than with non-members when participating in the organization as an on-going concern.

In concrete social systems, the greater the interaction between members, the easier it is to ascertain who is part and who is not part of the system; that is, to ascertain the boundaries of the system. For some systems, such as communities composed of family-sized farms, the interaction and loyalties of members are so often diffused throughout other systems that only a crisis will reveal some aspects of the community system. Even in the case of a simpler system, such as a family or a school, there are usually a central system and various sub-systems. For the typical family of the Western world there may be the conjugal core composed of father, mother, and children, and others related to the core—for example, grandparents, uncles, aunts, and cousins. For a labor union or a farmers' organization, the local may be the unit of observation and may be considered a system, or the whole organization with its central organizational core may be considered a system and the various state, county, and local units sub-systems. Obviously, even when we are studying organizations as on-going concerns, we must focus upon relevant sociological aspects of social interaction.

In the second place, a social system may be viewed as a more abstract unit, or one in which patterns of relationships prevail from generation to generation and from region to region. Social systems consisting of persistent patterns do not require that specific persons be considered as parts of the system. A Catholic Church official of a given order and position, for example, could easily fit into or adjust to Catholic sub-systems in different parts of the world. Furthermore, he could imagine himself as fitting into the same sub-system of earlier generations.

Social systems, whether studied as going concerns in the present or from a historical point of view, are composed of social interactions and the cultural factors which structure these interactions. As the significant unit of social systems, we accept Sorokin's "meaningful interaction of two or more human individuals" and his requirement that interaction be an event "by which one party tangibly influences the overt actions or state of mind of the other."[1] We also accept Parson's observation that "Participation of an actor in a patterned interactive relationship . . . is for many purposes the most significant unit of the social system."[2]

What do such apparently diverse social systems as a local

[1] P. A. Sorokin, *Society, Culture, and Personality: Their Structure and Dynamics* (New York: Harper and Brothers, 1947), p. 40. Social scientists like other scientists differ in their approaches to the subject matter of their fields. Just as geologists and physicists may approach the study of the earth's surface with conceptual schemes that are not identical, so also will social scientists undertake the study of interaction differently. The political scientist may pay particular attention to power relations, the human geographer to relations in space. Within each discipline or field, including sociology, there will be differences of interest and efforts. Although all sociologists consider interaction to be their primary interest, some want to focus attention on conflict, some want to focus on team work and integration, some want to focus on "what is taken for granted" in interaction, some on the selves of subject and object in role taking. In fact a myriad of such emphases are possible. Even so, to the extent that the investigator finds uniformities and regularities in his studies that enable him to explain and/or predict, he consciously or unconsciously thinks in system terms.

[2] Talcott Parsons, *The Social System* (Glencoe: The Free Press, 1951), p. 25.

church, a cooperative purchasing association, a local school, the X family of Middletown, or the old fellows clique in rural Ireland have in common? What instructions should a stranger be given so that he can identify such systems? What instructions should be given organization experts who specialize in introducing innovations through such systems? What are the significant differences in such systems? Volumes have been written in attempts to answer these questions, and key elements of concern to those interested in understanding social change and social interaction may be outlined.

ELEMENTS OF SOCIAL SYSTEMS[3]

Ends or objectives. Those changes that members of the social system expect to accomplish through the operation of the system are considered ends or objectives. In some instances systems have as an end or objective the retaining of the *status quo.* The prevailing objectives of a family may be broad and diffuse—those of a bank more specific. A family may strive to provide all its members with a level of living compatible with its standards, and this may be the family's end or objective. A bank may direct its activities toward the end of increasing its earnings which may often be measured in dollars and cents.

Norms. The rules or guiding standards that prescribe what is socially acceptable or unacceptable are the norms of a system. Hence norms govern the application of means in the attainment of ends or objectives. In everyday terminology, they are "rules of the game" and, as such, play a major part in establishing expectancy patterns for action in a given system. Norms as we use the term are more inclusive than written rules, regulations, or laws. They constitute the standards determining what is right and wrong or good and bad in given situations with respect to

[3] In all subsequent chapters, the elements of social systems will be treated. The nature and extent of treatment, however, will be variable, depending upon the treatment seeming most appropriate for a given social system. In some instances, both the elements and social processes are treated in separate sections of a given chapter; in others they will be discussed in conjunction with illustrative cases. Furthermore, in some instances, all of the elements and processes do not appear in discussion of certain social systems, in order to avoid unnecessary duplication and for other reasons. In the present discussion of elements of social systems, compare Charles P. Loomis, *Social Systems—Essays on Their Persistence and Change* (Princeton, New Jersey: D. VanNostrand, 1960).

relationships with teammates and fellows as well as with opponents and non-members. In athletics involving team play, the
norms not only include what is specified in the rule book, but
also what is included in such concepts as "fair play" and "good
sportsmanship." Both ends, as discussed in the previous section,
and norms are sometimes mentioned as the most important social values held by actors in social systems. In one social process, namely, evaluation, norms play a special function. In evaluation norms are the standards by which varying positive and
negative priorities or values are assigned to elements, processes,
other concepts, ideas, objects, actors, collectives or events, and
activities either past, present, or future. This is one reason why
Sorokin[4] states that what he calls "law norms" are the most
important component of social systems and social life. Having
discussed elements of value orientation, we now turn to components of the social structure.

*Status-role as a unit incorporating both element and pro-
cess.* The two-term entity, status-role, contains the concept,
status, a structural element which implies position; and the concept, role, a functional process. Both are important determinants
of what is to be expected from an incumbent and how the role is
performed by him as he occupies the position.

Evaluation was just mentioned as a process carried on
through reference to norms or standards, thus linking an element and a process. In the case of the term status-role an element and a process are built into action of social systems with
more interdependence than is common to other components. The
use of the double term status-role eliminates from consideration psychological concepts of role, such as the Milquetoast, Don
Juan, and glamour girl roles, which do not require membership
or participation in definite groups. We may illustrate the difference in status and role as we combine the two by the Judeo-
Christian commandment, "Honor thy father and thy mother
. . ." which specifies role behavior of children as actors toward
the incumbents of the parents' statuses or positions. The role
activity of parents toward incumbents of the child role is specified in the folk adage, "Spare the rod and spoil the child." The
active aspects of status-role may be illustrated by what is expected of farm or peasant fathers and mothers. It is usually ex-

[4] Sorokin, *Society, Culture, and Personality.*

pected that the father as a part of his role will do the heavy labor in the fields and that the mother as part of her role will prepare the meals. Surprise would be expressed if these activities were regularly reversed.

Power. Power, as we use the term, is control over others. Power has many components, which we classify under two major headings: legitimized power designated as authority and non-legitimized power which may take the form of influence or coercive force.

Authority may be defined as the right, as determined by the system, to control the actions of others. Implied in this concept of authority is the uncritical acceptance of this right on the part of subordinates and certain immunities from influence on the part of the superiors. Sanctions, as outlined later, also are implied.

Non-legitimized power may be regarded as control over others which is of a non-authoritative nature. Such influence may be based upon skills in human relations or social capital resulting from such things as past favors, superior knowledge of interrelations of members, certain types of wealth, or even outright blackmail. Some aspects of non-authoritative influence in a given social system may be derived from relationships outside of the system. Generally, the active aspects of a status-role or position held by a member articulate his authority. Even when a university president or a dean is known to have much more power than an instructor, it is usually the instructor of a particular student, not the dean or the president, who may award a grade or change a grade once it is recorded.

Social rank. Social rank of members of systems is based upon consensus as to what is to be rated high and what low insofar as this is relevant to the system under consideration. In conformity with our meaning, the term "standing" could be used instead of rank. As we use the term, it must refer to *a* system, i.e., rank in the Methodist Church, rank in Wagon Mound community, or rank in Family X. A member's rank in a given social system may be derived from more than one status-role in the system, from status-roles outside the system (insofar as these influence his value to the system), and power and wealth both inside and outside the system. Various personal factors not directly related to the elements just mentioned, such as personal appearance and morals, may also be important.

As we use the term, social rank results from an overall appraisal. When applied to an individual in a relevant system (let
us say, a neighborhood), it may involve evaluations related to
and based upon the following: (1) The non-active aspects of positions (often called status) which one has in the neighborhood.
These may be the status of adult, male, father, husband, farmer,
worker, church member, and farm organization officer. From
these non-active aspects of positions one derives *prestige.* (2)
Status-role performance in the neighborhood. From one's performance one derives *esteem.* (3) Prestige and esteem from
status-roles outside the neighborhood (insofar as these influence one's evaluation in the neighborhood). (4) Power.

It will be noted that social rank as used here is the social value
placed by members on these four items relating to the specific
reference group. This sociological concept of rank is comparable
to the economic concept of price. Price is a summary term which
expresses money value of an object due to utility and scarcity. In
fact, the money value or price of a professional baseball player
to his club is not unlike our concept of rank evaluations. Used in
this manner, social rank is a summary term that is quite different from the other elements of social systems we are employing.
Members of social systems evaluate sub-systems so that groups
as well as individuals have social rank. Individuals derive their
rank in the community from various reference groups in which
they place themselves and are placed, using a society, nation, or
large system as the most pertinent reference groups. Individuals
of the same rank make up the strata of systems. Such strata may
be in the nature of castes determined by birth or ascription. As
we shall see, the family and clique to which a person belongs are
very important in the status evaluation of individuals and larger systems.

Sanctions. Those potential satisfaction-giving or -depriving
mechanisms at the disposal of the system, which induce com-
pliance with ends and norms, are considered sanctions. Sanctions may be positive or negative. Positive sanctions are the *rewards* available to members from the system, including prestige
resulting from authority, rights, privileges, esteem, and other
social or economic returns. Negative sanctions are the *penalties*
or the deprivation of those items just mentioned as rewards at
the disposal of the system.

Facilities. Facilities are the means used by members of the system to attain its ends. The concept facility as used here is a residual category and not intended to include phenomena more correctly associated with the elements outlined previously. For a farm or ranch family, facilities involve property, such as equipment, livestock and real estate used in the farming operation; for schools, facilities include the plant, books, and equipment. Only when human beings are treated as "things" and as in the case of slaves, bought and sold, should they be considered as facilities.

IMPORTANT PROCESSES INVOLVED IN SOCIAL ACTION

Although the activities and social processes of evaluation and role playing have been mentioned above, the emphasis has been on the elements or the constituent parts of interaction at one point in time. We now turn to important processes of social action. Regardless of the diversities of the processes to be discussed, each is characterized by a consistent quality of regular and uniform sequences and is distinguishable by virtue of its orderliness. Even though a given actor may view events as being chaotic, an objective observer may note a social process through which transition from one social condition to another is accomplished. As the elements of social systems previously discussed are articulated in social action, the processes of communication, decision-making, boundary maintenance,[5] and systemic linkage are of special importance.

It is convenient in discussing change to differentiate what is called the "change-agent system" from the "target system." The former is the person or agency attempting to introduce or effect a change; the latter is the group which the agent and his system is attempting to change. If, for example, the Extension Service in a given community is attempting to organize the cotton growers into a one-variety cotton community, the Extension Service is the change-agent system and the community involved, the target system.

Communication. By communication we mean the process by which information, decisions, and directives pass through a social system, and the ways in which knowledge, opinions, and attitudes are formed or modified. Communication may be car-

[5] Charles P. Loomis, "In Defense of Integration—For One Nation and For One World," *The Centennial Review,* Vol. XIV, No. 2, (Spring 1970).

ried out through mass media, such as radio, television, and motion pictures, in which the agency receiving the communication cannot interact directly with the agency imparting the information. Mass media provide one-way communication from imparter to receiver. Communication may be carried on through formal and informal social channels which usually provide the opportunity for two-way interaction in which individuals are both imparters and receivers of information. An illustration of how the communication process operates in some rural areas is the telephone "company ring" or community signal and message. In cities events such as the coming of a tornado or flood may be communicated by telephone, radio, or television to large groups. Usually not all people are listening to such communications but the messages are further spread by word of mouth.

Decision-making. This is the process whereby alternate courses of action available are reduced. If a family in a flood or cyclone area is notified that staying will be dangerous, decisions must be made concerning evacuation. In many peasant families much decision-making occurs at mealtime. In patriarchal families much family decision-making rests with the father, who has greater power than other members.

The strategy of change involves decision-making on the part of the change agent in terms of the allocation of effort, facilities, and personnel in relation to status-roles, patterns of power, and social rank of the target system. Decisions concerning such allocations must be made with a view to maximizing the possibility of cooperation on the part of the target system and minimizing "costs" to the change system. The decision-making of the change agent should result in effective timing of events which requires intimate knowledge of the functioning of the change target in terms of social structure, value orientation, and the important processes related to change.

Boundary maintenance. This is the process whereby members of the system retain their identity and interaction pattern; that is, retain system equilibrium[6] involving both integration

---

[6] Kingsley Davis, *Human Society* (New York: The Macmillan Company, 1949), pp. 633ff. and Parsons, *The Social System,* p. 493. Karl Marx's use of both equilibrium and system analysis is well known. "The different spheres of production . . . constantly tend to an equilibrium . . ." *Capital,* (Moscow: Foreign Languages Publishing House, 1961) Vol. 1, p. 355. ". . . equilibrium would be restored under all circumstances . . ." Ibid. Vol. III, p. 248. More recently Frank M. Young re-

and solidarity. Boundary maintenance may be illustrated by various folk admonitions concerning an outsider taking the part of one member in a family quarrel. These proverbs usually imply that the quarreling family members will unite and turn on the outsider no matter how just his cause for supporting one side of the dispute. Folk beliefs and scientific findings show that members of systems challenged from outside defend their values.

Boundary maintenance signifies activity to retain the identity, value orientation, and interaction pattern of a social system. When the system engages in the process of boundary maintenance, it actively resists forces that tend to destroy the identity and interaction pattern. If integration is present, we say the system is functioning as a team. That is, individual effort contributes to the whole effort which moves the system toward its goal. Solidarity refers to the extent to which members are agreed as to the ends and norms of the system, and the extent to which members identify with the system as a value in and of itself. Our conception of social systems as boundary maintaining units implies that changes may be expected to set up strains in the existing systems. Strain sets up reequilibrating processes, but resistance must be expected, especially if the change interferes with the basic values guiding action.

Systemic linkage. This is the process whereby the elements of at least two systems come to be articulated so that in some ways they function as a unit. Thus, systemic linkage usually requires that the value orientation and the social structure of the change-agent system and the target system are brought together in at least temporary closure. In order to be effective, a teacher must have his role accepted by students; and the teacher, in turn, must accept the students in their roles as students. When a family borrows money from a bank, systemic linkage is accomplished between the two systems and the roles of debtor and creditor express this linkage.

Systemic linkage involves the following three processes: initiation, legitimation, and execution. Initiation is the process whereby members of the change system bring the proposed or

views his own, Bo Anderson's, Johan Galtung's and others' use of the concept, equilibrium. "Reactive Subsystems," *American Sociological Review,* Vol. 35, No. 2, (April 1970), pp. 297ff. See also Dorwin Cartwright and Frank Harvey, "Structural Balance: A Generalization of Heider's Theory," *Psychological Review,* Vol. 63, (September 1956), pp. 277-293.

advocated change to the attention of the members of the target system. Legitimation is the process whereby the proposed change is made "rightful" to the target system. Prestigeful sponsors, rituals, prayers, and other legitimizing procedures are used in the strategy of change. Execution is the process whereby the systemic linkage is put into effect.

CONDITIONS OF SOCIAL ACTION

As processes such as communication, decision-making, boundary maintenance, and systemic linkage take place, the elements of social systems are articulated. Although the elements involved in social action just discussed are under the control of actors, not everything important in the study of social processes and social change is controlled. The most important of the attributes of social action and change not under the control of actors we call the conditions. Among the conditions of social action the most important are those involving time, and space which we call territoriality.

Territoriality. The spatial arrangements and requirements of a social system are considered territoriality. It is obvious that all social systems are influenced by spatial considerations. The mere fact that a number of related families live in one house, for example, poses different problems than where each related family lives in its own house, separated by space.

Time. Time as a condition of social action is inexorable and cannot be made to stand still or to be completely controlled by man. Even though man is the only animal that bridges the generations through the transmission of culture, he is nonetheless timebound, a circumstance reflected in all studies of social and cultural change. In fact there are few considerations more important in the study of change than the part time plays in interrelationships and use of facilities. During the period immediately preceding the communization of China, an outstanding Chinese lecturer and change agent used to hold western audiences in suspense by posing the following: "China has more of something than your country has and by this I do not mean people or square miles of terrain. What is this that China has in greater abundance than you have?" After a few moments of intense silence this speaker gave his answer: "Time." Those of us who have worked in Latin America have heard many discussions of *hora española* (Spanish time) and *mañana* (tomorrow) as typifying this region and its people and *hora inglesa* (Anglo time) typifying, in comparison, England, the United States and by implication other industrialized societies. Of course, such comparative terms are only relative in so far as they were once true in the past. As societies industrialize, commercialize and adopt efficient technology, time perspectives change.

Since social action and human life constitute a totality, all conceivable segments of which are inextricably interrelated, categories such as those mentioned are not mutually exclusive. The value of the concepts can be determined only by their usefulness. Since we are concerned with directed social change in addition to considering the above elements, we must be aware of the nature of social change in general.

SOCIAL CHANGE

What is conceived as social change depends upon the observation point (more correctly called the point of reference), and the scope of one's vision. This may be illustrated by the differences in conception of what is going on when a fire fighting crew deploys to get a large and fast moving forest fire under control. The view of the superintendent directing the fight from a helicopter is different from that of the individual fire fighter working on the ground near the fire. The wild life specialist may be expected to view the situation in a different way than the mineralogist or the specialist in wood utilization. The view of the sociologist or anthropologist would be different from that of other specialists. In our analysis of change, we hope we may have under consideration the more important sociological aspects of both systems and sub-systems. However, our frame of reference is limited, since we are focusing primarily upon guided change in the most common social systems.

Although somewhat over-simplified, the following example may serve to illustrate the process of boundary maintenance and an effort to establish systemic linkage. An attempt was made in Costa Rica to change status-roles of village school teachers to include tasks other than the mere teaching of reading, writing and arithmetic in the classroom. The change in the teacher's status-role, designed to improve village life, involved and added responsibility of teachers to give instruction in improved sanitation, simple health and agricultural practices through activities inside and outside the classroom. The inspectors who supervised the teachers had no standards by which to appraise the new activities and resisted this change. The villagers also resisted. Many villagers said that the privies, installed through the teachers' efforts, were not the proper concern of the teacher. In this attempt to change a status-role, the norms of the villagers were involved. Forces within the school system and related external forces exerted pressure to reestablish earlier arrangements, or in our terms maintain boundaries.

In our considerations of social change, we are not focusing attention upon whole cultures, civilizations, or societies as have Sorokin,[7] Toynbee,[8] and Spengler.[9] Perhaps the most interesting aspect of change as described by these writers is the reaction or counteraction of large units to major changes. Sorokin describes the weakening of what he calls the sensate culture, in which the primary objective is that of satisfying the senses.[10] According to Sorokin, the sensate culture in the West which grew out of its counterpart, the ideational culture of the Middle Ages, must pass through a crisis before the ideational type is reestablished. In describing the reaction of the East to the invasion of western culture, Toynbee in 1947 wrote what appears to us to be a prophetic paragraph:

> The Russians have taken up a Western secular social philosophy, Marxism; you might equally well call Marxism a Christian heresy, a leaf torn out of the book of Christianity and treated as if it were the whole gospel. The Russians have taken up this Western heretical religion, transformed it into something of their own, and are now shooting it back at us. This is the first shot in the anti-Western counter-offensive; but this Russian counter-discharge in the form of Communism may come to seem a small affair when the probably far more potent civilizations of India and China respond in their turn to our Western challenge. In the long run India

[7] P. A. Sorokin, *Social and Cultural Dynamics* (New York: American Book Company, 1937), Vols. 1-4.

[8] Arnold J. Toynbee, *A Study of History* (London: Oxford University Press, 1934-54).

[9] Oswald Spengler, *The Decline of the West* (New York: Alfred A. Knopf, Inc., 1926).

[10] P. A. Sorokin, *The Crisis of Our Age, The Social and Cultural Outlook* (New York: E. P. Dutton and Company, 1942).

and China seem likely to produce much deeper effects on our Western life than Russia can ever hope to produce with her Communism. But even the comparatively feeble native civilization of Mexico is beginning to react ... and what is happening today in Mexico may happen tomorrow in the seats of the native civilization of South America: in Peru, Bolivia, Ecuador, and Colombia.[11]

Although we recognize the importance of the broad kinds of change just described, our attention will not be directed to social and cultural changes involving systems of such great magnitude as those considered by Sorokin, Toynbee and Spengler. We shall focus our attention on social systems such as the family, friendship group, school, and church—systems which were also considered by the great theorists. Changes in these smaller units are related to changes involving whole cultures and societies, but we shall not attempt to specify in detail the nature of these relationships.

Rate of change. It is possible to compare rates of change as reflected in vital statistics when such data are available. One may say, for example, that the birth rate is falling more rapidly in Japan than in Puerto Rico, or that the suicide rate is increasing more rapidly among rural than urban residents. What the causes and consequences of these rates in terms of social and cultural systems may be, however, are very difficult to determine. To compare rates of social and cultural change under the best conditions is not easy. Perhaps the most difficult comparisons to make are between systems of entirely different types. The theory of "cultural lag" maintains that one segment "lags" behind another. It is maintained that forms of material culture—houses, factories, machines, raw materials, foodstuffs,—change more rapidly than non-material things—beliefs, philosophies, laws.[12] Davis argues that such comparisons are of dubious validity and that "it may seem absurd to speak of relative rates of change in such noncomparable matters—like asking if a giraffe moves faster than a cell divides—but it is some- -

---

[11] Arnold J. Toynbee, "Encounters Between Civilizations," *Harper's Magazine,* 194 (April, 1947), pp. 289-294.

[12] William F. Ogburn, *Social Change* (New York: Viking Press, Inc., 1928), pp. 200 ff.

times done.''[13] It is more meaningful to compare rates of change of similar traits or items in varied settings, than to compare the rates of change of entirely different traits or items, even in the same setting.

Ideal types of social action—Gemeinschaft and Gesellschaft.[14] Types of social systems and relationships which are Gemeinschaft-like are those in which the relationship is an end in itself, as contrasted to those which are Gesellschaft-like in which the relationships are means to ends. That part of life which is rationally or instrumentally oriented is Gesellschaft-like in the sense that people and facilities are considered means to ends rather than ends in themselves. In general under given conditions, a process is rational when specified action results in a unit producing the most for the least effort or cost. Thus, a factory which is Gesellschaft-like will adopt a process that turns out a more valuable product at minimal cost.

Thus we say that Gesellschaft-like activity or systems are more instrumental than those which are Gemeinschaft-like. Activities and systems the functions of which are integrative or moral are sacred, or Gemeinschaft-like. In summary, for a given system instrumental or rational action is primarily Gesellschaft-like, whereas integrative or moral action is primarily Gemeinschaft-like.

Gemeinschaft-like relationships. Gemeinschaft-like relationships and systems are characterized by functional diffuseness. This means that one actor (for instance, a mother) reacts to another (for instance, her child) in such a way that *all* concerns and desires of the child are pertinent to the actor who is held responsible for them. Gemeinschaft-like relationships and systems are determined by norms that are personal or particularistic. The relationship itself, not duty or responsibility to larger reference systems, determines what is done. Relationships within systems which are considered Gemeinschaft-like are characterized as emotional or affective, and as solidary, with members constituting a kind of "community of fate."

Gemeinschaft-like compared with Gesellschaft-like relation-

<hr/>

[13] Davis, *Human Society,* p. 627.

[14] Ferdinand Toennies, *Community and Society—Gemeinschaft and Gesellshaft.* Translated by Charles P. Loomis (New York: Harper and Row, 1957, paper. Also Michigan State University Press, 1957).

ships. The Gemeinschaft-like system has been described as one in which the norms are in many ways opposed to the Gesell-like system.[15] The peasant family has been characterized as being Gemeinschaft-like in nature; a military unit as being Gesellschaft-like in nature. In the peasant family, the scope of interest of an actor for his object is diffuse, while in the military unit it is specific. The norms that determine the relationships are personal and particularistic in the instance of the peasant family; they are impersonal, universalistic and not bound to specific persons or relationships in the military unit. Furthermore, relationships are conditioned by emotion or affectivity in the family, while they lack emotion and are governed by affective neutrality in the military unit. Treatment of the actor as object is based upon ascription in the first instance; upon achievement or performance in the second case. In the first there are few relationships that are private or individual. Each individual is bound to fellow members of his system by personal relations of a diffuse nature, many of which are established at birth by ascription in the peasant family.

Direction of change. As underdeveloped societies adopt Western culture, the tendency is for various social systems involved in rational or instrumental activities to become Gesellschaft-like. In general, the rational or instrumental action (such as that found in bureaucracies), the traits of specificity, achievement, universalism, and affective neutrality are linked. Therefore, the blanket term *Gesellschaft* has meaning in considering the direction of social change. Also, as in the case of the family, diffuseness, ascription, particularism, and affectivity are linked, and therefore, the blanket term *Gemeinschaft* has meaning. There may be variations in the extent of linkage, as for example when the relations between father and son approach affective neutrality, but these exceptions can be described as they are encountered.[16] The specific directed changes we discuss will involve primarily rational or instrumental action. Such action is characteristic of Gesellschaft-like systems, and is action which is neither recreational nor religious. Insofar as we treat the direction of change in general, it will be on the continuum of activities which are Gemeinschaft-like at one extreme and Gesell-

---

[15]Loomis, *Social Systems,* Essay 2.
[16] Parsons, *The Social System,* p. 17.

schaft-like at the other extreme. We consider modern, Western, urban, technological society more Gesellschaft-like than that of the developing societies.

It is possible to appraise the relative emphasis members of a society or system place upon various types of activity at one time as compared with a later period. Assuming that the ends of a system are expressed in the amount of time used by the members in various types of activities, we may note how these change in time. One could study the time devoted by different segments of the population to recreation or other expressive pursuits that are ends in and of themselves. Redfield, for example, found that people in Tepoztlan, Mexico, spend one third of their time in fiestas and holidays.[17] The time devoted to religious activities which the social scientist might say serves the function of reinforcing the values of the group, could be measured. The time devoted to the production of goods and services as distinct from expressive or religious activities may also be measured. If one had a measure of the time spent by sample groups at different epochs in history one could rank them in primacy of orientation. Using Parsons' terminology, one could classify the sample groups in relation to action which was: (1) instrumentally, (2) expressively, or (3) morally oriented.

Types of social change. Social change may be classified according to various principles. We are more concerned here with directed change, or that which a change agent is consciously attempting to introduce. The social changes transpiring at any moment in a community are usually directed in part and non-directed in part. In either case changes may result from any one or combination of the following: (1) Changing the relative importance of the different social systems in society. The school, for example, may take over functions previously performed by the church or by a craft. Factories may take over the functions performed by families. (2) Creating new social systems. A government sponsored health insurance program for example, may be organized in a country which formerly did not have one. (3) Changing the elements of the systems and their relation to one another as well as creating new elements. Thus, the role of the school teacher may be changed to include community respon-

<hr>

[17] Robert Redfield, *Tepoztlan—A Mexican Village* (Chicago: University of Chicago Press, 1926).

sibilities such as those mentioned in the discussion of boundary maintenance and systemic linkage. An informal friendship group may become formal, as when a group of friends organize a cooperative.

If the use of an iron corn grinder, to turn from human relationships to material things, requires less effort than the *metate* or stone corn grinder, the former will be substituted for the latter, provided only rational or instrumental considerations are involved. However, if the activities organized about the use of the *metate* are ends in and of themselves (or Gemeinschaft-like) in that they may be recreational or expressive, or if they serve moral or integrative functions (such as religious symbols), they are less likely to be discontinued merely because they are less efficient. Experience indicates that group acceptance of more efficient means is not inevitable if the activities being changed or displaced are expressive, because it is more difficult to demonstrate the efficacy or result of the proposed change. Changes involving activities related to the basic values threaten group solidarity and may be resisted, even if their efficiency can be easily demonstrated. This is true because such change is thought to threaten the security of both individuals and groups.

A series of hypotheses concerning the importance of social factors in social change as related to these possibilities may be developed.[18] To cite only one: "Individuals of lower prestige accept culture traits from those of high prestige more readily than the reverse."[19]

Types of cultural change. Cultural change is a category of change broader than social change,[20] including changes in technology, philosophy, belief systems, systems of expressive symbols or art, and systems of values. Although few societal changes do not involve both social and cultural changes, one may think of them as being separated. The introduction of the germ theory of disease to a people who had no previous knowledge of it, would normally bring changes in the social systems dealing with sickness and disease prevention. Adding or changing clinics and hospitals may be used as examples of both cul-

[18] Charles P. Loomis, et al., *Turrialba, Social Systems and the Introduction of Change* (Glencoe: The Free Press, 1953).

[19] Ronald Freedman, et al., *Principles of Sociology* (New York: Henry Holt and Company, 1952), p. 319.

[20] Davis, *Human Society,* p. 622.

tural and social change. Changes in systems of mathematics or scientific procedures are cultural changes, and may be studied *per se* in the same way that changes in armies, churches, clinics and governments as social systems may be studied.

In discussing change, Ralph Beals writes: "If I were to rate the acculturative forces I have seen at work in various communities, I think I would suggest that one road is worth about three schools and about fifty administrators."[21] This statement, as well as our knowledge of change, suggests several hypotheses. The greater the felt need for a cultural item, for example, the easier it is to relate a proposed change to the ends of the system involved. Further, the better a cultural trait is understood, the easier it will be to introduce the change. If two cultural items are available, the one which costs the least in effort and yields the greatest satisfaction will be accepted.[22] "The developmental administrator . . .[should] expose villagers to change so that they will become less resistant to change . . . [and] he must do this without exceeding the 'trauma point' where added change will be rejected by most of the target population."[23] According to others, cultural traits of one group will probably show greater compatibility to a neighboring culture than to a distant one.

The greater the functional need of a system for a trait, the easier and more rapid will be its acceptance.[24] It is the felt, not "real" need in terms of various scientific standards, that is set against the apparent or latent incompatibility that determines acceptance or non-acceptance. Five gallon oil cans, for example, have displaced pottery containers for liquids among preliterate peoples, generally because users believe them superior. Machetes, sewing machines, and corn grinders spread more generally among indigenous Latin American peoples than bed springs or water sterilization. In considering agencies and in-

[21] Sol Tax et al., *Heritage of Conquest—The Ethnology of Middle America* (Glencoe: The Free Press, 1952), p. 232.

[22] Parsons, *The Social System*, p. 499. "There is indeed an ultimate strain to consistency in the total system of cognitive orientation in a society, and developments in science will have their long-run repercussions on philosophy, ideologies and religious beliefs as well as vice versa."

[23] Freedman, et al., *Principles*, p. 318. Fred Frey, "Developmental Administration," in J. Paul Leagans and Charles P. Loomis, eds., *Behavioral Change in Agriculture: Concepts and Strategies for Influencing Innovations* (Ithaca, New York: Cornell University Press, 1971) p. 271.

[24] Ibid, p. 317.

fluence of change, we usually do not separate the social from the cultural. Thus, the germ theory of disease, a cultural item, is not separated from hospital organizations, medical organizations, and schools which are considered by some to be social.

AN ILLUSTRATION OF A SOCIAL SYSTEM AND SOCIAL CHANGE: ELEMENTS AND PROCESSES

A football team.   The concepts we have discussed as elements of systems may be effectively illustrated by a football team.[25] Change and systemic linkage may be illustrated by the description of the attempts of coaches and schools to accept a new trait, such as the split-T formation. Directed change may be illustrated by the processes whereby the coaching staff as a system brings the team into its participation orbit.

In a football team, as with other athletic teams, each separate position clearly represents a different status-role, as we have defined the term. Full-backs perform different functions than guards because their status-roles are different. Authority may be illustrated by the general control coaches exercise over the players, particularly the quarterbacks to whom coaches delegate considerable authority during the game. Non-authoritative power, or influence, may be illustrated by human relations and leadership skills on the part of exceptional coaches and players. Sanctions, in the form of rewards, may be illustrated by letters, plaques, and citations received by the team or individual players. Rewards may also take the form of prestige and esteem, and bids to play professional football. Negative sanctions for violating norms may result in team penalties or individual penalties. Social rank may be illustrated when the team members select the "most valuable" player. Immediate ends such as those of winning games are rather obvious in the case of athletic teams. Norms or the rules of the game as prescribed in the rule book are also obvious, but other norms such as those falling under the heading of sportsmanship are less obvious. Norms concerning rewards a player may or may not receive and how players may or may not be recruited, are also important. Territoriality, or

[25] In this suggestion we precede Andrew M. Greeley's apt metaphorization by 13 years. See his "Comment on . . . Immoral Rhetoric" in the *American Sociologist,* Vol. 5, No. 4, (Nov. 1970), p. 370. See also Peter L. Berger, *Invitation to Sociology—Humanistic Perspective* (Garden City: Doubleday, 1963) p. 64.

spatial relationships, may be illustrated by the requirements of the various positions in relation to one another and the boundaries of the field. Facilities, including field house, practice fields and equipment, are also obvious.

The social processes whereby athletic teams develop superiority and high morale are not well understood by sociologists, but the same processes involved in effective operation of other social systems may well be applicable. Communication involving the means whereby teams are prepared for high level performance should constitute a profitable area of study for those who wish to understand human organization. No doubt high morale or the willingness to sacrifice for an organization, as well as confidence in its capacity to achieve its goals, are related to the decision-making process on and off the field. The degree to which members believe allocation of rewards, roles, authority, and rank square with existing norms is very important.

SELECTED REFERENCES

Berger, Peter L. *Invitation to Sociology: A Humanistic Perspective.* Garden City, N. Y.: Doubleday and Company, Inc., 1963.

Braithwaite, R. B. *Scientific Explanation—A Study of the Function of Theory, Probability and Law in Science.* New York: Harper and Brothers, 1960.

Davis, Kingsley. *Human Society.* New York: The Macmillan Co., 1949.

Foster, George M. *Applied Anthropology.* Boston: Little, Brown and Company, 1969.

Hathaway, Dale E., J. Allan Beegle and W. Keith Bryant. *People of Rural America.* Washington, D. C.: U. S. Bureau of the Census, Government Printing Office, 1968.

Lazarsfeld, Paul F. et al., eds. *The Uses of Sociology,* New York: Basic Books, Inc., 1967.

Leagans, J. Paul and Charles P. Loomis, eds. *Behavioral Change in Agriculture: Concepts and Strategies for Influencing Innovations.* Ithaca, New York: Cornell University Press, 1971.

Loomis, C. P. *Social Systems—Essays on Their Persistence and Change.* Princeton, N. J.: D. Van Nostrand, 1960.

Merton, Robert K. *Theory and Social Structure.* Glencoe, Ill.: The Free Press, 1949.

Miller, Paul A., et al. *Community Health Action.* East Lansing, Michigan: Michigan State University Press, 1953.

Moore, Wilbert E. *Social Change.* Englewood Cliffs, New Jersey: Prentice-Hall, Inc., 1963.

Parsons, Talcott. *The Social System.* Glencoe: The Free Press, 1951.

Sorokin, P. A. *Society, Culture, and Personality: Their Structure and Dynamics.* New York: Harper and Brothers, 1947.

Toennies, Ferdinand. *Community and Society, Gemeinschaft and Gesellschaft,* translated and introduced by C. P. Loomis. East Lansing: The Michigan State University Press, 1956.

2

Locality Systems

Despite the existence of efficient means of transportation, most rural and urban persons are rooted in localities which they consider to be home. Although Americans move about much more than their parents, the most meaningful ties and social interactions generally transpire within the confines of the local community.

THE COMMUNITY AS A SOCIAL SYSTEM

The community may be defined as a social system encompassing a territorial unit within which members carry on most of their day-to-day activities necessary in meeting common needs. Since the beginning of human existence, there have been families or kinship systems. The only other universal grouping or system is the locality group, frequently called the community. Historically, the community has been and still is the "local group, an aggregation of families and unattached males who habitually live together."[1] How and why the territorial aspect of the community has decreased in importance will be discussed later in the chapter.

Many of those who decry the state of the modern community have in mind a closed system, like the athletic team described in Chapter 1, as the ideal. Some would make each member of the community responsible to a common authority.[2] Relatively complete power in all spheres, for example, might be delegated to the governmental sub-system. Likewise, the educational system, within which the major needs of faculty and students are met,

[1] Ralph Linton, *The Study of Man* (New York: D. Appleton-Century Co., 1936), p. 209; Murdock in his study of more than 150 societies throughout the world found none without locality groupings which he called communities. George Peter Murdock, *Social Structure* (New York: The Macmillan Co., 1949).

[2] See R. M. MacIver, *The Web of Government* (New York: The Macmillan Co., 1952), p. 407.

might possess a monopoly of power. Large convents or monasteries may be thought of as communities in which the religious sub-systems of the larger society have a monopoly of power. Factory or mill towns and some large agricultural collectives or estates may constitute communities in which power is monopolized by economic or production sub-systems. Most American communities, unlike the examples cited, may seem disorganized, since power is most frequently diffused among several systems. This and other features of the community will become apparent in the discussion of its elements.

THE ELEMENTS OF COMMUNITY SOCIAL SYSTEMS

Ends, objectives, and norms.   The ends of the community differ in various ways from the ends of the sub-systems which compose the community. Likewise, the norms of communities tend to resemble those of society more than is true of other sub-systems. An agricultural or commercial enterprise may have as its primary goal that of making the greatest profit; a school may have as its end improving the skills and knowledge of the pupils. The ends of all these separate sub-systems are included and transcended in the ends of the community. This convergence of ends and norms furnishes the basis of community solidarity.

If all the systems and members of a community believe in the worthwhileness of the community goals and stand ready to sacrifice for them, a "fund of goodwill"[3] is said to reside in the community. This fund of goodwill is an expression and measure of the meaningfulness of the whole for its parts. Its measure is the extent to which sub-systems and members sacrifice for the whole. Consciously or unconsciously members of most sub-systems in the community try to tap this fund. The leaders of change systems who can relate their programs to the fund of goodwill in such a manner that the elements of the structure may be utilized should have little difficulty legitimizing and carrying out their programs. When members of various community organizations involved in an action related to the attain-

---

[3] See Christopher Sower, John Holland, Kenneth Tiedke, and Walter Freeman, *Patterns of Community Involvement* (Glencoe, Illinois: The Free Press, 1957). For early uses of this term see Charles P. and Zona K. Loomis, *Modern Social Theories* (Princeton, N.J.: D. Van Nostrand, 1961), p. 577.

ment of community ends or goals are questioned concerning their motives for assisting, the following answers are common: "I thought it was for the good of the community." "My organization believes it is for the good of our community." "I didn't want to do it, in fact, I doubted that it was necessary but I knew the community felt we should do it, so I did it."

The extent and nature of the fund of goodwill existing in communities vary greatly. It is probable that the fund of goodwill is less in communities having ethnic or occupational cleavages than in communities where such cleavages do not exist.

It is very difficult for the community to differentiate ends (the desired future states that the system is undertaking to bring about) from norms (the rules and principles whereby the means and facilities may be applied to attain these ends). Community ends and norms tend to fuse. Whereas much of the action of subsystems, such as business enterprises, may be rational or instrumental, much community action is often expressive, integrative, or both. In instrumental action it is easier to differentiate ends and norms than in other forms of action. The fiesta tends to be more expressive; the ritual of Memorial Day or certain court proceedings tend to be integrative or moral.

Changes in value orientation (the ends and norms of systems) are of extreme importance. The emerging rural community in America looks to the city, as though there were one-way windows between the farm and the trade center and between the trade center and the metropolis. The city, not the neighborhood or village, will "call the signals" for the future.[4] The metropolitan areas are swallowing up the old farm villages in the wake of a countrywide expansion. One instance of this invasion of the countryside is depicted in Figure 1. The importance and reality of this invasion due to the highway and automobile is evidenced by the following: "Prior to it, [the advent of the highway] in the waterway era and in the railroad era, the city was in very large degree autonomous of its own rural hinterland. One who journeyed from the center of a metropolis outward would always en-

<hr />

[4] Dale E. Hathaway, J. Allan Beegle and W. Keith Bryant, *People of Rural America* (Washington, D.C.: U.S. Government Printing Office, 1968). "The underlying hypothesis of this monograph, [is] that of metropolitan dominance" p. 123. For other than demographic considerations see Arthur J. Vidich and Joseph Bensman, *Small Town in Mass Society*. (Princeton, N.J.: Princeton University Press, 1968).

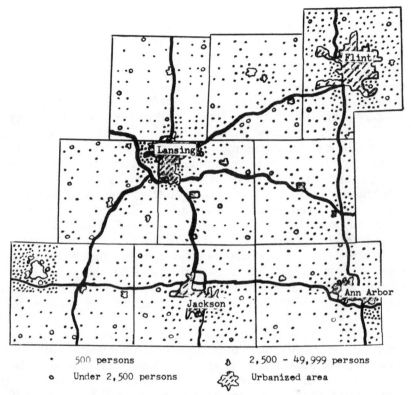

| • | 500 persons | ♪ | 2,500 - 49,999 persons |
| o | Under 2,500 persons | | Urbanized area |

FIGURE 1. Population distribution in relation to urbanized areas and highways in southern Michigan.

counter an abrupt, precipitous transition to unspoiled country-side. Socially and culturally, the transition was just as abrupt. The city was truly a state of mind; the country was another and very different state of mind. Between them there was an abyss."[5]

All this has changed, especially in the industrial, free-enterprise societies. Roland L. Warren[6] believes the changes require a

[5] Walter Firey, J. Allan Beegle, and Charles P. Loomis, "The Highway in Rural Areas," *The Highway in Our National Life,* edited by the Bureau of Urban Research (Princeton: Princeton University Press, 1951), p. 61.

[6] Roland L. Warren, "Toward a Reformulation of Community" in Roland L. Warren, ed., *Perspectives on the American Community* (Chicago: Rand McNally and Company, 1966), pp. 71-72.

"reformulation of community theory." Earlier theory which treated communities as sort of desert island cultures having been based upon "the factor of locality [with] common interests, life, associations, and institutions [must be changed because] this factor. . . . is becoming progressively weaker." Increasingly outside large-scale organizations bring independent and sometimes conflicting programs to communities. "Thus, the size of the new post office door. . . . [is] determined by national policy . . ." Similar decisions affect a Masonic Lodge, a Catholic Church, or a Grange meeting; and while leaders in the United Fund may plead for only one money-raising campaign, various national organizations carry on their own drives.

Status-roles. In small communities the division of labor and definition of functions of members are usually not as specific as in various subsystems, such as the school and church. There is no universal status-role comparable to the father in the family, the teacher in the school, or the deacon in the church. Some organization specialists have attempted to give the small community an integrated status-role system through the establishment of community councils, but the death rate of such mechanisms is very high.

Generally in the United States (outside of New England), if the rural community surrounds an incorporated trade center, an organized social system with specific status-roles (mayor, treasurer, and so on) exists for the center but seldom for the rural hinterland that often has more members than the center itself. Often two antagonistic systems, one urban and another rural, develop to express different interests in taxation, zoning, and school services.[7] There are a great variety of ways in which rural communities are related to the political structure. Smith advocates the Brazilian system in which the surrounding countryside is included in the corporate area.[8] At the same time, Wagley describes the great amount of rural-urban conflict in the same nation.[9] Regardless of the relationship between the rural and town systems, frictions and cleavages exist between the town and the country people in most areas of the world.

[7] Solon Kimball, "A Case Study in Township Zoning," *Michigan AES Quarterly Bulletin,* Vol. 28 (1946), pp. 253-269.

[8] T. Lynn Smith, *Brazil: People and Institutions* (Baton Rouge: Louisiana State University Press, 1946), p. 147.

[9] Charles Wagley, *Amazon Town—A Study of Man in the Tropics* (New York: The MacMillan Co., 1953), p. 267.

Those status-roles that articulate the affairs of the rural community system, except where the New England town form of government formalizes relationships, may be characterized as carrying responsibilities that are personal and informal. The different status-roles in communities often reveal a "lady bountiful" who assists in case of need, a "watchdog" who keeps school enthusiasts and others from increasing taxes, *patrones* in the Southwest who "look after their people," and *caciques* or informal rural "ward bosses" in Latin America and many other areas. Such status-roles are essentially different from that of city manager, whose duties are more specific and whose relationships may be more professional and less personal.

There are certainly logical as well as emotional reasons for concern about the declining importance of systems such as the neighborhood and community. As MacIver asserts, those who "yearn for a value which is not in the fleeting lives of men—a value that is not embodied merely in the successive members of successive generations . . ."[10] are yearning for what we call the community in its Gemeinschaft forms. If we assume with Mead that we are socialized as we learn to play the status-roles of others and "call out in ourselves the response of the community,"[11] the opportunity to learn the structure of society must suffer seriously when there is no semblance of the neighborhood and community.

Role playing, of course, conditions personality development, especially in the emergence of and interaction with a "generalized other." Immobile peasant villagers with tradition-directed personalities (in David Riesman's sense) prevent change through rigid adherence to traditional norms and by either eliminating or relegating innovators and deviants to existing status-roles such as that of the shaman. As early capitalism or communism bring into existence the inner-directed farmers, middle-class business men, communist officials and bureaucrats, rational action is fostered. Such inner-directed individuals are

[10] MacIver, *The Web of Government*, p. 419. For the linkage of informal clique structures see Herbert F. Lionberger and Gary D. Copus, "Structuring Influence of Social Cliques on Farm-information-seeking Relationships within Two Missouri Communities," *Rural Sociology*, Vol. 37, No. 1, (March, 1972).

[11] George Herbert Mead, *Mind, Self and Society: From the Standpoint of a Social Behaviorist,* edited by Charles W. Morriss (Chicago: University of Chicago Press, 1934), pp. 178-179.

guided by an inner "moral voice" and are motivated by rationality and independence which serves stable communities well while initiating basic changes, but they fare badly as social mobility increases. Thus as people shuffle about without a permanent home base and as relationships in the community lose their value as ends in and of themselves in the Gemeinschaft sense a different personality type is required. Riesman's other-directed personality type then emerges and serves to reduce fear of "being conspicuous," "unconventional" and "old-fashioned."[12]

All of the human interaction which goes into the process of personality formation is articulated in the small community. The adult as well as the child has most of his important needs met in the community. The community provides necessary rites which ease and legitimize critical periods in the life cycle; it provides a setting in which most status-roles may be internalized.

Power. Most people in industrialized societies do not carry on their day to day activities in communities under the domination of a single subsystem of society. Rather, they live in what we may call power-diffused communities, in the sense that no single social system monopolizes power. In most communities, however, only a few people hold the offices and control the formal organizations.[13]

As indicated previously, when one sub-system of a community is dominant, as in the case of the Latin American hacienda, that sub-system supplies the role structure and articulates the power for the whole community. Also, the more specific and visible will be the power relationships, and the more universal their application in that individual relationships are not as important as general principles. For communities in which no single sub-system has a monopoly of power, power tends to be gained and held in accordance with the value system of the culture. We may hypothesize that the more rural a society, the more power, includ-

---

[12] David Riesman, et al., *The Lonely Crowd* (New Haven: Yale University Press, 1950); C. P. Loomis and J. A. Beegle, *Rural Social Systems* (New York: Prentice-Hall, 1950), p. 27 (noted independently) and Rudolf Heberle, "A Note on Riesman's *The Lonely Crowd,*" *American Journal of Sociology,* 72, (July 1956), pp. 35-36.

[13] Don Martindale and R. G. Hanson, *Small Town and the Nation* (Westport, Conn.: Greenwood Publishing Corp., 1969), pp. 76-77. See also Paul D. Richardson and Ward W. Bauder, *Participation in Organized Activities in a Kentucky Rural Community* (Lexington: Kentucky AES Bulletin 598, 1953), p. 27.

ing authority and influence, will be dependent upon inherited position and wealth; conversely, the more urban and westernized the society, the more important achievement will be in the attainment of power.

Social Rank. Social ranking in communities is dependent upon several factors, all rooted in the values of the community under consideration and the society at large. The most important considerations in the social rank of individual members are the status-roles he occupies, the power he possesses, and the prestige and esteem that come from these and other sources. In a study of how communities acquired hospitals, persons of influence were referred to as follows: "He isn't rich and he has no high offices but the people look to him for leadership because he is the symbol of what is good in this community."[14] This person symbolized the norms and ends of the system.

Clear-cut class systems in rural America are more easily distinguished in the South, especially on the plantation and among divergent racial and ethnic groups, than elsewhere. The class differences between laborers and non-laborers, however, are obvious on the factory farms and other large scale farming enterprises in the United States. As Western technology spreads, social rank becomes increasingly dependent upon achievement. The larger the social systems which compose the communities remaining after mechanization and urbanization, and the more differentiated the status-roles composing these systems, the more distinction there will be between people, and the greater the tendency for systems based upon social rank to emerge. The essential difference which increased mechanization, commercialization, and bureaucratization brings is a kind of stratification based to a considerable degree upon achievement rather than upon ascription.

Sanctions. In general the more solidary the community system in terms of the acceptance of the ends and norms, the more effective the sanction system will be in enforcing the basic values upon which this solidarity and the accompanying fund of goodwill rests. As Durkheim observed, punishment among other measures, is the community's means of reinforcing its own belief in its values.[15]

[14] Paul A. Miller, *Community Health Action* (East Lansing: The Michigan State College Press, 1953).

[15] Emile Durkheim, *The Division of Labor in Society,* translated by George

The allocation of rewards in terms of social rank or other satisfactions provides a basis for the recruitment of personnel in the community systems. Contrariwise, the various mechanisms whereby members and groups are penalized for deviance from norms comprise the punishment system. Thus, in a well-integrated, solidary community, the reward-punishment system applies to all members a two-way dispenser of gratification and pain. It also provides the dynamics whereby citizens who go in the "right" direction derive the most satisfactions. Penalities may take the form of extreme punishment, such as lynching and physical and mental torture. Rewards may come in the form of great wealth, power, privilege, and access to satisfactions of all kinds.

CONDITIONS OF SOCIAL ACTION

Time. The significance of time in social relations may be found in the folk-sayings of all cultures. Several examples illustrate the diversity: "The longest way round is the shortest way home," "He who travels alone travels fastest" and "A stitch in time saves nine."

Few sociologists have captured the different perspectives of time held by traditionalistic rural and modern urban people more effectively than Simmel and Toennies. For Simmel "punctuality, calculability, exactness are forced upon life by the complexity and extension of metropolitan existence . . . These traits favor the exclusion of those irrational, instinctive, sovereign traits and impulses which aim at determining the mode of life from within, instead of receiving the general and precisely schematized form of life from without. . . .[The metropolis creates] that blasé attitude which, in fact, every metropolitan child shows when compared with children of quieter and less changeable milieus . . . [Such] self preservation . . . is bought at the price of devaluating the whole objective world, a devaluation which in the end unavoidably drags one's own personality down into a feeling of the same worthlessness."[16] Toennies thought

---

Simpson, (Glencoe: The Free Press, 1933), pp. 139ff. Also see an exposition of this in Talcott Parsons, *The Structure of Social Action* (New York: McGraw Hill Book Co., 1937), pp. 309, 318-39, 402, 403.

[16] George Simmel, "The Metropolis and Mental Life," in Paul K. Hatt and Albert J. Reiss, eds. *Cities and Society* (Glencoe: The Free Press, 1957), pp. 638-639.

that the impersonality and rationality of social relations brought about by the passing of the Gemeinschaft and the development of the Gesellschaft as peasant societies became modern created the actor ruled by rational will or the other-directed person in David Riesman's sense and the blasé in Simmel's sense.[17]

Territoriality.   Obviously territoriality is of prime importance in the comparison of locality groupings both in time and space. Although modern means of communication have lessened the importance of space and geographical factors, they are still important. It still requires less effort and expense to visit over the back fence with a neighbor than with an intimate friend a hundred miles away. Intimacy rarely can develop except in face-to-face relationships and it is retained over long periods and distances only through the expenditure of considerable time and effort. How intelligent use of the energy required to satisfy needs leads to a hierarchy of market and service areas will be discussed under systemic linkage and boundary maintenance.

The territorial constraints of the community are lessened as activities and services are differentiated and organizations are enlarged and centralized. Basic to these developments are technological changes which likewise reduce the importance of space in interaction. However, no movement of people, goods and services takes place without the use of energy and the consequent potential pollution of the environment. If all rural and urban populations were reorganized to minimize pollution of the environment, the importance of space would probably become much more important. For those living in industrialized societies the thought of carrying on most activities on foot or bicycle is staggering.

Intimacy and Territoriality.   On almost all dimensions, communities vary greatly from society to society, region to region, and epoch to epoch. The various physical forms of the rural community have been treated in some detail in *Rural Social Systems.*[18]

Among the most important variations among communities is the extent to which interaction is intimate. At one end of the continuum, one may find examples of the "community . . . as . . .

---

[17] Charles P. Loomis, *Social Systems—Essays in Their Persistence and Change* (Princeton: D. Van Nostrand, 1960), pp. 115-116.

[18] Loomis and Beegle, *Rural Social Systems,* Chapter 7.

a group of neighbors who know one another face to face."[19] Most contacts, in terms of intimacy and intensity of interaction, resemble those of the highly integrated and self-sufficient family. There are neighborhood communities such as El Cerrito, New Mexico, which when one of the authors first lived there was composed of several dozen families who, in many respects, behaved like an extended family.[20] At the other end of the continuum, one may find areas in which neighbors are strangers who rarely interact. Although some think of the large city as exemplifying this condition, it can occur in both urban and rural areas.

Between these extremes are to be found most of the rural communities of the United States and other countries of the urbanized Western World. Probably the most important change in the rural life of the Western World, and one which affects vitally the interaction of community members, is the decreasing importance of the smaller neighborhood-centered community. In its place we find the larger trade-centered community. This change, brought about by the advent of improved highways and the use of motor vehicles, has made the automobile rather than the "team haul" the determining factor in interaction and community size. There are also areas in which neighborhoods have relatively little significance and families travel many miles in order to associate with close friends. Many social philosophers and students of society believe that the modern community in Western society is its weakest link. "Instead of belonging to a community with its close spontaneous personal ties," according to MacIver, "modern man belongs to a heterogeneous array of de-personalized associations."[21]

[19] Baker Brownell, *The Human Community—Its Philosophy and Practice for a Time of Crisis* (New York: Harper and Brothers, 1950), p. 198. Brownell maintains that the community is also "a rather small group, such as the family, village, or small town, in which each person can know a number of others as whole persons, not as functional fragments."

[20] Olen Leonard and Charles P. Loomis, *Culture of a Contemporary Rural Community, El Cerrito, New Mexico,* reprinted in Charles P. Loomis, *Studies of Rural Social Organization* (East Lansing: State College Book Store, 1945), Chapter 16.

[21] MacIver, *Web of Government,* pp. 432-433. For an excellent critique of the concept "Neighborhood" as used in eight rural sociology texts, see Walter L. Slocum and Herman M. Case, "Are Neighborhoods Meaningful Social Groups Throughout Rural America?" *Rural Sociology,* Vol. 18, No. 1 (March, 1953), pp. 52-59.

A neighborhood is an area in which people "neighbor" with one another; that is, the area in which people visit, borrow, exchange tools and equipment, and cooperate in various ways. Typically, neighborhoods include from half a dozen to several dozen families. After the family, it is the smallest locality group. The great sociologist, Cooley,[22] looked upon the neighborhood, the family and the play group as being primary. These groups he considered to be extremely important in the development of personality.

The trade-centered community, which appears to be replacing the neighborhood community in rural areas of Western society, is a locality grouping including a hamlet, village, town, or city as center, and the surrounding farm and non-farm populations that interact in business as well as non-business pursuits. In typical rural areas, the families which patronize the center outnumber the families in the center. Although it is the trade center of 2,500 and over that is becoming increasingly important in American rural life, various rural sociologists have found that small service units, especially for bulky goods and general services, continue to persist.[23] While some farmers or ranchers may travel a hundred miles to their service centers, most rural families do not travel more than seven or eight miles for their main services. The trade-centered community, including hundreds of

[22] Charles H. Cooley, *Social Organization* (New York: Charles Scribner's Sons, 1909), Chapter 3.

[23] For a penetrating and significant modern treatment see Ruth C. Young and Olaf F. Larson, "The Social Ecology of a Rural Community," *Rural Sociology,* Vol. 35, No. 3, (September 1970). Here what the present authors would call a dialectic between systemic linkage with existing or emerging trade centers and boundary maintenance of original neighborhoods is described. "Social density" and other factors are considered, but for a south-central New York State Community "the most powerful factor in determining . . . structural perception is where the individual lives relative to the village center." Those living in neighborhoods more than three miles from such a center, other things equal, tend to maintain neighborhood boundaries. Those living less than three miles from the village center tend to link to the center and boundary maintenance of the neighborhood lessens. "Local units that are not sufficiently tied into a larger structure have no communication with and do not influence the larger unit . . . [and] they are aliented. Situations without local organization [as in urban ghettos] leave fringe persons totally out of any social structure." For those caught in the dialectic of change toward what the progressives call "bigger and better" and who are denied or left out of meaningful relationships, "the social importance of neighborhood groups takes on new meaning."

people who may be unacquainted or interact only for business purposes, tends to become Gesellschaft-like. However, both neighborhoods and trade center communities in which residents have strong social bonds in kinship, religion, recreation and work may continue to persist. The meaningfulness of the bonds is important for their persistence and neighborhoods which are close to trade centers tend to die as their functions are absorbed by larger places.[24]

A comparison of two areas well known to the authors may serve to illustrate the processes and consequences of changes in locality group structure. One area is the trade center community of Turrialba, Costa Rica, with a population of approximately 19,000. It is typical of many trade center communities in the underdeveloped areas of the world, particularly in Latin America. The other area is Livingston County, Michigan, with a population of 26,700 in 1950 but more than twice that number today. In the Turrialba trade center area, thirty-four percent live in Turrialba (the trade center) as compared with about sixteen percent in Howell (the trade center of the Livingston County area). Most of the interaction of the people in Turrialba is confined to the thirty-two villages outlined in Figure 2. Although most people live only one and one-half hours by foot from Turrialba, the trade center, only a relatively small portion of the interaction takes place here.

As indicated by Figure 3, nearly half of the rural people and about half of the area of Livingston County in which rural families live, were without identifiable neighborhoods at the time the study was made. Typically, the people of Livingston County who did not reside in neighborhoods lived near the trade center or along the heavily traveled highway running from Lansing to Detroit. The county population now has more than doubled since 1950 with large proportions of residents commuting to work in Detroit, Flint, and Ann Arbor. Newcomers now outnumber long-time residents. New interstate highways crossing this county make it possible for many to use the local area for little more than residence. Most of the social interaction occurs outside the county. In contrast, interaction in the Turrialba area is condi-

[24] Ruth C. Young and Olaf F. Larson, Ibid. See also William J. Haga and Clinton Folse, "Trade Patterns and Community Identity," *Rural Sociology*, Vol. 36, No. 1, (March 1971), pp. 42ff.

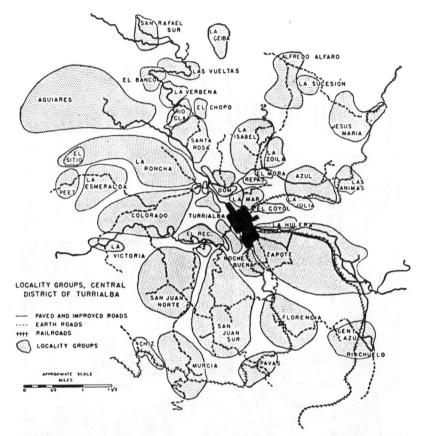

FIGURE 2. Locality groupings in the Turrialba area of Costa Rica. Delineation of the 32 locality groups depicted was done through interviews and observation.

tioned by transportation by ox cart or by foot and is largely confined to the outlying village neighborhoods.

Territoriality in Gemeinschaft- and Gesellschaft-like Societies.

The changes in social structure and value orientation that technology brought to the urbanized cultures of the world is reflected in the contrasting neighborhood communities of Livingston County, Michigan (Figure 3) and of Turrialba, Costa Rica (Figure 2). A generation ago, the neighborhoods of Livingston County resembled those of Turrialba, and the process that resulted in the present situation is going on everywhere. As the status-roles that members occupy are differentiated, and as free

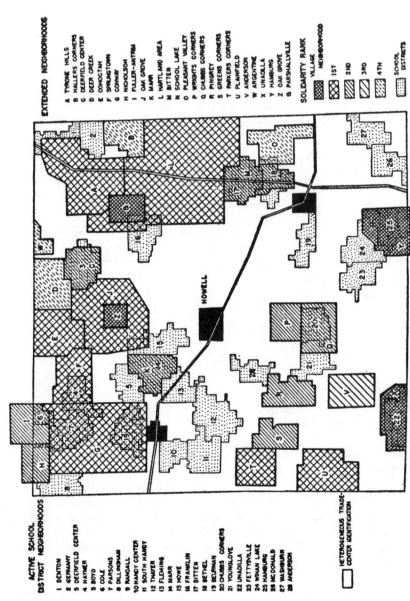

FIGURE 3. Locality groups in Livingston county, Michigan. Twenty-seven "extended neighborhoods" as well as school districts were identifiable in the late '40s.

mobility occurs, more social and economic activities leave the neighborhood for larger centers. In this process the latter grow at the expense of the smaller centers. Whereas people in the neighborhoods of the Turrialba trade center area know intimately and interact with most members, residents in a large segment of Livingston County already twenty years ago identified with no neighborhood and carried on their interaction with friends and relatives over a wide area. In many instances, the neighbors in the spatial sense are strangers, often rural residents who work in the towns and cities. Neighborhoods which once were "communities of fate," in that all shared good and bad fortune, no longer are bound by the same ties. In rural America, the neighborhoods and other locality groups are increasingly assuming the aspects of the Gesellschaft. Responsibilities among interacting neighbors in areas such as Livingston County are increasingly specific, rather than diffuse, as is the case among neighbors in Turrialba. Relationships in Turrialba are to a larger extent ends in and of themselves. It is fair to say that probably no social system has undergone more change than the community in areas in which technological diffusion has been extensive. Each of the sub-systems such as the church and school has changed, and these changes have apparently accumulated geometrically in the total system, the community.

General Spatial Patterns.   Flying over an area, one can see the spatial arrangement of individual homes, the division of the land, the system of roads, and the relation of communities to each other. Over much of France, for example, one observes the long strips of land with the farm dwellings along a road or stream. The dwellings are so close that they constitute line villages resembling the string settlements along highways in the United States. Although found in areas originally settled by French colonists, such as portions of Canada and Louisiana, the line village is not confined to such areas. Smith[25] reports that it is common in Brazil.

The Spanish and Portuguese village, as established in the Americas, consists of a core unit, the plaza, and is laid out in square blocks with straight streets, differing from the villages of Germanic and English origin. The New England village was

[25] Smith, *Brazil: People and Institutions,* Chapter 13.

highly influenced by the Germanic form. (See Figure 4). Villages in New England were nucleated in that the buildings were grouped about a core, with crooked streets and outlying fields and pasture land.

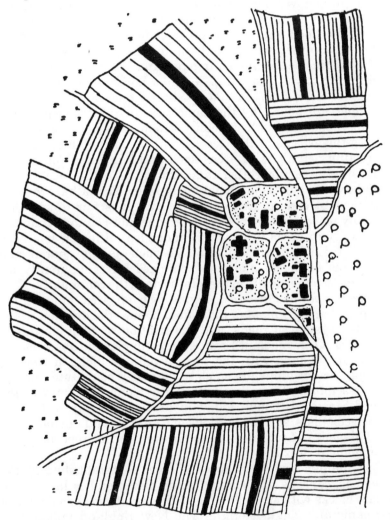

FIGURE 4. The German Gewanndorf in which residents form a compact village group. Due to the variable quality of land, each resident is assigned segmented strips of land. This village form was found in areas of southern Sweden, Denmark, Schleswig-Holstein, and southern Germany.

With the passage of the Northwest Ordinance of 1785, land was divided into townships of 36 sections, each with 640 acres. Gradually the rectangular form of land division was adopted over much of the land area of the United States. This type of division resulted in the land being laid out in sections one mile square, and is often referred to as the "checkerboard" pattern. This system spread over most of the area west of the Ohio-Pennsylvania line, with few exceptions.[26] Since roads in these areas were laid out on the township or section boundaries, they were straight and ran east and west and north and south. This explains why neighborhood and community boundaries in these areas, as in Figure 3, tend to be rectangular. In the underdeveloped areas of the world, the community boundary forms shown in Figure 2 are more typical than the Michigan pattern shown in Figure 3.

Locality Systems for "Field" and "Center" Activities. Human activities, from an ecological point of view, may be classified as "field" and "center" pursuits. The former are organized in communities involving the production of food, fiber, minerals, and raw materials. Such pursuits ordinarily require high land-man ratios, and populations are usually dispersed over large areas. In general, field-centered activities may be considered "rural." The "center" activities, on the other hand, are concerned with processing and distributing. In general, such activities are supported by populations in densely settled aggregates and may be regarded as "urban."

The relation of the locality groupings, within which field activities are carried on, to the locality groupings of the center, often gives the whole society a special character. In industrialized countries, such as the United States, metropolitan areas usually consist of one or two very large centers with many overlapping locality systems of numerous sizes. In non-industrialized countries, the change from city to country is often more abrupt. In Latin American countries, for example, a relatively large proportion of the people live in the largest city. In industrialized countries, such as the United States, the proportion living in the largest city is much smaller.

Demographic Definition of Territorial Systems. One of the

[26] T. Lynn Smith, *The Sociology of Rural Life* (New York: Harper & Brothers, 1953), pp. 262-263.

basic classifications used by the Bureau of the Census allocates the population according to residence. The usual place of abode is categorized as "urban" and "rural," with the latter subdivided into "rural-farm" and "rural-nonfarm." Since these categories are fundamental in understanding the data concerning residence, a brief explanation is essential. The urban definition in 1970 comprises all persons residing in areas determined to be urbanized areas or in places 2,500 or more outside urbanized areas. Specifically urban includes: (1) population in the central cities of urbanized areas; (2) population in the urban fringe of urbanized areas but not in central cities; and (3) population in places of 2,500 or more outside urbanized areas. The remainder then is rural population. The rural-farm population is that residing on farms as determined from responses to a question on acreage and dollar sales of farm products. Persons are classified as living on farms if they live on places of ten or more acres from which sales of crops, livestock and other farm products amounted to $50 or more in the previous calendar year, or places of less than ten acres from which sales of farm products amounted to $250 or more. The rural-nonfarm population is the remainder, or those residing in rural territory but not on farms.[27]

Thus, the rural-farm population includes all those qualified on the basis of acreage and sales without regard to occupation. The rural-nonfarm population includes those living in hamlets, villages and small towns under 2,500 as well as those living in the open-country who do not meet the farm criteria.

Despite the rapid growth in the American population, the rural population has remained relatively stable. In 1970 approximately three-fourths was classified as urban and about one-fourth was rural. The rural-farm segment of the rural population, however, declined from about 16 million (8.7 percent) in 1960 to less than 10 million (4.8 percent) in 1970.[28] The increasing urbanization of the population is illustrated in Table 1.

Migration Between Field and Center Systems. In America, as elsewhere in the world, the rural population supplies human resources to the urban areas through migration. In contrast to

[27] U. S. Bureau of the Census, *1970 Census Users Guide* (Washington: U. S. Government Printing Office, 1970), pp. 93-94.

[28] Economic Research Service, *The Economic and Social Conditions of Rural America in the 1970s* (Washington: U.S. Government Printing Office, 1971), pp. 2-4.

TABLE 1

Percent of Population in Rural Areas and in Four Urban Size Classes, U.S., 1950-1970

		Urban Size Class			
Year	Rural	I Under 100,000	II 100,000 to 499,999	III 500,000 to 999,999	IV 1,000,000 or more
1950	36.0	20.1	12.8	6.1	25.0
1960	30.1	19.4	13.3	8.5	28.7
1970	24.8	16.9	13.3	7.5	37.6

Source: Kingsley Davis, *World Urbanization 1950-1970, Vol. I: Basic Data for Cities, Counties and Regions,* (Berkeley: Institute of International Studies, 1969), p. 120.

many areas of the world, rural persons in the United States have frequent contacts with the cities, and few legal restrictions hamper movement. Due to these factors, adjustment problems of the migrant to cities may be less severe than in many parts of the world.

While the average net migration rate from the farm population has been high for many years, the numbers have dwindled as the size of farm population has diminished. This trend is shown graphically in Figure 5. Even though the farm population was only about 10 million, the average annual net outmigration between 1965 and 1969 amounted to more than one-half million.

The Fringe Between Field and Center. The area of destination of many rural migrants, of course, is the suburban and fringe area surrounding the large cities. In part, however, suburban and fringe growths represent a decentralization of the large urban aggregates. Areas surrounding the large cities in the last several decades increased at a much faster rate than the urban centers themselves. Farm lands in such areas have been subdivided for housing and other non-agricultural uses.

The location of the farm population of the U. S. in relation to the nearest metropolitan area is summarized in Table 2. More than one-third of the farm population is either located in or within 50 miles of an SMSA. Slightly less than half is between 50 and 100 miles from the nearest metropolitan area.

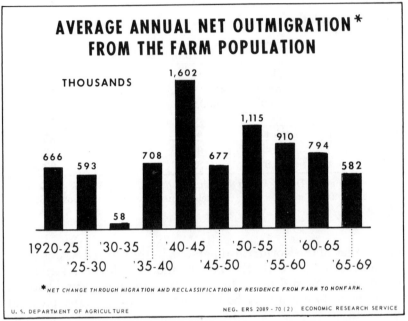

FIGURE 5.   Average annual net out-migration from the farm population.

TABLE 2
Percent Distribution of the Rural-Farm Population by Distance from
the Nearest SMSA for Conterminous United States, by Color, 1960

Distance from Nearest SMSA	Percentage of Rural-Farm Population in 1960		
	Total	White	Nonwhite
Total	100.0	100.0	100.0
Inside SMSA Counties	12.4	13.2	6.8
Less than 50 miles	23.3	23.7	20.2
50 to 99 miles	45.8	43.8	61.1
100 to 149 miles	12.8	13.2	10.0
150 to 199 miles	2.9	3.2	0.6
200 miles or more	2.8	2.9	1.3

Source: U.S. Bureau of the Census, *People of Rural America*, by Dale E. Hathaway, J. Allan Beegle, and W. Keith Bryant (A 1960 Census Monograph) (Washington: U.S. Government Printing Office, 1968), p. 243. SMSA
refers to an area comprising one or more counties in which there is at least one
city of 50,000 or more.

In some of the early work on suburban areas, Kimball viewed the fringe as a "new social frontier." Firey pointed to the high proportion of young adults with many children and the inadequate social life and organizational facilities as essential characteristics.[29]

Beegle and Schroeder found a lack of many of the usual urban services in their study of a Lansing, Michigan fringe area. But they also found that fringe residents were happy with life in the fringe neighborhood and most frequently cited "more space for a garden" as the chief advantage of living there.[30]

THE SOCIAL PROCESSES IN THE COMMUNITY

Communication. Communication refers to the manner in which information passes through social systems and the manner in which opinions and attitudes concerning information are formed or modified. Obviously, communication is related to all the elements we have discussed. From research and experience, we know that the attitudes of individuals are shaped from interaction in social systems. This is not to deny the importance of individual personality, but various experiments in group dynamics and "brain washing" demonstrate that most normal people are influenced by the social interaction in which they are involved. The Gemeinschaft-like kinship and friendship systems give the rural resident his principal attitudinal motivations. Ordinarily, it is more pleasant to be a conforming member of a group. An old saying has it that "birds of a feather flock together." The processes of coming and being together as equals on an intimate basis seem to make the attitudinal characteristics of people similar.

The importance of the printed word, the motion picture, the radio, and television in community action is closely related to the extent to which the communities urbanize, westernize, and possess a high level of living. Any social system that has the

[29] Solon T. Kimball, *The New Social Frontier: The Fringe* (East Lansing: Michigan AES Special Bulletin 360, 1949); Walter Firey, *Social Aspects of Land-Use Planning in the Country-City Fringe: The Case of Flint, Michigan* (East Lansing: Michigan AES Special Bulletin 339, 1946).

[30] J. Allan Beegle and Widick Schroeder, *Social Organization and Land-Use in the North Lansing Fringe* (East Lansing: Michigan AES Technical Bulletin 251, 1955).

power to control the stimuli that reach decision makers has an important advantage in the determination of action.

Systemic Linkage. Of great importance in the nature of the linkage between those who carry on the field and the center activities of a society. Whether the farms, ranches or large scale agricultural operations are laid out in checkerboard pattern or in other patterns, and whether the society is traditional or modern, the service centers are of different sizes and composition and their location is not happenstance or random. In rural Iowa today the typical rural resident may have linkages of various kinds with a large "regional capital" which reaches out 40 miles or more for customers, and provides most goods and services for those who do not live far away. The regional center services smaller places—small cities, towns, villages and hamlets each of which is linked to the regional capital and other centers. Small Iowa villages of about 500 people usually serve an equal number in the surrounding area who come a maximum of approximately five miles for goods and services.[31] Typically such villages offer 25 or so kinds of services which are housed in about 40 separate stores or businesses. Such villages commonly have a gas station, bar, restaurant, post office, farm elevator and church.

Towns typically have over twice as many inhabitants as the villages and about twice as many kinds of business and business services. Towns serve nearly three times as many people in the hinterland as within their boundaries. They reach out a maximum of eight miles on the average and offer the same services as villages plus hardware, furniture, complete drug store service, appliance store, doctor, dentist, dry cleaner, bank, insurance agent and funeral parlor.

Small cities which are some six times the size of the towns, offer twice as many kinds of services and three or four times as many separate establishments. These small cities serve people in a radius of less than twenty miles and in addition to the goods and services carried in villages and towns also typically publish a newspaper, have a movie, county government offices, stores for jewelry, shoes, clothing of all kinds, flowers, new and used autos, auto accessories and the like.

Hamlets, the smallest places with less than one hundred in-

---

[31] For this and the following three paragraphs the authors draw heavily from Brian J. L. Berry, *Geography of Market Centers and Retail Distribution* (Englewood Cliffs, N.J.: Prentice-Hall, 1967), pp. 13ff.

habitants, seldom have more than a general store, farm elevator, gas station, roadside restaurant and bulk fuel depot. The optimum territorial arrangement of the hamlets, villages, towns, small and large cities to one another and in relation to the open-country population is of great importance for rural sociology. For example, in which of the centers should schools, hospitals, churches, and other agencies for rural people be located? Unequivocal answers are not possible but experts planning for schools and hospitals generally maintain that, other things equal, those located in places having less than 50,000 in the trade center community will usually be handicapped.[32]

Boundary Maintenance. Hawley writes: "The human community is more than just an organization of functional relationships, and to that extent there are limitations to the scope of human ecology. Man's collective life involves, in greater or lesser degree, a psychological and a moral as well as a functional integration."[33]

Based on 36 rural villages in two central Illinois areas, Haga and Folse demonstrate that the Marxian notion that economic activities are the prime sources of identity for locality groupings does not hold. They find that "a class of nonfunctional relationships—affectual relationships—was more related to community identity choices than was a set of purely functional relationships."[34]

There is certainly no consensus among participating residents of modern societies about the advantages of rural vs urban community facilities and life. As would be expected studies have shown that both rural and urban residents acknowledge the general urban advantage in quality and quantity of shopping and medical facilities, teacher ability, employment opportunities and entertainment facilities. Nevertheless, there is also general recognition that smaller-size rural communities offer more opportunities for participatory democracy in the management of local affairs and that the closer dependence of rural agencies on their clients "sensitizes rural residents to the bounties of their natural milieu."[35]

[32] C. P. Loomis and J. A. Beegle, *Rural Sociology, The Strategy of Change* (New York: Prentice-Hall, Inc., 1957), p. 243.

[33] Amos Hawley, *Human Ecology* (New York: Ronald Press, 1950), pp. 73-74.

[34] Haga and Folse, "Trade Patterns," p. 50.

[35] Ronald L. Johnson and Edward Knop, "Rural-Urban Differentials in Com-

On one hand, communities are going concerns in the sense that social action results in the achievement of goals through the functioning of the various elements we have described. On the other, members attempt to maintain territorial boundaries and to counteract forces that may weaken the general acceptance of the values of the system. In more concrete terms, communities not only resist loss of territory, but they resist "fifth column" activities, propaganda, new ideas, or other influences which members feel will weaken them.

Communities vary greatly in their facility for boundary maintenance. The Amish communities, for example, have special mechanisms designed for boundary maintenance. At an early age children are taught that the Amish are a chosen but a persecuted people and that many types of activities involving non-Amish people are sinful. Tales of immorality in the high schools of surrounding communities are circulated to prevent children from wanting to attend and to prevent adults from acceding to the state laws requiring attendance. The distinctive dress, grooming, and taboos on travel and interaction of the Amish are all mechanisms which assist the communities and the whole sub-culture in boundary maintenance. The case of the Amish may be considered exceptional, but similar mechanisms may be observed in most communities.

The community whose members do not think that it is superior may be said to have low morale. Education develops a broadmindedness which counteracts provincialism, but strong communities always have boundary maintenance mechanisms which resist changes that may be at variance with the accepted ends and norms. It has been observed that the greater linkage a community has with modern Western urban culture, the less the emphasis upon boundary maintenance. Communities such as those of the Amish near large cities require special mechanisms built into their systems to maintain their ideological and social boundaries.

Gesellschaft-like or rationally efficient use of space and boundary maintenance. If one tries to maximize the returns

---

munity Satisfaction," *Rural Sociology,* Vol. 35, No. 4, (December 1970), pp. 544ff. The great differences in services offered in Sweden and America is dramatically described by Jules J. Wanderer and George R. Smart, "The Structure of Service Institutions in Rural and Urban Communities of Colorado and Sweden," *Rural Sociology,* Vol. 34, No. 3, (September 1969), pp. 368ff.

from expenditure of human energy and to this end sets forth "the most radical [and hence simplest] of the assumptions made in constructing . . . [models], the landscape in question is an isotropic plain on which resources of all kinds are uniformly distributed."[36] Following this assumption and basing his reasoning on that of Christaller[37] and Loesch,[38] Skinner summarizes the rationale for the hexagon model in Figure 6. He says that "as you move from the least advantaged position to the most advantageous position around the rim of the marketing area, the differential is maximal for triangular areas, intermediate for square areas, and minimal for hexagon areas." For any given region one can compare the territorial arrangements of the hamlets, villages, towns, small cities and regional centers mentioned above to the "ideal typological model."

If one accepts the assumption concerning the isotropicality of the landscape and certain other assumptions, reasons for deviations in the actual existing arrangements from the Gesellschaft-like or rationally efficient marketing and distribution model depicted in Figure 6 may be investigated. Plans for the relationships and locations of centers may also be developed for the future.[39] Like the economists who find many reasons why perfect competition seldom exists and that few buyers and sellers always behave as "economic men," so rural sociologists and geographers find many reasons why patterns of marketing arrangements across the landscape are not perfectly Gesellschaft-like or rationally efficient.

Among the most important reasons that rural areas fail to use space and time according to Gesellschaft-like or rationally efficient principles lies in the culture of the actors. Their beliefs, sentiments, norms and goals affect their marketing, transportation arrangements, and facilities. This is brought into sharp focus by a study of the use of service centers by "modern" Canadians and

[36] G. William Skinner, "Marketing and Social Structure in Rural China," *Journal of Asian Studies,* Vol. XXIV, Nos. 1-4, (November 1964-August 1965), p. 32.

[37] Walter Christaller, *The Central Places of Southern Germany.* Translated by C. Baskin, (Englewood Cliffs, N.J.: Prentice-Hall, 1966).

[38] August Loesch, *The Economics of Location,* Translated by W. H. Woglom and W. F. Stolper, (New Haven: Yale University Press, 1954).

[39] Perhaps the best example of such planning is found in Lalit K. Sen, et al., *Planning Rural Growth Centers for Integrated Area Development* (Hyderabad, India: National Institute of Community Development, 1971).

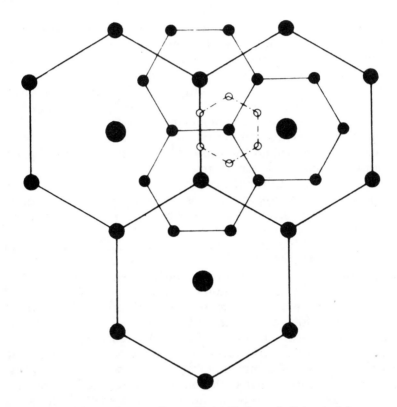

FIGURE 6. A hierarchy according to Christaller's marketing principle.

Old Order Mennonites in an area in Ontario.[40] The two groups did use space in the same way in satisfying needs for such Gesellschaft-like activities as banking. However, since the Old Order Mennonites travel by horse and buggy and wear garments prescribed by religious norms that have allowed little change since the Reformation, their behavior in the purchase of clothing and yard-goods is not related to size of center as it is in the case of the "modern" Canadians. Whereas the latter buy such goods in cities, the former buy them largely in nearby hamlets, villages, and towns.

[40] Robert A. Murdie, "Cultural Differences in Consumer Travel," *Economic Geography,* Vol. 41, (July 1965), pp. 211-33. After Berry, *Geography of Market Centers,* pp. 92-93.

The differences depicted in Figure 7 exemplify basic differences in value orientation, the "modern" Canadians demonstrating predisposition for systemic linkage and the Old Order

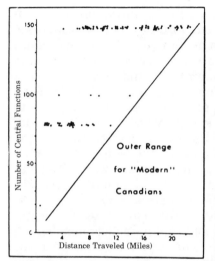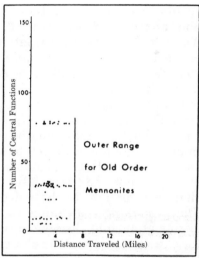

FIGURE 7. Differences in the range for clothing and yard-goods purchases.

Mennonites demonstrating predisposition for boundary maintenance. For the Old Order Mennonites as for the Amish,[41] cities are wicked, as are most of the occupations practiced there. Only farming and a few other occupations are acceptable to God for them as His chosen people. The "Plain People" in many places in the Western Hemisphere have resisted the rationalization and secularization of their ways of life. Despite this resistance they have been able to attain relatively high standards of living. Their achievement in this regard has led some to question the need for ever-increasing urbanization, industrialization, and commercialization. In view of our concern with the use of time and space, it may seem ironic that the Plain People consider it wicked to use tractors and automobiles while some environmentalists speak of the danger of human genocide from pollution.

[41] Charles P. Loomis, *Social Systems,* Essay 5.

Decision-Making and Change. Are there certain general principles to be followed by change agents in attempting to effect community change? For the most part, the authors believe that most change agents go by rule of thumb and experience. In terms of the concepts we have been using, most effective change agents carry their operations through the initiation, legitimation, and execution stages without formally stated principles. We wish to observe that initiation of change requires good "sales procedures." That is, the initiator·must see that the change is identified with the goals of the community and he must attempt to tap the fund of good will of the community. Members of the initiation group really function as salesmen. They attempt to bring the members of the target system who possess power into a favorable frame of mind about the proposed change. Once the initiation group has started this process, the legitimation group may be formed. Here, speaking again in general terms, the roles of the solicitor and the statesman come to the fore. The proposed change is brought to those decision-makers whose function is that of making the change rightful and legitimate. The legitimizing group may, like the initiating group, include members of the change agent and the change target systems. But, when the legitimation process is taking place, all are a part of the community system. Once the change has been legitimized as a "rightful" thing, the execution may go into effect. In carrying out the change, the roles of the administrator and the executive are more important than those of the salesman and the solicitor.

In the strategy of change the processes of initiation, legitimation, and execution are not distinct and separate processes. All may proceed at the same time. There may be different or similar persons in the systems which carry out initiation, legitimation, and execution. It is important to recognize, however, that each process may call for different qualities on the part of the agent.

The decision-making, communication, and boundary maintenance processes as related to pertinent status-roles, patterns of rank and power, ends, and norms of the target system must, of course, be understood by the change agent. In systemic linkage, few considerations are more important than decision-making with respect to timing of the sequence of events and distribution of effort and personnel, often called the strategy of change. How this is accomplished will be illustrated by a case study in this and in succeeding chapters.

INDUSTRY COMES TO A RURAL COMMUNITY

Few rural communities across the nation have not felt influences of industry either on a small or large scale. In fact, many rural communities look to industry as a means of stemming population loss and improving the quality of life. For many rural communities, of course, such hopes are unrealistic and can only lead to disillusionment.

The case study that is excerpted in the following pages is not unlike literally thousands of similar instances throughout the country. The details of each instance contain elements that are unique but in all cases the community experiences change. The present case is condensed to reflect changes in the local community and social action resulting from the introduction of industry. While this case dates from the mid-fifties, it retains a relevance for today.

Mohawk, Michigan[42]

The Pre-Industrial Community. Prior to the coming of a major industry in 1934, the community of Mohawk was a prosperous rural trade center in the southern part of Michigan. The town, established in 1824, formed the center of the community. By 1840, there were approximately 2,500 people in the town. After that the population declined to some extent, reaching a low point in 1894 when 2,210 inhabitants were reported.

Mohawk, however, did not share the fate of several other towns which had been established during the second quarter of the nineteenth century. Some disappeared entirely or became small neighborhood centers as their economy was exhausted, or competition from other towns drew trade away from their stores.

Mohawk was fortunate in being surrounded with fertile farm land. This advantage, along with a few small industries, kept the population of the community fairly close to the 2,500 mark until after 1930. Though serious, even the depression of the thirties did not disrupt the basic economy and way of life to which the people had become accustomed.

Even before 1934, however, the community experienced the effect of industrial experimentation. Many farmers in the area

[42] Charles R. Hoffer and Walter E. Freeman, *Social Action Resulting from Industrial Development.* East Lansing: Michigan AES Special Bulletin 401, September 1955). Excerpted from pages 6 through 24.

were being urged to sell their land to real estate agents who did not clearly identify the actual purchaser. Many did sell. It eventually became known that this land was purchased by the Ford Motor Company, because Henry Ford wished to experiment with manufacturing small parts in a factory to be located in the community.

According to Ford, the people living on the farms could work in the factory during the winter and on the farm in the summer, thereby avoiding the problem of seasonal unemployment, troublesome to employer and employee alike. An industry was actually started in an old factory building, and the "Ford interests" became an important influence in the community until about 1940, when their activities in the community declined. The farms were resold, and the factory building was bought by a button manufacturer. Thus Mohawk, with some favorable and some unfavorable impressions of its contacts with industrialization, was ready to resume its customary way of life. But fate had decreed otherwise.

A New Industry Begins.   A casual visitor in Mohawk today will soon hear about Mohawk Products. It is a thriving industry, employing approximately 4,000 people. The factory started on a small scale in 1934, but has grown rapidly since 1942 when war contracts made it necessary to enlarge the plant. The company now makes compression units for deep freezers and electrical refrigerators.

The Mohawk Products Company was started in Mohawk by four men: a production engineer, an inventor of a new type of compressor, a man who financed the invention, and another who had manufacturing experince. These men chose Mohawk to begin operations. They had only a small sum of money, so it was necessary for the community to help in every possible way. An old timer and factory worker commented as follows about the beginning of the "Products":

> We all worked together when they first came in. The church ladies furnished us with hot soup at lunch time, and we worked long hours getting the factory set up. They didn't even have enough money to pay us at first. I think I have a record of my old pay checks and I'd bet you would find that there were times that I'd get paid less than a dollar for twelve hours work.

From this small beginning, the factory grew to be a major economic influence in the community. In fact, in 1953, the local weekly paper reported that the factory payroll was $19,355,000 for that year. By 1954, the company was operating branch factories in two other states and had completed plans to have a third branch in still another state. A number of other industries are also active in Mohawk, but they are small in comparison with Mohawk Products. There are twelve such industries, and their combined payrolls amounted to $2,418,613 in 1953.

The Present Community. A traveller approaching the Mohawk community on the main highway which goes through the town would see fertile fields and modern-appearing farmsteads. As he gets near the trade center, some new "suburban" developments would become visible. Closer to the center of the town there are dwellings and some store buildings whose appearance clearly indicates that they belong to another era. Occasionally, however, a new, modern business place will be evident, and some of the older store buildings will have modernized fronts. Thus, the old and the new are intermixed in the architecture of the community even as they are in the attitudes and experiences of the inhabitants themselves.

The estimated population of the community (city and trade area) in 1950 was 8,000. According to the U.S. Census report, about half of these people lived within the corporate limits of the town with the remainder living in the trade area on farms or in recently developed housing projects. The trade area includes about thirty-five square miles. [*Territorial limits of the community*]. According to calculations from census data, the population within the town itself increased 37.3 percent from 1940 to 1950. No other Michigan town (exclusive of suburbs) of similar size in 1940 had nearly so great an increase. One place in the northern part of the lower peninsula increased 26 percent, but the population increase of the eight remaining towns used in comparison was less than 15 percent.

The term "native white" would include a high percentage of the population in both the trade center and on the farms. In the town itself, this group constitutes 96.6 percent of the total. Foreign-born whites totaled 3.3 percent of the population. There were only four persons classified in the U. S. Census as "other races" living in the community. Many residents can trace their ancestors back to the eastern part of the United States. A small percentage of the workers in the factories had come recently from south of the Ohio River. In the trade area outside the town there are a few Mexican families who came to work as farm laborers and remained in the community. . . .

The U. S. Census classification by major industrial groups of employed workers living in Mohawk shows that 64.5 percent of the males were working in manufacturing. A total of 16 percent were engaged in wholesale and retail trade. Except for manufacturing, this was the largest group in the town. Nearly 4 percent were classified in professional and related services. About 3 percent were construction workers, and another 3 percent were employed in transportation, communication, and other public utilities. All other industrial groups had less than 3 percent.

The importance of manufacturing in the community is clearly indicated. In actual numbers, the total of all employed males was 1,223. However, a considerable number of persons who worked in Mohawk lived in residences adjacent to the town, the surrounding rural area, or in other towns.

All of the factory workers in the Mohawk Products Company are members of a company union. When a worker is hired, he is put on a 30-day probationary period. At the completion of the probationary period, the worker must become a member of the union if he is to be considered a desirable employee. After becoming a member, his layoffs are union and management problems.

The Products Company also sponsors a plan for payment of hospital bills at the local hospital for employees and their families. There is no deduction in the pay check for this insurance, which is part of a "care" program that has been carried on since the founding of the company. The sales force of Mohawk Products receives the same benefits. Thus, it is clearly evident that Mohawk Products in one way or another constitutes an important, if not dominant, part of the community economy.

The owners and managers of other businesses in the community usually were described as old roots. In several instances, the businesses have been handed down from one generation to another. Many do not care to indulge in any great speculation to increase their profits, and consequently are content to leave their stores or other places of business much as they were years ago. In this group of "main streeters", as some of the newcomers call them, are many respected and influential leaders in the community. [*Power resides in this group*]

Eleven churches are located in the town. These represent the following denominations: Episcopal, Friends, Methodist, Presbyterian, Catholic, Evangelical Lutheran, Baptist, Christian Science Society, Lower Light Mission, Church of Christ, and Assembly of God. Among these, however, the following have most of the membership: Presbyterian, Catholic, Methodist, Baptist, Lutheran, Episcopal, and Friends. Each of the remaining denominations have a membership of less than one hundred; for several, it is less than fifty.

A four-year high-school and four elementary schools are located in the town. A parent-teacher association is active, and community support of schools has been excellent. In 1954, a Catholic parochial school was organized. It is expected that between sixty and eighty pupils will transfer from the public school to the parochial school in 1954-55.

Numerous associations were active in the community at the time of the study. . . . One-half of the associations have been formed since 1942 when the rapid growth of Mohawk Products occurred.

The foregoing paragraphs clearly indicate that as the Mohawk community has increased in population during the last decade, trade and service organizations have been established to meet the needs of the people. Numerous associations were also organized as various members of the community sought expression for their interests or tried to meet certain needs. . . .

Social Action in the Community. Out of a total of eight major action programs, four were initiated by newcomers, three by newcomers and old-timers jointly, and one by outsiders. (See Table) Once these proposals were initiated, opposition developed in six instances. [*Evidence of boundary maintenance activity.*] Active opposition was expressed by old roots five times, and by newcomers and old roots in one instance—the change from village to city form of government.

It is important to note that gaining of approval for social action by the community was accomplished in six instances by old roots and newcomers. The two exceptions were the Ford industry, which was essentially an activity of outsiders and old roots, and the addition to the hospital which was the gift of a newcomer. The name of the hospital was eventually changed to honor this individual.

Once these activities were accepted by the community, they

TABLE
Selected Types of Recent Social Action in Mohawk

Activity	Making the Proposal for Action	Approving the Proposed Action by Groups having Power and Influence	Taking the Necessary Steps to Make the Proposed Action a Certainty
Aspect of Action Involved	INITIATION	LEGITIMATION	EXECUTION
Ford Industries	Outsiders	Old roots (sale of land)	Outsiders (real estate agents) (purchase of land)
Mohawk Products	Outsiders and old roots	Cooperation of newcomers and old roots in getting the factory started	Newcomers (building factory)
Modernization of Main Street	Old roots and newcomers	Newcomers and old roots endorsed the proposal	Newcomers and old roots (construction and improvement of store buildings)

Building Hospital	Old roots and newcomers	Newcomers and influential old roots approved the idea	Newcomers and old roots (contributing funds)
Addition to Hospital	Newcomers	Newcomers approved the proposal	Newcomers (contributing funds)
Charter Change from Village to City Form of Organization	Newcomers and old roots	Newcomers and old roots discussed and approved the change	Newcomers and old roots voting at an election
Addition to School Building	Newcomers	Newcomers and old roots (both favored the addition of more classrooms)	Approving bond issue at election
Fluoridation of Water	Newcomers	Newcomers and old roots (gained approval of city council)	Not approved by city election

were carried out by newcomers and old roots working together in five instances. In one instance, that of the addition to the hospital, approval for the action was achieved by newcomers who were representatives of Mohawk Products. The purchase of farm land in the community, as previously explained, was accomplished by outsiders. One proposed action, the fluoridation of water, was defeated in an election and hence the execution phase of this project did not materialize.

The foregoing paragraphs present in a very brief way certain community action programs. Each one involved months of planning and many more months of voluntary effort on the part of many people in the community. Why did particular projects succeed while others failed? A review of each type of action may answer this question in part. The sociological frame of reference which will be used in making the analysis will be the aspects of social action indicated in the Table, namely initiation, legitimation, and execution, sometimes designated as goal achievement.

Designated in this manner, it may appear that these aspects of community action are relatively distinct and separate. Actually they are not. They are interrelated parts of a continuous social process. It is advantageous, however, to consider them separately because if any one is neglected, the success of programs of community action is less certain. Social action in a community is never a simple process. Many people and social systems are always involved. [*The equilibrium of rank and status roles would be disturbed.*]

The practicability of using these concepts for purposes of analysis is fairly obvious. No project in community change can occur unless someone initiates it. Usually those who initiate action are the community leaders or at least leaders in various community groups, as was true in Mohawk. Initiation of action or proposals for action is a relatively simple matter, but initiation alone is not sufficient. The action must be legitimized; that is, it must have approval of the groups in the community who have social power (authority and influence) to stop the proposed action if they happen to disapprove.

A few examples will help to clarify the meaning of this phase of the action process. In Mohawk, the approval of the modernization of Main Street was gained through the Chamber of Commerce and was supported by both old-timers and newcomers. Another kind of community action, the changing from village to city form of government, was preceded by six years of discussion on the part of all of the major groups in the community.

To initiate action without having reasonable assurance of approval, or at least absence of opposition, on the part of power groups in the community is risky, and the proposed action may never get beyond the initiation stage. Sources of opposition are as numerous and varied as community life itself. A proposed action in one part of community life is almost certain to affect other parts, either directly or indirectly. Hence, opposition is a potential threat to any kind of community action, no matter how necessary or desirable it may be.

The problem of those interested in achieving any type of community action, therefore, is to neutralize opposition as much as possible through publicity and get support of groups having social power with reference to the proposed action. Thus, for example, health programs need the support of medical groups. Matters involving governmental action or expenditure of public funds certainly will be more likely to be accepted if they have the approval of political groups.

Carrying out the proposed action until it is a certainty is a third aspect of the process. This is designated in the Table as execution. Many problems arise in this connection and numerous decisions must be made by the sponsors. In fact, the selection of sponsorship itself may involve important decisions and after it is determined, attention must be given to organization methods, public relations techniques, and methods of financing.

SELECTED REFERENCES

Arensberg, Conrad M. and Solon T. Kimball. *Family and Community in Ireland.* Cambridge: Harvard University Press, 1940.

Beegle, J. Allan and Widick Schroeder. *Social Organization and Land-Use in the North Lansing Fringe.* East Lansing: Michigan Agr. Expt. Sta. Bull. 251 September, 1955.

Berry, Brian J. L. *Geography of Market Centers and Retail Distribution.* Englewood Cliffs, N.J.: Prentice-Hall, 1967.

Duncan, Otis Dudley. *Metropolis and Region.* Baltimore: Johns Hopkins University Press, 1960.

Hathaway, Dale E., J. Allan Beegle and W. Keith Bryant. *People of Rural America.* Washington, D. C.: U.S. Government Printing Office, 1968.

Firey, Walter. *Social Aspects of Land-Use Planning in the Country-City Fringe: The Case of Flint, Michigan.* East Lansing: Michigan Agr. Expt. Sta. Bull. 339, 1946.

Galpin, C. J. *The Social Anatomy of an Agricultural Community.* Madison, Wisconsin: Wisconsin Agr. Expt. Sta. Bull. 34, 1915.

Hughes, Everett C. *French-Canada in Transition.* Chicago: University of Chicago Press, 1943.

Kimball, Solon. *The New Social Frontier: The Fringe.* East Lansing: Michigan Agr. Expt. Sta. Bull. 360, 1949.

Polanyi, Karl. *Trade and Markets in the Early Empires.* Glencoe, Ill.: Free Press, 1957.

Rural Life Studies. *Culture of a Contemporary Rural Community.* Washington: U. S. Dept. of Agri., Bur. of Agr. Econ. (This series contains six separate studies: El Cerrito, New Mexico; Sublette, Kansas; Irwin, Iowa; Lancaster, Pennsylvania; Landaff, New Hampshire, and Harmony, Georgia.)

Sanders, Irwin T. *Making Good Communities Better.* Lexington: University of Kentucky Press, 1950.

Sorokin, Pitirim and Carle C. Zimmerman. *Principles of Rural-Urban Sociology,* New York: Henry Holt and Co., 1929.

Vidich, Arthur J. and Joseph Bensman. *Small Town in Mass Society.* Princeton, N.J.: Princeton University Press, 1968.

Wileden, Arthur F. *Community Development: The Dynamics of Planned Change.* Totowa, N.J.: The Bedminister Press, 1970.

Zimmerman, Carle C., and Garry W. Moneo. *The Prairie Community System.* Ottawa: Agricultural Economics Research Council of Canada, 1971.

Zipf, G. K. *National Unity and Disunity.* Bloomington: Principia Press, 1941.

3

Family and Kinship Systems

In many ways strong families resemble strong communities. The ends or objectives of families are diffuse. They are not often specific enough so that a member can tell another exactly what its purpose is. A typical father will not say that his family exists in order to produce food or to help society control relations between the sexes. Much of the interaction within the family is not rational or instrumental in that it is a mere means to the attainment of specific objectives, as is the case of interaction in a factory run for profit. To the mother, the child is an end in and of itself, and most of the relationships within the family are of this order. Because of these characteristics the family is one of the best examples of Gemeinschaft-like groups.

FAMILY FUNCTIONS

Whether or not family members are conscious of them, the family performs four very important functions in society. First, the family produces children. Second, it provides nourishment and maintenance for its members, a function of special importance while children are still young. Third, it provides the individual of one generation with the most important linkage with the social and cultural systems of previous generations, permitting him to internalize the ends, norms, status-roles, and authority patterns of these systems. In other words, it provides situations, experiences, and affectual relationships whereby socialization may take place. And fourth, it provides each member with an important reference, identification, or placement, ascribing at least during the early part of life specific status-roles and social rank not only in the family, but also in the community. In the words of Murdock, "No society, in short, has succeeded in finding an adequate substitute for the nuclear family."[1]

[1] George Peter Murdock, *Social Structure* (New York: The Macmillan Company, 1949), p. 11.

Murdock and Davis[2] have commented not only upon the universality of these functions of the family, but also upon the fact that the four functions within one social system gives the family system special qualities. These functions are not so inextricably interrelated that they could not be carried on by separate social systems. Procreation, for example, could be a function of those who have nothing to do with the subsequent socialization of the child. Support and maintenance, as in the case of orphanages, may be provided by social benefactors who have no direct part in nourishing or socializing the child. Ascription or placement, although closely connected with socialization is not necessarily and inseparably linked to it. The link between the social and biological functions of the family is cogently expressed by Smith: "Mating and procreation provide for the continuity of the biological species, while socialization relates it to the equally important continuity of social structure and cultural pattern. It has been argued on both theoretical and empirical grounds that the primary function of the family is socialization, so that an intimate relation is established between biological and social processes, a relation which is reflected in the dependence of demographic trends upon social custom."[3]

The family, the group that performs these four functions, differs from all other groupings in society. It is a social system that depends to considerable extent upon biological factors for its solidarity, in that there are sexual relations between two members and biological linkages between all members, or, in the case of adoption, equated biological relations. It is also a work group, a fact too often ignored by many modern students of the family.[4] In the developing areas of the world, it is often the most important production system. A large portion of the population of the world would die of starvation if the family, as a cooperative system that provides food for its members, were to be impaired.

Because of childhood dependency and the slowness of human

[2] Kingsley Davis, *Human Society* (New York: The Macmillan Company, 1949), pp. 395-396; Murdock, *Social Structure,* pp. 11 and 295.

[3] Raymond T. Smith in *International Encyclopedia of the Social Sciences* (New York: The Macmillan Company and The Free Press, 1968), Volume 5, p. 302.

[4] Murdock, *Social Structure,* p. 7. Refer also to Leslie White, "The Definition and Prohibition of Incest," *American Anthropologist,* Vol. 50, No. 3, Part I (1948), pp. 416-434. Carle C. Zimmerman, *Family and Society* (New York: D. Van Nostrand, 1955), Chapter 22.

maturation and socialization, the family must be a relatively permanent group. Perhaps more important, the relationships within the family must be intimate. In all societies the family is an important, if not the most important, source of affectional relationships. This appears to be very important in personality development. Apparently a child must be loved and made to feel secure in order to internalize effectively the elements of the society in which he must live as a more independent adult. It has been inferred that those qualities that make it possible for a member to internalize the native culture and to adjust to adult society can be developed only if during childhood that individual is loved.[5] This is true if the individual is to fill any status-role in modern society, but is more especially true of status-roles, such as those of executives and professionals, characterized by stress. In more general and abstract terms, we may say that ability to function in emotionally neutral relationships, to direct one's life according to universal rather than personal norms, to compete for achieved status, and to fit into status-roles that are very specific in their requirements, necessitates affectional relations during childhood. Throughout human history the family has been the social system upon which society has most consistently relied for the nurturing of these affectional relationships so necessary in the development of stable personalities and the transmission of culture from generation to generation.

VARIATION IN FAMILY FORMS

Although the family is a universal phenomenon, its form is highly variable. The status-roles occupied by family members are specific to a given culture at a given time. What is defined as man's work in one culture may be woman's work in another. Even the status-roles of children vary in many ways from one culture or one epoch to another, especially with regard to the degree of permissiveness considered proper.

[5] Talcott Parsons, *The Social System* (Glencoe: The Free Press, 1951). Parsons maintains that "A need-disposition for diffuse affective attachments is presumably a component of the basic personality structure of all normal people in our society." (p. 238.) "We may say that very generally there are underlying need-dispositions to regress into passive dependency. . . . For example, the reaction to latent dependency needs may be particularly important in the dynamics of a society like our own where the expectations of individualistic achievement are particularly pronounced." (p. 262.)

Hierarchical patterns exhibited in families in all cultures are seldom identical in every respect. Two hierarchical patterns, however, are well known. The patriarchal family is that in which the father is the central authority. The matriarchal family, in which descent is usually traced through the mother, represents a pattern in which the mother exercises great authority in decisions affecting family members.

The family also is not identical throughout the world with regard to the composition of adult members. In some cultures there may be more than one wife for each husband, a form called polygyny; in others more than one husband for each wife, a form known as polyandry; and in others, one husband for one wife, a form called monogamy. Regardless of the particular family form, all cultures possess norms regarding what persons may marry. No culture known possesses norms sanctioning universal promiscuity.

Most families as a social system in all societies tend to be Gemeinschaft-like in that relationships within the family tend to be affectual; responsibilities among members tend to be functionally diffuse and personal, or particularistic; and status-roles and social rank are determined largely by ascription rather than by achievement. However, with regard to these and other Gemeinschaft-like characteristics, there are variations among families in various societies and among various sub-groupings in any one society. Therefore, although it would be improper to classify the families of any known society as Gesellschaft-like, it may be proper to describe the relationships within typical families of a given society as less Gemeinschaft-like than typical families of another given society.

In societies in which the most Gemeinschaft-like families are found, great authority usually resides in one status-role, either in that of the father or the mother. Furthermore, the older generation dominates the younger members who have little to say about the partners chosen for them, or the age at which they will take partners. There is little place for romantic love in the society which relies upon tradition as a source of norms. Social rank is determined almost entirely by ascription, that is, by kinship, age, and sex. If there is geographical mobility in such societies, as among the nomads, the larger family moves as a unit, thus preventing the disintegration of the control of the community over the various family units and adult members over the youth. In the less Gemeinschaft-like family this type of domination may be less prevalent. Families which fall toward the Gemein-schaft pole on various continua are comparable to the consan-guine type of family as developed by Linton; families in which the less Gemeinschaft-like or more Gesellschaft-like characteris-tics prevail may resemble Linton's conjugal type.[6]

In the dichotomy of consanguine and conjugal family types the former consists of a nucleus of blood relatives surrounded by a number of married persons and their children, while the latter consists of married persons and their children. In the consan-guine family, as it was found in pre-communist China, for exam-ple, the most important status-roles are the grandfather, son, and grandson. In societies where this type of family prevails, the change agent cannot ignore the dominant line, whether it be male as in the case of China, or female as in certain other societies.

In the conjugal families solidarity and authority reside with the conjugal pair, and in the typical case both husband and wife are important for the change agent who may ignore such "fringe" elements as grandparents. This type of family, common in western societies and more often in urban than rural areas, is highly mobile and adapted to changing social conditions. It is less efficient than the consanguine type, however, with respect to care for aged, perpetuation of property, and care of children in the event of death of parents.[7]

A different classification of families than those mentioned above is that of the family of orientation (the family into which one is born), and the family of procreation (the family which is created when one is married). Obviously, all types of families mentioned represent both families of orientation and procrea-tion. A typical conjugal family in the United States, for example, represents a family of orientation from the point of reference of the children of the family; it would represent a family of procrea-tion from the point of reference of the father and mother.

Apparently most family systems in the world are moving to-

---

[6] Ralph Linton, *The Study of Man* (New York: D. Appleton-Century Co., 1936), pp. 160-162.

[7] Murdock's nuclear family obviously resembles Linton's conjugal type; his extended family resembles Linton's consanguine type. See Murdock, Chapter 1 and p. 39. As indicated above, families as social systems, whether conjugal or consanguine, nuclear or extended, are more Gemeinschaft-like than they are Ges-ellschaft-like; see also *International Encyclopedia of the Social Sciences*, pp. 301-32.

ward a small-family system similar to the nuclear (conjugal) type. ". . . a reduction of functions in the extended family is accompanied by a reduction in the rights and obligations among extended kin that constitute the extended family system. This reduction in the significance of blood relationships shifts the emphasis from the extended family to the nuclear family."[8]

LARGER KINSHIP SYSTEMS

The larger family having Gemeinschaft-like characteristics seems to lose its solidarity when large structures bearing Western technology develop. The more Gesellschaft-like family form appears to be more compatible with the constellation of bureaucratic social structures that accompany westernization and the introduction of modern technology. The pre-communist Chinese family, grouped into clans which sometimes contained as many as 200,000 to 300,000 members, until recently retained its Gemeinschaft-like character.[9] These families and other clan-like organizations throughout the world also formed large cooperative social systems built from smaller units or building blocks. Apparently the larger consanguine or Gemeinschaft-like families do not constitute suitable building blocks from which to organize modern bureaucracies.

In the larger kinship systems the important building principle is always the manner in which families of orientation are linked to families of procreation. The building principles permit including and excluding individuals who are biologically related to the core of the larger unit. Murdock[10] has described three types: (1) the residential, (2) the consanguineal, and (3) the composite of these, the clan. The residential and consanguineal types are obviously related respectively to Linton's conjugal and consanguineal family types mentioned previously. The residential type includes husband and wife, but not brother and sister. The consanguineal includes both brother and sister and other blood relatives as determined by the rule of descent, but almost never both husband and wife. Since it has these characteristics

---

[8] Robert Winch in *International Encyclopedia of the Social Sciences,* Volume 5, pp. 1-8.

[9] Linton, *Study of Man,* p. 201.

[10] Murdock, *Social Structure,* pp. 65-68.

it can seldom be a residential unit. The residential kinship system's nature is determined primarily by the prevailing rule of residence. The groom may leave his parental home to live with his bride, either in the house of her parents or in a dwelling nearby, a form known as matrilocal residence. The bride may move to or near the parental home of the groom, a form known as patrilocal residence; or the couple may establish residence in or near either the groom's parents or those of the of the bride, a form which is called bilocal. If, as in the United States, the new pair goes to the location of neither family of orientation, a form which has been called neolocal is established. Of the 250 primitive rural peoples studied by Murdock, the following forms appeared: 146 patrilocal, thirty-eight matrilocal, twenty-two matripatrilocal (a form which requires periodic change of residence alternating between the parents of the father and mother), nineteen bilocal, seventeen neolocal and eight avunculocal (a form which prevails in a few societies which prescribe that a married couple shall reside with or near a maternal uncle of the groom).[11]

Whereas the residential kinship system is based upon the prevailing rule of residence, the consanguineal type is based upon the prevailing rule of descent. In other words, it is based upon the cultural principle whereby an individual is socially allocated to a specific group of consanguineal kinsmen. Building blocks for larger systems are created by eliminating the significance to the child of certain members of kin groups. In patrilineal descent, the culture discards the mother's kin group and allows the child to become affiliated exclusively with the father's kin. In matrilineal descent, it is the father's relatives who are discarded. In bilateral descent, such as that of our own society, some of the relatives of both mother and father are discarded. It may be noted that the bilateral descent form has certain disadvantages.

> One result of this peculiarity [failure to designate definite, clearly differentiated, isolatable, discrete kin groups which never overlap with others of their kind] is that the kindred, though it serves adequately to define the jural rights of an individual, can rarely act as a collectivity....
> A particular disadvantage of the kindred appears in the instances in which an individual belongs to the kindreds of

[11] Ibid., p. 17.

two other persons and thereby becomes involved in conflicting or incompatible obligations....

Under unilinear descent such conflicts could never arise....
This advantage may well account in considerable measure for the marked preponderance of unilinear descent throughout the world.[12]

Of the 250 different societies studied by Murdock, 105 were patrilineal, fifty-two were matrilineal, and the remainder were of other types.

The social system based upon both the rule of residence and the rule of descent, the clan, is important in those parts of the world to which Western bureaucratic and instrumental technology has not spread. Of 228 societies for which Murdock had data, units larger than the residential or consanguineal family, called the clan, were absent in 131.

Clans may perform many functions that the immediate family is not of sufficient size to perform. Such functions include military protection, political and governmental operations, organization of religious activities, and maintenance and operation of economic and instrumental enterprises. Clans "tend to arise in a stable, rural society and to disappear when urbanism and industrialism arise. They have played a tremendous role in the history of human society, and even today millions of persons live in clan societies, and many more in societies with a clannish tendency."[13]

DISRUPTION AND THE INCEST TABOO

Since two of man's more important needs are those of sustenance and affectual relations, both of which are provided for in large measure in the family, it is logical to expect that the cooperative relationships that satisfy these needs will be protected by special norms. The incest taboo, the most universal of norms, in reality is a mechanism which apparently prevents disruption of the family or kinship system, the most important production and consumption unit during most of man's existence as a social being. To quote Davis:

[12] Ibid., pp. 61-62.
[13] Davis, *Human Society*, p. 409.

If sexual relations between parent and child were permitted, sexual rivalry between mother and daughter and between father and son would almost surely arise, and this rivalry would be incompatible with the sentiments necessary between the two. Should children be born the confusion of statuses would be phenomenal. The incestuous child of a father-daughter union, for example, would be a brother of his own mother, i.e., the son of his own sister; a stepson of his own grandmother; possibly a brother of his own uncle; and certainly a grandson of his own father. This confusion of generations would be contrary to the authoritarian relations so essential to the fulfillment of parental duties.[14]

Although the functions of the incest taboo as described are largely speculative,[15] there are good logical grounds at least for believing that they are not essentially different from the functions of the norms which guard status-role and social rank in organizations such as bureaucracies.

In a recent popular periodical, the story is told of the president of a large university taking the door off his office so that any college employee could enter at will. According to the periodical, a spirit of democracy prevailed in the office. However, elsewhere it was observed that very few of the students and non-administrative staff members availed themselves of the opportunity of talking with the president. Although encouraged to interact with the president, non-administrative faculty members said they would not feel right about going to the president directly.

It is noteworthy that certain status-roles in the authority structure of a system usually require that the most important interaction be confined to certain specific status-roles. Most frequently, such interaction involves persons of equal rank or of rank immediately above or immediately below. The point we are trying to make is that such interaction is regulated. If it is not regulated, persons in the intermediate status-roles will be placed in stressful positions. Only in exceptional circumstances will a dean feel secure if faculty and staff interact more frequently

[14] Ibid., p. 403. "In no known society is it conventional or even permissible for father and daughter, mother and son, or brother and sister to have sexual intercourse or to marry." Murdock, *Social Structure*, p. 12. See the rare exceptions, p. 13.

[15] Harry C. Bredemeier, "The Methodology of Functionalism," *American Sociological Review*, Vol. 20, No. 2 (April, 1955), pp. 173 ff.

with the president than he does. The dean might say that the situation was developing to a point where there were "wheels within wheels" and that he was getting "the squeeze." In the same manner, in a family, if what is defined as incest were permitted, the father (or mother) presumably exercising authority over the child would find his own prerogative usurped by the child whom he outranks. Thus the incest taboo, the most universal of the norms, appears to prevent disruption. Since for the most of the rural peoples of the world the effective cooperation of the family members in a work team is necessary for existence, it is not difficult to understand why the sanctions against its violation are usually very drastic.

CHARACTERISTICS OF RURAL AND URBAN FAMILIES

We have seen from the preceding discussion that the family system is universal, but that there are many variations in its form and that the form in existence at a given place at a given time tends to represent an adaptation to the circumstances existing at that place and that time. The conjugal family characteristic of this country has numerous Gesellschaft-like traits. But just as there are rural and urban differences in American society, so there are important demographic differences between rural and urban families which will be treated under the following headings: (1) the birth rate; (2) the infant mortality rate; (3) household composition; and (4) age and sex structure.

The birth rate. Among the marked differences between agrarian and industrial societies is the level of the birth rate. Likewise, the farm population in most industrial societies tends to have larger families than the urban population. While this difference is still true in the United States, the rural-urban fertility differential has narrowed materially. Grabill, Kiser and Whelpton[16] comment that the rural-urban fertility differential in

[16] W. H. Grabill, C. V. Kiser, and P. K. Whelpton, *The Fertility of American Women* (New York: Wiley and Sons, Inc., 1958), p. 288. See also Bernard Okun *Trends in Birth Rates in the United States Since 1870* (Baltimore: The Johns Hopkins Press, 1958); Dale E. Hathaway, J. Allan Beegle and W. Keith Bryant, *People of Rural America* (Washington, D. C.: Government Printing Office, 1968), Chapters IV and V; and J. Allan Beegle, "Social Structure and Changing Fertility of the Farm Population," *Rural Sociology,* Vol. XXXI, No. 4 (December, 1966), pp. 415-427.

this country will likely continue to converge since differences in the style of life between rural and urban residents are already small indeed.

In developing societies that are still largely rural, and perhaps to some degree even in the American farm communities, large families are functional. That is, in relation to urban, industrial environments, the rural family is a production unit. Due to high levels of mechanization and specialization on American farms, however, manpower requirements have been reduced. Just as with the urban family, rural families need to be mobile and readily adaptable to change. No longer can farm parents anticipate that their children will remain in agriculture nor in the community in which they grew up.

While birthrates in rural areas remain somewhat higher than in urban areas, it should not be surprising that differences are not great. Several plausible explanations have been proposed for this contraction in the birth rate: (1) the spread of contraception through all strata, a process that has virtually eliminated the differential use of contraception as a basis of differences; (2) the high degree of consensus among Americans that the ideal family size should be from two to four children;[17] and (3) the blurring of class differences as virtually all social segments assume middle class characteristics and as the function of children becomes similar in different social strata.[18]

Over long periods of time, the birth rate in Western societies, in both rural and urban parts, has been declining. The pattern of decline generally is that urban birth rates fall first, followed by those of the rural residents. The most rural portions of a given country, those most isolated from cities, are usually the most resistant to change, including change in the birth rate.

Trends in the marriage and birth rates in the recent past for the United States are shown in Figure 1. The marriage rate reached a peak in the mid-40's, after which it fell to a low in the late 50's. Since that time the marriage rate has been rising. As

[17] Judith Blake, "Ideal Family Size Among White Americans: A Quarter of a Century of Evidence," *Demography*, III, No. 1, (1966), pp. 154-73.

[18] Robin M. Williams, "American Society in Transition: Trends and Emerging Development in Social and Cultural Systems," in James H. Copp, *Our Changing Rural Society* (Ames: Iowa State University Press, 1964), pp. 23-24; also Norman Ryder, "Variability and Convergence in the American Population," *Phi Kappa Deltan*, XLI (June 1960), pp. 379-383.

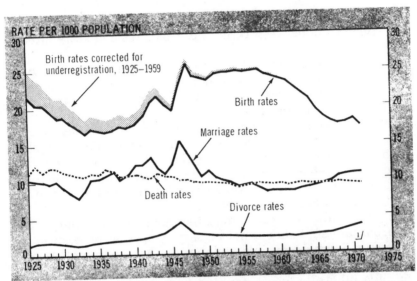

FIGURE 1.   Vital statistics rates for the U.S., 1925 to 1971. (Birth and death rates for 1969, and all data for 1970 and 1971, preliminary.)

shown in Figure 1, live births per thousand total population increased from a low of 17.9 in 1940 to a peak of 25.0 in 1957. Since that time the birth rate has fallen steadily, reaching a low of less than 17.0 in 1972 (provisional data.) The annual number of registered live births exceeded 4 million for the first time in 1954 and remained in excess of that number until 1965.[19] Despite the low birth rate and reduced number of births in the recent past, the population continues to grow at the rate of about 1 percent per year.

Previously we have alluded to the persistence of higher fertility among rural than urban populations as well as the narrowing of group differences in fertility. Tables 1 and 2 serve to make these assertions more concrete. Table 1 shows fertility levels for the urban, rural-nonfarm, and rural-farm parts of counties in conterminous United States in 1960. The measure of fertility is the number of children ever born per 1,000 ever-married white

[19] Robert D. Grove and Alice M. Hetzel, *Vital Statistics Rates in the United States 1940-1960* (Washington, D. C.: U. S. Department of Health, Education and Welfare, 1968), Tables 19 and 80; *Monthly Vital Statistics Report,* Vol. 18, No. 11, Supplement, January 30, 1970.

TABLE 1
Percentage Distribution of Low and High Fertility Rates for White Women, by Residence Components of Counties, Conterminous United States and Divisions, 1960

| U.S. and Divisions | Children Ever Born per 1000 Ever-Married White Women 15 to 44 years old | | | | | | | | |
| | Urban Parts of Counties | | | Rural-Nonfarm Parts of Counties | | | Rural-Farm Parts of Counties | | |
	N	Percent under 2,000	Percent 3,000 & over	N	Percent under 2,000	Percent 3,000 & over	N	Percent under 2,000	Percent 3,000 & over
United States	2,124	19.2	1.3	2,996	2.0	8.0	2,712	0.6	28.6
New England	59	—	—	66	—	3.0	58	—	32.7
Middle Atlantic	143	16.1	—	142	1.4	—	127	1.6	21.3
East North Central	369	5.7	0.5	435	0.5	3.4	418	—	33.5
West North Central	344	10.8	1.2	595	1.0	8.9	603	0.2	34.8
South Atlantic	374	40.6	—	547	4.9	4.4	452	1.8	17.4
East South Central	226	44.7	—	361	2.2	8.8	349	0.6	25.8
West South Central	346	19.1	2.9	456	1.3	8.8	397	0.5	26.5
Mountain	153	2.0	7.2	263	2.7	27.4	194	0.5	44.8
Pacific	110	3.6	—	131	0.8	0.8	114	0.9	16.7

Source: Rodger R. Rice and J. Allan Beegle, *Differential Fertility in a Metropolitan Society*, Rural Sociological Society Monograph, Number 1, 1972.

TABLE 2
Selected Characteristics of Ever-Married Women 15 to 49 Years Old, by Number of Own Children Under 5 years Old, 1968.

Subject	Children under 5 per 1000 ever-married women 15 to 49 years old		
	All Races	White	Negro
U.S. Total	514	504	590
Farm—Nonfarm Residence			
Nonfarm	518	509	584
Farm	428	395	790
Metropolitan—Nonmetropolitan Residence			
Metropolitan	497	488	562
In central cities	491	474	558
Outside central cities	502	497	578
Nonmetropolitan	547	535	672
Years of School Completed			
Elementary: Less than 8 years	516	527	494
Elementary: 8 years	466	434	628
High School: 1 to 3 years	555	529	699
High School: 4 years	510	504	569
College: 1 to 3 years	508	510	532
College: 4 years or more	482	486	384
Labor Force Status			
In labor force	299	277	437
Not in labor force	687	677	793

Source: Current Population Reports, *Women by Number of Own Children Under 5 Years Old, 1968 and 1967,* Series P-20, No. 184, June 16, 1969.

women from 15 to 44 years of age. About one-fifth (19.2 percent) of all urban parts of counties have a low index of fertility (under 2,000) while less than 1 percent of the rural-farm parts of counties have this low index of fertility. On the other hand, 1.3 percent of the urban parts as compared to 28.6 percent of the rural-farm parts of counties exhibit high fertility (3000 and over). The rural-nonfarm portions of counties are intermediate between these extremes. The patterns just outlined are characteristic of all divisions of the United States.

Table 2 shows selected group differences in fertility, by color. The measure used is the number of own children under 5 per 1000 ever-married women from 15 to 49 years of age. In most categories, Negroes exhibit substantially higher fertility levels than whites. Among those with some college education, however, differences are very small. The anticipated rural-urban difference holds true for the metropolitan-nonmetropolitan breakdown but not for the farm-nonfarm breakdown. It is probable that the low fertility level for the farm population merely reflects the high proportion of older women in this population. Hence, this measure of fertility may be spurious since correction for differing age structures should be introduced.

The infant mortality rate. One of the best indexes of the standard of living of a people is the rate of infant mortality. In certain developing areas of the world, it is not uncommon for one-fifth of the children to die during the first year of life. As these societies introduce modern health practices, the general death rate, including the infant mortality rate, will fall. Indeed, just this has occurred in many portions of the developing world and large population increases are occurring.

The infant mortality rate of the United States (number of deaths under 1 year of age per 1,000 live births) has declined over a long period, and since 1960 has continued its decline each year. The infant mortality rate in 1968 stood at 21.8. However, the rate for nonwhites was 34.5 as compared with 19.2 for whites in that year. By 1972, the provisional infant mortality rate had fallen to 18.9.[20]

In general, the more remote rural and economically-deprived areas and regions of the United States exhibit higher infant mortality rates. However, the gap in rates in metropolitan and nonmetropolitan areas has narrowed and varies less than formerly. For example, infant mortality rates in 1968 ranged from a low of 16.9 in North Dakota to 35.5 in Mississippi. However, only seven states had rates under 19.0 (North Dakota, Utah, Nebraska, Hawaii, Idaho, Minnesota, and New Hampshire), and only five states had rates over 26.0 (North Carolina, Nevada, Alabama, South Carolina, and Mississippi).[21]

Recent improvements in infant mortality in the United States,

[20] *Monthly Vital Statistics Report,* Vol. 19, No. 5, Supplement, August 26, 1970, and Vol. 21, No. 3, May 24, 1972.
[21] Ibid.

however, have not kept pace with those in many Northern and Western European countries. It would seem paradoxical that such small improvements have occurred in a period of expanding allocation of resources to medical care and increased migration from rural areas with high mortality rates and relatively poor medical facilities. In considering this problem, a Public Health Service report says: ". . . . Some of the very conditions which, on the surface, might be taken as harbingers of improvement had the reverse result. An outstanding example is the migration of nonwhite persons to large metropolitan areas; in these areas, then, infant mortality increased. The explanation is complex, encompassing many social and program issues. High on the list might well be a lag in community facilities in accommodating themselves to the change and a delay in the adaptation of the in-migrant group to their new medical care and social environment."[22]

Household composition. In addition to the fact that farm families are larger than urban families, they differ in marital status and in other characteristics. Table 3 summarizes some of the differences in regard to family type and composition. "Husband-wife" families are found in larger proportions in farm than nonfarm areas. While about 11 percent of nonfarm families are headed by a female, less than 5 percent of farm families are of this type. In both farm and nonfarm areas, there is a high incidence of female-headed families among Negroes. The mean number of family members by age reflects the older age structure of the farm population. This condition reflects the residual influence of selective out-migration to urban areas over a long period of time.

Table 4 shows the marital status distribution of farm males and females in relation to other segments of the total population. In general, relatively large proportions of farm males are single and small proportions married in relation to other population segments. Small proportions of males are found in most of the marital disruption categories. In contrast, large proportions of farm females are married and very small proportions are found in the marital disruption categories. Some of the differences found are linked to the preponderance of males in the farm pop-

---

[22] *Infant and Perinatal Mortality in the United States,* National Center for Health Statistics, Series 3, Number 4, (Washington, D. C.: U.S. Department of Health, Education, and Welfare, 1965), p. 56.

TABLE 3
Characteristics of Families by Type and Race of Head for the United States, Farm and Nonfarm, March 1969

Subject	Total United States			Nonfarm			Farm		
	Total	Husband-Wife Families	Families with Female Head	Total	Husband-Wife Families	Families with Female Head	Total	Husband-Wife Families	Families with Female Head
Number in Thousands									
All Families	50,510	43,482	5,439	47,880	41,432	5,312	2,630	2,410	128
White Families	45,437	40,355	4,053	42,982	38,083	3,955	2,455	2,273	98
Negro Families	4,646	3,141	1,327	4,489	3,020	1,297	157	120	30
Means									
Mean Size of Family	3.64	3.70	3.32	3.63	3.69	3.31	3.77	3.83	3.49
Mean Number of Members under 18	1.39	1.40	1.47	1.39	1.40	1.47	1.37	1.42	1.25
Mean Number of Members 18-64	1.99	2.06	1.51	1.99	2.06	1.51	2.00	2.05	1.62
Mean Number of Members 65 and over	0.26	0.25	0.34	0.26	0.24	0.33	0.39	0.36	0.63

Note: This table omits "Other families with Male head" and "Other Nonwhite" families.
Source: U.S. Bureau of the Census, *Current Population Reports*, Series P-20, No. 200, "Household and Family Characteristics: March 1969", U.S. Government Printing Office, Washington, D.C., 1970, Table 1.

TABLE 4

Percentage Distribution of Marital Status for the Population 14 Years Old and Over, by Sex and Race for the Total U. S. Population and by Sex for the U.S. Farm Population, 1969

Marital Status and Sex	Total			
			Negro and Other	All
	Both	White	Races	Farm
Male	100.0	100.0	100.0	100.0
Single	27.4	26.4	35.8	32.0
Married, wife present	64.6	66.5	48.9	62.0
Married, wife absent	2.5	1.9	7.4	1.1
Separated	1.4	0.9	5.2	0.4
Other	1.1	1.0	2.2	0.8
Widowed	3.3	3.0	5.3	3.4
Divorced	2.3	2.2	2.6	1.4
Female	100.0	100.0	100.0	100.0
Single	21.8	21.1	27.8	23.6
Married, husband present	58.6	60.6	43.0	66.3
Married, husband absent	3.7	2.7	11.6	1.5
Separated	2.3	1.5	9.2	0.7
Husband in armed forces	0.5	0.5	0.7	0.4
Other	0.9	0.8	1.6	0.4
Widowed	12.5	12.4	13.6	7.9
Divorced	3.3	3.2	4.0	0.6

Source: Current Population Reports, *Marital Status and Family Status: March 1969,* Series P-20, No. 198, March 25, 1970.

ulation, a condition brought about by the selectivity of females in rural-urban migration.

Figure 2 displays the proportions of farm and nonfarm males and females in the marital status category "married, wife present." This figure shows clearly the larger proportions of farm than nonfarm persons in this marital status category at most ages. For all age groups of males beginning with age group 35 to 39 and for all age groups of females beginning with the age group 25 to 29, the farm percentages exceed the nonfarm percentages.

Our data suggest that the American conjugal family has been more resistant to changes in the rural areas. While the family in

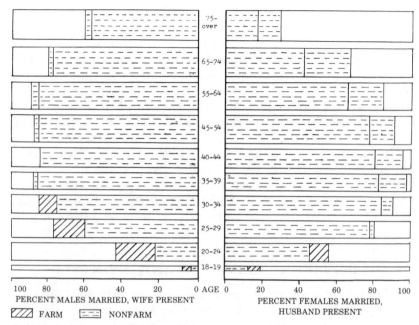

FIGURE 2. Percentage of farm and nonfarm males and females "married, spouse present," U.S., 1969.

rural areas is undergoing changes, evidence of disruption is much less noteworthy than elsewhere.

Age and sex structure. One of the most significant differences between the agrarian, developing areas of the world and the western, industrial societies is their age structure. The respective age structures of the two type areas are in sharp contrast primarily as a consequence of different birth and death rates. Briefly, developing areas have relatively large proportions of young and small proportions of economically-productive and older age groups.

In the United States, the farm population age structure for whites and nonwhites presents a picture of high proportions of youth and older adults, and low proportions of young adults. At most points in this generalized picture, these characteristics are reversed in the urban population. The age features of the rural-nonfarm population are usually intermediate, except for high percentages of children under 5 and low percentages of elderly. Large proportions of males at most ages are typical of the farm population; small proportions at most ages in the urban population.

In general, the proportions of young in the rural population increase as the distance from a Standard Metropolitan Statistical Area increases; the proportions of elderly decrease. Likewise sex ratios (males per 100 females) tend to increase with increased distance from an SMSA. Thus, youth dependency loads are heavier in the more remote, isolated and often economically depressed rural areas.[23]

The difference in the age structure of the farm and urban population is dramatically demonstrated by the age of heads of households. In 1969, 28.5 percent of farm household heads were under 45 years of age while 71.5 percent were 45 years old and over. The comparable urban proportions were 44.6 percent and 45.4 percent.[24]

THE LIFE CYCLE OF FAMILY SYSTEMS

All family systems pass through life cycles, although the consanguine type of family has a much longer existence than the conjugal family because replacement of members in the latter does not provide for the perpetuation of continuous interaction.[25] The conjugal family begins its life cycle at marriage. With the addition of children, the family grows in size until children begin to leave home for employment or marriage. From the period that the last child is born to the time the first leaves home, the family is usually relatively constant in size. As the children leave the parental home the unit decreases, and with the death of the last parent it passes out of existence.

If we examine changes in the life cycle of the American family, we may gain some idea of the changes that the introduction of Western technology may bring to the underdeveloped areas of the world. Table 5 summarizes the recent work of Glick and his associates on life cycle changes. This table shows the average number of years between selected events for women born between 1880 and 1939. Glick and Parke summarize their findings as follows: "Changes during the twentieth century in age at

[23] Hathaway, Beegle, and Bryant, *People*, Chapter III.

[24] *Current Population Reports,* Series P-20, No. 200, Table 17.

[25] See Charles P. Loomis, "Studies of Family Life Cycles," in *Studies of Rural Social Organization* (East Lansing: College Book Store, 1945), pp. 151-152.

TABLE 5

Median Number of Years Between Selected Events in the Family Life
Cycle for Women Born from 1880 to 1939

Subject	Year of Birth (Birth Cohort) of Woman					
	1880 to 1889	1890 to 1899	1900 to 1909	1910 to 1919	1920 to 1929	1930 to 1939
For all Couples:						
First marriage to birth of last child	11.3	9.7	9.3	9.8	9.2-10.2	NA
First marriage to death of one spouse	35.4	38.0	41.2	42.0	43.6	44.5
For Couples Surviving to Marriage of Last Child:						
First marriage of couple to marriage of last child	43.6	32.1	30.8	31.3	30.7-31.7	NA
First marriage of last child to death of one spouse	13.0	14.6	15.9	15.2	15.2-16.2	NA

Source: Paul C. Glick and Robert Parke, Jr., "New Approaches in Studying the
Life Cycle of the Family," *Demography,* Volume 2, 1965, p. 192.

marriage, size of completed family, spacing of children, and life
expectancy have had substantial effects on the life cycle of the
average family. The youngest women for whom data are available compare as follows, on the average, with women who are
forty to sixty years older: The youngest women marry one to two
years younger; their age at the marriage of their last child is four
to five years younger, and their length of married life is about
nine years longer. . . ."[26]

The importance of understanding the life cycle of the families

[26] Paul C. Glick and Robert Parke, "New Approaches in Studying the Life Cycle of the Family," *Demography,* Volume 2, (1965), p. 196.

with which a change agent works should be obvious. Unfortunately, many agencies do not differentiate between families which are in different stages of the life cycle. Blackwell's[27] study of families on relief during the Great Depression indicated that relief agencies gave relatively little assistance to families when there were young children, no doubt because the parents were considered to be more able. These families felt the "pinch" of hard times more than families in other stages of the life cycle which received relatively more relief.

Elsewhere, details have been presented concerning the differences in consumption and production patterns of families in various stages of the life cycle.[28] Such differences are worthy of note for social workers, family suppliers, and adult educators, since the success or failure of their programs is often dependent upon the proportion of families at a given stage of the life cycle. For example, after several county agents told the authors that they had particular difficulties with their programs in certain areas of their counties, we noted from census materials that a large proportion of the farmers were old and that many young adults had left the areas. Areas like these are becoming more common in the United States and pose special problems. Parenthetically, it is interesting to note how few programs in rural areas are designed for older people, even though it is known that the farm population is aging and fewer families are in the early stages of the life cycle.

No social system is as important in the creation of personality and in training for social life as the family. Although social sciences recognize that it is not yet possible to specify exactly how the wide range of personalities encountered in society is formed and how much of the personality is formed by biological inheritance, no one doubts the importance of the family as a socializing agency. For the vast majority of people throughout the world, the family is the first social system experienced, and it is here that many of the lifelong aspirations, expectations, and social understandings or misunderstandings are produced. Even the basic pattern of interaction of individuals is developed in the family.

[27] G. W. Blackwell, "Correlates of Stage of Family Development Among Farm Families on Relief," *Rural Sociology,* Vol. VII, No. 2 (1942), pp. 161-174.

[28] C. P. Loomis and J. A. Beegle, *Rural Social Systems* (New York: Prentice-Hall, Inc., 1950), p. 78 ff.

Ends and objectives. Fichte, the great German philosopher, posed the question: "What noble-minded person does not want as a result of his efforts to view his own life repeated anew in his children and again in his grandchildren in an improved, ennobled and perfected form long after he has died?[29] He is probably correct in expecting the general answer, "none," but the concrete ends of individuals differ from class to class and group to group in each society. Some set as the prime goal a happy family. Others, although relatively successful in their status-roles as family members, judged by the standards of their peers, commit suicide when they fail to achieve in their occupations according to the standards or norms they and their families have learned. Although all socially sensitive people orient their lives to the groups that are most important to them, there is considerable variation in the alternatives chosen, due in no small measure to early training in the family.

Throughout the world, the rural societies generally place a high value on having a family and children. The families of various cultures inculcate in the youth the ends in accordance with the requirements of the system. In the original Hindu family, for the women, "pride in their son became the main consolation of their life but attendance upon their husband remained their chief duty."[30] They also believed that one who does not marry goes to hell. In pre-communist China, few goals were more important for the individual than perpetuating the family. In all cultures, and particularly in rural cultures, the important goals of individuals are instilled in the family.

Norms. Not only does the family implant the goals toward which the individual will later strive, but also the standards by which they may be attained. He internalizes the standards defining what is right and what is wrong, what is good and what is bad. Unfortunately, not enough data are available on rural and urban families to draw conclusive generalizations concerning norms in the two situations. However, the social systems to which rural people belong less frequently impose conflicting norms, partly because they are influenced by fewer reference groups having varying ends and norms. For example, urban parents may attempt to inculcate truthfulness and respect for

[29] Fichte, *Rede an die deutsche Nation.*
[30] Davis, *Human Society,* p. 421.

the property of others as universal norms. At the same time boys' gangs may set the stage for stealing from and lying to those outside these gangs. Such conflicts, although they do exist, are less frequent in most non-urbanized societies.

In all societies the norms of the lower classes differ from those of the upper classes. Since vertical mobility in general is of less magnitude in rural than in urban society, the norms imposed on rural people from birth to death vary less than those imposed in urban society. In fact, cities having heavy rates of in-migration, part of which comes from rural areas, often exhibit high suicide rates. This is, in part at least, explained by problems involved with conflicting values or with a loss, during migration, of reference groups which served to impose norms and ends. Migrants are often like driftwood on the sea. They may have no clear objectives or destination, and they may be confused about their norms or methods of reaching goals.

Societies vary in the amount of emphasis placed upon norms in contrast to ends; in what one might call the *how* as contrasted with the *what* of action. In all societies it is more honorable to have achieved power and wealth according to the norms of the society than by violating them, but in some societies it is more widespread to make the good or rightful life an end in and of itself than in others. The societies which lay great stress upon norms or rightful ways are "sacred" cultures, while others may be more "secular." In general, many of the norms inculcated by the family are ends in and of themselves. Rural societies tend to be more sacred; the ends less frequently justify the means in rural than in urban societies.

These considerations are important for the change agent working in rural society. Often effective procedures and organization are resisted because the old ways are the "right" ways, and new, more efficient ways may be considered sinful, especially if they violate sacred taboos. Although resistance to change is more common in rural than urban areas, it is maintained throughout this book that urbanization is spreading to rural areas throughout the world. The reasons for this have been summarized by Parsons and Bales.

> With the development of modern type of occupational structure in industrialized societies, there must also be a change in family structure if only because the same person, e.g., the husband-father, plays crucially important roles in both

structures, and because children must be socialized for roles in both.[31]

Status-roles. It is in the family and play groups that the individual learns the basic components of the most important status-roles of society. George Herbert Mead and others have observed that the very essence of personality grows out of practice in playing roles to which one must react. Certain family status-roles furnish a reference point which one carries throughout life. It is on the basis of these patterns that fraternal orders and sororities function. In sickness the patient may appreciate the nurse who appears motherly to him, and such imposition of status-roles may be important in the healing arts. In fact the basic status-roles are projected to the unknown and we pray, "Our Father Who art in Heaven. . . ." Religious orders have fathers, brothers and many other status-roles based upon the family pattern. The importance of the family as a prototype of a system of status-roles is obvious. The following expressions are revealing in reference to family status-roles: "He was more like a father to me than a boss"; "He talked to me like a Dutch Uncle and I resolved not to do that again"; or "He acted like a babe-in-arms."

An institution known as the *compadrazgo* establishes status-roles in Latin American communities which appears to function as an integrating agency among the various kinship and class systems.[32] At the birth of a child or sometimes as soon as pregnancy is certain the parents choose a godfather *(padrino)* and a godmother *(madrina)* for the child. These godparents arrange for the baptism of the child, accompany him to the ceremony, and pay for the ritual. In many rural areas the godparents serve as co-parents *(compadres)* and have a lifelong interest in the welfare of the godchild. Thus the institution links two families, providing the godchild a social family of orientation in addition to the biological family of orientation. If a child's biological parents die, it is the duty of the godparents to take the godchild to their home and rear him as their own. Redfield found that urbanization tended to weaken the *compadrazgo* relationships.[33]

In Mexico and most other Latin American countries many

[31] Talcott Parsons and Robert F. Bales, *Family, Socialization, and Interaction Process* (Glencoe: The Free Press, 1955), p. 390.

[32] Sol Tax, et al., *Heritage of Conquest—The Ethnology of Middle America* (Glencoe: The Free Press, 1952), p. 101.

[33] Robert Redfield, *The Folk Culture of Yucatan* (Chicago: University of Chicago Press, 1941), p. 211.

children, particularly those of domestic servants, are born out of wedlock. The authors have advanced the hypothesis that this practice is self-perpetuating, not only for economic reasons, but also because children have no opportunity to internalize the father's status-role, since they may never know their biological father or any other man in the status-role of father.[34]

The status-roles of the members of rural families are usually relatively fixed with age and sex being the principal determinants. What is the status-role of the man in our society may be the status-role of the woman in another; what is done by adults in one may be done by children in others. But in any specific rural society, certain status-roles are prescribed according to age and sex. When activities are rationalized, it is often found that there is no intrinsic reason for the division of labor, and activities which in the rural hinterland are women's work may become men's work in the cities. Rural males from outlying districts in this country may be surprised to find male cooks, male bakers, or male dress designers in city establishments.

Any male agricultural agent, especially in Latin American but in most underdeveloped areas where there is separation of the sexes, may find it difficult to change practices in the home, because as males they are not permitted interaction with the women who occupy housekeeping status-roles. The status-roles of physician and priest, in part at least, have met the difficulty of bridging sex status-roles in that the church father and the medical doctor advise women in the province of their status-roles. These examples are mentioned merely to stress the importance of knowledge of the status-role structure of families and society if change is to be understood. The part of the women in cultural change in the so-called backward areas may be great indeed. In areas in Latin America which are relatively untouched by modern Western technological culture, the acceptance and use of the sewing machine and corn grinder by women is more general than other types of acculturation and has demonstrated women's importance in cultural change.

[34] In this connection, the convergence of research done by Bales and by Parsons has significance for rural sociology. The former differentiated two types of leaders which cannot be alternated, namely the "task or instrumental leader" and the "popular or expressive leader." Parsons delineates the "male-instrumental" and "female-expressive" status roles. Parsons and Bales, *Family,* Chapter 1, 5, and 7.

Power. The authority and rights of the members of families are prescribed by law and custom in all societies and furnish the basic pattern of control. In Freudian and neo-Freudian psychological theory, the father figure which may represent a strictly disciplinarian role is internalized and may furnish the generalized basis whereby individuals respond to and occupy roles of authority. Of course, from a broad anthropological and sociological viewpoint, in many cultures the biological father is not the disciplinarian at all. In all societies, however, one status-role, whether it be the biological father, the biological mother, or the uncle, has more authority over family members than other status-roles. Regardless of what status-role articulates authority, that role extends and receives less affection than more expressive status-roles. In societies in which grandparents relinquish control over sons and daughters who marry and have children, the grandparent-grandchildren relationship is usually warm and indulgent; in societies in which such control is not relinquished, this relationship is usually more formal.[35]

In general, we may say that the activities of different family members in large measure determine the authority within the family. The pattern of authority and immunity from authority within the family is related to the evaluation members place upon given status-roles. Among the Eskimos, for example, the women prepare food and clothing while the men are fishing and hunting away from the igloos. This indispensable division of labor and resultant status-roles permits little opportunity for either sex to become dominant.[36]

The observation has been made repeatedly that the children of immigrants to the United States are relatively immune from the influence of authoritarian parents, owing in large measure to more complete assimilation of the children and their economic importance to the family unit. Humphrey[37] reports that Mexican girls in Detroit often declare their independence from their fa-

[35] For a comparative discussion of affinal relationships, see Gloria A. Marshall in *International Encyclopedia of the Social Sciences,* Volume 10, pp. 8-18.

[36] Loomis and Beegle, *Rural Social Systems,* p. 46. Based upon a study of family systems by Zelditch, Parsons and Bales, it is concluded that most nuclear families differentiate between status-roles characterized by task leadership and power on one hand and by expressive functions on the other. In the American middle class "the cult of the warm, giving 'mom' stands in contrast to the 'capable,' 'go-getting' male." Parsons and Bales, *Family,* p. 339.

[37] N. D. Humphrey, "The Changing Structure of the Detroit Mexican Family,

thers, partly because of their economic value. Girls can earn money in Detroit, whereas in Mexico it is more difficult. In the economic life of the typical Mexican family in Mexico, the young girl is often an economic loss and has little chance for an independent existence outside the family. In all of the societies from which modern Western urban technological culture developed, the biological father is the chief authority.

For any change agent attempting to change farm and home practices, it is important to know to whom and under what circumstances action is initiated in the ordinary family. When agents attempted to introduce improved home practices into Macedonia, for instance, the men said women would become immoral if they had more time through the use of improved practices.[38]

Of course, the general authority structure of the family in a given society is never enough for a change agent to know. Very frequently, even where the society pronounces the father as the "lord and master," the intelligent wife may have every aspect of the home and farm "under her thumb." This is obvious in all societies, and makes it possible to illustrate the difference between authority, or the right to influence others, and influence that is not necessarily based upon this right. In this connection, we may mention the problem of deviancy in the matter of family control. In any society in which the husband is supposed to be in control and is not, he is certain to occupy a stressful position. In our own culture, where achievement is rated highly, mediocre men married to successful professional women almost universally betray evidence of stress from this source by overacting, false claims, and in many other ways.

Social rank.   As indicated previously, one of the most important functions of the family of orientation is that of placement of the members in the larger society. Marriage establishes the social rank in the general society for members of the family of procreation. Here we are most concerned with the rank of the members within the family, but it should be remarked that in general the rank or standing in the family given to individuals because

---

An Index of Acculturation," *American Sociological Review,* Vol. IX, No. 6 (December, 1944), pp. 622-626.

[38] H. B. Allen, *Come Over into Macedonia* (New Brunswick, N.J.: Rutgers University Press, 1943).

of sex and age is carried into the larger society. For instance, "the rule of residence helps explain the 'low' position of Hindu women. Since daughters were destined to leave the household at an early age, they were not valued as highly as were the permanent male members. The incoming daughters-in-law, young strangers from another household, were equally disvalued. They were felt to be of a lesser order than the males of the household. Not until they bore a son did they gain respect in their adopted home."[39]

Sanctions. We may observe that generally the more desired resources a system has to offer as rewards to its members, the more effectively it may enforce its norms on its members. It has been observed that the small urban middle class family enforces its norms upon the children more effectively than the urban lower class family, in part because of the available rewards such as toys, costly pleasures, and the like, which may be withheld in case of disobedience.

Davis and Havighurst claim that ". . . the culture of middle class Europeans and Americans probably exerts more severe pressure upon the young child—upon both his bodily processes and his emotional development—than does the culture of any other people in the world."[40] These writers claim to have evidence that children from the middle class, families whose patterns are the pace-setters for the Western world and increasingly for the whole world, suffer from this imposition. They may develop thumb sucking, nail biting, hay fever, asthma, and other manifestations. Possibly without sufficient proof, these writers imply that rural and urban conditions lead to entirely different personality structures. Some of the claims about the influence of early child training in respect to toilet training have been questioned.[41] The rural family has available, perhaps, greater opportunity to apply the sanction system than the urban family.

[39] Davis, *Human Society,* p. 421.

[40] W. Allison Davis and Robert J. Havighurst, *Father of the Man* (New York: Houghton-Mifflin Co., The Riverside Press, 1947), p. 10.

[41] William H. Sewell, "Infant Training and the Personality of the Child," *The American Journal of Sociology,* Vol. 58, No. 2 (September, 1952), pp. 150 ff. See also W. H. Sewell, P. H. Mossen, and C. W. Harris, "Relationships Among Child Training Practices," *American Sociological Review,* Vol. 20, No. 2 (April, 1955), pp. 137-148. Britton K. Ruebush, "Childhood Mental Disorders," *International Encyclopedia of the Social Sciences,* Vol. 10, pp. 161-2.

Sanctions are applied to reward assistance in achieving the family's goals or to penalize failure in this respect. When the father must pay for hired labor at present rates, he and his son can easily see what the son contributes to the enterprise when he works effectively. Also, the mother who must buy food if the chickens and garden do not produce can see the contribution she and her daughter make to the home. In most urban situations it is more difficult to arrange reward sanctions according to contribution to the attainment of family goals.

Change agents have long recognized the importance of the sanction system in introducing change. Often the skeptical father has permitted the son to have a 4-H Club or Future Farmers of America project, such as a purebred calf or a plot for a special crop. Many changes in farm practices have resulted when the son's project demonstrated the value of the new methods.

Facilities. The social rank of a farm family is very closely related to its facilities, or the means of attaining its ends. Within each type of farming area a different pattern of enterprise exists, and the principal variations are the facilities, or the means employed in earning a living. In the range-livestock areas, for example, the size of the ranch and the number of livestock are important. In the dairy areas, the quality and size of the herd and the general farm layout, including feeding and milk handling facilities, are important. In general, facilities and their use are the subjects of farm management and we shall not go into them in detail here. We shall, however, make the claim that in attaining a given level of living with a given family-sized farm or ranch organization, the facilities available are not more important in the operation of the system than the team work of the members in the various status-roles of the enterprise.

Territoriality. We have discussed the important influence of the norms of culture dealing with the residence of pairs after marriage. Of course, kinship systems in which it is the custom of the wife to live with the family of the husband may be expected to differ in structure from those in which the husband goes to live with the wife's family. Both of these types may differ in structure from the family formed when the husband and wife, upon marriage, establish their own homestead separate from the families of orientation of both husband and wife. In societies throughout the world, the most prevalent types are the patrolocal and the neolocal.

The effect of territoriality upon who will marry is of interest to sociologists. Even in highly mobile Western urban societies, parents may predict that most of their children will marry those they meet in their immediate or adjacent communities. Originally in most rural societies, the individual "stayed put" spatially, married, and produced children whose grandparents lived not far distant, possibly even in the same house. Now, in the areas which have come under the influence of modern Western technology, two giant forces, one the occupational system and the other the family system, struggle to gain control of the individual. So compelling is the occupational force and so great the distances to which it dispatches its victims that now millions of children in these societies grow up without even knowing their grandparents. Other millions are almost completely out of contact with their parents, brothers, and sisters.

SOCIAL PROCESSES IN THE FAMILY

Communication.   Few social systems offer better opportunity for the study of social factors in communication than the family. In all societies, the elements we have just discussed are of vital importance to communication. Among the Navajos, for example, the husband must not communicate with the mother-in-law as he does with others. In fact, he must turn away as soon as he learns of her presence near him. Generally throughout the world, different words and ideas may be expressed only within given age and sex groupings. This restriction on interaction and communication appears to be a device provided by culture to prevent persons in status-roles between which there is tension from expressing their feelings in open conflict. In our society, boys may tell jokes or use language which is inappropriate to use when their sisters are present even though recent changes have reduced these differences.

Joking relationships and joking subjects such as the mother-in-law joke are more closely associated with some status-roles in the family system than with others. All of these phenomena are the manifestations of potential stressful relations in the system involved, and demonstrate the impossibility in organized society for everyone to treat and to be treated alike. In the interest of effective attainment of its ends, each family system has developed certain norms which control communication between members in the various status-roles of the system. Also each family has certain experiences and related forms of communication not transferred to the outside.

In general, as rural families come under the influence of modern urban technological culture, the various social factors making for differentiation in communication between one pair of status-roles as compared with that between another is lessened. In these respects, there is considerable variation from class to class and group to group in rural as well as urban culture. Wives come to share the jokes and profanity of their husbands, and children may share certain aspects of the adult world of discourse at an earlier age. Whether this is because the various status-roles come to have more equal rank, or because the family is relatively less important in attaining individual goals and hence does not require these inhibitions, is not known. Also the equalizing and leveling effect of urbanization should not be overestimated. In all industrialized societies there are differences in the manner in which members in different status-roles within the family are expected to communicate with one another. Because of the different functions of the different status-roles, it is probable that these differences will always remain. No man can internalize all the experiences of a woman and vice-versa, and for this reason communication between mothers and daughters may be expected to be different than that between fathers and sons. This, we predict, will remain true in cities where men may wash dishes or change diapers. In rural areas, where the differentiation in status-roles is greater, urbanization will probably tend toward, but not accomplish, equalization of status-roles.

Decision-making.   One of the authors, after accompanying a rural sociological investigator on one of his visits, described decision-making in a Dutch orthodox family living in South Holland, Illinois, as follows: "After we finished the evening meal the father reached under the table, pulled out a Bible, and read a few verses while all listened in subdued silence. As he calmly slipped the Bible back in place, all heads were bowed, and a prayer was pronounced supplicating the Almighty to sustain and purify the family, and us, the guests. Then there was a brief period of friendly discussion, involving events of the day and what would be done tomorrow. This ended abruptly when the father's gaze swept past all the children's eyes and moved with theirs to fasten on the clock with its hour hand at eight and min-

ute hand at twelve. The eyes of the children came back to the
father, then to us, the guests, as if to say, 'Does their being here
make a difference?' No word was spoken. The father's gaze settled this question by moving toward the stairs and immediately
every child rose, placed his chair under the table, said good-by
and good night, and filed off upstairs to bed."[42]

There should be no question who was the chief decision-maker in this instance. Based upon patriarchal control, a pattern
was articulated which is much more common in rural societies
than in modern industrialized urban cultures. Throughout most
of the rural peasant cultures of the world, the father or the oldest
male most frequently wields the greatest power. As modern urban technology engulfs rural society, the mother and children
may come to have more power and to play more important parts
in decision-making in the family. But in no industrial society is
the husband and father, insofar as he is a functional member of
the family, not a decision-maker. The pattern and pressure of his
occupation may make him almost a stranger to his family, but
still in important matters such as where the family will live and
what the occupational activity will be, his is the greatest influence. In fact, if the basic assumptions upon which we base our
theory of social systems is correct, the effective articulation of
the two basic systems, the family and occupational systems, requires that the husband and father make basic decisions. Since
the factories, commercial establishments, and other bureaucracies and organizations of the Western world must be manned
by family members, social rank in family systems and occupational systems must be coordinate. As a general pattern, either
the man or the woman must "wear the pants" in both systems;
otherwise, decision-making tensions would develop which would
disrupt one or the other system. If our assumptions are correct,
since men and women cannot change places in the family in
production of children, statuses of men and women are not likely
to be equal, even in an industrial society.

Boundary maintenance. Waller has observed that the family
"has two elements of strength, the one, that it is private, the
other, that it is public, and from neither of these is the group

---

[42] Notes made by C. P. Loomis while supervising the field work which
resulted in the publication: *Social Relationships and Institutions in an Established Rurban Community, South Holland, Illinois,* by L. S. Dodson. Social Research Report No. 16, (Washington, D. C., BAE, USDA 1938).

outside altogether excluded."[43] Culture provides social systems, such as the family, with institutions which make it possible for outsiders to interact with at least some family members. The status-roles of the friend, the guest, the stranger, the outsider, and the host are all available to determine behavior within the situation. Literature is full of instances whereby the family maintains its boundaries on the one hand, but at the same time acts out its function in the total society by maintaining standards of hospitality.[44] Thus, in most societies, socialized individuals learn at an early age that it is not only impolite as an outsider to become embroiled in family squabbles, but is often unsafe. The family quarrelers may turn on the intruder, offering an example of boundary maintenance reflected in the proverb: "Blood is thicker than water." On the other hand, norms of hospitality which function to make larger groupings in society possible may require that a person, while in the home of the host, be treated with the utmost consideration even when his behavior is insulting, both parties knowing that once the guest leaves a struggle may ensue.

Perhaps no norms differ more from culture to culture than those that make possible boundary maintenance and hospitality, two apparently opposing processes. Obviously, such norms are of great importance to change agents attempting to introduce improved health and other practices. In some cultures, such as those in Latin America, it is difficult for outsiders to become intimate with families, a fact which is of utmost importance, since intimacy is usually necessary to effect the adoption of change. Tax writes, "A new means of making a living—a new crop, a new industry, or a new business—spreads first to relatives and neighbors, thus eventually becomes widespread in one community before it diffuses to a second . . ."[45] For the developing areas of the world, most improved practices must be incorporated in the family. All social systems, and particularly the family, have boundary maintenance mechanisms. In most societies with solidary families, it goes without saying that boundary maintenance is strong. Change agents must expect resistance to

[43] Willard Waller, *The Old Love and the New* (New York: Liveright Publishing Corporation, 1930), pp. 106-107.

[44] See Charles Lamb, "A Bachelor's Complaint on the Behavior of Married People" for example.

[45] Tax, et al., *Heritage of Conquest*, p. 46.

change, particularly if the change is thought to threaten the solidarity of the family.

Systemic linkage. The role of the family as a change system has been very great throughout history. A revealing manner in which to weigh its importance in America would be through the analysis of the comparative impact upon the society of immigrants coming as family units as compared with immigrants coming as individuals. The family and social customs of every state in the United States have been affected by this type of systemic linkage. However, in terms of relative numbers or any other criterion, those coming as families have produced greater changes than those coming singly. In fact it is difficult to trace a single change in the basic family structure of the United States due to the thousands of blacks from Africa who came without families or who were separated from their families. In view of the fact that the family systems in which the blacks had lived differed so greatly from those in the areas to which they came, and in view of the large numbers which came to this country, it would seem plausible to assume that had they come as families their influence even with their low social rank would have been greater. The fact that no apparent influences from African forms of the family were enduring supports our theory that the influence of single individuals apart from their families has less effect in social change than families as units. The experience in Haiti and Brazil, where more family unity was permitted and where African traits persist, seems also to support this view. Perhaps the most interesting description of systemic linkage of family systems is recorded in the literature describing the impact of Spanish and Portuguese family systems upon the Indians of Latin America. We suggest the following hypothesis concerning this particular linkage: Other things being equal, the larger the proportions of immigrants migrating as families from the mother country, the more completely the Iberian family institutions are now found in the new country. (Costa Rica and Eastern Bolivia readily illustrate this point.)

A CASE OF SYSTEMIC LINKAGE

In the following case, one of the authors reports an event in his youth which it is hoped will make the concepts we are using meaningful and illustrate the process of systemic linkage.

The italicized comments are intended to relate the events to the elements and processes involved in systemic linkage.

Crisis in Harvest Season

My family lived on a farm in western Nebraska on the irrigated margins of the range-livestock and the wheat areas. One of the main crops was sugar beets, and the events relevant to the case history occurred during the annual beet harvest.

Beet harvests were periods of strenuous and continuous work against time—against the impending bitter cold weather which would freeze the beets in and prevent even the best beet lifter from pulling them. The general pattern was for us children to stay out of school to help in the harvest, and extra hands were also hired. Father ran the beet puller, and sometimes when he was ahead of the toppers he helped with the hauling. Mother and the younger children were toppers who knocked the dirt off the beets by hitting them together, then cut the tops off, and threw the beets into neat piles for the haulers. When I was about twelve, I joined the three hired hands as a hauler. The haulers loaded the beets into horse-drawn wagons and drove them three miles to the nearest railroad where they were dumped into railroad cars from a beet dump. [*The status-roles which came into play in the family beet harvesting operations were the toppers, haulers, and a puller. The power structure, including the authority and influence patterns, was somewhat complicated as will be indicated by the following.*]

The hired men called father the boss, and once when father asked me to tell the hired men what to do, something which he did fairly frequently, one hired man said, "When I took this job I didn't know I'd be takin' orders from a kid." [*The father, not the rest of the family, had authority to give orders.*]

Work started early, and it was always difficult for father to get the hired men up early enough. The three hired men and my younger brother and I slept in the upstairs which was one large room over the rest of the house. The other members of the family slept downstairs. At 4:00 each morning father got up, made the fire in the cook stove, and lit the lanterns. Before going to the barn to start feeding, currying, and harnessing the horses and milking the cows, he always tried to awaken the men. He yelled loudly enough to be heard a quarter of a mile, "Charles, get up! It's time to do the chores!" Of course, this implied that everyone was supposed to get up. [*Communication was indirect.*]

One time after father yelled, Slim from Wyoming yawned and said, "Charlie, does your dad think them beets is alive an' gonna run off if we don't sneak up on 'em in the dark?"

One year just after World War I, when I was fourteen, a crisis arose. That fall the banker and one of the farmer members of the board of directors of the bank, a man of high *social rank* in the community and highly respected, paid a visit to the farm. They recommended to father that he borrow money on a loan on the farm and buy feeder stock to fatten during the winter. Father had never fed cattle or sheep before, but he knew the advantages of the operation in terms of the manure for the beet land. However, father was not aware of the availability of credit for the operation. The banker explained how much money could be made by feeding out the sheep on the beet tops, alfalfa hay, and corn grown on the farm. After the visitors left, father visited several farmers who had fed stock previously, talked it over with mother, and decided to take the banker's advice. He would borrow the money, sign the mortgage on the farm and buy about 3,000 sheep to feed out.

[*Here the bank was the principal change agent and the family was the change target. What we have called systemic linkage was achieved when the money was borrowed. As in the case of most family operations, the facilities are often difficult to differentiate from the ends or objectives. The various facilities are interrelated. A loan would increase soil fertility through the purchase of livestock.*]

[*The banker's tactics involved initiation of the plan with the chief decision-maker of the family, the father, and relating the ends of the proposed change to the ends of the family and the bank. Part of the strategy involved having the farmer board member, whom father respected, present when the banker talked. Positive sanction or rewards such as money income, fertilizer to bring increased yields, and better returns for the other products of the farm as well as use of the facilities of the farm during the idle winter months were stressed. The decision-making involved the judgment of the banker which the father respected, the advice of the farmers whom the father visited, and finally the mother. She said the decision was not hers, but father would probably not have decided as he did if she had opposed him, because she had influence in such matters. So far as the bank was concerned, the processes of legitimation and execution were one. When father signed the mortgage to borrow the mon-*]

ey, the action was legitimized. The change system (the bank) and the target system (the family) had merged. Systemic linkage was accomplished. This merging of systems gave legal basis for new status-roles—father became a debtor, the banker his creditor. Later, when the depression came on, we were all made to feel our status-roles as debtors. Our social rank in the community was affected adversely.]

The decision to buy sheep led father to go south to Texas to buy the sheep in the middle of the beet harvest. Father doubted the wisdom of being away during the harvest for the two or three weeks the trip would require. The beet harvest was the most important farm operation in the region, and the beets must be harvested before the winter, which comes rapidly and severely on the northern great plains.

After father left, mother became the boss, but I at fourteen was carrying part of the supervisory load. Mother sent me to carry instructions and to find out how things were going at the various points of activity. The general work pattern of everyone was the same after father left, except that before going he hired another man to run the beet puller. Also, this year he had hired a different set of beet haulers than he had the year before. The informal leader of the men was a young Russian-German from the area, named Jake. *[Jake had non-authoritarian influence over the men.]* Jake was always saying, "Women should not wear the pants" and claiming that if he ever married he would be the boss of his family. The others were also single and from the cattle country of Wyoming.

Things went all right for a few days. Then the haulers began failing to get up when mother called them. This put the workers in the field an hour late, but mother was willing to put up with it since father should be home before too long.

It was customary Saturday nights, when the men were paid, for the boss's family to drive them into a neighboring town. The first Saturday after father left, mother had me drive the men to town in the Ford. I went to the movie, and when I came back to the place where I had parked the car it was missing. I waited around a long time, then went home very much worried. Mother was terribly upset and none of the family could sleep the rest of the night. About four o'clock in the morning Jake and the men came driving the car home. They had taken girls out and had been drinking. After mother sized up the situation, she fired all the men and they left without going to bed. [*As was common among farm families in the area, our family was what may be called Puritanical. No one drank or smoked. Thus this drinking as well as the stealing of the car violated the family norms. The car was something the hired men at this period were never permitted to use. Mother used negative sanctions by discharging them. Although the men seemed to resent her authority previously, they had no doubt of her right to discharge them, thus demonstrating that her authority to discharge was legitimate. Obviously, discharging the men was a boundary maintenance reaction.*]

During the next days we feverishly hunted for help up and down the valley and learned that there were no haulers available anywhere. We became frantic, with winter coming and most of our crop still in the field. Mother called her brother, Frank, who ran a farm similar to ours three miles away. He could not spare any of his help. Knowing that the men mother had fired were still in town unemployed and that if we didn't push ahead with our harvest we would lose our crop, he advised mother to rehire the men. Mother resisted. She said she thought this would be practically immoral, since it would make the men think that their actions of drinking and stealing were all right. However, she finally gave in on condition Uncle Frank would give the men a "talking to."

Uncle Frank, instead of bawling the men out as mother expected him to, told them, unknown to her, that they had a responsibility to get the beets out and that this was about the best place to work in the valley. They couldn't get better pay or food and the hauls were so long that the work wasn't hard. [*Allocation of rewards, positive rather than negative sanctions, were stressed.*]

The men complained about taking orders from "women" and "kids." Uncle Frank told them he'd drop over as often as he could to supervise the work, and this seemed to satisfy them. [*In other words, he provided more legitimate authority.*] Actually Uncle Frank lived too far away to get over often. [Here *spatial arrangements or territoriality were important in preventing his authority from functioning.*] No real trouble developed, but I was always aware of the fact that the men thought neither mother nor I had the right to direct them.

After father returned, everyone engaged in the big sheep drive from town to our farm. Even the Wyoming cowhands who usually had nothing but curses for sheep and sheep herders enthusiastically helped get the sheep out to the farm. After we listened to father's tall tales of Texas ranching, the beet harvest got under way in earnest. Everything ran quite smoothly, and all the beets were out before the ground froze solid.

SELECTED REFERENCES

Agrarian Societies in Transition, The Annals, Vol. 305, (May 1956). See especially "Economic Change and the Extended Family," by Jean L. Comhaire, and "The Unpredicted Pattern of Population Change," by Kingsley Davis.

Bultena, Gordon L. "Rural-Urban Differences in the Familial Interaction of the Aged," *Rural Sociology,* Vol. 34, (March 1969).

Brown, James. *The Farm Family in a Kentucky Mountain Neighborhood* and *The Family Group in a Kentucky Mountain Farming Community.* Lexington: Kentucky Agr. Expt. Sta. Bull. 587 and 588, August-June, 1952.

Copp, James, ed. *Our Changing Rural Society: Perspectives and Trends.* Ames: Iowa State University Press, 1964.

Economic Research Service, U.S.D.A. *The Economic and Social Condition of Rural America in the 1970's.* Washington: U.S. Government Printing Office, 1971.

Glick, Paul C. "The Family Cycle," *American Sociological Review,* 12, No. 2, (April 1947).

Kollmorgen, Walter. *Culture of a Contemporary Rural Community, The Older Order Amish of Lancaster County, Pennsylvania. Rural Life Studies.* Washington, D. C.: U. S. Dept. Agr., September, 1942.

Lewis, Oscar. "Husbands and Wives in a Mexican Village," *American Anthropologist,* 51, (1949). Reprinted in Olen E. Leonard and Charles P. Loomis. *Readings in Latin American Social Organizations and Institutions.* East Lansing: Michigan State College Press, 1953.

Linton, Ralph. *The Study of Man.* New York: D. Appleton-Century Co., 1936.

Martindale, Don and R. Galen Hanson. *Small Town and the Nation.* Westport, Conn.: Greenwood Publishing Corporation, 1969.

Mirande, Alfred M. "Extended Kinship Ties, Friendship Relations and Community Size: An Exploratory Enquiry," *Rural Sociology,* Vol. 35, (June, 1970).

Murdock, George Peter. *Social Structure.* New York: The Macmillan Co., 1949.

Rice, Rodger R. and J. Allan Beegle. *Differential Fertility in a Metropolitan Society.* Rural Sociological Society Monograph, Number 1, 1972.

Schwarzweller, Harry K., James S. Brown, and J. S. Mangalam. *Mountain Families in Transition.* University Park: The Pennsylvania State University Press, 1971.

Strauss, Murray A. "Social Class and Farm-City Differences in Interaction with Kin in Relation to Societal Modernization," *Rural Sociology,* Vol. 34, (December, 1969).

Shapiro, Sam, Edward R. Schlesinger, and Robert E. Nesbitt, Jr. *Infant, Perinatal, Maternal and Childhood Mortality in the United States.* Cambridge: Harvard University Press, 1968.

U. S. Department of Health, Education and Welfare. *Health Resources Statistics.* Rockville, Md., February, 1972.

4

Informal Social Systems

Throughout the world, networks of informal social relations play an important role in the lives of people. Informal groupings such as the play group and congeniality groupings are important to personality formation and, outside the family, often supply the security necessary to normal mental and emotional development.

DEFINITION OF INFORMAL GROUPS

Before proceeding with the discussion of informal social systems, it is appropriate to make explicit the meaning of clique groupings. In the literature dealing with informal social systems, terms such as "informal," "congeniality," "friendship," "mutual-aid," and "clique" groups are often used interchangeably. For our purposes, no distinction will be made between them. The group, as used in this chapter, is most often a nonkinship grouping and is defined in the same way as Warner and his associates use the term "clique." To quote Warner:

> ... membership ... may vary in numbers from two to thirty or more people ... When it approaches the latter figure in size, it ordinarily breaks up into several smaller cliques. The clique is an informal association because it has no explicit rules of entrance, of membership, or of exit. The clique does have very exacting rules of custom which govern the relations of its members .... Members speak of others in the community as outsiders. Feelings of unity may even reach such a pitch of intensity that a clique member can and does act in ways contrary to the best interests of his own family. . . . Its activities vary according to the social position and relative wealth of its members.[1]

[1] W. Lloyd Warner and Paul S. Lunt, *The Social Life of a Modern Community* (New Haven: Yale University Press, 1941), pp. 110-111.

The informal group is found everywhere as an essential part of social organization. The family and the neighborhood in rural areas have been studied extensively, but informal groups of friends and neighbors have often been overlooked.[2]

While small friendship groups of many kinds may be found in rural areas today, the mutual-aid groups of the past furnish excellent examples of informal group behavior. Although mutual-aid activities in rural areas have not totally disappeared, they have certainly declined in importance. The "threshing ring," the "apple-butter boil," "the butchering exchange," and the "husking bee" as mutual-aid activities of friends and neighbors are no longer essential ingredients in the social life of American farm communities. In their place are informal clique groupings organized to a large extent on the basis of mutual interest, similarity of age, and social class.

IMPORTANCE, FUNCTION, AND CHARACTERISTICS OF INFORMAL SOCIAL SYSTEMS

Importance of informal groups. As suggested previously, informal groups may be found everywhere—in all societies, in urban areas, and in rural areas. They are found among all age groups and among all social classes. They may be found within formal organizations, often controlling and shaping important policies and decisions.

It is essential for the action agent or anyone else interested in understanding social organization to identify and comprehend the nature and function of informal groupings. More frequently than not, the power to make community decisions rests with a small, informal clique group and not with the community as a

[2] For a study that focuses on the function of cliques in the diffusion of information see Herbert F. Lionberger and Gary D. Copus, "Structuring Influence of Social Cliques on Farm-Information-Seeking Relationships with Agricultural Elites and Nonelites in Two Missouri Communities," *Rural Sociology,* Vol. 37, No. 1, (March 1972), pp. 73ff. See also Lalit K. Sen, *Opinion Leadership in India: A Study of Interpersonal Communication in Eight Villages* (Hyderabad: National Institute of Community Development, 1969). For earlier studies see C. P. Loomis and J. A. Beegle, *Rural Sociology* (Englewood Cliffs: Prentice-Hall, Inc., 1957), p. 104 and Charles P. Loomis, *Studies of Rural Social Organization in the United States, Latin America, and Germany* (East Lansing: State College Book Store, 1945).

whole—or even with a formal organization from which the "official" decision may emanate. Those who wish to introduce change or influence others through their leaders need to observe carefully the patterns of interaction on the part of small groups.

In order to illustrate some of these considerations, Figure 1 is

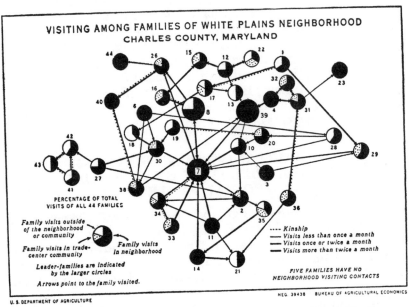

FIGURE 1. Visiting among families in White Plains neighborhood, Charles county, Maryland.

presented. This sociogram shows family visiting for all families in a neighborhood, that of White Plains, Maryland.[3] Each family is represented by a circle, the size of which varies according to the number of visits received, and is placed on the sociogram in approximately correct geographical relation one to the other. Of

[3] Charles P. Loomis, Douglas Ensminger, and Jane Woolley, "Neighborhoods and Communities in County Planning," *Rural Sociology*, Vol. VI, No. 4 (1941), pp. 339-341. Also published in Charles P. Loomis, *Studies in Applied and Theoretical Social Science* (East Lansing: The Michigan State College Press, 1950), Chapter 3. In the latter, the remarkable history of this sociogram, first used by Loomis, Ensminger, and Woolley is documented.

considerable importance is the fact that visits inside the neighborhood are distinguished from those to the trade-center community and those outside the neighborhood. Kinship visiting may also be distinguished from non-kinship visiting.

The central position of family number 7, the family having the largest number of visiting contacts, is dramatized, giving the possible impression that the White Plains neighborhood is a single clique group. This is not the case, however, as careful inspection will reveal. Approximately one-third of all visiting contacts on the part of the forty-four white families in White Plains were outside the neighborhood. One-eighth of the outside contacts were within the trade-center community comprising White Plains and one-fifth were visits to families in Baltimore or Washington, both of which are at least twenty-five miles away. Five families in the neighborhood reported no visiting within the neighborhood.

The largest circles shown in Figure 1 represent families, the heads of which the farmers in the neighborhood name most frequently as those most capable of representing them in agricultural, marketing, and public affairs. The heads of families 7, 39, and 8 are prestige leaders, and families 7 and 39 are also "grass roots" leaders. They have few, if any, visiting contacts outside the neighborhood, but are popular in the neighborhood. They occupy key positions in the interaction and communication systems of the White Plains neighborhood.

Functions of informal groups. Among the essential attributes of informal groups such as those we have been discussing is their intimacy. For clique group members, association is often an end in itself. In many clique groups, association is based upon the joy of association and "emotional" inclination to be together, not upon a rational evaluation of the value to be derived from association. In short, the clique group is a primary group ranking next to the family and kinship groupings in degree of intimacy.

From this basic character of the informal group stems one of its most important functions, namely, that of providing socialization and orientation for the individual. As Cooley remarks: "Primary groups are primary in the sense that they give the individual his earliest and completest experience of social unity, and also in the sense that they do not change in the same degree

as more elaborate relations, but form a comparatively permanent source out of which the latter are ever springing."[4]

It is within an atmosphere of intimacy and confidence that the
individual acquires his attitudes, models his behavior, and
gains his impressions of the social world about him. While the
family assumes this function for the young and may continue it
as family members grow older, the clique group assumes this
function alongside the family, especially in the play group,
sometimes reinforcing and sometimes challenging the authority
of the family. It is probable, although evidence is incomplete,
that the informal groups, during and after adolescence, play a
more important role in American society than the kinship
groups.

The importance of friendship groups in the changing of farm
practices is suggested by various studies. In one study it was
found that farmers claimed they had been most influenced in
changing practices by farm papers and magazines, the county
agent, friends, and neighbors, in the order named.[5]

A Social Science Research Council survey[6] reported that 25
percent of the adult book users got their books from the public
libraries, 20 percent from friends, 35 percent from purchase and
home libraries, about 8 percent from rental libraries, and about
10 percent from other sources. A study of Michigan cooperatives
by the Social Research Service of Michigan State University involving a sample of 500 farmers revealed that one-half of the
member informants stated that their "farmer friends and farmer
relatives in this community [are] all members of co-ops." Moreover, 29 percent stated that within the past year they had tried to
interest non-member friends in joining a co-op.[7] Kolb and Mar-

[4] Charles Horton Cooley, *Social Organization* (New York: Charles Scribner's
Sons, 1909), p. 27.

[5] *The Extension Service in Vermont, Part One: Farmers and the Extension
Service,* (Washington, D.C.: U.S.D.A., July, 1947), pp. 20 and 30. For more recent
studies see H. F. Lionberger and G. D. Copus and L. K. Sen, (Footnote 2).

[6] Survey Research Center, *The Public Library and the People* (Ann Arbor:
Univ. of Michigan, April, 1948). For a study of potential influence of informal
groups on marriage see: John E. Mayer, "The Self-Restraint of Friends: A
Mechanism in Family Transition," *Social Forces,* XXXV (1957), pp. 230-38.

[7] Duane Gibson, *Co-Ops as the Farmer Sees Them, Membership Relations of
Michigan Farmers' Cooperatives,* A Report by the Social Research Service of
Michigan State University to the annual meeting of the Michigan Association of
Farmers' Cooperatives (October 30, 1947).

shall[8] found that families which exchange work tend to visit one another. Those who exchange work also tend to be related, to have the same nationality background, and to share the same church affiliation. Studies have shown that the diffusion rate of improved practices is influenced by the culture embodied in both neighborhood and family which influence the structure and function of communication and cliques.[9]

In the words of Dubin, "people develop informal patterns of interaction in order to do the work required of them most expeditiously." Although the writer was speaking primarily of informal relations in bureaucratic organizations, especially in industry, this function of clique groupings is applicable to a wide variety of informal groupings. To quote further: "An organization would soon break down if everybody in it did only what his formal job descriptions called for, and did it 'according to the book.' "[10]

In a social order becoming increasingly bureaucratic, it would seem that one of the important functions served by informal patterns of association is that of minimizing frustration created by working within rigid, formal organizations. In such an atmosphere, the informal group may well provide a measure of security to the individual. The informal structure may, in many instances, support and buttress the formal structure and value orientation. In such cases, morale may be said to be high. Again, the informal structure may be at odds with the formal structure, in which case morale is likely to be low. In the latter case, it would seem that one of the functions of the informal group is that of altering and modifying the formal structure and value orientation. In fact, the cost in terms of human energy of operating formal organizations such as community or health councils is so great that members sometimes create or improve informal

---

[8] John H. Kolb and Douglas G. Marshall, *Neighborhood-Community Relationships in Rural Society* (Madison: Wisconsin AES Research Bulletin 154, November, 1944), p. 24. See also C. P. Loomis and J. A. Beegle, *Rural Social Systems* (New York: Prentice-Hall, 1950), Chapter 5, for other examples of the importance of clique groups.

[9] C. Milton Coughenour, "The Rate of Technological Diffusion among Locality Groups," *American Journal of Sociology,* LXIX (1964), 324-339 and Eugene Wilkening, *Adoption of Improved Farm Practices as Related to Family Factors* (Madison: Wisconsin AES Research Bulletin 183, 1953).

[10] Robert Dubin, *Human Relations in Administration* (Englewood Cliffs, N.J.: Prentice-Hall, Inc., 1951), p. 57.

organizations so that the larger formal organizations are not necessary. Often the death of a health or community council or an organization for fund-raising means that informal contacts and communication have become sufficient to carry on functions which formal organizations carried on at a higher cost of human energy.[11]

Characteristics of members of informal groups. Although clique groups are diverse, it may be said that members of a given clique or informal group are usually similar in that they belong to the same sub-group or follow the same life style. Several studies[12] support this statement. In resettlement groups, it was found that associating families resemble each other in economic status, as represented by total value of family living. Interacting families also are similar in money spent for social activities, recreation, reading material, and clothing. They are also similar in the number of religious and non-religious organizations in which they participate. Other studies show that the membership of clique groups is often age-graded, composed only of males or females, and similar in ethnic or racial composition. Still other studies show distance to be an important element, clique members generally coming from the same locality. While special-purpose informal groups having heterogeneous membership exist, the nature and function of most clique groups militate against great heterogeneity among the membership. In rural and urban resettlement, both propinquity (closeness of residence) and similarity of backgrounds and interests were found to be determining factors in the establishment and maintenance of informal relationships. Thus, Loomis and Liell[13] found that for several years after first arrival the proportions of families which visited

[11] Christopher Sower, John Holland, Kenneth Tiedke, and Walter Freeman, *Community Involvement* (Glencoe: The Free Press, 1957).

[12] See Loomis and Beegle, *Rural Social Systems,* p. 153; also C. P. Loomis, "Visiting Patterns and Miscegenation at Oxapampa, Peru," *Rural Sociology,* Vol. IX, No. 1 (1944), p. 68; and Dale Faunce and J. Allan Beegle, "An Experiment in Decreasing Cleavages in a Relatively Homogeneous Group of Rural Youth Members of the Michigan Junior Farm Bureau," *Sociometry,* Vol. XI, No. 3 (1948), pp. 207ff.

[13] Loomis, *Studies in Rural Social Organization,* pp. 41-123, and John T. Liell, "Propinquity and Selectivity as Processes of Informal Community Organization: A Study in the Formation of Levittown, New York," paper presented at the 1955 Annual Meeting of the Ohio Valley Sociological Society, Cleveland, Ohio.

and associated with next-door neighbors or families living close by gradually declined as families became acquainted with other families in the community. However, in all newly-formed communities studied, a large proportion of the associations are with families living close-by—the more homogeneous the new community, the larger the proportions of associates who live adjacent will be, and the longer the propinquous relationships will tend to persist. In less homogeneous communities, desires to associate with persons of similar religion or social class and many other factors result in the scattering of members of informal groups in modern mobile society.[14]

METHODS OF DISCOVERING INFORMAL GROUPS

Two methods are most commonly used in discovering the existence and structure of informal groupings. The first is that of observation. Ideally, all interaction between members over a long period of time should be observed. Furthermore, some judgment of the quality of the interaction often needs to be made. The observation method is often slow, and many observers are insufficiently trained to determine adequately the essential nature of the clique group structure.

The most commonly used method of determining clique structure is by means of the sociometric test. The population under observation is requested to answer certain questions designed to reveal the nature and quality of interaction patterns. For example, informants may list in the order of frequency the persons with whom they visit, including data concerning the nature of friendship ties. In addition, certain background data such as age, sex, religion, and income are often requested. Sociometric data may be secured through personal interviews or on questionnaires that the participants fill out themselves. The results of such a sociometric test are then analyzed. A sociogram, such as Figure 1, is often constructed in order to assist in visualizing the

[14] Leon Festinger, Stanley Schachter, and Kurt Back, *Social Pressures in Informal Groups, A Study of Human Factors in Housing* (New York: Harper and Brothers, 1950), p. 58; Theodore Caplow and Robert Forman, "Neighborhood Interaction in a Homogeneous Community," *American Sociological Review,* Vol. 15, No. 3 (1950), pp. 357-366; and W. H. Form, "Stratification in Low and Middle Income Housing," *Journal of Social Issues,* Vol. 7, Nos. 1 and 2 (1951), pp. 109-131.

nature of the informal groupings in the population being studied.

EXAMPLES OF INFORMAL SOCIAL SYSTEMS

Two of the best documented examples of informal social systems are the *cuaird,* or "old fellows clique," in rural Ireland and the Norton Street Gang, composed of second-generation Italians in Boston. We shall refer to these groups as we discuss the elements and processes of informal groupings. In order that the reader may understand the settings in which these two informal groups function, a brief description is necessary.

Old Fellows clique in rural Ireland.[15] In the rural communities of Ireland, it is common for the older men to meet more or less regularly at homes in informal groups. The meetings are called by different names in different parts of the country, but congeniality is one of the prime purposes everywhere. "For instance, the 'old fellows' went out on *cuaird,* as they called their visiting, to join one another. They followed a deep-set regular habit. As they phrased it 'a man would feel lonely if he didn't go out on *cuaird.*' "[16]

The seven men in the *cuaird* described by Arensberg have nicknames related to their roles, such as judge, prosecutor, and senator. The younger men do not come to *cuaird* until they attain the responsibility of operating a farm. Younger men attaining a place in the old men's group feel insecure at first. Prior to attaining full status in the old men's group, the younger men usually exhibit behavior common to marginal persons who are neither completely of the one group or of the other. Cliques such as these furnish the basis of some of the formal organization in Ireland. In the political sphere, for example, "It is here . . . that the community reaches unanimity in party voting."[17]

The Norton Street Gang.[18]   This gang, studied in the depres-

---

[15] Conrad M. Arensberg and Solon T. Kimball, *Family and Community in Ireland,* 2nd ed. (Cambridge: Harvard University Press, 1968) and Conrad M. Arensberg, *The Irish Countryman, An Anthropological Study* (New York: The Macmillan Co., 1937), pp. 125ff.

[16] Ibid., p. 125.

[17] Ibid., p. 138.

[18] William Foote Whyte, *Street Corner Society* (Chicago: University of Chicago Press, 1943).

sion of the thirties, was composed of young men from twenty to twenty-nine years of age. The hangout of the Norton gang was the streets of East Boston. This gang or clique was active in athletics (especially bowling), took girls out on dates, and engaged in political campaigns. The area in which the gang operated had been first inhabited by people of English origin and later by the Irish. These ethnic groups moved away to other locations as they bettered their social and economic conditions, and the area when studied was inhabited by Italians. The young men habitually spent little time at home. Most of their time was spent at work or hanging out with the gangs. Since the depression prevented them from working, most of their time was spent with the gang.

In the following pages we will often contrast the Norton Street clique with that of the "old fellows" in Ireland. Cliques of the Norton Street type are less common in rural than in urban areas. In rural areas, cliques often tend to be extensions of the family.

ELEMENTS OF INFORMAL SOCIAL SYSTEMS

Ends and objectives. An important end of the old men's clique in Ireland, viewed from the standpoint of the individual, is that of congeniality. One would feel lonely if he did not attend. The function, viewed by one interested in its relation to the community, is reflected by one of the members who says: "There is never any bad blood between any of the village, and one reason is because we talk things over." According to Arensberg, "The community reaches agreement upon its internal affairs, too, through the old men's discussions. It is in just this type of activity that one can at last put one's finger upon that nebulous force among men: public opinion."[19]

Any change agent attempting to improve agriculture, health, or other services in Ireland would certainly have to take his case before the jury of the old fellows. Although the informal groupings which pass final judgment may be younger or differently composed in other societies, sooner or later the recommendations of the change agent will come before similar groupings. One function of the informal group is that of assisting the individual in judging that which is new.

[19] Arensberg, *Irish Countryman,* pp. 126 and 139.

The ends of the Norton Street Gang in Boston may be different in specifics from those of the old fellows in rural Ireland. However, both provide their members with fellowship. Both render mutual aid and provide the individual with a means of relating himself to his group members and to outsiders. In the Norton Street Gang, opportunity for athletic participation, mutual aid, and economic and social assistance were among the expressed ends of the group. Members would spend their last cent to help other members close to them.

The real ends of informal groupings may be overlooked if one does not investigate the meaning in terms of interpersonal relations. On one occasion Doc, the leader of the Norton Street Gang, asked for help from Whyte, who had become one of the gang as a participant observer. Whyte replied that Doc had done so much for him that he was glad to be able to do something in return. Doc objected, saying, "I don't want it that way. I want you to do this for me because you're my friend. That's all." For the Nortons, such relations were extremely important. They were poor and unimportant people. Insofar as they were to have the advantages of the larger society, they had to come in contact with the important people who ran this society. Little people cannot do this directly. Cliques function as intermediaries whereby this linkage is made. As Whyte says, "The interaction of big shots, intermediaries, and little guys builds up a hierarchy of personal relations based upon a system of reciprocal obligations."[20]

In the consideration of the ends of informal groups, perhaps it will be more meaningful if the reader asks himself, "With whom would I enjoy associating?"[21] When answering this question, the groups and the relationships one anticipates having are often

[20] Whyte, *Street Corner Society,* p. 272.

[21] Jennings has described the groupings which would form on this basis as psyche-groups. Psyche-groups "most want to express and share and enjoy with others who would view it [the self] with understanding and cherish it *just as it is."* (Italics added). For her the socio-group, on the other hand, imposes requirements on the individual for this or that objective which the group may have. See Helen Hall Jennings, *Leadership and Isolation—A Study of Personality in Inter-Personal Relations,* Second Edition (New York: Longmans, Green and Co., 1950), pp. 275-276. Actually the psyche-group and the socio-group may be composed of the same members. The independent discovery of Bales that successful small groups almost always have two types of leaders, namely, the "task or instrumental leader" who is the more powerful and a "popular or expressive lead-

ends in and of themselves. Normal individuals need the interaction of others, and in situations where strangers are thrown together—on the American frontier, in resettlement projects, or in new army encampments—considerable activity involves finding people with whom one is congenial. In such situations there is relatively little effort at first to "keep people in their places," relatively little "snubbing" or other activity designed to keep established congeniality groups intact. Before long, however, cliques form, and many become less outgoing and more satisfied with their companions. In short, through a process of selection and elimination, most people become members of congeniality or clique groups. Usually these groupings are formed more or less spontaneously in the normal course of events. Few people set out to build friendship groups for themselves; groups are built out of the interaction one engages in during his day-to-day activities.

It should not be assumed that informal social systems do not have ends and objectives other than congeniality. Generally such groups protect members from anxiety, loneliness, lack of recognition, and unfavorable response, as well as extend all kinds of mutual assistance to members. They may engage in production or trade and still remain relatively informal. Many of the protective societies on the frontier, voluntary urban and farm organizations, and business concerns of many types began as informal groupings. But as the informal congeniality groups attempt to achieve objectives, they become more formal. They may develop specific status-roles for the members, elect officers, and discuss policy. At this point, they usually become formal organizations. Membership of informal groups is determined through mutual attraction of personalities, and an organization grows out of the need to plan and execute group activities. As soon as several functions must be coordinated, the fixing of responsibility becomes necessary. There is a direct relationship between the nature and scope of group activities and the organizational structure.[22] Thus, if an informal group of farmers who

er" who will lose his popularity if he attempts to assume the task role is important here.

[22] See Coughenour, *"Technological Diffusion,"* and Hurley H. Doddy, *Informal Groups and the Community, A Research Study of the Institute of Adult Education* (New York: Bureau of Publications, Teachers College, Columbia University, 1952), pp. 14-15.

came together by chance were to attempt to build a barn or organize to fight a fire, it is very dubious that the group would remain informal. However, formality and informality as we use the terms are relative concepts.

Norms. Merely because informal groups do not have written constitutions, procedure manuals, bylaws, and similar devices to guide action, does not mean that they are without norms. On the contrary, informal groups may be singularly ruthless in enforcing agreed-upon or accepted ways of behaving.

In the old fellows clique in Ireland great emphasis is placed upon deliberation and decision, and the norms of the group favor conformity. When one of the clique members, in a discussion with Arensberg, expressed political views differing from those of the group, he made Arensberg promise not to let these deviant views be known. Since the old fellows deliberate, the norms permit no one to belong who cannot control his temper while engaging in the process. For example, O'Brien who otherwise is eligible, "is a man of moody temper, given to gusts of anger. He goes out very little at all; when he does it is to the young men's gambles."[23] The norms of the old fellows clique are different from those of the young fellows. The latter ". . . gather in at Jack Roche's and they laugh and joke and play cards; they talk about the next gamble and the next dance, and that is all they know."[24]

The Norton Street Gang also has its norms. As will be indicated in the discussion of social rank, those who conform most closely to the norms of the clique have the highest rank. The norms prescribe how the members participate and reciprocate. Great emphasis is placed upon living up to personal obligations, and members are required to help friends when possible. The leaders always give more money to other members than they receive from members. The norms of cliques such as the Norton Street Gang require that men "make" girls if they can. Perhaps more important for our immediate discussion, corner boys are not permitted to have sexual intercourse with relatives of other members.[25] A corner boy would not usually go steady or marry a girl who was "no good"; if he did, he would be considered a "sucker".

[23] Arensberg, *Irish Countryman,* p. 137.
[24] Ibid., pp. 125-126.
[25] W. F. Whyte, "A Slum Sex Code," *American Journal of Sociology,* Vol. XLIX (1943), pp. 24-31.

The description of the norms of the Norton Street Gang provides some of the best materials on norms as used in the social-pychological sense. The organization of the Norton Street clique is oriented to achievement, so that those members who are the best athletes or have the most money are in an advantageous position. Leaders generally direct their activities to those things in which they excel and away from situations in which they would be at a disadvantage. When participation is required in an activity in which the leader may be inferior, the group finds its own way of retaining its leadership structure. When bowling was a sign of distinction in the Norton Street Gang, high performance of top-ranking members was accepted as natural and was encouraged. This was not the case for high performance of members with low standing in the groups. When their performance surpassed that of high-ranking members, it was said to be due to luck or some chance factor. Sherif, who has specialized in this aspect of social norms, summarizes Whyte's data as follows: "Take the case of Frank, a member with rather low standing. Frank was a good player in his own right, yet 'he made a miserable showing' while playing in his own group. In Frank's words: 'I can't seem to play ball when I am playing with fellows I know, like that bunch. I do much better when I am playing for the Stanley A. C. against some team in Dexter, Westland, or out of town.' "[26] Whyte concludes as follows: "Accustomed to filling an inferior position, Frank was unable to star even in his favorite sport when he was competing against members of his own group."[27] In the Norton Street Gang, leadership and follower patterns became so firmly fixed that it was difficult for some members to dissociate themselves from these status-roles and rankings, regardless of the nature of the situation.

Attitudes as related to ends and norms. It is our thesis that the chief components of social attitudes are the internalized ends and norms of the group. Next to the family, the informal social systems or reference groups are the most important sources of attitudes of individuals. As Sherif states, ". . . it may be safe to assert that the formation and effectiveness of attitudes cannot be properly accounted for without relating them to their group matrix. . . ."[28]

[26] Muzafer Sherif, *An Outline of Social Psychology* (New York: Harper and Brothers, 1948), p. 128. See also Chapters 6 and 7.

[27] Whyte, *Street Corner Society,* p. 19.

[28] Sherif, *An Outline,* p. 138.

In a study of the spread of "planted rumor" involving informal groups, the conclusion was reached that "Groups can induce members to work hard or to be lazy, to vote democratic or not to vote at all, to dress for dinner or to lead a 'bohemian life' . . . ." To quote further, "An opinion or attitude which is not reinforced by others of the same opinion will become unstable generally. . . . The 'reality' which settles the question in the case of social attitudes and opinions is the degree to which others with whom one is in communication are believed to share these same attitudes and opinions."[29]

Important for our discussion are the differences in rural and urban attitudes. Such differences are to be explained by differences of reference groups in rural and urban society. In fact, in the United States, the reference groups of well-to-do farmers and businessmen impose similar attitudes concerning many aspects of life. Despite a general trend in the direction of greater similarity in the attitudes of farm and urban people, several differences in basic attitudes may be said to persist. Needless to say, there are differences of considerable magnitude between the attitudes held by rural people of different class levels, regions, and periods of time.

Hour for hour, less activity in cities is moral or integrative than in farm and peasant communities. Social systems of farm and peasant people place more emphasis on religious or moral activity. This is especially true in the underdeveloped areas of the world. In the United States, the relatively more sacred attitudes of rural people are objectively manifested in greater interest in religious activities, and in greater interest in religious programs and religious music over the radio.[30]

Status-roles. A discussion of status-roles in informal social systems brings to light many differences in formal and informal groups. By definition, informal groups do not have a specific set of status-roles which are articulated in action as in the case of typical formal organizations. Nevertheless, it is one of the prime rules of group life that, in order to achieve group goals, not all people can do the same thing simultaneously. There must be differentiation. Therefore, expectancy patterns grow up for mem-

[29] Festinger, Schachter and Back, *Informal Groups,* pp. 165, 168-169.

[30] Carl C. Taylor, et al., *Rural Life in the United States* (New York: Alfred A. Knopf, 1949), p. 504, and *Attitudes of Rural People Toward Radio Service* (Washington: U.S.D.A., Bur. Agr. Econ.; January, 1946), pp. 12 and 69.

bers of informal groups, and these may combine group needs and the characteristics of the individual personality. From the following discussion it is evident that the personalities of individuals are more important in the expectancy patterns of informal groups than of formal groups.

In the field of group dynamics, terminology and ideals for group behavior, especially for discussion groups, have been developed. We cannot go into detail here, but leaders in the field of group dynamics maintain that, for most effective group effort in many situations, different individuals should function in various roles, so that all feel more or less as equals in the process. For example, the following are specified as possible task roles: activity initiator, information seeker, opinion seeker, information giver, opinion giver, elaborator, coordinator, summarizer, and feasibility tester. As group-maintenance roles, the following are suggested: encourager, gate keeper, standard setter, follower, expresser of group feeling, and tension reliever. As being either task or group-maintenance roles, the following are suggested: evaluator, diagnostician, consensus tester, and mediator. The following roles are suggested as non-functional: aggressor, blocker, self-confessor, competitor, sympathy seeker, special pleader, playboy, recognition seeker, and withdrawer.[31]

The following discussion of the old fellows clique will indicate that informal groups that have been in existence for considerable periods of time do not rotate status-roles and are not leaderless.[32] Normally, the needs of groups, the needs of the individual members, and the individual competencies are woven into a system in such a manner that it is far from being leaderless and non-rotating roles usually become established. Note that in the following discussion of status-roles, we treat territoriality as we describe the status-roles. In many informal groupings, as in

[31] "Kinds of Member Roles," *Adult Leadership,* Vol. 1, No. 8 (January, 1953), pp. 17-23. This issue features member roles, and there is a bibliography. The following were among those who participated in the preparation of the issue or prepared pertinent material on roles: Jack R. Gibb, Malcolm S. Knowles, Kenneth D. Benne, Ronald Lippitt, Herbert A. Thelen, Leland P. Bradford, Paul Sheets, Paul L. Essert, D. M. Hall, and Norman R. F. Maier.

[32] The research of Robert F. Bales indicates that most groups develop at least two leadership roles, the task leader who implements goals and instrumental activity and the more popular leader who functions as an integrator of the system. See Talcott Parsons, Robert F. Bales, et al., *Working Papers* (Glencoe: The Free Press, 1953).

formal groupings such as athletic teams, the spatial relationships of the members are important. They may imply the rank of
the member, or they may indicate his access to others.

Status-roles in the old fellows clique.   The parts played by
members are well portrayed in the following excerpt:

> Soon after supper they begin to gather . . . stride across the
> threshold with a "God bless all here" and take their accus-
> tomed places.
>
> O'Donoghue has the place of honour. He sits in the chair to
> the right of the fire . . . is the "judge" in this gathering. . . . He
> is regarded as a wise man. All must defer to his opinions. . . .
> He initiates nothing. . . . He rarely generalizes; when he does,
> his theme is the "old times."
>
> Silent as this shrewd old man is, his is the central position in
> the group. Comments and questions are phrased through
> him. He takes the proffered verbal bit and passes it on
> among the others. And, when agreement is finally reached,
> it is his quiet "so it is" that settles the point for good.
>
> O'Halloran sits on the hob across the hearth from him. He is
> the "drawer down". . . . O'Halloran seeks information. Most
> frequently it is he who brings up points of interest and ques-
> tions of the day. These he addresses to O'Donoghue, who
> passes them on for general discussion. Like all the rest of
> them, he is most at home in finding apt illustrations in def-
> inite, precisely told anecdotes. But his chief role is to "draw
> the talk down" to common levels of interest.
>
> O'Loughlin usually occupies the other hob. . . . He is silent
> nearly all the time . . . just as he has no voice here, he has no
> title either.
>
> Roche, the "public prosecutor" sits in the chair before the
> hearth opposite the old man O'Donoghue. . . . Roche demands
> "Why," he forces one to parade one's best arguments, he pur-
> sues a point relentlessly to its final conclusion. There his in-
> terest stops, and he makes way for O'Donoghue, who sums
> up the agreement of the group. Roche earns his title well; he
> tests one's mettle. No one takes offense at his "prosecution."
> It clears the issue and brings out the right and the wrong
> upon which all can agree and O'Donoghue phrase judgment.
>
> Behind these two, a little further into the middle of the room,
> sits Cullinan, the "senator.". . . . The "senator" is a
> "weighty" man. His part here is in character. . . . Cullinan's
> memory of persons and happenings, slowly and accurately,

even pompously phrased, gives "weight" to the evening's discussions.

Still further behind them, and, often perched upon settle or table in this kitchen, are two other *habitués*. The elder of them is Ruin. . . . Privately, at least, the others think Ruin "a bit of a fool" . . . his role at *cuaird* is not a weighty one. Ruin is a very voluble man; he can be counted upon at all times to enliven the gathering with a deal of opinion upon all subjects. His volubility makes him more vulnerable than the rest to the "public prosecutor's" relentless logic. Nevertheless, it helps to keep the conversation alive and active. Consequently, though he has no important title, Ruin is a member of long standing.[33]

The other man sitting in the back of this kitchen was Quinn, who at the beginning of the study was changing from the role of member in a young man's clique, which he still attended, to the role of member in this *cuaird*. At the beginning of this transition the members of the old fellows clique thought of him as a "bit of a playboy." At one meeting he would be silent, at another "ready to joke, to render a song, to break into playful banter. . . ." In other words he had not yet established his role in the group. A year later the investigator reports that he was making progress. He had dropped the younger set of earlier acquaintances. "O'Donoghue, 'the judge,' passed judgment one evening which affirmed his new place. 'He's a bit of a playboy,' he said, 'but he has a good head on him.' "[34]

Status roles in the Norton Street Gang. A study of the role behavior of city cliques comparable to studies of rural cliques would probably reveal status-roles such as those we have discussed but having different functions. All the studies of city gangs have described leaders who often depend to a considerable extent upon force for their position.[35] The Nortons had a leader in Doc, and two lieutenants, Mike and Danny. The data available indicate that Doc played many roles, such as those designated as judge, senator, and public prosecutor in the old fellows clique, plus combat leader and strategist, all rolled into one person.

[33] Arensberg, *Irish Countryman*, pp. 130-134.
[34] Ibid., p. 135.
[35] These studies are cited by Sherif, *An Outline*, p. 124.

As will be shown in the discussion of power, interaction is strictly channelled in clique groups. Among such groups there is no such thing as the ideal discussion group, as described by the proponents of group dynamics, in which most roles are interchangeable and positions of influence are rotated so that the person who is most competent in a given operation has the most influence. In such cliques, leaders usually lead regardless of their competence, but as previously indicated they attempt to keep the group engaged in activities in which they excel.

Power and its components — authority and influence. In the old fellows clique, it is obvious that the "judge" has the greatest power. He controls communication. Everything that is to be discussed by the group passes through him, and he determines when and how the discussion of a particular topic is terminated. The person of least power in this clique is O'Laughlin, who has no voice in the group, even though he always attends.

There is no doubt about who is the most powerful in the Norton Street Gang. It is Doc. Figure 2 indicates the relative status, based primarily on power, or what Whyte calls influence. The chart indicates the lines of influence of the members. The principal difference between power in informal and formal systems is the relatively greater importance of authority in formal systems and the relatively greater importance of non-authorative power in informal systems. If the power held by Doc and his lieutenants were authority as in the case of the army, it would not only be marked by symbols on the uniforms, but Doc would have the right to give directives and have them carried out. These would be enforced by the customs and before the courts of the larger system and would have the sanctions of police power. As we have defined the terms, Doc has non-authorative power; the authority he does possess is confined to his group. It cannot be enforced logically by external sanction systems.

As indicated previously, the counterparts of city gangs which are relatively free of family influence as described by Thrasher, Zorbaugh, Shaw, and Whyte[36] are rural groupings based upon kinship. In some societies, these relationships may be structured into clans, in which case the leader will have an authoritative position defined by the law-norms. In the rural areas most influenced by modern, technological culture, those groupings

---

[36] See Sherif's summarization of this material, *An Outline,* pp. 124ff.

THE NORTONS
SPRING AND SUMMER 1937

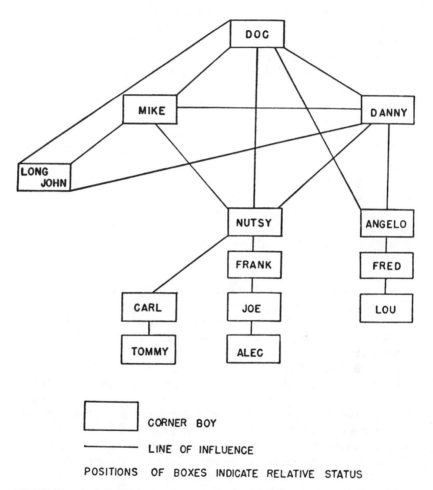

FIGURE 2. Differences in rank among members of the Norton Street gang.

which are larger than the immediate families are informal in the sense that the specific elements we use to define systems—status-roles, authority patterns, sanctions, and so on—are not specified by the larger community. Although data are lacking for traditional rural groupings comparable to city gangs, we hypothesize the following:

1. Leadership or power is less pyramidal, less dictatorial, and less absolute in rural than in urban groups. In interpreting Whyte's data on gangs, Homans says, "The more severe the environment in which the group must survive—ships and armies are examples again—the more likely it is that interaction will be strictly channelled."[37]

In respect to "severity of environment," urban middle class friendship groups are probably more comparable to rural cliques than are lower class urban gangs. No doubt, cultural factors, including class and environment, are responsible for these differences. The hold of the rural family over its members is probably as important as any other factor in restricting the growth and power of gangs in traditional rural societies.

2. Non-family clique groupings which compete with the family for control of members are less common in traditional rural than in urban areas, and they constitute a less important reference group for their members than comparable groupings in cities.

Social Rank. In the description of the old fellows clique in Ireland, differences in social rank have been apparent. In order to be a member of this group, a certain social rank is acquired. "The old men's house includes all the farm-fathers of complete families. It is made up of those who are married and . . . 'have a responsibility on them'. Informal as it is, it nevertheless unites these men of full status within the community and unites them, too, in such a way as to crystallize and canalize the influence their status gives them."[38] Each culture will hold different factors important in the rank of both groups and individuals, but most agrarian cultures, like that of the Irish, emphasize age, the family, the farm operation, tenure, and size of farm. The more important the status-role a member plays in the system, the higher will be his rank. Also, the more individuals he may influence, the higher his rank will be.

Rank differences among the members of the Norton Street

[37] George C. Homans, *The Human Group* (New York: Harcourt, Brace and Co., 1950), p. 184.
[38] Arensberg, *Irish Countryman,* p. 137.

Gang are represented in Figure 2. In this system rank is determined completely by the influence one has over fellow members of the system. Nevertheless, the leaders of the gang are those who most completely realize the norms the group values most highly.[39] They have more contacts outside the system, and they not only do not violate the norms of the group but they personalize and enforce them.

Although cultural standards are important in the informal groupings, effectiveness in personal relations, whether attained or ascribed, has importance in determining social rank. The personality of the individual is measured against the norms of the system, and the value measuring stick is applied to specify the social rank. Of course, differences of rank in informal groups are not great, because by definition members believe themselves to be near equals. Within the group, however, personality factors not involving status-role, wealth, and authority are reckoned in the equation. The change agent who must deal with informal groups will need to know the peculiarities of each, especially the criteria for social rank, if he is to use them in plans involving the introduction of new elements.

Sanctions.   As is illustrated by both the old fellows clique in Ireland and the Norton Street Gang in Boston, much of the motivating force involves the rewards incorporated within these systems themselves. The power and social rank achieved by the judge or by Doc may be considered rewards from within the system. When Doc ran for political office his group supported and worked very hard for him. Negative or penalty sanctions were applied when later, because of outside complications, he withdrew from an election and the gang members felt "let down" and "sold out." The gang fell apart, later regrouping around another leader and refusing to let Doc be the leader when he finally tried again.

Informal groups have informal sanction systems that do not require the specialized enforcement status roles of police officers. Arensberg, for example, says this of public opinion as applied to the old men's cliques of Ireland: "That force is not implemented; it is merely the power of gossip and censure; only in critical

[39] These ideas specified with qualifications by George C. Homans may be found in his *Social Behavior: Its Elementary Forms* (New York: Harcourt, Brace and World, Inc., 1961), p. 112.

days, as in the time of land agitation, can it rise to action, as a last resort, and win itself an international name: the boycott. But it is nonetheless powerful."[40]

All those acquainted with traditional rural life know the power of informal sanction systems. The rural school teacher who comes from the liberal circles of the city, the politician with upper or lower class city values who is dependent upon rural votes, and the extension worker who may have more liberal morals are examples of people to whom sanctions are likely to be applied. The power of gossip is particularly dangerous for change agents working in those communities that are in a stage of transition from the neighborhood to urban orientations. In such situations the protection one has in his occupational and professional cliques and formal systems of communication is not yet present.

Facilities.   Informal groups in traditional rural areas seldom avail themselves of extensive facilities as we have defined them. However, Whyte's account of the relation of city gangs to facilities during the depression is of interest to change agents working in both rural and urban areas. Not only were the settlement houses, facilities offered by middle class persons, not frequented by the Italian gangs, but gang members stole equipment, threw stones through the windows, and otherwise damaged the buildings. At the suggestion of Whyte, Doc—the unemployed leader of the Norton Street Gang—was put in a responsible position in one of the settlement house projects. The pilfering and destruction stopped. Once systemic linkage between the settlement house project and the gangs occurred, its facilities were treated as their facilities. They were not to be destroyed or stolen. However, they used their own norms for the use of facilities owned by houses that were not linked to their system.[41]

Territoriality.   In discussing the old men's clique as a going concern, we indicated the customary spatial relationships of the members. Any effective change agent learns to evaluate such relationships. Sometimes in larger groupings the members of highest social rank sit informally together in a given place. In concert halls, for example, the cost of admission may separate informal groups by rank.

Territoriality is frequently important in informal groups, be-

[40] Arensberg, *Irish Countryman,* p. 139.
[41] William F. Whyte, "The Social Role of the Settlement House," *Applied Anthropology,* Vol. 1, No. 1 (October-December, 1941), pp. 14-19.

cause other aspects of formal structure are lacking. A given corner or place in a building may be the chief referent. In his review of the study of the Norton Street Gang, Homans says:

> Besides its own corner, it often has a regular evening meeting place, a cafeteria or a tavern, where the gang goes at about nine o'clock for coffee or beer before going home. "Positions at the tables are fixed by custom. Night after night each group gathers around the same tables. The right to these positions is recognized by other Cornerville groups." A corner boy never gets far away from his own corner and his own routine.[42]

The importance of spatial relationships in the functioning and formation of informal and clique groups, particularly in newly settled rural areas, is very great. Perhaps the most interesting description of the operation of cliques is one reported in a study of Dyess Colony, Arkansas. The clique groupings, shortly after the formation of this resettlement project, were based primarily upon geographical location. Visiting and mutual-aid activities occurred most frequently between near neighbors. After a two-year period had elapsed, however, the clique groupings had changed markedly and realignments of cliques had occurred. The importance of clique groupings in this resettlement project was very great, since the decision to leave the project or to stay seemed to be determined more largely by clique groups than by rational decisions on the part of individuals. In a very real sense, it was clique groups that moved and clique groups that stayed.

Because of need for interaction at frequent intervals, nearness in a geographical sense is essential to the operation of clique groups. Although clique groups may exist where members are distant, generally such groups have a restricted territorial basis. High and intense rates of interaction between members are seldom possible except in restricted space. However, in upper and middle class rural and urban society, mobility is relatively great and clique groups include members from several neighborhoods. Cosmopolitan individuals and members of such groups as "jet sets" may live in widely separated places. Relatively few farm people belong to such groups. The more homogeneous the popu-

---

[42] Homans, *Human Group,* pp. 159-160.

lation of a community the higher the probability that close associates will be neighbors.[43]

SOCIAL PROCESSES IN INFORMAL
SOCIAL SYSTEMS

Communication. Difficulties of communication are often at a minimum within informal social systems: "The more intimate the friendship, the greater the range of content which flows through this communication channel and the lower the restraining forces against communication."[44] The symbols that permit reciprocal interaction of members on the basis of shared experiences are so well internalized that each can almost exactly predict what another will do under given circumstances. Often a word or gesture unintelligible to outsiders is sufficient to convey to fellow members meanings of consequence for the group. Many clique groups develop their own vocabularies.

This fact often forces outsiders, such as change agents who attempt to influence the system or its members, to use more formal and conventional means of communication and to remain outsiders. Informal agrarian groups also are influenced by the cultural system and tradition, and resist change because of inertia. In discussing the old fellows clique, Arensberg writes as follows about a member in the group: ". . . the countryman's way of life exerts its strongest sway upon him . . . Agriculture, perhaps, comes first. Times of sowing, reaping and harvesting are debated. Prices are compared, innovations tested. Traditional methods receive their strongest support here, in the web of legend, proverb and reference to the past the speakers throw round them."[45] In almost all clique groups, in traditional societies, the change agent must expect resistance to change, and change that affects the ends and norms will be resisted most.

Homan's conclusions about communication should be of interest to the change agent. "We can say then that the more nearly equal in social rank a number of men are, the more frequently they will interact with one another . . . . We can say then that the

[43] Loomis, *Studies of Rural Social Organization,* pp. 41-123; and Liell, "Propinquity and Selectivity."

[44] Festinger, Schacter, and Back, *Informal Groups,* p. 167.

[45] Arensberg, *Irish Countryman,* p. 138.

higher a man's social rank, the more frequently he interacts with persons outside his own group. . . . the higher a man's social rank, the larger the number of persons for whom he originates interaction, either directly or through intermediaries."[46]

As will be indicated in our discussion of systemic linkage, special problems always are involved in the linkage of informal with formal systems. "What factors will determine what is and what is not communicated within a social group? It is probably that, other things being equal, there will be more communication in a social group on matters which affect the behavior of the members in the context of that particular group than on matters which are not immediately relevant to the group's functioning. The direction of the communication flow will be toward those members for whose social behavior the content of the communication is especially relevant."[47]

Ramsϕy[48] maintains that friends rarely are as dependent on leadership or as separated from non-friends as the Corner Boys. He maintains that the group was in part the product of lower-class environment of second-generation immigrants in a depression. However, the fact remains that similar groupings are common throughout free-enterprise countries both in depression and in affluence. As in the case of blacks and poor whites, many from the rural South now in American ghettos may experience alienation. It is not to be expected that agrarian informal groups will carry the same type of information through their channels of communication as urban groups. Members of the old fellows clique in rural Ireland would not be likely to discuss the same thing as the Norton Street Gang, even if they had the same cultural background.

Decision-making. Although probably the most important functions of clique groupings in both agricultural and urban areas may be those of giving meaning and worth to the individual member and mitigating loneliness, decision-making also is an important function. The old fellows clique in Ireland is built around discussion and decision for the community at large. The Norton Street Gang engaged less in this kind of interaction, but

---

[46] Homans, *Human Group,* pp. 182, 184 and 185-6.

[47] Festinger, Schachter, and Back, *Informal Groups,* p. 171.

[48] Odd Ramsϕy, "Friendship," *International Encyclopedia of Social Sciences,* Vol. 6, pp. 12-17.

the four leaders discussed alternative courses of action at great length.

Homans' summary description of Figure 2 indicates the decision-making process of the gang: "The diagram . . . shows two things at once. In the first place, the lines between the members of the gang are lines of 'influence.' In actual behavior this seems to mean that if Doc felt the group ought to take a particular line of action, he was apt to talk the matter over first with Mike and Danny and perhaps Long John. If the decision reached Long John it went no further; he influenced no one. But if it reached Mike, he was apt to pass it on to Nutsy, and through Nutsy it reached Frank, Joe, Alec, Carl, and Tommy. Or Doc could influence Nutsy directly. As for influence in the opposite direction, if Tommy, for instance, had an idea that the gang ought to take a certain step, the idea was apt to get to Doc through Carl and Nutsy . . . Doc was the acknowledged leader of the Nortons, Mike and Danny serving as his lieutenants; the rest of the men were followers."[49] Decisions made by Doc had the advantage of these discussions, and they had to conform to the norms of the group or they were not accepted.

Even in informal groups, such as gangs, where the power is centralized in one person, there is always a great amount of two-way action. That is, there are followers making suggestions as well as leaders giving directives. In decision-making in informal groups, it is usually more difficult for participants to hide private interests and claim public interests. In informal groups, each member usually knows intimately the private needs and wishes of the others, and, if these are at variance with the larger system, it is usually more difficult to conceal this fact than in most formal systems.

Boundary Maintenance. Perhaps the easiest way to observe the manner in which an informal group maintains its boundaries is to observe its activities when in contact with opposing systems, when new members are being initiated into the system, and when members are expelled from the system. Cliques, such as the Norton Street Gang, establish territorial boundaries and fight other groups who enter these boundaries. Individuals who are being considered for membership must demonstrate that they have the same values, and frequently initiation involves proving or developing these. Members may be expelled and

---

[49] Homans, *Human Group,* pp. 160-162.

sanctions applied when they violate the central norms or do not accept the group values. In discussing the Norton Street Gang, Whyte describes how some members began going with girls having higher social rank. This led to frustrations not only because gang members did not have money enough to manage relationships on the higher level, but because it excluded some members and brought those involved into relation with other gangs. The leaders, when they saw that the group was threatened, used the device of "symbol manipulation" to discontinue the interaction. Although relations were good between the pairs involved, the girls were branded as "snooty," "tactless," and as thinking themselves too good for the Nortons. In the previous discussion of norms, the manner in which the incest taboos are applied to maintain integration and solidarity has been mentioned. Of course, informal groups on all levels use such devices as snubbing, derision, ridicule, mockery, and the like for purposes of boundary maintenance. Informal groups of higher social rank may be able to maintain boundaries by providing physical barriers, such as special compartments in vehicles or in public places, which limit interaction with those in other informal groupings.

Systemic linkage.   Informal social systems, when considered in relation to directed social change, are usually target systems, not change agents or systems. A change agent or system, such as a fund raising organization with ends which require it to introduce change into other systems, in nearly all cases is a formal system. Of course, within the formal change systems there are cliques and other informal groupings, but schools, government public health services, military units, and technical cooperation missions are formal organizations. They frequently attempt to change those who are organized in informal systems.

As will be indicated later, all attempts to carry out programs which involve changes in practices and attitudes involve informal systems. However, possibly the most difficult problem in the strategy of change is the matter of an effective linkage of the formal change system with the informal target system. This may be illustrated by two instances related by a former director of the Extension Service:

> In another county where I was agent for a time, we almost lost the name of the thing we were trying to get accepted. We

were trying to introduce a new and improved variety of rye. This was a long time ago, but that variety was then much superior in productivity per acre and care required than any we had in the county. In a short time it was adopted by most of the farmers, but it was not called variety X rye, the designation which the college and I gave it. One group of farmers called it White's rye, another called it Arnold's rye, and it went by the names of several farmers who were the leaders of various groups in the county.

In this instance the college and the extension service had effected a merger of their systems with the local informal groups of farmers. These groups had retained their original structures, including their leaders.

I am interested in these informal groups and leaders you are talking about. It is my impression that organizations can destroy them. I remember when I was county agent in X County. That was some years ago, but the Service began a vigorous campaign of designating food farmers and citizens in communities as Master Farmers. Often these had been effective leaders in their groups and people had never thought of them and they never thought of themselves as exceptional, except that they were good farmers and always helpful to others. When they were publicly acclaimed Master Farmers, it sort of set them apart. They were often not much good as local leaders any more.

Convergence of the change system and the target system was not accomplished in the above case. On the contrary, the Master Farmer was deprived of his position in the target system and more or less absorbed into the change system. The Master Farmer is comparable perhaps to the local clique leader who is elected to high office in the state or national government. If he becomes too involved in his activities and status-role in the larger system and does not "keep his fences mended," he may lose the support of the local system.

Successful strategy of change involving leaders of informal cliques can be illustrated by a case described by Whyte. In Boston, as elsewhere, settlement houses were designed for lower class minority groups suffering from poverty. The funds and administration of such organizations were from the social classes above those whom they were designed to serve. The local street gangs were considered by those who operated these projects to be "roughnecks" and the "tough element" which seemed to be unreachable. When ordinary fellows from these groups took jobs in the settlement houses, it was an indication to corner boys, such as those in the Norton Street Gang, that they were too good for them and trying to leave their kind through social climbing. On the other hand, the corner boys called those from their own ranks who worked at the settlement house or in any way cooperated "stooges," "flunkeys" and "yes-men" for the social workers.

When the settlement houses launched a project of establishing recreation centers in vacant stores, one director agreed as an experiment to place Doc, leader of the Norton Street Gang, in charge of one unit. Because Doc, in contrast to the middle class leaders, knew "Cornerville society," particularly the leaders and power relations in all of the gangs, and because of his other abilities, his unit became the most successful by all standards. When things were stolen or when the corner boys threw stones at his center, Doc did not attempt to deal directly with those who were thought to be involved. He negotiated with or used force on their leaders. Doc's center was successful, not only in athletics, but also in so-called "constructive work" such as art, publication of a house paper, and similar activities.

This experiment indicates an approximate fusion of two systems and systemic linkage. Doc's success was due to knowledge of the systems of the corner boys and his own system supported him. Through Doc's work, Mr. Kendall, head of the boy's work at the settlement house, came to know the corner boys of the area. Prior to this time, he and other settlement house leaders had been known as friends of the rich and identified with the Republican party. Then the corner gangs began to come to Mr. Kendall personally; they identified him as a man who was interested in helping the corner boys. At their requests Mr. Kendall was able to obtain a city appropriation for improvement of the park facilities, the first appropriation of this type that had appeared in the city budget for seven years. Without the voting power of the Cornerville boys and their friends, Mr. Kendall could not have brought sufficient pressure on the city government to get such facilities. The linkage of the informal systems with the settlement house program had lasting results. In the words of Whyte, "The recreation center then not only brought about a change in the corner boys' attitude toward the Cornerville House, but it also made Mr. Kendall a powerful man in the local community...."[50]

[50] Whyte, "The Social Role of the Settlement House," p. 19.

SELECTED REFERENCES

Arensberg, Conrad M. *The Irish Countryman.* New York: The Macmillan Co., 1937.

Hare, A. Paul, Edgar F. Borgatta and Robert F. Bales, (ed.). *Small Groups: Studies in Social Interaction.* New York: Alfred A. Knopf, 1955.

Homans, George C. *The Human Group.* New York: Harcourt, Brace and Co., 1950, and *Social Behavior: Its Elementary Forms.* New York: Harcourt, Brace & World, Inc. 1961.

Leonard, Olen and C.P. Loomis. *Culture of a Contemporary Rural Community: El Cerrito, New Mexico.* Washington, D.C.: U.S. Dept. Agr., 1941.

Lindzey, Gardner (ed.). *Handbook of Social Psychology.* Cambridge: Addison Wesley Press, 1954. See especially "Sociometric Measurement," by Gardner Lindzey and Edgar Borgatta.

Lionberger, Herbert F. *Adoption of New Ideas and Practices.* Ames: Iowa State University Press, 1960.

Lionberger, Herbert F. "The Relation of Informal Social Groups to the Diffusion of Farm Information in a Northeast Missouri Farm Community," *Rural Sociology,* 19, No. 3, (September, 1954).

Loomis, C.P. *Studies of Rural Social Organization.* Chap. 2. East Lansing: Michigan State Book Store, 1945.

Loomis, C.P. and J.A. Beegle. *Rural Social Systems.* Chap. 5. New York: Prentice Hall, Inc., 1950.

Moreno, J.L. *Who Shall Survive?* rev. ed. New York: Beacon House, 1953, and J.L. Moreno. *The Sociometry Reader.* Glencoe, The Free Press, 1960.

Ramsφy, Odd, "Friendship" in *International Encyclopedia of the Social Sciences.* New York: Macmillan Company and The Free Press, 1968, Vol. 6, pp. 12-17.

Rogers, Everett M. *Diffusion of Innovations.* New York: The Free Press of Glencoe and Macmillan, 1962.

Whyte, William Foote. *Street Corner Society.* Chicago: University of Chicago Press, 1943.

5

Systems of Agricultural Production

As traditional cultures and societies undergo modernization, fewer and fewer of the important social relations take place in enterprises owned and controlled or operated as family units. Economies of scale that bring about the substitution of the factory-type unit for the family unit, however, have appeared more slowly in agriculture than in other production areas. Such crises as economic depression and other disturbances accompanying back-to-the-land movements in the past may reverse trends that weaken family farming enterprises. Thus, during the great industrial depressions, the bombardment in World War II, and during some revolutions and civil wars, migrations from field to center have been reversed. Such reversals may have significant consequences for attitudes and thinking.

Soon after the last great depression the author polled rural sociologists and agricultural economists to get data for an article entitled "The American Rural Culture of the Future—What the Rural Sociologists and Agricultural Economists Think It Should and Will Be."[1] Respondents were asked to indicate extent of agreement or disagreement with the following statement: "The small family-sized farm, operated by an owner-farmer even though he has only a small cash income, should be the goal of American agriculture." Seventy one percent of the rural sociologists and 41 percent of the agricultural economists agreed. The reason for disagreement may be the inclusion of the word "small" in the statement. The two groups also were requested to respond to the statement: "The major issues in agriculture are

[1] Charles P. Loomis and Carl C. Taylor, *Farm Population, Rural Life Activities,* Bureau of Agricultural Economics, Vol. XI, No. 1, January 1937; Reprinted in Charles P. Loomis, *Studies of Rural Social Organization in the United States, Latin America and Germany* (East Lansing: Michigan State College Book Store, 1945), pp. 178ff.

economic and must be solved by better farm management and marketing practices." Seventy-two percent of the agricultural economists but only 27 percent of the rural sociologists agreed. Although neither group would admit that a sizable income resulting from economies of scale or a social milieu conducive to healthy mental and physical growth and development are unimportant, sociologists would be expected to stress the latter and would tend to disagree that sizable incomes from large scale operations would assure it.

Bigness tends, even in family-centered operations, to nurture Gesellschaft-like, non-familistic rather than Gemeinschaft-like, familistic features in individuals and societies. Both rural sociologists and agricultural economists agreed on various aspects of the subject matter of the present chapter. To the statement: "There are traits peculiar to rural culture which, because of their value as a stabilizing influence, should be retained at almost any cost," 82 percent of the sociologists and 71 percent of the economists agreed. To the statement: "Even an approximately self-sufficient peasant culture is more to be desired than our sharecropper system," 87 percent of the sociologists and 79 percent of the economists agreed.

In the evaluation of peasants, neither the sociologists nor the economists seemed to accept the "idiocy of peasantry" view of Marx and Engels as expressed in the *Communist Manifesto,* nor the governing-class view expressed by Lenski that they are "essentially subhuman . . . a peasant's children were not his *familia,* but his *sequela,* meaning 'brood' or 'litter'."[2] (Peasants were often listed with livestock in estate records in Europe, Asia, and America.)

Since rural sociologists throughout the world as well as those knowledgeable about rural America take a very different view of yeoman farmers and peasants than Marx or Lenski, it seems appropriate to turn our attention to the historical background from which these evaluations come. In this discussion it should be noted that the writers believe in the virtues of farm life, favor the free enterprise system as it developed in the West, and oppose forms of large agricultural holdings on which most of the work is done by sharecroppers and wage hands. We also oppose the splintering of once independent yeoman and family farms

[2] Gerhard Lenski, *Human Societies* (New York: McGraw-Hill, 1970), pp. 270-271.

into minifundia or tiny holdings too small to provide the farm family a respectable level of living.

THE YEOMAN AND FAMILY FARMER IN PERSPECTIVE

Various analysts have mistakenly assumed that peasant societies are always centers of inequality and exploitation. This may be explained by the fact that the peasant society is usually divided into "two parts; that is, the peasant culture is not capable of survival without joining with other part-cultures to make up a large entity. Peasants . . . self-sufficient in many ways, depend on traders to bring them products (salt, perhaps) . . . and on political authorities (earls, perhaps) to protect them."[3] Although some peasant groups armed with sickles and scythes have defended their freedom against power grabbing robber barons, empire builders, and others, in general they are no match for those who make a speciality out of conquest and war. Thus, the Roman colonate and the feudal system spread over wide areas as the common man in rural areas bought survival for himself and his family at the cost of his freedom.

Although other potentates brought subjugation and degradation to peasants, we shall give special but brief attention here to the processes of feudalization by feudal lords and collectivization by the Marxian communists. Against the widespread processes of feudalization of earlier times and collectivization of modern times, we wish to stress the importance of the fact that when and if yeomen and family farmers retain their independence they are, as Thomas Jefferson knew, a bulwark against oppression, submission and servility. When they become an important part of democratic societies where each has a vote, as in the United States, Canada, Switzerland, Costa Rica, and other countries, the characterizations "idiocy of peasantry" and "peasants as subhumans" are false. But let us briefly review the development of feudalism.

As Prawer and Eisenstadt[4] note, "The specific features of feudalism were the outcome of the encounter of two types of soci-

[3] Paul Bohannan, "Our Two Story Culture," *Saturday Review*, (September 2, 1972), p. 40.

[4] Joshua Prawer and Shumel N. Eisenstadt, "Feudalism," *International Encyclopedia of Social Sciences*, (New York: Macmillan Co., 1968), Vol. 5, pp. 394ff.

ety, the Romanized and the Germanic. . . ." Feudalism in its most concentrated form centering in northern France and dating from the eleventh to the thirteenth centuries, resulted from an earlier linkage of the Roman colonate, (a rigid factory-like governmental system of the late Roman and Romanized Western society) and the family and locality groupings of German tribes who "were basically a society of free men with a charismatic and hereditary chieftainship." Out of this latter culture came much of what is idealized by Americans who write about the free yeoman peasant. As Sorokin[5] notes, while the economy of the Roman Empire was decaying, a strait-jacket system of controls including the colonate was fastened over most activities and relationships making them compulsory and Gesellschaft-like. The fusion of the German culture with this totalitarian system of the declining Roman society brought more familistic and Gemeinschaft-like ties, but freedom of action remained restricted. With mounting insecurity everywhere "peasants—and often whole villages—commended themselves into the protection of the powerful, relinquishing their property and receiving it back as a 'precarium' . . . a possession (later hereditary tenure) burdened by certain economic obligations."[6] In those communities onto which feudalism fastened itself, only the authorities and a professional cast of warriors remained "free men". The majority sank into serfdom and submitted to social degradation and exclusion from the community of free men. However, in those areas in which free yeomen retained their freedom as in Upper Bavaria, Swabia, Thuringia, Saxony, Frisia, and Holstein, the yeomen idealized by Thomas Jefferson and others, held their own. Even in feudal societies such as Russia with its communal villages, small independent farmers emerged. When writers such as Le Play, Toennies, Sorokin, Weber, and others described rural social relations among yeoman and peasants in Gemeinschaft and familistic terms, they had such people in mind. Likewise a seldom-quoted piece from Marxist-Engels literature reports a cultural infusion of no mean importance for this background: "Let us . . . not forget that . . . English law is the only one which has preserved through ages, and transmitted to America and the colonies, the best part that old German person-

---

[5] Pitirim A. Sorokin, *Social Cultural Dynamics* (New York: American Book, 1937), Vol. 3, p. 202.

[6] Prawer and Eisenstadt, "Feudalism," p. 395.

al freedom, local self-government and the independence from all interference but that of the law courts, which on the Continent has been lost during the period of absolute monarchy, and has nowhere been as yet fully recovered."[7]

Unfortunately, serfdom and monarchy were not the only forces to weaken the independence of free yeomen and peasants. As feudalism passed, the revival of money economy, renewal of city life, trade, commerce and other results of the twelfth-century "urban revolution" brought disorder, change and suffering. Rural dwellers in many areas fell into a state of semi-shock and without the necessary knowledge or institutional protection to meet the new order lost much of the freedom and security they had. The emerging capitalistic class along with some feudal lords used their power to initiate changes such as the enclosures in England which deprived villagers and peasants of rights to communal property that had been theirs by custom. Along the Baltic coast in Mecklenburg and Holstein, and in Pomerania, peasants lost grazing and grass lands because they lacked power to hold what was by custom theirs to use. Even the ownership by fee simple and transfer of property worked against the many and for the richer few. Where fee simple ownership could have protected the yeoman peasant it often was not available. It was in fact not achieved for peasants in the French Revolution and due in part to this fact half of the land of France, Italy and Spain came to be worked by tenants and sharecroppers.[8] Ownership by family farmers and yeomen of the type referred to by Jefferson was much more common in Germany and in the Scandinavian kingdoms whose agricultural operations were close to the "ideal type" free yeoman family farmers.

PEASANTS—RURAL IDIOTS OR THE BACKBONE OF DEMOCRACY?

In no two societies are there greater differences in evaluations as reflected in claims for the strengths and weaknesses of the family-owned and operated agricultural enterprise than those

[7] Frederick Engels, "Socialism: Utopian and Scientific," in Karl Marx and Frederick Engels, *Selected Works* (Moscow: Foreign Languages Publishing House, 1949-1950), Vol. 1, p. 108.

[8] C. von Dietze, "Peasantry," *Encyclopedia of the Social Sciences,* (New York: Macmillan Co., 1937), Vol. 12, pp. 48-53.

held by agriculturists and politicians in the USA and the USSR. The institution of feudalism is of considerable importance in this regard. Marx and Engels who furnished the basic ideology for Russian communism saw the capitalistic system based upon private property as an intermediate and necessary stage in the movement from feudalism toward communism. During the capitalistic stage small enterprises such as the yeoman or family farm would be overcome by larger enterprises, in part at least because of the advantages accruing to the latter from economies of scale. It is our contention that despite his great scholarship, Marx, along with some other scholars such as Durkheim and Oscar Lewis, never understood nor sympathized with rural people and rural life. In this respect they stand in opposition to sociologists such as Toennies, Sorokin, and Le Play who understood peasants and respected their virtues.

It is doubtful that any single denunciation and related ideology has led to more suffering than that of Marx and Engels in proclaiming the "idiocy of peasantry." The liquidation of kulaks (small family farmers) along with the communal *mir* is one of the cruelest pages in human history. Since this action converted Russia from one of the important food exporting nations to a society visited by chronic food shortages and even famine, there appears to be plenty of evidence that "idiocy" resides not alone in the peasantry. As Mitrany in his *Marx Against the Peasant*[9] shows, yeoman farmers of Europe and the United States had proven themselves economically viable even before the liquidation of family farming in Russia and later in satellite countries after World War II. In Russia this evaluation and action both altered and defined the nature of the Soviet interpretation of socialism. "The collective farm [which replaced the peasant holding] become the single most important symbol of the Soviet system."[10] Marx, who denounced peasant life as rural idiocy, "bequeathed this prejudice to the socialist parties of Western Europe,"[11] and despite the continued vitality of European peas-

[9] David Mitrany, *Marx Against the Peasant—A Study in Social Dogmatism* (Chapel Hill: University of North Carolina Press, 1951).

[10] Philip M. Raup, "Societal Goals in Farm Size," in A. Gordon Ball and Earl O. Heady, eds., *Size, Structure, and Future of Farms* (Ames, Iowa: Iowa State University Press, 1971), p. 3.

[11] Daniel Thorner, "Peasantry," *International Encyclopedia of the Social Sciences* (New York: Macmillan Co., 1968), Vol. 2, p. 508.

antry in the early 1890's after Marx's death Engels insisted on the soundness of Marx's analysis and his prediction. Thus "Engels cut the ground out from under the social politicians of the day who were hoping to make an alliance with the peasantry against the landlords and industrialists."[12] Because peasants were well organized and because the dangers of food shortage following collectivization had been learned by native Marxist leaders, Poland and Yugoslavia did not follow Russia in liquidating peasant farms and villages. To national leaders who still rely on the family work unit as the chief production and consumption unit in rural areas falls the lot of proving the fallacy of Marx's prediction concerning the inevitability of factory farms.

As Mao and other Marxist leaders attempted to advance their revolution in China, little progress was made with city laborers. This led to a "dramatically different Marxist evaluation of the political possibilities of the peasantry, particularly in refernce to the Far East and Latin America . . . The road to power, according to the theory which the Chinese Communists elaborated, was no longer urban but rural."[13] Should we say that the agriculturalist who was once the idiot is now the hero? Hardly, because Marxism has no place for private property. But it must be noted that the place of the peasant in the secular religion of Marxism has changed drastically. Of course, rural sociologists have noted that the role of the peasant in general thinking changes. In cycles of urban prosperity peasants tend to be considered ignorant and uncouth. During periods of urban depression and instability the peasant may be romanticized as was the case after the French Revolution[14] and during the period of Nazism in Germany.

The United States, Australia and New Zealand never had a peasantry or the feudal remains of the peasantry. The enclosure movement in England and other experiences led early settlers to these countries (outside the plantation areas) to establish family farms where possible. Also, colonists resisted efforts by England to impose a quasi-feudalistic system on them. It was common for both rural and urban people to speak of the free-holding yeoman farmer as the backbone of democracy. After World War II conquered areas of large estates under American control were

[12] Ibid.
[13] Ibid., p. 509.
[14] Ibid., p. 508.

changed from large to small family farming units. In addition, the family farming unit is important in many other areas of the world including Canada, parts of Western Europe, Costa Rica, Chile, Brazil, Colombia, Turkey, India, Bangladesh, Japan and Korea.

Large estates, latifundia, haciendas, and other forms of non-family farming operations frequently arose out of feudal manors. In one such area in what was East Prussia before World War II one of the authors studied German efforts to change very large scale agricultural enterprises into family-sized units. Several German studies indicated that as these great estates, many of which were originally feudal manors, were broken down and reorganized as family-sized units, the basic nature of the economic enterprises changed. Agriculture became more intensive, more livestock was produced, and the density of population increased. More food, including that consumed by the farm families as well as more food delivered to the market came from the family-sized farms than from the previous estates.[15] This change from large factory-farm operations manned by wage laborers and/or sharecroppers under administrators to a family farming economy brought improved levels of living for most agricultural workers involved. The change also brought alterations in community and family life. The value orientation and attitudes of those living in the areas changed and population increased.

For those concerned with urban deterioration and pollution of various kinds, it is of interest to note that family farm enterprises support more people and support them at higher standards of living than do large farm enterprises. Family farmers and peasants also tend to vote for officials and measures that are relatively conservative whereas the reverse was true at least in Germany for the large estate laborers. Of course, this is one reason that Marxists have opposed the yeoman and family farmers.[16] Various studies have shown that when compared with factory farm communities, family farm communities have more

[15] Charles P. Loomis and J. Allan Beegle, *Rural Social Systems* (New York: Prentice-Hall, 1950), p. 294. See also Charles P. Loomis, *The Modern Settlement Movement in Germany* (Washington, D.C.: Bureau of Agricultural Economics, United States Department of Agriculture, 1935).

[16] Charles P. Loomis, "Political and Occupational Cleavages in a Hanoverian Village, Germany," *Sociometry*, Vol. IX, No. 4, (November 1946), p. 322 and

and better schooling as well as other social and economic facilities such as newspaper, business establishments, service and commercial clubs, and churches.[17] Also important is that people in family farming areas have pluralistic or diffuse power relations to neighborhood and community influentials. The relationships are more Gemeinschaft-like and less power centered than comparable relationships in communities and neighborhoods where large scale relationships prevail whether the latter be collective farms, factory-farms, haciendas or other forms.[18] As indicated in Chapter 14, successful plans for introducing improved practices into family farming communities must be very different in the two settings.

THE PROBLEM IN EFFICIENCY FOR EFFICIENCY'S SAKE

Only a few thousand farms will be needed to produce an excess of food and fiber for the nation. Heady and Ball believe that even under present available technology as few as 300,000 farms and 3 percent of the nation's labor force could achieve this.[19] With technology and organization envisioned by some for the future, less than 1 percent of the labor force of the nation could produce all the food and fiber needed. However, as sociologists who believe in the importance of socialization for future Americans as human beings, we suggest that the American family farm is indispensable.

Charles P. Loomis and J. Allan Beegle, "The Spread of German Nazism in Rural Areas," *American Sociological Review,* Vol. II, No. 6, (December 1946).

[17] Walter R. Goldschmidt, *Small Business and the Community: A Study in Central Valley of California on Effects of Scale of Farm Operations.* Report of the Special Committee to Study Problems of American Small Business, United States Senate, December 23, 1946, (Washington, D.C.: U.S. Government Printing Office, 1946). See an effort to update results of this study by Bruce L. LaRose, "Arvin and Dinuba Revisited: A New Look at Community Structure and the Effects of Scale of Farm Operations" in *Farmworkers in Rural America, 1971-1972,* Hearings Before the Committee on Migratory Labor of the Committee on Labor and Public Welfare, United States Senate, (Washington: U.S. Government Printing Office, 1972), pp. 3355-3363.

[18] Charles P. Loomis and John C. McKinney, "Systemic Differences Between Latin-American Communities of Family Farms and Large Estates," *American Journal of Sociology,* Vol. 61, No. 5, (March 1956).

[19] E. O. Heady and A. G. Ball, "Public Policy, Means and Alternatives," in Ball and Heady, *Size, Structure and Future,* p. 396.

Some economists and journalists eulogize the large non-family farm agricultural enterprises. One recent example is: "How Fred Andrew Tills the Soil with a Computer."[20] As such enterprises gobble up family farms one may laud the economies of scale introduced and the easy introduction of improved technology. One can hardly envy the once independent family farmers who face the possible prospect of becoming wage laborers. Should efficiency and economy of production of food and fiber and their marketing be the only goals? Why, one might ask, stop at elimination of family enterprises? Why not intensify and extend the working day or introduce other means of getting cheaper non-human output from the human input? For instance, prison labor on diets containing work-inducing drugs. Of course, we do not believe that such methods under the direction of managers will be used on any large scale in agriculture. But this suggestion is intended to emphasize the fact that the United States (and many other areas of the world) is at the cross-roads on the issue of "What price efficiency and technology?" Don Paarlberg of the USDA correctly poses the question, shall we "sacrifice a form of agricultural production that has produced good people as well as good crops and livestock [adding that the question is] 'social and political as well as economic' ".[21] We can hope with Secretary of Agriculture, Earl Butz, that 'we're always going to remain a nation of family farms."[22] Such statements have always been vote getters in the past. For us and many others the issue in addition to being social, political and economic, is moral.

We believe that probably no arena provides a better setting for the development of the work ethic in both children and adults in free enterprise societies than the family farm. The entrepreneurial ability required by such societies, independence with the desire to get ahead in the world, is nurtured through socialization of children (who live and work in families) whose parents own and operate a family farm. Although details concerning the socialization process here implied are very important, space requires that we restrict our discussion. We believe that the case at

[20] Dick Hubert and Peter Hauck, "How Fred Andrew Tills the Soil with a Computer," *Saturday Review of the Society,* March, 1973, p. 52ff.

[21] Ibid., p. 58.

[22] Ibid.

the end of the chapter on Family and Kinship Systems illustrates the dimensions of the problem. One of the authors has upon occasion briefly described the team activity of his own family in stacking hay when he, the oldest, worked with his father on the stack. His mother and the brother next to him in age pushed the hay onto the stacker with horse-powered hay bucks. Either his youngest brother or his sister drove the stacker team which brought the hay to the top of the stack with an overshot stacker. After explaining to college classes how important the action of each person was in the operation of the team, the authors asked students if they knew of work settings that offered comparable opportunity to develop ability to cooperate, take initiative, and make decisions. Few students were able to describe comparable family work operations that did not involve activities on family farms.

As area after area came under communistic control in Russia, China, Eastern Europe, Cuba, North Korea, North Vietnam, etc. and as collectives, communes and other agricultural forms were introduced, most family-oriented productive efforts were liquidated. We believe communism brings the greatest changes to farming enterprises and institutions. When various large estate and non-family farms are collectivized, the features of family farming are not lost since they never existed. In the many areas in which excessive subdivision has left only tiny scattered units or minifundia, collectivization also does not negate the important personality development that occurs when family farms are the victims. In our judgment, however, collectivized large estates and minifundia are poor substitutes for family farms either in the production of food and fiber or well-adjusted, independent personalities. We recognize that agricultural societies of minifundia or units too small to support families with adequate levels of living are very common in underdeveloped areas. In such societies poverty presses so heavily that only earlier exploitation by feudal masters prevented "economic surplus . . . [from being] swallowed up by population growth."[23] "Technological advance [was largely] . . . cancelled out by the system of social organization."[24] However, these do not represent the societies of yeoman peasant farmers idealized by Thomas Jeffer-

[23] Lenski, *Human Societies,* p. 236.
[24] Ibid., p. 327.

son. The yeoman family farmers were able to avoid feudal domination, but it appears now that the forces of both capitalism and communism threaten their continued existence.

THE FAMILY FARMING ENTERPRISES IN AMERICA

Philip Raup, an agricultural economist, has presented a lucid historical background for societal goals regarding farm size in the United States. "For Jefferson and the men of the eighteenth century who championed small farms the reasons were largely political and (as we would recognize today) sociological: freedom, independence, self-reliance, ability to resist oppressors, these were the qualities of the small property-owning farmers and husbandmen that most impressed Jefferson."[25] The sociologist Lowry Nelson writes that "the family farm can be said to represent the 'American ideal' of farm organization . . . Despite numerous variations and the difficulty of precise definition, the term 'family farm' is in general use and there is a common understanding as to its meaning."[26] Unfortunately, the agreement concerning its meaning is less common than earlier. But is the family farm still an American ideal?

In 1970, rural Michigan residents over the age of 21 were asked in a survey: "How important do you think it is to preserve the family farm as a basic unit of American agriculture?" Seventy-seven percent of the respondents said they thought it was "quite" or "very" important and only 2 percent thought it was not important at all.[27] The same respondents were also asked:

[25] Raup, "Societal Goals," pp. 4-5.

[26] Lowry Nelson, *Rural Sociology* (New York: American Book Company, 1948), p. 265.

[27] Richard D. Rodefeld and E. A. Wilkening, *Wisconsin Incorporated Farms I: Types, Characteristics and Trends* (Madison: Wisconsin Department of Rural Sociology, 1972), p. 1. See also Tom Koebernick and J. Allan Beegle, *Selected Attitudes and Opinions of Michigan's Rural Population* (East Lansing, Michigan: Agricultural Experiment Station Research Report 169, June 1972). Although we cannot claim that a cross-section sample of the United States general public would yield comparable results, in previous studies on comparable items, the sample of Michigan's rural population was surprisingly similar to that of the general public of the United States, including both rural and urban residents. See Charles P. Loomis, et al., *Linkages of Mexico and the United States* (East Lansing, Michigan: Agricultural Experiment Station, Research Bulletin 14, 1966).

"What do you think is best for American agriculture—large corporation farms, large commercialized family farms or small family farms?" Approximately 47 percent endorsed large commercial family farms and 47 percent favored small family farms. Only 6 percent endorsed large corporation farms. A larger proportion of the rural respondents who were farmers (63 percent) than the rural-nonfarm population favored the small family farm. This is true despite the fact that in 1970 the average farm stood at 387 acres as compared with 147 acres 50 years earlier—a growth making it 2.6 times larger.[28] There seems little doubt from this and other studies that the family farm remains an American ideal.

Recently, two rural sociologists and an agricultural economist, while underlining the American farm as an ideal, went further to proclaim that it is in remarkably sound economic health. The sociologists write, "The growth of . . . [the family farm] and the rural social system of which it is the central feature are unparallel as instruments making for the well-being of the agricultural population . . . Mechanization has made the family-sized farm in the United States increasingly efficient . . . Efficiency, expansion of size and income, and the characteristics of the genuine family-sized farm all are thoroughly compatible features and all continue to be viable parts of American agriculture. No factors have been identified that might cause all this to change in the future."[29] As will become evident the last sentence in this statement is becoming increasingly dubious, but let us see how an agricultural economist attempts to give the family farm a clear bill of health: "Family farms, those using predominantly family labor, make up about 95 percent of all farms and produce 65 percent of all farm products sold in the United States . . . Although these percentages have fluctuated slightly, they have been substantially the same for the last 30 years, despite the decline in total farm numbers . . . We have fewer than three million farms in the United States today, a little less than half the number we had 30 years ago . . . The major decline in numbers has been among those farms with value of sales of less than $10,000 per year. Their numbers dropped from nearly 5 million in 1939 to 1.8 million in 1970. Three-eights of the farms had sales of

[28] Ball and Heady, *Size, Structure, and Future,* p. 44.
[29] T. Lynn Smith and Paul E. Zopf, Jr., *Principles of Inductive Rural Sociology* (Philadelphia: F. A. Davis Co., 1970), p. 206.

$10,000 or more in 1970 . . . they currently account for about 90 percent of receipts from marketing. The smaller farms in this group—those with sales of $10,000 to $20,000—accounted for just over one-sixth of all farms . . . The largest farms—those with sales of $100,000 or more—comprise less than 2 percent of the total number, but they account for nearly one-third of marketings and more than one-third of farm production expenses."[30] Later in the same testimony Campbell argued that nonfamily types of corporations have low involvement in agriculture and denied any "takeover" by outside corporations.

As opposed to the position just expressed, we would support Richard Rodefeld, who is concerned about the vigor and health of the family farm and the invasion of agriculture by large-scale enterprises.

In his analysis of the situation, Rodefeld says: ". . . those who have maintained that 'family' farms are declining and 'corporate' or 'industrial type' farms are increasing are a good deal closer the truth than the USDA and others who have supported its position. If a family farm is defined as an owner operated family sized farm, then this type of farm has not predominated in farm sales since at least 1959 . . . 'Nonfamily' farms can be viewed as insignificant in U.S. society only if one is willing not to attach very much import to farm types which account for more than 50 percent of all sales, even though they only accounted for 21 percent of the farms and farm operators in 1964. 'Corporate' and 'industrial type' farms can be viewed as insignificant only if 10 percent of all farm sales in 1964, and undoubtedly those 9 years later, is also viewed as insignificant. There has, in fact, been a systematic, uninterrupted 20-year decline in the proportion of all farm sales accounted for by family sized farms over the same 20-year period."[31]

Even though they may favor the family farm, many economists give first priority to the freedom of all to compete in the

[30] J. Phil Campbell, Under Secretary of Agriculture, before the Antitrust Subcommittee of the Judiciary, U.S. House of Representatives, March 22, 1972 on HR 11654, *The Family Farm Act,* mimeographed version.

[31] Richard D. Rodefeld, "A Reassessment of the Status and Trends in 'Family' and 'Corporate' Farms in U.S. Society," paper presented for First National Conference on Land Reform, April 25-28, 1973, San Francisco, mimeographed, pp. 30-31. See Rodefeld, "The Current Status of U.S. 'Corporate' Farm Research," in *Farmworkers in Rural America,* pp. 3244-3305.

market. After demonstrating that the big operators use more credit than the small ones (those with sales of $100,000 or more had debts equal to 24 percent of their assets as compared with only 15 percent for those with gross sales of less than $5,000 in 1970), Campbell points out that the smaller farm operators earn money in off-farm activities. The statement that "two or more sources of income is a way of life for many Americans' seems gratuitous, especially because off-farm work is forced upon farmers by the cost-price squeeze and other pressures on farming. Once partly out of agriculture, these "farmers" become more interested in such things as union wages and, as Heady and Ball note, "just don't care that much" about legislation and other means of helping agriculture.

The great reduction in the number of family farms in recent years, the fact that only 5 percent of all farms which are defined as non-family farms now produce more than 35 percent of the farm products sold, the large volume of off-farm employment especially by small farmers, and other facts, lead us to believe the family farm, once proclaimed as the backbone of the nation, is weakening. Certainly future generations produced in a family farm environment are likely to be small indeed if the number of people involved is decreasing significantly.

The percentage decrease of people on farms was 14.6 between 1966 and 1970.[32] When farms are classified by value of products sold, the number of people living on those producing over $20,000 increased. This increase stood at 33.8 percent for those farms selling over $40,000 in products and 12.0 percent for those selling from $20,000 to $40,000 worth of products. In the same period, percentage decreases in population living on farms selling $2,500-$4,999, $5,000-$9,999, and $10,000-$19,999 were 19.3, 29.7, and 21.8 respectively. Such great losses in population on these farms do not prompt us to proclaim robust health of the family farm as we have known it.

Remembering that the same proportion (47 percent) of the rural people in Michigan favored preserving *small* and *large* family farms, the data of Table 1 leave little doubt that a value in America is being lost. The type of farm on which most rural so-

---

[32] These and the following figures on population change are from Vera J. Banks and Calvin L. Beale, *Farm Population by Race, Tenure, and Economic Scale of Farming, 1966 and 1970* (Washington, D.C.: U.S. Department of Agriculture, Agricultural Economic Report No. 228).

TABLE 1.

Comparison of the Concentration of Number of Farms and Value of Products Sold, 1929 (Adjusted to 1964 Prices), 1964 and 1969.

1964 Census Class (Value of Products sold)	Percent of Total Number			Percent of Total Sales		
	1929 adj.	1964	1969	1929 adj.	1964	1969
$20,000 & over	1.2	12.7	20.2	14.9	64.4	75.8
10,000-19,999	2.7	14.8	14.5	12.4	19.2	14.9
5,000- 9,999	7.9	16.0	14.3	17.9	10.6	5.4
2,500- 4,999	23.8	14.1	16.7	30.0	4.7	1.9
Less than 2,500	64.4	42.5	34.3	24.8	1.1	2.0

Calculations for 1929, 1964, and 1969 by Leonard R. Kyle based on U.S. Census of Agriculture.

ciologists and agricultural economists were raised is disappearing. To those agricultural economists and others who say about the family farm that it is not in danger but merely getting larger, we must dissent. What is accomplished if the family farm as an institution is preserved "in the same sense that DuPont is a family business?"[33] It is time that the technology and economy polluting the air and water and eliminating the favorable environments in which to live and raise children be placed under human control.

Although USSR officials report that the large state farms and the collectives demonstrate the economy of bigness, there are not solid facts to support it. As has been observed by critics of such reports, if there were economies that favored bigness it would lie not in technical economies but rather "in a dearth of well trained under-managers and that the way to get over improvements is by using such highly skilled managers as you have and spread them over a wide area ... In our country ... [the United Kingdom] a man of high skill and the gimmicks that the others haven't got can acquire land and operate a larger area."[34]

The input of technology certainly is not the only force promot-

[33] Hubert and Hauck, "How Fred Andrew Tills," p. 58.

[34] Ford Sturrock, in his discussion of S. Sergeyev's paper, "Methods of Economic Analysis of Large Soviet Agricultural Enterprises," *Papers and Reports, Fourteenth International Conference of Agricultural Economists, Minsk, USSR* (Oxford: Institute of Agrarian Affairs, 1971), p. 179.

ing bigness. This is highlighted by the fact that in the United States the highly mechanized family farm is over 300 acres in size whereas in Japan highly mechanized farms average about three acres. Obviously the form of technology can be adapted both to human and non-human components of a system. If training and experience in management skills would help the many smaller farmers compete more effectively, perhaps what Max Weber called the "iron cage" of rational efficiency does not necessarily lead to ever larger agricultural operations. As Madden and Partenheimer note, the function of size of operation and highest profit combination is very complex: "The size of farm currently attracting the greatest increase in cropland is not as small as the most efficient size nor as large as the most profitable size, but . . . somewhere in between."[35] A few advantages of smaller operations noted by these writers are the following: (1) Large operations may have to pay for roads and other facilities paid for by the public in the case of smaller operations; (2) Large operations may be greater polluters as in the case of beef feedlots and come under public pressure to furnish disposal not required of smaller operators; (3) Unionization of laborers is more pressing on larger farms and labor costs may be higher. Despite these facts and the generally favorable American public attitude to the small family farm "the optimum-size farm in terms of sales is becoming larger and larger, and the scope for the family farm is restricted in the process."[36]

WHY IS THE FAMILY FARM IN TROUBLE?

If, as the writers we have quoted and the attitude surveys indicate, the family farm is a value cherished by Americans, why is it in danger? If most staff members of Land Grant Colleges and Universities in service abroad are candid when they say that no farmers in the world have more helpful services than those provided in the U.S. through various agricultural research and extension services, it seems incredible that the family farm is in danger of disappearing. However, we believe that it is and we

[35] J. Patrick Madden and Earl J. Partenheimer, "Evidence of Economies and Diseconomies of Farm Size," in Ball and Heady, *Size, Structure, and Future,* p. 97.

[36] Peter G. Helmberger, "Markets, Farm Size, and Integration," in Ball and Heady, *Size, Structure, and Future,* p. 115.

believe with Moore and Dean that "past public research and extension has hastened the demise of small farms."[37] Publicly supported research, perhaps to a larger extent in the United States than Japan, has resulted in technical innovations of various kinds, most of which have increased the pressures from economies of scale. Also the effect is selective. It is the larger operators who gain most from improved technology because they tend to be the first to learn of it and use it, thereby gaining a windfall before resulting increases in production reduce prices. Therefore, if "the public wishes to foster family farms, its public research and extension agencies . . . must . . . [become more efficient in reaching] these farms."[38] Various governmental programs such as the Resettlement Administration, Farm Security Administration, and Farmers Home Administration with their explicit policies to favor family-sized farms along with the vocational agriculture program, the Extension Service and the Soil Conservation Service have had little impact on farm size.[39] However, with the price and income support programs it is a different matter.

Quance and Tweeten maintain that all public programs in the four decades before 1970 increased farm size and that commodity programs designed to improve incomes while retiring land, produced conditions such that, "the bigger the farm, the greater is the opportunity to take advantage of program benefits."[40] Thus in 1970 as a result of price support programs those farms with gross sales of over $40,000 constituted only 7.6 percent of all farms but received 30.4 percent of all payments.[41] Although the manner by which this is brought about is complex, the lesson is there. A nation cherishes the family farm, yet designs governmental programs that do not favor it, especially in its smaller forms. What rural sociologist has not been ridiculed by an economist for suggesting that, other things equal, the effort

[37] Charles V. Moore and Gerald W. Dean, "Industrialized Farming," in Ball and Heady, *Size, Structure, and Future*, p. 230.

[38] Ibid.

[39] Leroy Quance and Luther G. Tweeten, "Policies, 1930-1970," in Ball and Heady, *Size, Structure, and Future*, p. 26.

[40] Ibid., p. 37.

[41] Leonard R. Kyle, et al., "Who Controls Agriculture Now?" in *Who Will Control U.S. Agriculture?*, North Central Public Policy Education Committee, (Urbana: Cooperative Extension Service, University of Illinois Special Publication 27), p. 8.

required by society to keep the small family farm should be made?

Even agricultural economists who maintain that the family farm, being "A durable and resilient institution . . . has survived a technological revolution"[42] admit that some agricultural products, as for example broilers, are no longer in any considerable amounts produced on family farms. In fact, less than 5 percent of the producers of broilers are independent. Three-fourths work in the corporate-integrated structure under contract with feed and other large enterprises, and the remainder are large outfits using hired labor. As with broilers, family farmers producing other products are often under heavy pressure to become subsidiary units in larger business organizations that are built upon merchandizing. It is estimated that in 1970 three-quarters or more of the output of the following crops had already fallen under such arrangements: broilers, seed crops, fluid milk, sugar crops, citrus fruit and processed vegetables. Many other products are not far behind in the extent they have fallen under such arrangements, ranging from 36 percent of all livestock and 40 percent of eggs, to 70 percent of potatoes and sweet potatoes. As yet the family farms producing wheat, corn, cotton, soybeans, cattle and hogs are relatively free from domination of such arrangements.

Two factors that work against the increase in the number and strength of farms in America are government acreage control programs and pressures by larger business organizations that bring family farmers under various forms of vertical, integrated structures. There are also many other pressures on the family farm. Some of these include: (1) The increasing technical complexity of farming; (2) Persistent pressure for volume production; (3) The scarcity of land, coupled with growing needs for land for purposes other than farming; (4) tax laws and rules making it relatively easy for nonfarm investors to outbid farmers for land;[43] (5) The ever-increasing need for firms and individuals with money to invest at interest or in stocks or property to hedge against inflation. An example of this need is the strategy of the Superior Oil Company of Houston, Texas, which, according to

---

[42] Donald Paarlberg, "The Forces Modernizing Farming," in the National Farm Institute, *Corporate Farming and the Family Farm* (Ames: Iowa State University Press, 1970), p. 118.

[43] Ball and Heady, *Size, Structure, and Future*, pp. 40-58.

eulogies of their manager, keeps getting computer print-outs advising the company to buy more land.[44] Publishers and writers accustomed to a semi-craft tradition of a few decades ago know all too well how the Texas oil and other millions transformed the book publishing world. The family farmer, less accustomed to dealing with big investors may be more easily victimized than the publishing world. The family farmer's fate may, as some writers forsee, be settled "in the mournful burial of its Jeffersonian past."[45] We fear this may happen before his friends know what took place.

From the first no single production enterprise in America could deliver more votes at the polls than agriculture. Accompanying the (from 6½ million in 1930 to 2/3 million in 1970)[46] great attrition in number of farms since 1930 is the increasing dependence of the reduced numbers of farmers on non-farm income, as depicted in Table 2. For almost two-thirds of the farmers of the nation the average off-farm income per farm operator is greater than the average realized net income per farm, including government payments. As a result of these conditions, "farmers who control farm organizations and commodity groups are the larger commercial operators of family-controlled farms"[47] and the smaller farmers who are more dependent on union wage rates and other sources and "just don't care that much[48] about farm legislation for the small farmer. Unless farmers who operate family farms, both large and small, can be activated to join others to protect the family farm, "the farmer as independent yeoman, more or less self-sufficient, tilling the soil, reaping the harvest, at peace with his God, at home in his . . . farmhouse, this persistent folk hero of a persistent pastoral legendry...[will be replaced by the] agri-businessman."[49]

The large scale non-family corporation farm. In terms of social organization, a non-family corporation farm is like any other non-family corporate enterprise, be it a factory or an insurance company. A manager is employed by the corporation.

---

[44] Hubert and Hauck, "How Fred Andrew Tills."

[45] Ibid.

[46] A. Gordon Ball and Earl O. Heady, "Trends in Farm and Enterprise and Scale," in Ball and Heady, *Size, Structure, and Future,* p. 43.

[47] Ibid., p. 394.

[48] Ibid.

[49] Hubert and Hauck, "How Fred Andrew Tills," p. 52.

TABLE 2
U.S. Farm Income Distribution by Sales Class, 1970

Selected Items	Farms with Sales of						All Farms
	$40,000 and more	$20,000 to 39,999	$10,000 to 19,999	$5,000 to 9,999	$2,500 to 4,999	Less than $2,500	
Number of farms (thousands)	223	374	513	370	260	1,184	2,924
Distribution (percent)	7.6	12.8	17.5	12.7	8.9	40.5	100
Cash receipts (percent distribution)	52.5	21.4	15.6	5.8	2.1	2.6	100
Average realized gross income per farm	$126,812	$32,096	$17,450	$9,324	$5,199	$2,148	$19,350
Average realized net income per farm*	$ 25,664	$ 9,962	$ 6,208	$3,492	$2,049	$1,059	$ 5,374
Average off-farm income per farm operator family	$ 5,803	$ 3,503	$ 3,452	$4,984	$5,465	$7,954	$ 5,833
Average direct government payments per farm	$ 5,067	$ 2,527	$ 1,715	$ 916	$ 592	$ 227	$ 1,271
Direct government payments (percent distribution)	30.4	25.5	23.7	9.1	4.1	7.2	100

*Includes government payments. Source: USDA, Economic Research Service, Farm Income Situation, July, 1971.

The final authority resides in the board of directors, but the status-role of manager carries authority in operating the enterprise within the policies and procedures defined by the board. Hired labor or tenants or both are used for manpower. Most large scale corporation farms, sometimes called "factories in the fields," produce specialty crops and are most often located in the Western Specialty-Crop Areas. Most other crops, however, are sometimes produced on corporation farms, with wheat, cotton, soy beans, cattle, and hogs being less involved than other major crops. Obviously the goal of such an enterprise is profit to the stockholders.

Norms and laws to prevent extreme exploitation of labor usually develop in cultures where labor organizations are prevalent. Nonetheless, it is difficult for the manager, not to mention the laborers, to make farming "a way of life". The manager and the laborers cannot become interested in developing a permanent home, for much of the labor requirement on such enterprises is seasonal. The status-role, social ranking, and sanction patterns in the corporation farm are not different from those in the rationalized plantation. In fact, some modern plantation owners have little more intimate contact with their plantations than most stockholders have with their corporations. For example, one of the authors spent some time on one of the largest corporation operations in the Peruvian Andes. Of the 150 stockholders living in Peru, only three had ever seen the operation. In the many years of its existence these three came only once and spent only a few hours there during which they were sick with *soroche* (mountain sickness). Operation decisions were left to the manager. That ownership and management status-roles may be separated in the case of large estates is well illustrated in this example.

As we note that "many farmers . . . deplore the lack of freedom which exists for the farmer who produces broilers under contract"[50] in large corporate structures, we are reminded of how the Roman colonate and the feudal system placed a strait-jacket on the free yeoman. Heffernan has compared two forms of large-scale broiler operation—the corporate-integrated structure in which families function under contract and the corporate-farmhand structure in which factory-like, wage-hand rela-

[50] Kyle, "Who Controls," p. 37. The percentages above are from this source.

tions prevail. Community involvement was lower and alienation higher in the factory-like,wage-hand system, but neither form of large scale integration provided the community participation and freedom from alienation of the family farm operation.[51] Those who rejoice in cheaper broilers, noting that "closer coordination between production and marketing processes . . . has been beneficial to both producers and consumers . . ."[52] need to think of the family farmers who have been driven out of business by this intrusion of big money and big business. Such persons need to face up to the fact the factory-like wage-hand system is here to stay and that unless the Land-Grant Colleges and others can bring farmers the coordination and other services needed while retaining the rural community base, American rural society will have disappeared. We agree with Richard Rodefeld[53] in his testimony criticizing the testimony made by J. Phil Campbell. Campbell claimed that the gigantic forms of integration that tie big industry and money into agricultural production provide employment opportunities for small farmers. However, not a word was said about the thousands of family-sized producers who are driven out of farming by these big establishments.

The plantation and hacienda. Where family farms and larger holdings exist side by side, the smaller units usually are on the poorer soils. Studies made by the Area Research Center of Michigan State University and the Inter-American Institute of Agricultural Sciences[54] show that in one area in Costa Rica agricultural production per acre on the family-sized farms was only one-third as great as on the haciendas in the same area. Even though the population density was the same, the level of living of those on family-sized holdings was not lower than for most persons living on the haciendas. Only hacienda owners, managers, and a few others had levels of living that excelled the poorer family farmers. Those living on the family-sized farms, howev-

[51] William D. Heffernan, "Sociological Dimensions of Agricultural Structures in the United States," Paper Presented to the Third World Congress for Rural Sociology, Baton Rouge, La., August 1972.

[52] J. Phil Campbell, on HR 11654, *The Family Farm Act.*

[53] Rodefeld, "Comments on the Statement of J. Phil Campbell," *Farmworkers in Rural America.*

[54] Charles P. Loomis, et al., *Turrialba* (Glencoe, Illinois: The Free Press, 1953), Chapters 13 and 14.

er, enjoyed the freedom and independence of being private entrepreneurs; that is, they were their own bosses.

Although there is a tendency for large estates to swallow the good land surrounding them, Smith[55] has shown that whether an area becomes dominated by family farms or large estates, the economy is largely determined by early land division. The original nonfamily-sized farm operation in the United States was the plantation. How the plantation operated as a social system and how it dominated much of the South has been described by Woofter and his collaborators. Woofter writes: "A plantation is defined . . . as a tract farmed by one owner or manager with five or more resident families. These may include the landlord, and laborers, share tenants, or renters. Except in the case of renters, the landlord exercises close supervision over operators, and except in the case of wage laborers each family cultivates a separate piece of land."[56] Woofter (writing in the 1930's) says that the typical plantation had fourteen families living on it. The average size of 646 plantations was 907 acres and each wage hand averaged forty-five acres and each tenant twenty-five acres.

Originally the plantation and feudal manor approached a self-contained community with slaughter and storage houses, spinning rooms, gins, grist mills, and similar processing units. The work force was relatively stable. Class lines were sharply drawn, with relatively few in the middle and upper groups. The thinking, planning, and security patterns in such areas of the Cotton Belt of previous decades depended upon a few owners and operators. This type of social system produced a large body of workers who were accustomed to having others initiate action. Workers were not expected to manifest great initiative. Most operations and decisions involved little resourcefulness or mental effort. Many never were involved in more complicated tasks than the use of a mule and a plow. Few engaged in concerted and formal group activity such as that involved in the organization and operation of a cooperative. Most of the formal organizations that did exist were in the nature of fundamentalistic churches requiring little deliberation on the part of the group.

Figure 1 is of special interest to those concerned with the ad-

[55] T. Lynn Smith, *The Sociology of Rural Life* (New York: Harper and Brothers, 1953), pp. 313-319.

[56] T. J. Woofter, Jr., *Landlord and Tenant on the Cotton Plantation,* Research Monograph V (Washington, D.C.: Works Progress Administration, 1936), p. 19.

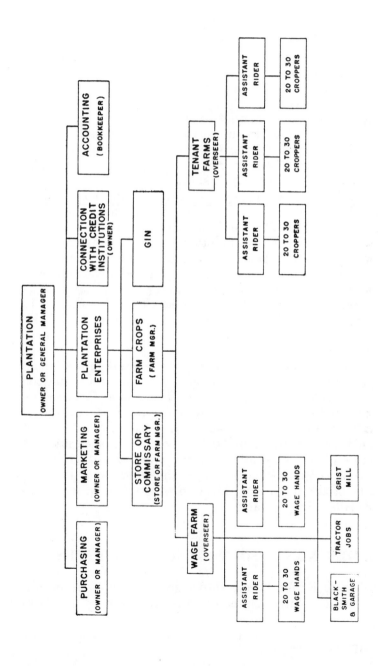

FIGURE 1. Organization of enterprises on a large and closely supervised plantation.

ministration of social systems. Although the organization grew out of the semi-feudal slave plantation, the formal organization chart indicates the authority patterns of factories. The resemblance may be limited to the organization chart, however, because in actual practice the factory and the plantation may operate quite differently.

The factory, of course, cannot be independent of the market and like all Gesellschaft-like enterprises has functionally specific status-roles, most of which are attained rather than ascribed. If non-rational or traditional norms are dominant, the factory in a market economy is not likely to survive. Under the conditions of the factory and modern factory farm, management usually has control over the workers only during working hours. On plantations and estates that are not governed by the economic stragegy of highest profit combination, the control may be more diffuse and the responsibility of those in positions of authority for those under their control may be much greater. Commercialization and mechanization and the accompanying universalistic norms bring functional specificity and affectual neutrality to the status-roles of large-scale agriculture. The social rank attached to status-roles in such situations depends largely upon performance.

Leonard and Loomis,[57] in a study made before the mechanical cotton picker was introduced, found the wage hands and the croppers of the Arkansas Delta to be highly mobile. Mobility frequently resulted in an attempt to improve living levels in spite of the fact that mobility is negatively correlated with the level of living. This study further indicated that owners pushed laborers and tenants off the plantation when it was advantageous for them to do so. Tenants and laborers, on the other hand, left in an attempt to better conditions. Mechanization and other forces continue to displace thousands.

OTHER NON-FAMILY-SIZED FARM TYPES

According to Eaton, "Cooperative group farming is indigeneous to America. Although today it is practiced more widely in

[57] C. P. Loomis and Olen Leonard in *Farm Population and Rural Life Activities,* Vol. XIII, No. 2 (April, 1939).

Russia, Mexico and Palestine, America was the principal location of its early development."[58] Although space does not permit an analysis of the various experiments and systems, these studies provide some interesting and significant sociological literature. Unfortunately few studies of such groups have been made that analyze them as social systems. Analyses of family farms and haciendas as social systems in Latin America, however, have been made.[59] Most of the cooperative farms may be classified as follows: (1) joint cultivation associations; (2) cooperative corporation farms; or (3) communal villages.

Joint cultivation associations. These associations bring the advantages of cooperative farming to families who remain individual family farmers but pool their machinery, land, livestock, and labor to produce collectively as a unit. These are common in areas recently brought under the domination of the Soviet Union. They were common in Russia during the period following the revolution but later most of them were transformed into collectives and state farms. Some of the Mexican *ejidos* are joint cultivation associations, some English farms, and many Jewish agricultural enterprises in Palestine, called *moschavei-ovdim,* are of this type.[60]

The cooperative corporation farm. This type of farm enterprise is owned or rented and operated jointly so that the returns are shared, usually in accordance with the work contributed. Much of Russian agriculture is carried on in this form and most of the Mexican *ejidos* are of this type. Some land in Palestine is operated under this arrangement. In this type of system private property plays an important role, since at least some of the products either of the total unit or the individual family are available to and/or consumed by each family. In many instances the families own their own homes.

One of the most interesting accounts of a cooperative corporation farm is a description of the attempt of the United States

[58] Joseph W. Eaton, *Exploring Tomorrow's Agriculture* (New York: Harper and Brothers, 1943), p. 207. For additional bibliography, see Joseph W. Eaton and Saul M. Katz, *Research Guide on Cooperative Group Farming* (New York: H. W. Wilson and Co., October 1942).

[59] Loomis, et al., *Turrialba,* Chapters 1 and 5; and Thomas L. Norris, "Decision-Making in Relation to Property on a Costa Rica Coffee Estate," Michigan State College Ph.D. Dissertation, (1952).

[60] Eaton, *Exploring,* p. 242.

Department of Agriculture to rehabilitate families, stranded during the depression, on a large irrigated farm near Casa Grande, Arizona. Banfield[61] attempts to use what he calls "Cooley's life study method" to describe *what* happened in such a way as to give insight into *why* it happened. Although the analysis is not made according to the categories used in this text as elements of social systems, it does provide evidence of their utility in understanding social processes.

What happened was that the Federal Government invested $1,000,000 and the time of expert farm managers, administrators, and home economists. Due to the war and prosperity, the material level of living of the families—mostly people from the drought-stricken western Cotton Belt—was raised beyond anything most of them had expected. Factionalism, based upon a bitter cleavage between pro-government and the anti-government groups, however, led to the liquidation of the project. The local lawyers who carried through the liquidation against governmental wishes received almost as much in proceeds as the settlers who had endured the anguish of frustration and conflict, and had put up with dictatorial officials. The project was a failure and as one settler put it, "We not only killed the goose that laid the golden egg, we even threw the . . . egg away."[62]

Why did it happen? Tugwell, the administrator who was chiefly responsible for the project, says that "after almost two decades it seems to me that we were doomed to failure from the start."[63] The implication seemed to be that the culture and character of Americans lacked that which was needed for the success of this type of venture.

The following seem to be the salient reasons for failure: 1. Insufficient and shifting definition of the situation. The status-roles, norms, rights, and responsibilities for individuals and groups on the project were not explicit. Members played the roles of both employers and employees. The manager, although restricted to the members in the selection of foremen and supervisors, was expected to strive for efficiency and profits, and, especially during the latter period of the project, he was expected to make a democratic community and a true cooperative. "In the

---

[61] Edward C. Banfield, *Government Project* (Glencoe, Illinois: The Free Press, 1951).
[62] Ibid., p. 217.
[63] Ibid., p. 11 (Foreword by Rexford G. Tugwell).

absence of conventions that would prescribe a 'right' way of looking at things, every man was forced to make up his own mind about the proprieties of almost every situation that arose."[64]

2. The lack of definition of the situation resulted in continuous struggle for power. Since incomes from the project were more or less equal, the only rewards left in the sytem were those of position. At the bottom of the social scale were the migrant cotton picker "Okies" whom the local people regarded as an "inferior species." Those who had never had anything better generally sided with the foremen and other pro-government members, who were only slightly better off economically and socially. A system such as this left only one way for those little better off than the sharecroppers to gain power and prestige—to lead in the fight against the government. "The chief avenue to status in the project situation was power in the management of the farm. This power could be secured in one of two ways: it could be had by joining forces with the government and serving as a foreman or informally as a supporter of management or it could be had by leading or participating in an anti-government faction . . . the government officials made the mistake of supposing that the settlers would act rationally in the manner of economic men. . . ."[65] In reality much of the struggle for power was "irrational," because of a need for power that the fluid nature of the project accentuated.

Although there have been many attempts to establish such cooperative farms in the United States, few have succeeded. The failure of the Casa Grande experiment throws in relief the necessity for administrators and planners to understand the basic nature of social systems and their elements. If new social systems with different value orientations and social structures are to be created, they must be articulated with the larger society.

Communal villages. In the communal villages, the importance of private property is eliminated. Need is the basis for the division of earnings, and the villages are usually held together by strong religious bonds and ideology. Communal villages are most common in Palestine where they are called *kvutzoth*. These differ from the other systems of this type in that they are secular

[64] Ibid., p. 129.
[65] Ibid., p. 233.

and, according to Eaton,[66] are the most successful group farms anywhere. Paradoxically such communities exist not in totalitarian nations but in the democracies.

Before the Amana Society in eastern Iowa with its seven villages, communal farms, and factories reorganized to become the largest cooperative corporation farm in the United States with assets of over $2,445,000, it was a communal agricultural community that called itself the "Community of True Inspiration." As in the case of the Hutterites, the members of The Amana Society were a religious sect who came to America to avoid persecution and practiced a collective form of community ownership and operation of all property.[67]

The largest group of communal farmers living in the United States is the Hutterite settlement in southeastern South Dakota. Most of the Hutterites are now located in Manitoba, Alberta, and Saskatchewan, where they migrated from the United States to avoid persecution by local South Dakota vigilantes during World War I. The first community was founded in 1528 in Moravia by a group of Anabaptists and pacifists who fled to escape the Peasants' Revolt in southern Germany and Switzerland. The group fled from Moravia to Slovakia, then to Hungary and Rumania, and finally to Russia. Some 250 immigrants established three communities in South Dakota between 1874 and 1879. In 1965 there were 170 Hutterite communities in the United States and Canada and approximately 16,500 persons.

THE ELEMENTS OF THE HUTTERITE SOCIAL SYSTEMS[68]

Ends and Objectives.   Although expressed ends are highly transcendental, the outsider is given the impression that preservation of the existing order is the most important goal. A classless society without individual income and property and the sup-

---

[66] Eaton, *Exploring,* p. 244.

[67] For a discussion and bibliography, see Paul Honigsheim, "Rural Collectivities" in Loomis and Beegle, *Rural Social Systems,* pp. 825-850 and John A. Hostetler and Gertrude E. Huntington, *The Hutterites in North America* (New York: Holt, Rinehart and Winston, 1967).

[68] Based upon Eaton, *Exploring,* p. 218ff and Hostetler and Huntington, *The Hutterites.*

porting structure and value orientation reinforce this goal. It leads to an extreme amount of energy and sacrifice in the interest of boundary maintenance of the group and its social system. The importance of material goods as an objective of life is denied. Of course, members do not deny that it is necessary to provide the minimum of material essentials of life. The farm enterprises of dairying, producing grain for livestock feed, and baking bread support the main ends of the group.

Norms. Communication with the "sinful" world is restricted. Established taboos have the following results: Movies are not attended, secular books are not read, radios are not owned, and no one votes in governmental elections. Individual income and property are forbidden. Modes of clothing, housing, food, and most behavior are the same for all of the same age group and sex. Special privileges for the performance of roles having authority are kept at a minimum and are theoretically non-existent.

Status-roles. The preacher-manager is elected for life and is both a temporal and spiritual head. There are preachers, elders, a business manager, farm manager and councilmen, female kitchen and garden bosses, and male farm bosses for cattle, sheep and hogs—all elected by popular oral vote. The same family roles prevalent in the Western nucleated family exist in the Hutterite family.

Power. The council, composed of five to seven men, elected by the voting members of the community carries on the executive functions. Usually four other men sit on the council. They are the head preacher, who is responsible for all aspects of community life, both economic and moral; the householder, who is responsible for the economic prosperity of the colony; the assistant minister, and the field manager. Although the first preacher has the highest leadership position, his actions are subject to review by the council. The first preacher, sometimes the assistant preacher, the field manager, and sometimes additional members constitute an informal sub-council, the members of which may lay out the day's work and check on one another and the other officials. Women are without voting rights and have little power.

Social rank. Rank or standing depends upon embodiment of the ends of the group, industry, and the ability to perform the many jobs associated with farming, shoemaking, and carpentry. Men have higher status than women and adults have higher status than children. "In the end all men are equal before God," the Hutterites say.

Sanctions. The most effective and only obvious negative sanction is the danger of having to leave the group. The most important and almost sole positive sanction is esteem by one's fellows and the promises of the hereafter.

Facilities. Individual property does not exist; and the land and machinery, much of which is modern, costly and efficient, and livestock are community property. Families are provided kitchenless apartments, the number of rooms being determined in accordance with the number of members. Members are supposed to eat in community kitchens, and work in and use goods produced in the community industries: the bakery, laundry, soap making room, creamery, blacksmith shop, carpentry shop, broom shop, shoe shop, and gristmill. Community facilities include the one-room schoolhouse which also serves as the center of worship.

Territoriality. The location of the Hutterite communities in space has always featured the theme of the minority group persecuted by the "sinful" majority group. Isolation was sought by the original settlers and present members attempt to maintain it. Homes and farm buildings are usually grouped together.

SOCIAL PROCESSES IN THE HUTTERITE COMMUNITY

Communication. As indicated before, every effort is made to prevent communication with the "sinful" outside world. "They live in as complete isolation as possible and do not participate in the rights and duties of citizenship. They do not own radios, attend movies, read secular books, vote in elections. . . ."[69] Interpersonal communication within the community is frequent and constant. Communal meals and work bring everyone together regularly.

Decision-making. As indicated previously, the first preacher makes most of the decisions. However, if there is a division of opinion concerning what should be done, the matter is discussed by the council informally or a community meeting is called. Generally this is not necessary because administrators do what they

[69] Ibid., p. 219.

know to be the "common will," based upon tradition and custom.

Boundary maintenance. Group norms, taboos, and other devices serve to maintain solidarity and integration of the group. Individual property, distinctive dress, grooming, and contacts with the outside world (except as permitted and institutionalized) are tabooed. Integration and isolation seem to be ends in and of themselves. The group image of itself as a chosen people persecuted by the "sinful" outsiders is internalized by individuals. The few who leave the Hutterite community usually return, because they find adjustment to the outside very difficult. Whereas socialization on family farms prepares members for the loneliness and competition of capitalistic society socialization among the Hutterite Brethren develops the socially dependent individual.

COMMUNAL FARMS VS. OTHER FARMS

The Hutterite communities were reviewed to indicate how the structure and value orientation of these systems differ from those in capitalistic economies and elsewhere. The Hutterites attempt to follow the Biblical pattern outlined in Acts 2:44-45, "And all that believed were together, and had all things in common, and sold all their possessions and goods and parted them to all men, as every man had need." The Hutterite system makes communal existence, structured into one more or less exclusive social system, an end in and of itself. Outsiders find life in the system intolerably dull because it is the communal system, not the individual or separate sub-systems such as families and associations, that is important. Relationships are Gemeinschaft-like with emphasis on first the community and then the family. Cultural standards and norms emphasize the collective, not the individual. Responsibility of the individual is broad and diffuse, having few of the specific, limited characteristics of individuals in bureaucracies; love and affectivity in interpersonal relationships is not only permitted but enjoined by the scriptures. Although the Biblical injunctions followed are universalistic in nature, the groups are small and the particular "needs" of the individual are stressed and met. Except for the higher ascribed rank accorded males, social rank is determined not by birth or ascription but by performance and achievement.

On a corporation farm or plantation that is more Gesellschaft-like, the standards stress specificity, affective neutrality, and achievement. Only in the case of achievement, as opposed to ascription, are the communities of the Hutterites and the corporation farms similar. In both cases achievement is emphasized but perhaps less so in the case of large estates than among the Hutterites.

The Hutterite community is used to highlight some of the differences to be found in types of farm organization. The Gemeinschaft-like structure of the Hutterite community is shown to contrast sharply with the more Gesellschaft-like structure of the plantation, corporation farm, or large estate. The family farm enterprise, characteristic of American agriculture, falls between the two extremes. However, it bears more resemblance to the Hutterite pattern than to the plantation pattern.

TYPE-OF-FARMING AREAS

Thus far in the present chapter the social make-up or the organizational form of the agricultural enterprise has been the central focus. Implied in this presentation is the logic that some social and economic factors such as economies of scale give some forms of organization, for example, the family enterprise or the Hutterite community, advantages or disadvantages over other farms. Thus economies of scale may impose restraints. We turn now to ecological and/or physical restraints. Some of these restraints may be too obvious to need discussion. For instance, it is known that bananas can be grown in the Arctic but at very great cost. In a market economy, however, the nature of the physical and geographical factors and their influence on production and life generally cannot be taken for granted.

The concept of type-of-farming area as used by the agricultural economist, the rural sociologist, and the social or cultural anthropologist is an excellent example of an entity that depends upon its cultural components for articulation. Cultural configurations such as dairy herds, milking machines, and cheese factories correspond closely to a given type-of-farming area, in this case the Dairy Area.

SOCIAL AND CULTURAL SYSTEMS

The type-of-farming areas of a nation must usually be expressed in terms of cultural traits, because they do not normally form separate and distinct social systems. Only in times of crisis, when those engaged in common production and marketing activities organize to accomplish an objective, are they true social systems possessing ends, norms, status-roles, and the other elements of social systems.

As used in the following pages, type-of-farming areas refer to those in which the major source of income on farms and/or ranches comes from a designated crop or from general agriculture.[70] Rural cultural regions are areas that are homogeneous with respect to certain cultural traits such as level of living, enterprise, farm tenancy, land value, extent of home consumption of farm produce, prevalence of nonfarm families in the rural areas, and, where pertinent, ethnic and racial factors. Figure 2 outlines the generalized type-of-farming areas in the U.S.

Lively and Almack,[71] pioneers in cultural region research, noted that among other items the fertility ratio and the level of living index moved together. In other words, when a county had a high fertility ratio it tended to have a low level of living index. Later Mangus used this relationship and others to plot cultural regions for the nation. He observed that "if, from the cards which record these factors for all counties in the United States, those that represent counties with the lowest plane of living and at the same time the highest ratio of children to women are sorted out, their regional pattern when plotted in a map is most striking... If the extreme opposites of these counties are plotted, that is, counties with highest plane of living and lowest population fertility, equally striking results appear."[72] An exception to this relationship is found in the Mormon culture, including Utah and contiguous areas where high birth rates are associated with a high level of living. This is accounted for by the value orientation of the Mormon religion.[73]

[70] Loomis and Beegle, *Rural Social Systems,* Chapter 8.

[71] C. E. Lively and R. M. Almack, "A Method of Determining Rural Social Sub-Areas with Application to Ohio," (Wooster: Ohio AES Mimeograph Bul. No. 106, January, 1938).

[72] A. R. Mangus, *Rural Regions of the United States* (Washington: Government Printing Office, 1940), pp. 81-82.

[73] Lowry Nelson, *The Mormon Village* (Salt Lake City: University of Utah Press, 1952), and "Education and the Changing Size of Mormon Families," *Rural Sociology,* Vol. 17, No. 4 (December, 1952). In the latter, Nelson shows that Mormons are becoming less exceptional in regard to differential fertility.

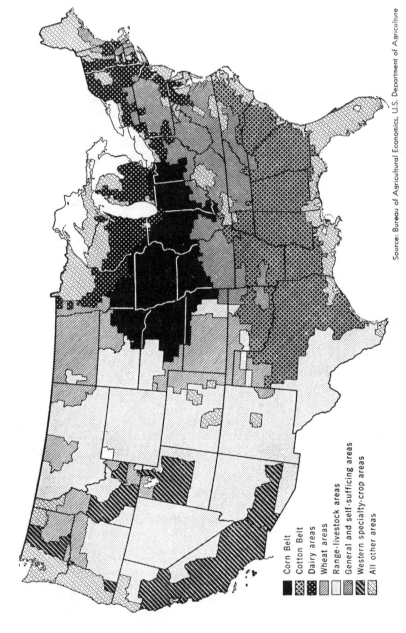

Corn Belt
Cotton Belt
Dairy areas
Wheat areas
Range-livestock areas
General and self-sufficing areas
Western specialty-crop areas
All other areas

Source: Bureau of Agricultural Economics, U.S. Department of Agriculture

FIGURE 2. Major type-of-farming areas in the United States.

TYPE-OF-FARMING AREAS
IN THE UNITED STATES

In his work on type-of-farming, Elliott emphasizes the economic basis and character of such areas. His position is well illustrated in the following quotation: "Types of farming are regional manifestations of the principle of economic specialization. They result from man's efforts to adjust himself and his resources to his environmental conditions. Type of farming, specifically, is a term descriptive of the kind of farming followed on a group of farms having a high degree of uniformity in the kind, relative amount, and proportion of the crops and livestock handled, and in the methods and practices followed in production. Types of farming are identified, therefore, by the form which the farm business takes with respect to size, productive factors used, lines of production of the business. When a type of farming is fairly well concentrated in one area, so that it is the prevailing or dominant type in that area, usually associated with a set of reasonably homogeneous, natural, and economic conditions occurring throughout a definite geographic area, an area so characterized may be called a type of farming area."[74]

The Cotton Belt.   No region has undergone greater change than the Cotton Belt. The whole nation is still reeling from some of the recent changes, particularly the exodus of literally millions of sharecroppers and wage-hands replaced by such machines as the cotton picker. For instance, from 1950 to 1960 each year about one-third million black Americans moved to central cities. From 1960 to 1968 this increment to cities approached one-half million. The result now is that over two-thirds of the blacks outside the South live in eight large northern cities and Los Angeles.[75] There also were comparable movements of whites to cities from rural areas, but the formation of black ghettoes and the riots of the 1960's dramatize the movement of the blacks.

In the study[76] of the attitudes of rural sociologists and agricultural economists made about 35 years ago prior to the great

[74] Foster F. Elliott, *Types of Farming in the United States* (Washington, D.C.: Government Printing Office, 1933), p. 1. The basic descriptions of major types-of-farming areas in the United States were developed by F. F. Elliott in the Bureau of Agricultural Economics, and this work remains a classic in the field.

[75] Charles C. Killingsworth, "Negro Unemployment: Causes and Cures," *The Centennial Review,* (Spring, 1966), p. 140.

[76] Loomis and Taylor, *Farm Population.*

exodus from the Cotton Belt, 44 percent of the sociologists and 40 percent of the economists agreed that: "The use of such a mechanical device as the cotton picker should be controlled by the government because it threatens the security of thousands of people." In the same study, 88 percent of the sociologists and 80 percent of the economists agreed with the statement: "If mechanization throws thousands of rural people out of work, it is the correct function of the Government to grant aid to those who have thus become unemployed."

The incidence of rural poverty today is especially high in the South despite the fact that rural poor can be found everywhere in the Nation. Even within a state, distinct areas with high concentrations of poverty may be identified, as for example, in the Delta and the hill country of Mississippi.[77]

There is striking convergence between the rural counties with exceptionally high replacement rates (four or more children for every married woman, 35-44 years old) and the concentration of cotton farms of the Deep South. This high replacement rate means that many rural blacks with less than about fourth grade educations, usually in inferior schools in these areas, will continue to flow into the ghettoes.[78] The "flight from the land" by those of low educational and cultural level, and especially by Negroes, can in large measure be charged to the heritage of the plantation system, slavery, and a farming system based on wage-hands and sharecroppers.

With the mechanization and diversification of the Cotton Belt some of its special features have disappeared. The various Delta regions remain the location of large holdings averaging 840 acres per unit in the Mississippi Delta as compared with 31 acres in northern Alabama.[79]

Tobacco is still produced in cotton-producing areas in South Carolina, peanuts have taken over some land previously planted

[77] A Report of the President's National Advisory Commission on Rural Poverty, *The People Left Behind* (Washington: Government Printing Office, 1967), p. 3-5.

[78] Dale E. Hathaway, J. Allan Beegle and W. Keith Bryant, *People of Rural America* (Washington, D.C., 1968), p. 140. In 1960 the median white male twenty-five years and over living on a farm in the South had 8.2 grades of education; the comparable Negro male had only 4.6.

[79] I. R. Starbird and B. L. French, "Costs of Producing Upland Cotton in the United States, 1969," Economic Research Service, USDA, Report No. 227, June 1972.

to cotton in southern Alabama and Georgia, and rice competes with cotton for land in Arkansas, Louisiana, and southeast Texas. The production of cattle and calves and to a lesser extent hogs now competes with cotton in most of the Cotton Belt. Cotton is no longer king throughout this area.

The Corn Belt.   The richest agricultural region because of the overall quality of soils and products is the Corn Belt. It has been the location of the family farm *par excellence,* but large agglomerations are making their inroads. In a booklet on *Corporate Farming and the Family Farm* a successful owner and operator of an Iowa family farm presents his own thinking, a product we believe of the family farm on which he was reared: "The real question in my mind [on whether the giants will provide better management than the family farmer] . . . is, will he manage himself, discipline himself to the degree necessary for success in farming in the future? Farming has always been known as an occupation that required long hours. New machinery and techniques . . . [can give time] for keeping records, attending short courses, improving skills and ability, arranging credit, supporting our cooperatives and farm organization, and plenty of hard thinking. The farmer who uses all of his time away from the hard work for bowling, cards or television probably cannot compete with the giants . . . We won't all be able to compete with the giants. But then, we haven't always been able to compete successfully with our neighbors."[80]

Because of the outstanding efficiency and prevalence of the family farm in the Corn Belt most agriculturalists and statesmen from Communist countries interested in agriculture visit this region. The optimum growing conditions for corn, coupled with livestock production are its source of wealth. Very heavy expenditures for gasoline and other petroleum products characterize the Corn Belt, indicating dependency on mechanization with resulting pollution.

The Wheat Areas.   Different from the Corn and Cotton Belts, as may be noted from Figure 2, wheat production is not centered in one contiguous area. Although wheat like corn is produced in small quantities in many parts of the country, especially in the eastern Corn Belt, it is produced in largest quantities where

---

[80] Dean Kleckner, "Competing with the Giants," in *Corporation Farming and the Family Farm* (Ames, Iowa: Iowa State University Press, 1970) p. 61.

other types of farm production are not possible. Although there are still some "suitcase" wheat farmers who work and live with their crops and machinery only during the planting and harvesting periods, the good operator should be a good mechanic able to weld and make minor machinery repairs. Slack periods can be spent profitably in "(1) repair work needed for an efficient operation, (2) record-keeping neglected during the busy season and keeping up on technology and other important relationships. Full land ownership is no longer the chief goal for the typical entrepreneur..."[81] Often the farm is inherited. Although wheat farms are not usually so large as livestock ranches in the high plains, they are relatively large. "In the drier areas [of Washington] for example where the wheat-fallow rotation is commonly practiced, the ideal farm ranges from 1,300 to 2,400 cropland acres."[82]

If farming were to be nationalized the easiest farm areas in the United States to place under large scale governmental bureaucratic control probably would be the western wheat areas. However, it is doubtful that the high levels of efficiency of production of the ablest farmers would be equalled. The business acumen required to effectively decide how much land to fallow, how much land to rent in addition to that owned, what costly machinery to buy, what varieties to grow, and other actions is great. Even on such large pieces of land the family farmer remembers particular attributes about one quarter section as compared with another. Not all managers would pay attention to such details, and it is doubtful that computers would supply the wisdom needed. Once the memory of the computer and useful analyses come to be relied upon in the large-scale production of wheat, the population of the area may be further reduced. Machinery is so expensive and is in use for such short periods that pressures for large scale operations become very great.

The Range-Livestock Areas. This area, most of which is arid, embraces approximately four percent of the total farm population, occupies the largest land area, and includes diverse cultural groups. (See Figure 2). Population density is low regardless of the fact that the areas are inhabited by Indians, Spanish-Americans, and Mormons, who have high birth rates. Neighborhoods

[81] P. Weisberger, *Commercial Wheat Production,* Economic Research Service, USDA, ERS-480, September 1971, p. 10.
[82] Ibid., p. 8.

usually are relatively weak. Outside the Indian and Spanish-speaking areas, incomes are relatively high. The livestock industry dominates the lives of the people, and the traditions of the "wild and woolly West" still survive. This dominant industry is well organized and constitutes a social, economic, and political power to be reckoned with. There is perhaps more leisure time in this area than others, but distances and population sparsity make many activities of county agricultural agents and other change agents very difficult.

The Dairy Areas. As in the case of the other areas, work in the dairy region influences most other activities. The high sanitary standards required make attention to farm buildings and equipment important. The twice-a-day milkings, even when highly mechanized, impose a routine followed year in and year out. These facts are basic wherever milk is produced. Although it is found in almost every farm area, dairying is concentrated especially in one region, the eastern and northern states. (Figure 2).

In the lake states portion of the Dairy Areas, the Scandinavian-American stocks are dominant; in the northeast, the Old American and Canadian stocks predominate. The value of products consumed at home is high, and a high rate of farm ownership prevails. The farms in this area are highly mechanized, with work loads relatively stable throughout the year. The New England heritage is more important in this region than in other areas of the United States. Many special interest groups exist, and producers' cooperatives are strong. The trade-centered village settlement pattern, which grew up in the border areas such as New York State, is common throughout the Dairy regions. Few farmers are more closely bound to their work routine, season in and season out, than the dairy farmer.

The Western Specialty-Crop Areas. The Specialty-Crop Areas comprise many small and non-contiguous areas. Factory farms are found in California where labor-management cleavages are important. The family farm prevails elsewhere, especially in the Mormon areas. The foreign population is large including Orientals, Spanish Americans and Europeans. High levels of living, high incomes and low birth rates are characteristic of most of this area. Harvest seasons require large labor forces and often pose special problems, especially when transient labor is necessary. In general uncertainty common to many areas is absent because of dependency upon irrigation. However, the crops are perishable, making harvesting and marketing critical periods. Especially in the factory farming areas, organized labor groups in recent years are pitted against organized farmers in wage and other disputes. These and other problems may forebode conditions that are in store in all farming regions unless the family farm is preserved.

The General and Self-Sufficing Areas.   Located mostly in the eastern part of the nation, this area includes the most mountainous terrain east of the Rockies. Many of the inhabitants trace their ancestry to northwestern European stock, especially English, Scotch, and Irish. As Schwarzweller, et al.,[83] note for Kentucky: "The family . . . was a working and consuming unit made strongly cohesive through the interdependencies of age and sex roles . . . daughters helped their mothers as apprentices for job-roles . . . The men worked mostly outdoors, plowing and planting, clearing land, looking after livestock, and 'raising coal.' Their sons were expected to help . . . [life is] basically not unlike . . .[that in] that of the modal American family . . . children both feared and respected their father, whereas they sought affection from their mother . . . most normal activities . . . carried the imprint of a familistic social organization . . . a 'gemeinschaft' type of social organization with its emphasis on primary groups and informal channels of communication [prevails]." Migration, especially to industrial areas to the North, has been great.

Lower levels of living, average machinery inventories, and relatively high birth rates characterize this area. Neighborhood, informal friendship or clique groups, churches, and other organizations support the family-centered life. The families of the area produce for home use to a larger extent than elsewhere. The family farm is dominant and the ownership rate is relatively high. In this area there is considerable time for non-work activities, especially during the winter.

Residual areas.   There are several smaller areas, not considered major type-of-farming regions, called residual areas. (See Figure 2). The Lake States Cut-Over Area is characterized by low incomes, relatively high birth rates, and large proportions of

[83] Harry K. Schwarzweller, James S. Brown and J. J. Mangalam, *Mountain Families in Transition* (University Park, Pennsylvania: Pennsylvania State University Press, 1971), pp. 211-213.

foreign-born. This section contains a large proportion of rural-nonfarm inhabitants who depend upon off-farm work, especially in the mines. In many respects, the lake states area is like the General and Self-Sufficing Areas. Additional sources of income are being opened by tourist and recreation industries.

LOW INCOME AS RELATED TO TYPE-OF-FARMING AREAS

Although low income farms may be found in all type-of-farming areas, they are most numerous in areas of high rural density, in areas of high birth rates, and in areas where off-farm employment possibilities are slight or where the land is not adapted to the use of machinery. As shown in Figure 3, an extensive serious problem area is found in the Range-Livestock Area of New Mexico. A moderately serious problem area is located in the Residual type-of-farming area of the northwest. In addition, the Great Lakes Cut-Over Areas of northern Minnesota, Wisconsin, and Michigan are classed as "substantial" or "moderate" problem areas.

Due to lack of space, the nature of the problems in Areas 1, 4, and 7 (Figure 3) will be treated briefly. Area 1—Appalachian Mountains and Border Areas—is mountainous, with little good tillable land and a large farm population. Burley and dark tobacco farms are the most common commercial enterprises, with livestock farms and general farming ranking next. The problem for this area arises from low average tobacco allotments and spotty or declining opportunities for off-farm work. Area 4—Mississippi Delta—is an area of fertile soil, high tenancy, and low levels of living. The main crops are cotton, rice, and sugar cane, produced under plantation conditions. The mechanization of cotton production and the attractiveness of urban employment is reducing the farm population of the Delta. Area 7—Northern Lake States—is a problem area in large part because of the exhaustion of timber and mineral resources. Dairying is the most frequent type-of-farming, but soils are shallow and distances to markets great. This area has been an area of heavy out-migration for a number of years.[84]

[84] For a thorough discussion of this out-migration phenomenon in the Upper Peninsula of Michigan, see Jon H. Rieger, J. Allan Beegle, and Philip N. Fulton,

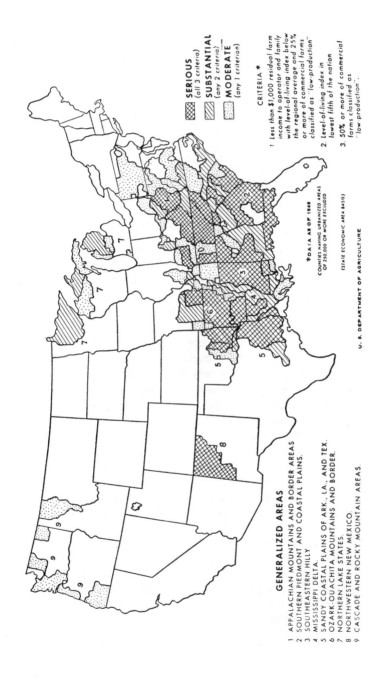

FIGURE 3. Rural Problem Areas in the United States.

VALUE ORIENTATION AND REGION

What influence do the activities and culture of the type-of-farming areas have upon the value orientation and attitudes of the people? Unfortunately we do not have detailed data concerning value orientation for various type-of-farming areas, but some regional comparisons are suggestive. A study[85] comprising a sample of 4,933 adults compares the attitudes of tolerance toward socialists, atheists, communists, or suspected communists in the West, the East, the Middle West, and the South. Unfortunately, these regional divisions embrace part or all of several types-of-farming areas. The differences in tolerance scores in these four regions, for places of different size, are shown in Table 3.

TABLE 3

Proportion Of Urban and Rural People Classified As More Tolerant, By Region and Place Of Residence

Region	Farm (Percent)	Small Town (Percent)	Other Cities (Percent)	Metropolitan (Percent)
West	35	34	46	54
East	18	35	31	47
Middle West	26	27	33	34
South	10	14	16	24

Source: Samuel A. Stouffer, *Communism, Conformity, and Civil Liberties* (Garden City, New York: Doubleday and Company, Inc. 1955), p. 118.

In general the South is least tolerant and the West most tolerant as determined by the Guttman type scale used in this study. Also farm and rural (small town) people are generally less tolerant in most of the regions than the urban people. Such differences generally hold for various levels of education and for certain specified leaders and the general population. The authors

---

Profiles of Rural Youth: A Decade of Migration and Social Mobility (East Lansing, Michigan: Agricultural Experiment Station Research Report 179, January 1973). See also footnote 77.

[85] Samuel A. Stouffer, *Communism, Conformity, and Civil Liberties: A Cross-Section of the Nation Speaks Its Mind* (Garden City, New York: Doubleday and Company, 1955), p. 118.

conclude that the more opportunity for travel and new experience, the more tolerant people are likely to become. Rural people and southerners appear to lack these broadening influences. Therefore, they manifest attitudes which we have described as related to boundary maintenance when confronted with threatening ideologies.

THE END OF THE TRAIL[86]

In trying to inform people at home and abroad about the American family farm, I have sometimes referred to my boyhood on the farm on which the incident discussed at the end of Chapter 3 took place. Until very recently, I have been proud of the poultry farm which my brother, Andy, two years younger than I, developed from scratch and operated for almost 25 years. In fact, when a special illustrated write-up of Andy's farm was published in *Western Farm Life* about ten years ago, I took a copy to Thomas Cowden, then Dean of Agriculture at Michigan State. As I prepare these lines, I note from the slip Cowden attached to the article when he returned it that he was impressed, and I know that neither of us thought it likely that someone would write about this farm as the "end of the trail."

The bitterness of this story came home to me at the last homecoming celebration at New Mexico State University, not far from Andy's poultry farm. Both Andy and I were especially interested in this home-coming at our alma mater; our brother, Clark, younger than Andy, was being honored as a distinguished alumnus by NMSU largely because he had founded a successful Town and Country Property Management firm in Santa Ana, California. As Andy, Clark, and I chatted with Professor George Dawson, Head of the Department of Agricultural Economics about poultry farms, property management businesses, and related matters, Dawson said that Andy should return to teaching at NMSU. Andy responded somewhat as follows: "What would I teach? You know I built up my poultry farm partly to show those ranch kids who took my poultry classes that poultry raising is a respectable and profitable business. Now that I've failed, what do I teach?" Dawson answered: "Teach students that nothing but large scale agriculture can

---

[86] A personal case written by Charles Loomis.

survive. You have the evidence." How bitter this advice was will be evident later as we note the dedication and love Andy had for this farm. But Andy agreed with Dawson, saying that the price war going on among the giant producers at the time was taking some of the fairly big firms along with some smaller concerns such as his own that did not have huge reserves to tide them over economic dips. Brother Clark, perhaps to comfort Andy, noted that the "big boys" were also trying to smash the small realtors. Many people in Las Cruces, New Mexico regret the demise of this family farm. Not only is Andy not doing what he can do best, but his in-laws who were so important in operating the farm must find other things to do. Of less importance but nevertheless to be mentioned is the fact that sister Elizabeth's family, their children and their grandchildren no longer have Loomis eggs and meat at "family" prices. Likewise, hundreds of others who had come to rely on the high quality eggs miss them. [*The family enterprise maintained systemic linkages not only with the "larger family" but to significant others in the community.*] Most stores carried them where they were sold at premium prices over those generally stocked through the various chain stores and other large scale arrangements.

Not to be overlooked in assigning causes for the failure are some which I call sociological, but, of course, they have their economic aspects. Las Cruces, the chief market for the eggs, is a city of 39,000. There is considerable turnover in the population and there are more newcomers each year. Thus there were increasing numbers toward the end who did not know the importance of the Loomis stamp on the egg cartons in quality terms. Of course, to the very end, members of the Lion's Club and Methodist Church where Andy and his family had always been staunch members and others bought the eggs willingly paying a premium for the quality. But as the size of the center increased, more strangers came and as the Gemeinschaft-like relations of earlier times were replaced by more impersonal, rationalistic and Gesellschaft-like relations, the problem of retailing quality eggs changed. As I argued with Andy on how to advertise his quality eggs, some of the difficulties emerged. It is one thing to have and maintain a reputation for quality produced in a small enterprise for a small public and quite another for large scale mass society. [*Norms by which personal trust and confidence are maintained are different among friends and neighbors in the*

Gemeinschaft than they are in the impersonal Gesellschaft.] In brief, strategy of establishing the reputation for "the beer that made Milwaukee famous" could scarcely be used for Loomis eggs in Las Cruces.

As a sociologist I see the greatest loss to Andy as a person. In the Lion's Club and in the Las Cruces community generally, until dismantling and sales of the houses began local small business men said, "Andy is different than some other professors out there at the college. He could teach it but he could do it, too." [*The status-roles in the "town system" and in the "gown system" differ in this small community. Andy had linked the two systems.*]

Actually as all poultry men know, to stay in this business one must keep up on many difficult and complicated areas of technology and learning—feeding, hybridization, and disease control, to name a few.

DDT vs. Feed Problems

I remember visiting in Las Cruces about 10 years ago when Andy's farming operations were in a state of crisis. Loomis eggs were famous in the community for shape, size, consistency in color, and overall high quality. The crisis that had kept Andy sleepless for almost two weeks was caused by a few eggs that had tiny traces of blood in the white. He had spent hundreds of hours checking on every possible source. A month earlier he had sprayed the feed bin with DDT, then a respected insecticide, but he had been very careful to make sure there was no moisture in the bin when the feed was put into it. While I was there on a visit he removed all feed and washed the walls and floors and then put in an entirely new mix of feed. Sure enough in a week the "beautiful" Loomis eggs were back again! But neither Andy nor the University was able to prove it was DDT. There were three or four possible causes that changing the feed could have relieved. Of course, there were many other crises. Wild birds flying over could have brought in disease. A poultry man can be wiped out in a matter of weeks by a new disease.

In the course of time dedication to perfection and a reputation for always providing this perfection becomes part of one's personality—one's "Who am I?", if you please. During this concentrated dedication to production of Loomis eggs, Andy about 15 years ago had dropped out of the University teaching to give his full time to the job, which it required. He became a dedicated family farmer, and like thousands of others he now has no job. In American society this produces great stress, identity crisis and other problems. But being an American with the entrepreneurial "know-how" he is busy developing other businesses and he will survive personally even though his love, professionally, is at the trail's end. [*The status-role of dedicated farmer, like that of the dedicated physician or attorney affects the personality. Great physicians have become great writers, but such changes are not easy.*]

Cecil Hellbusch, a writer, in *Western Farm Life* described the salient features of Andy's poultry farm. We shall omit some technical detail and rely on his description which he calls, *Excellent Eggs—Profitably Produced:*

"Producing eggs 1961 style demands the knowledge and skills of a professional. It is not a business for the amateur, or the retired business man with a few dollars to invest in what he might call a hobby for mom and me.

"The point is well proved by Andy Loomis, owner and operator of the Loomis Poultry Farm, near Las Cruces, New Mexico. Loomis is a professional and runs a successful egg laying plant of 12,000 hens. [*Note emphasis on 'professional' status-role.*]

"It is a well integrated business with Loomis buying Rothway double inbred cross chicks from a hatchery and growing them into the laying house.

"The reason Loomis is a professional and a successful egg producer is because of his educational background and his love for the business. He is a former vocational agriculture instructor, Soil Conservation employee, and served four years as associate professor of Poultry Husbandry at New Mexico State University. . . . He presently runs 12,000 [later expanded to 15,000] hens and says he does not plan to expand any more.

"Loomis buys new chicks every month, except June and July when it is too hot for chicks to do well. Chicks going into the brooder in April will go into the laying house in late August or early September. They keep maximum production for about ten months and then are replaced.

"Egg quality is the replacement factor. When the egg white begins to weaken, hens are replaced. About 1/3 of the disposal hens are sold to individuals who put them in cold storage lockers. Retailers buy some, but the bulk of the disposal hens are bought by poultry and produce jobbers who have a market for dressed birds. Loomis receives an average of 9 to 10 cents per pound, or about 40 cents per bird. Chicks cost about 45 cents each, so the disposal hens almost offset the cost of replacements.

"Loomis markets his own eggs, gathering them four times daily and immediately puts them into an air conditioned egg room where a 70 degree temperature is maintained. The eggs are placed under blowers to insure rapid cooling.

"All candling, grading, packaging and selling to chain stores and other retail outlets in his area are done by Loomis, his mother, and his in-laws, and his employees. Loomis sells AA grade eggs in all sizes to retail outlets and Grade A eggs are sold mainly to commercial firms.

"The demand is strong for Loomis eggs. 'People are quality minded when it comes to eggs. Even the so-called low-income customers demand quality eggs,' says Loomis. Generally AA grade eggs sell for a 10 cent per dozen premium over the price of grade A commercial eggs sold retail.

"The net income of the Loomis layout valued at $60,000 capital investment return, is about $1 per hen profit per year, or figured another way about 5 cents net per dozen eggs sold."

As the cost price squeeze recently closed in on this family farm the net income dropped to 15 cents per hen per year. Of course, Andy recognized that this was an especially low return due to various factors. These included competition among the big concerns, difficulty in marketing eggs at their quality value because some large chainstores which were linked with poultry plants monopolized all sales outlets, and improvement in the quality of mass-produced eggs. [*Note that systemic linkage resulting from vertical integration and other sources can squeeze out the family farmer.*] In all probability the market will improve and eventually make it possible to continue operation with a little profit after all labor including family labor is paid. However, in the nature of the poultry industry losses cannot be postponed but must be absorbed as they come. The actual salvage return for the dismanteled $60,000 plant was approximately $40,000. From the poultry operation in the last year there was a loss of about $20,000. Such losses could not have been absorbed had the farm not done relatively well earlier.

SELECTED REFERENCES

Ackerman, Joseph and Marshall Harris. *Family Farm Policy*. Chicago: University of Chicago Press, 1947.

Ball, A. Gordon and Earl O. Heady, eds. *Size, Structure and Future of Farms*. Ames, Iowa: Iowa State University Press, 1971.

Elliott, Foster F. *Types of Farming in the United States*. Washington, D.C.: Government Printing Office, 1933.

Farmworkers in Rural America 1971-1972. Hearings Before the Subcommittee on Migratory Labor of the Committee on Labor and Public Welfare, United States Senate. Washington: Government Printing Office, 1972, especially Parts 2 and 3A.

Goldschmidt, Walter R. *Small Business and the Community: A Study in Central Valley of Effects of Scale of Farm Organizations*. Report of the Special Committee to Study Problems of American Small Business, U. S. Senate, December 23, 1946. Washington, D.C.: United States Government Printing Office.

Hostetler, John A. and Gertrude E. Huntington. *The Hutterites in North America*. New York: Holt, Rinehart and Winston, 1967.

Johnson, Sherman E., et al. *Generalized Types of Farming in the United States*. Agricultural Information Bulletin No. 3. Washington, D.C.: United States Department of Agriculture, 1950.

Kraenzel, Carl F. *The Great Plains in Transition*. Norman: University of Oklahoma Press, 1955.

Lenski, Gerhard. *Human Societies*. New York: McGraw-Hill, 1970.

Loomis, Charles P. "Rural Society, Contemporary," *Encylcopaedia Britannica,* 1964. "Social Organization in Agriculture," *International Encylopedia of the Social Sciences,* 1968, Vol. 1.

Mangus, A. R. *Rural Regions of the United States*. Washington, D.C.: Government Printing Office, 1940.

Osipov, G. V., ed. *Town, Country and People*. Studies in Soviet Society, Vol. 2. London: Tavistock Publications, 1969.

Rodefeld, Richard D. and E. A. Wilkening. *Wisconsin Incorporated Farms*. Madison: Department of Rural Sociology, University of Wisconsin, 1971.

Schwarzweller, H. K., James S. Brown, and J. J. Mangalam. *Mountain Families in Transition*. University Park: Pennsylvania State University Press, 1971.

Skrabanek, R. L. "Commercial Farming in the United States," *Rural Sociology,* 19, No. 2, (June, 1954).

6

Hierarchical Social Systems

As pointed out by Lipset, stratification has been conceptualized by sociologists in multidimensional terms that can be grouped as follows: "(1) *Objective* status, or aspects of stratification that structure environments differently enough to evoke differences in behavior; (2) *Accorded* status, or the prestige accorded to individuals and groups by others; (3) *Subjective* status, or the personal sense of location within the social hierarchy felt by various individuals."[1] In this chapter, we are primarily concerned with accorded status but not to the exclusion of the other types.

In all societies there are differences in social rank, standing, or honor accorded various groups and individuals. The social rank or honor accorded depends upon the standards rooted in the values of the social system. These standards form the basis of an evaluating process whereby each system and each member attains a given social standing. In a given community there are usually many reference groups that provide their members social rank and honor. The members of some systems devote much time and effort to this evaluation process and its maintenance.

The proverb, "There is no honor among thieves," is only true if the thieves do not belong to a social system, for each group has its rank or honor system. In a rural community a gang of cattle rustlers may accord rank to its members that contrast sharply with that accorded them by other community members. In speaking of social rank, therefore, it is always necessary to specify the social system which is the referent.[2] Unfortunately many of the studies of social rank are less specific than they should be.

---

[1] Seymour M. Lipset, "Social Class" in *International Encyclopedia of the Social Sciences* (New York: The Macmillan Co., 1968) Vol. 15, p. 310.

[2] Ibid., pp. 310-315; and Harold F. Kaufman, Otis Dudley Duncan, Neal Gross, and William H. Sewell, "Social Stratification in Rural Society," *Rural Sociology*, Vol. 18, No. 1 (March, 1953), pp. 12-24.

HIERARCHICAL GROUPS AS SOCIAL SYSTEMS

In the preceding chapters and those to follow, social rank has been treated as an element of social systems. In this chapter, at the risk of doing violence to the organizational framework of the book, we attempt to view primarily hierarchical groups as social systems. While we are aware of the logical difficulties arising from this decision, the importance of social stratification to social science has dictated our choice. To treat hierarchical groups as social systems, however, is not unjustified.[3]

In discussing stratification, Sorokin poses the question as to whether or not there is a "specific multibonded group, different from the family, tribe, caste, order, or nation, that in modern times has exerted a powerful influence." His answer is yes, and he suggests that we may have to call it "X" to avoid confusion. "There has been and is such a group. Its formula is as follows: It is (1) legally open, but actually semiclosed; (2) 'normal'; (3) solidary; (4) antagonistic to certain other groups (social classes) of the same general nature, X; (5) partly organized but mainly quasi-organized; (6) partly aware of its own unity and existence and partly not; (7) characteristic of the Western society of the eighteenth, nineteenth, and twentieth centuries; (8) a multibonded group bound together by two unibonded ties, occupational and economic (both taken in their broad sense), and by one bond of social stratification in the sense of the totality of its essential rights and duties as contrasted with essential different rights and duties of other groups (social classes) of the same general nature, X."[4]

It is Sorokin's judgment that from a "macroscopic viewpoint" the following major classes in the Western society of the past two or three centuries may be observed: "(a) the industrial-labor, or proletarian, class; (b) the peasant-farmer class; (c) the dwindling class of large landowners; (d) the capitalistic class, now being transformed into the managerial class."[5] Each has subclasses and there are other smaller classes. Others[6] have de-

---

[3] Pitirim A. Sorokin, *Society, Culture, and Personality: Their Structure and Dynamics* (New York: Harper and Brothers, 1947), pp. 271 ff.

[4] Ibid., p. 271.

[5] Ibid., p. 273.

[6] See Gregory P. Stone and William H. Form, "Instabilities in Status: The Problem of Hierarchy in the Community Study of Status Arrangements," *American Sociological Review,* Vol. 18, No. 2 (April, 1953), pp. 149-162.

scribed "status aggregates," which are not closed systems but nonetheless function to maintain ranking or standing. It is such aggregates that we treat as social systems in this chapter.

SOCIAL RANK SYSTEMS

Caste, estate, and open-class as a continuum. Although every social system evaluates its members and is evaluated by the larger system of which it is a part, certain social systems are more actively engaged in according and maintaining social rank than others. At one extreme are the caste systems, which use various sanctions to prevent individuals from leaving the groups into which they are born. The most extreme example of caste is to be found in India where over a period of twenty centuries there has existed "the most thorough-going attempt known in human history to introduce inherited inequality as the guiding principle in social relationships."[7] Endogamous relations, designated occupations, segregation, special dress, and food requirements are among the characteristics of caste systems.

Estates. No Western nation has such a caste system. The social stratification system of Europe, of areas in Latin America, and of the Eastern world, however, places persons in broad classes or estates that may be changed or into which persons may be allowed to pass according to fixed rules and rites of passage. Sons of peons and serfs have been known to achieve high social rank, but such is not the rule. The different estates, or *Staende,* as they are called in Germany, specify the roles, rights, privileges, and responsibilities of members, and institutionalize the means of entry or expulsion by a kind of ritual. Social rank is largely ascribed but less completely than in a caste system.[8] The estates are usually associated with hereditary nobility, freemen, and serfs. The system is known only in relatively rural societies and seems to have been broken down by the growth of modern business, commerce, and industry.

[7] Kingsley Davis, *Human Society* (New York: The Macmillan Co., 1949), p. 377.

[8] See Ferdinand Toennies, *Staende und Klassen* (Stuttgart: Ferdinand Enke Verlag, 1931), pp. 617-638. Here Toennies characterizes the estate as being a Gemeinschaft-like collective and class as Gesellschaft-like. See also Max Weber's treatment of these status groups: Max Weber, *Wirtschaft und Gesellschaft* (Tubingen: Mohr, 1922), pp. 130-140, 179-180, and 724-752.

Open-class. As used here, a truly open-class system is a theoretically possible system in which all persons find their places according to the skills and technical competence they possess. Urban cultures usually possess more features of the open-class system than the surrounding rural cultures. Where an open-class system prevails, such considerations as the family into which one is born, "color or previous condition of servitude," class position, age, sex, and similar factors have no bearing on one's status, except insofar as they may enhance or interfere with one's technical competence in performing the duties required by one's role in the society.

No completely open-class society exists, but of all societies, the white American population, particularly in urban centers and commercialized farming areas, probably comes nearest to having an open-class system. Actually, there is good evidence to indicate that if such a society were to exist, the family would be very weak. If men, women, and children were ranked solely on the basis of their competence, the family system would have difficulty maintaining a uniform ranking system. Women who outrank their husbands or children who outrank their parents, are not likely to submit to the authority of persons they outrank.[9] Where the productive and kinship systems are one and the same, as in the family farm economy, conflicts involved in various standards of rank for the two systems must be reconciled. In rural society this is frequently done by giving the family status-roles greater importance than others.

Caste in the United States. Figure 1 shows Warner's[10] schematic portrayal of the class and caste system in the Cotton

---

[9] Parsons indicates that the relatively low rank of women in the occupational world, despite the various opposing movements, persists as society's attempt to preserve the family. Talcott Parsons, "An Analytical Approach to the Theory of Social Stratification," *American Journal of Sociology,* Vol. XLV, No. 6 (May, 1940), pp. 841-862.

[10] W. Lloyd Warner, "American Caste and Class," *American Journal of Sociology,* Vol. XLII, No. 2 (September, 1936), pp. 234-237. See also Oliver C. Cox, *Caste, Class, and Race: A Study in Social Dynamics* (New York: Doubleday & Co., Inc.,1948), p. 519, and C. P. Loomis and J. A. Beegle, *Rural Social Systems* (New York: Prentice-Hall, Inc., 1950), pp. 353 ff. Studies in which the Bogardus Social Distance scale was used to measure caste rejections of outsiders sheds doubt on the assumption that caste relationships in the United States are comparable to those in India. See Charles P. Loomis, "In Defense of Integration," *The Centennial Review,* Vol. XIV, No. 2, (Spring 1970), pp. 147-150.

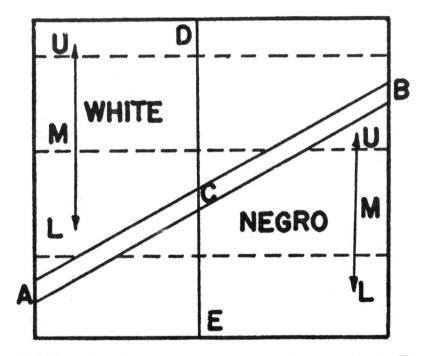

FIGURE 1. Warner's schematic diagram of class and caste in America. The diagonal lines (AB) separate the Negro from the white caste. The dashed lines within each caste distinguish upper, middle, and lower classes. The line (DE) indicates a hypothetical position to which the diagonal (AB) may move.

Belt, where approximately one-third of the farm population of the nation lives. Since approximately one-fifth of the total population in this region is black, it is of particular importance to understand the bases for social ranking and stratification in the South.

It may be noted that a diagonal bar separates the black and white castes in Figure 1. The arrangement of this bar expresses the fact that the more restrictions are removed, the more bar *AB* will move on the axis *C* until it approximates the vertical line *DE*. If the restrictions are increased and if the black's rights and privileges are decreased so that no black group, not even those who had the highest rank in the community, are higher than the lowest white group, then the bar *AB* would become horizontal, with only blacks below and only whites above.

TYPE OF ENTERPRISE AND PATTERNS OF STRATIFICATION

While many may argue that improved social rank among blacks has been unduly slow, the evidence is that gains have been made, especially in the '60s. In a report jointly prepared by the Bureau of Census and the Bureau of Labor Statistics, the changing status of Negroes in regard to income, education, and occupation is summarized as follows: "Median family income of Negro and other races, in 1970, was about $6,520, about 50 percent higher than in 1960. The ratio of Negro and other races to white median family income was 64 percent in 1970, a significant increase from the 53 percent ratio in 1961-63. This increase was preceded by a decade in which there had been no significant narrowing of the income differentials. . . . In 1970, 56 percent of all young adult blacks 25 to 29 years old had completed high school compared with 38 percent 10 years ago. By 1970, about 17 percent had at least 1 year of college. Approximately 78 percent of the comparable group of whites had a high school education and about one-third had received some college training. . . . Between 1960 and 1970, total employment of Negro and other races increased 22 percent, but their employment in professional, technical, and clerical occupations doubled."[11]

Another measure of recent progress made by blacks is reflected in the changing number and character of the low-income population. While the number and percentage of all low income persons declined between 1959 and 1971, the rate of decline was slower for Negroes. "The number of white persons below the low-income level has decreased by about 38 percent between 1959 and 1971 as compared to a 29 percent decrease for low-income Negroes. . . . By 1971, about one-third of all Negroes were below the low-income level, compared to one-tenth of all whites."[12]

The changing distribution of employed persons, white and nonwhite, is shown in Table 1. Between 1960 and 1970, blacks and other races made dramatic gains in white collar occupa-

[11] "The Social and Economic Status of Negroes in the United States, 1970," BLS Report No. 394 and *Current Population Reports,* Series P-23, No. 38, (Washington, 1971) p. 1-3.

[12] U. S. Bureau of the Census, *Current Population Reports,* P-60, No. 86, "Characteristics of the Low-Income Population, 1971," (Washington: U.S. Government Printing Office, 1972), p. 1-2.

TABLE 1.
Percentage Distribution of Employed Persons by Occupation and
Race, 1960 and 1970

Occupation	Negro and Other Races		White	
	1960	1970	1960	1970
Total Employed in Thousands	6,927	8,445	58,850	70,182
Percent	100.0	100.0	100.0	100.0
White Collar Workers	16.1	27.1	46.6	50.8
Professional, technical & kindred	4.8	9.1	12.1	14.8
Managers, administrators, exc. farm	2.6	3.5	11.7	11.4
Salesworkers	1.5	2.1	7.0	6.7
Clerical workers	7.3	13.2	15.7	18.0
Blue Collar Workers	40.1	42.2	36.2	34.5
Craftsmen and foremen	6.0	8.2	13.8	13.5
Operatives	20.4	23.7	17.9	17.0
Nonfarm laborers	13.7	10.3	4.4	4.1
Service Industries	31.7	26.0	9.9	10.7
Private household workers	14.2	7.7	1.7	1.3
Service workers, exc. priv. hsld.	17.5	18.3	8.2	9.4
Farmworkers	12.1	3.9	7.4	4.0
Farmers and farm managers	3.2	1.0	4.3	2.4
Farm laborers and foremen	9.0	2.9	3.0	1.6
Paid workers	6.6	2.6	1.7	1.0
Unpaid family workers	2.4	0.3	1.3	0.7

Source: Bureau of Labor Statistics, *Employment and Earnings, Statistical Abstract of the U.S., 1972,* p. 231

tions, particularly in professional and clerical categories. At the
same time, the proportions of nonwhites declined in service occupations and as farmworkers. Farmworkers, both white and
nonwhite, declined markedly between 1960 and 1970. Nonwhite
farmworkers accounted for about 12 percent of all nonwhite
employed persons in 1960 and less than 4 percent in 1970. Comparable proportions of white persons so employed at the two
time periods were 7.4 and 4.0 percent.

Although many reference systems are important in determining the social rank of individuals and groups, the production
systems discussed in the previous chapter are important in
determining the pattern of stratification. Thus, a society domi-

nated by large agricultural enterprises on which many unrelated families provide labor to the management or entrepreneurial function will have a different type of stratification pattern than one in which the family farm is the unit of production. In Chapters 2 and 5 we indicated that societies having large-scale agricultural operations as the most common production unit are likely to be located in "power-centered" rural communities. In societies in which the family farm has primacy, the communities are characterized as "power-diffused."[13] We will suggest here the probable structure of stratification systems in these divergent types of agricultural communities. Barber summarizes overall trends as follows: ". . . the rankings tend to show some, and often a considerable, degree of hierarchy, which manifests itself in a tapering toward the top of the various stratification structures. If some tapering is universal, the shape of the rest of the structure is more variable. There seem to be two basic shapes, the pyramid and the diamond. The latter is the typical pattern for modernized societies, where there are strong pressures toward social equality as well as a need for increasing numbers of middle-ranking functionaries. In other types of societies, where the opposite forces prevail, the standard shape o: the stratification structures has been more pyramidal, the ma jority of roles (and therefore the individuals who occupy them ranking very low."[14]

Stratification in "power-centered" communities. The basi pattern of stratification or social ranking in a community mad up of large estates is not essentially different from that of ar army, a factory, or a college in which the authority relations o those in control are constantly articulated through the structure. In rural societies dominated by the large agricultural enterprise, at least three distinct classes, all of which are separate subsystems, can be discerned. At the top is the very small proprietary class receiving the greatest honor and respect and having

---

[13] Studies of stratification in areas of Latin America in which family-sized farm communities exist near those of large estates lead to this characterization. For analyses of rural communities with these differences, see C. P. Loomis, et al., *Turrialba* (Glencoe, Ill.: The Free Press, 1953), Chapter 3; see also Victor K. Ray, *The Corporate Invasion of American Agriculture* (Denver: National Farmers Union, 1968), especially pp. 41-53.

[14] Bernard Barber, "Social Stratification", *International Encyclopedia of the Social Sciences* (New York: The Macmillan Co., 1968) Vol. 15, p. 295.

the greatest power. Next to the proprietary class is a somewhat larger stratum composed of the supervisors, professionals, artisans, and some skilled workers. Beneath this stratum is the large group of families that furnishes the labor for the large estate. This group often constitutes more than three-fourths of the total population. Although in rural societies there is considerable informal interaction not directly related to the articulation of the authority structure of the system, the classes constitute sub-systems in that more interaction takes place among families within each system than among families across class lines.

Figure 2 represents an attempt to generalize the pattern of

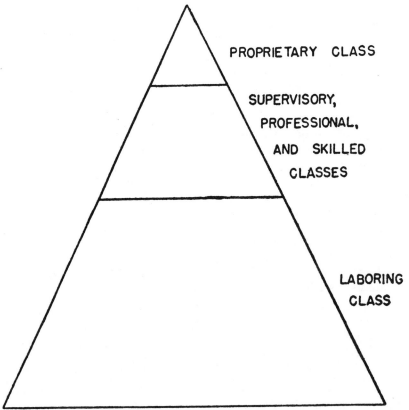

FIGURE 2. Generalized and simplified diagram of the class structure of rural communities in which large non-family farming enterprises are dominant.

stratification in rural societies where large agricultural enterprises are dominant. This large-scale pattern is becoming increasingly prevalent in many rural areas of the Nation, but especially in California, Arizona and Texas.

Stratification in family-sized farm communities.[15] Figure 3
describes the stratification hierarchy as revealed in studies of
power-diffused communities. Fewer families in such areas come
under the authority of the larger production system than on
haciendas or large estates.

Note that in Figure 3 the lines separating the hypothetical
strata are shown by a dotted line. This indicates that in the case
of family-sized farming areas the system on which ranking is
based is less definite and that interaction among families at
various levels may be great. In general, families at the top are
large, well-to-do owners who interact as equals with the professional and business families in the trade centers. As the case at
the end of this chapter implies, communities of family-sized
farmers have little place for non-middle class people. Some are
"gentlemen farmers." Such farmers will be more at home where
the ethos of the family farm is weak or where the larger-than-
family farm operation is prevalent. Families in the upper part of
the diagram hold offices of importance in the counties in which
they live and help control the schools, churches, and other formal organizations. The families at the bottom of the diagram
are generally laborers and poorer families. Usually there are
some families in this group who are considered by the classes
above them to "live like animals." They may be accused of stealing, lack of cleanliness, and shiftlessness. Between the families
at the bottom and at the top of the diagram are the majority of
families in American rural society. They consider themselves to
be the good, honest, self-respecting, average, everyday working
people.[16] Usually it is people from this class who support the
churches, farm organizations, and larger social systems of rural
America. Kaufman[17] found that when families in a New York

---

[15] The authors have described social stratification in rural communities of the
various regions of the United States in *Rural Social Systems,* Chapt. 11.

[16] James West, *Plainville, U.S.A.* (New York: Columbia University Press,
1948), p. 117. Also see *Plainville Fifteen Years Later* by Art Gallaher, Jr. (New
York: Columbia University Press, 1961).

[17] Harold F. Kaufman, *Prestige Classes in a New York Rural Community*
(Ithaca: Cornell AES Memoir 260, March, 1944), p. 39.

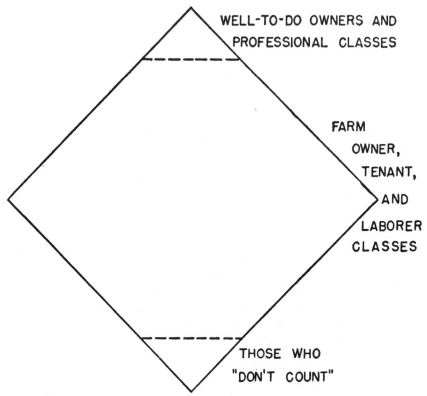

FIGURE 3.   Generalized and simplified diagram of the class structure of rural communities in which the family farm enterprises are dominant.

rural community were rated by their "standing," "reputation," or "respect," the result was a form not unlike Figure 3. Although the people have different rank, as is indicated by the diagram, there is considerable interaction between all levels. Various studies participated in by the authors have led them to conclude that there is generally a less rigid class structure in communities of family-sized farms than is found in communities of large estates.[18] Since it was this type of society out of which the Agri-

[18] See Loomis, et al., *Turrialba,* and "Social Status and Communication in Costa Rican Rural Communities," in Olen E. Leonard and Charles P. Loomis, *Readings in Latin American Social Organization and Institutions* (East Lansing: The Michigan State College Press, 1953), pp. 183 ff.

cultural Extension Service developed, it is not difficult to understand why attempts to transplant it without alteration to underdeveloped areas with an entirely different stratification system have sometimes met with little success.

SOCIAL RANK AND INTERACTION

We contend that the rural family in America increasingly shares the attributes of the urban middle class family and that the rural community has become increasingly heterogeneous occupationally. As a consequence, a number of changes affecting rural areas complicate the ranking and stratification systems. Among the important changes are: (1) school consolidation which enhances the opportunity for interaction between farm and nonfarm youth; (2) the high incidence of off-farm work which increases the interaction and involvement outside the community of residence; and (3) the increased use of rural areas by nonfarm people for residential and recreational purposes.

While social class rank remains an important basis for social interaction in rural areas, the significance of neighborhood and kinship has receded markedly. Irrespective of the social class position of rural people, important friendship ties likely include urbanites, special interest group participation, and other forms of interaction outside the local area, often at considerable distance. Neighboring *per se* in rural areas has declined significantly, along with other locality-based interaction such as silo-filling and labor exchange. Bracey, an Englishman, makes an interesting observation regarding neighboring (including borrowing) in the United States. He says: "Shopping in bulk is a necessity when your farm is fifty miles from the nearest store; this kind of situation obtains over large areas of the United States and it is with this pattern of buying that many present-day town Americans were brought up. When borrowing from your neighbor is a necessity it is not regarded as a vice, or admission of weakness, but a neighborly act and this feeling seems to persist in America even where the conditions of supply make it less necessary."[19]

As pointed out by Larson and Rogers,[20] the growing numbers

[19] Howard E. Bracey, *Neighbours* (Baton Rouge: Louisiana State University Press, 1964), p. 85.

[20] Olaf F. Larson and Everett M. Rogers, "Rural Society in Transition: The

of farm family members working off the farm are caused in part by the differences in farm and non-farm income. Numbers of persons commuting to work at non-farm jobs has assumed massive proportions in most rural areas. As one would expect, the percentage of income from off-farm sources declines for farm operator families as the value of farm sales increases. This fact is portrayed in Table 2. For farm operator families on farms whose sales are under $2,500, 88 percent of the total income was

TABLE 2

Income per Farm-Operator Family, by Value of Sales Class, and Percentage from Non-Farm Source, 1960 and 1970

Sales Class	1960		1970	
	Total Income[1]	Percent from Off-farm Source	Total Income[1]	Percent from Off-farm Source
All Farms	$ 5,102	41.9	$11,207	52.0
Less than $2,500	3,581	76.3	9,013	88.3
$2,500-$4,999	3,810	48.5	7,514	72.7
$5,000-$9,999	4,878	32.2	7,476	58.8
$10,000-$19,999	6,626	19.0	9,660	35.7
$20,000-$39,999	10,330	16.2	13,465	26.0
$40,000 & over	21,132	10.3	31,467	18.4

[1] Includes government payments and nonmoney income from farm food and housing

Source: U.S.D.A., *The Farm Income Situation, Statistical Abstract of the United States, 1972*, p. 587.

derived from nonfarm sources in 1970. In fact, nonfarm sources account for one-fourth of farm operator family income even when the farm sales fall between $20,000 and $39,999. Off-farm sources for all value of sales classes of farms increased markedly between 1960 and 1970. Hence, it would seem that the smaller, lower and middle class groups in American agriculture become commuters in the largest proportions. Off-farm work is often the mechanism through which they can retain farm residence and

American Setting" in James H. Copp, ed., *Our Changing Rural Society: Perspectives and Trends* (Ames: Iowa State University Press, 1964), p. 48.

delay the time they must leave agriculture. At the same time, off-farm work experience may serve as a bridge between rural and urban life, and may often serve to diminish adjustment problems when migration occurs.

There is evidence that populations in areas beyond the feasibility of commuting are deprived in many ways. Non-commuter areas need more adequate income, better housing, and acceptable public services.[21] An estimated 12 percent of the total population (farm, non farm and urban) reside in non-commuter counties. Non-commuter counties are a residual after defining: (1) urban employment centers, counties with 25,000 or more urban population or 10,000 or more nonfarm wage and salary jobs in 1970, and (2) commuter counties, those from which 10 percent or more of all workers commuted to jobs located within the urban employment centers. About half of the non-commuter populations in 1970 lived in the South. The average income gap between non-commuter and U. S. average per capita income level was $931 in 1967. In the East South Central states this gap amounted to $1,478.[22]

THE FUNCTION OF SOCIAL RANK

The evaluative process that results in variations in social rank, according to functional theory, permits social systems to reward groups and individuals in accordance with the utility and scarcity of their services. There are no systems in which certain activities or qualities are not rewarded in accordance with their social value, that is, their utility and scarcity to the system. This makes it possible to recruit people of the necessary ability and training for the various status-roles in society and to reward them in accordance with the importance of their status-roles and the effectiveness of their role performance.

The social ranking mechanisms also have the function of making those in important status-roles more conspicuous than others, thus forcing greater responsibility upon them for conforming to certain norms. Of course, the rewards for individuals placed in important status-roles may be in the form of rights to

[21] Economic Research Service, *Characteristics of U. S. Rural Areas with Non-commuting Population* (Washington: U. S. Government Printing Office, 1972), p. 1.

[22] Ibid., pp. 3-4 and 22-23.

ignore some norms. There may be a certain element of truth in the saying "The king can do no wrong;" nevertheless, when he does violate the norms more people are likely to learn about the violation because of its importance to them and because of his visibility.

When the social system is considered as a "going concern," effective social ranking systems have a very important function that is often overlooked. That is, assuring maximum effectiveness of communication within systems and sub-systems. The ease with which people communicate both information and feelings is dependent in large part upon similarities of experience, aspirations, and backgrounds. Certainly, friends and kinfolk can usually communicate with each other experiences and feelings more easily than they can with strangers. Usually, people feel more at ease and derive greater satisfaction from participation with those who understand and sympathize with them. The foregoing may be symbolized by the often used expression applied to newcomers almost everywhere, namely, "Make yourself at home." What is really meant is "Formalities aren't necessary; be comfortable and feel as secure as though you were in your own home." Of course, security and comfort depend upon understanding and common expectancy patterns.

Through boundary maintenance mechanisms large systems such as nations, factories, and large scale agricultural operations provide means by which relatively intensive interaction among equals can take place. In this way, the larger system, containing many homogeneous sub-systems of varying ranks, can move toward its general objectives. In settings in which people from various backgrounds and various social ranks must interact, people cannot "feel at home" as they can in familistic Gemeinschaft-like settings. For example, in foreign embassy receptions, where people from many cultures and social systems must interact, tolerable expectancy patterns are forced upon the participants by various institutionalized formalities of speech, action, and behavior. At any time when persons of different rank must interact, the situation must be formal and the invitation "make yourself at home" becomes a hollow gesture.

Those sociologists who condemn the above explanation of rank in functional terms often claim that such explanations are conjured up by the conservative to legitimize the establishment. It is tempting to take their arguments and condemn the low rank of farmers and peasants throughout the world. Unfortunately, too many "anti-functionalist" theorists, perhaps influenced by the same factors that led Marx and Engels to write of the "idiocy of the peasantry" have little concern for their low rank. We now turn to this problem.

SOCIAL RANK OF FARM FAMILIES

In most societies of the world, farm or peasant families have relatively low social rank. As Nelson[23] has remarked, the farmer's or peasant's status in the Western world is often characterized in derogatory terms that carry connotations of slavery and serfdom. In most societies, when the support of the people from the countryside is sought, politicians and others talk of the "embattled farmer" or call him the "backbone" of the nation. But even in the United States this apparently is praise with ulterior motives.

No one would explain the relatively low status of the farm and peasant families of the world by their lack of importance to society. All will agree that few occupations are more important than those that supply food and fiber. Nor can the low status of agriculture be explained on the basis of the knowledge or skill required. Any urbanite accustomed to shifting among urban occupations would find that farming, particularly the managerial and entrepreneurial functions, requires great knowledge and skill, despite the fact that much is learned by apprenticeship.

Census Bureau reports indicated that in 1970, median white family income of those living on farms outside metropolitan areas was $6,819 as compared with $11,203 for white families in metropolitan areas. Comparable black family incomes on farms and in metropolitan areas were $3,106 and $7,022, respectively.[24]

Various studies have shown that children of farm families, in terms of IQ's or school grades, make lower scores than children of some other groups in society, notably professionals.[25] Farm children in general have access to poorer educational facilities

[23] Lowry Nelson, *Rural Sociology* (New York: American Book Co., 1949), p. 210.

[24] Bureau of the Census, *Current Population Reports,* Series P-60, No. 80, *Statistical Abstract of the United States,* 1972, p. 323.

[25] For a review and listing of several of these studies, see Nelson, *Rural Sociology,* pp. 209 and 210.

than nonfarm children. Furthermore, testing does not usually present an opportunity for the farm-reared child to demonstrate the knowledge and ability gained from his farm experience.

LAND TENURE AND SOCIAL RANK

Land tenure means customary and legal rights in land. Social rank is closely related to the type of tenure relations a given individual has in land. The owner of a large estate who has the right to use or dispose of his land at will and who controls the lives of those attached to the land ordinarily outranks the peon who has fewer rights in the land. In all agricultural societies status-role designations are related to variations in the rights to use and control land.[26]

Early land tenure. Various social ranks existed in medieval European rural society, from which our own tenure system evolved. One group was slaves who could be sold. Another group, serfs, such as cotters and villeins, had certain land rights and, although they could be transferred with the estate, their status remained the same. Still other landed classes were the lesser gentry, the nobility, and royalty.[27] One's tenure rank or relation to the land determined the conditions of marriage, the services and payments one was expected to render, and the conditions under which one could leave the estate.[28]

Most Americans are so accustomed to land held under fee simple that they do not understand other systems. Although efforts were made to establish feudal tenure systems in Maryland, the Carolinas, and New York, for example, such attempts did not survive and disappeared after the American Revolution.[29]

Land tenure in the United States. According to the 1969 Census of Agriculture, there were 2,730,000 farms in the United States. Of this total, 62.5 percent were operated by full owners,

[26] Irvine remarks that in most rural places of medieval Europe there was "no place for a landless man." All persons who had any rights were related to the land through some tenure status. Helen D. Irvine, *The Making of Modern Europe* (New York: E. P. Dutton and Company, 1923), pp. 11-22.

[27] Irvine estimates that in 1300, two-thirds of the population of England were villeins. Ibid., p. 23.

[28] For the situation in England see George C. Homans, *English Villagers of the 13th Century* (Cambridge: Harvard University Press, 1941), pp. 232-252.

[29] Irving Mark, "Agrarian Conflicts in New York and the American Revolution," *Rural Sociology,* Vol. VII, No. 3 (September, 1942), pp. 275-293.

24.6 percent by part owners, and 12.9 percent were operated by tenants. As shown in Table 3, the rate of tenancy has declined sharply, from 38.8 percent in 1940. The rate of tenancy has also declined sharply in the South, a region having high rates for many years, but as shown in the table, the tenancy rate in 1969 was below national average. The incidence of tenancy for minority race farms has been high in all years shown, and in 1969 amounted to about one-fifth of farms operated by blacks, Chicanos, and others.

TABLE 3
Percentage of Tenancy in the U.S. for Selected Dates

| Year | Tenant Operated | | | |
	Percent of all Farms	Percent of Farms in South	Percent of Minority Race Farms	Percent of Land Acreage in Farms
1940	38.8	48.2	74.6	29.4
1950	26.9	34.1	65.5	18.3
1959	20.5	23.1	51.9	14.9
1964	17.1	18.5	44.3	13.1
1969	12.9	11.7	20.2	13.0

Source: U.S. Census of Agriculture, *Statistical Abstract of the United States, 1972*, p. 587.

Economic class of farms. One view of the scale of farm operations in the United States may be gained from the classification of farms by the Census of Agriculture based upon the value of farm products sold. As shown in Table 4, Economic class contains three major categories: Farms with sales of $2,500 or more, the more commercialized farms; farms with sales of less than $2,500, including "part-time" and "part-retirement" farms, and "abnormal" farms. About 64 percent of farms in the nation have sales of $2,500 or more. Most of the remaining farms, or approximately 36 percent have sales of less than $2,500. Only about 2,000 farms are classed as abnormal. They include institutional farms operated by hospitals, penitentiaries, schools, government agencies, etc.

As indicated in Table 4, average acreage per farm rises as the value of sales increases for farms with sales of $2,500 or more. Farms with sales of $2,500-4,999 average 192 acres as compared

TABLE 4
Number of Farms, Acreage, and Value of Sales, by Economic Class, 1969

Economic Class of Farms (Value of farm products sold)	Number of Farms in Thousands	Average Acreage per Farm	Average Value of Sales per Farm	Percent Distribution		
				Farms	Acreage Total	Value of Sales, Total
Farms with sales of $2,500 or more	1,734	530	$25,680	100.0	100.0	100.0
$2,500-$4,999	395	192	3,406	22.8	8.3	3.0
5,000-9,999	390	274	7,208	22.5	11.6	6.3
10,000-19,999	395	433	14,396	22.8	18.6	12.8
20,000-39,999	331	626	27,990	19.1	22.6	20.8
40,000 and over	222	1,611	114,579	12.8	38.9	57.1
Farms with sales less than $2,500	994	90	940	100.0	100.0	100.0
$50-2,499	193	96	977	19.4	20.6	20.1
Part-time	575	86	926	57.8	54.9	56.9
Part-retirement	227	97	947	22.9	24.5	23.0
Abnormal	2	26,174	72,267	100.0	100.0	100.0

Source: U.S. Census of Agriculture, vol. II., *Statistical Abstract of the United States, 1972*, p. 588.

with 1,600 acres in the case of farms in the $40,000 or over category. Farm size averaged 90 acres for farms with sales of less than $2,500.

The data found in Table 4 lead one to the correct conclusion that the farms in the United States exhibit extraordinary diversity, that economic scale alone would produce large variations in social rank. Of all commercial farms, for example, the 13 percent having sales of $40,000 or more account for 57 percent of the total farm sales. At the other extreme, the more than one-fifth of all farms in the $2,500 to $4,999 category account for only 3 percent of the value of farm sales.

While the data for economic class of farms are revealing, they fail to portray the growing invasion of agriculture by large-scale corporations and conglomerates. These developments have proceeded in the West, particularly in California, to a greater extent than elsewhere. California, however, leads the nation in food production. This state provides one-fourth of the table foods and one-third of the nation's canned and frozen vegetables and fruits. Eight of the top ten counties in value of farm products sold are in California.[30] Krebs, in his testimony on land ownership, use and distribution, before the 92nd Congress, had this to say concerning California agriculture: "From its beginning— through a combination of massive land grabs, violence, foreign exploitation, political intrigue, slave labor, greed, the frequent ignoring of state and federal laws, and giant growing, processing and packaging conglomerates (like the Del Monte Corp., Tenneco Inc., DiGiorgio Corp., and Sunkist Growers, Inc., with their interconnecting directorates) who control a vertically integrated flow of food from the field to the table—California's agribusiness has grown wealthier, more elite, and more powerful."[31]

Land as a value in and of itself. The more the land is used as a means of making money rather than as a value in and of itself, the more it will be misused. The tenancy rate is likely to be high-

[30] *Farm Workers in Rural America, 1971-1972,* Hearings before the Subcommittee on Migratory Labor, 92nd Congress, A.V. Krebs, "Agribusiness and Land in California" (Washington: Government Printing Office, 1972), Part 3A, p. 734-735.

[31] Ibid., p. 735. Also see Peter Barnes, "The Great American Land Grab," "The Vanishing Small Farmer," and "The Case for Redistribution," *New Republic,* (June 5, June 12, June 19, 1971).

er, and the equity of farm operators in the land will be smaller. As Firey[32] has shown, land can be the symbol of group integration and social status in a large city. Beacon Hill, a residential area of upper-class Bostonians, should have changed to commercial uses from an economic point of view. Group solidarity held this residential area intact, even though it is an area which ordinarily would have been given over to business. Through zoning and other devices available to the upper class, the area retains such characterizations as "this sacred eminence," "stately old-time appearance," and "age-old quaintness and charm."

In most peasant and noncommercial agricultural economies, land has a value other than its profit potential. Land often provides the basis for the social rank of all related to it. There are still some areas in the United States in which farm land means more than other tools of production having equal cost. Kollmorgen[33] has shown that the Old Order Amish place a high value on land near the center of their settlement and that the true Amish farmer hopes to be able to buy farms for all his sons near the center. Peripheral areas, although having comparable fertility and other economic advantages are usually worth much less than the lands at the center of the Amish settlement, away from the evil influences of the "worldly."

DISADVANTAGED GROUPS IN RURAL AREAS

The rural areas of the United States, the wealthiest nation in history, contain a disproportionate share of the deprived, poverty-stricken people. Based upon data for the mid-sixties, the President's Commission on Rural Poverty estimated that 41 percent of all poor persons resided in the rural areas even though the rural population accounted for only one-fourth of the total.[34] A survey of the low-income population in 1971 reinforces this conclusion. Approximately 11 million, or about 43 percent of all poor

---

[32] Walter Firey, *Land Use in Central Boston* (Cambridge: Harvard University Press, 1947).

[33] Walter M. Kollmorgen, *Culture of a Contemporary Rural Community: The Old Order Amish of Lancaster County, Pennsylvania* (Washington, D. C.: U.S.D.A., 1942).

[34] *The People Left Behind,* A Report of the President's National Advisory Commission on Rural Poverty (Washington: Government Printing Office, 1967), pp. 1-9.

persons, lived in nonmetropolitan areas and about 8 percent of all poor lived on farms. The proportions of poor whites living in nonmetropolitan areas exceeded the proportions of poor blacks in nonmetropolitan areas, the percentages being about 45 and 38.[35] The disadvantaged groups in rural America include the blacks, especially in the South, the Spanish-Americans, particularly in the Southwest and often important in migratory labor streams, the Indians, and poor whites found in certain "pockets of poverty" but also distributed throughout most rural areas of the nation.

Much has been written about the flight from the land on the part of the Southern blacks. Nonetheless, large numbers remain on farms and in nonmetropolitan areas of the South. Howard Taft Bailey, a black farmer from Lexington, Mississippi, gave this lucid picture before the National Advisory Commission on Rural Poverty:

> Farm mechanization seems to have a tendency to make the median income a little lower because it causes people to be shifted from the farm, unemployed; and some are moving into the small towns, you might say urban areas. They are unskilled and don't have no experience—which you know that the plantation system has created dire need for the rural participants on the plantation—and they don't have the skill nor the ambition . . . to make for themselves a way in this society . . . We need more family farms. Too many families have lost their farms and have shifted from the farms, and there are many who never had a chance to own farms and had no place on the plantation where they live . . . We feel that if we could break into the plantations and buy land and help these people on the farm they could help themselves in production, cattle, things that would make life more secure for them. And they might be able to take a place in the society.[36]

Despite the progress of blacks in the past decade, blacks have not achieved equality with whites, whether in urban or rural areas. Blacks hold a disproportionate share of low ranking jobs

[35] U.S. Bureau of the Census, *Current Population Reports,* P-60, No. 86, p. 35. The low-income threshold in 1971 for a nonfarm family of four was $4,137 and the farm threshold was set at 85 percent of that figure.

[36] Hearings before the National Advisory Commission on Rural Poverty, Memphis, Tennessee, February 2 and 3, 1967, (Washington, D.C., 1967), pp. 1-4.

in rural areas and many join the streams of seasonal farm laborers.

About 2.4 million, or 26 percent of the persons who identified themselves as being of Spanish origin (predominantly Mexican) were below the low income level in 1971. A large number of the Spanish-Americans who have moved to the large cities are a part of the migrant agricultural work force. The Commission on Rural Poverty concludes that traditionally the Spanish-Americans have been "objects of discrimination and exploitation." A study of housing conditions among Spanish-Americans in New Mexico revealed that while 89 percent had homes with electricity, only one-third had water piped into the house, only slightly more than one-fourth had flush toilets, and only about one-eighth had a telephone.[37]

The American Indians certainly are among the most deprived groups in the United States, and a large number reside in rural areas. Indian housing is grossly inadequate on the reservations and trust lands, a large share of the housing being dilapidated and overcrowded. Clyde Warrior, president of the National Indian Youth Council, described the circumstances of American Indians before the Commission on Rural Poverty. The following are excerpts of his testimony:

> ... if there is one thing that characterizes Indian life today it is poverty of the spirit. We still have human passion and depth of feeling ... but we are poor in spirit because we are not free in the most basic sense of the word. We as American Indians are not allowed to make those basic human choices and decisions about our personal life and about the best need of our communities, which is the mark of free, mature people ... Those of us who live in nonreservation areas have our lives controlled by local white power elites. We have many rulers. They are called social workers, 'cops', school teachers, churches, etc., and recently OEO employees, because in the meeting they tell us what is good for us and how they programmed us, and their manners are not what one would call polite by Indian standards, or perhaps by any standards. We are rarely accorded respect as fellow human beings. Our children come home from school to us with shame in their hearts and a sneer on their lips for their home and parents. We are the 'poverty problem', and that is true;

[37] *The People Left Behind,* pp. 98-99.

and perhaps it is also true that our lack of reasonable choices, our lack of freedom, our poverty of spirit is not unconnected with our national poverty.[38]

While the blacks, Chicanos, and Indians are perhaps more visible racially and culturally, disadvantaged whites can be found throughout rural America. Rural whites, too, bear similar scars left by material and status deprivation.

THE HIRED FARM WORKING FORCE

We once noted that "large proportions of agricultural workers were living with their employers in the same households at the time of the regular census in 1940."[39] This picture has changed markedly. At present only slightly more than one out of four persons who do at least some farm work for pay live on farms and very few live with farm families where they do such work. In 1948-49, 65 percent of the 3,946,000 who did some labor for pay for farmers said that their home address was a farm. Again we write as we did in 1950: "Those who lament the passing of what has been here referred to as familistic Gemeinschaft-like type of society, recall when the farm laborer outside the Cotton Belt was not a mere wage hand. Social distance between farmer and laborer was small, the laborer being treated as a member of the family. The laborer and the members of the farm family ate at the same table and slept under the same roof. Then the status of farm laborer was a rung on the agricultural ladder to ownership . . ."[40] Actually, the farm laborer is still treated as a member of the family in some parts of the country.

The hired farm working force of 1972 consisted of about 2.8 million persons 14 years of age and over who did some farm work for cash wages during the year. These workers did about 247 million man-days of work on farms in 1972—about one-fourth of the total number of days of labor on farms. Of these workers only 24 percent were engaged chiefly in farm wagework. Of these 367,000 were year-round workers who averaged 306 days and earned $4,358. About 52 percent (primarily

[38] Hearings before the National Advisory Commission on Rural Poverty, p. 144.

[39] Loomis and Beegle, *Rural Social Systems,* pp. 118-119.

[40] Ibid., p. 338.

housewives and students) were not in the labor force most of the year. About 183,000 or 7 percent of the total were migratory workers.[41]

MIGRATORY FARM WORKERS

Migratory farm workers, among them large numbers of Spanish-Americans and blacks, occupy the lowest position in the status hierarchy. While the number of persons employed at farm work for any period of time has fluctuated from about 3 to 3.5 million annually in recent years, migratory farmworkers have averaged fewer than 400,000 annually, or about 9 percent of the total.[42] A large share of the migratory workers are employed in the harvest of fruits and vegetables. Characteristically they are employed in farm areas requiring large numbers of hired workers for brief periods or seasonal peaks and they move on as the season advances.

Migratory agricultural workers follow three major routes, all of which originate along the southern border. As shown in Figure 4, the main stream moves north and west from Texas and covers most of the vast area west of the Mississippi river as well as the East North Central states. This stream comprises many Mexican-Americans, many of whom were born in southern Texas. The second migratory stream originates in Florida and other southern states and moves north along the Atlantic Seacoast into the Middle Atlantic and New England states. A large proportion of this stream is made up of blacks. The third stream starts in southern California and moves northward to the state of Washington. Like the first, this stream is heavily composed of Mexican-Americans.

While migratory farm workers are employed in practically all states, five states, California, Florida, Michigan, Texas, and Washington, account for about half of the man-hours of employment. Migratory workes are used particularly to harvest the following fruits and vegetables: strawberries, tomatoes, beans, lettuce, cherries, grapes, peaches, and melons. As technological

[41] *The Hired Farm Working Force of 1972—A Statistical Report,* Economic Research Service, U.S. D.A., Agr. Economic Report No. 239.

[42] *The Migratory Farm Labor Problem in the United States,* 1969 report of the Committee on Labor and Public Welfare (Washington: Government Printing Office, 1969), pp. 1-4.

TRAVEL PATTERNS OF SEASONAL
MIGRATORY AGRICULTURAL WORKERS

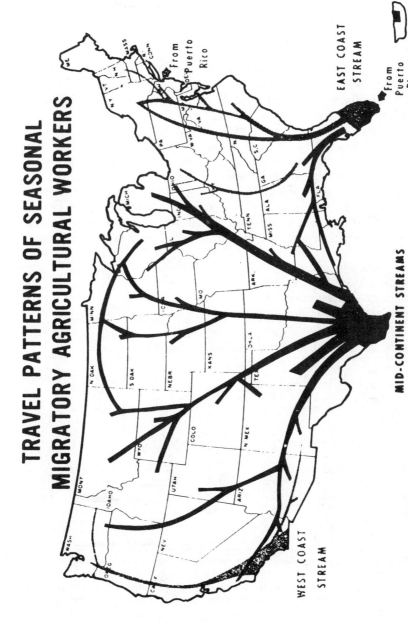

FIGURE 4. Major routes followed by seasonal farm workers in the United States.

innovations take place, the need for migratory workers may diminish rapidly as in the case of cherry harvesting in Michigan.

The seasonal peak in the employment of migratory farm labor, of course, varies as to regional location and type of crop. Nationally, the seasonal peak occurs in the summer months as shown in Table 5. However, seasonality of employment varies substantially in the five states having the greatest employment of migratory farm workers.

It is difficult to imagine a set of circumstances that would increase the assault on human sensibilities more than those now endured by migratory farm workers. The work is backbreaking; housing and sanitation are usually below reasonable standards; the farm worker is a stranger in a strange land, often removed from friends and relatives; and he is without power and prestige. Of migrant farm workers, Robert Coles, a psychiatrist says: "It is rather obvious that migrants live demeaned, undig-

TABLE 5
Estimated Employment of Farm Workers for the United States and Selected States, by Month, 1968

Month	U.S. Total	California	Florida	Michigan	Texas	Washington
			(In Thousands)			
January	35.3	11.2	20.2	0	0.1	0.2
February	38.5	12.2	21.5	0	0	0.8
March	40.7	14.0	19.2	0	0.2	1.9
April	59.8	20.2	19.0	0.7	1.3	4.0
May	115.2	37.9	18.7	3.7	2.2	6.6
June	203.9	38.3	7.3	23.2	10.0	12.5
July	208.3	35.5	1.8	27.3	19.8	7.8
August	235.6	51.5	0.5	40.0	14.7	5.8
September	202.3	62.5	0.9	13.6	6.4	7.9
October	134.9	38.7	5.0	10.3	6.2	9.8
November	48.1	14.6	12.0	0.6	6.1	0.7
December	44.9	12.7	18.6	0	7.5	0

Note: Due to rounding, figures may not add to totals; in some cases, 0 represents less than 50 workers.

Source: *Federal and State Statutes Related to Farmworkers,* Subcommittee on Migratory Labor, 92nd Congress, (Washington: U.S. Government Printing Office, 1972), p. 201.

nified, and impoverished lives, as do many poor people in our rural areas and our cities . . . they are also very much different from any other group of American citizens, because they lack a place of residence—with all that goes with membership in a community—and ironically, they give up that rather ultimate possession in order to seek out and find work."[43]

Federal and state benefit welfare programs exclude farm workers entirely or in part. In many instances, the migratory status of workers magnifies the exclusions. The wages received by migrant farm-workers are low in part because many are not covered under the minimum wage law. Farmworkers were not included under the minimum wage provision of the Fair Labor Standards Act until 1966 and even then at a lower rate than the national minimum wage. Furthermore, only farm employers who use 500 man-days of agricultural labor in any quarter of the previous year and who engage in interstate commerce, are compelled to pay the minimum wage. Thus, a large number of farmworkers are excluded from the provisions of the Act.[44]

Farm workers were covered by social security after 1956, if the worker received cash wages of at least $150 from one employer during the year. A farm worker may also qualify for OASDI benefits when he works for one employer 20 days or more for cash computed on a time basis rather than on a piece-rate basis. Often the migrant worker and others fail to meet the requirements for coverage, and consequently lack any retirement benefits, survivors, disability, or medicare protection. Part of the problem is the failure of migrants themselves to know what is legally due them and to conform with the bureaucratic demands.[45]

While farmworkers need insurance protection against unemployment as much as workers in other industries, most farmworkers lack this form of insurance. The argument that most

[43] Paper submitted by Robert Coles and excerpted in *Federal and State Statutes Relating to Farmworkers*, prepared for the Subcommittee on Migratory Labor, U.S. Senate (Washington: Government Printing Office, 1972), p. 210. Rushing finds non-English Spanish speaking workers less alienated than Anglo-American, with bilingual workers intermediate. See William A. Rushing, *Class, Culture and Alienation* (Lexington, Mass.: D.C. Heath, 1972).

[44] Raymond Schmitt, *The Migrant Farmworker Situation in the U.S.*, March 16, 1972, reprinted in *Federal and State Statutes Relating to Farmworkers*, 92nd Congress, pp. 389-390.

[45] Ibid., pp. 394-395.

agricultural employers have small enterprises and lack book-keeping and management skills has not been altered, and the Federal Unemployment Tax excludes farm workers. Individual states control workmen's compensation. In contrast to industrial workers who are almost completely covered by Workmen's Compensation laws, farm occupations remain largely excluded from coverage. This condition is especially serious in view of the hazardous nature of agricultural operations, especially since modern agriculture is highly mechanized and makes use of dangerous chemicals and pesticides. Some 22 states provide for voluntary Workmen's Compensation and specifically include agricultural workers.[46]

The unionization of farm workers for the purpose of collective bargaining over wages and working conditions, though attempted in the early 1900's by the IWW, has not been remarkably successful on a nationwide scale. Efforts in California, Hawaii, and Florida are exceptions. "The scattering of many workers over a large number of farms, the relatively small size of farm establishments, the short duration of much of the work, the frequent movement of workers from one job to another, and the temporary attachment of many workers to farming have generally made it difficult to organize stable unions and to persuade employers to bargain with them collectively."[47]

SOCIAL PROCESSES AND HIERARCHICAL SOCIAL SYSTEMS

Communication. Reference has already been made to the function of social rank in facilitating communication within sub-systems. A change agent working in an open-class system is confronted with a very different situation than when working in a society dominated by castes or estates and where ethnic or similar groups are strong subsystems. In the open-class system, a general procedure in efforts to introduce improved practices in agriculture or health is to attempt to gain adoption by individuals and groups of high rank, with the expectation that these practices will spread downward. Downward diffusion is less likely to take place in societies that are stratified into castes and estates. If persons of higher rank adopt a change, those of lower

46 Ibid., pp. 398-401.
47 Ibid., p. 396.

rank are frequently not motivated to accept the change because those above are "supposed to be different." In such societies, acceptance on the lower level may preclude upward spread, because the new practice may symbolize the lower rank and carry a negative connotation for those of higher rank. Although there are many exceptions, plans to introduce change into highly stratified societies usually require separate personnel and procedures for the different strata. The tenant purchase programs, supervised loans, and similar devices which were effective in improving the standard of living of sharecroppers, for example, could hardly be effective in improving the practices of plantation owners.

Decision-making. Whether the society is highly stratified or not, more decision-making power resides with the higher ranking groups and individuals. However, outside of large systems such as plantations and other large-scale enterprises, there is no general institutionalized decision-making mechanism for rural areas. The manner in which decisions in a given area of life are made varies greatly from culture to culture. In Latin American cultures where the "*patron* configuration" exists, much important decision-making rests in the higher ranks in both highly stratified and less stratified communities. In societies in which authority and power are played down, on the other hand, individualism may impel persons and groups to resist the decision-making of higher rank individuals.

Boundary maintenance. In the novel and short story, few themes are used more extensively than those involving attempts to improve social rank against the opposition of others. The boundary maintenance mechanisms of hierarchical systems are different from other systems because the honor of the person is involved in a more conspicuous manner. When a person attempts to "move up," those above may feel that their social rank will be degraded and those in the same social rank may feel rejected. All the sentiments involved in the maintenance of social rank are of importance for the change agent attempting to introduce new practices into the whole community or any particular stratum. The change agent's social rank may be more important than any other factor in the success of a plan involving social change. His ability to identify with various hierarchical groups and at the same time provide prestige to those who adopt the change are often critical problems.

Systemic linkage. In the writings of social scientists, no single subject has been of more concern than stratification and social rank. In part, this is due to a pervading assumption that, if social rank is understood, at least a major segment of human motivation would be understood. It is often assumed that most people strive to behave like those they consider to be their "betters", or those they accept as having higher social rank, both within their own social system and outside.

Most cultural change, whether involving beliefs, the adoption of practices, or the acquisition of material objects, spreads downward from systems having higher social rank. Under conditions in which the ranking systems are congeries of cultural sub-systems, this is particularly true. Where caste conditions exist or the values of one system are not articulated to another system, a quite different state of affairs exists. Therefore, it is important that the change agent knows the nature of the social structure within which he is working. If the change system has higher social rank than the target system, the change agent may find means of bringing the two systems together in integrated action. If the system has lower rank than the target system, the change agent may resort to various strategies. Labor and farm organizations, for instance, have exerted influence through voting and economic power. The poor whites in the South may get support of higher rank whites in the South when caste problems are involved by evoking caste identification. Through symbol manipulation the change agent may force the upper rank white caste to identify with the lower rank white caste and become involved in actions they ordinarily oppose. Similar symbol manipulation may force higher rank persons to act against certain ethical principles, as when loaded terms such as "communist," "radical," and the like are used.

THE WEALTHY NEWCOMER

The following case is included not only for its portrayal of social rank under conditions of threat but also for its vignettes of the social life and norms in a small Midwestern community. This case, the student will quickly recognize, would be equally appropriate for the chapter considering types of farming organizations. A few italicized insertions will be used to relate this case to the author's conceptual scheme.

THEY'RE DESTROYING OUR SMALL TOWNS[48]

Odebolt is in western Iowa, in an area that has been blessed with rich soil and good weather. A drouth comes only about every 20 years—in 1936 and 1956, folks recall—and then only for a year at a time.

The town is centrally located in the triangle of Omaha, Sioux Falls, and Des Moines. Temperatures in January average about 19 degrees, immobilizing the organic matter that makes the soil dark and rich, and it rises to an average of a warm molecule-activating 74 degrees in July. The last killing frost ordinarily comes about May 4 and the first killing frost in the fall comes about October 2. Extremes can go above a hundred degrees in the summer and well below zero in the winter. The average growing season is an ideal 151 days; average rainfall is 30 inches a year.

The land rolls gently, lending itself to full cultivation; the topography is kinder than the river bluffs area to the west. Houses sit squarely, conservatively tending to face straight east, south, west or north. The architectural angles are modest squares, rectangles, and safely peaked roofs. Many of the houses are two-story, with one-story lean-to additions to accommodate growing families. Barns are rugged, painted against the extremes of weather, many with hay fork-supporting hip roofs.

A sign at the outskirts says that Odebolt is the "Star in the Crown of Iowa." Nearby is an extraordinarily neat cemetery, noticeably well cared for in this state which seems to care for its dead with unusual reverence.

There is a comfortable, intimate triteness about the business district. A story of one Iowa town tells of the theater owner who built a new movie palace, with a red carpet out to the sidewalk. But when it was finished, attendance declined. In desperation, he hired a consultant to find out why. It was the red carpet. Folks didn't feel comfortable coming in off the street, with their dusty shoes, stepping on the fine red carpet. Attendance was restored when the carpet was removed.

It is easy to believe that it could have happened in Odebolt. The people of Odebolt are too considerate to track dirt into a

---

[48] Victor K. Ray, *The Corporate Invasion*, pp. 41-47.

neighbor's home or business, or to complain at the absence of a foot scraper at the door, or about a pretentious thick carpet inside. [*Norms and Values not uncommon in genuinely rural areas.*]

There are, then, things not visible in the prosaic facade of neat, proud homes that sit along the tree-covered streets of Odebolt; shadows not apparent in the enormous elms that cool the lawns and churchyards; messages not communicated by a hurrying housewife stewing along on an errand or the businessman crossing the empty street to the bank for his daily deposit.

But there is a subject they discuss among themselves. It is something that angers, confuses, makes them envious, and saddens them. In the diversity that characterizes even the small towns of America, it is likely that you can also find people who are delighted and proud of this phenomenon. But one thing is for sure. It is something they cannot forget. Some think it is an economic cancer that is sickening the body and soul of the community—worse, a form of malignancy that is threatening to spread.

The topic is Shinrone Farms, Inc., 6,000 acres that surround the town on the south and west sides. It sits there, always visible, dominating the heart and mind, choking off the bloodstream of pride of the community, showing to the people of Odebolt every day of the year the presence of an invader of their way of life. The wealth of its owners seduces the youngsters. Its presence robs businessmen of hope for the future. [*Change in the stratification system and its impact on the community is the issue.*] It hovers there, its headquarters spreading away at the end of a mile-and-a-half tunnel of road lined and covered by magnificent elms that meet high above its center. But even the elms are sick, as though made ill by a contagion of the invader. The trees betray their illness in a telltale white substance that streaks down the trunks, the deadly symptoms of Dutch Elm disease. When they are gone, Shinrone will be even more visible to the town.

It was the Adams Ranch, and is still called that despite its recent new ownership and its interesting new name. Odeboltians look at the gleaming white tractors and combines and other farm equipment—$250,000 worth, according to the Des Moines Register—and see in the green shamrock on the radiators the flag of an alien force. The farm equipment was not bought locally. A businessman says with some bitterness that it was bought direct from the manufacturer; although a dealer at the county seat, Sac City, may be involved "in order to service the equipment." [*What can be done to preserve the Community System?*]

The new owner is William Oldfield Bridge, whom few citizens of Odebolt have seen. He has a sentimentality about Ireland, as the shamrocks attest. Bridge is a Detroit trucking executive, operating a vast automobile hauling agency—the Baker Driveaway Company.

They say that Bridge and his wife may move to Odebolt and, if they do, it will be a most natural choice. For this beautiful community and its friendly people must be a temptation to a family accustomed to the ugly roar and impersonal grind of Detroit. It must be better to live in Odebolt than even in the spacious suburb of Bloomfield Hills, Michigan, where the papers say the Bridges now reside. Besides, Bridge is interested in horses, the newspapers say, and Shinrone will be glamorized by the presence of fine horses.

It is doubtful that anyone in Odebolt will convey to the Bridges what a barrier they must surmount if they find the natural friendliness they expect. It is unlikely that a single resident of this considerate little city will speak frankly with these strangers. Indeed, there are few who would like to face this own hostile feelings in the matter, for those who have met Bridge say that he seems to be a decent sort, friendly and sociable. [*How can communication take place when the social rank chasm is so great?*]

But implacable history must be overcome if the Bridges find welcome in Odebolt. The Adams Ranch has a wall around it—scar tissue that has hardened in response to its alien presence in this area where families have farmed their own land, their children have grown up together, visited in each other's homes, gone to the same churches, and shared the same pleasures, dissatisfactions, the tedium of lonesome days, and have longed together for the adventure of life.

The character of the Adamses, much of it, has been dimmed in the rushing years that have included wars and disasters and murders. Some of the older folks remember. William Adams was "a pretty good man," they recall, "known and respected in the town." Somehow he managed to buy the land around the turn of the century from somebody who had acquired it for $3 an acre or less from a railroad. Then the Adams' name is further confused by the fact that three generations came and went. William Adams' son, Robert, was an odd one, they say. "He wanted to buy the whole town," somebody says.

"You mean, literally, he wanted to buy the town?" you ask.

"Well, it was the same thing. He said that if folks would rename the town 'Adamsville,' he would pave the streets."

They turned him down.

It may be that as a result they even invested the town name, Odebolt, with a romantic history in response to Adams' suggestion, because nobody seems quite certain how it really got its name. But the story they tell is that in the early days when the Germans and the Scandinavians were coming overland in wagons, two old fellows were making their way across the rolling prairie. The strain proved too much for the bolt in the tongue of the wagon and, suddenly, the team of horses broke loose, causing one of the men to exclaim, "oh de bolt!" They stopped to repair the wagon, and thus were the first settlers of Odebolt. It sounds rather unlikely, but it is better than selling one's heritage for a concrete pavement. [*A newcomer who does not understand the cultural heritage embodied in the norms and values.*]

And then there was the time an Adams (was it Robert, or his son, William II?) made a deal with the local elevator to sell some corn. On the day it was to be delivered, a disastrous storm covered the roads and the trees and the streets with a sheet of ice. There was conversation with the elevator manager who said, "Bring the corn another day."

"No, we've got a deal. We'll deliver it today."

Then, they say Adams ordered his hired hands—who would have liked to be in by the fire on such a day—to haul manure from the barnlots and spread it on the road to town so the loads of grain could be delivered. Inevitably the ice melted, but the manure—and its odor—remained and spread across the town, insulting the people. It was as if Adams had made a statement to the town, letting them know his contempt. [*An obvious misuse of power.*]

A new pastor arrived and observed the bitterness. When William Adams II walked down the street, nobody spoke. The pastor met him one morning and said, "Good morning, Mr. Adams." The young man just looked the other way.

The most recent owner before the Bridges was Charles Lakin.

He mixed with farmers and bought some things locally. His wife was a member of St. Martin's Catholic Church.

But among the first things you will hear about Lakin was that he received $241,000 in payments under the Agricultural Stabilization and Conservation Service program in 1966. "What right has a millionaire got receiving that kind of payment from the government?" they ask.

Mostly, Odebolt hides its shame from the world. But among themselves they talk about it. In fact, it seems "they talk about nothing else," somebody said. And now other farms are consolidating; other acreages are growing. They see it all as a part of the materialism that seems to obsess the new America.

Father Linus Eisenbacher of St. Martin's Church is a short man with a pock-marked face and a rounding middle. Despite his name, he seems to speak in an Irish accent.

He tells the story of St. Martin's—"named for St. Martin of Tours, a soldier who became disgusted with war. One day he met a beggar and cut his cloak in two, giving half to the beggar and, in a dream that night, he saw that the beggar was actually the Lord." He was made a Saint for his vision.

Father Eisenbacher can appreciate the idealism of St. Martin's. "The whole thing," he says (meaning the pressures that are taking people off the farms) "is affecting our people adversely. People are money hungry. They are secular. Spiritual values have gone down the drain."

"Rural people live close to God," he continues. "The rain and the sunshine and the good weather. The farmer is reminded every day that he is dependent on God. But people who draw a salary don't care about such things. They just begin to live at night . . . I was born and raised on a farm. You could tell something about the season just by looking. There was the thunder and lightning with the storms. Here, even in this little town, you can't see a storm until it's on you."

St. Martin's has had a 30- to 50-percent drop in participation of its members in the seven years Father Eisenbacher has been there. "Religious attitudes are directly related to the land," he said.

"The small farmer can't compete," he added bitterly. "The government doesn't do a thing for the small farmer."

Not far from Odebolt, an Omaha resident took her 80-year-old mother for a Sunday afternoon drive to their home community.

The old woman looked at the empty houses as they drove along
the country roads and became so upset she began crying. Her
daughter had to drive her home. What was to have been a
pleasant Sunday afternoon was spoiled.

The Snow-White Tractors

And now William Oldfield Bridge has bought Shinrone, hoping, perhaps, to find the peace that comes from walking in the
plowed ground, involving oneself in the processes of creation.
But he arrived at the wrong time in history at a place already
ruined, and he arrived under the wrong circumstances.

The whole matter came to the attention of his neighbors-to-be
in Odebolt on March 17, 1968, when the Des Moines Sunday
Register carried a story Shinrone, Inc. that dominated the front
page of its farm section. The story told of a shipment of new
machinery coming to Shinrone:

"Folks blink a bit in this community at the sight of snow-
white farm tractors, combines, implements and the like—all
painted this somewhat unusual (for farm equipment) color. The
white machinery is a part of the new look at what once was the
'Adams Ranch', then the 'Lakin Ranch' and now Shinrone
Farms. There will be about $250,000 worth of such white-painted
farm tractors, combines, and equipment brought to the famous
Sac County farming spread." [*Conspicuous symbols of rank and
power.*]

The story went on to identify Bridge and tell of the history of
the farm, pointing out that it had sold to Lakin in 1962 for an
estimated $2.5 million; and that Lakin had receipted payments
from the U.S. Department of Agriculture in 1966 amounting to
$241,000—more than anybody else in Iowa. The story said that
Bridge had visited Shinrone three or four times.

If folks in Odebolt were blinking at the big equipment purchase, their eyes really popped open three days later when the
Des Moines Register returned to Shinrone and William O.
Bridge. The paper printed a lengthy Associated Press story date-
lined Washington by Harry Rosenthal and Gaylor Shaw. The
headline was an attention-getter: "He settles $594,398 Tax for
$110,000."

They were talking about William Oldfield Bridge. The story
quoted Harry Snyder, chief of the Internal Revenue Service collection division, at length, about how the IRS had decided to set-

tle for less than 20 percent of its claim. "If I were a gambling man, I would bet we got all we can," said Snyder.

The article continued:

"On Oct. 5 (1967) while Bridge's compromise was being processed, four newspapers—including the largest in Iowa and Nebraska—carried stories that the 6,000-acre Lakin Ranch near Odebolt, Iowa had been sold to a Delaware corporation headed by F. G. Bridge."

The story quoted Snyder as saying that the IRS was unaware of the articles (although the IRS maintains a 10,000-man field staff whose duties include clipping newspapers for items).

The story continued:

"On September 27, 14 days after initial approval of the compromise, a company named Shinrone, Inc. filed incorporation papers in Delaware. Shinrone's first annual report listed F.G. Bridge of Bloomfield Hills, Michigan as president and one of three directors, and W. O. Bridge as another director. It stated that 5,000 shares of stock had been issued at $100 par value—a total of $500,000.

"On September 29, Shinrone, Inc. reached an agreement to buy the Iowa ranch from Charles E. and Florence Lakin.

"On October 19, Shinrone, Inc. applied to the Iowa secretary of state for authority to transact business in that state, saying it was among other things 'to acquire farm properties and other real estate'.

"On October 10 at 2:40 p.m. an official memorandum and notice of the sale of the Lakin Ranch to Shinrone, Inc. was filed with June Rheinfrank, Sac County, Iowa, recorder. The document referred to the September 29 sale agreement.

"Shinrone took possession of the ranch on March 1. Sale price was not disclosed, but an expert on land values estimated the farm is worth $3 million or more. He based this on the going price for farmland in Sac County—$500 to $700 an acre."

The Associated Press story went on to quote the IRS examiner as saying that Bridge did not own any property, that it was all in his wife's name.

Odebolt folks were interested to read that the Bridges have a number of corporations and that their home in Bloomfield Hills is on a 50-acre plot, assessed for tax purposes at $147,000 (Michigan law required that property be assessed at 50 percent of its true market value). Frances Bridge was listed as the owner. The

IRS examiner said that Bridge told him his assets were only $100 cash and a life insurance policy with a surrender value of $10,668.

It was a sobering story to the folks in Odebolt, most of whom work hard for their money and who have never thought of contesting the Internal Revenue Service and have never, in their most unrestrained dreams, visualized owning a $3 million ranch.

Odebolt, Iowa—with its incipient illness already taking its toll —is the first chapter in a story that has already been written in other parts of America. You can read it in the empty stores and offices along the main streets, the deteriorated shacks that were once called home, the purposeless old people who are left behind and whose only meaningful days come once a month when social security or welfare checks arrive at the postoffice.

Worse, there being no jobs in town, the younger ones have loaded their possessions in old cars, or boarded buses, bound for the urban centers where the disease is more advanced, where the body of social values has rotted, where the stench will not be ignored. Sometimes they are called, contemptuously by their neighbors, Okies and Arkies, even though they may be from Iowa or Missouri or Nebraska. It means only that they are country folks. (In the San Joaquin Valley, they refer to the second generation of these people as "CIO's"—the initials stand for California Improved Okies.)

The so-called Okies and Arkies, labeled by some as products of rural America, are not authentic representatives of the culture. They are representatives of the culture of poverty, of economic and social disenfranchisement. At home, on their own land, they were honest, hardworking, church-going citizens. But without their land, and without the stability of the familiar social values, they can become—as their haughty new neighbors say—whiskey-drinking, prejudiced, and often improvident Americans.

They, along with Negroes, most of whom never had the stability of property, the integrity of self-respect, the security of their own economic and social system, form a new problem in the cities of America. We are only now learning the enormity of that problem.

The tragedy is that we are learning it so late.

We were warned.

SELECTED REFERENCES

A Report by the President's National Advisory Commission on Rural Poverty. *The People Left Behind.* Washington: U.S. Government Printing Office, 1967.

Economic Development Division, U.S.D.A. *Characteristics of U.S. Rural Areas with Non-Commuting Population.* Washington: U.S. Government Printing Office, 1972.

Economic Development Division, U.S.D.A. *The Economic and Social Conditions of Rural America in the 1970's.* Washington: U.S. Government Printing Office, 1971.

Farmworkers in Rural America, 1971-1972. Hearings before the subcommittee on Migratory Labor of the Committee on Labor and Public Welfare, U.S. Senate, 92nd. Congress. Part 1, *Farmworkers in Rural Poverty.* Part 2, *Who owns the Land?* Part 3a, *Land Ownership, Use, and Distribution.* Washington: U.S. Government Printing Office, 1972.

Federal and State Statutes Relating to Farmworkers, A Compilation. Prepared for the Subcommittee on Migratory Labor of the Committee on Labor and Public Welfare, United States Senate. Washington: U.S. Government Printing Office, 1972.

International Encyclopedia of the Social Sciences. "Social Stratification," Volume 15. New York: Macmillan Co., 1968, pp. 288-337.

Kaufman, Harold F. *Prestige Classes in a New York Rural Community.* Ithaca: Cornell Agr. Expt. Sta. Memoir 260, March, 1944.

Kaufman, Harold F., Otis Dudley Duncan, Neal Gross and William H. Sewell. "Social Stratification in Rural Society," *Rural Sociology,* 18, No. 1. (March, 1953).

Loomis, C.P., et al. *Turrialba: Social Systems and the Introduction of Change.* Glencoe, Ill.: The Free Press, 1953. See especially Chap. 3, "Social Status and Communication," By C.P. Loomis, Thomas L. Norris, and Charles Proctor.

Stone, Gregory, and William Form. "Instabilities in Status: The Problem of Hierarchy in the Community Study of Status Arrangements," *American Sociological Review,* 18, No. 2, (April, 1953).

U.S. Bureau of the Census. "Characteristics of the Low-Income Population, 1971." *Current Population Reports,* P-60, No. 86, Washington: U.S. Government Printing Office, 1972.

U.S. Department of Commerce/Bureau of the Census. *Current Population Reports.* P-23, No. 38. Special Studies. "The Social and Economic Status of Negroes in the United States, 1970." Washington: U.S. Government Printing Office, 1971.

7

Religious Social Systems*

All societies, no matter how primitive or advanced, hold religious beliefs and carry on religious activities. In few social systems, however, is there greater variety in form and practice. Some societies have shamans or religious functionaries who give only part of their time to religious activities. Others, including the more complex societies such as our own, as well as some simpler cultures, have fulltime religious functionaries.[1] Some societies have simple religions cults, characterized by elementary dogma and beliefs; others possess complex dogma and elaborate ritual. Some religions support norms of moderation or even negation in the satisfaction of the senses; others, at least on occasion, permit indulgence in mass orgies of eating, dancing, and sexual license.

Definition and Function of Religion

Religion has always been an important, integral part of culture. "Throughout the greater part of mankind's history, in all ages and states of society", Dawson asserts, "religion has been the great central unifying force in culture. It has been the guardian of tradition, the preserver of the moral law, the educator and the teacher of wisdom."[2] Although not all persons in a given society may consider themselves to be "religious", and this is certainly true in twentieth century rural America, religious values are pervasive and modify the behavior of most individuals and social systems.[3] Vernon makes this point when he says:

*The authors wish to acknowledge the assistance of Louis Ploch, University of Maine, in the revision of this chapter.

[1] Ralph L. Beals and Harry Hoijer, *An Introduction to Anthropology* (New York: The Macmillan Co., 1953), pp. 485-493.

[2] Christopher Dawson, *Religion and Culture* (Cleveland: The World Publishing Company, 1958), p. 49. Also see p. 56.

[3] John L. Thomas, *Religion and the American People* (Westminster: The Newman Press, 1963), p. 7.

"[Religion] is always part of an ongoing, dynamic social system in which it influences and is influenced by other social factors."[4] This fact will become apparent when the interrelationships involved in social change are discussed in this chapter.

Although religion can be defined in many ways, the writers feel that at least three forms of human activity and belief are to be subsumed under the term religion. These are a distinction between that which is considered sacred and that which is considered profane, belief in a superior power or powers, and a pattern of worship. A major function of religion is to provide integration and solidarity in group life.[5] It thus serves to establish and reaffirm group ends and norms and, except when groups with different religions are locked in conflict, helps to prevent disruption of social systems. Religious systems provide collective ritual and other means to reinforce the legitimacy of their particular ends and norms. Sacred objects that are not intrinsically different from secular objects are accorded respect, reverence, and awe. In sacred objects, concrete references are provided for the values reflected in group ends and norms. These sacred objects also provide a basis for mobilizing and rallying those who share the ends and norms of a particular group.

Adjustment to the Unexpected

Normal social interaction among members may often be interrupted, even in solidary societies or systems. Individuals are disturbed and interaction patterns may be shattered when loved or respected associates die, when leaders pass on or change, or when crises develop from unexpected catastrophes. In almost all fields, even in instrumental or technological action, the most competent and diligent person may fail due to unpredictable and uncontrollable forces. In the world of human affairs, arduous, diligent, and conscientious effort may not only fail to bring the expected rewards but may result in tragedy. At any moment death may snatch away those who make life meaningful; conflicts in status-roles and ends may turn friends into enemies; the just may be punished and the unjust rewarded; and earthquakes, cyclones and war may play havoc with normal social life. In such cases religion provides a means for retaining in-

---

[4] Glen M. Vernon, *Sociology of Religion* (New York: McGraw-Hill Book Company, Inc., 1962), p. 7.

[5] Beals and Hoijer, *An Introduction,* pp. 485-493.

tegration. Injustices in this world may be corrected in the hereafter, and for personal and group catastrophes there are rites of passage and intensification.

Success in farming and ranching cannot be attributed solely to ability and effort, since climate, diseases of plants and animals, and prices cannot always be effectively predicted or controlled by the farm operator. In most rural areas, religious beliefs and practices provide security in those realms that have not been brought completely under human control.

An important function of religion and religious leaders is to reestablish interaction in periods of crisis or in periods during which normal interaction of individuals has been disrupted. Cooperative activity, including farming operations, requires that individuals be organized into social systems and that they function in roles according to norms and standards. Any change such as birth, marriage, illness or death will alter the previous equilibrium and interaction. Various rites associated with events that cause disequilibrium are known as rites of passage and intensification. Many of these rites are carried out by religious leaders to restore interaction, to initiate recruits into the group, and to restore equilibrium to the system.[6]

Anomie, Social Disequilibrium, or Disorganization

When the ends and norms become meaningless for the individual, leaving him without motivation; when the customary patterns of interaction among members of a system deteriorate; when the existing interaction patterns fail to provide the individual with a significant status-role; or when the ends and norms to which he responds are in serious conflict, *anomie* or social disequilibrium results.[7] The manifestations are high suicide rates and the rapid growth of religious sects. The relationship between the spread of Nazism and the insecurity brought about by rapid changes accompanying industrialization and commercialization of the family-sized farming areas of rural Germany, for instance, has also been shown.[8]

[6] E. D. Chapple and C. S. Coon, *Principles of Anthropology* (New York: Henry Holt and Co., 1942).

[7] Emile Durkheim, *Division of Labor in Society,* translated by George Simpson (New York: The Macmillan Company, 1933), Book III, Chapter 1.

[8] C. P. Loomis and J. Allan Beegle, *Rural Social Systems* (New York: Prentice-Hall, Inc., 1950), pp. 401ff. H. M. Nelson and H. P. Whitt in their analysis of data from the Detroit Area Study and the Southern Appalachian Studies in "Religion and the Migrant in the City: A Test of Holt's Cultural Shock Thesis," *Social*

Although the evidence is inconclusive, it appears that religious sects or political organizations that perform many of the functions of the sects tend to appear where anomie exists. Such organizations furnish individuals with motivation by providing meaningful ends, norms and status-roles, and may often develop a powerful *esprit de corps*. In order that members may attain economic security and at the same time achieve integration, the sect often becomes uncompromising with the value orientations of other social systems in society. With the passing of time, the sect may achieve solidarity as well as economic well-being for its members and begins to rise in rank in the community. Finally sects may lose their "separateness" from the community and assume the aspects of typical church organization.[9] The development, as described by Niebuhr is as follows: ". . . One phase of the history of denominationalism reveals itself as the story of the religiously neglected poor, who fashion a new type of Christianity which corresponds to their distinctive needs, who rise in the economic scale under the influence of religious discipline, and who, in the midst of a freshly acquired cultural respectability, neglect the new poor succeeding them on the lower plane. This pattern recurs with remarkable regularity in the history of Christianity. Anabaptists, Quakers, Methodists, Salvation Army, and more recent sects of like type illustrate this rise and progress of the churches of the disinherited."[10]

Forces, Vol. 50, (March 1972), find no support for Holt's claim made 30 years earlier that the sect was a "shock absorber" for migrants. Holt's study was supported by others, however. Nelson and Whitt are probably correct in noting that migration shock may be absorbed "by insulating mechanisms such as the presence of others in similar situations", (p. 384) or "cultural bridges" provided by kin, friends and others. Nelson and Whitt neglect the adaptation of denominations in systemic linkage as churches become more Gemeinschaft-like or communal. See C. P. Loomis, *Social Systems-Essays on Their Persistence and Change* (Princeton: D. Van Nostrand, 1960), p. 171.

[9] Leopold von Wiese, *Systematic Sociology,* adapted and amplified by Howard Becker (New York: John Wiley & Sons, Inc., 1932), see pages 624-642 especially for a more specifically defined typology including the concepts "ecclesia", "sect", "denomination", and "cult". The authors have condensed these types into two main types, namely sects, and non-sects which we call denominations and churches.

[10] J. Milton Yinger, *Religion in the Struggle for Power* (Durham: Duke University Press, 1946), p. 28, as quoted from H. R. Niebuhr, *The Social Sources of Denominationalism* (New York: Henry Holt and Company, 1929). See also A. B. Hollingshead, "The Life Cycle of Nebraska Rural Churches," *Rural Sociology,* Volume 11, No. 2 (1937), pp. 180-191.

This type of development is important for all areas subjected to the rapid changes brought about by the introduction of modern technology. This is especially true in areas where the social systems were organized and established on a Gemeinschaft-like basis. In Gemeinschaft-like societies before the introduction of Western technology, the long established ends and norms were reinforced by religious ritual and ceremony. In the non-primitive areas, the church has become denominational and organized into structures comparable to other bureaucratic social systems. With the impact of modern technology in both primitive and advanced cultures, the individual may be torn from his reference and membership groups, including his family, his neighborhood, and, of course, his local church. A state of *anomie* may result. In areas where the religious social systems have not evolved from the sect to the denominational or church state, the impact may be different, but the same disorganizing influences will be present.

THE RURAL CHURCH IN THE UNITED STATES

One of the most striking structural features of American society is the large number of religious bodies that coexist in relative harmony. For many years, the *Yearbook of American Churches* has reported approximately 250 religious bodies in the United States. The edition for 1969 is no exception.[11] It is likely, however, that the 250 figure greatly understates the actual number of separate church entities. In 1949 Clark estimated that there were more than 400 different religious groups in this country, many of them very small groups having less than 7,000 adherents each.[12]

The regional diversity in religious preference is shown in Table 1. The data are for white respondents and are based on four Gallup Polls taken from December, 1963, to March, 1965. Protestants are substantially over-represented in the South while Catholics are substantially over-represented in New England and the Middle Atlantic states. Seven out of 10 Jews are found in the Middle Atlantic states. Persons with no religious preference are most heavily concentrated in the Pacific states. This may be due in part to the high rates of migration into these states.

[11] Louis B. Whitman, ed., *Yearbook of American Churches for 1969* (New York: National Council of Churches of Christ in the United States of America, 1969).

[12] Elmer T. Clark, *The Small Sects in America,* rev. ed. (New York: Abingdon-Cokesbury Press, 1949), p. 9.

TABLE 1
Percent Distribution of Religious Preference of White
Respondents to Four Gallup Polls, by Region

Region	Protes- tants	Cath- olics	Jews	No Re- ligion	Total
New England	2.5	12.3	7.8	5.8	5.0
Middle Atlantic	16.7	39.0	70.1	11.9	23.6
East Central	18.4	18.6	5.7	18.4	18.0
West Central	12.7	8.4	1.1	8.3	11.2
South	34.4	7.8	7.1	14.8	26.9
Rocky Mountain	4.3	3.2	0.9	12.3	4.1
Pacific	10.9	10.6	7.1	28.5	11.1
Total	100.0	100.0	100.0	100.0	100.0
N	9,099	2,940	435	277	12,751

Source: Norval D. Glenn and Ruth Hyland, "Religious Preference and Worldly Success: Some Evidence from National Surveys," *American Sociological Review* Vol. 32, No. 1 (February 1967), pp. 73-85.

While rural populations are less heterogeneous than urban populations, rural areas in the United States are characterized by a high degree of diversity in religious expression and belief systems. Among the possible explanations of this diversity may be the following: a desire among many of the early colonists for religious freedom; the subsequent passage (1791) of the first amendment to the Constitution guaranteeing individuals free access to religion and proscribing a state church; the diversity of migrants in terms of ethnicity, language, occupation, education, and religious heritage; and especially in rural areas, the establishment of socially isolated communities.

Religious systems in the United States also exhibit a variety of institutional forms, most of which are commonly categorized as denominations, sects, and cults. Denominations are generally considered to be those larger religious institutions that have accommodated to the ends, goals, and values of the society of which they are a part. There is, of course, some diversity among the major denominations in the United States. In fact, the major denominations could be placed on a scale ranging from highly structured to loosely structured. Among the highly structured in both a hierarchical and a liturgical sense are the Roman Catholic and Protestant Episcopal churches. The Methodists and Presby-

terians, both of which have centralized structures and a degree
of central control, would be placed near the center of the distribution. The Baptists and Congregationalists would fall at the other extreme. In general, the denominations are relatively "liberal" in their stands on theological, social, economic, and political
issues. Here again, there is diversity within the denominational
families and between churches. The United Methodist Church
generally takes liberal positions on many issues. Other denominations with "Methodist" in their names do not. This kind of
variation is also true of the several types of Presbyterians, Baptists, and Lutherans.

Sects are generally considered to be religious protest groups.
They grow out of dissatisfaction with the status quo. The following passage from Clark presents a graphic picture of the dynamics of sect growth and development:

> All denominations began as sects, and the evolution of a sect
> into a church has followed a routine. In the background of
> nearly all sects there is a strong economic influence. These
> groups originate mainly among the religiously neglected
> poor, who find the conventional religion of their day un-
> suited to their social and psychological needs. This is true of
> Christianity itself, which was three hundred years old before
> it attracted considerable numbers of the socially well-placed.
> Finding themselves ill at ease in the presence of an effete
> and prosperous *bourgeoisie,* their emotional natures unsat-
> isfied by the middle class complacency, their economic prob-
> lems disregarded by those who have no such problems to
> meet, and their naive faith and simple interpretations
> smiled upon by their more cultured fellows, the poor and ig-
> norant revolt and draw apart into groups which are more
> congenial. They elevate the necessities of their class—fru-
> gality, humility, and industry—into moral virtues and re-
> gard as sins the practices they are debarred from embracing.
> Those pinched by economic circumstances look askance at
> theatergoing, card playing, and "putting on of gold and cost-
> ly apparel" but indulge in the same when their earthly for-
> tunes improve. Their standards of conduct are invented from
> the simple lives they are compelled at all events to lead and
> which are congenial to their simplicity. They give free rein to
> their emotions and attribute the pleasant thrills thereof to a
> divine agency. They look for an escape from their hard lot
> into a heaven of bliss and comfort which is foreign to their

workaday existence, and usually picture a coming time
when the judgments of society shall be reversed and they
shall change places with the prosperous and comfortable,
who shall be cast down while the pious poor shall be exalted.
They espouse their tenets with almost fanatical devotion
and regard themselves as the true beloved of God. Thus the
sect is born, out of combination of spiritual need and economic forces.[13]

It is possible that no true sect groups exist in the United
States. The Old Order Amish is an example of a sect whose members, despite living intermixed with non-Amishmen, have maintained their own separate religion as a way of life. The Amish
differ from most sect groups which, as they become more economically affluent, tend to drop their isolation from the larger
society. For a time, at least, sects remain theologically fundamentalist and at the same time they accomodate to societal
norms. It is for this reason that in several places in this chapter
the term "sect-like" will be used to denote religious groups that
may have originated as sects but do not presently constitute an
exclusive, completely social-psychologically isolated religious
system. By "sect-like" then we mean religious systems that are
relatively loosely structured, theologically conservative and uncompromising in their social and moral codes, usually emotional
in their religious behavior, and comprised of members who rank
relatively low in society.

Cults are religious groups in which the emphasis is placed upon the personal ecstasy of the individual. There is usually a charismatic leader who exerts considerable control. In their religious behavior cultists are likely to be both emotional and
uninhibited. In the more rural areas cultism may involve a ritual
such as snake-handling.[14]

Church Members

The great number of church bodies in the United States parallels a high rate of church membership. Although church membership reflects various definitions used by the many religious
groups, the trend in membership has been upward for over 100

[13] Ibid., p. 16.
[14] Everett M. Rogers and Rabel J. Burdge, *Social Change in Rural Societies*
(New York: Appleton-Century-Crofts, 1972), pp. 222-225.

years. Since 1850, church membership as a percentage of population has been as follows:[15]

1850		16	percent
1900		36	percent
1940		49	percent
1950		57	percent
1960		64	percent
1970		62.4	percent

Church Attendance

Despite the growth in church membership in the post World War II period church attendance has not demonstrated a comparable increase.[16] For example, Gallup polls show that adults indicating that they had attended church during the week preceding the interview amounted to 41 percent in 1939, 45 percent in 1947, and ranged from 44 percent to 49 percent for each of the years from 1954 through 1967. During this period the low of 44 percent was reached in 1965 and 1966. The high of 49 percent was reached in 1955.[17]

In discussing the disparity between church growth and attendance, Gordis concludes: ". . . what we are witnessing is less a revival of religion than a revival of interest in religion . . . Its most public expression is to be found in the notion that religion is good for the country and that the absence of some kind of faith, it matters little what its faith, or content, or character is somehow subversive of society."[18] The churches that have shown the most rapid recent growth rate, tend to be those in which there is a great stress placed on the individual. The greatest gains were made by the more conservative Lutheran bodies,

[15] Charles Y. Glock and Rodney Stark, *Religion and Society in Tension* (Chicago: Rand McNally and Company, 1965), p. 79. The 1970 percentage is based on a Gallup poll.

[16] A strange concomitant to the increase in church membership is the increasing proportion of persons who reply "yes" to the Gallup Poll question "Is religion losing its influence?" In 1957, 14 per cent responded "Yes"; in 1962, 31 per cent; in 1965, 45 per cent; in 1967, 57 percent; in 1968, 67 per cent. See Whitman, *American Churches,* p. 206.

[17] Whitman, *American Churches,* p. 205.

[18] Robert Gordis, *A Faith for Moderns* (New York: Block Publishing Co., 1960), p. viii.

the Latter Day Saints (Mormons), the Baptists generally, the Church of Christ, the Methodist, and Adventist bodies.[19]

The noted religionist, Will Herberg, believes that an increase in religious interest is associated with the growth of mass society and particularly with rural to urban migration. Salisbury, in paraphrasing Herberg, says: "As the typical individual finds himself increasingly isolated in the 'Lonely Crowd' he discovers a need for 'belonging'. Many recover this sense in a religious group whose various 'fellowship' experiences take the place of the face-to-face organization of the small town and rural community."[20] As rural areas undergo out-migration with an attendant loss of persons engaged in agriculture, or experience industrialization and population growth, there are often those who discover a "need for belonging." Increasingly the sect-like church provides this need. It should be noted that in communities with universities many modern sect-like groups have been formed.

INTERCHURCH COOPERATION AS A LINKAGE PROBLEM

Because of the intricate ways in which religious bodies are interrelated with their social environment, the changes taking place in rural life have been reflected in the number, type, and distribution of rural churches. In many parts of the United States as the number of farmers and farm families have decreased, the membership and support of rural churches have also decreased. One of the consequences of such changes has been a movement toward consolidation or some other type of interrelationship between church bodies.

Since the 1930's and 1940's one of the more common types of inter-church cooperation has been the so-called larger parish plan.[21] Although there have been many variations, the larger parish often consists of several churches in a larger community working through an elected parish council and a hired, diver-

[19] Benson Y. Landis, "Trends in Church Membership in the United States", *The Annals,* Vol. 332, (November 1960), p. 6.

[20] W. Seward Salisbury, *Religion in American Culture—A Sociological Interpretation* (Homewood: The Dorsey Press, 1964), p. 79.

[21] Mark Rich, *The Larger Parish* (Ithaca: Cornell Extension Bulletin, 1939).

sified, professional staff. A major motivation of the larger parish plan is to provide a more effective ministry to the community. To reach this goal, the smaller, weaker, more inaccessible churches may be closed. The number of professional leaders required in the larger parish plan may often be reduced. Those who are retained or who are newly hired are likely to be more highly trained than those persons who have been replaced. Usually each church in the parish is represented on the parish council by one or more members.

The larger parish plan would seem appropriate in rural areas having a dispersed population. This plan can provide a more effective ministry, better educational programs, more professional music, and more efficient use of property. Despite such advantages and although some larger parishes have succeeded, failure is not uncommon. Among the reasons for failure of some larger parishes have been frictions over the membership in the parish council, problems involving which churches should be closed and which kept open, division among the constituent congregations over the allocation of parish expenses, and interpersonal problems among the staff.

Perhaps the most common form of interchurch cooperation is the federated church. As the name implies, the degree of linkage between and among the two or more churches is less than complete union. As with the larger parish the variation in this type of arrangement is great. Generally the churches agree to jointly hire a minister, or in a few cases a more elaborate staff. If the churches are of different denominations, as many are, a common practice is for each church to take its turn in selecting the minister. In some cases, such as described by Vidich and Bensman, a single minister preaches in churches affiliated with different denominations but conducts the services in accordance with the tenets of that church in which he is preaching.[22]

Among other types of interchurch cooperation are the affiliated church and the community church. The affiliated church takes many forms. Most commonly two or more churches merge organically and give up direct ties with the original denominational hierarchies. However, it is often quite difficult for congregations to relinquish connections with a larger church body.

[22] Arthur J. Vidich and Joseph Bensman, *Small Town in Mass Society* (New York: Doubleday, 1958).

There are the problems of ministerial supply, religious educational materials, and mission support. A loose linkage with a denomination can solve these problems while retaining a large share of independence for the local congregation.

The nondenominational community church is similar to the affiliated church. It may have a flexible arrangement with one or more denominations. Its distinctive feature is that it welcomes all persons into its fold. Its norms are usually Protestant but generally very few bars are placed upon membership. Almost always in this type of system dual membership is permitted. That is, a person is free to retain membership in another church while at the same time he enters into full, but perhaps temporary, fellowship in the community church. This type of church is particularly well suited to communities with a highly mobile population, such as is now frequently the case in rural areas which are experiencing industrialization and suburbanization or to which a military base or a college is being added.

In summary, local interchurch cooperation is one way the religious system has met drastic shifts in population size and composition and other crisis-like situations in rural areas. Because of the strong boundary maintenance aspects of the rural church, relatively few churches do enter into close interrelationships except under threat of crisis.

ELEMENTS OF RELIGIOUS SOCIAL SYSTEMS

Ends, Objectives, and Norms

The ends and objectives of rural religious social systems are extremely complex and difficult to conceptualize.[23] In part this is due to two components of any religious system—the spiritual and the social. It is also partly due to the problem of accurately conceptualizing the linkages of religious systems of local churches as they are interrelated with the church at large. Thus, Ford has indicated on the basis of research in Appalachia, that the values of the local church are not always those of the larger

---

[23] For a critique of the opinion held by a number of churchmen and scholars that American religion has become homogenized see, especially chapter 5, "The New Denominationalism" in Glock and Stark, *Religion and Society.* For a discussion of values and evaluation as related to ends and norms see Loomis, *Social Systems,* pp. 184ff.

system.[24] Ashbrook states the problem as follows: "Local churches present a double characteristic. They represent both a social phenomenon and a sacred system. They are marked by an external, outwardly institutional dimension and by an internal, inwardly communal dimension. They are permeated by the dilemma of relating external institutional requirements with internal communal demands."[25]

Local churches, particularly if they are affiliated with one of the more episcopal (hierarchical) denominations are likely to follow the requirements of the denomination quite closely. Their ministers will most often be trained in a denominational seminary, and the form of the worship service, educational program, and the missionary efforts will be in conformity with denominational principles. However, as Ford concluded, each is likely to have a local flavor. As in the case of many rural churches, to the degree that the congregation represents a homogeneous system—racial, ethnic, and regional—which is not representative of the denomination as an entity, the expression of ends and objects is likely to be largely locally influenced.

A not uncommon factor in the establishment of new sect-like churches is the disagreement within the congregation about some important internal ends or norms. In a rural central Pennsylvania community one relatively conservative church experienced a split and the formation of a new splinter sect over whether a common or individual communion cup would be used. A number of years later a controversy occurred in the newer church over whether music should be part of the religious service. The conservative "no music" dissenters withdrew and established their own congregation.

In a well-documented study in California, Glock and Stark have demonstrated that relatively great differences exist among denominations about beliefs usually considered basic to Christianity and certain behaviors and attitudes subsumed under the rubric of the "puritan ethic."[26] Responses revealed that Congregationalists tend to be the least positive about their belief

---

[24] Thomas R. Ford, "Status, Residence, and Fundamental Religious Belief in the Southern Appalachians," *Social Forces* (October, 1960), p. 42.

[25] James B. Ashbrook, "The Relationship of Church Members to Church Organization," *Journal for the Scientific Study of Religion,* Vol. 5, No. 3, (Fall 1966), p. 397.

[26] Glock and Stark, *Religion and Society.*

as to basic Christian dogma. The response patterns of Methodists and Episcopalians tended to follow that of the Congregationalists. The Missouri Lutherans, Southern Baptists, and Catholics were much more sure of the reality of God, the divinity of Jesus, and of the life beyond death than were the Congregationalists, Methodists, and Episcopalians. The most sure of all were the members of the sects.[27]

Although no comprehensive data are available, it is well known that most denominations attempt to perpetuate their existence and thus their ends and objectives by subsidizing local churches. In some cases new churches are subsidized for a limited period until they can become self-sufficient. In other cases churches that would probably otherwise cease to exist receive financial help from the denomination. Sometimes aid is received directly from the other churches of the same denomination. In this way the ends and goals of the denomination are extended to more parishioners. At one time denominations more or less indiscriminately "planted" churches in developing areas, urban and rural. Currently in most states the major Protestant denominations work through a state council of churches or similar organization to attempt to prevent excessive competition among churches. The sect-like churches, more independent of both denominational superstructure and centralized interdenominational bodies, tend to build congregations wherever a minimum number of persons are committed to the religious ends and objectives of that religious body.

Status-Roles

If one wishes to understand the functioning of a religious system, or if a change agent wishes to inaugurate a program of change, it is necessary to be sensitive to the configuration of status-roles in that system. Important status-roles exist on at least

[27]In a similar study but using a national sample Stark and Glock found similar variations between the various denominations and the sects but the respondents were considerably less dogmatic in their responses than were the California respondents. This difference may well reflect a relatively more conservative religious climate in California than in the United States generally. See particularly Table 8, page 38 in Rodney Stark and Charles Y. Glock's *American Piety: The Nature of Religious Commitments* (Berkeley: University of California Press, 1968). A study reported by Thomas also contains a more positive set of responses than the Glock and Stark study, but the variation by denomination is retained. See John L. Thomas, *Religion and the American People.*

three levels for denominationally related churches—denominational, ministerial, and lay. In the sect-like church, because of a generally less definitive relationship to a supra-institutional body, the crucial status-roles are likely to be confined to the ministerial and lay levels. The episcopal or hierarchical denominations by definition are characterized by a set of highly structured status-roles. The more hierarchical the system, the more meaningful the system of denominational-designated status-roles is to the local church and its congregation. The ends, goals, and norms of the larger system are funneled into and made operative at the local level by means of the status-role hierarchy.

In some instances the presidency of a church-related organization may be considered more important than being a church officer. Particularly in the more rural communities that lack social activities, one of the few opportunities to assume meaningful status-roles outside the family or occupation is in church-related organizations.

It is well-documented that church members are more likely to belong to voluntary organizations. Furthermore, it has been shown that church related organizations form the bulk of participational opportunities for rural people. Typically in rural areas non-church members belong to few other organizations. In a study of several communities in a Midwestern county, Schroeder and Obenhaus found that: "Non-participators tended to avoid all types of institutional involvements . . . non-church members belonged to the fewest voluntary associations."[28] It can be concluded that participation in a church, particularly one with a congregational structure and relatively liberal theology, is one way in which many rural persons expand their status-roles. Within some communities simply being a member of a church is still a significant status-role.

In most rural areas the status-role of the minister or clergyman is important. Within highly structured churches the formal role of the clergyman is well defined. With certain exceptions the formal status-role of the Roman Catholic or Episcopal priest would be similar from church to church. Salisbury in his study of churches and their clergy in upstate New York concludes that:

[28] Widick Schroeder and Victor Obenhaus, *Religion in American Culture—Unity and Disunity in a Midwestern County* (New York: The Free Press of Glencoe, 1964). See especially p. 49 and p. 52.

"A liturgical church, Catholic or Protestant, may roll on in spite of its professional leader."[29]

While Blizzard's research on the roles of the rural Protestant minister is the most comprehensive,[30] his sample is confined to college and seminary trained clergymen. The less formally trained ministers of the more rural churches, particularly the sect-like type, are not included. Blizzard emphasizes the importance of the clergyman's "prophetic role" in a changing rural community. In this role the minister seeks to help parishioners and others in the community as they become aware of and make adjustments to a changed community and cultural environment.[31] Blizzard's sample of rural ministers in the role of counselors reported the following, in order of frequency: community problems (31 per cent); general social-ethical problems (29 per cent); and specific personal problems (29 per cent).

Power

In the more structured religious systems, as in the school or factory, power is institutionalized and is vested in status-roles in the form of authority. Each official and member has rights of which the change agent will want to be aware. The authority structure is often clear cut. However, the power structure does not necessarily conform to the formal table of organization. The President of the Ladies' Guild, because she is the wife of a successful farmer and because her father was instrumental in founding the church, may have more power and influence than does the Chairman of the Board of Trustees.

The more homogeneous and the more isolated a local religious social system is from the larger society, the more powerful the clergyman is likely to be. In the coal-producing ethnic communities of rural Pennsylvania, in the fishing communities of the Louisiana Bayous, and in the agricultural and lumbering communities of northern New England, the Catholic priest traditionally exerted power beyond his strictly religious or spiritual

[29] Salisbury, *Religion in American Culture*, p. 166.

[30] Salisbury, *Religion in American Culture*, contains a good summary of Blizzard's work as well as a set of minister self-defined roles which include those of preacher, administrator, pastor, counselor, educator, and organizer-promoter. See pp. 219-223.

[31] Samuel W. Blizzard, "The Role of the Rural Minister in Community and Cultural Change." Address delivered at the National Convocation on the Church in Town and County, St. Louis, Missouri, 1956 (Memeo.).

role. In a number of communities in the French-Canadian rural areas of northern Maine, the local priest continues to exert great influence in matters other than those directly related to the church.[32]

In the more sect-like churches, the minister is also likely to exert great influence. He often possesses a charismatic personality. In extreme cases he is considered to have God-like, and in some cases, God-ordained attributes. Because sect-like churches are not usually highly integrated into community life, the sect-like clergyman's power is likely to be more confined to his own congregation than is the power and influence of other clergymen. The power and influence of the sect-like minister can, however, have community relevant effects in given circumstances. In a rural community in Pennsylvania interviewers were refused interviews by members of a sect-like group who were the majority residents in a remote, open-country section of the community. The refusals were based on the belief that because the study included questions about participation in a variety of volunteer activities it was "other worldly" and thus taboo to members of the sect. After the minister was located and the purposes of the study explained to him, he agreed that there was no intrinsic harm in it. Within a few days the interviewers were welcomed into homes to which they previously had been denied access.

As indicated in the section on status-roles, organizational participation in community affairs is often confined to the church. This concentration of activities in the religious system is a source of power for the church. Those who are active in church activities tend to be the same persons who have power and influence in other systems. Vidich and Bensman document this situation for Springdale. They also conclude that while only a small proportion of the total population of approximately 1700 adults directly participate in community affairs, ". . . the multiplication of the activities of these 400 people, by participation in numerous church programs and social activities, is so great as to give the appearance of dominating the whole of the public life of the community."[33]

[32] For an insight into the role of the Catholic priest in the affairs of the com-
[33] Vidich and Bensman, *Small Town,* p. 229.

Social Rank

As previously noted one is more likely to find Methodist and Baptist churches in American rural areas than Protestant Episcopal or Presbyterian churches. The former are less likely than the latter to attract persons of higher socio-economic status. In almost all rural areas there is at least a sprinkling of sect-like churches. In some areas they are the predominant type. Thus, the income, education, and occupational levels prevalent in rural areas and communities is reflected in the denominations, and consequently in the ranking of their members.

In the typical American rural community, the many religious organizations are likely to reflect, to promote, and to perpetuate a system of social differentiation or social ranking. It would be inaccurate to assume that all rural churches have memberships representative of a very narrow segment of the social strata in a given community. Vidich and Bensman demonstrate for Springdale that although a specific church may rank higher on the socio-economic scale than another, each may contain something of a cross-section of the community. They also indicate, however, that one occupational grouping may dominate a specific church: "Prosperous farmers provide the core membership of the Methodist Church and are scattered throughout other churches."[34]

In Springdale the traditional, small, unprogressive farmers unlike their more prosperous counterparts are not church members or church participators: "Their traditional family affiliations are to country churches which have fallen into disuse and they have not been willing to shift their membership to a village church. They do not participate because of their incapability to adjust to the twentieth century trend to centralize churches."[35] In some communities persons like the Springdale traditional farmers who have lost a church identification and who are also on the economic margin of the community are attracted to, and sometimes establish, sect-like churches.

The stronger identification with organized religion, as indicated by church attendance, by persons with occupations that are generally accorded higher social rank is evident in Table 2. Among both Protestants and Catholics, persons in the white col-

[34] Ibid., pp. 229-230.
[35] Ibid., pp. 229-230.

TABLE 2
Frequency of Church Attendance by Occupation of Family Head*

Religious Groups	Sample Size	Frequency of Church Attendance				Total (%)
		Regu-larly	Often	Seldom	Never	
Protestants						
Professions	372	47	23	23	7	100
Owners, managers & officials	502	41	22	30	7	100
Clerical and sales	419	43	23	29	5	100
Skilled	711	35	21	36	7	100
Semiskilled	628	34	23	36	7	100
Unskilled	411	35	27	31	7	100
Farmers	410	44	30	20	6	100
Roman Catholics						
Professions	106	81	11	7	1	100
Owners, managers & officials	139	83	8	5	4	100
Clerical and sales	132	81	11	5	3	100
Skilled	279	68	15	13	4	100
Semiskilled	254	66	16	13	5	100
Unskilled	131	62	21	11	6	100
Farmers	51	67	9	20	4	100

*Bernard Lazerwitz, "Religion and Social Structure in the United States," pp. 426-430

lar groups are more likely to be church attenders than persons with blue collar jobs. Catholic and Protestant farmers differ little in church attendance.

The relationship between educational attainment and church attendance is usually positive. One study for example, indicates that for Protestants the proportion attending church "regularly" is 33 per cent for those with no more than eight grades of schooling; for those with four or more years of college the figure is 52 per cent. The same relationship holds for Catholics.[36]

One exception to the relationship between education and church attendance should be noted. Members of sect-like

[36] Bernard Lazerwitz, "Religion and Social Structure in the United States" in Louis Schneider, ed., *Religion, Culture, and Society* (New York: John Wiley & Sons, Inc., 1964), pp. 426-439.

churches generally attend church with great frequency. In many of the churches the core members attend service twice on Sunday and once during the week. As previously indicated, the members of most sect-like churches are likely to have attained fewer years of education and have lower social rank than members of non-sect churches.

In a study of mobility among Mennonite church members, Hostetler has shown for this somewhat sect-like group that membership is related to upward social mobility.[37] The data indicate that persons joining the Mennonite church have fewer years of education, lower incomes, and are less likely to have white collar occupations than are those persons who leave the church.[38] The position of the Mennonite church somewhere in the center of the church-sect typology is also demonstrated in Hostetler's data. The converts to the Mennonite church are more likely to have no previous religious affiliation, or had been members of sect-like churches including the Old Order Amish sect, than were persons who left the Mennonite church. Those who left the Mennonite church were quite likely to join "General American" (Hostetler's term) denominations.

An understanding of the social rank of churches and their members is important to the change agents who may wish to use them as channels of communication. If the class structure of a community is 'open', it is assumed that an item which a change agent wishes to introduce would spread more rapidly if the members of the congregation with the highest rank adopted the item first. Those items that are first accepted by the lower social rank may be thought to possess low social prestige and value. If lower class persons—say sect members—are first to adopt an item, the spread upward may be extraordinarily slow.

Sanctions

Deviation from religions norms not only may evoke the wrath of church officials and one's fellow church members but also may incite the displeasure of some supernatural force. While the fears of "fire and brimstone" and "damnation and Hell", may not be as real as they once were, the possibility of punishment for norm deviation still exists. The more sect-like the church and

[37] John A. Hostetler, "Religious Mobility in a Sect Group: The Mennonite Church," *Rural Sociology*, Volume 19, Number 3, (September, 1954), pp. 244-255.
[38] Ibid. Tables 9, 10, 11, 12.

the more fundamental the interpretation of biblical injunctions, the more likely the sanctioning system is to have meaning for parishioners. The norms of sect-like churches often assume the form of "Thou shall not" rather than "Thou may." The most universal of the "shall nots" in addition to the ten commandments are "the insistence on temperance and opposition to the liquor traffic.[39] According to Clark, as a result of strict norms and consequent sanctions, members of the most strict sects ". . . seem to have settled down into a state of resignation, and they expect God to reward them in the world during the millenium or in Heaven after death."[40] For many persons who belong to sect-like churches the day of judgment is not far in the future. In his analysis of a study of the Southern Appalachians, Ford indicated that the proportion of people who believe that the world will end soon is twice as high among rural respondents (30 per cent) as among urban respondents (15 per cent).[41]

Among rural groups in the United States, perhaps the strongest sanctions against religious deviation exists among the Amish. One of the authors, when working with Kollmorgen in the study of an Old Order Amish community in Lancaster County, Pennsylvania was told a tragic account of a family who had violated one of the norms. The Old Order Amish, who think of themselves as a people apart—God's plain people—have traditionally banned the use of automobiles, trucks, electric lights, radios, telephones, and "fancy" clothing. Through seven years of hard work one Amish family had built up a milk route in a nearby city. Disappointment after disappointment followed the hiring of non-Amish persons to furnish the truck and deliver the milk. When it appeared that the route would be lost and after spending many hours in prayer, the family decided to purchase a milk truck in order to make their own deliveries. After the congregation met, evaluated the nature of this "sin" and decided the sanction, the family was "shunned" by other members of the Amish sect. The family, after much anguish, renounced the sect and joined another that permitted the use of a truck. No one in communication with a family during a period when its members are shunned can fail to appreciate the power of religious sanctions of the sects.

[39] Clark, *Small Sect,* p. 219.
[40] Ibid.
[41] Ford, "Status, Residence, and Fundamental Religions Belief."

Change agents must be particularly aware of the system of sanctions within religious systems. The agent could introduce or guide a change for which sanctions might be invoked. Many successful change agents have learned to avoid the imposition of sanctions upon themselves and members of the target system by learning about and consulting with key figures in relevant religious social systems.

Facilities

At least until the post World War II period when a wave of modernism became endemic in church building, the type of church edifice indicated region, the size and wealth of the congregation, and degree of sectarianism. The simple, white, spired church nestled in a hamlet immortalized on Christmas cards reflects some aspects of Protestantism in rural New England a half century or more ago. These churches were sturdy, functional, largely built by local labor out of local materials, and were usually paid for by members of the resident congregation.

Sect-like churches are likely to be small, unadorned, and inexpensive, reflecting the economic status of the congregation. Unlike most of the more denominational churches, many sect-like churches are considered to be houses of worship only. They lack kitchens, dining rooms, recreation facilities and other non-religiously oriented accoutrements. It would seem to be a valid hypothesis that the extent of non-religious recreational use of the church building is correlated with the degree of liberality of the congregation. A characteristic of the Old Order Amish is that no church is permitted—meetings are held in homes and barns—which is believed to bring God and man together in worship and in life.

Particularly among sectarian churches internal conflict can erupt over the use or non-use of certain facilities. The conflict over the type of communion cup cited earlier is a case in point. In another rural central Pennsylvania federated church, of denominational type, the more theologically and socially conservative parishioners were in conflict with other parishioners over the addition of a kitchen to the church. At the culmination of a service dedicating the new facility by a denominational official it was discovered that members of the conservative group had padlocked the door and refused to allow the kitchen to be used.

The increase in church membership resulted in a church building boom. During the 1950's approximately 10,000 new congregations were established each year. Most of the congregations built new, often elaborate facilities. Except in the most conservative churches it has become standard practice for numerous facilities to be made an integral part of the new structures. In addition to the usual kitchens and meeting rooms, gymnasiums, recreation rooms, and even swimming pools are not uncommon.

It should be noted that all church expansion has not resulted in elaborate building programs. One of the new religious features of the 1950's and 1960's was the establishment of the "drive-in church". In many cases it has been the more conservative, less socially-conscious churches that have instituted church services in movie drive-ins and other similar locations on Sunday morning. In some cases these services are interdenominationally sponsored. Because of the space requirement of drive-in theaters, such facilities are located on the periphery of an urban area, often in rural communities.

Territoriality

The territorial component of rural religious systems varies with differences in the social structure, the ends, goals, and norms, of the system. In general the spatial extent of the denominational churches allows for considerable freedom in choice of church. In the most structured denominations, the Roman Catholic for example, the boundaries of parishes are determined by the church hierarchy. This has the effect, particularly in those areas in which only one church exists (the rural French-Canadian areas of northern New England for example) to create the community around the church. The spatial aspect of the church parish is, in effect, the community social system. In the horse and buggy days not only did the majority of the rural congregation live relatively close to the church, but also the more active participants tended to be those persons who lived closest to the church. The old neighborhood church is a thing of the past in many rural areas.

It is generally assumed that rural areas of the United States are predominantly Protestant. The data in Table 3 show the relationship between size of place and the prevalence of the major faiths. Protestants are not only over-represented in rural areas but in the smaller cities as well.

The way in which religion, in its institutionalized forms, is

TABLE 3

Percent Distribution of Major Faiths, by Size of Place

City Size	Major Faiths				
	Protes-tant	Roman Catholic	Jewish	None or Other	U.S. Totals (all groups)
U.S. Total	68	23	3	6	100
Over 1 million	43	37	13	7	100
100,000-1 million	61	27	4	8	100
25,000-100,000	60	33	2	5	100
10,000-25,000	76	19	2	3	100
Under 10,000	76	17	2	5	100
Rural	82	13	*	5	100

*Less than one-half of one percent.
Source: Thomas, *Religion and the American People,* p. 37.

interrelated with territoriality is suggested by Hartzell Spence in *The Story of America's Religions.*[42] He points out that the Church of England fostered a country-gentleman tradition in the pre-Civil War South, that Roman Catholicism found roots in Louisiana, New Mexico and California, that the Baptists shaped the Deep South, that Lutheranism took root in the upper Midwest, and that the Methodists crossed the Alleghenies with the early pioneers. In each instance, the particular religious culture has left its mark, still in evidence today.

Schnuker asserts that in many instances there were too many rural churches, far beyond the need of the population. He also concluded that "Churches became neighborhood churches instead of serving a large area. Families and close knit racial groups rallied around each local church. Their ties were so close that when the time came for change, and it was manifest that changes should be made, neighborhood groups resisted it."[43]

Communication

Communication of course takes place in religious social sys-

[42] Hartzell Spence, *The Story of America's Religions* (New York: Holt, Rinehart, and Winston, 1960), p. viii.

[43] Calvin Schnucker, *How to Plan the Rural Church Program* (Philadelphia: The Westminster Press, 1954), p. 40.

tems. At least once a week a significantly large segment of the membership assembles. A message for which many of them have been prepared by a lifetime of formal and informal training is delivered. In most of the denominational churches, and in some of the sect-like churches, the person who delivers the message has training in communication appropriate for his status-role. In the larger seminaries homiletics, the art of preaching, is a required subject. The speaker and the message are thought to have behind them the weight of the Bible and the authority of a divine force.

Status incongruence sometimes makes communication through the sermon ineffective. In the denominational churches in which the congregation is predominantly lower middle or working class, one of the difficulties may be the disparity in educational attainment between the minister and parishioner. While the parishioner sitting on the Board of Trustees may insist on a theologically trained minister, such a minister may not find communication with the congregation easy. Communication in the sect-like church may not suffer from this difficulty which is more characteristic of the denominational churches. Not only do many of the sect leaders possess charismatic personalities, their social characteristics are likely to be similar to those of their congregation. The minister may work with some of his church members in a factory or he may be a fellow farmer.

All of the more formally organized religious systems use a variety of printed media to communicate with members. To a large extent these materials, while they are deemed to be educational are also boundary maintenance devices. The "right" messages are transmitted, especially the case in church school publications. In the following excerpt Schroeder and Obenhaus express some concern about limitations of religious media communication:

> A perusal of literature directed toward church members indicates the relatively high level of competence which writers usually presuppose. Further, denominational strategies to communicate theological and ethical understanding seem frequently to minimize the limited potential of most of the members of the churches in such areas. Two related phenomena are involved. On the one hand, the level at which material is focused is too high for much of the church membership. On the other hand, minimal attention has been di-

rected to the small group possessing the potential to appropriate cognitive dimensions of the faith for whom the current programs are not particularly illuminating or helpful.[44]

Problems of denominations in communicating with members are reported on by Obenhaus and Schroeder.[45] They asked the question "Do you know of any social issues on which your denomination has taken a stand?" With the exception of a group of Catholics in one of the towns of the sample midwestern county, more than 75 percent of the respondents had no knowledge of any position their respective denominations had taken on any social issue. There were no significant differences in the responses of persons judged to have high or low intellectual abilities or between white and blue collar workers.

Decision-Making

Except for beliefs and dogma, few differences among religious systems are greater than those involving decision-making procedures. In terms of degree of involvement of laymen in decision-making, the range extends all the way from the Quakers for whom consensus in the local congregation is essential, to the Catholic Church where the decision of high officials, often far removed from the local system, is very important. Decision-making tends to be more dependent upon particularistic elements (especially those involving influential local persons) in the sects than in the churches or denominations. In the denomination or church there is more place for principles of universality, functional specificity, and affective neutrality.

In the more structured denominations, the very life of the local church can be in the hands of presiding officials. They can make the decision to keep a faltering church open, to subsidize it with denominational funds, to send in the type of clergyman who has a history of "saving" churches. Churches die slowly, but the decision when death comes can be in the hands of persons outside the local, interactive religious social system. However, the ability on the part of the local congregation to control important decisions in the life of the church in less structured systems in both rural and non-rural areas is not uncommon.

[44] Schroeder and Obenhaus, *Religion in American Culture*, p. 243.
[45] Ibid, pp. 243-244.

Although women are more likely to be in attendance at rural church services than are men, it is the latter who are more likely to be the decision-makers in matters of church-wide importance. Vidich and Bensman point out that it is men who are highly involved in the decision-making process within the church, but these tend to be the same men who are involved in political decisions outside the church.[46]

In the case of the larger denominations any change agent would normally have to deal with local churches through the official hierarchy. His arguments would have to be sound and rational and generalizable to most local situations. In dealing with the less structured groups the change agent's task is to locate the decision-makers and to build a case which makes sense from a local point of view.

Boundary Maintenance

Few social systems offer better opportunity to study boundary maintenance than do religious systems, especially those that are sect-like. Boundary maintaining activities take many forms but since they aim to preserve group solidarity and integrity, they are often considered evidences of rigidity. The reluctance to change is considered a prime attribute of rural religious groups. Ford says that communicants of all churches, whatever their denomination, in the remote Appalachian mountain areas are extremely conservative and are not representative of a given denomination elsewhere.[47]

As indicated previously, the boundary maintenance techniques of the sects and the sect-like churches are powerful and important. The Old Order Amish of Lancaster County, Pennsylvania, offers an excellent example. This group of highly devoted plain people has maintained its solidarity in the heart of an industrial and commercial farming area since colonial times. Among the devices used in achieving this remarkable feat is one common to many systems engaged in boundary maintenance, namely, that of internalized expectations of persecution from the outside.

Living as they do intermingled with non-Amish persons, the Amish have an increasingly difficult time in keeping young people in normative roles. An illustration of the ways in which the

---

[46] Vidich and Bensman, *Small Town,* p. 232.
[47] Ford, "Status, Residence, and Fundamental Religious Belief."

Amish take advantage of the fear of outside persecution is illustrated from the following excerpts from the notes of one of the authors when he was living and working with an Amish family:

> An intelligent and alert youth of nineteen years of age kept asking the investigator about motion pictures which are tabooed by the Amish. The investigator asked him why he did not go and see for himself. He said his dress and beard would give him away and everyone would know about it. He related a story about how some boys had sold some of their parents' chickens to get money to sneak into the movies in Lancaster. When the parents heard about it they had the local sheriff arrest the frightened boys for chicken stealing. The boys were permitted to leave the jail only after the parents interceded. This, said the nineteen year old boy, was enough to keep them from trying to learn more about movies.

Although the Amish may have exceptional boundary maintenance procedures, most religious systems have similar devices. The change agent who attempts to introduce change into an Amish community must know the taboos concerning going to movies, owning a radio, and using a camera, since they are related to group solidarity. If change agents are to use the religious systems as channels of communication, the values as well as the boundary maintenance devices must be known.

Systemic Linkage

In the denominational churches there are regularized linkages between the individual churches and the hierarchical structure. As previously noted there are also linkages between churches. For these reasons, once a chance agent makes contact with church authorities, change affecting multiple church units may well be involved. The lack of superstructure of most sect-like churches tends to set them apart from other church units. Instead of seeking social linkage, the sect-like churches, by virtue of their "other worldly" orientation, tend to have only minimal contact with agencies and systems of the larger society.

Perhaps the best known and extensive linkage of organized religion has been with the educational system. Denominations and sects ranging from the highly structured to the most sect-like have supported parochial schools in the United States. In the 1950's and early 1960's one of the strong arguments against federal aid to education was one based on fear that parochial schools would be unfairly and unconstitutionally aided.[48]

The most dramatic action related to the linkage between religion and education occurred when the Supreme Court, in a series of decisions, banned the reading of the Bible and other religious practices in the public schools.[49] An immediate reaction took place. The editorial columns of newspapers and magazines were filled with opinions pro and con. Many of the right wing American religious groups felt that the banning of school prayers was connected with a Communist conspiracy. This belief is consistent with the opinions of many that any change in traditional American practices, especially if and when religion is involved, is being promoted by anti-American forces.

While the conservative religious adherents differ from the "liberal" point of view on many political and social issues, they do so selectively. On the issues of the income tax and federal aid to education members of conservative churches, in general, do not take the extreme position of the right wing. Gary Marx attributes this attitude to the working class status of the membership of the theologically conservative churches, noting ". . . that the working class tends to take a liberal stand on matters affecting their own life chances."[50]

Perhaps the most obvious example of systemic linkage on the part of organized religion is the so-called ecumenical movement. Church leaders from Pope John XXIII to local clergymen were calling for a reunification of churches of the Christian faith. Among the Protestants action toward inter-church cooperation and union was primarily among the more denominational or-

[48] An interesting sidelight in the relationship between government and religion, and one which indicates the complexity of our society, is the joint sponsorship of Soil Stewardship Sunday by the Soil Conservation Service, United States Department of Agriculture and the National Council of Churches.

[49] For an analysis of the Supreme Court decisions regarding the banning of religious practices in public schools see William R. Ball, "Religion and Public Education - The Post Schempp Years" in Theodore R. Sizer, editor, *Religion and Public Education* (Boston: Houghton-Mifflin Co., 1967), pp. 144-163.

[50] In the Marx Study, 64 per cent of our theologically neo-orthodox respondents reported that they minister to predominantly working class congregations. See Gary T. Marx, "Religion: Opiate or Inspiration of Civil Rights Militancy Among Negroes?" *American Sociological Review*, Vol. 32, No. 1, (February, 1967), pp. 64-72.

ganizations rather than among the more conservative churches. Roy reports:

> Since the early 1940's, top fundamentalist leaders have sought to form a single co-operative group. The National Association of Evangelicals, a cluster of thirty denominations with a total membership of more than a million, through its affiliates claims to serve 10,000 Protestants . . . while many fundamentalists support the ecumenical movement, as represented in the National Council of Churches and the World Council of Churches, others are critical. They fear that the church-unity movement will completely abandon 'old-time religion'. A few dread the emergence of a 'super-church'.[51]

The degree to which systemic linkage can be achieved among religious systems is a function of how strong boundary maintenance may be. As indicated earlier, the more isolated systems are most likely to resort to boundary maintenance and thus resist linkage. The great economic changes taking place in rural areas, the high degree of mobility of the population, and the general reduction of isolation in both a territorial and psychological sense will no doubt contribute to an increase in the linkages of rural religious systems.

AN AMISH CHURCH ADOPTS THE AUTOMOBILE: A CASE OF SUCCESSFUL SYSTEMIC LINKAGE[52]

As in every instance of evaluation and decision making, the adoption of the automobile by the Old Order Amish, which we shall call the Hoog Church, has a particular history. The Hoog group was one of four House Amish religious communities in Pennsylvania County. The House Amish groups were more con-

---

[51] Ralph Lord Roy, *Apostles of Discord* (Boston: The Beacon Press, 1953), p. 183. In his book *Why Conservative Churches are Growing,* Dean M. Kelley notes that Anabaptists, Mormons, Jehovah's Witnesses and Wesleyan Revivalists increase in number at the expense of churches which are "tolerant." (New York: Harper and Row, 1972).

[52] This case resulted from field research carried on by John A. Hostetler who wrote the original case. Hostetler, a former Amishman who became a Mennonite, is a sociologist and an authority on the "plain people." This adaptation of the original case was made by the author and previously published in Loomis, *Social Systems,* Essay 5.

servative than the four Church Amish groups in the County. The Hoog group was the most progressive of the House Amish, resembling the most conservative of the Church Amish as much as they did the next most progressive group of House Amish. The Hoog group originated fifty years ago as an offshoot of the then most progressive of the House Amish. While the group shares the same general culture as other Amish in the territory the details differ considerably. Shirts, suspenders, and in some instances broadfall trousers are purchased when available at the nearby store. Buttons are permitted on work jackets. The men's hair extends over part of the ear, which is considerably shorter than the hair length for men in the next most progressive group. Tractors, including those with rubber tires, are used for farming operations. The brims of men's hats are smaller than those of all other Amish. Until the acceptance of automobiles carriage tops were black. The ban on the use of electricity was lifted 10 years ago; since that time farms have been modernized considerably. Farming is completely modern and tractor-oriented but religion centers in house worship. [*Norms and boundary maintenance devices had already been relaxed. Partial systemic linkage with the larger society in agricultural practices had already been achieved.*]

For a number of years members of the Hoog Group used tractors in the field and for farm work. With the appearance of pneumatic tires, they were also used on the road, to pull wagons to town and to run errands to nearby farms. Several members installed high speed transmissions especially for road work. During deer hunting season tractors could be seen on the mountain where they were parked while their operators were hunting. The tractors were equipped with huge platforms on the rear for hauling milk. Boxes were also attached in which Amish youngsters were transported. One church official of the group commented to the writer: "This seemed inconsistent to me and I was afraid to be seen on the road anymore with the tractor." [*The objective of occupational efficiency was added and was sometimes in conflict with the old objective of remaining "God's peculiar people." New norms were institutionalized, new facilities added to accomplish the old objective of making money, an objective given a higher priority by the evaluative process.*]

Some of the younger members commented on the inconsistency of driving rubber-tired farm tractors on the road, but using horses for transportation to church. One informant predicted, "It won't be long until some change will have to be made. When the youngsters grow up they will not understand why horses must be used on Sunday, when rubber-tired tractors can be used during the week."

Members often traveled long distances, to and from other Amish settlements in the state or even beyond in order to maintain contact with relatives who had migrated. They often hired taxicabs or the service of a neighboring Church Amish member for whom automobiles were not taboo. [*Communication and interaction patterns could not be maintained under the old norms. Strain resulted.*] One of the bishops of the Church Amish informed a minister of the group: "You cannot expect to keep up this practice."

Some of the parents bought or financed autos for the young men who had become members of the Church Amish. There were no dominant negative sanctions for such generous acts on the part of the House Amish father to his Church Amish son as there was in stricter Amish groups. In this way the entire family had transportation. [*Note that members of the same family held memberships in two different church groups, a type of systemic linkage.*]

The desire for automobiles became dominant in informal conversation among some of the members. One farm hand in particular constantly kept ribbing his employer, a minister of the group, about inconsistency, and the difficulty of hitching up horses. Horses were too much trouble, too slow a form of transportation, and besides it was dangerous to drive a carriage on the open highway. This informal conversation and "egging" undoubtedly played a significant part in preparing the minister for a favorable decision later when the time came for a nod in the church. [*Communication about new norms to a person holding a status-role vested with power was important.*]

No amount of informal conversation concerning the desire for an automobile could make the subject legitimate for discussion in church. Only if some person violated the restriction could it be discussed. Early one spring a young man of a well-thought-of family became the first offender. Without the consent of his family and church he purchased a used automobile under considerable pressure from a used-car dealer. The youngster had secured a learner's permit; he drove the automobile to the home of his parents. The father objected to having the car on his property, and after a good deal of persuasion on the part of his parents, the sixteen-year-old boy returned the car to the dealer with the promise from his parents that he could have it back if the church should come to a favorable decision whenever the subject came up for discussion. [*The objective of full fellowship was important to the family as was the Godliness represented by the Church.*]

In the following week, a young married man who was employed in the nearby village purchased a new automobile. He kept it at the place of his employment, continuing to use his tractor to commute to and from work. With the aid of another friend he had taken a driver's test and satisfactorily passed it.

In the latter instance the offender was immediately excommunicated for purchasing a car, and in order to be received again into full fellowship he was advised to put it away until the church could come to a unanimous decision on the ownership of automobiles. He sold his new auto to a friend for one dollar, and after the church had approved, he took it back. Meanwhile, a brother of the young married man was offended that his brother was excommunicated; in retaliation he also purchased an automobile. Like his brother, he too was promptly excommunicated. [*Rank is evidenced here; evidently the two excommunicated brothers had lower rank than the first offender who was granted an immunity from the negative sanctions.*] By this time the officials of the church had enough justification to bring up the question for discussion and taking the "Rot" or vote of the membership. [*The status-role of the officials is here articulated. They use their power to initiate the evaluation and decision-making processes.*]

Following the excommunications, informal discussions continued. Meetings were held informally in the homes. The second offender, in desperation for help, on a Sunday afternoon went to see the bishop of one of the Mennonite (Church Amish) congregations. He informed the bishop of his predicament and stated his desire to become a member of the Mennonite Church. The bishop advised him not to be in a hurry about joining another church. The next day the third offender came to the same bishop stating his desire to join the Mennonite Church. The bishop suggested to him that he call a meeting with other persons who, like himself, wanted to have an automobile. About 30 persons both men and women came to the meeting which was held in a private home. [*Members intimately acquainted and sharing the same need, continue to reinforce sentiments and opinions and evaluate action through informal communication.*] The bishop, accompanied by one of his assistant ministers, stated his position and read the Bible and led prayer. He explained that for people to join a church because they want an auto "usually doesn't help the church they jump into." He advised them to take the matter to their own ministers and see whether they couldn't come to some solution. The bishop's position was that in the previous years he had received many of the Amish members for no other reason than that they wanted automobiles. He was not interested in having more members of that kind, or just for that reason. [*The bishop realized that his church as a social system was a complex of belief, sentiments, objectives and norms. Agreement on one norm, perhaps this one concerning automobiles in particular, is not enough to insure dedication to the whole system.*]

The six ordained men of the Hoog group in the meantime had counselled with each other informally. None of them opposed the on-coming automobile question, but one wife did. "Where will this lead to, if our young people are given the privilege of going wherever they want?" was the chief objection she raised. [*Sentiments and opinions were formed and modified by the communication process.*]

The decision finally came before the assembled church. The process of decision making has been defined as the reduction of the alternate courses of action available so that some course of action can take place. Since the Amish church provides that each district maintain its own regulations and discipline it was up to the Hoog group to decide.

The "Rot" is usually taken at the members' meeting following the worship service. The two deacons polled the church, one taking the vote among the men and the other among the women. The bishop as a rule states the opinion of the ministry on any issue up for consideration, after which the membership affirms the minister's decisions, disapproves of them, or remains neutral on the question. [*The process of decision making had become institutionalized.*] The terms used to describe the outcome of the vote may be three: unanimous, practically unanimous, or not unanimous. In this case the report was practically unanimous in favor. Only four persons did not give assent, and they chose to join a stricter conservative Amish Church in the community. [*Those in conflict with the new norms sought a group whose objectives, norms and sentiments would be like theirs.*]

On the following Sunday at worship services eight automobiles were present. Several weeks later most of the members came in automobiles, and today from 40-50 automobiles are parked in a single barnyard with perhaps one or two carriages present. Only four of a total of 70 household heads have not purchased autos, and all of these are old people. Members were advised to secure only black automobiles or to have them painted black, and they were not to drive trucks.

The bishop had his own view of what had happened. The general practice of using tractors for road work and business trips to towns helped to bring on the automobile. The bishop felt it was not so much the fault of the young people as it was the fault of the parents—those who purchased automobiles for their boys who were either not yet members or were members of Church Amish groups. The frequent practice of young drivers dropping their parents off at preaching and then returning for them after the service was a primary reason for the innovation, according to the bishop.

[*The legitimation of the automobile by the Amish Church is a case of successful linkage of the Amish social system with that of the outside world. The change agent in this case was the group of Amish "young Turks" who advocated and successfully introduced the automobile into the Amish community. The target system, as the recipient of the "egging" and the direct attempts at innovation, was the Amish community represented by the ministers whose objectives, at first, were the maintenance of the status quo.*]

The results of the systemic linkage which brought the automobile to the Hoog group will take some time to manifest themselves. After all, the boundary maintenance devices failed to prevent the invasion of sacred norms, and in a matter of weeks forces were released which in the larger society required half a century to partially regularize and to control through continuous institutionalization. Except for infrequent and expensive "taxi" rides, the community had been the chief arena of interaction; now the interaction arena has been increased in size to cover the eastern part of the nation. Young people who formerly courted in prescribed ways now have the automobile, a facility viewed with mixed feelings by almost every parent with children of courting age even in the larger society. Such are the problems which the automobile has brought to the Hoog group.

SELECTED REFERENCES

Ford, Thomas R. "Status, Residence, and Fundamental Religious Belief in the Southern Appalachians," *Social Forces.* Vol. 39, No. 1. (October, 1960).

Glock, Charles Y. and Rodney Stark, *Religion and Society in Tension.* Chicago: Rand McNally and Company, 1965.

Hassinger, Edward W. and John S. Holik, "Changes in the Number of Rural Churches in Missouri, 1952-1967," *Rural Sociology* 35, No. 3, (September, 1970), pp. 354-366.

Hostetler, John A. "Religious Mobility in a Sect Group: The Mennonite Church," *Rural Sociology* 9, No. 3 (September, 1954), pp. 244-255.

Landis, Benson Y. "Trends in Church Membership in the United States," *Annals of the American Academy of Political and Social Science,* No. 332 (November, 1960), pp. 1-8.

Rogers, Everett M. and Rabel J. Burdge, *Social Change in Rural Societies.* New York: Appleton-Century-Crofts, 1972, Chapter 8.

Salisbury, W. Seward. *Religion in American Culture—A Sociological Interpretation.* Homewood: The Dorsey Press, 1964.

Schneider, Louis, ed. *Religion, Culture, and Society.* New York: John Wiley & Sons, Inc., 1964.

Schroeder, Widick W. and Victor Obenhaus, *Religion in American Culture.* Glencoe, Ill.: The Free Press, 1964.

Smith, T. Lynn and Paul Zopf, *Principles of Inductive Rural Sociology.* Philadelphia: F. A. Davis Co., 1970, Chapter 14.

8

Educational Social Systems

Among the important tasks in all societies is that of educating
the new generation. The family and informal groups in every
society assume part of the responsibility, but no "modern" society permits the entire task to be assumed by these groups. As
Clark points out, "All social systems, large or small, contain occasions for learning and participate to some degree in transmit-
ting culture and in socializing the individual. But the degree of
educational involvement is often minor, since many systems of
regular transaction leave instruction undifferentiated and inci-
dental and are not characterized by their educational effort."[1] In
all Western societies elaborate systems have been built for the
explicit purpose of educating the young. The character of such
an educational system reflects the value orientation of the society producing it.

By education we mean the process by which the cultural heritage is transmitted. Included in cultural heritage are ". . . skills,
ideas, reaction patterns, moral values, social attitudes, and the
beliefs which constitute citizenship and personality."[2] Since the
educational role of the family and clique is treated elsewhere,
this chapter will be concerned primarily with those formalized
systems established for the purpose of education.

IMPORTANCE OF EDUCATION AS A
SOCIAL SYSTEM

All but a small fraction of the population comes under the influence of the American educational systems for greater or lesser

[1] Burton R. Clark, "The Study of Educational Systems" in *International Encyclopedia of the Social Sciences,* Vol. 4, p. 510.

[2] Bronislaw Malinowski, "The Pan-African Problem of Culture Contact,"
American Journal of Sociology, Vol. XLVIII, No. 6 (1943), pp. 649-665; see also C.
P. Loomis and J. A. Beegle, *Rural Social Systems* (New York: Prentice-Hall, Inc.,
1950), p. 457.

periods of time. The magnitude of the educational enterprise, as reflected by school enrollments, is impressive. In 1970, about 6 of of 10 persons between 5 and 34 years of age in the United States were in school. More than 99 percent of all youth, white and non-white, in the age group from 7 to 14 were in school. And approximately one-fifth of whites and about one-sixth of Negroes between 20 and 24 years old were in school.[3] Even a large proportion (37.5 percent) of preprimary children 3 to 5 years old were in school in 1970. This percentage is much larger than in 1965 when slightly more than one-fourth (27.1) were enrolled.[4]

For a large segment of the population school begins the initiation into the larger society. For many children, especially in rural areas, preschool social interaction has been restricted largely to family and kinship groupings and to the play group. In the environment of the school, the child learns, often for the first time, to respond to a more impersonal type of authority than he had previously encountered. It is here also that he learns new status-roles—those of student, teacher, and school-mate, for example. Furthermore, he is in a position to learn the bases of new social ranking systems, not only those within the school system, but also those established by his peers. Even the least perceptive student will observe that a ranking system exists among the teachers themselves, and that the teachers use different criteria to ascertain rank or standing in school work. Therefore, the school must be regarded as a training ground, completely apart from substantive training, for the social order to which the child must eventually adapt.

The school is also a training ground of another variety, for the school supplies a meeting ground for diverse racial, ethnic, cultural, and social class groups. The child's first contact with groups other than his own often occurs at school. The provision of an opportunity for youth to interact with various segments of the community appears to be an extremely important function of the school system.

The feeling is strong in America that education is the answer to most problems. The degree to which education is sought and the amount of money spent for education support this conten-

[3] Bureau of the Census, *Current Population Reports,* Series P-20 and unpublished data.

[4] Department of Health, Education and Welfare, Office of Education, Annual Report, *Preprimary Enrollment Trends of Children Under 6.*

tion. In the words of Wissler: "Our culture is characterized by an overruling belief in something we call education—a kind of mechanism to propitiate the intent of nature in the manifestation of culture. Our implicit faith that this formula, or method, will cause this purpose to be more happily fulfilled, is our real religion."[5]

NEIGHBORHOOD SCHOOLS VS. TRADE-CENTER COMMUNITY SCHOOLS

"School-days, school-days, dear old golden rule days, Readin' and 'Ritin' and 'Rithmetic, Taught to the tune of a hick'ry stick," —the familiar lines obviously were intended to eulogize the one-room country school. And certainly for many people the neighborhood school is remembered as a place of warm sympathy and cherished memories. The first children on the frontier were taught in neighborhood schools. The organization and construction of a school and the employment payment and arrangements for boarding the teacher, were among the first collective acts on the frontier. The neighborhood district school, usually with one room and one teacher, is a prototype of Gemeinschaft-like relations. It has always been one of the purest examples of American democracy, representing its weaknesses and strengths.[6]

The original pattern of the school system as developed on the frontier by the American farmer and rancher established the principle of local autonomy firmly in the social fabric. Even today the hiring of teachers and the choice of curricula in both rural and urban areas are the responsibility of local people through democratically elected school boards. Notwithstanding the important function of the norms and standards of state accrediting agencies, in few nations of the world do local people have more direct control over the schools. Where rural neighborhood schools still exist, this control is generally greatest.

The point was made earlier that the most important change in

[5] Clark Wissler, *Man and Culture* (New York: Thomas Y. Crowell Co.,1932), p. 8. Christopher Jencks and associates argue that quality education will not reduce socioeconomic inequality. Mary Jo Bane and Christopher Jencks, "The Schools and Equal Opportunity," *Saturday Review,* (October 1972), pp. 37-42.

[6] Charles P. Loomis, et al., *Rural Social Systems and Adult Education* (East Lansing: Michigan State College Press, 1953), pp. 24-25.

rural locality groups has been the weakening of the intimate neighborhoods and the concomitant growth and increasing importance of the more impersonal trade-center community—a change resulting in large part from the advent of the automobile and improved highways. At the time that the neighborhood school was dominant in rural education, the neighborhood was, of course, the chief focus of mutual-aid of all kinds. House raising, threshing, husking, and many other types of cooperative activities were common neighborhood affairs. New families moving into a neighborhood for the first time were visited by their neighbors, welcoming them into membership in the neighborhood. Likewise, the rural teacher was in a very real sense a member, even though the occupant of a special status-role. Frequently he or she boarded with families in the neighborhood, and occupied the status-role of neighbor as well as teacher. Indeed the use of the "hick'ry stick" in these schools can be correctly understood only as a delegation of the parent's status-role to the teacher. In this respect the parental surrogate was not supposed to manifest the affectually neutral and bureaucratic motivation of the large system.

THE RURAL SCHOOL AS A SOCIAL SYSTEM

Ends and Objectives

"The fundamental purpose of the schools in every instance is the same—to provide an educational program that will stimulate and guide each individual in developing his abilities to their fullest extent for useful, satisfying living."[7] These are indeed broad objectives. Formerly the ends and objectives of the rural neighborhood school were understood to be the teaching of the three R's. With the growing complexity of modern society and the increasing contact between rural and urban areas, the school's objectives have been broadened and redefined. "As a society undergoes industrialization and modernization, its instruction of the young becomes extensively differentiated, internally complex, and elaborately connected with other features of society."[8]

Considering the broad aims of modern education in relation to

---

[7] *Your School District, The Report of the National Commission of School District Reorganization,* (Washington: National Education Association, 1948), p. 73.

[8] Clark, "The Study of Educational Systems," p. 510.

achievement, the least satisfactory schools in the United States are found for the most part in rural areas. The President's National Advisory Commission on Rural Poverty summarizes the current situation as follows: "Rural adults and youth are the product of an educational system that has historically short-changed rural people. The extent to which rural people have been denied equality of educational opportunity is evident from both the products of the educational system and the resources that go into the system. On both counts, the quality of rural education ranks low."[9] It is not difficult to understand this condition. In a period of rapid urbanization with consequent disruption in rural areas, it is not surprising that the ends and objectives of rural schools were not rapidly reoriented to the needs of a non-rural society.

Norms

The norms of a number of social systems influence teacher and teacher-student relationships. This is true, of course, of many important status-roles in rural and urban areas. A factory foreman, for instance, may be a member of a family, bowling team, a church, and possibly several other groups that impose different norms of behavior.[10] As will be indicated in the discussion of sanctions, the teacher may give primacy to the norms of (1) the community, (2) the immediate social system of the school, or (3) the professional organizations and groupings of colleagues. The early neighborhood school was rooted in the neighborhood community and in many respects functioned as an extension of the family. The norms of the school system *per se* and the profession were generally less important than those of the neighborhood community. School discipline, like family discipline, tended to be strict and would now be considered authoritarian. But there is evidence that rigorous discipline as a part of a general expectancy pattern yields different results than when applied in the impersonal atmosphere of a larger bureaucratic organization. In the neighborhood school motivation was based more largely upon the personal and often affectual appeal of the

[9] *The People Left Behind,* A report of the President's National Advisory Commission on Rural Poverty, (Washington, D. C.: Government Printing Office, 1967), p. 41.

[10] Delbert Miller and William Form, *Industrial Sociology* (New York: Harper and Brothers, 1951), pp. 208ff.

teacher than in the trade-center community school. Norms and standards of achievement varied greatly from neighborhood to neighborhood. The instances of teachers being bullied by lower class ruffians in frontier communities attest to the fact that the neighborhood schools were not always controlled as exclusively by the norms of the middle class as they are today.

The neighborhood school, like the church, tends to function as a conserver of values rather than an initiator of change. Many adults today remember the Scopes trial and how many school authorities attempted to prevent the teaching of evolution. Some educators see the reflection of enlightenment in the leadership of modern schools. Stouffer, for example, found that the presidents of school boards and of Parent-Teacher Associations (although in general less tolerant of communists, socialists, atheists, and persons accused of radicalism than were some other leaders, such as presidents of library boards, industrial leaders, and newspaper publishers) were much more tolerant than the average citizen. "Not only are more of the people who are moving from youth to middle age better educated than their elders," says Stouffer, "but also they are products both of child-rearing practices and of a school system which is more apt to foster tolerance."[11] For any age group, no factor analyzed was as important in producing tolerance as education—the more education the greater the tolerance. Farm and rural areas and those regions with lower educational attainment and standards, such as the South, were more intolerant than urban areas and areas of higher educational attainment, such as the West and East.

Status-Roles

The most important status-roles in all school systems are those of the student and teacher. We shall center our discussion here on the teacher role and the relationship between teacher and student. Numerous classifications of teacher roles have been outlined but we will utilize that developed by Kinney to illustrate the multi-faceted complexity of the teacher's status-roles.[12] The six roles specified by Kinney are described as follows: (1) Director of learning; (2) Guidance and counseling per-

---

[11] Samuel A. Stouffer, *Communism, Conformity, and Civil Liberties, A Cross-Section of the Nation Speaks Its Mind* (Garden City, New York: Doubleday and Co., 1955), p. 107.

[12] Havighurst and Neugarten, for example, provide a classification of "roles in relation to adults in school system" such as employee, colleague, leader and of

son; (3) Mediator of culture; (4) Member of the school community; (5) Liaison between school and community; and (6) Member of the profession.[13] While most teachers occupy the roles specified, there is great variation in the extent to which each is performed and importance attached to each role. Fishburn found that there was specialization with respect to these roles. Furthermore, he found that high school teachers ranked "mediator of the culture" as most important and "member of a profession" least important.[14]

The neighborhood teacher has frequently been characterized as a "baby-sitter" who, under the authority of the family and neighborhood community, has charge of the children for a few hours five days a week. In more recent times the larger systems have nurtured the growth of a certain amount of professionalism which permits affectually neutral relationships between student and teacher, at least in the more advanced grades. Under such conditions the teacher is held responsible for only specific functions at specific times, is judged by performance and is rewarded by more universalistic standards of achievement than in the neighborhood school.

Even in the larger, more bureaucratic school systems, however, teachers and school administrators find it necessary to involve the parents. Through participation in the Parent-Teachers Associations and other groups, ways have been developed to keep teachers in the social systems of the community. This is necessary if adequate financial support is to be made available and social linkage between community and school maintained.

It should be emphasized that although the size of the locality to which the school is articulated has changed, the teacher continues to be held accountable to the community. School board members and others in the community often disapprove failure to attend church, playing cards for money, and residence outside the community. We may safely conclude that the rural commu-

---

"roles in relation to pupils" such as mediator of learning, disciplinarian, parent substitute. R. J. Havighurst and B. L. Neugarten, *Society and Education* (Boston: Allyn & Bacon, Inc., 1957).

[13] L. B. Kinney, *Measure of a Good Teacher* (San Francisco: California Teachers Association, 1952).

[14] C. E. Fishburn, "Teacher Role Perception in the Secondary Schools of One Community," *Dissertation Abstracts* 1955, pp. 1798-1799.

nity exercises more powerful controls over the teacher than the urban community.

As pointed out by Goslin, "the ultimate unit of the educational process is the two-person group made up of the teacher and the student."[15] While this teacher-student relationship may vary widely in regard to frequency of interaction and the degree to which the relationship is expressive or affectively neutral, certain stable characteristics can be cited. As Goslin observes, the teacher-student relationship is ordinarily one of status inequality in which the teacher is expected to make more demands on the behavior of the student than vice versa. In addition, only one of the participants (the student) in the relationship is expected to change behavior during the course of the relationship. Further, the teacher role requires that the student be induced to change behavior in some respect. "There can be little doubt," Goslin argues, "that many of the problems that teachers as well as students encounter in the establishment of an integrated and productive role relationship result from a lack of agreement on the amount of specificity in the system of mutual expectations about each other's behavior."[16]

Unfortunately, the better salaries in the cities attract many of the better rural teachers. The turnover of teachers, for example, has been much higher in rural than in city schools. The more rural and the lower the economic status of counties, the lower the number of years of education teachers have beyond high school. The elementary school teacher in rural areas is often a young, unmarried girl, who has only recently left college.

Less than one-third of all public elementary and secondary school teachers in the United States are males. Historically, a large proportion of school teachers at this level have been women. Since 1920, the proportion of male elementary and secondary school teachers has risen gradually from 14.1% at that date to 31.5% in 1968.[17] Although the function of the woman teacher in American society is not completely understood, Parsons has hypothesized that it is the female teacher who may have "a sig-

[15] David A. Goslin, *The School in Contemporary Society* (Glenview: Scott, Foresman and Co., 1965), p. 20.

[16] Ibid., p. 22.

[17] U.S. Bureau of the Census, *Statistical Abstract of the United States* (Washington, 1971), p. 113.

nificance connected with the process of emancipation from earlier attachments to the mother." This he believes to be of particular importance because "dependence on the mother is particularly intense in the American kinship system . . ."[18]

Power

Although the modern large school system is more often under the domination of the elite of the community than many other systems, the rights of the teacher and administrators have increased as the trade-center community school has supplanted the neighborhood school. Both student and teacher are more subject to the impersonal nature of bureaucracy than ever before. Much has been written[19] about the relative merits of what has been called the authoritarian versus the democratic relationships within the classroom and within the authority structure of the staff of the school system. Brookover observes that ". . . it may be suggested that at the lower-grade levels, children respond to the authoritarian or dominating teacher with resistance and patterns of domination in relation to their peers. At the same level the children respond to the integrative, democratic teacher with initiative, spontaneous contributions, and cooperation. The secondary school youth express unfavorable reactions to the authoritarian teacher, but learn more from him. The opposite is true of their reactions to the friendly, democratic teacher."[20]

The greatest weakness in the current treatment of power in relation to its effect within social systems is the failure to analyze in a systematic manner the situations within which power is applied. The strict teacher in the neighborhood school of earlier times usually conformed to the expectancy patterns of the community, and teachers who behaved in ways that are now called democratic and friendly, were often ridiculed. Their permissiveness usually caused frustration, because students were unaccustomed to or could not predict their behavior. In general, the authority of the typical neighborhood teacher was more

---

[18] Talcott Parsons, *The Social System* (Glencoe: The Free Press, 1951), p. 241.

[19] See N. L. Gage, ed., *Handbook of Research on Teaching* (Chicago: Rand McNally and Co., 1963), Chapters 10 and 11. See also Ronald Lippitt, "An Experimental Study of Authoritarian and Democratic Group Atmospheres," *University of Iowa Studies in Child Welfare,* Vol. 3 (1940).

[20] W. B. Brookover, *The Sociology of Education* (New York: American Book Co., 1955), p. 311.

Gemeinschaft-like. By this we mean that teacher-student relations were more affectual, more personal or particularistic, and responsibilities were more diffuse. In the larger more bureaucratized trade-center school system, the authority of the teacher in teacher-student relations is more affectually neutral, less personal and more universalistic, and responsibilities are more specific. Attainment of positions of authority is more dependent upon achievement in the profession. Thus, power in the older neighborhood school is of a different order than power in the large school systems.

Social Rank

Although the rural teacher in the trade-center community school may have higher social rank than the neighborhood school teacher, the status-role of public school teacher does not have high social rank in American society. In fact, of ninety occupations selected from a national cross-section study, there were twenty-nine occupations having higher rank. The public school teacher (thirtieth in rank) was only somewhat higher than the farm owner and operator (forty-third in rank).[21] Nevertheless, the rural teacher's social rank is higher than the power attached to the rank. This is in part, no doubt, due to the relatively great respect in American society for those having learning.

Education is widely regarded throughout the United States as a mechanism through which the individual may improve his social standing. For many rural people, education is a requisite in the process of migration and eventual urban adjustment. Education also assists in the process of advancing middle class values. The interrelations of social rank and education are numerous, and thus far a complete study of the ramifications has not been made.

One of the most direct and readily observable associations between social class and education is that all social classes do not have free access to education. Access to equal educational opportunity, as we have pointed out before is a major problem for most children growing up in rural areas. An especially succinct statement of the dynamics of the "opportunity gap" is found in

[21] Robert W. Hodge, Paul M. Siegel, and Peter B. Rossi, "Occupational Prestige in the United States, 1925-1963," *American Journal of Sociology,* 70 (November 1964), pp. 286-302. See also Melvin L. Defleur, William V. D'Antonio and Lois B. Defleur, *Sociology: Man in Society* (Glenview: Scott, Foresman and Co., 1971), p. 228.

Schools and Inequality. The authors point out that both the family and society invest larger sums in the growth and development of the high than the low socio-economic status (SES) child. Whether rural or urban, the low SES child is more likely to suffer prenatal malnutrition and to be exposed to inadequate medical and dental care. He is also more likely to live in a modest physical environment in which the family income precludes exposure to a whole host of enriching and stimulating experiences. Parental attention is likely to be less and the lower educational attainment of the parents severely restricts the knowledge that can be transmitted to the low SES child.[22]

It is generally accepted that teachers are usually recruited from the middle class and represent middle class values. Their social class background leads them to select these traits in students for praise and approval.

Sanctions

The rewards for teaching, particularly salaries, are low considering the training and intelligence required for the status-role. This is particularly true for rural teachers. In part due to unionization, the salaries of teachers have increased greatly. While the following salaries have not been adjusted for price changes, approximately 88% of public elementary and secondary teachers received under $6,500 in 1960; about 58 percent received this salary in 1966, and only 8.7 percent received this amount in 1971. About 41 percent of all teachers in public schools received salaries of $9,500 or more in 1971.[23]

In a study of involvement as related to teacher stress, Washburne[24] attempted to appraise the importance of: (1) economic gain and security; (2) status in the community; (3) authority or recognition and approval by varying agents of authority within the school system; and (4) professional status of orientation toward teaching as a profession. Obviously, achievement in any one of these areas might be regarded as rewarding; failure to achieve might be regarded as penalizing. The important fact is that attempting to achieve in all areas simultaneously might well bring

[22] James W. Guthrie, George B. Kleindorfer, Henry M. Levin, and Robert T. Stout, *Schools and Inequality* (Cambridge: The MIT Press, 1971), pp. 141-142.

[23] *Statistical Abstract, 1971.*

[24] Chandler Washburne, *Involvement as a Basis for Stress Analysis: A Study of High-School Teachers* (East Lansing: Michigan State College doctoral dissertation, 1953).

stress. Washburne's study of a small group of men teachers in a city school concludes that a teacher "is caught in the center of a confused mixture of orders which place conflicting demands on him. Stated over-simply: He is caught between the structural demands of bureaucratic organization, the traditional demands of the community, and a series of 'ideal' demands associated with the profession."[25] It is our thesis that the pressures from the community are greater in the rural schools. Brookover supports this thesis when he says: "The chances of stress are probably less in large school systems, where authority is more clearly defined in a bureaucratic structure and where the teacher's relations with the community are less personal. At the other extreme, the teachers of the small, one-room rural school can also probably identify with a predominant source of authority more easily. It is in the great number of town and village schools that role conflict seems most likely to occur."[26]

Facilities

With respect to facilities of all kinds we think rural schools lag a decade behind the urban schools. And the rural neighborhood schools are more disadvantaged than the larger rural schools. In the United States as a whole, even the reorganized, consolidated rural schools are inferior to those in urban areas. Teachers' salaries are lower, teachers' preparation inferior, school terms shorter, library services poorer, health services and remedial care more limited, and high school training more inadequate.

Territoriality

In the United States a realistic discussion of school reorganization and development must differentiate between attendance units and administrative units. In the early days of the frontier the neighborhood school often embraced a single attendance and administrative unit, controlled for the most part by a popularly elected school board.

In 1917 and 1918, 196,037 public schools or 71 percent were one-teacher elementary schools, most of which were in rural areas. Thirty years later, the number of one-teacher elementary schools had decreased to 74,944. Nine states—South Dakota, Nebraska, Wisconsin, Illinois, Missouri, Minnesota, Iowa, Kentucky, and Kansas—account for over half of these one-room

25 Ibid., p. 118.
26 Brookover, *The Sociology of Education*, p. 284.

schools, which are for the most part rural neighborhood schools.[27] In the late sixties there were only about 10,000 one-room schools, mostly in rural America.[28]

Many professional educators recognize the necessity of retaining the Gemeinschaft-like characteristics of the old neighborhood school through planning attendance areas that correspond to the more dynamic locality groupings. This means that as the older neighborhoods decrease in population and lose their vigor, the attendance area must shift from the neighborhood to the trade-center community. How to retain the advantages of the intimate neighborhood associations and at the same time to take advantage of the efficiencies of larger attendance areas is a crucial problem in rural life.

Through rapid school consolidation in rural areas, school children are being drawn from increasingly larger spatial areas. Many rural young people spend several hours on a school bus each day. The reasons for consolidation may be obvious. Among them are reduced cost per pupil, inability of small units to support education, and a more adequate, more specialized training.[29] Important in the process of consolidation have been the standards and guidelines established by the National Commission on School District Reorganization in 1948.[30]

In many rural communities throughout the nation, the school is a primary integrative agency. In the light of this consideration it would seem obvious that school district reorganization should exercise care to preserve boundaries of communities which are true systems of social interaction. "The high school attendance area should, insofar as possible, be identified with the area in which people associate together in aspects of community life."[31]

Smith and Zopf argue cogently that rural schools be consolidated *within the community.* ". . . school consolidation should

---

[27] Walter H. Gaumitz and David T. Blose, *The One-Teacher School—Its Mid-century Status* (Washington, D. C.: U.S. Government Printing Office, 1950), p. 30.

[28] *The People Left Behind,* p. 41.

[29] See E. M. Rogers and Rabel Burdge, *Social Change in Rural Societies* (New York: Appleton-Century-Crofts, 1972), Chapter 9.

[30] *Your School District.*

[31] Shirley Cooper, "Characteristics of Satisfactory Attendance Units," in *Characteristics of Good School Districts,* School of Education, University of Wisconsin (Madison: University of Wisconsin, 1948), p. 13.

accompany, but not anticipate, the expansion of the community area; and the first few grades might well be handled on a different basis from the upper grades. In the consolidation of schools, the ignoring of community interests and boundaries and of the fact that the community is the locality grouping that embraces virtually all aspects of the lives of its people, might well result in a form of educational absenteeism fully as vicious as absentee landownership."[32]

Communication

One of the primary functions of the school, whether rural or urban, is to provide an arena for communication. It is clear that learning will not occur if the teacher fails to communicate with pupils. Of great importance in the learning process is the communication among students. Barriers to interaction and communication among peers include numerous hierarchical cleavages most often based upon social class, color, and ethnic origin. Cliques composed of like-minded peers are found in all school systems and are not only often serious barriers to interaction but may also effectively isolate certain students in and outside the classroom.

One may think of numerous other kinds of communication involving the school. There must be reciprocal communication between school administrators and teachers. When school systems become large, communication often becomes impersonal—through mimeographed announcements and directives. In such systems teachers may feel that they do not have adequate access to the principal. There is also the need for the school to communicate with the community of which it is a part. And of course, communication in the opposite direction is also necessary.

Coincident with school consolidation, school children from rural areas find themselves in classes with town and city children. Historically, pupils from rural areas are generally regarded as inferior by those living in the towns and cities. Such cleavages based upon residence may be severe, but most commonly today the initial bias tends to be transitory.[33] Ethnic cleavages

[32] T. Lynn Smith and Paul E. Zopf, *Principles of Inductive Rural Sociology* (Philadelphia: F. A. Davis Co., 1970), p. 332.

[33] See Charles P. Loomis, *Studies in Applied and Theoretical Social Science* (East Lansing: Michigan State College Press, 1950), Chapter 12.

and consequent interaction and breakdown of communication remain important in rural and urban schools.

Decision-making

Most reports reveal that rural people are not as active as the town people in decision-making affecting school policy. Many factors are responsible for this, one of the most important being that other nonfarm economic and social agencies, such as banks, stores, and businesses, are usually owned and operated by townspeople. When no reorganization takes place, and high school attendance areas develop based on the size of the trade-center school and ability of neighborhood districts to pay tuition, the middle class in the trade-center rather than the rural people are in control. Under these conditions rural people are disenfranchised.

In most large centers the school teachers and administrative staff are not as important in decision-making for the school and community as are the businessmen and political leaders. In general, the teachers, often with superior knowledge and frequently with considerable experience, have relatively little power in the community. Their power is also not great in the final determination of school support and facilities.[34] School administrators, however, must have access to those with power in order to operate the schools. To be successful, they must establish working relationships with potentates in the communities.

Vidich and Bensman, in *Small Town in Mass Society* recount the paternal dynamics of decision-making between the principal and a country-dominated school board. The principal successfully attained the status of technical expert and administrator of board policies. In effect, the school board simply rubber-stamped the principal's prior decisions. His strategy, according to Vidich and Bensman, was as follows:

1. Become aware of all the facts in the case.
2. On the basis of these facts, paying special attention to the reactions of the significant people involved, reach a decision.

[34] Floyd Hunter, *Community Power Structure—A Study of Decision-Makers* (Chapel Hill: University of North Carolina Press, 1953).

3. Formulate a definite plan of action based on the decision, implementing every step of action in detail.
4. Come to the board meeting fully prepared with the detailed solution of the problem and then present the problem as though you just realized the problem existed and 'could the board help you with some advice since you are new and inexperienced in Springdale and they are familiar with the precedent.'
5. Let the board knock it about for a while while you sit back and size up their individual stands on the issue.
6. Present the facts and the carefully worked out solution, countering every argument with a better one, being, of course, very tactful.
7. Wait for Jones to make the motion that your plan be adopted.[35]

Boundary maintenance

With respect to boundary maintenance, the school as a system seems to be in a very difficult position. Since the professional and administrative personnel have relatively little power in the community, great emphasis must be placed upon gaining community support. This means that the professional status of the teacher and the school administrator in many instances is less important than being on good terms with persons influential in the community and with influential parents. Moreover, the public school and those who support it attempt to prevent the system establishing closure through boundary maintenance. Thus, community colleges often find it difficult to develop high standards for academic freedom because of community linkage with the educational system. An attempt is made to have parents participate in programs, visit classes, and insofar as possible determine policy. Since support for the school depends upon good public relations, and since the teacher and administrator have not established their own areas of competence as superior to those of the citizens, there is usually much greater interference with the teacher's performance of his role by those outside of the school system than would be permitted by such professional groups as doctors and lawyers.

[35] Arthur J. Vidich and Joseph Bensman, *Small Town in Mass Society* (Princeton: Princeton University Press, 1968), p. 193.

Systemic Linkage

Few social systems are used more by change agents to reach out into the community than the schools. The school population is a "captive audience," assembled for considerable time over long intervals. It is obvious that change agents in both developed and developing societies see the school population as an economical target to reach large numbers of parents and friends directly, or indirectly. A project carried on by the Inter-American Institute of Agricultural Sciences, for example, made the rural school teacher the chief change agent for all community activities.[36]

PATTERNS OF RURAL AND URBAN ATTAINMENT

Levels of educational attainment, of course, are lower among farm than among urban people. Since farming is less professionalized and bureaucratized, schooling is generally thought to be less essential than in many urban-centered occupations. Irrespective of the measure used to assess educational achievement, rural people rarely measure up in that respect to the urban population. Levels of schooling for the adult population 25 years old and over, whites and Negroes, are shown in Tables 1 and 2. As measured by the median number of school years completed (Table 1), adults in metropolitan areas have an average of 12.3 years as compared with 10.7 for adults residing on farms. Levels of schooling for nonmetropolitan nonfarm residents are intermediate between the extremes. Differences among residence categories shown, it will be noted, hold true for whites as well as Negroes and for males as well as females. Interestingly, differences in achievement for females among residence groups are not great.

Table 2 summarizes levels of school completion for adults who are young (25 to 44 years) and older (45 years old and over). When we use the percentage of adults who have completed elementary school and college or more, the high urban and low farm achievement found in Table 1 is repeated. Both whites and Negroes exhibit the same pattern. The table shows the dramatic rise in educational level for all categories regardless of resi-

[36] Charles P. Loomis, et al., *Turrialba: Social Systems and the Introduction of Change* (Glencoe, Ill.: The Free Press, 1953). See Chapter 10, "Educational Systems," by Eduardo Arze and Roy A. Clifford.

TABLE 1

Median Years of School Completed by Persons 25 Years Old and Over
by Residence, Race and Sex, March 1971

Residence and Race	Median School Years Completed		
	Both	Males	Females
Total, 25 years old and over	12.2	12.2	12.2
Metropolitan Areas	12.3	12.3	12.2
Nonmetropolitan Areas	11.9	11.6	12.0
Nonfarm	12.0	11.9	12.0
Farm	10.7	9.7	11.8
Whites, 25 years old and over	12.2	12.3	12.2
Metropolitan Areas	12.3	12.4	12.3
Nonmetropolitan Areas	12.1	12.0	12.1
Nonfarm	12.1	12.1	12.1
Farm	11.2	10.2	12.0
Negroes, 25 years old and over	10.0	9.7	10.3
Metropolitan Areas	10.8	10.6	10.9
Nonmetropolitan Areas	8.3	7.9	8.5
Nonfarm	8.4	8.2	8.6
Farm	6.1	5.1	7.2

Source: U.S. Bureau of the Census, *Current Population Reports,* Series P-20,
No. 229, "Educational Attainment: March 1971," U. S. Government Printing
Office, Washington, D. C., 1971, Table 2.

dence. One-fifth (20.7 percent) of farm residents aged 25 to 44
had completed 8 grades or less, while more than half (52.0 percent) of those 45 years old and over had completed this low level
of schooling.

The well known association between income and level of
schooling is depicted in Table 3. For each broad occupational
category of employed males, the median level of schooling rises
with each increment in income. The pattern holds true of farm
workers as well as each of the urban, industrial worker occupations. Blue collar workers and farm workers exhibit similar
patterns.

As is well known, introduction to schooling in American society is occurring at increasingly early ages. The proportions of
children enrolled in pre-primary school, by residence and other

TABLE 2
Percent Completing 8 Years or Less of School and 4 or More
Years of College by Persons 25 Years Old and Over, by
Residence, Race, and Age Group, March 1971

Residence and Race	Percent Completing 8 Grades or Less		Percent Completing 4 or More Years of College	
	25-44 Years	45 Years and Over	25-44 Years	45 Years and Over
Total, 25 years old and over	12.3	38.0	14.9	8.7
Metropolitan Areas	10.4	33.6	17.0	10.0
Nonmetropolitan Areas	16.2	45.8	10.8	6.2
Non-farm	15.8	44.7	11.3	6.6
Farm	20.7	52.0	4.9	3.8
Whites, 25 years old and over	11.3	35.7	15.7	9.2
Metropolitan Areas	9.4	31.4	18.1	10.7
Non-metropolitan Areas	14.7	43.3	11.3	6.5
Non-farm	14.2	42.1	12.0	6.9
Farm	18.4	49.7	5.1	3.9
Negroes, 25 years old and over	21.1	62.0	5.8	3.2
Metropolitan Areas	16.9	54.7	6.6	3.6
Nonmetropolitan Areas	33.4	77.3	3.2	2.4
Non-farm	31.6	86.2	3.3	2.5
Farm	58.3	87.2	1.6	1.5

Source: U. S. Bureau of the Census, *Current Population Reports,* Series P-20, No. 229, "Educational Attainment: March 1971," U. S. Government Printing Office, Washington, D. C., 1971, Table 2.

socio-economic factors, are shown in Table 4. The percentages of children enrolled in pre-primary school are lowest for those residing in nonmetropolitan areas and for those whose parents are in farming. All categories shown in Table 4 have increased sharply in the 5-year period shown. In part, the relative position of rural school children is due to spatial and income problems of families residing outside metropolitan areas.

The relatively high rates of scholastic retardation of rural and ethnic children are shown in Table 5. Scholastic retardation re-

TABLE 3
Median School Years Completed by Employed Males 25 to 64
Years Old, by Income in 1970 and Broad Occupation Group,
March 1971

Income		Median School Years Completed			
	Total	White Collar Workers	Blue Collar Workers	Service Workers	Farm Workers
All Employed Males					
25 to 64 Years Old	12.4	13.9	11.7	11.9	10.1
Under $3,000	10.0	12.7	9.3	8.9	8.6
$3,000 to $5,999	11.0	12.7	9.8	9.6	10.0
$6,000 to $9,999	12.2	12.8	11.6	12.1	12.1
$10,000 to $14,999	12.6	13.9	12.2	12.4	12.2
$15,000 and over	15.6	16.2	12.3	12.8	12.4

Source: U. S. Bureau of the Census, *Current Population Reports,* Series P-20, No. 229, "Educational Attainment: March 1971," U. S. Government Printing Office, Washington, D. C., 1971, Table 7.

fers, of course, to enrollment in a grade below the modal grades for a person at a given age. As shown in this table, retardation was highest in rural-nonfarm areas, and lowest in the suburb of urban areas. Retardation rates are very high for Indian and Negro children and lowest of all for Japanese and Chinese children. How well a child keeps up with his age peers is closely related to family status, education, occupation and income of parents.[37]

Considerable variation exists among the states in wealth and expenditures for education. In general, expenditure per pupil in public schools is directly related to per capita income. With few exceptions, each of these variables is lower in the more rural than in the more urban states. (See Table 6.) The majority of those states ranking highest in expenditures per pupil are highly urban states. In contrast, the majority of those states ranking lowest in per pupil expenditures are relatively rural, and all, except Idaho, are in the South.

[37] See John K. Folger and Charles B. Nam, *Education of the American Population* (Washington: U.S. Govt., Printing Office, 1967), pp. 52-59.

TABLE 4

Pre-primary School Enrollment of Children 3 to 5 Years Old, by
Selected Characteristics, 1965 and 1970

Race, Residence and Socio-economic Status	Percent Enrolled	
	1965	1970
Total, 3-5 years of Age	27.1	37.5
White	27.9	37.8
Negro and Other	23.3	35.7
Family Income		
Less than $3,000	14.4	24.4
$3,000—$4,999	21.0	29.9
$5,000—$7,499	26.3	32.4
$7,500—$9,999	$\left\{37.4\right.$	36.9
$10,000 and over		47.5
Residence		
Metropolitan Areas		
Central Cities	29.9	39.4
Outside Central Cities	32.5	43.2
Nonmetropolitan Areas	19.4	30.2
Occupation of Family Head		
White Collar	36.3	47.0
Manual or Service	23.2	32.1
Farm	9.6	23.6
Unemployed or not in Labor Force	24.3	34.2

Source: Department of Health, Education and Welfare, Office of Education;
Annual Report, *Pre-Primary Enrollment Trends of Children Under Six.*

EDUCATION, MIGRATION AND SOCIAL MOBILITY[38]

The accelerating rate of technological and social change in recent decades has affected all areas of our national life. Not only
have such changes provided new opportunities and a higher
standard of living for many people, but they have also meant
new challenges and problems. Nowhere can this be better seen
than in rural areas. Improvements in agricultural technology
and the reduction in the demand for agricultural labor, consoli-

[38] Jon H. Rieger, J. Allan Beegle and Philip N. Fulton, *Profiles of Rural Youth:
A Decade of Migration and Social Mobility,* Michigan AES Research Report 179
(East Lansing: Michigan State University Press, 1973), pp. 20-22. This "case" is
a summary of a longitudinal study of rural youth from a relatively remote low
income area in Michigan's Upper Peninsula.

TABLE 5

Percent Scholastically Retarded for Youth 10 to 17 Years
Old, by Age, Residence, and Ethnic Status, 1960

Residence and Ethnic Status	Percent Retarded by Age		
	10-13 Years Old	14 & 15 Years Old	16 & 17 Years Old
United States	9.8	14.6	15.1
Residence			
Urban	8.2	12.1	13.2
Urbanized Areas	7.6	11.1	12.5
Other Urban	10.3	15.2	15.2
Rural	13.0	19.3	18.8
Nonfarm	13.2	19.9	19.3
Farm	12.8	17.9	17.6
Ethnic Status			
White	8.2	12.5	12.9
Native-white	8.1	12.3	12.7
Foreign-born white	15.6	21.6	28.0
Nonwhite	21.1	30.2	33.3
Negro	21.6	31.1	34.4
Indian	29.2	41.5	43.3
Japanese and Chinese	4.9	4.3	6.9
Other Races	11.2	15.2	17.5

Source: U. S. Bureau of the Census, *Education of the American Population* by John K. Folger and Charles B. Nam (A 1960 Census Monograph), U. S. Government Printing Office, Washington, D. C., 1967, p. 52.

dation of farm units, and the increasingly intricate linkage of the rural to the urban-industrial economy, have had an important impact on rural communities and on the careers of their young people. Rapidly changing conditions continually modify the career alternatives of these young people, and have required a high degree of adaptability on their part in obtaining education and employment and in deciding where they would like to live.

This study focused on some problems associated with migration and social mobility of rural youth. Our canvas was confined to a crucial period of the life cycle, from about 18 to 28. During this time span numerous decisions converge concerning migration, further education, marriage, and career. Our research strategy was longitudinal in that we solicited information from the

TABLE 6
Income Per Capita, 1969, and Current Expenditures Per
Pupil in Public Schools, 1971

Rank in Expenditures Per Pupil		Amount	Rank in Personal Income Per Capita	Amount
Highest 10 States:				
Alaska	1	$1,429	2	$4,460
New York	2	1,370	4	4,442
New Jersey	3	1,088	7	4,241
Vermont	4	1,061	32	3,247
Minnesota	5	1,021	18	3,635
Connecticut	6	997	1	4,595
Rhode Island	7	983	13	3,858
Wisconsin	8	977	19	3,632
Maryland	9	968	10	4,073
Delaware	10	954	9	4,107
Lowest 10 States				
North Carolina	41	642	42	2,888
Texas	42	636	31	3,259
Georgia	43	634	34	3,071
Idaho	44	629	40	2,953
West Virginia	45	624	47	2,603
Kentucky	46	621	43	2,847
Tennessee	47	601	44	2,808
Arkansas	48	578	49	2,488
Mississippi	49	521	50	2,218
Alabama	50	489	48	2,582

Source: Department of Commerce, Office of Business Economics, Department of Health, Education, and Welfare, and U.S. Office of Education.

subjects at two points in time—once near the end of high school and again about ten years later.

The research site was a remote county in Michigan's Upper Peninsula. At one time its economy was among the thriving economies in the state. Today, while copper mining is still very important, the area fails to sustain a fully-developed, modern economy.

We chose this site for two reasons. First, we wished to maximize the rural outmigration phenomenon. Based on regional averages, Ontonagon County had a low level of living and a small proportion employed in manufacturing. It also had a long history of net outmigration. Second, we wanted to minimize the difficulty of data retrieval in the follow-up study. We felt that the informal network of friends and kin present in the Ontonagon County area would make it possible to readily locate our informants ten years after graduation from high school. [*That is, a Gemeinschaft-like environment supported by restricted territoriality*].

The situation of the present sample of students in 1957, as it emerges from our data, is that of a critical stage in their careers. It is a time of assessment of the many factors involved in, and the decisions affecting, later experience. There is a widespread, realistic anticipation of the necessity of leaving the area to obtain adequate employment or to get further education or training. Some of the students planned to leave on the basis of the simple intuition that such experience would be instrumental to their growth and independence. Although some had the familiar complaints about a local area ("people don't mind their own business"), certain of their attitudes had basis in objective fact. The post-high school education and vocational opportunities in the immediate area were inadequate or nonexistent. The students' sense of gloom about the area (only one-third felt their community's future looked bright) reflected the sentiment of many local people. Most of the parents would agree to their children leaving for other places and expressed willingness to provide assistance during the process. [*Instead of insisting on boundary-maintaining activities, linkage with outside systems was viewed favorably*].

This is not to say, of course, that the students disliked the community in which they had grown up. Evidence points to a substantial attachment. While a majority expected to leave the area after high school, only a minority of them were actually looking forward to the prospect. Moreover, their residential preferences twenty years into the future reveal a considerable sentiment for the Ontonagon County area.

Many of these young people exhibited exceedingly high occupational aspirations. Their migration expectations were instrumental in their attempts to realize high occupational goals and thus an integral part of their overall career strategy. [*Migration is viewed as a means to gain high status-roles*].

A majority of the subjects did subsequently move away from

their home communities. Only a small number stayed in the area throughout the post high school decade. Most of those who left did so within the first several years. Many subjects moved initially for the direct purpose of obtaining further education, their destination being college towns. Others went to urban areas in the state and along the south-western shore of Lake Michigan to find work.

The amount of mobility is quite surprising, with most of these young people having moved five or more times during the decade. Some had moved eight or more times. A considerable amount of back-and-forth movement occurred between Ontonagon County and other places: about half the subjects moved away from, and back to, the county one or more times during the decade.

A little more than half the males, and even a few females, served in the armed forces. More than half completed some form of additional training or education after high school, with almost one-third of the entire group obtaining college training. Over 50 percent of those who attended a college finished a 4-year degree, and about half of these subsequently obtained advanced education.

By 1968, the subjects were dispersed throughout the occupational structure. A goodly number had attained professional status. Both skilled and semi-skilled occupations were also well represented. Among females the highest proportion had worked in clerical jobs, while others had been employed in service trades and some professional and technical jobs. By the end of the 10-year period, however, only about one-third of the women were working outside the home. [*A reflection of the changing status-roles of women*].

Occupational achievement was related to residence. Not only did persons who left their home communities generally do better than those who did not, but the level of the migrants' occupations varied with the size of the community in which they were living. Persons who lived in urban areas seemed to be faring better than those living in rural areas. Among the men, those living in small cities exhibited the highest level of occupational achievement.

Nearly half the subjects had attained incomes of $8,000 or more within ten years of high school graduation. Fewer than 10 percent report incomes similar to those of their parents ten years before. Even allowing for inflation, such trends imply a comparatively high overall degree of success among these former rural high school students.

Most of the young people had married during the decade, many within the first several years after high school. Mate choice and the timing of marriage was related to geographic mobility and occupational achievement. In general, the earlier the marriage took place after high school the more likely the mate would be from the home area. Persons who married early also tended to have children sooner after marriage and to have somewhat larger families, both absolutely and in the number of children born per year. Moreover, early marriage was associated with lower rates of migration out of the local area and with relatively modest educational and occupational achievement. It is easy to see a causal linkage in this sequence of events. It is a pattern in which earlier events tend to impose limits on later alternatives. Early marriage tends to be accompanied by early dependency, which results in reduced mobility and the advantages it makes possible, particularly further education and a wider range of occupational choice.

Most of our informants felt, in retrospect, that it is necessary for young people to leave the area after high school to pursue desirable career objectives. In addition, some evidently feel that such departure is important in establishing onself as an independent adult and in gaining some degree of sophistication. While many seemed to leave the door open for returning, few specifically urged it as an objective. This would tend to reinforce the impression that many of these young people themselves will be more or less permanently located away from the local area, despite their widely expressed nostalgia and sentiment for Ontonagon County.

The literature on rural-urban migration presents two essentially incompatible views of the potential migrant. In one view the migrant is seen as the prototype of economic man, ready to move to whatever destination in response to financial advantage. In the other, the migrant is seen as enmeshed in a network of friends, relatives, and kin. He is viewed as being firmly tied to his birthplace and the process of migration is considered painful and socially costly.

Our data suggest that each view is an exaggerated characterization of contemporary migrants. We find that migration is generally viewed as normative behavior, and the process of migration is not considered unduly painful nor socially costly. It is also clear that many parents prepare their children for this event and expect they will move away.

We found attachment to the local area and to kin strong among many of the migrants. But this attachment, alleviated by occasional return trips, correspondence, telephone, and other sporadic contacts, was not viewed as incompatible with residence elsewhere, often a great distance away. Satisfactory adjustment of most migrants in destination areas appears to have been made with relatively little difficulty. At the same time, a large proportion benefited from the mediation of friends and relatives in the areas of destination [*an important facility in achieving desired ends.*]

A considerable body of literature finds the rural migrant to the city at a disadvantage in the urban labor market. This disadvantage accrues, according to the literature, to those inadequately trained and inadequately attuned to urban life. We cannot unequivocally challenge these findings, but our cohort of youth exhibits remarkable achievement in income and status. There is reason to believe that the cohort studied may differ somewhat from other rural young people in the value placed on education as a medium for social mobility.

The existing literature on rural-urban migration rarely does justice to the phenomenon of return-migration. When the return-migrant is considered, he is often viewed as a failure in the urban labor market. Our data challenge the notion that the return-migrant has simply failed to adapt successfully elsewhere. A large proportion had returned for carefully calculated reasons, in some instances to render badly needed services in the local area. Few had been failures elsewhere. Not an insignificant proportion of the return-migrants were, in reality, "multiple migrants." That is, they had moved away, then returned for various periods of time, only to move away again.

The overall record of our informants is one of a high frequency of mobility and an unusually high level of achievement, both educational and occupational. This is in contrast to the findings typically reported for rural youth in the literature, and offers considerable encouragement in terms of the capacity of such young people, at least from areas like Ontonagon County, to cope with the many challenges and problems in finding a niche in a rapidly changing and increasingly urban society.

SELECTED REFERENCES

Folger, John K. and Charles B. Nam. *Education of the American Population,* A 1960 Census Monograph. Washington: Government Printing Office, 1967.

Gaumitz, Walter H. and David T. Blose. *The One-Teacher School—Its Midcentury Status.* Washington: Government Printing Office, 1950.

Goslin, David A. *The School in Contemporary Society.* Glenview, Ill.: Scott, Foresman and Company, 1965.

Guthrie, James W., George B. Kleindorfer, Henry M. Levin, and Robert T. Stout. *Schools and Inequality.* Cambridge: The MIT Press, 1971.

International Encyclopedia of the Social Sciences, "Education", articles by Burton R. Clark, C. Arnold Anderson, and A. H. Halsey. New York: The MacMillan Company and The Free Press, 1968 Volume 4, pp. 509-533.

Martindale, Don and R. Galen Hanson. *Small Town and the Nation.* Westport, Conn.: Greenwood Publishing Corporation, 1969.

Rogers, Everett M. and Rabel Burdge. *Social Change in Rural Societies.* New York: Appleton-Century-Crofts, 1972, Chapter 9.

Smith, T. Lynn and Paul E. Zopf. *Principles of Inductive Rural Sociology.* Philadelphia: F. A. Davis Co., 1970, Chapter 13.

Vidich, Arthur J. and Joseph Bensman. *Small Town in Mass Society.* Revised Edition. Princeton: Princeton University Press, 1968.

9

Governmental Social Systems

In no society is there unrestricted freedom to resort to force. At the same time, no society has been able to eliminate the use of force completely. The most important function of government is that of institutionalizing the use of force among individuals and groups, to the end that law and order is established and certain services provided. According to Parsons, "No society can subsist unless there is a basis for 'counting on' some control of the use of force. . ."[1]

Usually the governmental unit or social system that provides law and order through the institutionalization of social power and the monopolization of authority includes a population occupying a specified land area within which this social system may exercise one or all of the following: right of taxation, eminent domain, police power, and penal power. The governmental system carries on one or all of the functions of law enforcement, education, public health, social welfare, highway construction and regulation, and promotion of welfare, in the fields of agriculture, labor, industry, and commerce. In the final analysis, since control over and exercise of force (as, for example, incarceration of criminals) are physical acts, most governmental social systems are territorial units bounded in space.

UNITS OF GOVERNMENT

The units of government and their systems may be thought of as functioning in tiers, all operating within specified geographic boundaries. In the United States the following units are prevalent, with the tiers or layers that cover the largest areas listed first:[2]

[1] Talcott Parsons, *The Social System* (Glencoe, Ill.: The Free Press, 1951), p. 162.

[2] William Anderson, *The Unit of Government in the United States* (Chicago: Public Administration Service, Publication No. 84, 1942), p. 10.

A. Units of central government
   1. The nation
   2. The states
B. Units of local government
   3. The counties (and parishes)
   4. Cities, villages, boroughs, incorporated towns, and townships
   5. School districts
   6. Other special districts

Primary attention is given local units of government in this chapter. Local government may be defined as an organization, the members of which are entitled and expected to make decisions involving people living with them in a subdivision of a state or national government.[3]

Figure 1 shows that few people in the United States are in intimate contact with more than two levels of local government, exclusive of those involving education and special districts. Table 1 presents a summary of the number of local governmental units in the United States from 1942 to 1967.

TABLE 1
Types of Government in the United States

Types of Government	Number of Units			
	1967	1962	1952	1942
Total	81,299	91,237	105,798	155,116
U.S. government	1	1	1	1
States	50	50	50	48
Counties	3,049	3,043	3,052	3,050
Municipalities	18,048	18,000	16,807	16,220
Townships and towns	17,105	17,142	17,202	18,919
School districts	21,782	34,678	56,346	108,579
Special districts	21,264	18,323	12,340	8,299

Source: Based on U. S. Bureau of the Census, *Governments in the United States, 1967*. The definition of special districts changed between 1952 and 1962 so as to include about 10 per cent more agencies within this category. The 1952 data are adjusted to include units in Alaska and Hawaii.

[3] Duane Lockard, "Local Government," *International Encyclopedia of the Social Sciences,* Vol. 9, p. 452.

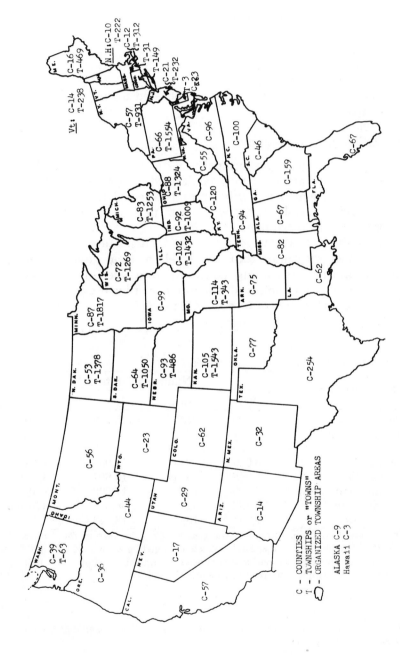

FIGURE 1. Number and location of County and Township governments, 1967.

C – COUNTIES
T – TOWNSHIPS or "TOWNS"
◯ – ORGANIZED TOWNSHIP AREAS

ALASKA C–9
Hawaii C–3

TYPES OF LOCAL GOVERNMENT

The local governing bodies in Australia, Canada, West Germany, Switzerland and the United States are similar in that the governments functioning at the national and intermediate levels allow local units a very broad range of discretionary authority and independence. So-called "home rule" does not by any means permit total autonomy because legislatures through general laws and the courts do restrain local government. Nevertheless, the idea of home rule originating as a legal concept in the late nineteenth century "contradicts the principle of municipal (and other local) inferiority that previously stood as a basic rule of law."[4] In fact local units "are authorized to undertake on their own responsibility many important functions. In such cases, local governments are far more than the ultimate administrative extensions of the national government. This viable type of local government exists in relatively few societies . . . with the forms found in the United States and Canada probably representing the most highly developed and by far the most successful in existence. In fact, the claim to 'democracy' in the United States rests fully as much upon the extent to which local governmental units are allowed to run their own affairs as upon any other basic factor."[5]

But as organizational complexities arise, local units in industrialized and differentiated societies often fail to use their legal rights to independence and autonomy.[6] In rural areas local government may be the weakest of the governmental systems. "In the United States (although there is great variation) the role of local government expanded greatly with the maturation of industrial society in the first half of the twentieth century; protective, regulatory, welfare, planning, economic promotion, cultural, and other activities were initiated or expanded . . . In smaller rural or suburban communities, local government ranges from the moribund to the fairly vital."[7]

Great Britain and the Scandinavian countries have local governments that Lockard calls, "unitary-decentralized systems."

[4] Ibid., p. 452.

[5] T. Lynn Smith and Paul E. Zopf, Jr., *Principles of Inductive Rural Sociology* (Philadelphia: F. A. Davis Co., 1970) p. 377.

[6] Arthur J. Vidich and Joseph Bensman, *Small Town in Mass Society* (Princeton, N.J.: Princeton University Press, 1958).

[7] Lockard, "Local Government," p. 453.

As early as the fifteenth century in England merchant guilds and borough councils originated the rudiments of local self government, one of the characteristics Max Weber noted as being absent in oriental and most other societies that remained traditional. In the Scandinavian nations a fair degree of autonomy has been allowed the local governments since the early nineteenth century. Although parliaments generally remain the supreme source of local authority in countries with "unitary-decentralized systems," local councils and other bodies have considerable decision-making authority.[8]

In France, the Mediterranean countries, Latin America (with the exception of Brazil which has a Federal System), and Japan the most common form of local government is carried through agents appointed and under the control of the central government.[9] Smith and Zopf[10] write that this is a common and widely distributed type, noting that the local agency is merely an extension of the arm of the central government as in Latin America, communist countries, and in earlier times among societies such as the Medes and Persians. In this form "orders . . . flow from the central government to the smallest of the local units . . ."[11]

The extent of centralization of some of these systems is surprising to students of organization accustomed to the federalized decentralized systems such as in the United States. One of the authors remembers with disbelief first learning how in Costa Rica, a relatively democratic country, the central government controlled the local schools to the extent that exactly the same lesson in arithmetic was being taught at the same hour every day from the smallest village to San Jose, and that the minister of education signed the salary check of each teacher.

In communist nations the area of local independence is narrow and extends to minor matters, but local agencies are extensive and their functions are rigorously applied. Treatment of local officials who apply funds to other purposes may be very harsh. The discipline of the Communist party is a means of detailed policy control. Lockard notes that this control is not greatly different from extreme forms of party boss control in some cities in the United States, except that in the latter the system depends

[8] Ibid., p. 454.
[9] Ibid.
[10] Smith and Zopf, Jr., *Inductive Rural Sociology.*
[11] Ibid. p. 379.

upon local insularity for control whereas under communism power resides with national party leaders.[12] In general it is maintained that control and government on all levels will become easier as "individualist attitudes" of capitalism are extinguished. If individualist attitudes survive, "it is necessary to change the basic structure of the farm as soon as possible and to set up multipurpose work teams or sections . . . (This) by itself will not necessarily lead to success . . . (But) it is necessary to maintain a constant improvement in all forms of educational work in the collective. This is the only way to create real collectivists."[13]

THE COUNTY AS A SOCIAL SYSTEM

Counties in the U.S. may range in population from one or two thousand to several million people; they range in area from one square mile to twenty thousand square miles; their governing boards have twenty-seven different titles and are composed of memberships ranging from one to fifty.[14]

Counties may also resemble each other. From the smallest to the largest they handle growing sums of money. They are charged with increasingly diverse duties and are proliferated with a growing number of special-function boards. Certain federal and state legislation, notably that dealing with public welfare, agriculture, and public health, depends upon the county for partial execution of its provisions and thus tends to standardize certain segments of county activity.

Except in New England, where the township prevails as an important local unit, the county is an agent of the state for law enforcement, judicial administration, the conducting of elections, highway provision and maintenance, educational administration, and other matters. Some counties have acquired additional functions such as the ownership and maintenance of airport facilities. All these functions are centered in the county seat. Slightly less than half of all county-seat towns have fewer

[12] Lockard, "Local Government," p. 456.

[13] O. I. Zotova and V. V. Novikov, "The Development of Collectivist Attitudes Among Agricultural Workers," in G.V. Osipov, ed., *Town, Country and People* (London: Tavistock Publications, 1969), p. 217.

[14] William Anderson and Edward W. Weidner, *State and Local Government in the United States* (New York: Henry Holt and Co., 1951), pp. 458-462.

than 2,500 inhabitants and about half of all counties are definitely rural.[15]

THE TOWNSHIP AND THE TOWN

Although many have idealized the town meeting and other features of the town in New England, the township and the town meeting as they exist today, find few supporters. Thus, Anderson and Weidner write: "Man has become too busy for town meetings. In an age of specialization, he demands that his representatives. do the principal debating and deciding. If town meetings are held, he responds in most instances by not attending."[16] In those states (New Jersey, New York, Michigan, and Wisconsin) where the coexistence of township and county tends to splinter local government, townships are besieged by two opposing ills. Many are too small, both in area and population, to have sufficient tax monies to perform services. Others are in fringe areas near large cities, endowed with population, resources, and tremendous need for services, but are unable to perform them adequately because of the limited duties turned over to townships by state law. In the one case there is not enough need to warrant a separate unit of government and in the other there is too much for the township to handle. It has been noted that over 85 percent of the 17,214 American townships in existence are rural local governments performing a limited range of services for nearly 11 million people.[17]

MUNICIPALITIES

Municipalities that are incorporated places possess the powers of general government and number more than 18,000 in the United States. Approximately 65 percent of the population lives in such incorporated places. Moreover, more than 75 percent of the municipalities have less than 2,500 inhabitants and are classified as rural-nonfarm. In the 13,000 municipalities of this category 9,500,000 inhabitants reside, but this number constitutes

[15] Alvin L. Bertrand, ed. *Rural Sociology* (New York: McGraw-Hill Co., 1959) p. 256.

[16] Anderson and Weidner, *State and Local Government,* p. 472.

[17] Bertrand, *Rural Sociology,* p. 257.

less than 10 percent of the total population of the municipalities.[18]

SCHOOL DISTRICTS

In keeping with the ideal of making education the service and responsibility of local people, American school districts have been formed throughout the nation that are relatively free from external political interference and influence. There were 21,782 school districts with independent status in 1967. Local boards, with their own taxing powers and subject to statutory and constitutional limitations, control them. More than 23,000 additional public school systems are operated as part of state, county, municipal or township governments. The independent school districts have decreased markedly in the last two decades due to consolidation, annexation, and abolition in rural areas. However, the basic principle of local control unique to America prevails, especially in rural areas.[19]

SPECIAL-FUNCTION BOARDS
AT THE COUNTY LEVEL

Perhaps the most important development in county government in the United States, especially in recent years, is the growth of special-function boards and commissions attached to the local units of government. Their growth as separate agencies related to the county governing boards is to be accounted for by the lack of trust higher levels of government have for the local units as well as by the desire on the part of the higher level units to retain control.

In the typical case, a state legislature vests in the county a function, such as health, welfare or planning, in which there is both state and local interest. It not only makes the performance of this function compulsory, but specifies that a structure such as a welfare board be established to administer the activity. The relation of the special-function board to the county governing body varies. At one extreme the governing body of the county may provide detailed supervision and financial control; at the

[18] Ibid., p. 256.
[19] Ibid.

other extreme the special-function board may be independent. The complexity and unwieldy nature of county government is certainly not improved by the proliferation of special-function boards and commissions, of which some counties now have as many as eight or ten.

The most recent special-function boards deal with airports, local planning and construction and maintenance of parks. Boards involving agriculture, assessment, election administration, finance, health, highways, hospitals, libraries, penal administration, personnel, recreation, schools, and welfare are also common. The proliferation of these special-function boards often proceeds to the extent that several separate units may be involved in administering one function. The existence of two boards administering welfare in a county is not uncommon. One administers the categorical aid program for the blind, aged and dependent children under the United States Social Security Act and one supervises the county's institutions.

SPECIAL DISTRICTS

In addition to special-function boards and commissions over which the governing bodies of the minor civil divisions exercise at least some control, the states have created many special or *ad hoc* districts for special purposes over which the local units may have no control. The most common unit of this type is the school district, but such units also exist for water control, irrigation, roads and bridges, urban improvements, urban utilities, public housing, soil conservation, port development and other purposes. Table 2 indicates the distribution of special districts, including special-function and *ad hoc* units. The soil conservation district, for instance, is a type of governmental unit—a social system of considerable importance in all states.

BASIC NATURE OF RURAL GOVERNMENTAL SOCIAL SYSTEMS

The bases of our local governmental units, laid down in an agricultural, comparatively non-mobile era are essentially Gemeinschaft-like in character. As our countryside has become more urbanized and the jobs we expect of government more varied and regulatory, the Gesellschaft-like influences have

TABLE 2
Number of Special Districts Other than School Districts in 1967, by State

Number of Districts	States
2,000 or more	California, Illinois
1,000 to 1,999	Kansas, Pennsylvania, Texas
500 to 999	Colorado, Idaho, Indiana, Missouri, Nebraska, New York, Oregon, Washington
250 to 499	Alabama, Arkansas, Florida, Georgia, Iowa, Kentucky, Louisiana, Mississippi, New Jersey, North Dakota, Tennessee
50 to 249	Arizona, Delaware, Maine, Maryland, Michigan, Minnesota, Montana, Nevada, New Hampshire, New Mexico, North Carolina, Ohio, Oklahoma, Rhode Island, South Carolina, South Dakota, Utah, Vermont, West Virginia, Wisconsin, Wyoming
Under 50	District of Columbia, Hawaii, Virginia
21,782	U.S. Total

Source: U. S. Bureau of the Census, Census of Governments: 1967, Vol. 1., *Governmental Organization.*

been felt. Our expectations of local government performance seem to be dual, and we alternately ride each horn of the dilemma.

> ... the traditional theory of democracy in the United States has emphasized the importance of keeping the conduct of the public services, which are the real ends of all local government, constantly under the scrutiny of the community.... On the other hand, it has become apparent that a multiplicity of governmental units tends to defeat efforts to obtain economy and efficiency in the conduct of public affairs. Communities are created which have neither the population nor the tax paying capacity to support the essential local services. Within these communities the ends of local self-government cannot be achieved and the democratic ideal becomes impossible of fulfillment.[20]

[20] William S. Carpenter, "The Problems of Service Levels," *The Annals,* Vol. 292 (May, 1954), p. 127.

The reader will at once recognize the Gemeinschaft concept in the ideal of constant community scrutiny of the conduct of public services. The citizen bent upon keeping tab on his local government will need contact with some board member or county supervisor; he will need officials who are not too busy to stop and chat in the post office, or board members who have time to set around the courthouse to hear most of what's going on, a person who's easy to say "hello" to, and who makes a man feel he has a right and a duty to hear all the news about what's happening in the courthouse. That is Gemeinschaft-like local government.

The reader will also recognize the Gesellschaft elements of the above quotation in "the efforts to obtain economy and efficiency in the conduct of public affairs." A man gets irritated at needless bungling. Any analysis of the local governmental social system can be successful only as long as the often contradictory character of local government is remembered.

The responsive official is obviously Gemeinschaft-oriented. His finger is on the pulse of his community; his ear is at the grass roots. He listens, he tells, and he acts. He tries very hard to act within the limits of broad acceptance of the majority of his constituents.

"The politicians dislike the aloof, technically competent, and sometimes condescending bureaucrats. The latter resent the hurly-burly methods and attitudes of the politicians and the pressure sometimes put on themselves to do favors for the politicians' friends. The politicians keep repeating that the bureaucrat has never won an election. (On the other hand) the bureaucrat criticizes the politician for his constant ear-to-the-ground attitude and his personal rather than impersonal approach to problems. Both types of competition, in fact, produce roughly the type of personality called for. The politician has to be responsive to his constituents even when they are in his opinion, wrong. He represents the human and the personal side of government..."[21]

The age of specialization, professionalization, and efficiency has not yet reached most of the counties in the United States. With a few notable exceptions, the atmosphere, organization, and procedures used in many rural counties, especially in regard

---

[21] Jessie Bernard, *American Community Behavior* (New York: Dryden Press, 1949), p. 240.

to elective offices, are very similar to those of fifty years ago. Most county coroners do not use modern methods of inquiring into deaths that seem to be questionable. Some assessors have improved their techniques, but many still resist the use of aerial surveys and other devices for checking property valuations for tax purposes. Registrars of deeds are likely to be painstakingly copying by hand various records that could be photographed or otherwised much more easily and efficiently. The sheriff is likely to be using old rule-of-thumb methods of crime detection.[22]

As the special jobs assigned to the county have become more numerous, the need has grown for the bureaucrat. Special boards, commissions and bureaus, generally with a special-purpose staff under their supervision, have become common on the county level.

The ends, objectives and norms of local government. Some of the objectives of local government have been suggested in the foregoing paragraphs. The institutionalizing of force and power is represented in the local governmental picture by the various law-enforcing branches of government. Other than this major objective, the local units concern themselves mostly with education, highways, public health, and welfare.

In a period when there is general disillusion especially by farmers concerning what some call the growth of the "welfare state" it may be well to remember that "the first effective non-business demands for action came from farmers . . . 'rugged individualists', they were the first major segment of the society to demand collective action."[23] The more moderate Granger movement increased the power of government and its services and, as noted in the chapter on farmer's organizations, other segments of the farmer's movement, particularly the Nonpartisan League, carried through programs which were radical even by contemporary leftist standards.

As several sociologists have noted, farm people in the United States tend to exercise the franchise in larger proportions than others and to believe in its efficacy. Farmers by and large stand for regulation of banks and corporations, such as those transporting goods they sell, and measures designed to promote

---

[22] Anderson and Weidner, *State and Local Government,* pp. 476-477.

[23] Charles R. Adrian, *Governing Our Fifty States and Their Communities* (New York: McGraw-Hill, 1967) p. 19.

honesty in government. They oppose minimum wage laws, softening of the criminal code, pensions for occupational groups, increases in taxation, civil rights legislation and workmen's compensation laws.[24] But since farmers are both owners hiring labor and themselves laborers they sometimes vote with laboring groups and other times with management. Buying of votes, "pork barrel" and "party boss" control of voting on an impersonal basis, are less common in rural than urban areas. In fact these practices result from the Gesellschaft-like nature of modern urban life.

In an activity so all-embracing as government, it is inevitable that individuals and sub-systems have their own objectives which they hope can be accomplished through the local governmental process. A drainage bill and appropriation might benefit many, but it may never have been initiated except for the somewhat selfish need for land drainage on the part of a few. Highways and roads certainly benefit all—even those who don't travel them. The maximum benefit from any one bit of road repair might accrue to the person near whose property the road lies. What is suggested here is that abstract "general welfare" is very difficult to embody in laws and that as long as a government needs individuals to set its direction, that direction will bear the marks of the individual concept of "good."[25] "One man's meat is another man's poison," an adage at least as old as Aesop, is the operating principle. The politician tries to see that what he serves is regarded by most as somewhat palatable, even though the dish is chiefly concocted according to his own taste. By and large, as long as the officials carry on the work of the government without violating openly the norms of their constituency, and as long as a number of people other than the officials benefit from the government's activity, the governmental body is within the area of acceptance of the populace.

Accounts are replete with the misfeasance, malfeasance and nonfeasance of office. Lancaster, for example, suggests that county government is largely in the hands of the "court house gang,"[26] a clique which monopolizes the control in its own inter-

[24] Smith and Zopf, Jr. *Inductive Rural Sociology*, p. 376.

[25] See David Truman, *The Governmental Process* (New York: Alfred A. Knopf, 1951) for a fuller discussion.

[26] Lane W. Lancaster, *Government in Rural America* (New York: D. Van Nostrand, Inc. 1937), p. 78.

est with little regard for the general welfare, let alone the universal principles by which this might be furthered. He notes that the process of getting re-elected, if there is competition, often requires that the office holder use his position not only to "feather his own nest" but to feather the nests of those he wishes to vote for him. What must be remembered is that the very lack of concern on the part of the citizenry shows that the office holder is not violating a principle held in great esteem by the populace. The office holder may not be the most efficient, he may cater only to his own selfish interests, but he must be sufficiently responsive to get re-elected, and that is essentially the number one political virtue. No system of written legalized norms can supersede those grounded in the mores of everyday living.

> It is fitting and proper for the community to expect higher standards among its public servants than in private life. But in the end administrative morality will reflect the morality of the community it serves. A society . . . in which the clever man who can make a "fast buck" is eulogized, and in which private speculation is often concealed in acts of so-called public policy, ought not to be surprised if an occasional bureaucrat strays from the straight and narrow path.[27]

The formal expression of norms is to be found in the ponderous compendia of election laws, in the "watch-dog" role of the political parties, and in the many non-official but formally organized groups such as municipal leagues, civic groups, and the League of Women Voters.

> From inability to control our complex of governments by the ballot box, we Americans have attempted to control government by means of parties and have then found it necessary to attempt control of the complex party mechanisms. Failing there, we have attempted to control by concerted shouting at them through the organized alertness of civic associations![28]

"In a country where the 'politician' is a symbol of corruption

---

[27] *Report of Sub-Committee on Labor and Public Welfare, Ethical Standards in Government,* U.S. Senate, 82nd Congress, 1st session, p. 10.

[28] Richard S. Childs, "Citizen Organization for Control of Government," *The Annals,* Vol. 292 (March, 1954), pp. 134-135.

and dishonesty, if not dishonor, where a large majority of parents, as reported by the Gallup poll, prefer *not* to have their children enter the public service, where the bureaucracy is regarded as a legitimate object of ridicule and even revulsion and the term 'bureaucrat' is a nasty name,"[29] who becomes the county official, what is his social rank?

SOCIAL RANK OF MEMBERS OF GOVERNING BODIES

The members of rural county governing bodies are predominantly farmers, with a few businessmen and retired persons. A distinct difference between the governing bodies of counties and those of city councils or state legislatures is the virtual absence of lawyers on the former. Professional persons, such as physicians and dentists, are also much less frequently represented on county governing bodies. The governing boards of counties are drawn heavily from the older age groups. Not more than 10 to 12 percent are under forty-five years of age. About half of them have more than an eighth-grade education and not more than 20 percent have ever attended colleges.[30]

In some states, members of the county governing body hold key positions in their political parties and in some cases are supported by their own politicial machines. In other states, however, members of the governing bodies take little or no part in political party activities. Through their power to grant or withhold favors of various kinds, the members of the county board exercise considerable influence over all county offices. In rural America, persons of high social rank are seldom represented on the county governing boards. Persons of high rank often rely upon informal means and pressures, including control of capital resources and credit, to influence the county boards on which persons of lower rank usually sit. In crisis situations or in areas where it is believed that the culture of the group in control may be threatened, representatives from "higher" community ranks are often elected to the governing boards. In a study of how rural communities obtained hospitals, an operation of considerable

[29] Peter H. Odegard, "Toward a Responsible Bureaucracy," *The Annals,* Vol. 292 (March, 1954), p. 29.
[30] Anderson and Weidner, pp. 458-462.

community importance, Miller[31] found that local government officials played less significant roles than self-employed businessmen, professional workers, employed managers, and farm owners and operators. Interestingly, the only regions which favored the civil government as sponsoring agents for the development of a hospital were the Southeast and the Southwest, areas in which it is claimed that governmental officials have relatively high rank, in part because of the historical importance of the race problem. Miller's study of social action in rural areas is a clear demonstration of how persons of high social rank in communities use the office holder of lower rank to obtain desired action or to prevent action not desired.

STATUS-ROLES AND POWER

Table 3 shows the elective county administrative offices in the United States. In general, these status-roles lack functional specificity. Although most county governing boards have devised formal and informal means of providing some central leadership, in general the county is left headless in the sense that authority is not centralized at one point.

In Michigan, Preiss asked seventy-four township supervisors, members of the governing bodies of their counties, what they considered to be their main duties. Table 4 indicates how little consensus these local officials have of their status-roles and how functionally-diffuse their status-roles really are. The difficulty rural governmental officials would have adhering to universalistic principles is revealed by Table 5, which presents the results of how township officials say they maintain contact with their constituents. Many said they let their constituents come to them.

In general, election to local governmental office is less dependent on technical competence than on knowing the right people. One writer described an effective local politician as follows: "He moved among the country people with the energy of a Henry Clay, smiling confidently, speaking to everybody, pausing frequently for a more intimate word."[32] Informants were questioned for an explanation of this man's success and the follow-

[31] Paul A. Miller, *Community Health Action—A Study of Community Contrast* (East Lansing: The Michigan State College Press, 1953), pp. 22 and 46.

[32] J. B. Harrison, "Anse Little: Successful Politician in Bloody Beaumont County, Kentucky," (Unpublished manuscript, Michigan State University.)

TABLE 3
Elective County Administrative Offices in the United States in
Addition to the Elected Executive, 1967

Office*	Number of States in which Found
Assessor	29
Attorney or solicitor	38
Auditor or comptroller	19
County clerk	23
Clerk of court	35
Collector or commissioner of taxes	14
Constable (as a county office)	28
Justice of the Peace	26
Coroner	27
Public administrator	6
Recorder	9
Registrar of deeds	18
Registrar of probate	3
Registrar of wills	3
Sheriff	46
Superintendent of schools	21
Surveyor or engineer	27
Treasurer	40

* Cases where the same person had dual functions, e.g., clerk-assessor, were counted as two offices; Townships in Connecticut and Rhode Island were treated as counties.

Source: U.S. Bureau of the Census, Census of Governments, 1967, Vol. 6, No. 1, *Popularly Elected Officials of State and Local Government,* 1968, Table 15.

ing summary was written: "It's because he has something to offer them and that's the only reason.... There's a Post Office in every hollow in this county and he's got all of these.... W.P.A. came along, about every other family was on relief and dependent on Little. You just can't beat a set-up like that."[33]

These examples stress the functionally-diffuse, particularistic, and affective nature of role performance and power in rural government and politics. Universalistic norms and procedures such as *Robert's Rules of Order* in decision-making, and civil service rules and regulations for employing and discharging functionaries, are uncommon. Responsibilities of incumbents in office,

[33] Ibid.

TABLE 4

Supervisors' Conception of Their Main Duties as Revealed by a Probing Study of Seventy-Four Township Supervisors in Michigan, 1952

Category	Number of Times Mentioned[1]
Assessment of property	47
Road and bridge maintenance	24
Taxation problems	25[2]
County and township committees	19
Health and welfare	12
Represent community wherever necessary	11
Drainage problems	7
Public school affairs	4
Attend to county business	4
Zoning	3
Building and construction	3
Listen to complaints	2
Keep people satisfied	2
No main duties	10

Source: Edward W. Weidner and Jack Preiss, "Rural Local Government and Politics and Adult Education," in C. P. Loomis, et al., *Rural Social Systems and Adult Education* (East Lansing: Michigan State College Press, 1953), p. 277.

[1] Respondents were free to name as many categories as they wished.

[2] Five supervisors believed their job was to keep taxes down.

far from being functionally specific with respect to duties, frequently require that friends, relatives, and powerful persons in the voting precinct be served. No doubt such functional diffuseness has caused county manager government, or a unified county executive, to be advocated by political scientists for several decades.

Some of the disadvantages in the headlessness of local governing bodies have been overcome in other ways. In some states, chairmen of governing bodies, such as probate judges, exercise managerial powers. In other counties, auditors have been appointed to exercise such functions. In Indiana and Minnesota the county auditor, and in Illinois the clerk, have considerable power and in some respects resemble county executives. According to Anderson and Weidner, "in a majority of the states and in a substantial number of counties (about 50 percent in Wisconsin, for example), there is a tendency to make an appointive or elective administrative official, or the chairman of the governing

TABLE 5

Ways in which Supervisors Contact Constituents, Seventy-four Michigan Township Supervisors, 1952

Category	Frequency of Mention
Personal contact and visiting in general	42
Visiting at assessment time (once a year)	26
Public meetings	22
People come with problems	15
Farm organization meetings	9
Through the township board	7
Telephone	9
Lodge or civic organization meetings	4
Regard meetings as generally ineffective	8
Used own judgment primarily	4
Few contacts with constituents	3

Source: Edward W. Weidner and Jack Preiss, "Rural Local Government and Politics and Adult Education," in C. P. Loomis, et. al., *Rural Social Systems and Adult Education* (East Lansing: Michigan State College Press, 1953), p. 289.

body, at least a limited county executive."[34] Other means of improving local government require the introduction of the merit system, modernization of purchasing methods, and the consolidating of departments.

SANCTIONS

In the functioning of governmental systems, both rewards and penalties are important. "At the very least the county governing body is a group that every county officer, whether directly elected or not, has to reckon with."[35] An account of how one local politician used penalties to achieve his ends is given by a local school teacher who refused to "kowtow." She reported: "Elias Johnson came around and told me I would have to contribute twenty-five dollars to Little's campaign fund. I told him I wouldn't be beholden to anybody, so I quit and went back to work in a war plant in Louisville. My aunt, though, said she had a family to raise, so she chipped in and is still teaching."[36] This

[34] Anderson and Weidner, p. 482.
[35] Ibid., p. 482.
[36] Harrison, "Anse Little."

incident illustrates the absence of or failure to enforce such universalistic criteria as civil service regulations for employment and promotion. However, such conditions are less common in the United States than in more Gemeinschaft-like societies in Latin America where particularism is much more important for professionals.

FACILITIES

The county courthouse and other facilities of local governmental systems in rural areas are often very poorly maintained and in contrast with local schools, churches, and business establishments appear dingy and untidy. Usually public facilities controlled by technicians and professionals such as hospitals, libraries, and highways are better maintained than the rural courthouse. Seldom are all the offices of the governing bodies and special function groups in the same buildings. Often officials of different agencies who deal with the same people daily do not know one another and have little occasion to discuss common problems, partially because they are often housed in widely separated places.

TERRITORIALITY

As counties range in area, population and taxable wealth, they also range tremendously in their ability to supply essential services effectively.

> Many communities simply cannot afford to provide a level of social services at all commensurate with the ideal of equality of opportunity. In spite of the fact that the poorer states and localities generally make a greater effort—in terms of their taxable resources—to raise revenue than do the richer units, they are not able to maintain satisfactory service standards.[37]

Independent studies in Minnesota, Texas, and California,[38] conclude that high per capita costs and low levels of services

[37] Alvin H. Hansen and Harvey S. Perloff, *State and Local Finance in the National Economy* (New York: W. W. Norton and Co., 1944), p. 15.

[38] "The Reorganization of Local Government in Minnesota," *Minnesota Municipalities*, Vol. 18 (February, 1933), p. 102; H. C. Bradshaw and L. P. Gabbard,

prevail in counties below the 30,000 to 50,000 population level. Fixed costs of the smallest government unit contribute to the relatively high costs of the small counties. Table 6 shows that most of the counties of the United States are under 50,000 in population. Although county reorganization and consolidation

TABLE 6
Frequency Distribution of Counties, by Size of Population, 1970

Size of County	Number of Counties	Percent of Total
Under 1,000	26	0.8
1,000 to 5,000	299	9.5
5,000 to 10,000	554	17.6
10,000 to 50,000	1,583	50.4
50,000 to 100,000	332	10.6
100,000 and Over	347	11.0
Total*	3,141	100.0

*Includes county equivalents.
Source: 1970 Census of Population, *Number of Inhabitants, United States Summary,* p. x.

have been persistently recommended for decades, only a few consolidations have taken place. According to Hansen and Perloff:

> The forces which stand in the way of the rationalization of local units of government are formidable. They include (a) local loyalties, which induce people to resist the dissolution of local governmental units regarded as their own; (b) tradition, or the tendency to think of arrangements made in the past as having an inherent rightness and permanence; (c) desire of local office holders to hold onto their jobs; (d) resistance of individuals and businesses that are getting special favors from existing local governments; (f) resistance of local units that stand to lose some of their taxable resources; (g) urban-rural antagonisms especially where it is felt that a change might involve additional burdens or a loss of power.[39]

"Possible Savings through Changes in Local Government," (College Station: Texas AES Bulletin 540, April, 1937); and Charles Aiken, "California—Proposed County Consolidation," *National Municipal Review,* Vol. 23 (June, 1934), p. 327.

[39] Hansen and Perloff, *State and Local Finance,* p. 95.

Such are the forces which have thus far maintained the status-quo of territoriality in county government. It is interesting to relate them to the concepts and the social factors treated in this chapter. Items a and b are Gemeinschaft-like, particularistic, and affective. Furthermore, they reflect sentiments held not only by special interest groups, but by large segments of the population, as does item f. Item c is an example of self-motivated interests on the part of the "politician" and the "bureaucrat," while d illustrates the same motive on the part of non-officials. Item e could well include those whose "nests were feathered" by the ingratiating politician. Item g probably reflects in part the strain where a Gemeinschaft-like way of life is yielding gradually to the more Gesellschaft-like behavior. All in all, the items provide a good example of the manner in which diverse and often opposing interests converge; they illustrate how the office holder can be selfish and corrupt, but nevertheless chooses a line of action harmonious with the will of the constituents; and how the democratic ideal of self-government can be valued beyond considerations of efficiency. The persistence of the county reorganization movement as well as the resistance of the population the country over are evidence of the tremendous importance of territoriality in the governmental social system. This resistance represents one of the best examples of boundary maintenance known to the authors.

PARTICULARISTIC VERSUS UNIVERSALISTIC GOVERNMENT: MEXICO AND THE UNITED STATES

If we place the governments of Mexico and the United States on a continuum with the Gesellshaft-like type at one pole and the Gemeinschaft-like type at the other pole, Mexico would fall toward the Gemeinschaft pole, the United States toward the Gesellschaft pole. The social relationships involved in rural government of both countries would fall nearer the Gemeinschaft pole than the relationships which are chiefly involved at the national level.[40]

---

[40] For a comparable analysis including the Dominican Republic and Pre-Castro Cuba see John C. McKinney and Charles P. Loomis in "Application of Gemeinschaft as Related to Other Typologies," in Introduction to *Community and*

Campbell and associates[41] studied the "sense of political efficacy," that is, the feeling that individual political action does or can have an impact upon political process, and "sense of citizen duty" in the United States, through a scientific national sample. Through the use of Guttman scaling devices they developed measures for these characteristics. In general, these measures were highly correlated with education and income, with farm operators having lower scores. That is, these groups felt that they and others had little personal political influence and had little sense of citizen duty. Farm operators and unskilled workers were at the lower end of the scale in this respect, followed in sequence by skilled and semiskilled workers, other white collar employees, and professional and managerial workers. In both cases the South, the most rural section of the country, ranked at the bottom. This study demonstrated that "the more strongly a person feels a sense of obligation to discharge his civic duties, the more likely he is to be politically active."[42] It was also demonstrated that members of friendship groups and families tended to have the same political preferences.

No similar study has been made of Mexico but it is well known that governmental relations on all levels are much more personal than in the United States and that bribery, graft, and extortion are much more common.[43] An insightful description of Mexican government is that of Tannenbaum, who summarized the present situation as follows: "The alternative to a strong president is rebellion. The alternative to political decisions made in detail and enforced by the president is decisions which no one can enforce. The fact of the matter is that the president must decide because no one else's decision will be accepted. The older tradition that the king rules has survived in modern dress: the president rules. He rules rather than governs, and must do so if

---

Society: Gemeinschaft and Gesellschaft, by Ferdinand Toennies, translated by Charles Loomis.

[41] Angus Campbell, et al., *The Voter Decides* (Evanston: Row, Peterson and Company, 1954), pp. 187 ff.

[42] Ibid., p. 199.

[43] Nathan L. Whetten, *Rural Mexico* (Chicago: University of Chicago Press, 1948) pp. 545 ff. For survey data based upon probability samples supporting this thesis, see Charles P. Loomis et al. *Linkages of Mexico and the United States,* (E. Lansing, Mich.: MSU Agricultural Experiment Station Research Bulletin 14, 1966) pp. 72 and 73.

he is to survive. . . ."[44] The president makes sure that his friends and his friends only control the Senate which decides who is the "rightfully elected governor." This is necessary because there is frequently more than one claimant. "The president controls the election of the members to the Congress and the Senate. No one can be elected to either without his consent and approval."[45] National elections for a future president are always controlled by the president in office. "The candidate who has official approval is certain of election . . . the election itself is never in doubt." Opposition members know "their people will probably not be permitted to vote; that if they do vote their vote will not be counted; that, if counted, and sent into the final test in the national Congress, it will be disregarded; and finally, that if elected by some strange accident, they could not govern."[46] An election for the "ins" provides the opportunity for candidates to travel, renew friendships, and build fences. For the "outs" it is a rehearsal and preparation for revolution.

"Watching Mexican politics closely, one begins to discern the drift of the new alignment by noting changes in the cabinet, and asking: Whose friends are they?"[47] The same holds for Congress and the manner in which the president shifts the generals of the army which is a final source of power. "Like a good father, the president cannot say no, and if he does, the no is not final. Surely the father's heart can be mellowed, his kindness reawakened, his true virtues as the father of his children brought to bear upon the issues in hand."[48] If this proves impossible, "It becomes essential to drive him from office. There is no alternative between personal government and revolution. Inefficiency, corruption, cruelty—if personal—are all acceptable. What is not acceptable is the cold, impersonal, efficient government."[49]

Although political behavior as manifest in elections in both the United States and Mexico tends to be less Gesellschaft-like than economic behavior such as one finds in the operation of banks, it is less Gemeinschaft-like in the United States than in

[44] Frank Tannenbaum, "The United States and Mexico," *Foreign Affairs,* Vol. 27, No. 1 (October, 1948), pp. 44-57.
[45] Ibid.
[46] Ibid.
[47] Ibid.
[48] Ibid.
[49] Ibid.

Mexico. The status-role of the Mexican official, whether local or national, makes relationships more affectual and is governed more by particularistic norms and ascription. Responsibilities are more functionally diffuse than in the United States. The two societies are more alike on the rural level and in the lower social class levels.

SELECTED REFERENCES

Adrian, Charles R. *Governing Our Fifty States and Their Communities.* New York: McGraw-Hill, 1967.

Adrian, Charles R. "Local Politics", *International Encyclopedia of the Social Sciences,* Vol. 9, pp. 459-464.

Anderson, William and Edward W. Weidner. *State and Local Government in the United States.* New York: Henry Holt and Co., 1951.

Baker, Gordon E. *Rural Versus Urban Political Power.* New York: Doubleday and Co., Inc., 1955.

Banfield, Edward C. *Government Project.* Glencoe: The Free Press, 1951.

Bertrand, Alvin L., ed. *Rural Sociology—An Analysis of Contemporary Rural Life.* New York: McGraw-Hill, 1958, Ch. 17.

Hardin, Charles M. *The Politics of Agriculture.* Glencoe: The Free Press, 1952.

Janowitz, Morris (ed.) *Community Political Systems.* New York: The Free Press, 1961.

Lancaster, Lane W. *Government in Rural America.* New York: D. Van Nostrand, Inc., 1937.

Lockard, Duane "Local Government", *International Encyclopedia of the Social Sciences,* Vol. 9, pp. 451-459.

Loomis, C. P., et. al. *Rural Social Systems and Adult Education.* East Lansing: Michigan State College Press, 1953. See Chapter 12, "Rural Local Government and Politics and Adult Education" by Edward W. Weidner and Jack Preiss.

Vidich, Arthur J. and Joseph Bensman. *Small Town in Mass Society.* Princeton: University Press, 1968.

10

Farmers' Organizations as Social Systems

Like many other occupational groups farmers are not without their organizations. The degree to which farmers have organized and the complexity of their organizations varies greatly. Farmers and peasants in many parts of the world are either without organizations or the existing organizations are ineffective agents either in a political or economic sense. In the United States, however, farmers' organizations are structurally complex and play significant economic, political, and social roles in the lives of rural people.

Most of the farmers' organizations in the United States today have not appeared suddenly and full-blown. The major farmers' organizations represent the culmination of what is often referred to as the "farmers' movement." Over the years, this movement has been a series of attempts, often inept and sometimes violent, on the part of farmers to secure relief from what they consider to be maladjustments. Often these attempts have been crude organizational efforts to obtain a hearing before legislative bodies. In the following quotation, Taylor places the farmers' movement in America in perspective:

> So long as American agriculture was largely a self-sufficient family economic enterprise and was largely represented by home-owning farmers, there was little occasion for a farmers' movement beyond general farmer protests against the quit rents imposed by England in colonial days. Theoretically the self-sufficient farmer had no market or price problems. His sole task was to produce year after year the products for his own food, clothing, and shelter, while he went without those things that he could not produce and, so to speak, let the world go by. But American agriculture never was fully self-sufficient. . . . Indeed, certain areas in Maryland and Virginia, at the very outset of their settlement, were con-

verted into commercialized agriculture, and interestingly enough the first farmers' revolt, as well as later ones, arose in highly commercialized agricultural areas.[1]

Thus, it would seem that the farmers' movement, in its beginning and to a certain extent today, represents an attempt on the part of farmers to adjust to a price and market regime.

In the brief space of this chapter, it is impossible to consider all the attempts of farmers to organize. The point should be made, however, that such attempts have been numerous, diverse, and often short-lived. It is necessary, therefore, to restrict much of the discussion to selected representatives of farmers' organizations today, namely, the Grange, the Farmers' Union, the Farm Bureau, National Farmers Organization (NFO), and farmers' cooperatives.

IMPORTANCE OF FARM ORGANIZATION SYSTEMS

For much of American history, farmers' organizations provided a means through which the individualistic farmer attempted to redress injustice as he saw it and to adjust to economic change. Shover comments as follows:

> The American family farm remained an isolated outpost of traditional free enterprise for long after the economic system passed it by. A common denominator in the panaceas rural America has produced, from sub-treasury and free silver to state administered crop insurance and state-owned elevators, has been an attempt to catch step with an economy characterized by rational price and production controls. Farmers through their protests [and organizations] won a series of transitory victories from the agents of corporate capitalism: fairer railroad rates, protection for cooperative marketing arrangements and even, in the Agricultural Adjustment Administration, a method of initiating production controls. But in the long run the family farmer has not persevered against the system itself. Technological improvements reducing the ratio of labor to output, heavy capital

[1] Carl C. Taylor, et al., *Rural Life in the United States* (New York: Alfred A. Knopf, 1949), pp. 510-511. For a definitive study of farmers' movements in America, see Carl C. Taylor, *The Farmers' Movement* (New York: American Book Company, 1953).

costs, and the advantages of mass production have brought to agriculture the same consolidation movement which long ago smothered the corner grocer and the local craftsmen.[2]

Thus, while numerical strength and objectives fluctuated from time to time, farmers' organizations represented sectors of the rural population politically and economically. They also furnished an arena for social and educational events.

Farmers' organizations as social systems. The crucial importance of the farmers' organizations in the network of social relationships and channels of communication reaching rural people is revealed in a national study.[3] Leaders of most rural organizations in 263 sample counties of the United States were requested to answer the following question:"What other organizations do you work with, or through, in your educational work with adults?" This question was followed by the request: "Check as many as apply," and a list of twenty organizational categories plus an "others (specify)" category.

The leaders of organizations (other than farmers' organizations) most frequently mentioned "farm organizations." The nonfarmers' organizations whose leaders mentioned "farmers' organizations" most frequently were the following: (1) The Cooperative Extension Service units and organizations, (2) Production and Marketing Administration, (3) Soil Conservation Service, (4) Farmers' Home Administration, (5) county supervisors, and (6) schools and libraries. The fact that farmers' organizations are mentioned more frequently than any other category as a channel through which organizations work in adult education programs demonstrates their importance for all change agents.

Functions of farm organizations. At least four functions of the farmers' organizations seem important to mention. Since the farmers' organizations grew up in response to the farmer's efforts to adjust to prices and related problems, one of the most important functions of these organizations has been and still is economic. The very earliest uprising on the part of farmers in the United States centered around the price of tobacco among the Virginia planters. According to Taylor,[4] a tobacco monopoly

---

[2] John L. Shover, *Cornbelt Rebellion* (Urbana: The University of Illinois Press, 1965), p. 1-2.

[3] C. P. Loomis, et al., *Rural Social Systems and Adult Education,* (East Lansing: Michigan State College Press, 1953), Chapter 4.

[4] Taylor, et al., *Rural Life,* p. 511.

was granted by King James I in 1620, but farmer protest was so great that the King withdrew the monopoly charter in the following year. Prices of tobacco were so low in the following two decades that farmers demanded price-fixing. In fact, so many tobacco planters were so deeply in debt that the Virginia Assembly declared that debts might be cancelled upon the payment of 40 per cent in terms of tobacco.

The first of the large farmers' organizations, the Grange, was organized shortly after the Civil War and reached its peak in membership when prices were relatively low. Relatively low farm prices also were associated with the rapid growth of the Farmers' Alliance in the latter part of the 1800's. Similarly, the Farmers' Educational and Cooperative Union, organized in Texas in 1902, and the American Society of Equity, organized in Indiana that same year, experienced their greatest growth in periods of low prices. Even the Farm Bureau and many of the cooperatives made their most significant advances when prices were low during the last great depression.[5]

The Farmers Holiday Association, among the most aggressive of farmers' organizations, centered in Iowa and adjacent states in the early 30's. Farmers picketed, halted milk and livestock deliveries to market, and intervened to prevent the foreclosure of farms. In the "penny auctions," bidders were friends and neighbors who returned the farm to the owner. Genuine bidders found themselves intimidated in various ways. Shover sees the Farmers Holiday Association as "a final attempt of the family farmer to save himself from absorption and annihilation."[6]

In addition to the economic function, the farm organizations constitute powerful pressure groups. In fact, the economic and political functions may be difficult to separate, for political activity often is solely economic in purpose. Throughout the history of the farmers' movement in this country political activity is in evidence. Unlike many of the European countries, however, no farmer or peasant party has persisted for a long period of time in this country.

The Nonpartisan League movement grew up in North Dakota and spread to surrounding states. This movement swept farmers into legislatures and took over banks, elevators, and warehouses

---

[5] See C. P. Loomis and J. A. Beegle, *Rural Social Systems* (New York: Prentice-Hall, Inc., 1950), pp. 627-628.

[6] Shover, *Cornbelt Rebellion,* p. 2.

as instruments of the state government. Due in part to insufficient political experience, however, the entry of the Nonpartisan League into politics was short-lived.[7] According to Taylor,[8] the Grange, Agricultural Wheel, and Farmers' Alliance made themselves felt at both state and national levels. Since 1900 the Farmers' Union, the American Society of Equity, the Nonpartisan League, and the Farm-Labor Party have given the farmer a voice, sometimes even at the national level.

The social and educational functions of these organizations are most readily observed in units at the local level. The local units of the Grange, Farm Bureau, and Farmers' Union provide a meeting ground for informal visiting, discussion, and entertainment on the part of the members. In addition to the informal interaction provided at local meetings, programs of an educational nature are often featured.

According to the findings of a study of adult education in rural areas,[9] 87 per cent of the general farmers' organizations reporting indicated that they were conducting programs and activities of an adult educational nature. A few random examples of educational programs reported in this study are the following: A Farm Bureau discussion group in Ohio considered the cost and administration of local welfare. A Subordinate Grange discussed the problem and decided to make a roadside park from a public dumping ground. The Arkansas Farmers' Union, the membership of which was 25 percent black, practiced democracy in local discussion groups and at the state conventions.

THE STRUCTURE OF THE FARMERS' ORGANIZATIONS

The Grange. The Grange, or technically, the Patrons of Husbandry, was organized in 1867 through the efforts of Oliver Hudson Kelley. The Grange grew rapidly in the next few years and attained a membership estimated at 850,000 in 1875. After 1880

[7] Charles E. Russell, *The Story of the Nonpartisan League* (New York: Harper and Brothers, 1920), pp. 280 ff.

[8] Carl C. Taylor, *Rural Sociology* (New York: Harper and Brothers, 1933), Chapters 27 and 28.

[9] Loomis, et al., *Rural Social Systems and Adult,* Chapter 5 "Adult Educational Programs or Activities of the General Farmers' Organizations and Cooperatives" by Wayne C. Rohrer and Carl C. Taylor, p. 100.

Grange membership declined, but in recent years it has again become as large as in 1875.

The Grange, the first of the large general farmers' organizations, is ritualistic. Membership consists of men, women, and children. Children up to the age of fourteen belong to the Juvenile Grange. The community unit, called the Subordinate Grange, may include all persons over fourteen. The Pomona Grange is the county or district unit, made up of the Subordinate bodies. In addition, there are the State Grange, made up of delegates from Subordinate Granges, and the National Grange, the delegates to which are composed of Masters of State Granges and their wives.

At its height in the 1870's the Grange entered commercial and manufacturing activities. Legislators and other political officials were elected from the organization. Haynes says: "The Granger movement began that radical but tedious revolution of American ideas which is slowly bringing industry under the political power of democracy!"[10] Although the Grange still engages in political activity, it is more restrained than formerly. The importance of social and educational activities, as well as certain cooperative activities, is being emphasized in the Grange today.

In his discussion of agrarian politics, Ziegler points out that the Grange which flourished early in the Midwest where crop specialization had progressed beyond that of most other areas, began to shift eastward. The growth of the Grange in New England and the Middle Atlantic states was related to greater agricultural diversification, a condition that tended to ameliorate the hazards of diversification. Ziegler says: "The shifting of membership of the Grange (two-thirds of its members are now located in New England) was accompanied by a toning down of its early radical indignation. Reflecting the restrained conservatism of farmers more favorably situated to markets than their prairie counterparts, the Grange gradually came to adopt a position in favor of keeping the government as far from the agricultural segment of the economy as possible."[11]

The Farmers' Union. The Farmers' Educational and Cooperative Union of America (the complete name of this organiza-

---

[10] Fred E. Haynes, *Social Politics in the United States* (Boston: Houghton Mifflin Co., 1924), p. 160.

[11] Harmon Ziegler, *Interest Groups in American Society* (Englewood Cliffs: Prentice-Hall, Inc., 1964), p. 171.

tion) was founded in Texas in 1902.[12] Although precise membership figures are difficult to obtain, it is estimated that 250,000 farm families were dues-paying members in 1969.[13] Families belong as units to the Union. Although the Farmers' Union was originally strong in Texas, Louisiana, and Arkansas and later in the South Atlantic states, its center of strength is now in the wheat areas of the Great Plains and in parts of the range-live-stock areas. North Dakota, Oklahoma, Nebraska, and South Dakota are the centers of the Farmers' Union's numerical strength.

The Farmers' Union is similar in structure to the Grange and is organized in local community unions, county unions, state and territorial unions, and a national union. Among the objectives of the Farmers' Union, those of maintaining and protecting the family-type farm, of expanding local and regional farmers' cooperatives, and of educating farm families concerning the economic, social, and cultural problems of agriculture have been especially important. Unlike the Grange, the Farmers' Union has little ritual and no degrees.

There are many strands in the Union's ideology but four are from the central core, according to Crampton. These are: the sense of disadvantage, pacifism, cooperativism, and the family farm ideal.[14] In defending the family farm, Crampton says, "the Union leans heavily on the rural myth, taken here to include reverence for and attachment to the land (which is seen as the ultimate value), respect for the stability arising from property ownership and a close-knit hierarchical family, high valuation on work, rigid morality, individualism, the view that the farmer makes the best citizen of a democracy, and a consciousness that in all these areas the farmer is set apart from (and above) the city man."[15]

The Farmers' Union member is typically a small middle-class, family farmer. While he is generally less affluent than Farm

[12] For a treatment of the early history of the Farmers' Union especially in the South, see Charles P. Loomis, "The Rise and Decline of the North Carolina Farmers' Union," and "Activities of the North Carolina Farmers' Union," *North Carolina Historical Review* (July and October, 1930), Vol. VII, Nos. 3 and 4.

[13] Everett M. Rogers and Rabel J. Burdge, *Social Change in Rural Societies* (New York: Appleton-Century-Crofts, 1972), p. 305.

[14] John A. Crampton, *The National Farmers' Union* (Lincoln: University of Nebraska Press, 1965), p. 7.

[15] Ibid., p. 39.

Bureau or Grange members, the Farmers' Union member is not impoverished.[16]

The National Farmers' Union and the National Board of Farm Organizations helped to secure such legislation as rural free delivery, parcel post, and rural credit. The Farmers' Union Grain Terminal Association in St. Paul is the largest grain-marketing association in the world, and the first cooperative hospital in the United States was the Farmers' Union Cooperative Hospital in Oklahoma.[17]

The Farm Bureau.   The American Farm Bureau Federation, in its earliest phases, was closely allied with the development of agricultural extension work in this country. Although county agents were first employed in the South as early as 1906, the first agent in the North was employed in Broome County, New York, in 1911. Two years later in this county farmers organized the first Farm Bureau Association in order to take a hand in the direction of county agent activities. Similar organizations were soon formed in other states, particularly in Illinois, Iowa, and West Virginia. In 1914 with the passage of the Smith-Lever Act, which made available funds to support extension work on a large scale, the organizational basis of this work had already been established in a number of states.

There were about 1,800,000 memberships in 1970, making it the largest of the farmers' organizations.[18] The major unit of the Farm Bureau is the county bureau, and organizations of the Farm Bureau are to be found in most of the states. In addition, in certain states, there are Junior Farm Bureaus and the Associated Women of the Farm Bureau Federation. The Farm Bureau is especially strong in such states as Illinois, Iowa, Indiana, New York, and Ohio as well as in many parts of the Cotton Belt.

Ziegler points out that during the period of Farm Bureau ascendancy (in the '20s and '30s), stratification within agriculture was increasing. Ziegler summarizes the situation as follows:

"The membership and policies of the Farm Bureau indicate

[16] Ibid., p. 55.

[17] For more complete discussion, see Loomis and Beegle, *Rural Social Systems,* pp. 633-635, and Dewitt C. Wing, "Trends in National Farm Organizations," *Yearbook of Agriculture, 1940* (Washington, D. C.: U. S. Government Printing Office, 1940), pp. 954-960.

[18] Rogers and Burdge, *Social Change,* p. 306.

quite clearly that it is primarily the representative of the upper strata of the farm population. In contrast to the sympathy of the earlier movements toward labor, the Farm Bureau's more prosperous membership identified with the values of business and the urban and small-town middle class. This orientation was immediately evident in the boasts of the Farm Bureau that it helped to keep down 'unrest' among the farmers in the 1920's and that it avoided any policy which would 'align organized farmers with the radicals of other organizations.' One of the early struggles in the Farm Bureau involved a decision on whether the organization should hold to the original purposes of the county farm bureaus—education for the average farmer—or whether the organization should operate as a business and legislative agency for larger farmers. The latter view won out and overt support from business groups signaled a major alteration in the course of farm politics."[19]

The National Farmers Organization (NFO). The NFO, an aggressive Holiday Association, was formed in 1955. It had its beginnings in Iowa where discontent was widespread among disadvantaged farmers over declining livestock prices. An Iowa farmer and a feed salesman, Wayne Jackson and Jay Loughry, are considered the founders.[20]

The NFO grew rapidly in Iowa, Missouri, and surrounding states but today has memberships outside the Midwest in such states as New York, Georgia, and Idaho. Initially the goals of NFO were aimed toward influencing legislation affecting farmers and farm prices. In the late '50s the NFO changed its tactics to embrace collective bargaining and withholding actions. It also raised its dues substantially and employed paid organizers.

In a study of farm organizations in Michigan in the mid-sixties, an attempt was made to construct profiles for farmers who were NFO, Farm Bureau and Grange members as well as for non-members. NFO and Farm Bureau members were found to be similar in important ways. However, NFO members, compared to other groups, were younger, more often had children at home, had better education, more often had a mortgage on the land

[19] Ziegler, *Interest Groups,* pp. 186-187.
[20] Rogers and Burdge, *Social Change,* pp. 306-308.

farmed, and averaged more off-farm income than Farm Bureau and Grange members.[21]

Table 1 shows the responses of farm organization members on selected items related to the causes and possible solutions to farm income problems.[22] For all items shown NFO members exhibit larger percentages who agree or smaller percentages who disagree. While differences are not large, a larger percentage of NFO than Farm Bureau or Grange members agree that "consumers ought to pay more for food" and that "consumers should pay enough for food to equalize farm and non farm income." On issues related to labor union tactics, NFO members tend to be most supportive and Grange members least supportive.

Farmers' cooperatives. Taylor has sketched the rise of farmers' cooperatives in this country in terms of the growth of commodity marketing associations, and regards their achievements as "the consistent long-time accomplishments of the farmers' movement."[23] According to the annual report of the Farmer Cooperative Service, there were 7,790 farmers' marketing and purchasing associations in 1970 in the United States. The membership of these associations amounted to over 6 million and their estimated business was about 19 billion. Table 2 shows some of the details for marketing and supply cooperatives and changes over time.

Compared with that of many Scandinavian and Western European countries, the cooperative movement of the United States is not strong. In terms of both number of associations and volume of business, the Midwest is the center of farmers' marketing and purchasing associations. Such associations are proportionately fewer throughout the southern and western states. Well over half of the number of associations, estimated membership and value of business is located in twelve states comprising the East and West North Central divisions.

Farm supply and marketing cooperatives were explored as a part of a state-wide survey of Michigan farmers in the mid-sixties. Considerable purchasing of farm supplies was reported by

[21] Dale E. Hathaway, Richard L. Feltner, James D. Shaffer and Denton Morrison, *Michigan Farmers in the Mid Sixties,* (East Lansing: Agricultural Experiment Station, 1966), pp. 52-55.

[22] Ibid., p. 57.

[23] Taylor, et al., *Rural Life,* p. 518.

TABLE 1

General Farm Organization Membership Related to Views of Some
Causes of and Possible Solutions to Farm Income Problems.

Item	All Farm- ers	Farm Bureau Mem- bers	Grange Mem- bers	NFO Mem- bers	Non- Mem- bers
			Percent Agreeing		
Consumers					
Consumers ought to pay more for food	63	64	67	70	60
Consumers should pay enough for food to equalize farm and nonfarm incomes	79	80	79	82	77
Organized Labor					
Make strikes against public interest illegal	67	72	77	44	65
Most labor union policies determined by rank and file members	48	40	36	62	54
Closed union shop a good idea	38	33	16	56	42
Farmers and the Farm Marketing System					
Farmers should produce, forget marketing problems	17	15	37	8	20
Farmers not earning satisfactory income at farming should leave farming	55	58	57	38	54

Source: Hathaway, et al., *Michigan Farmers in the Mid-Sixties*, p. 57.
These items are selected from tabular materials prepared by Denton Morrison.

the 804 farmers included in the total sample. Twenty-four percent of the farmers purchased fertilizer from a cooperative only,
57 percent from a private source only, and only 7 percent purchased fertilizer from both a cooperative and private source.
Twelve percent purchased no fertilizer. Seeds, petroleum prod-

TABLE 2
Number, Memberships and Business of Farmers' Cooperatives, Selected Dates, 1950 to 1970.

Year	Cooperatives			Membership** in Thousands			Business*** in Million Dollars		
	Total	Mar-keting*	Farm Supply	Total	Mar-keting*	Farm Supply	Total	Mar-keting*	Farm Supply
1950	10,035	6,922	3,113	6,584	4,075	2,509	8,726	7,083	1,643
1960	9,345	6,048	3,297	7,273	3,673	3,600	12,036	9,628	2,408
1965	8,583	5,498	3,085	7,082	3,831	3,251	14,742	11,832	2,910
1970 (prel.)	7,790	5,015	2,775	6,355	3,133	3,222	19,078	15,207	3,871

* Includes service associations

** Excludes nonvoting patrons

*** Value of commodities sold or purchased for patrons and charges for rendering other services in marketing or purchasing. Beginning in 1960, adjusted for duplication resulting from intercooperative business.

Source: *Statistical Abstract of the United States*, 1972, p. 588. Data from U.S.D.A., Farmer Cooperative Services, *Statistics of Farmer Cooperatives*, Annual.

ucts, and mixed feeds were purchased through a "cooperative only" by more than 10 percent of the sample of farmers.[24]

The authors also attempted to measure attitudes toward cooperatives through a series of questions. They conclude that, "in general, farmers do not regard supply cooperatives as institutions which are likely to have any great positive influence upon the profitability of their farm operation."[25]

About 43 percent of the Michigan farmers interviewed had sold products through a marketing organization during the past three years. A higher percentage of Farm Bureau than NFO members (51 and 44 percent, respectively) had used cooperative marketing facilities. In general, cooperative marketing organization enjoys a more positive image than cooperative supply organization among Michigan farmers.[26]

In their study of the Finnish cooperative movements in this country Kercher and associates have this to say:

> It has been in the intimate, neighborly, social setting of the hamlet, village, or small town that the cooperatives as a whole have had their firmest roots. Here occupational and other class differences are minor factors, and consequently economic wants are sufficiently commonplace and uniform to be served by a relatively simple institutional structure. Furthermore, the face-to-face contacts of everyday life provide the ideal social experience for the development of common understanding and formation of attitudes of group solidarity so essential to voluntary cooperative effort.[27]

VALUE ORIENTATION OF FARMERS' ORGANIZATIONS

Ends. As previously indicated, the various farmers' organizations have attempted to satisfy various needs—economic, social, and political. It is true that some farmers' organizations —such as commodity agencies, special interest groups, certain cooperatives, and some locals of larger organizations—have

---

[24] Hathaway, et al., *Michigan Farmers,* pp. 10-11.

[25] Ibid., p. 14.

[26] Ibid., pp. 15-16

[27] L. C. Kercher, V. W. Kebker, and W. C. Leland, Jr., *Consumers' Cooperatives in the North Central States* (Minneapolis: University of Minnesota Press, 1941), pp. 119-120.

rather specific objectives, but the farmers' movement as a whole and most local organizations have functionally diffuse ends. At the local level, for example, an important function may be that of providing fellowship for members. In any case, the objectives of farm organizations are not functionally as specific as in most bureaucratic organizations.

Norms. The farmers' organizations strive to obtain their economic, political, or other objectives within the framework of the American legal system and customary procedure. Even in the more radical movements such as the Nonpartisan League, the existing structure and norms were followed. Few, if any, agricultural parties or organizations in America have recommended the abolition of private property or private initiative, except as the farmer might be prevented from obtaining what he believed to be his share of the total proceeds from his products. Almost no agricultural movement or party in any society has recommended the abolition of private property in land, and frequent early revolts and movements were designed to strengthen the farmers' control and power over use of the land. Only in the early peasants' revolts was violence advocated and used.[28]

Several large organizations have followed the system of signing contracts to control production and prices. This is, of course, compatible with American norms. Several such contractual schemes have failed in the past because farmers did not abide by the contracts they had signed. It has been successful only among commercial fruit growers in California and in areas in which farmers are accustomed to the impersonal Gesellschaft-like nature of contractual agreements. On the other hand, the "sign-up campaign" of the Tri-State Tobacco Growers Cooperative Marketing Association in North Carolina, Virginia, and South Carolina, which claimed 90,000 members in 1923, failed and went into the hands of receivers. The farmers of these areas were less accustomed to Gesellschaft-like institutions, such as contracts, and they did not conform.

In summarizing our discussion of the value orientation of farmers' organizations, we may say that for the most part, except where only business interests were involved, a Gemeinschaft-like orientation has been maintained. Almost universally

---

[28] For a brief account of these uprisings see Loomis and Beegle, *Rural Social Systems,* pp. 616 ff.

the organizations have recognized the importance of the family and the community in their organizational structures. "The Grange, . . . Farmers' Union, some labor unions, a few industrial corporations, and in some states the American Farm Bureau, are built around the importance of the community and family. They too may recognize the danger to America in the current decline of the primary groups."[29]

Before the spread of the civic organizations into the country, the general farm organizations furnished the first and sometimes only experience rural people had in organizational life outside the church and school. In most areas the organizational experience acquired in farmers' organizations, as in all Gemeinschaft-like systems, emphasizes friendly affectivity as opposed to the reserved affective neutrality of special interest, business, or governmental bureaucracies.[30]

The farmers' organizations, especially the Grange with its secret ritual, are traditional rather than rational and secular. A change agent attempting to reach farmers through the farmers' organizations can be more effective if his appeal is to the basic values of the rural people than if it is merely utilitarian. Morality, community, solidarity, fair play, enlightenment, bountiful living, opportunities for the young, international understanding, just prices, improving international relations—all are objectives that appeal to farmers' organizations and are supported in their programs.

Social structure of farmers' organizations. Among the farmers' organizations, the Grange has the most elaborated status-role development. It is a secret, fraternal organization, and members call one another "brother" and "sister," thus symbolizing, if not completely achieving, an extension of the family to the organization. The official status-role designations are, in order of their importance: master, overseer, lecturer, treasurer, secretary, chaplain, steward, assistant steward, lady assistant steward, Pomona, Ceres, Flora, and gatekeeper. Rank in the Grange organization is in no small manner related to mastery of ritual which is rewarded by the granting of degrees.

[29] Baker Brownell, *The Human Community—Its Philosophy and Practice for a Time of Crisis* (New York: Harper and Brothers, 1950), p. 100.

[30] See, for example, C. P. Loomis and J. A. Beegle, "The Spread of German Nazism in Rural Areas," *American Sociological Review,* Vol. XI, No. 6 (December, 1946), pp. 724-734.

The Farmers' Union is also a secret organization but employs much less ritual than the Grange and has no degrees. The American Farm Bureau Federation and its affiliates are neither secret nor fraternal. The power and rank of members of the farmers' organizations are usually based upon criteria not different from those held in the rural communities generally and in the other social systems of importance in these communities. Farmers who are influential in local farmers' organizations are usually also influential in the local community, school, church, and similar groups.

PROCESSES INVOLVING SOCIAL ACTION IN FARMERS' ORGANIZATIONS

Communication. The most important communication in the various farmers' organizations is carried on by informal interaction between neighbors in communities. Thus, in a study of 500 farms in Michigan, Gibson[31] found that face-to-face contacts furnished the most important source of information these farmers had concerning cooperatives. The farmers' organizations have other more formal means of establishing communication on the various levels.[32]

Each of these organizations has a paper that goes to its membership. A wide range of subjects including international affairs, the economy, and democracy are covered. Many organizations publish monthly or quarterly publications for local board members, field employees, and others in agriculture. The GTA Digest of the Grain Terminal Association in St. Paul is such a publication. This Digest does not deal solely with technical subjects but attempts to get people to think broadly on such issues as land reform in Italy or famine in India. The monthly magazine of the Ohio Farm Bureau is an example of a publication, originating at the state level and featuring a broad editorial and news policy. Other media including radio, TV, and films are also widely used by farm organizations.

Decision-making. It is important for the change agent work-

---

[31] Duane L. Gibson, *News for Farmer Cooperatives* (November, 1948). See also Duane L. Gibson, *Membership Relations of Farmers' Milk Marketing Organizations in New York State* (Ithaca: Cornell University, doctoral Dissertation, 1940).

[32] Loomis, et al., *Rural Social Systems and Adult,* pp. 114 ff.

ing in the local community to know how official policy is determined. The records and minutes of farmers' organizations are full of progressive action supported and made possible by them.[33] On the other hand, in many cases local farmers' organizations have blocked action which was in the interest of the community.[34] In general, decision-making on the local level in the farmers' organizations is according to American democratic organizational procedures and is subject to the same limitations and advantages common to all organizations on the community level. However, most observers are very much impressed with the manner in which decisions from local levels in farm organizations pass to higher levels.

In all these volunteer membership organizations, policy is made by the democratic and educational process of resolutions. Each organization lays great stress on this fact. Each has well ordered procedures by which resolutions are presented, debated, and finally approved. At each organizational level, committees discuss and carefully frame resolutions dealing with local, state, national, and international issues. In the national conventions, resolutions are again debated, refined, and adopted. Once approved, they become the policies of the organizations. These policy statements then travel back down the organizational channels and become materials for program discussion in state and local meetings. Resolutions finally approved are distributed to members and others through newspapers, printed pamphlets, and by word of mouth at state and local meetings.

Resolutions become an educational technique in still another way. Inasmuch as formal resolutions cannot cover every issue and variation of issue, and because resolutions are the basis for action following adoption, leaders of these organizations must interpret resolutions in fulfilling their roles. Leaders' interpretations of resolutions stimulate members to think and act on mat-

[33] Paul A. Miller, *Community Health Action—A Study of Community Contrast,* (East Lansing: The Michigan State College Press, 1953), Chapter V. In this case the Farm Bureau played a very important role in initiating and obtaining a community hospital.

[34] A. B. Hollingshead, *Elmtown's Youth* (New York: John Wiley & Sons, 1949), p. 144. Hollingshead reports the actions which followed when a high school in Illinois lost its status as an accredited school in the North Central Association of Schools and Colleges. Owners of medium-sized farms, "working against the proposal through a secret Farm Bureau Committee," tried to prevent an increase in taxes needed to accomplish the reinstatement of the school.

ters of interest to the organizations. Interpretation of resolutions culminating in action is of educational value.

Boundary maintenance. No definitive study has ever been made of boundary maintenance by the farmers' organizations at the various levels, although it is one of the most interesting aspects of these organizations and would comprise an important area of sociological inquiry. Most of the great farmers' organizations have either been swallowed up or have avoided with great difficulty being swallowed up in political organizations and campaigns. The largest farm organization ever to appear, the Farmers' Alliance, rose to its height in the United States in the depression years of the 1890's, entered politics, and then passed out of existence. The Grange grew to 850,000 members in 1875, entered politics, declined to a little over 100,000 members, and only at the turn of the century began its return to influence. The Farmers' Union continually warns its members and locals to keep out of politics, frequently referring to the experience of the earlier organizations. The Nonpartisan League attained its greatest power in the 1920's and took over the state government of North Dakota for a period but has now lost most of its members. Because of the various experiences in politics, the organizational literature of most of the farm organizations warns locals against the danger of being made into political organizations. The ritual of both the Grange and the Farmers' Union are boundary maintenance mechanisms making them more or less inaccessible to non-members and especially to non-farmers.

Systemic Linkage. Historically, the farmers' organizations represented an important link in the communication network of rural communities. In earlier periods they also provided important linkages to non-rural sectors and to legislatures. In certain areas of the nation these same linkages remain important today.

The Cooperative Extension Service, various government bureaus, and other organizations use the farmers' organizations as channels of communication for their programs. Most change agents working in rural communities can rarely afford to ignore farm organizations in understanding community structure and manner in which communication takes place.

SOCIAL ACTION IN THE CANADIAN MARITIME PROVINCES

The following case study is an excellent example of the benefits achieved through cooperation. It is revealing in that it shows the power of an effective organization produced by the efforts of the church and university.

Antigonish for Potatoes and Fish[35]

"Here's your party. Go ahead please."

Sandy McTaggart hadn't fancied being the one to do the talking, but they had elected him. He didn't know why it was so hard to begin. The six men crowding around the telephone with him here in the parish priest's house were his friends, lobstermen like himself off this Nova Scotia coast—all except the man from the university who had made hard, cold sense in his talk, but who dealt in new ideas.

The "professor" claimed they should all go back to school. Study classes for grown men! But he also said he thought he could show them how to get more money for their lobsters, and that part had sounded all right.

In his free hand Sandy held a sheet torn from the *Fisherman's Gazette*. One flinty thumb poked clear through the paper, serving the purpose of underscoring the name of Matt Skelly of Boston, Massachusetts. Mr. Skelly's street address and phone number were there.

The man from the university had insisted they would get more out of it if they did everything for themselves than if he did it for them, and they had emptied their work-pants pockets of nickels, pennies, and a few dimes, pooling the money to make this long-distance call. Their first venture in working together, he had said. An investment in their future—a step that might end up in changing the lives of everybody on this starvation coast. It sounded like a big order. If you took into account the Magdalena Islands, there were 8,000 miles of this kind of coast in the Canadian Maritime provinces.

Through the small-paned window Sandy could look out on a rocky chunk of it. Without craning his neck he could see nearly the whole of the straggling town in all its gray bleakness. He could see his own house. It had two rooms and no paint, and it was lashed by a rusty cable to granite boulders to keep his wife and five children from being blown out to sea in winter storms. Beyond the house, salt water lapped at the pilings of a gray,

[35] Ryerson Johnson, "Antigonish for Potatoes and Fish," *Adult Leadership*, Vol. 4, No. 4 (1955), p. 5 ff.

sagging wharf, and put a scuffing of white against seaweed ledges in the cove. The operator's insistent vioce came again over the wire, "Here's your party—"

Sandy felt his arm nudged gently by the man from Antigonish—the Extension Department of St. Francis Xavier University there. "Go ahead, Sandy." The man smiled in encouragement. "It won't bite."

In blunt succession then, they all heard Sandy McTaggart say:

"Are you Mr. Skelly? . . ."

"It says in the *Fisherman's Gazette* you buy live lobsters . . ."

"Will you buy ours? . . ."

"How much you payin'? . . ."

"All right, we'll send you some."

That's all there was to it. Sandy forked the receiver against the side of the old-fashioned wooden phone box while they stared with misgivings. They had spent their precious pennies for—what? It had all sounded too brisk and inconclusive. They pressed him with questions.

"How much's he payin'?"

"Payin' market, he said."

"How much is market in Boston?"

Sandy stared sheepishly. "Clean forgot to ask."

"You didn't even tell him our names!"

"Don't matter," Sandy defended himself. "He can read our names on the shippin' tag."

The doubt remained on their faces. One spoke for all of them. "We undertake to ship our own lobsters, Jim Wallace won't like that."

Jim Wallace was the local buyer of all sea products, the on-the-spot representative of "outside interests." He was the local seller, too, of salt, twine, food, clothing, boat gear—everything a fisherman needed to try and stay alive and keep his family alive.

There was a trader like Jim Wallace in every town on the coast —the region's lone contact with the outside world of commerce. The trader set his own prices for the things he sold, and for the things he bought. The spread between these prices wasn't quite enough to let a man, however frugal, stay out of debt. The trader carried him on the books from year to year; he remained always just a little bit owing. This was little short of slavery, the university man had insisted. They hadn't called it anything themselves. It was just a way of life—a way of hunger and misery, but the only way they knew.

One of the lobstermen registered their undercurrent fear. "If we try and sell over Jim's head, might make him so mad he'd quit carryin' us. What'd we do then?"

"Carry ourselves, I figger." Sandy looked to the university man for support, and got it in the glow deep in the man's eyes . . .

This was 26 years ago—and folks of the Canadian Maritime Provinces have been "carrying themselves" ever since.

Here's How it Grew

Twenty-six years ago Eastern Canada was economically desolate, the people starving and rebellious—and talking communism. Then came the telephone incident (almost word-for-word as recorded here, except that the names of people involved have been changed). The action dramatized the beginning of what has come to be called the Antigonish Movement—a continuous program of self-help that is permitting fishermen, farmers, and industrial workers to solve their economic and social problems through education and planned action.

The Antigonish Movement began with nothing more revolutionary than discussion groups—study clubs, they called them —organized along windswept granite shores. It started with the cooperative marketing of a single crate of lobsters, and went on to change the economy of Maritime Canada and the temper of a people. Today the cooperative shipping and processing of lobsters alone is a multimillion dollar business . . . and from Cheticamp and Grand Etang on the island of Cape Breton, from Port Beckerton, Larry's River, and Canso on the isolated shores of Nova Scotia trailer trucks make scheduled trips from all manner of cooperative fish plants to the great marketing centers of New York and Montreal.

This is but a small part of the change that has come about. The well-being and the dignity of the individual have been raised to such a level that today retail stores owned and operated by fishermen, farmers, and miners serve some 220 Martime communities. Wholesale cooperatives, in turn, serve the consumer stores. Nearly 100,000 people are pooling their savings in 420 credit unions with assets of more than 13 million dollars—credit unions that have loaned vastly more than this to their members for such significant things as fishing gear, a repair job on a boat, a milk cow, a farm tractor, a doctor's bill, new shingles on a house. And there are successful ventures into such things as insurance and cooperative housing.

To the Extension Department of St. Francis Xavier University at Antigonish, Nova Scotia, goes much of the credit. The Dominion Departments of Agriculture and Fisheries have played an important part, too. But it was the men of Antigonish who put sparks to the endeavor and for 26 years fanned the flames. [*Note that the Extension Department of St. Francis Xavier University and the Dominion Departments of Agriculture and Fisheries are change agents instrumental in achieving systemic linkage with the Antigonish group.*]

How has this remarkably widespread program of self help been accomplished, and just where does adult education come into the picture? Let's have a look at the initial planning.

The largest vocational group in the Maritimes is farmers. Fishermen come second. Facing the same peculiar hazards and living in close-knit communities, fishermen in general are more inclined toward cooperative action than farmers. It was decided by the men of Antigonish to begin with the fishermen. [*Territorial considerations among others were important.*]

But commercial fishing is a different kind of business for nearly every kind of fish. The ground-shore fisherman's problems are different from the smelt fisherman's, the herring fisherman's, the lobsterman's, and so on. A decision was made to concentrate first on the lobster business since the price of lobsters had always been uniformly high in city markets, and there was less complexity in handling and shipping than with the more perishable cod, haddock, salmon, mackerel, shellfish. . . Success with lobsters, they thought, would spur cooperative efforts in the more complex fields.

And so it proved.

This takes us back to the apprehensive lobstermen of 26 years ago making the long distance telephone call. [*The initiation step in the systemic linkage.*] They made up a crate of lobsters and shipped it to Mr. Skelly in Boston.

Time went by and nothing happened. A subject of gibes from their more timid neighbors, and gnawed by fear of economic reprisals from the local trader, they met every night to draw strength from each other and to talk it over. A crate of lobsters weighs about 140 pounds. The local trader was paying seven cents a pound. Seven times 140 figures out at $9.80. Maybe they should have been content with the trader's $9.80.

And so they waited and doubted.

When the check came it was for $32.

As soon as news got around that men on the Canso coast had broken tradition by shipping their own lobsters, thereby realizing better than three times the local price, it became immeasurably easier for the Extension people at Antigonish to peddle their dream of relating the academic findings of their university to the close-up, immediate needs of people.

We must deal in specifics. . . If we are to make an idealist of the common man we must first satisfy his realism.

So affirms Dr. M. M. Coady, Director of Extension Work at St. Francis Xavier from the day the department was established in 1928. Sometimes he says it in another way: "You have to fill a man's belly before you can fill his head—or his heart or his soul."

The Men of Antigonish

It can be said of Dr. Coady: "He wants nothing for himself; he wants everything for everybody else." A big and hearty individual—his human warmth, his uncompromising sincerity, his salty talk and vigorous manner have turned despair into hope, and started men and women up the path to effective social action in a thousand places in the Canadian Maritimes. Director Emeritus since 1951, Dr. Coady in his own time has become legendary in the annals of adult education.

He (and men like Dr. A. B. McDonald who worked with him at Antigonish, and Father "Jimmy" Tompkins before them both) thought it was not enough for a university to offer good academic and classical training. He foresaw a university that would exert influences in contemporary society far beyond its traditional constituency, reaching out in active fight against ignorance and injustice where it found them. If the people wouldn't —or couldn't—go to the university, then the university, through its extension department, would go to the people. It would involve them in the educational process by meeting them on their own level of interest. [*Note the details concerning important status-roles and social rank attached to them.*]

But let Dr. Coady speak for himself:

Any sound philosophy should teach that education is an instrument to unlock life to all the people. . . Our present educational procedure does not do this. We are robbing our rural and industrial population of their natural leaders. The bright boys and girls are educated and leave their people. They enter the so-called vocations and professions. Their interests are now different from what they would be back home...

We need a new kind of education that will give the people life where they are, and through the callings in which they find themselves. It cannot be done in the old way. . . . No scheme of education conceived in terms of a preparation for life is going to do the job. Children do not run society. Clearly, the techniques by which we can improve the social order and hold an educated generation of our youth, must be achieved by the adult population. This means, then, the necessity of finding a scientific and effective technique by which all the adult people of our land can be mobilized in an adult education program.

This is what the Extension Department at St. Francis Xavier has been concerned with all these years. It has developed an adult education program of which economic cooperation is the first stage. The core of the Antigonish Movement has been the study groups—study groups established to pave the way for self help through credit unions and cooperative enterprises.

It was early discovered that men who came to lecture could not change things very much, however inspiringly they spoke. The people had to do it for themselves. There was no sugar coating of this reality. From the first it was stressed that there was no easy way—but that there was a way. The people had to develop their own leaders. They had to study—and then act.

This they did. Let's look at how it was done . . . how it is still being done. We can perhaps do this best by following a field worker from the Extension Department as he goes into a typical Maritime fishing community. It could be any one of a thousand drab and apathetic towns, peopled with fisher folk of whom lobsterman Sandy McTaggart is a prototype.

The First Mass Meeting

There has been some preliminary advertising through press and pulpit, enough to let the villagers know that there will be a mass meeting in their interests, featuring an out-of-town speaker. This mass meeting is the ice breaker for the whole program [*The necessity of setting a stage upon which communication may take place.*] Here, the personality of the speaker is all-important. He has to set the stage for change and leave the people with enough enthusiasm to carry on the more prosaic part of the program—the learning part that precedes action—after he has gone.

In his talk he stresses basic, down-to-earth philosophies. He tells stories of what people have done for themselves in other places. (The story about the men who realized $32 for their crate of lobsters when the going price on the Canso coast was $9.80, was effective, as might be imagined. Forest and farm, mine, and mill towns supplied similar success stories as the program gathered momentum.)

The point is made and remade of the importance of brain working in double-harness with brawn. (Dr. Coady has been quoted as jarring village folks out of their apathy in this way: "There are those who oppose education for grown men. They prefer to trust to native ability—to horse sense, as they say. It is well named. Because of this thinking, three-fourths of the human race are on a level of living very little above that of the good old horse.")

Since the mass meeting in a backward locality has as its first task the breaking down of apathy, if not outright suspicion and hostility, the field worker who forearms himself with some knowledge of people's everyday lives is in an immensely better position to make his talk effective. Suppose, for instance, that among the specialized bits of information that have come to his attention is this: a fisherman who bends all day hauling up lobster traps—or cod or pollock lines—from water that stays only a few degrees above freezing summer and winter, grows a protective covering of skin on his hands so thick that he has to take a knife sometimes and cut away the callouses on the inside of his finger joints so he can keep bending his fingers.

The field worker who calls attention to his homely reality has a ready-made channel to the topic closest his heart. "A man grows callouses on his brain too," the field man may remark. "Only not from working his brain too hard. That's the difference between hand callouses and brain callouses. A man grows callouses on his brain from not working it. The cure is easy. You cut away the brain callouses with a book. With a little study. You can even make a start by asking a few questions, or by setting your mind to answering another fellow's questions."

Included in the field man's talk are some of the fundamentals of credit unions, and of cooperative buying and selling; a hint of the promise they hold out in terms of human betterment. Just the bare outlines here, because it is hard to sell the idea of self betterment to people who all their lives have been struggling only for survival. They have so small a purchase on life already they are slow to take chances with anything different.

To help break down this attitude, and in answer to those who might question whether such things were within the province of fishermen or miners or farmers, Dr. Coady has been known to thunder: "We ask the people of Canada to run the biggest business in the country, the political state. Are you in the same breath going to declare that they are not competent to run their own grocery store?"

When faint hearts till shrink at the complexity of the thing, complaining that there have been cooperative ventures that failed: "Of course there have been co-ops that failed," Dr. Coady readily agrees. Then he drives in his clincher. "They failed because there wasn't enough education behind them. People hadn't studied it out. They didn't rightly know what they were doing. That's why I say first we study and then we act."

When School's Out

Study never stops in the Maritimes, but there does come a day when to the study phase action is added and people start their stores, their processing factories, their marketing organizations ... and these have continued in successful operation for 26 years now, with their numbers and their influence steadily growing.

It is a stirring thing, and one worth many words of exposition and glowing description, to drive along the roads that wind through the Canadian Maritimes, through all the little towns, and see the weatherbeaten structures—no more than shacks in some instances—in which people first started putting to the test their laboriously acquired notions of how to run a grocery store; a stirring thing to see that in town after town these grubby little stores have been boarded up and abandoned now as inadequate for serving the expanding needs of a vigorous people, while next door or across the street, their gleamingly new, efficient consumers cooperative has arisen. The stores, both the old and the new, stand as monuments to the faith of the pioneer planners who believed that people everywhere had within themselves the capacity to help themselves, and who clung stubbornly to the revolutionary concept that if people wouldn't or couldn't go to the university, then the university had a responsibility to carry its findings to the people.

And this is not the end. As Dr. Coady reminds us, economic cooperation is only the first step. [*Other ends and objectives supersede the short-run ends.*] In all phases of the Antigonish Movement pains have been taken to assure that study club members understand why St. Francis Xavier promotes study clubs and encourages definite action to follow the study.

As they plainly say in one of their bulletins, "The efforts of the individual member are meaningless unless he realizes that he is working, not merely to become a member of a credit union, not merely to live in a better house, or buy his groceries cooperatively, or sell the products of his labor cooperatively, but that by his organized reading, thought, discussion, and action, he is striking his little blow toward building up a true democratic society in which he will have a voice according to the extent to which he has prepared himself to speak."

SELECTED REFERENCES

Buck, S. J. *The Granger Movement.* Cambridge: Harvard University Press, 1913.

Crampton, John A. *The National Farmers' Union.* Lincoln: University of Nebraska Press, 1965.

Folkman, William S. *Membership Relations in Farmers' Purchasing Cooperatives.* Fayetteville: Arkansas Agr. Expt. Sta. Bull. 566, June 1955.

Hathaway, Dale E., Feltner, Richard L., Shaffer, James D., and Morrison, Denton. *Michigan Farmers in the Mid-Sixties.* East Lansing: Michigan Agr. Expt. Sta. Bull. 1966.

Hicks, John D. *The Populist Revolt.* Minneapolis: University of Minnesota Press, 1931.

Kile, Orville M. *The Farm Bureau Movement.* New York: The Macmillan Company, 1921.

Rogers, Everett M. and Rabel Burdge. *Social Change in Rural Societies,* Second Edition. New York: Appleton-Century Crofts, 1972.

Rohrer, Wayne C. and Louis H. Douglas. *The Agrarian Transition in America.* Indianapolis: The Bobbs-Merrill Company, 1969.

Shover, John L. *Cornbelt Rebellion: The Farmers' Holiday Association.* Urbana: The University of Illinois Press, 1965.

Taylor, Carl C. *The Farmers' Movement.* New York: American Book Company, 1953.
Taylor, Carl C., et al., *Rural Life in the United States.* New York: Alfred Knopf, 1949. Chapter 29.
Ziegler, Harmon. *Interest Groups in American Society.* Englewood Cliffs: Prentice-Hall, Inc., 1964. Chapter 6.

11

Social Systems in Health

Two quotations, one from the National Academy of Science study of the consequences and policy implications of rapid population growth, and the other from the 1951 Commission on the Health Needs of the Nation, are appropriate in introducing the subject matter of this chapter. Not only do they express the importance of health to individual and national welfare but they also view health as a mirror of man's adjustment to his environment.

"Health—in the traditional sense of the absence of disease and disability or in the ideal of complete physical, mental, and social well-being—has long been one of man's aspirations. Reducing mortality and prolonging life are goals that are rarely in open conflict with other national objectives. . . The proportion of national income devoted to health services has tended to be small, with primary emphasis on alleviating disease and disability, not on preventing them."[1]

"Health reflects dynamically the measure of man's control over his environment and his ever-changing adjustment to it. Health makes possible the maximum self-expression and self-development of man. . . Failure to safeguard health, whether through ignorance, neglect, or the lack of means, exposes the individual to suffering, incapacity, or death. National neglect of proper measures for the preservation of health exposes the country to weakness and destruction."[2]

In no field of human organization is the optimum balance between Gemeinschaft-like and Gesellschaft-like relationships more important than in the administration of the healing arts. This is manifest in the following: "Good health service is never

[1] The National Academy of Science, *Rapid Population Growth: Consequences and Policy Implications* (Baltimore: The Johns Hopkins Press, 1971), p. 368.

[2] *Building America's Health, The President's Commission on the Health Needs of the Nation,* Vol. 1 (Washington, D.C.: U.S. Government Printing Office, 1951), p. 1.

mechanical; it stems from the educated mind, the warm heart, and the practiced hands of our many health workers."[3] Anyone who has been hospitalized with a serious illness knows the importance of organizational efficiency. He also knows the importance of what Parsons[4] calls the "collectivity-orientation" which requires the doctor or nurse to place "the 'welfare of the patient' above his personal interests."[5] The patient-doctor relationship, although rational and secular does permit a certain amount of affect and particularism, both characteristics of the Gemein-schaft.[6]

Numerous types of social systems in American society are concerned with health. The doctor and the patient constitute one such system; the patient and a variety of health personnel—the nurse, the dentist, the medical social worker, the pharmacist, and even the receptionist—constitute others. In a collective sense, "the public" or "the community", together with the public health personnel, comprise social systems. Two types can be discerned here—the personal, confidential, *vis-a-vis* relationship of the patient and the doctor alone in his office, on the one hand, and hundreds of people lined up for mass inoculations on the other. In actual practice there is a range between these polar types. The physician's nurse or consulting physicians may be present with the patient and doctor, thus altering somewhat the highly intimate nature of the social system. The public health nurse, on a family visit, may make a contact fully as intimate and confidential as the physician in his office. One objective of this chapter is to analyze a few of the prototype social systems, and by means of supporting data, attempt to give an overall view of the sociological aspects of health systems.

Patient-doctor relationship. The idealization of this social system is found in the concept of "the family doctor." He minis-

---

[3] Ibid, p. 11.

[4] Talcott Parsons, *The Social System* (Glencoe: The Free Press, 1951), p. 435.

[5] No doubt Parsons is correct in calling attention to this feature as differentiating the patient-doctor relationship from relationships in business. However, there is ample evidence that similar relationships exist in business, as between salesman and client. See G. P. Stone, "City Shoppers and Urban Identification: Observation on the Social Psychology of City Life," *American Journal of Sociology,* Vol. LX, No. 1 (July, 1954), pp. 36ff. Nevertheless, in the healing arts the patient-doctor relationship is all important.

[6] C. P. Loomis and J. A. Beegle, *Rural Social Systems* (New York: Prentice-Hall, Inc., 1950), pp. 714ff.

ters to the physical, the mental, and the spiritual needs; to the individual, the family, and the community. An excellent example of this relationship is found in "A Doctor of the Old School," from which the following excerpts are taken:

> Before and behind his saddle were strapped the instruments and medicines the doctor might want, for he never knew what was before him. There were no specialists in Drumtochty, so this man had to do everything as best he could, and as quickly. He was chest doctor, and doctor for every other organ as well; he was accoucheur and surgeon; he was oculist and aurist; he was dentist and chloroformist, besides being chemist and druggist. It was often told how he was far up Glen Urtach when the feeders of the threshing mill caught young Burnbrae, and how he only stopped to change horses at his house, and galloped all the way to Burnbrae, and flung himself off his horse and amputated the arm, and saved the lad's life.

On another trip of mercy the old doctor tries to console the desperate husband:

> Ye needna plead wi' me, Tammas, to dae the best a' can for yir wife. Man, a' kent her lang afore ye ever luved her; a' brocht her intae the warld, and a' saw her through the fever when she wes a bit lassikie; a' closed her mither's een, and it wes me hed tae tell her she wes an orphan, an' nae man wes better pleased when she got a gude husband, and a' helpit her wi' her fower bairns. A've naither wife nor bairns o' ma own, an' a' coont a' the fouk o' the Glen ma family. Div ye think a' wudna save Annie if I cud?[7]

Here the patient-doctor relationship manifests a functional diffuseness that contrasts sharply with that of most modern specialists. It should not be surprising if the particularistic, affective behavior of Gemeinschaft-like rural communities convey some of these qualities and, therefore, stands in sharp contrast with the rational, secular health systems that accompany societies as they become Gesellschaft-like. The specialization of the healing arts and the recent growth of group practice is characteristic of the present day.

[7] Ian Maclaren, *Beside the Bonnie Brier Bush* (New York: Dodd, Mead & Company, Inc., 1895), pp. 162 and 173.

"Group practice is a natural outgrowth of the development of modern medicine. Since the turn of the century rapid advances in medical research have produced a vast and complex science, one which is too tremendous and complicated to be grasped and applied by any one individual. This has led to an increase in specialization until today twenty-three different classifications of specialists and sub-specialists are certified by the various American Medical Specialty Boards. In addition, the medical team includes members from allied professional fields—the dentist, the nurse, the social worker, the physical therapist, the health educator, the dietitian, the psychologist, and the laboratory technician, to mention but a few. The physician accounts for only one in ten of those engaged in health work. To provide complete medical care of high caliber, the individual doctor calls upon numerous medical specialists for consultation and assistance, and also enlists the aid of workers in these many allied fields. . .

"As medical practice has progressed in effectiveness and complexity, it has at times lost sight of the 'patient as a person.' There has been a tendency to accord greater prestige to superspecialization than to general practice, to place more emphasis upon the disease or the affected organ than upon the individual. A full understanding of the patient, including his personal problems and the impact of these upon his well-being or response to treatment, has often been neglected. In education and in daily practice the medical group can provide the most favorable environment for consideration of health service in its entirety. . ."[8]

Patient-nurse relationship. The patient-nurse relationship, perhaps even more than the patient-doctor relationship, combines the characteristics of the Gemeinschaft and the Gesellschaft.

The essential qualities of the nurse, rooted in the person of Florence Nightingale, are those of saintliness, humility, self-sacrifice and self-denial. More so than the doctor, the nurse is often romantically viewed as rendering services as an end in and of themselves. Whittaker and Olesen point out that the nursing profession is often referred to as a "calling" and retains sen-

[8] Dean A. Clark and Cozette Hapney, "Group Practice," *The Annals,* Vol. 273 (January, 1951), pp. 43-44.

timentalized rituals like capping, notions of dedicating one's life and being "ministering angels."[9] A personal testimony from a nurse about to retire suggests that these elements have not fully disappeared. "One risks the tag of maudlin sentimentality by a bold confession of love and concern for people in pain, but that is the sum and substance of nursing's lure. Scientific detachment and analytic attitude are certainly laudable, but I pray that such qualities, without personal concern for the individual, may never be the ultimate attributes of the nurse."[10] Among the major problems in the patient-nurse relationship, especially in large hospitals with specialized health care roles, is to retain at least some elements that are Gemeinschaft-like.

Public health agency and community relations. The local public health service is perhaps the most Gesellschaft-like of all the systems dealing with the healing arts. Emerson, long a spokesman for public health services, recognizes two resources available to a public health program—authority under statute or ordinance and the power of education. Emerson says:

> . . . . The resources are granted by the expressed will of the people. The health officer, the executive, generally a physician, is employed by civil government to make effective use of both authority and education for the benefit of all the people. His patient is the community, not an individual.[11]

Although the dispenser and the recipient of the healing arts in this case are of a completely different order from patient and doctor, nevertheless there is a mutuality of activity.

ELEMENTS OF SOCIAL SYSTEMS CONCERNED WITH HEALTH

Ends and Objectives. We have cited only three of the many

[9] E. W. Whittaker and Virginia L. Oleson, "Why Florence Nightingale?" *American Journal of Nursing,* (November 1967), pp. 2338-2339.

[10] Ruth LaGanga, "To Nursing with Love", *American Journal of Nursing,* (December 1967), p. 2557. The nurse-patient relationship, having a heavy component of the mother role, may be less functionally specific than many. See Sam Schulman, "Basic Functional Roles in Nursing: Mother Surrogate and Healer", in E. Gartly Jaco, ed., *Patients, Physicians and Illness* (Glencoe, Illinois: The Free Press, 1958).

[11] Haven Emerson, "Essential Local Public Health Services," *The Annals,* Vol. 273 (January, 1951), p. 19.

health systems which constitute the health organization in the United States. We will now scrutinize them in relation to the elements of all social systems. Their objectives are alike. We can discern, from the following description of objectives, that they were the goals of the "doctor of the old school," that they are the ends of the specialists, of the group practitioners, of the general practitioners, of the nurse, and of the departments of public health. Of the latter, Emerson explains:

> Its purpose is to apply the sciences of preventive medicine, prevent disease, develop a healthy population, and safeguard life at all ages so that the optimum of longevity may be attained.[12]

Somewhat more inclusive is the goal:

> . . . that medical care of highest qualitative and quantitative standards should be available to everybody . . . From the viewpoint of social organization of health service, the term denotes the systematic organization of all the personal services by members of the various health professions and all the clinic, hospital, and related facilities necessary to attain the highest level of health, prevent disease, cure or mitigate illness, and reduce if not prevent disability, economic insecurity, and dependency associated with illness.[13]

Few, if any, thoughtful people in the health field are complacent about the attainment of their goals. It is recognized by many medical and public health officers that much progress remains to be made in the rural areas of our country.

Norms. The medical profession has long been regarded as possessing a model system of ethics. The Oath of Hippocrates marked the beginning of what has been a twenty-five-hundred year evolution of standards of conduct for the medical profession. The "doctor of the old school," were he practicing today, would be far from sure that he was doing the "right thing." He might well say with the Fittses: "We do not share the view that a code of ethics should be inviolate and unchanging. Moral truths may be unchanging but their application varies as social and

---

[12] Ibid., p. 19.

[13] Franz Goldmann and Hugh R. Leavell, "The Problems of Medical Care," *The Annals,* Vol. 273 (January 1951), p. 1.

economic factors change."[14] They see as chief among the variations the splintering of medical knowledge into specialties leading to group practice and in turn changing the patient-doctor relationship. They list as other factors demanding a reappraisal of the classical modes of conduct, the insurance principle in medicine with its uniform fee scales in a non-uniform field, and the radical treatment of serious disease which sometimes verges upon human experimentation. To quote Fitts and Fitts:

> The essence of the doctor-patient relationship is the promise of the doctor to take complete responsibility for a patient once he has accepted his care, and the freedom of the patient in the choice of his physician. Once the physician's responsibility is divided between consultants, other specialists, and laboratory physicians, the strength of the doctor-patient relationship is weakened. Multiple practice is effecting a virtual revolution in medicine because of the fragmentation in responsibility that goes with it. . . To replace this loss of an intense individual responsibility, it will probably be necessary to develop a greater sense of the collective responsibility of the profession to society. The absorption of the average physician in his own demanding practice has made him peculiarly blind to the inadvertent gaps in medical care that have arisen through social and economic forces outside his immediate acquaintance. This passive attitude toward the public in general, as opposed to his patient in particular, may be deeply rooted in the nature and history of medical care. In a world where it was impossible to cure more than a few of the sick and dying, the physician unconsciously and in self-protection closed his ears to all but the few he could help.[15]

In rural areas, where the family doctor may still be found and where group practice is less prevalent, the bitter struggles over professional ethics are not so intense. For all areas, however, they are in the offing, "and the two major areas of controversy (which are really two sides of the same coin) are: how to divide responsibility *for* the patient and how to divide fees *from* the patient."[16] These considerations will serve to illustrate the neces-

[14] T. Fitts, Jr. and Barbara Fitts, "Ethical Standards of the Medical Profession, *The Annals,* Vol. 297 (January 1955), p. 28.

[15] Ibid., pp. 26-27.

[16] Ibid., p. 21.

sity in this field as in others, for the continuous establishment of norms so that they may function in a manner appropriate to the society to which they are to be applied.

Status-roles. The simple patient-doctor relationship is Gesellschaft-like in that it is governed by norms that are universalistic, as opposed to particularistic or personal; in that responsibilities are specific, not blanket or general; and in that affection must be subordinated. It is Gemeinschaft-like in that it is a community of fate—it is collectivity oriented. Besides bearing a relationship to each other, both doctor and patient bear relationships to the community at large.

> When an individual behaves in a certain manner with reference to a doctor he is characterized in the role of patient. Any social role is always defined in a social relationshp, i.e., with reference to the interactive behavior of a plurality of individuals. Thus, "the patient" is defined in the relationship between himself and his physician. However, he is also perceived by the larger community—his friends and associates, the doctor's staff and colleagues—as a patient. In the complete depiction of the patient role, then the sociologist must immediately broaden his view so that the doctor-patient relationship is transcended and the patient is seen in a community context.[17]

In the community context, the authors then suggest that inquiry be made into how the patient role is initiated, how different people behave as patients in different social contexts, and how the individual "leaves" the patient role. These considerations suggest certain differences in the patient role from those of most others: "One may say that it is in a certain sense a 'negatively achieved' role, through failure to 'keep well,' though, of course positive motivations also operate, which by that very token must be motivations to deviance."[18] It is not inevitable as contrasted with the status-role in the family into which one is born; it is capriciously intermittent as contrasted with a controlled intermittency of the status-role in an informal group.

[17] Department of Sociology and Anthropology, Michigan State College, "The Patient-Doctor Relationship," in *Needed Research in Health and Medical Care,* by Cecil G. Sheps and Eugene E. Taylor (Chapel Hill: University of North Carolina Press, 1954), pp. 194-195.

[18] Parsons, *The Social System,* p. 538.

It is obvious that the doctor role is defined in his relationship with patients. However, the doctor is a highly visible person in the American community. As a doctor he is expected to participate in various civic affairs, and he is expected to live a particular kind of "social" life. His relationships with colleagues in the different contexts of private practice, the hospital, public health programs, and the like are also crucial for characterizing him in the role of doctor. In a sense, then, the mere depiction of the doctor role in a sociological investigation is more complex than the depiction of the patient role.[19]

The visibility of the patient and the doctor roles is doubtless greater in the rural and small town settings. Who the ailing are and how they conduct themselves, who the doctor is and what he says and does are not nearly so visible in New York City as in Four Corners.

Power, authority and influence. The public health official is in possession of legitimized authority. He operates within statutes or ordinances and is charged with specific duties for which his authority is spelled out. The authority of the practitioner in relation to his patient is absolute once the doctor has accepted the case; it is illustrated in the expression "doctor's orders."[20] The private practitioner wields much power. From his social rank one would expect that his influence would be great. People listen to him on medical and health matters, where he is an authority, but he is not without influence on many civic boards and commissions dealing in matters for which he has no specialized training.

Social rank. In a nationwide study[21] that sought to establish

[19] Sheps and Taylor, "The Patient-Doctor Relationship," p. 196.

[20] However, "Doctor's orders" or power based upon technical competence should be distinguished from that based on rational-legal authority of office. The physician in "getting his orders obeyed depends entirely on securing the voluntary consent of his patient to submit to them", not on coercive powers. For Parsons' well known criticism of Max Weber for having failed to differentiate these two types of power and authority, see Max Weber, *The Theory of Social and Economic Organization,* tr. by A. M. Henderson and Talcott Parsons, with an introduction by Talcott Parsons (N.Y.: Oxford University Press, 1947), p. 59.

[21] Robert W. Hodge, Paul M. Siegel, and Peter H. Rossi, "Occupational Prestige in the United States 1925-1963," *American Journal of Sociology* 70 (November, 1964) pp. 286-302. See Melvin L. Defleur, William V. D'Antonio and Lois B. Defleur, *Sociology: Man in Society* (Glenview, Ill: Scott, Foresman and Co. 1971), p. 228.

the popular evaluation of occupations, the chief factors making for high prestige seemed to be specialized training and responsibility for public welfare. The physician was thought by the respondents to rank very high, second place among the ninety categories listed. The U.S. Supreme Court Justice was the only occupation that was rated higher. Other health-related jobs which fell in the upper half of the ranking were dentist in thirteenth place, psychologist in sixteenth place, biologist in twenty-fifth place, and sociologist in twenty-sixth place.

Sanctions. Positive sanctions for the medical profession operate much like those of other organized groups. Election to local, county, state, and national office within the various associations, appointments of varying rank to hospital staffs, selection by an elect group such as American College of Surgeons, are rewards and recognition. Negative sanctions differ from most other groups in that they are almost entirely meted out by the profession itself and are virtually free from lay control.

"But perhaps the most conspicuous fact is that even their own professional associations do not play a really important part in the control of medical practice and its potential abuses through formal channels. It is true that medical associations do have committees on ethics and disciplinary procedures. But it is exceedingly rare for cases to be brought into that formal disciplinary procedure.

"Thus the well-known reluctance of physicians to testify against other physicians in cases of malpractice, in the courts, has its parallel in the reluctance of physicians to resort to the formal disciplinary procedures of their own associations, which do not involve 'washing their dirty linen' before laymen. . . .

"As one physician put it, 'Who is going to throw the first stone? We are all vulnerable. We have all been in situations where what we did could be made to look very bad.' "[22]

Territoriality. It will be remembered that one of the chief objectives of America's health program is adequate service to *all.* Much of the explanation for the exclusion from adequate service is territorial. In every important aspect of service, whether it be doctor, nurse, dentist, hospital, or public health department, the rural resident finds himself disadvantaged. Some of the regional

[22] Parsons, *The Social System,* pp. 470-471.

and territorial aspects of selected services and health measures will be treated in subsequent paragraphs.

The spatial problems in relation to health services in rural areas was highlighted among the recommendations of the President's National Advisory Commission on Rural Poverty. "The use of helicopters, small planes, and two-way radios for emergency care service as well as regular medical service in the outlying areas should be extended. Moreover, the increasing potential of computerized communication systems could be of crucial importance in the organization and delivery of health care in outlying areas. The use of closed-circuit television, telephone transmission of electrocardiogram tracings, electronic analysis of electrocardiograms, rapid recall of individual health records and the like should be explored."[23]

One sensitive measure of the quality of health services is the infant mortality rate. Table 1 shows these rates for whites and nonwhites residing in counties classified by degree of rurality and income level of the states. From this table it is clear that infant mortality rates are related to residence as well as income level: Rates are highest in the most rural and poverty stricken areas. Isolated rural counties exhibit markedly higher infant mortality rates than the metropolitan counties. While nonwhite rates are often twice as high as white rates, their relationship to rurality holds true.

The territorial spread of physicians, nurses, and hospital beds places isolated rural populations at a disadvantage. A crude indication of this fact is found in Table 2. The incidence of physicians, nurses, and hospital beds per population is shown for the ten most urban and the ten most rural states (based on the percentage urban in 1970). In general, the incidence of active non-Federal physicians and employed nurses is associated with urbanity. Active physicians, for example, range from 200 per 100,000 population in New York to only 64 per 100,000 population in Alaska. All except two of the most rural states have less than 100 active physicians per 100,000 population. Much the same pattern applies to active nurses. Only three urban states

---

[23] A Report by the President's National Advisory Commission on Rural Poverty, *The People Left Behind*, (Washington: Government Printing Office, 1967), p. 71.

TABLE 1

Infant Mortality Rate by Color, County Group, and Per
Capita Income Group of States: United States, 1961-65.

County group	United States	High (17 States)[1]	Middle (17 States)	Low (17 States)
Total infants:				
All county groups	25.1	23.5	24.7	29.3
Metropolitan	24.1	23.5	24.2	27.1
Greater[2]	24.0	24.0	23.9	25.5
Lesser[3]	24.2	22.7	26.8	27.2
Adjacent	25.5	22.5	25.0	29.9
Isolated	28.1	24.6	25.9	31.1
Semirural[4]	27.9	24.0	25.7	31.1
Rural	29.2	30.4	26.8	30.7
White infants:				
All county groups	22.0	21.3	22.3	23.3
Metropolitan	21.4	21.1	21.7	21.8
Greater[2]	21.0	20.9	21.1	21.3
Lesser[3]	22.5	21.8	22.2	21.8
Adjacent	22.6	21.8	23.0	23.7
Isolated	23.8	22.8	23.4	24.5
Semirural[4]	23.6	22.7	23.4	24.4
Rural	24.2	23.6	23.5	24.8
Nonwhite infants:				
All county groups	41.1	37.0	41.7	45.3
Metropolitan	38.2	36.7	39.4	41.1
Greater[2]	37.7	37.5	38.2	38.5
Lesser[3]	38.9	33.9	41.0	41.3
Adjacent	45.0	38.6	45.9	46.0
Isolated	48.1	43.8	47.7	48.7
Semirural[4]	47.8	39.1	48.1	48.8
Rural	49.5	63.8	47.0	48.8

(Exclusive of fetal deaths; rate is deaths under 1 year per 1,000 live
births; per capita income group of states, 1963-65).

[1] Includes District of Columbia.

[2] Population of 1,000,000 or more.

[3] Population of 50,000 to 1,000,000.

[4] Contains an incorporated place of 2,500 or more.

Source: Department of Health, Education, and Welfare, National Center for
Health Statistics, August 1966.

TABLE 2
Incidence of Physicians (Active, Non-Federal Providing
Patient Care), Employed Active Nurses, and General Medical
and Surgical Hospital Beds in 10 Most Urban and 10 Most
Rural States, 1970

State	Active Non-Federal M.D.'s and D.O.'s Providing Patient Care per 100,000 Population	Employed Nurses per 100,000 Population (Adjusted)	General Medical and Surgical Hospital Beds per 1,000 Population
United States	130	313	5.0
Ten Most Urban States			
California	169	312	4.6
Florida	122	369	5.1
Hawaii	128	321	4.6
Illinois	121	330	5.2
Massachusetts	168	532	4.9
Nevada	103	246	4.9
New Jersey	133	362	4.1
New York	200	408	5.0
Rhode Island	140	409	7.3
Utah	119	233	4.3
Washington	128	374	4.4
Ten Least Urban States			
Alaska	64	223	5.9
Arkansas	80	133	5.2
Mississippi	74	157	5.3
New Hampshire	116	521	4.5
North Carolina	92	244	4.4
North Dakota	84	329	7.6
South Carolina	80	217	4.8
South Dakota	77	308	6.9
Vermont	155	447	5.0
West Virginia	97	260	6.1

Source: U.S. Department of Health, Education, and Welfare, National Center
for Health Statistics, *Health Resources Statistics,* (Rockville, Maryland:
February 1972), Tables 85, 95, and 184. Most of the data relate to a year near 1970.
States are selected on the basis of the percentage urban in a state population.

fall below national average in the number of employed nurses per 100,000; only three rural states fall above national average. With respect to general medical and surgical hospital beds, sharp differences between the rural and urban states do not emerge. In fact, North Dakota, a rural state, has the largest number of general hospital beds per 1,000 population. Specialty hospitals, including psychiatric, tuberculosis, and others, of course, are not included in the data of Table 2, and such facilities tend to be located in large population centers.

Data from the National Health Survey are suggestive of the role played by residential location in relation to actual visits to physicians and dentists. Other factors as well are related to the use of physicians and dentists, as shown in Table 3. For residents of Standard Metropolitan Statistical Area (SMSA) counties, an average of 4.4 physician visits and 1.6 dentist visits per person per year are made. In contrast, for farm residents outside SMSA counties, the averages are only 3.1 and 1.1, respectively. This table also shows much larger percentages of the SMSA than the farm populations reporting one or more visits to the physician and dentist within the year of interview. As shown in the table the incidence of physician and dentist visits is greater for females than males, greater for whites than nonwhites, and greater for those in families whose head has more education.

Facilities. In the preceding section, we have stressed the disadvantaged position of many rural people in regard to health care due to residential location. In addition to spatial problems relating to health care, two demographic characteristics—the large proportion of young and old in rural populations—not only magnify but give a special character to these problems for rural people. Facilities for health care, initiated or expanded in the 1960's, will be singled out for brief comment because of their obvious relevance to health care in rural areas. They include nursing home care, ambulance service, and community comprehensive health service programs for the mentally ill, the poor, and the migrants.

The 1965 amendments to the Social Security Act (Medicare), and Title 19 of the same Act (Medicaid) gave impetus to development of new skilled nursing care facilities and the modification of existing facilities. In 1939 there were 1,200 nursing, convalescent and rest homes with about 25,000 beds. In 1969 there were 18,910 establishments providing nursing or personal care with

TABLE 3
Physician and Dentist Visits for Selected Segments of the U.S.
Population, 1969

Characteristic	Physician Visits		Dentist Visits	
	Number of Visits*	Percent with 1 or More Visits**	Number of Visits*	Percent with 1 or More Visits**
All Persons	4.3	69.4	1.5	45.0
Sex				
Male	3.7	66.7	1.4	43.8
Female	4.7	71.9	1.6	46.1
Color				
White	4.4	70.3	1.6	47.3
All Others	3.5	62.9	0.7	28.3
Education of Head of Family				
Under 5 years	4.1	61.2	0.6	21.0
5-8 years	4.0	63.4	0.9	29.9
9-12 years	4.2	69.7	1.5	45.3
13 years and over	4.7	76.2	2.2	62.9
Place of Residence				
All SMSA	4.4	70.8	1.6	47.2
Outside SMSA:				
Nonfarm	4.0	67.6	1.2	40.9
Farm	3.1	60.5	1.1	39.9

*Number of visits per person per year.
**Percentage of population with one or more visits within year of interview.

Source: U.S. Department of Health, Education and Welfare, National Center for Health Statistics, *Physician Visits*. (Series 10, Number 75) and *Dental Visits* (Series 10, Number 76), Rockville, Maryland, July 1972.

about 944,000 beds. See Table 4. While these nursing care facilities vary widely in the nature and quality of care provided, they tend to be evenly distributed throughout the nation.[24]

Of special significance to rural, dispersed population is the provision of emergency ambulance service. While ambulance services are widespread many rural residents are without such services. In 1971 it was estimated that about 13,000 ambulance services operated in the United States, in 49 states and the Dis-

[24] U.S. Department of Health, Education and Welfare, *Health Resources Statistics 1971*, (Rockville, Md.: February, 1972), pp. 317-330.

TABLE 4

Number and Beds in Nursing Care and Related Homes, 1963 and 1969

Type of Nursing Care and Related Homes	Number		Beds	
	1963	1969	1963	1969
Total	16,701	18,910	568,560	943,876
Nursing Care	8,128	11,484	319,224	704,217
Personal Care Homes with Nursing	4,958	3,514	188,306	174,874
Personal Care Homes without Nursing	2,927	3,792	48,962	63,532
Domiciliary Care	688	120	12,068	1,253

Source: U.S. Department of Health, Education and Welfare, *Health Resources Statistics 1971,* (Rockville, Maryland: February 1972), p. 320.

trict of Columbia. Ambulance services are operated by a great variety of organizations, including funeral homes, police and fire departments, volunteer community groups, welfare departments, and gasoline service stations. In addition, there is great diversity in vehicles used, equipment and training of attendants. About half of the states regulate the operation of ambulances and emergency vehicles.

In 1963, Congress passed the Mental Retardation and Community Mental Health Centers Construction Act, which marked the beginning of financial assistance for construction and staffing of mental health centers. About 500 centers have been established since that time. The mental health center may be a separate physical entity or it may be a network of services. Federally funded centers are unequally dispersed throughout the regions. Slightly more than one-third are in the South, the most rural region, but California led all states with 40 centers in 1971.[25]

The neighborhood health centers, revived in the 1960's, which help solve the out-of-hospital health problems of the poor, are sponsored by numerous groups such as hospitals, citizens groups, and departments of health. The neighborhood health center emphasizes preventive care and diagnosis and usually includes medical and dental, X-ray, laboratory, and pharmacy services. It is estimated that about 2,000 such centers are functioning in the United States. Comprehensive neighborhood health service programs federally funded through the Public Health Service or the Office of Economic Opportunity numbered 83 in

[25] Ibid., pp. 355-356.

1970. Alabama, Mississippi and North Carolina each reported two such centers. About one fourth, however, were located in New York and California.[26]

Historically, health services for migrant farm workers were virtually non-existent. In 1962, Congress passed the Migrant Health Act, which was broadened in 1970. This Act authorized the Public Health Service to make grants to State and local agencies for health services to migrants and their families as well us to nonmigrant seasonal farm workers. In 1971 there were 120 migrant health programs in operation and they were concentrated in those states having large migrant worker populations.[27]

CHANGES IN HEALTH STATUS INDICATORS

A variety of indicators demonstrate success in reducing the mortality rate and in altering the major causes of death. The experience of the United States has had parallels among most of the industrialized nations in moving from high to low birth and death rates. With relatively minor exceptions, both rural and urban populations have participated in major changes in the patterns of mortality.

As shown in Table 5, the crude death rate in the United States fell from 17.2 per 1,000 population in 1900 to 9.4 per 1,000 in 1970. Despite the continuous aging of the population in this period, the overall death rate continued to decline. During this period there has been a significant change in the major causes of death. In essence, the shift has been from the communicable group of causes to those considered degenerative. In 1900, influenza and pneumonia, tuberculosis, and gastritis ranked 1, 2, and 3, and were responsible for slightly less than one-third of all deaths. As shown in Table 6, heart disease in 1971 alone accounted for about 39 percent of all deaths. This table shows the ten leading causes of death in 1971, death rates per 100,000 and the percentage of all deaths attributable to each cause.

While we have alluded previously to high infant mortality rates in rural areas, we cannot assert unequivocally that all health status measures place rural populations in a disadvantageous position. In fact, it is probable that other characteris-

[26] Ibid., p. 356-360.
[27] Ibid., p. 356-357.

TABLE 5

Death Rate Per 1,000 Population for the United States, 1900 to 1970

Year	Death Rate Per 1,000 Populations
1900	17.2
1910	14.7
1920	13.0
1930	11.3
1940	10.8
1950	9.6
1960	9.5
1965	9.4
1970	9.4

Source: Department of Health, Education and Welfare, Public Health Service, *Vital Statistics of the United States.*

TABLE 6

Death Rates for the 10 Leading Causes of Death, United States, 1971

Rank	Cause of Death	Death Rate per 100,000	Percent of Total Deaths
	All Causes	929.0	100.0
1	Diseases of heart	358.4	38.6
2	Malignant neoplasms, including neoplasms of lymphatic and hematopoietic tissue	160.9	17.3
3	Cerebro-vascular diseases	100.6	10.8
4	Accidents	53.8	5.8
5	Influenza and pneumonia	27.2	2.9
6	Certain causes of mortality in early infancy	19.2	2.1
7	Diabetes mellitus	18.2	2.0
8	Cirrhosis of liver	15.5	1.7
9	Arteriosclerosis	15.5	1.7
10	Bronchitis, emphysema, and asthma	14.5	1.6
	All Other Causes	145.3	15.6

Source: U.S. Department of Health, Education and Welfare, Public Health Service, *Monthly Vital Statistics Report,* Vol. 20, No. 13, August 30, 1972. (Based on 10 percent sample of deaths).

tics such as income and education are more important than rural or urban residence in accounting for variations in health and mortality.

In his review of the relationship between crowding and health, Cassel explores residential differentials in death and mortality rates in the United States. He found death rates from all causes to be higher in urban than rural areas before 1950 and that by 1960 the situation had reversed. Since 1960 the ratio of rural to urban deaths he found to be increasing. Cassel speculates as follows about the reasons:

> Paradoxically, even though cities have been increasing in size since 1940, death rates have fallen more rapidly in these crowded circumstances than in the more sparsely populated rural areas. Part of this phenomenon may be due to improved medical care and sanitation in the cities and part to the migration of younger people to the cities, which leaves an older, more susceptible population behind in rural areas. These processes, it could be argued, might overwhelm or obscure the effects of crowding. That they can be only partial explanations for this reversal in the rural-urban health ratios is evident from the data. . . . The rural excess in incidence from typhoid fever, for example, may well be due to differences in sanitation, and the more effective immunization programs in cities may account for the lower urban rates of diphtheria and pertussis. However, the rural excess in the incidence of scarlet fever can hardly be due to either of these processes, as we do not as yet possess any means to prevent the occurrence of streptococcal infections. Similarly, as far as the migration hypothesis is concerned, this could not explain the excess mortality rates in rural children both black and white, male and female.[28]

The most elaborate analysis of childhood mortality by metropolitan and nonmetropolitan residence is provided in the American Public Health Association's Vital and Health Statistics Monograph published in 1968. Major findings relative to childhood mortality (ages 1-14) may be summarized as follows:[29]

[28] John Cassel, "Health Consequences of Population Density and Crowding" in *Rapid Population Growth,* pp. 463-464.

[29] Sam Shapiro, Edward R. Schlesinger, and Robert E. L. Nesbitt, Jr., *Infant, Perinatal, Maternal and Childhood Mortality in the United States* (Cambridge: Harvard University Press, 1968), pp. 201-203.

1. Mortality among pre-school and school age children is higher in nonmetropolitan than in metropolitan counties of the Nation.

2. The mortality excess in nonmetropolitan areas amounts to about 22 percent. This excess is applicable to whites and nonwhites but the difference is greater for nonwhites.

3. Excess male mortality is found in metropolitan and nonmetropolitan counties and for whites and nonwhites.

4. The excess nonmetropolitan mortality rates hold true for all nine geographic regions, but are small in the Middle Atlantic and North Central areas.

The authors make the following observations on their findings:

"The 22 percent excess in the overall childhood (1-14 years) mortality rate in the nonmetropolitan counties over the metropolitan counties of the United States (all races) was related mainly to the higher mortality rates from accidents and infectious diseases in the nonmetropolitan counties. The 52 percent excess in the accident rate in the nonmetropolitan counties accounted for 73 percent of the differences in the rates between the two groups of counties. . . .

"Most of the remaining difference in the childhood mortality rates was traceable to the higher rates for infectious diseases in the nonmetropolitan counties. The greatest difference was observed in the death rate from gastroenteritis, which was nearly twice as high (89 percent excess) in the nonmetropolitan counties. . . .

"The differentials in rates by cause of death suggest some of the reasons for the overall higher mortality outside the metropolitan counties. Adverse environmental conditions in the nonmetropolitan counties would tend to be associated with the considerably higher death rates from fires and explosions of combustible materials and from gastroenteritis and, to a lesser extent, other infectious diseases. The relative inadequacy of medical care and other health services in nonmetropolitan areas receives some confirmation from the lower recorded death rates from malignant diseases and congenital malformations in these areas; the most obvious explanation for these differences lies in the less adequate diagnosis of these conditions outside the metropolitan counties."[30]

[30] Ibid., pp. 203-204.

SOCIAL ORGANIZATION AND THE DIFFUSION OF THE HEALING ARTS

Gaining an understanding of the processes involved in the adoption and diffusion of improved practices in health in underdeveloped areas provides the social scientist with challenging opportunities. Unquestionably, there is untold suffering and millions of needless deaths throughout the world because the scientific achievements of the advanced countries have not been brought into active use in the less favored areas. Actually, many die in the United States for the same reason. The authors hope that the following analysis of an early unsuccessful attempt to bring medical facilities to a major segment of the population of the United States will help to explain some of the problems involved in improving health.

THE TAOS COUNTY COOPERATION HEALTH ASSOCIATION

The Taos County Cooperative Health Association,[31] if it had been successful, would have had great significance for the two and a half to three million Spanish-speaking people in the five southwestern states at that time. The Association was formally organized in 1942 and began to give service to 907 paid-up member families. It had the formal approval and active support of the Taos County Medical Society. And it was supported by the Taos County Project, an experiment in adult education started in 1940 by the University of New Mexico and the Harwood Foundation with support from the Carnegie Corporation. It also received financial support and other assistance from the Farm Security Administration. After the Association was incorporated in 1942, the FSA made a grant of $47,000. During the first year of operation the 1,145 families enrolled paid $38.03 per family, 80 percent of which was covered by a subsidy from the FSA. Under the subsidy no family paid less than $1 and none more than $32, each family paying in relation to ability. Medical care

---

[31] Charles P. Loomis, "Putting a Cooperative Health Association Over to Spanish Speaking Villagers," in *Studies of Rural Social Organization* (East Lansing: State College Book Store, 1945), Chapter 18; and "The Taos County Project of New Mexico—An Experiment in Local Cooperation Among Bureaus, Private Agencies, and Rural People," in *Studies in Applied and Theoretical Social Science* (East Lansing: The Michigan State College Press, 1950), Chapter 7.

was made available for less than $8 per person of which the FSA bore all but 15 percent.

Need for health facilities. At the time the Association was formed, Taos County had great need for more adequate medical care. The infant mortality rate was as high as for any county in the nation.[32] In the period from 1937-1939, 64 percent of the deaths reported were listed as "cause unknown," an indication that no physician handled the case at the time of death. In 1941 no death certificates had been issued for 62 percent of those who died, likewise indicating that no physician was present. In the 1937-1939 period, 1,629 births occurred and of these 1,122 were delivered by midwives with little or no formal training, and 193 by other persons with doubtful training.[33] An investigation of human nutrition found diets so poor in one of the villages that children walking to school and playing at recess had such a tissue deficiency of oxygen that the remainder of the day was required to make it up. The same investigator found that whole villages were sometimes so infected with intestinal parasites that school lunches had no effect on physical performance until a village-wide parasite elimination campaign was conducted.[34]

Great ingenuity was used to involve the rural people in the program of the Association. This included the utilization of local leaders, an educational program, and as previously stated, a heavy subsidy. The University of New Mexico, through its Extension Division, the Taos Project, and the various cooperating agencies, especially the Farm Security Administration, applied unbelievable energy and ingenuity in order to make the Association a success. "Here, it would seem, was an enterprise that could not fail. Here was a serious medical need that an organization had been set up to meet. Here was good medical care made available at a cost (including the Farm Security Administration's subsidy) of less than $8.00 a year per person. And yet, in spite of tremendous efforts, membership in the Association steadily declined until, in 1948, it ceased to function."[35] Why had

[32] An infant mortality rate of 108 per 1,000 live births, traceable mainly to diarrhea and enteritis, was reported.

[33] Lyle Saunders, *Cultural Difference and Medical Care* (New York: Russell Sage Foundation, 1954), p. 175.

[34] Michael Pijoan, "Food Availability and Social Function," *New Mexico Quarterly Review,* Vol. XII, No. 4 (November, 1942).

[35] Saunders, *Cultural Difference,* p. 177.

this operation failed? We cannot specify all the reasons. We shall, however, attempt to provide some of the reasons in the following analysis.

STRATEGY OF CHANGE INVOLVING TWO CONTRASTING SOCIAL SYSTEMS

As Saunders writes, "one major cause was that the Association attempted to provide Anglo medical care to a people who were not yet culturally ready to receive or support it."[36] In 1944, it had been noted that although 95 percent of the people of Taos County spoke Spanish, all of the physicians and most of the professionals and business people in the county were Anglos. United States Department of Agriculture investigators,[37] after the Association had operated a year, found that 80 percent of the families knew little of the purpose for which it was organized, 40 percent did not know the manager, only 40 percent could name one or more of the members, and 22 percent did not know it had a board of directors. No doubt, as Saunders implies, his lack of information about the Association is in part responsible for its failure. But even this is related to the difficulties involved in an attempt to link the value systems of the families and communities of the rural Spanish-speaking people on one hand, and the social systems which carry Anglo medicine, on the other. One year after the establishment of the Association, 15 percent of a sample of member families interviewed had paid for a midwife's services and approximately six percent had used a native medicine man, even though hospitalization and delivery by a physician were included in the Association membership. These facts point to the necessity for comparative analysis of the Spanish-American social system and the Anglo system. We now attempt to explain some aspects of the failure of the change system, the Taos Project, which attempted to attain systemic linkage with the target system, the Taos County Cooperative Health Association.

The medical social system incorporated in the Association was organized around specific roles, namely, doctors, nurses,

[36] Ibid., p. 177.

[37] T. Wilson Longmore and Theodore L. Vaughan, *Taos County Cooperative Health Association, 1942* (Little Rock: Bureau of Agricultured Economics, U.S.D.A., September 1944), mimeo.

and auxiliary personnel. It was an Anglo system that had worked effectively in Anglo communities but that had not been adapted to Spanish-American culture. Some cultural differences pertinent to the analysis of the failure of the Taos Association will be indicated here. These are essentially differences in the ends and norms of social systems and individuals.

Relative importance of the family.   The nuclear and extended families are much more important in the motivation and value orientation of individuals in the Spanish-American than in the Anglo culture. Physicians and hospital administrators who have had experience with Spanish-Americans as patients have commented upon the great difficulty of retaining them in the patient role, especially when family crises or celebrations are involved. Thus, to quote Saunders:

> One Spanish-American woman, for example, has a record of having left a tuberculosis ward seven times against medical advice. Each time a minor family crisis was involved. . . . Another instance is that of a Spanish-American woman who was injured in an automobile accident and was confined to a hospital with two broken bones. After a few days she and her husband decided that she should go home. Physicians argued that the woman needed to be in traction if the bones were to heal properly and that she also required specialized care that could not be given in the home.[38]

This was to no avail. Rural Spanish-Americans desire home treatment with family members present even when not as effective as hospital treatment. Probably because of the strength of the family, many hospitals in Latin America are equipped with beds for relatives of patients.

Dependency vs. independency.   In an analysis of the patient-doctor relationship, Parsons described functionally important aspects of the physician's roles that prevent slipping out of the doctor role. Thus, some of the characteristics of the relationships, namely, "universalism, functional specificity, and affective neutrality, are to enable the physician to 'penetrate' sufficiently into the private affairs, or the 'particular nexus' of his patients to perform his function,"[39] and at the same time avoid

[38] Saunders, *Cultural Difference,* pp. 210-211.
[39] Parsons, *The Social System,* p. 459.

slipping out of his role as physician. Such an institutionalization requires that the physician not permit the patient to become dependent in any way outside the limits of his status-role. Anglos in general, and Anglo doctors in particular, put much greater stress upon independence in interrelationships than do Spanish-Americans. Numerous studies[40] have emphasized the importance of dependence rather than independence in nonfamily as well as family social systems in the Spanish-American culture. In relying on the institutional protection of their status-roles and as a consequence avoiding dependence, Anglo doctors may fail to give the degree of satisfaction provided by local medicine men, who do not value independence, Anglo doctors may fail to give the degree of satisfaction provided by local medicine men, who do not value independence so highly. The apparent need for personal dependence on the part of persons in the Spanish-American culture is in sharp conflict with the general Anglo emphasis on ability to "stand on one's own feet" and to be "beholden to no one."

Personalism and particularism. In the Spanish-American culture particularism, or personal relations as ends in and of themselves, has greater importance than in the Anglo culture. Whether or not another person is *simpatico* (a word for which there is no exact English equivalent but which indicates the quality of increasing others' self-esteem on personal grounds in interaction) is of great importance to Spanish-Americans. Although doctors may emphasize such behavior as "the bedside manner," the emphasis on professional competency is much greater. The local medicine man and *curanderos* who depend extensively upon personal appeal and who do not need to guard against the patient becoming dependent upon them have a distinct advantage over Anglo physicians because of the great emphasis in the Spanish-American culture on personal relationships.

Dislike for bureaucracy. A number of scholars have incorrectly considered the Spanish-American to be individualistic

[40] Loomis, *Studies in Rural Social Organization*, p. 385. Here the *peon-patron* relationship is described. This is related to the paternalism subconfiguration of the *familia* configuration as developed by Florence Kluckhohn in *Los Atarquenos, A Study of Patterns and Configurations in a New Mexico Village*, (Cambridge, Mass.: Radcliffe College doctoral dissertation, 1941). See especially Saunders, *Cultural Difference*, pp. 133ff.

and have stressed his preference for informality.[41] These terms may correctly describe the Spanish-American if applied to specific large-scale, bureaucratic, or Gesellschaft-like reference groups. However, the great sacrifices Spanish-Americans make for family and friends and the effective cooperation carried on through these groups belie any individualism so far as these reference systems are concerned. Thus, a father or other family member who acts in a manner unbecoming to his status-role is condemned, perhaps more in Spanish-American than in Anglo culture. Actually what has been incorrectly called individualism and dislike for formal groups is in reality lack of intimate acquaintance with and distaste for bureaucracy or large scale Gesellschaft-like organizations. In the field of health this is expressed in the resistance to hospitalization.

Acceptance and resignation vs. work and efficiency. As Saunders emphasizes, the Anglo lives in the future; the Spanish-American in the present. "The Spanish-speaking ideal is *to be* rather than *to do.*"[42] This leads to behavior which the Anglo may consider as laziness or lack of "gumption." The rural Spanish-Americans generally accept sickness as inevitable. It is not something that effort may remedy.

Differences in orientation to time. Most American students of Spanish-American culture have observed a basic distaste for discipline in the timing of events. In Latin America *hora Inglesa* means time by the clock as contrasted to time in the everyday sense. Florence Kluckhohn[43] has described the Spanish-American orientation to time as the *mañana* configuration. The rural Spanish-American finds the Anglo medical time schedules and requirements for punctual appointments disagreeable and frustrating. Thus, Saunders writes that "in dealing with Spanish-speaking patients it may prove wise not to expect rigid adherence to time schedules. . . . Long-in-the-future appointments should be avoided. . . ."[44]

Fear and anxiety. A vague fear of the unknown or of unpredictable forces on the part of Spanish-Americans is another cul-

[41] Saunders, *Cultural Difference,* p. 136 and Parsons, *The Social System,* p. 199.

[42] Saunders, p. 126. See also Arthur L. Campa, "Mañana is Today," *New Mexico Quarterly,* Vol. 5(1939); and Loomis, *Studies of Rural Social Organization,* pp. 385ff.

[43] Kluckhohn, *Los Atarquenos.*

[44] Saunders, *Cultural Difference,* p. 220.

tural configuration. Young women, for example are supposed to be afraid of the dark. This general feature of Spanish-American culture is mentioned because it accentuates the feelings of insecurity that most people have in the unfamiliar surroundings of the clinic or hospital. Saunders[45] reports the case of a Spanish-American woman who so feared the hospital, and particularly the delivery table, that she delivered the child herself in a corner of the room rather than ring for attendants.

PATIENT-FOLK PRACTITIONER COMPARED WITH THE PATIENT-PHYSICIAN RELATIONSHIP

For the rural Spanish-American, the local medicine man (*curandero*) and local untrained midwife *(partera)* compete with the Anglo physician. All three are specialists, although the Anglo physician is more specialized than his competitors, the *curanderos* and *parteras*. For the Spanish-Americans certain major differences exist which are more important than the differences in specialized training. The local folk practitioners do not charge as much as the Anglo doctor. They ply their skills and knowledge in the homes of sick persons and do not require special facilities such as hospitals. Their approach is more personal or particularistic. They may be related through kinship to the family, and they speak the same mother tongue as the patient.

The basic relations of the folk practitioner with his patient falls closer to the Gemeinschaft end of the continuum than those of the physician with his patient. Since the Spanish-American culture carries with it the particularistic-ascriptive patterns, it does not find modern medical practice based upon opposite and more Gesellschaft-like patterns compatible. These are among the reasons why the Taos County Cooperative Health Association failed. They are also reasons why modern medical science is not in as great demand in many rural cultures as in most urban cultures.

EXPLANATION OF FAILURE

We may now briefly review the discussion to this point specifically mentioning the relevant elements and processes involving Anglo medical practice and the Spanish-American people.

[45] Ibid, p. 20.

Ends and norms.   For the Anglo medical system the chief end was improving the health of the people. The normative orientation of the Association required that improved health be accomplished through the application of science in accordance with universalistic standards and in such a manner as to retain the independence of the practitioner. Affective involvement was to be avoided. The practitioner held himself responsible for only specific activities of the patient, namely, those related to his health. Thus, the practitioner maintained a nonpersonal, nonaffective, and specific as opposed to diffuse orientation.

The Spanish-American people desired a highly personalized service in which the practitioner assumed responsibility for economic and general well being as well as health, and in which "care" meant affection. The Anglo physicians, when compared with the medicine men and midwives in these respects, were found less satisfying.

Status-roles.   The doctor, nurse, and other roles in the social system that brought medical practice to the Latin American villager fit less readily into the status-role prototypes of the family, the chief social system of the villager, than did the medicine men and midwives. Not only did the latter not require the impersonal, anxiety-producing hospital, but also they could often assume the status-roles of fathers, mothers, aunts, or uncles.

Power.   The power implied in "doctor's orders" for the Anglos simply did not apply for the Spanish-Americans. Many cases of complete disregard for the orders and prescriptions of the doctors and nurses, even when disregard led to great danger and even pain, are on record. In the Spanish-American society the priest exercises far more power than the medical doctor; in Anglo society the reverse is true. Social rank in this instance is closely related to power. Among the Latin Americans in New Mexico, the doctor's social rank depended less upon his technical competence than upon other factors, including income and local influence.

Sanctions.   The local medicine men, because of their reputation for control over the natural and supernatural, could apply at least imaginary positive and negative sanctions that were not available to the medical practitioner. The more adequate facilities available to the latter did not overcome the advantages that the belief system gave to the non-medical practitioner.

Territoriality.   The fact that the medical doctor's service was restricted to the hospitals and the clinics that were often long distances from the people must be considered important, especially for women and children who are customarily closely confined to the home and village. The hospitals that did not accomodate family members of the sick patient were anxiety-producing because they offered little to which the Spanish-Americans were accustomed. Spanish-Americans might be expected to visit a priest whose residence was as distant as that of the doctor, but his powers are not thought to be space-bound as in the case of the doctor.

FAILURE TO ESTABLISH SYSTEMIC LINKAGE

When one of the authors studied the Taos County Cooperative Health Association in 1942 there were three clinics in the towns of Taos, Questa, and Penasco, each staffed by a full-time registered nurse and visited on a regular schedule by physicians and dentists. The waiting rooms of these clinics were usually full of Spanish-American people off the farms and ranches with ailments ranging from broken bones to minor illnesses and injuries. At this time systemic linkage seemed to be in process. When he returned in 1949 after the Association had failed, the doors and windows of the clinics in Questa and Penasco were boarded up and the expensive equipment was idle. The Taos clinic, now a private doctor's office, was empty. There were few patients in any of the private doctors' offices. The people who filled the clinics had returned to the local *curanderos* and to resigned suffering. Systemic linkage had not been achieved.

Communication. The fact that few of the health practitioners spoke Spanish, of course, was an important factor in the failure of the Association. Not to be overlooked when two cultures merge are basic differences in value orientation which lead to misunderstanding, perhaps more important than language barriers. For instance, one of the doctors who helped support the Association before it was organized, while under the influence of liquor in one of the community saloons, shouted something to the effect that the trouble with Taos County was that there were too many "dirty Greasers." This was frequently mentioned by local people when the Association was discussed.

Decision-making. The Association was established with a board of seven directors elected at the annual membership meetings of the Association. The treasurer-manager and the staff of the Association was employed by the board of directors. In the Taos Association, the participation of Spanish-Americans in the decision-making of their Association was feeble. With their dislike for formal meetings and with their lack of experience in large scale organizations, the Spanish-Americans lost interest in attending after the start. This meant that the employed staff made most of the decisions. In view of the tendency on the part of Spanish-Americans to stress personal relationships, such a development was to be expected.

Boundary maintenance. The two systems, the Anglo staff, and the Spanish-speaking members of the Association continued to hold to their own value orientations. These basic differences in the value orientations of the Spanish-Americans and the Anglos in large measure explain the failure of the Association. Before an Association such as this can succeed, acculturation of the Spanish-Americans to Anglo ways must proceed further than it had in 1949, or the Anglo medical system must adjust itself to the value orientation of the Spanish-Americans.

SELECTED REFERENCES

Economic Research Service, U.S.D.A. *The Economic and Social Condition of Rural America in the 1970's.* Washington: Government Printing Office, 1971, Part III.

Hitt, Homer L., and Paul H. Price. *Health in Rural Louisiana at Mid-Century.* Baton Rouge: Louisiana Agr. Expt. Sta. Bull. No. 492, June, 1954.

Hoffer, C. R., et al. *Health Needs and Health Care in Michigan.* East Lansing: Michigan Agr. Expt. Sta. Spec. Bull. 365, June, 1950.

Loomis, Charles P. "Social Systems for Health," in *Social Systems—Their Persistence and Change.* Princeton: D. van Nostrand, 1960, Essay 6.

Miller, Paul A., et al. *Community Health Action.* East Lansing: Michigan State College Press, 1953.

Paul, Benjamin D., ed. *Health, Culture, and Community.* New York: Russell Sage Foundation, 1955. See Chapter 14, "A Medical Care Program in a Colorado County," by Lyle Saunders and Julian Samora.

Report by the President's National Advisory Commission on Rural

Poverty. *The People Left Behind.* Washington: Government Printing Office, 1967, Chapter 6.

Saunders, Lyle. *Cultural Differences and Medical Care.* New York: Russell Sage Foundation, 1954.

Shapiro, Sam, Edward R. Schlesinger, and Robert E. Nesbitt, Jr. *Infant, Perinatal, Maternal and Childhood Mortality in the United States.* Cambridge: Harvard University Press, 1968.

U.S. Department of Health, Education, and Welfare. *Health Resources Statistics,* Rockville, Md., February, 1972.

12

Federal Agency Systems

Except for the Extension Service, the growth of governmental agencies providing services to farmers is confined largely to the past forty years. Hence, bureaucracy in the form of numerous governmental agencies has made its debut relatively recently in rural communities throughout the United States. With regard to bureaucracy, Hardin says: "Our government is heavily obligated to defend the country, to keep order, to regulate and promote the economy, and to provide social security and other services. To fulfill these ends requires a formidable organization of power that is symbolized in the term 'bureaucracy' . . ."[1]

Federal government outlays for agricultural and rural development functions have been substantial for many years. Since 1960 the support of these functions has amounted to about 3 percent of total outlays. In 1972 the outlay for agricultural purposes compared favorably with that for education and manpower (3.1 percent as compared with 4.3 percent).[2] A number of agricultural agencies, many of them arms of the U.S. Department of Agriculture, are also organized on a state, district, and/or county level.

Among the important agencies designed to serve the needs of rural people are: The Cooperative Extension Service, the Agricultural Experiment Station, Vocational Agriculture and Homemaking, the Soil Conservation Service, The Forest Service, the Agriculture Stabilization and Conservation Service, the Farmers Home Administration, the Farm Credit Administration, and the Rural Electrification Administration. Each has a particular function and organization. We will consider the Extension Service in some detail and select others for brief comment.

[1] Charles M. Hardin, *Freedom in Agricultural Education* (Chicago: University of Chicago Press, 1955).

[2] *Statistical Abstract of The United States,* 1972 (Washington: Government Printing Office, 1972), pp. 384-385.

THE COOPERATIVE EXTENSION SERVICE
AS A SOCIAL SYSTEM

The work of the Extension Service involves many and varied social systems. Those to whom service is rendered deal chiefly with the county agricultural agent, the home demonstration agent, and the 4-H Club worker. In addition to their relations with the public, extension personnel have a network of relationships with the Extension Division of the Land Grant Colleges that in turn is related to the national program. Typical social systems will be presented and analyzed in terms of the elements of social systems. The case at the end of this chapter illustrates these elements and the processes involved in change.

County agent-farm family relationships. The Gemeinschaft-like nature of the scene when agricultural extension began is typified in the following fictionalized excerpt concerning pre-extension work in an inaccessible area of the Kentucky mountains at the turn of the century. Aunt Ailsie is impressed with the demonstrations of bread-making, table-setting, and sewing but is shocked because the young women conducting the demonstrations are unmarried. Uncle Lot, her husband, falling back upon the Bible and Solomon, sees the workers as "furrin" women. After a lively exchange involving manners, morals, and theology, he says: "Them women may be quare and furrin and fotched-on, but, in my opinion, they hain't runaway wives."[3]

Many of the relationships of extension personnel with farm families today are Gemeinschaft-like. A home demonstration agent, for example, may plan a kitchen with a local leader who in turn may teach the lesson in neighborhood groups. She often knows in detail the habits of a given family, the balance of farm and housework expected of the mother, and the day-to-day routine of the father. On the other hand, the relationships may be more Gesellschaft-like. The county agent on a platform surrounded by sixty or seventy men, demonstrating how to cull chickens exemplifies relatively Gesellschaft-like situations in extension work.

County agent-agricultural college extension division relationships. Formality and informality, friendship and business, all

[3] Lucy Furman, *The Quare Women* (Boston: Atlantic Monthly Press, 1923), pp. 7-44.

exist in the interrelations between the personnel of the Extension organization itself. A county agent may feel close to one of the subject matter specialists, for example, and seek his assistance more often than that of a specialist whom he knows only in more formal relationships. In groups of counties and especially in districts, the agents often have a decided in-group feeling. Problems, personal and professional, are often discussed in such groups as one would with old friends. The relations of the agents with officials at the higher echelons are unlikely to be entirely uninhibited, since standards, promotions, salary, and policy generally are controlled at this level. However, many times there are personal friendships and friendly relationships between the lowest and the highest echelons. One Extension director made it a point to make conferences with all staff members lengthy, filled with witty stories and small talk. Much of the interaction up and down the hierarchy, however, is restricted to impersonal memos, reports, and other formalized means of transacting business in a bureaucracy.

Objectives. Several legislative acts furnish the foundation for the Cooperative Extension Service created and defined by the Smith-Lever Act of 1914. The Morrill Act which established the colleges of agriculture in the United States was passed in 1862. This was followed by the Hatch Act of 1887 which provided for the establishment of the Agricultural Experiment Stations. In addition, the Adams Act of 1906 should be mentioned, since it provided funds for agricultural research.

The objective of the Cooperative Extension Service, as described in the Smith-Lever Act, was "to aid in the diffusing among the people of the United States useful and practical information on agriculture and home economics and to encourage the application of the same through field demonstrations, publication, and otherwise." The Extension Service, as related by Knapp, "may be considered a system of rural education for boys and adults by which a readjustment of country life can be effected and placed upon a higher plane of profit, comfort, culture, influence, and power."[4]

Probably the most important unfulfilled objective is that of reaching all of the people. The accusation is made that extension

[4] Seaman A. Knapp, "The Farmers' Cooperative Demonstration Work," *Yearbook of the United States Department of Agriculture, 1909* (Washington, D.C.: Government Printing Office, 1910), p. 160.

programs reach the upper third of the people and that they generally are the ones who "don't need it." In an open-class society such as ours, the lower classes should profit from the gains of the upper classes as improved practices diffuse downward. The reason for the accusation is discussed in connection with social rank.

Norms. The county agent is beset with a number of normative decisions peculiar to his profession. One such decision revolves around the balance necessary between the will of the people and the agent's technical knowledge. A home demonstration agent giving a demonstration on preserving huckleberries, for instance, was confronted with folk knowledge of a canning method in which cold water and aspirin were used. There was no scientific basis for using this method. Approval of "any process that works" would have given scientific and professional approval to an unscientific folk practice. In this instance it was not difficult to be loyal to the scientific training of the profession. In other cases, however, a county agent may give approval to a project that has no scientific basis, but which is advocated by an important power group.

Extension personnel are also subjected to divided loyalties—to the State Extension Service, on one hand, and to the county on the other. The following example illustrates such divided loyalty:

"FL had unenthusiastically organized a county Agricultural Advisory Council at the behest of the State Extension office, but he felt it was unnecessary in the county. It took months to get organizations to designate representatives, and it was hard to find meeting times when a majority could or would appear. The sessions themselves were strained and awkward, since many council members were cautious about each other, and preferred to operate via old accustomed channels. After a few unproductive meetings, FL decided the group was too unwieldy, and ceased to schedule any more. He knew the state office was disturbed by this outcome, but felt he had made a genuine effort to make the organization work. He believed its failure was not his fault, but was simply due to the impracticality of the idea at the county level."[5]

[5] Jack J. Preiss, "Functions of Relevant Power and Authority Groups in the Evaluation of County Agent Performance," Unpublished doctoral dissertation (Michigan State College, 1954), p. 236.

Any effective county agent inevitably builds up a large group of friends and supporters who would be an asset if the agent were to get into politics. The framers of the Hatch Act foresaw this possibility and this act prohibits political activity by Extension personnel. Besides this legal prohibition, however, a strong ethic regarding nonparticipation in politics prevails within the Service.

Status-roles. Although Figure 1 indicates the main organizational outlines of the State Extension Service, it fails to emphasize sufficiently the local nature of the organization. While the county agent is subject to the authority of those at the state level, the position he occupies in his own county is not that of an inconspicuous cog of a large state bureau. He has subject-matter and organizational status-roles which mark him in most of his activities. It is hard for him to be just another member in the Farm Bureau, for example. Here his knowledge of agricultural practices in the county and his coterie of supporters cause him to act and be expected to act in a manner consistent with his status-role as county agricultural agent. Because he has the responsibility for continually reinforcing the organization of the county, every program that relies upon rural organization sees in him a possible ally. The Red Cross in making rural collections in its finance drive, the county library in planning the location of its branches, the health service in disseminating information are all likely to want to rely upon him or upon the sub-organizations his agency has created to render assistance. Since the subjects he and his staff deal with concern the farm, the home, and the family, the agent's style of life as well as that of his family is expected to reflect the best teachings of the Extension Service. Although he may have majored in a special field of agriculture, he no longer is a specialist when he becomes a county agent. While his love might be soil science, his practice must be shared among dairy, farm management, and many other interests. He becomes the personification of scientific agricultural practices on the one hand, and an integrative rural organizer on the other.

Just as the county agent occupies a conspicuous status-role, the clientele of the Service is also likely to be more visible in the community than are members in most organizations. To the extent that the client is an innovator, he is watched by non-clients so that they may copy if the innovation is successful or laugh at

THE COUNTY EXTENSION OFFICE
How People Use It

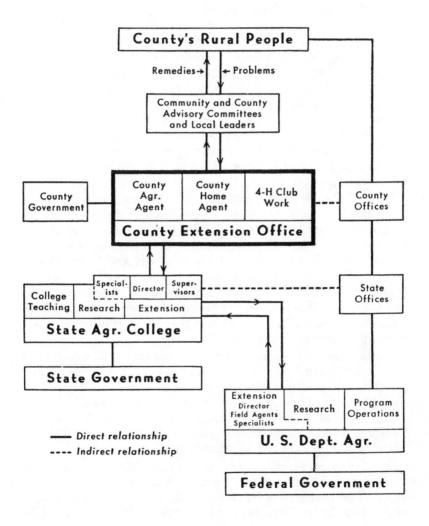

FIGURE 1. Organizational chart of the Cooperative Extension Service.

the innovation if it fails. One farmer comments upon the county agent as follows:

"Well, a lot of people criticize him, but he knows what he's doing. They laugh at him sometimes, and at me for all the things I try, but I'll tell you, mister, if it wasn't for FH I wouldn't be on this farm today. The ones who gripe are the ones who just barely keep a-going. The progressive farmers are all behind him."[6]

Power, authority and influence. From the beginning, the Cooperative Extension Service has been a quasi-governmental organization, with stipulated relations to the United States Department of Agriculture. Each County Extension Service has its share of this authority. Each County Extension Service has its share of this authority. It is a branch of the State Extension Service in a Land Grant College and in turn is related to the Federal Extension Service.

In 1962 the Federal Extension Service was reorganized into the following: (1) Division of Agricultural Service, Technology and Management; (2) Division of Marketing and Utilization; (3) Division of Resource Development and Public Affairs; (4) Division of Home Economics; (5) Division of 4-H and Youth Development; (6) Division of Information ; (7) Division of Extension Research and Training; and (8) Division of Management Operations. Each of these divisions maintains administrative liaison with the states and interprets and prepares resources for use in the state extension programs.

At the county level there is a legal authority, the county governing body, and frequently a number of federal agricultural agencies carrying out directives from national headquarters on a county basis. The agent's ability to identify himself with a sufficient number of the power groups and to maintain satisfactory relations with the authority groups seems to determine the power he wields in doing an effective job.

Preiss'[7] analysis of county agent case histories shows that there is little local power inherent in the position of the county agent. The real power resides in the locally organized groups such as the Dairy Herd Improvement Association, the Artificial

[6] Ibid., p. 166.
[7] Ibid., p. 168.

Insemination Association, the Farm Bureau, and the Beet Growers Association. The organizations with which extension agents work are indicated in Table 1.

Social rank. Preiss' study of county agent performance reveals that the support of the local power groups is more important than carrying out assignments and the "proper relations" to superiors in attaining high rank in the state Extension system. A national study of the ranking of occupations places the county agent in the upper half (40th) of the ninety occupations ranked. This rank is shared by the railroad engineer and the electrician. Ranking relatively near but below the county agent is the farm owner and operator (43rd).[8] Functionally, this indicates that the county agent is approximately at the social level of the people with whom he works. "A few of the top farmers and leaders could meet FH as a status 'equal' and could feel that he depended upon their support fully as much as they depended on him,"[9] Preiss reports in one of his county case studies.

Various studies have demonstrated that although the contacts of the Extension Service personnel are broad, the frequency of contact and acquaintance with Service personnel are closely correlated with income and social rank.[10] In fact, the Cooperative Extension Service has been criticized severely in recent years for neglecting low income and minority groups in rural areas. The National Commission on Rural Poverty, in addressing the need

[8] Robert W. Hodge, Paul M. Siegel and Peter H. Rossi, "Occupational Prestige in the United States: 1925-1963," *American Journal of Sociology,* Vol. 70, No. 3, (November 1964), pp. 286-302. The argument of status equality between extension agents and farmers is difficult to sustain since the farm group in this research is a "catch-all" group having great variance. That is some farmers would outrank the agent while others would not. However, most agents were born and reared as farmers or in small towns and villages which would tend to offset the effects of status differences.

[9] Preiss, "Functions of Relevant Power," p. 168.

[10] For early studies supporting this generalization, see D. L. Gibson, "The Clientele of the Agricultural Extension Service," *Michigan AES Quarterly Bulletin,* Vol. XXVI, No. 4 (May, 1944); C. R. Hoffer, *Selected Social Factors Affecting Participation of Farmers in Agricultural Extension Work,* (East Lansing: Michigan AES Special Bulletin 331, 1944); and James West, *Plainville, U. S. A.* (New York: Columbia University Press, 1945), p. 224. More recently see A Report of the President's National Advisory Commission on Rural Poverty, *The People Left*

TABLE 1
Organizations that Extension Agents Work With Most in
Educational Activities for Adults

Organizations Worked With	Percentage of Agents Naming Specified Organizations
Farm Organizations	96
Schools	90
Colleges and Universities	79
Women's Clubs	70
Federal and/or State Government Bureaus	69
Churches and Religious Organizations	66
Community Councils	57
Parent's Organizations	56
Elected or Appointed Government Bodies	46
Civic and Service Organizations	45
Welfare Councils	36
Libraries	36
Inter-Agency Councils	36
Patriotic and Veterans Organizations	34
Fraternal Organizations	19
UNESCO Organizations	13

Source: Joseph L. Matthews in C. P. Loomis, et al., *Rural Social Systems and Adult Education* (East Lansing: The Michigan State College Press, 1953), p. 68.

for informal education in rural America says: "the Cooperative Extension Service . . . must have its mission clearly identified with the problems of low income rural families."[11] The report also includes specific recommendations to modify and alleviate the status of rural blacks, Chicanos, and American Indians.

Acquaintance with personnel and use of the Service are also positively correlated with educational attainment and the extent of acculturation to American ways. Farmers between the ages of forty and sixty use the Service more than either older or younger

---

Behind (Washington: Government Printing Office, 1967), and L. Watson, J. Gatehouse and E. Dorsey, *Failing the People* (Washington: Agricultural Policy Accountability Project, 1972).

[11] Ibid., *The People Left Behind,* p. 54.

farmers. The realities of social class to a large extent dictate the makeup of the county agent's clientele and pose great difficulties in the actual realization of the objective of reaching everyone.

Sanctions. The chief sanctions applied to the county agent come in the nature of rewards (higher salary and ranking) or penalties (increased inspection of work and possible dismissal) from the Extension Service. The chief sanctions applied by the county agent are his to give or withhold chiefly insofar as he has allied himself with the power structure of his community. Preiss reports:

> He has several techniques for controlling membership on most boards. If he felt he wanted to remove a man in a leadership position, he began asking questions about him all over the county. He would drop hints that perhaps the marked individual wasn't carrying out his job as well as he might. Eventually the man would find himself replaced by a new director. Conversely, if FH wanted to get a particular person elected, he campaigned indirectly by describing the best man for the post without actually naming him. Pretty soon people got the idea who was being groomed for a job.[12]

It must be recognized, however, that a county agent who had not effectively worked himself into the local power groups would have very little effect in dealing out such sanctions.

Facilities. The Agricultural Experiment Stations and the staff of subject-matter specialists must be regarded as sub-systems of a larger system. These are facilities for the county agent in his work in the county. Professional Extension workers also have the assistance of about one million unpaid voluntary leaders who give a great deal of their time to Extension work. The help of voluntary leader, valued at a rate for unskilled labor, would probably exceed the amount of the entire budget. This budget is the largest of any adult educational organization, either public or private. The demonstration situation provided by the individual client in a county also is a facility. A demonstration of crop rotation, a laminated barn roof, or a particular breeding practice are all important facilities to the county agent as well as to the farmers.

[12] Preiss, "Functions of Relevant Power," pp. 170-171.

Territoriality. There are more than 3,000 county Extension Services in the fifty states of the United States. The Extension Service is the only adult education organization having a local unit in almost every county of the United States. Territoriality is the factor that affects the work of the county agent in respect to the geographic area he covers as well as to the diversity of his projects. A one mile square county in Virginia with primarily tobacco production would be very different, for example, from a 20,000 square mile county in California encompassing desert grazing, intensive cultivation on irrigated land, and multiple crop raising in mountainous terrain.

SOCIAL PROCESSES AND EXTENSION WORK

Communication. It is one of the explicit features of the Extension Service that it furnishes a channel of communication for rural people and the Land Grant Colleges, enhancing the possibility of organizing research, teaching, and extension activities in a more relevant way. As indicated in the discussion of power, communication in the Extension Service tends to be more personal than in many governmental organizations. Because the agent is usually located at considerable distance from the administrative center at the Land Grant College, each county office has considerable autonomy. The administrative center evaluates the work through inspection by supervisors, formal and informal reports, and contacts with the local organizations, especially the farm organizations in the respective countries.

The mark of a professional extension worker, according to Sanders, is "to know when, where, and how to provide each learning experience to best advantage . . . persons may be contacted individually, in group, or through mass-communication media."[13] Communication may be on an individual basis and include visits, office calls, telephone calls, and mail requests. Communication may be provided in groups and include the results of demonstration meetings, general meetings, tours and field days, workshop, clinics, schools, short courses, non-credit classes, and achievement days, contests, and camps.

Decision-making. The programs of few rural bureaucracies

[13] H. C. Sanders, ed., *The Cooperative Extension Service* (Englewood Cliffs: Prentice-Hall, Inc., 1966) p. 111.

are as complete a blend of local needs expressed through the organizations of the people and of the plans and policies developed at the state level as are those of the Extension Service. As indicated in the discussion of power, the agents on the county level who articulate their activities and programs effectively with the powerful local social systems may ignore more frequently the decisions and directives from the state level than those who do not. Generally the county offices attempt to work with advisory groups, but the form of this type of linkage varies from state to state and within the states. In general, the most successful agents involve the relevant power groups in their decision-making at the local level.

Boundary maintenance. During and following the major depression, many new federal agencies were created that at one time or another threatened the Cooperative Extension Service and its chief supporting farm organization, the American Farm Bureau. "Under the early Agricultural Adjustment Administration program," for example, "a farmer would have to take some of his land out of wheat in order to qualify for a rehabilitation loan. But whether he took the land out of wheat or left it in wheat, it might blow away; therefore, the Soil Conservation Service might advise him to restore the land to grass. The Bureau of Plant Industy and State Experiment Station might be telling him not to plant wheat that year, because recent research showed that the crop would be a failure unless there was a certain amount of moisture in the soil at seeding time. Yet he could borrow the money for seed and, by attempting to grow some wheat, would qualify for a benefit payment on reduced acreage."[14] ". . . New and powerful Federal agencies were barging into almost every local community administering action programs that strongly affected local affairs and dealt with things which were far from being noncontroversial."[15] Not only were some of those competing local and federal agencies considered by the Cooperative Extension Service as threats to its existence and power, but the Bureau of Agricultural Economics of the USDA, which later was given the responsibility of integrating the programs through the device of county and state

[14] Milton S. Eisenhower and Roy I. Kimmel, "Old and New in Agricultural Organization," *1940 Yearbook of Agriculture* (Washington, D. C.: United States Government Printing Office, 1940), p. 1130.

[15] Ibid., p. 1131.

planning agencies, was considered in many cases an even greater threat.

How the conservative farmers' organizations and the Land
Grant Colleges were able to eliminate these planning agencies,
strengthen the Extension Service, and in many cases weaken or
eliminate the threatening organizations is one of the best examples of boundary maintenance in American rural life. Thus, in
1953 the most powerful of the bureaus of the USDA, the Production and Marketing Administration (called the AAA until 1945),
was abolished. Its major functions were divided among three
agencies. Marketing was given to the new Agricultural Marketing Service, which also absorbed many of the functions of the
Bureau of Agricultural Economics, the agency that earlier attempted to plan for the department and integrate its programs.
Production control, storage, and related activities were given to
the Commodity Stabilization Service. The Agricultural Conservation Program was given to the Federal-State relations group
of organizations. Thousands of elected community committee-
men who originally directed the program lost their administrative functions. This once powerful committee system has been
renamed the Agricultural Stabilization and Conservation committee system.

In the struggle for primacy and social rank in rural America
the Cooperative Extension Service has not been without its supporters. "The Farm Bureau has traditionally supported agricultural colleges and especially the Extension Services, seeking to
augment their appropriations and to transfer programs into
their hands."[16]

Systemic linkage. In the above discussion and in the case at
the end of this chapter there is ample evidence of linkages between the Agricultural Extension Service and the other systems
on all levels in the various states. To quote Hardin:

> Agricultural research and extension workers operate in re-
> lation to their clientele with an intimacy which is difficult
> for their more cloistered colleagues to understand . . . Exten-
> sion specialists from the state colleges find their local meet-
> ings blazoned in press headlines, and the county farm and
> home demonstration agents are continuously on the firing
> line. It would be hard to imagine a more striking contrast to

[16] Hardin, *Freedom in Agricultural Education,* p. 29.

the experience of the typical academician, whose influence works slowly (if at all!) through his library and study, his class rooms and publications, and perhaps enjoys a perceptible effect in a generation of so.[17]

BUREAUCRACY AND THE COMMUNITY

We have seen that the county agent tends to have Gemeinschaft-like relations with his clientele and his community, whereas his relationship with his own bureaucratic organization is often more Gesellschaft-like. The strain on the individual who tries to meet the requirements of both the community and the bureaucratic organization was treated briefly under norms. Research on this question might reveal that functionaries working in bureaucratic organizations that do not require community participation for the success of their programs suffer less stress than do functionaries working in systems that require the worker to balance the requirements of his Gesellschaft-like employing organization with the Gemeinschaft-like requirements of families and communities. In a small way this represents a crucial problem of our age: how to relate Gesellschaft-like bureaucratic action that requires efficient service in all fields to Gemeinschaft-like families and communities. The Cooperative Extension Service is an agency for which local reference groups are extremely important and bureaucratic procedures emanating from administrative centers are relatively unimportant. This is particularly true in comparison with such agencies as the Forest Service and Soil Conservation Service.

Each of the following agencies can be analyzed as a social system in a manner similar to that just employed in analyzing the Extension Service. Probably the major differences are variations in degree of decentralization and differences in power structure. The following agencies will be briefly described.

THE AGRICULTURAL EXPERIMENT STATIONS

As mentioned earlier, a system of Land-Grant Colleges of Agriculture was created by the Morrill Act in 1862.[18] In 1887 the

[17] Ibid., p. 7.

[18] Land-Grant Colleges and Universities are found in all 50 states and Puerto Rico. In addition, there are 17 land-grant colleges for blacks in the South known as "The 1890 Schools."

Hatch Act provided for the establishment of Agricultural Experiment Stations in each state. The intent of Congress is revealed in the following excerpt from the Hatch Act: ". . . That in order to aid in acquiring and diffusing among the people of the United States useful and practical information on subjects connected with agriculture, and to promote scientific investigation and experiment respecting the principles and applications of agricultural science, there shall be established, under direction of the college or colleges or agricultural department of colleges in each State or Territory . . . a department to be known and designated as an Agricultural Experiment Station . . ."[19] Thus, the research function became an integral part of the colleges of agriculture.

The basic philosophy that the research work would nourish the teaching program on campus as well as provide research results to be disseminated through the Extension Service has played an important part in the technological revolution in rural America. New fertilizers, pesticides and insecticides, improved livestock, and innovative farm machinery have come from Experiment Station research. Bayley expresses the importance of agricultural research as follows: "We are all familiar with the phenomenal increase in crop yields over the past several years. The fantastic increases in efficiency of soil preparation, crop cultivation and harvesting . . . the spectacular technological revolution in the poultry industry. . . the steadily growing productivity of dairy and beef cattle and swine. We have long grown used to the convenience of high-quality products in frozen potatoes, and powdered milk. The housewife now expects—and generally gets—fresh leafy vegetables and fruits at economical prices during all seasons. The results of research have been essential to all these developments . . ."[20]

While acknowledging the enormous achievements of the Land-Grant complex, questions are being raised as to whether the achievements outweigh the failures—whether benefits are wiped out by the costs. The Agribusiness Accountability Project, a public interest research and advocacy group, argues that Ex-

[19] The Hatch Act, as quoted in Sanders, *Cooperative Extension Service*, p. 26-27.

[20] Ned D. Bayley in *Farmworkers in Rural America, 1971-1972*. Hearings before the Subcommittee on Migratory Labor of the Committee on Labor and Public Welfare, U.S. Senate (Washington: Government Printing Office, 1972), p. 2147.

periment Station research has been captured by technology and places first priority on economic efficiency, not human beings. In *Hard Tomatoes, Hard Times* it is pointed out that in 1969 only 289 out of 6,000 scientific man years were spent on "people-oriented" research. Thus, less than 5% of the total research effort of the State Experiment Stations was allocated to research related to people.

In an abbreviated summary of his book, Hightower says:

> There is nothing inevitable about the growth of Agribusiness in rural America. While this country enjoys an abundance of relatively cheap food, it is not more food, not cheaper food and certainly not better food than that which can be produced by a system of family agriculture. And more than food rolls off the agribusiness assembly line—rural refugees, boarded-up businesses, deserted churches, abandoned towns, broiling urban ghettos and dozens of other tragic social and cultural costs also are products of agribusiness.
>
> Had the land grant community chosen to put its time, its money, its expertise and its technology into the family farm, rather than into corporate pockets, then rural America today would be a place where millions could live and work in dignity.[21]

THE SOIL CONSERVATION SERVICE

The Soil Conservation Service, a bureau of the United States Department of Agriculture, gives assistance to farmers and ranchers chiefly through soil conservation districts which farmers and rachers organize and operate under state laws. The Soil Conservation Service technicians help local individuals and groups in conservation, surveying, planning and application of suitable soil and water conserving practices on individual farms, watersheds, or other areas having common problems. The activities of the Soil Conservation Service are designed to prevent soil erosion, preserve natural resources, control floods, prevent destruction of reservoirs, maintain the navigability of rivers and harbors, and protect public health.

The Soil Conservation Service is a more centralized organiza-

---

[21] Jim Hightower, "A Summary of Hard Tomatoes, Hard Times," in *Farmworkers in Rural America,* p. 2226.

tion than the Cooperative Extension Service. The highest authority resides in the administrative offices in Washington. Next in importance are the state and area offices. Below the state level, there are some 3,000 soil conservation districts covering about 82 percent of the land in the United States. However, only about 23 percent of the land in these districts is covered by conservation plans.[22] The district, rather than a county or "natural group," is the unit through which the technical and educational information of the Soil Conservation Service is channeled.

Most conservation districts are large and encompass too many families for the limited number of conservationists to work on an individual basis. If the conservationists can gain group acceptance of their program, the sanctions, goals, and norms of such groups often govern individual action in conservation work. The Soil Conservation Service has directed its employees to use the "group approach." Since most conservationists have had little acquaintance with social science, the instructions from the regional offices and Washington are often phrased in lay rather than social science terminology. To quote from one pamphlet: "If there is to be any 'big shot' it should be the local neighborhood leader and just to the extent that his followers make it so."[23] For the Soil Conservation Service, the neighbor group is limited in number, not over fifteen or twenty, living in close proximity to one another and bound together by mutual likes and interests. The so-called "neighbor-group leaders" are those looked to for advice, and if they try something, are most likely to be copied by their neighbors.

THE FOREST SERVICE

Major forested areas, which cover one-third of the land area of the United States, are located largely outside the Corn Belt, Wheat Areas, and the eastern portions of the Range Livestock Areas. During their careers with the Forest Service, those who have been reared and trained in one area may work in totally

[22] Everett M. Rogers and Rabel Burdge, *Social Change in Rural Societies* (New York: Appleton-Century-Crofts, 1972), p. 335.

[23] *Group Action in Soil Conservation: Upper Mississippi Valley, Region III* (Milwaukee: United States Department of Agriculture, Soil Conservation Service, March, 1947).

different social and cultural regions. In the Forest Service, as in other bureaucracies, personnel are frequently transferred from one region to another to develop administrators who will know overall problems. The forested areas cover 754,000,000 acres, of which 500,000,000 acres are considered commercial lands. As shown in Table 2, slightly less than half of all forest land is located in the Western region. Of the total commercial forest land, about 27 percent is owned by federal, state and local governments.

TABLE 2
Total and Commercial Acreage of Forest Land
in the United States, 1970

Region	Commercial Forest Land, Ownership[1]				
	Total Forest Land	All Owner- ship	Federally Owned & Managed	State, County, & Municipal	Private
	In Millions of Acres				
U.S. Total	754	500	107	29	364
North	186	178	12	30	146
South	212	193	14	3	175
West	355	129	81	6	42

[1] Comprises all land which was (a) producing or physically capable of producing, usable crops of wood, (b) economically available on date shown or prospectively, and (c) not withdrawn from timber utilization.
Source: U.S.D.A., Forest Service, *Statistical Abstract of the U.S., 1972*, p. 625.

The Forest Service makes decisions having important consequences for the local community. Many of its decisions are made in a context of conflicting demands and expectations on the part of environmental groups, on one hand, and industrial interests on the other. The Forest Service activities, for instance, include reforestation, the development and preservation of wildlife habitats, and the leasing of grazing lands to ranchers.

According to the Forest Service, there were more than 110,000 forest fires which burned more than 4.5 million acres in 1971. During the same year, fire protection expenditures were estimated at 12.5 million dollars.[24] A large percentage of forest fires

[24] U.S.D.A., Forest Service, *Statistical Abstract of the U.S., 1972*, p. 629.

are set by man, many deliberately. Of all forest fires on protected areas in 1971, arson was the leading cause and accounted for about one-fourth of all fires. Burning of debris was only slightly less important than arson as a cause. Other important causes included smoking, campfires, and fires from the use of equipment. Lightning, a natural cause, accounted for slightly less than 10 percent of forest fires in 1971.[25] Since the management of the forests and the ranges they cover must be carried on by residents in them, it is obvious that foresters must deal with human problems of the first magnitude.

AGRICULTURAL STABILIZATION AND CONSERVATION SERVICE

The ASCS is a line action agency established in the 1930's as the Agricultural Adjustment Administration (AAA). The major purposes of the ASCS are to control food surpluses, to maintain farm prices, and to support the adoption of soil conservation practices by farmers.

In order to exercise some control over food surpluses and maintain farm prices, the ASCS restricts crop acreage and purchases surplus production. This agency also pays farmers for conservation measures such as contour farming, farm ponds, and application of lime. In 1971, the value of price support commodities purchased by the government amounted to $1.2 billion. This total included 370 million bushels of wheat valued at $488 million; 92 million bushels of corn valued at $103 million; 78 million bushels of sorghum grain valued at $79 million; and 396 thousand bales of cotton valued at $48 million.[26]

Rogers and Burdge feel that the ASCS has had limited success in modifying farm production and maintaining farm price levels. They point out that farmers can apply more fertilizer and seed to acreage not withheld from production, thus approaching the level of production from the total acreage. Furthermore, not all farmers participate in crop acreage allotments under the ASCS program, hence limiting the overall effectiveness. Finally, there is little "cross-compliance" in that a farmer can grow wheat on vacated corn land in a given state, for example, even

[25] Ibid., p. 629.
[26] U.S. Agricultural Stabilization and Conservation Service, *Statistical Abstract of the U.S., 1972*, p. 597.

though these crops are under acreage allotments in other states.[27]

THE FARMERS' HOME ADMINISTRATION

Historically, the Farmers' Home Administration, established in 1946, stems from the Resettlement Administration and the Farm Security Administration, both of which appeared in the depression years of the 1930's. The latter agencies sponsored such action programs as those involving experiments in the establishment of communities, collective farming, group medicine, tenant purchase programs, and family rehabilitation. The FHA offers credit services to farm families unable to borrow on reasonable terms from other agencies. Loans are made for farm operation, for building or repairing farm structures, for purchase of family-type farms or developing uneconomic farms, and for water facilities in all states.[28]

Although the FHA program is centralized in Washington, most loanmaking authority is delegated to field offices. Farmers make contacts with the agency through county supervisors and each county FHA office is advised on loans by a local committee of three persons, at least two of whom are farmers.

The developing of the supervised farm and loan plan and working with families as units are perhaps the most significant contributions to program administration made by the FHA. FHA supervisors not only make arrangements by which monies are lent but they also provide skilled advice.

Operating loans for purchase of equipment, feed, seed, fertilizer, livestock, and other farming needs are made to help small farmers. The repayment period is from one to seven years. Farm Ownership loans are made to help farmers buy, enlarge, develop, or improve family-type farms. Such loans are to be amortized for periods not to exceed forty years but can be repaid earlier. In designated areas, emergency loans can be made to enable farmers to continue operation. Special livestock loans are made to help livestock farmers maintain their normal livestock operations. These loans are repaid in one to three years.

[27] Rogers and Burdge, *Social Change,* pp. 336-338.
[28] See "Agricultural Credit" in *International Encyclopedia of the Social Sciences,* Vol. III, p. 470.

THE RURAL ELECTRIFICATION ADMINISTRATION

The Rural Electrification Administration, established in 1935, serves the following functions: (1) to administer loans for rural electrification facilities and (2) to administer loans for extension and improvement of rural telephone service. At the time of the establishment of the REA, only 10 percent of American farmers had central-station electrical service as compared with 95 percent in France, and 85 percent in Denmark.[29] Since 1935, rural electrification in the United States has been rapid. By 1953 about 9 out of 10 farms were being served and by 1963 about 98 percent of all farms in the U.S. had electricity. The REA policy has been to provide "area coverage," thus extending service into the fringe areas of cities. Hence, a large portion of the REA clientele is nonfarm residents, the major source of recent growth.[30]

The local unit of the REA is a cooperative association. In 1971 the REA had loaned approximately $7.8 billion to borrowers and had energized 1.7 million miles of lines serving 6.7 million customers. The number of customers had risen from 4.8 million in 1960.[31]

HOME DEMONSTRATION WORK, AND RESISTANCE TO CHANGE

The following case is introduced to illustrate the problems that change agents may encounter in rural areas. The Home Demonstration Agent in Smith County, Michigan, attempted to organize a Home Demonstration Club in Bayone Township. In a county noted for the spectacular growth of its Home Demonstration program, Bayone Township was unique because of lack of participation.

Pleasant Corners[32]

Located in Bayone Township is the small neighborhood of Pleasant Corners, consisting of some thirty families. The nucleus

[29] "Rural Electrification," *Yearbook of Agriculture 1940* (Washington, D.C.: Government Printing Office, 1940), p. 790.

[30] *Encyclopedia of the Social Sciences,* Vol. III, p. 470.

[31] U.S. Rural Electrification Administration, *Statistical Abstract of the U.S., 1972,* p. 513.

[32] Condensed by Elizabeth Williams Nall from an unpublished manuscript en-

of Pleasant Corners is a Fundamentalist Church, established late in the nineteenth century, the majority of whose members come from the old, traditional families in Pleasant Corners.

Three networks of human relationships exist in Pleasant Corners. One network consists of old families of long residence in the area who are closely affiliated with Pleasant Church. The second, connected to the first by ties of kinship, consists of those families of long residence many of whom are younger and not affiliated with the church. The third is composed of those families who are relative newcomers to the neighborhood, many of whom are "fringe" residents. . . .

The families closely affiliated with Pleasant Church believe that it is the most important basis of life in the local neighborhood. Supported by church belief and doctrine, members of the church insist that the church and its sub-groups be maintained as solely religious organizations. Church members are encouraged by church policy to participate actively in secular affairs, but they do so as individuals and not as members or officials of the church.

Those families of long residence not affiliated with the church are typically second generation members of older church affiliated families, linked to the first group by ties of kinship. Examples of this are Mr. A and Mrs. B, brother and sister, both of whom do not actively participate in the local church and whose interests are oriented away from the neighborhood. They are bound to the church affiliated group, however, for their 80-year-old mother has been all her life a pillar in Pleasant Church.

Those families who have more recently arrived in the neighborhood have in general moved out from nearby cities and continue to work in those cities. Thus their interest in the neighborhood is of a different nature. Such families commonly express their concern over the existing blockage in gaining access to affairs of the neighborhood. One wife reported, "This is the awfullest place to get acquainted in that I have ever seen, and it is the churchiest place that you could find." Another reported, "Rural communities are really more selfish than those in

---

titled "Pleasant Corners: A Case of Failure at the Crossroads" by Paul A. Miller, Charles P. Loomis, and Francis M. Sim, Department of Sociology and Anthropology, Michigan State University.

the city. The people around here will laugh when some of us new ones do something wrong, but you don't see them jumping over the fence to help you."

The older families likewise indicated that newcomers had difficulty in entering the affairs of Pleasant Corners. One woman remarked, "It is just like some women who are sometimes too quick to buy a new broom for an old one. We like to take our time in seeing how newcomers behave before we go and make ourselves known."

Another factor relevant for this case study is the existence of a Ladies' Service Society affiliated with the Church. In existence for sixty years, the Society is composed of some twenty members and has the manifest function of serving the "needy" of the neighborhood. The president, Mrs. E, has been a member for 57 years, and several other members have belonged for over half a century. The mother of Mrs. B was a charter member. Mrs. B herself, however, is not active in the Society, remarking, "One reason why I don't like to go up to the Ladies' Service Society is because they won't gossip. Now in the Club (another Home Demonstration Club) that I belonged to, when someone had it coming, we really took them apart."

The strategy used by the Home Demonstration Agent, the change agent in this case, in attempting to organize the new Club was to persuade Mrs. B and Mrs. E to form the nucleus of it. Mrs. B is the wife of an outstanding farmer in the neighborhood and exerts a great deal of influence among the women of the neighborhood. Presumably she would provide excellent leadership for the new Club and would attract other women to join. Mrs. E was noted for her active work in the church, serving as Sunday School superintendent as well as president of the Ladies' Service Society.

Technically, Mrs. B did not meet the resident requirements, for she lived just south of the township line in Comstock Township. She already belonged to a Home Demonstration Club in Comstock Township but was persuaded to transfer her membership to the new club.

The Home Demonstration Agent proceeded to contact other prospective members for the new Club, attempting to demonstrate the need for a Home Demonstration Club in Bayone Township. As a result, ten women living in or near Pleasant Corners agreed to attend the meetings. The new Club was duly formed and Mrs. B. was elected secretary. Two meetings were held and the Home Demonstration Agent was encouraged by the manifest interest of the ten members. After the third meeting, however, Mrs. B informed the Home Demonstration Agent that the group wished to disband. The decision had been made without consulting the Home Demonstration Agent and came as a great surprise to her. When she attempted to ascertain the reason lying back of the decision, she was given the cryptic response, "We did not take into account what was to the north of us."

Thus this is a case of an unsuccessful systemic linkage of the system of the Cooperative Extension Service with that of the neighborhood of Pleasant Corners. Within each system involved in the attempted linkage various primary elements were operative. Within the target system of the neighborhood were the following sub-systems: the church group, those of long residence who although not affiliated with the church were related by kinship to its members, and the more nebulous grouping of the newcomers. Each may be described in terms of (1) ends or objectives, (2) norms, (3) status-roles, (4) power, involving both authority and influence, (5) social rank, (6) sanctions, (7) facilities, and (8) territoriality. Insofar as the embryonic Home Demonstration Club was operative, it had these components. In this analysis these elements will be discussed in relation to the systemic linkage being attempted.

Ends and objectives. In attempting to introduce the Home Demonstration Club into the neighborhood of Pleasant Corners the Agent here, as elsewhere, stressed improved homemaking as the objective. Although the manifest objective in most demonstration clubs is improved homemaking, also important are such latent objectives on the part of members as visiting, exchanging experiences, enjoying the favorable self-images or feelings of personal warmth resulting from interaction among those who are mutually known and respected, and even of opportunity for upward social mobility. Such organizations often serve an integrative function in the neighborhood.

The Home Demonstration Agent's ends were in line with those of her agency, the Cooperative Extension Service. The church group, however, was already engaged in "quilting," which some members thought to be not unlike the objective of the Home Demonstration Club. Moreover, the group placed religious objectives above all else. They were more interested in retaining the traditional way of life than in introducing improved home practices, that is, their objective was the retaining of the status quo. The other older people in the community who were not church members were committed to the church group's ends by kinship ties. Although they would not actively support the religious objectives of the church group, they would not oppose them. They valued neighborhood solidarity and would rather support the church group than align themselves with the newcomers.

Norms. The church group was accustomed to meetings which were permeated with religious ritual not altogether approved by the newcomers or the Home Demonstration Agent. Although those in the church would not oppose the introduction of improved home practices, most believed the church was the agency which should influence the home. The church way was the "right way and for them the only way." They definitely opposed having an outside agency taking over activities of the church. Again many of the older non-church members would not support the church view but neither would they oppose it. The newcomers would probably be willing to oppose the church and some might be interested in Home Demonstration work, but they were not organized.

Status-Roles. The status-roles most significantly involved in the attempted systemic linkage being described were those of the Home Demonstration Agent and the leaders, Mrs. B and Mrs. E. Had the organization of the Home Demonstration Club been a success, all of these roles and others would have been articulated into a new social system. The status-role of the Home Demonstration Agent would have in many ways become a part of the neighborhood and its systems. However, during the time the embryonic club existed, the Home Demonstration Agent was regarded as an outsider who was bringing in an activity which, if not competing, was unnecessary. She was no doubt regarded by some of the older non-church members as one who might bring a cleavage in the neighborhood. Mrs. E, functioning in her capacity as leader of the church group, played the role of one interested in the good of the neighborhood but so devoted to her church that she could not have a functional role in the new organization. Mrs. B, functioning as a leader of the older non-church women, was so much linked by kinship to the church group and by affiliation to another Home Demonstration Club, that she decided that the Home Demonstration Club for Bayone Township was not necessary. Thus, her leadership role referred to the neighborhood and not to the new organization. All three principals, the Home Demonstration Agent, Mrs. E., and Mrs. B, played their roles with reference to the social systems to which they owed their primary loyalty, and the new social system, the Home Demonstration Club of Bayone Township, never came into being.

Power. In terms of influence, the four leader families, A, B, C, and E are central in the neighborhood. In terms of authority, exercised on the local level, both Mrs. E, representing the church group in the three meetings of the Club, and the Home Demonstration Agent were the chief actors. Since boundary maintenance efforts of the church group placed Mrs. E in a position which would not allow her to give firm support to the Club, and since Mrs. B had strong ties by kinship to the church group, the Home Demonstration Agent obviously did not have the basis for articulating the power structure of the community with the organization of the Club.

Social Rank. It is important that all the women of high rank in the neighborhood are older people. The manifest objective of the Home Demonstration Club did not appeal sufficiently to these older people who had already established the groups from which they derived the social satisfactions which constitute the latent functions of such groups as the Ladies' Service Society and the Home Demonstration Club.˙

Sanctions. Those sanctions which are usually operative were not available for the Home Demonstration Agent to invoke during the three meetings of the new Club's existence. In other clubs she had organized, members saw in the early meetings the possibility of learning improved homemaking practices, of making important contacts in the county seat, of achieving prestige and rank among the people whom they respected. The members of the Ladies' Service Society, engaged in quilting and similar activities, were deriving rewards from their membership in this organization. Also, certain facilities such as booklets, visual aids, and workshops for leaders which could help a club attain its objectives were not used by the new Club. Nor were any negative sanctions operating. Even such a mild penalty as anxiety about possibly disappointing the Agent was not available. Neither the Home Demonstration Agent nor any of the members of the county or state Cooperative Extension staffs were well enough known by the principals to make this possible.

Territoriality. The considerations of spatial relations were quite important in this case, as they frequently are in other attempts to organize social systems. In general, the basic ecological pattern of Home Demonstration Clubs is one club for one area. Thus, in this case, one club was planned for women of all ages, all social ranks or classes, and all types of religious orientation and affiliation. This meant that a larger area could not be used in order to obtain membership support of separate clubs for the church people, the older non-church people, and the newcomers. Neither could there be provision for the younger and older women or other groupings to meet separately.

There were other complications of a spatial nature. The neighborhood consisting of approximately 30 families which the Home Demonstration Agent attempted to make the center of the Bayone Township Home Demonstration Club was bisected by a township line. Thus Mrs. B said at a time considerably after the disbanding of the Club, "It makes a lot of difference around here whether you are in Bayone or Comstock Township. I don't have anything against those people, but I have never wanted them to get credit for contributions that I make—I want my own township to get the credit."

Systemic linkage was not established because the boundary maintenance mechanisms of the existing systems functioned so that the leaders involved made unfavorable decisions for such action. Pleasant Corners was not only an operative social system but it likewise was the target system for the Cooperative Extension Service. The basic problem involved in the present instance of attempted change and systemic linkage was that of the persistence of Pleasant Corners in maintaining itself as a social system, against both the complications of three internal sub-systems and of external change systems, such as the Cooperative Extension Service.

SELECTED REFERENCES

A Report by the President's National Advisory Commission on Rural Poverty, *The People Left Behind.* Washington: Government Printing Office, 1967.

Baker, Gladys. *The County Agent.* Chicago: University of Chicago Press, 1939.

Beal, George M. and Joe M. Bohlen. *How Farm People Accept New Ideas.* Ames: Agr. Ext. Serv. Spec. Report No. 15, November, 1955.

Farmworkers in Rural America 1971-1972. Hearings before the subcommittee on Migratory Labor of the Committee on Labor and Public Welfare, United States Senate, on The Role of Land-Grant Colleges, parts 4-A and 4-B, Washington: Government Printing Office, 1972.

Hardin, Charles M. *Freedom in Agricultural Education.* Chicago: University of Chicago Press, 1955.

Hightower, Jim. *Hard Tomatoes, Hard Times.* Washington: Agribusiness Accountability Project, 1972.

Leagans, J. Paul and Charles P. Loomis, eds. *Behavioral Change in Agriculture—Concepts and Strategies for Influencing Transition.* Ithaca, New York: Cornell University Press, 1971.

Lionberger, Herbert F., and Edward Hassinger. "Neighborhoods as a Factor in the Diffusion of Farm Information in a Northeast Missouri Farming Community," *Rural Sociology,* 19, No. 4 (December, 1954).

Loomis, Charles P. "Social Organization in Agriculture." *International Encyclopedia of Social Sciences.* New York: Macmillan and The Free Press, 1968, Vol. 1, pp. 208ff.

Preiss, Jack J. *Functions of Relevant Power and Authority Groups in the Evaluation of County Agent Performance.* East Lansing: Michigan State University doctoral dissertation, 1954.

Rogers, Everett M. and Rabel Burdge. *Social Change in Rural Societies.* New York: Appleton-Century-Crofts, 1972, Chapter 12.

Sanders, H. C., ed. *The Cooperative Extension Service.* Englewood Cliffs: Prentice-Hall, Inc., 1966.

13

Library and Mass Media Systems

The public library will be analyzed as a social system through which various mass media are disseminated to the public. The mass media such as the radio and television industries, the news gathering, printing and publishing industries, and the film industries will be analyzed as social systems that function to form the communications network of a society. The mass media are Gesellschaft-like. The initiators of interaction are separated from the recipients by mechanical devices, or by time and space. The interaction is one-sided in that the flow is much more from initiator to recipient than *vice versa,* and there is little or no face-to-face contact. As compared with the mass media, the public library is relatively Gemeinschaft-like.

THE PUBLIC LIBRARY

Public libraries exhibit a range of characteristics, some being essentially Gemeinschaft-like and others predominantly Gesellschaft-like. The librarian who orders and prepares materials with an individual patron in mind and who calls the attention of this patron to what is awaiting his selection is rendering Gemeinschaft-like service. On the other hand, the anonymous voice asking a reference question or the anonymous customer at the checkout desk is part of a Gesellschaft-like relationship not unlike that of a typical commercial enterprise. Diverse locations on the Gemeinschaft-Gesellschaft continuum can be anticipated in light of the diversity of objectives characteristic of the public library.

Objectives. Any consideration of the goals of the public library in the United States is a study in contrasts. There is, for example, the contrast between its historical purpose and its emerging purpose. There was no equivocation about the goals of the public libraries at the time of their greatest expansion: opportunities for self-education for thousands of immigrants and literate, aspiring native citizens. High social mobility was a characteristic of the times and the urge to pull "one's self up by his own boot-straps" was strong. Means for fulfilling such goals have gradually become bureaucratized and institutionalized. The upwardly mobile individual is less frequently forced to carve out a learning program on his own. Community colleges, junior colleges, industry-sponsored training centers, more accessible universities, a publishing industry capable of providing cheap books, night classes, and a more affluent society have combined to reduce the number of people who would map out for themselves a reading program designed to expand their cultural horizons and increase their job potentials.[1] That sense of mission lingers among librarians and is reflected in the objectives to which they believe they should be committed.

There is a contrast between the provision of an efficient service for those who know exactly what they want and the provision of an atmosphere in which a curious individual can explore diverse subject matter at will. Nathan Glazer says: "Bookworms must browse." There is a chasm between the ideal atmosphere for browsing and the ideal nerve center of a communications network that links the stockpile of knowledge with all points demanding information and all points generating information. Yet the latter ideal is viewed as a high priority public library objective by thoughtful librarians and social critics.[2] The public library's goal of being a vast storehouse of knowledge and information capable of instantaneous retrieval is increasingly evident. With a proliferation of knowledge, reports, specialities, inventions, regulations, and research findings, no segment of society knows what many other segments are doing. Investigators in one part of the world may pursue inquiries into subjects already thoroughly researched by another group of investigators which may bring about needless duplication. Hence the objective develops of providing a master-tape on which all would be recorded, retrievable for any fact of a given subject. But the notion that "bookworms must browse" also retains its vitality. The

[1] Nathan Glazer, "The Library in the Community," in Ralph W. Conant, *The Public Library and the City* (Cambridge: MIT Press, 1965), p. 67ff.

[2] Richard L. Meier, "The Library: An Instrument for Metropolitan Communication" in Conant, *The Public Library*, pp. 82ff.

idea that modern man needs a place to retreat to be alone—just by himself, his ideas and lots of books—has vitality, too. To that end "The library . . . [must be a place for] being alone with a book, or with a lot of books—and not for the efficiency of the librarian, or the art exhibit—or the lecture discussions. [It should be encouraged] to hold onto the records of civilizations, and to hold onto them whether anyone wants to use them or not."[3]

Some feel that the library has a special obligation to those with special needs, especially if those needs cannot be filled elsewhere. Students, foreign-born readers, the non-reader and the culturally-deprived are all groups regarded by some as the most deserving patrons of library service, even if they must be served by "non-library" materials, and even if they must be cajoled into wanting library service.[4] Others oppose such an idea. There are natural publics for the library, they claim, the most deserving and ill-served public being the serious reader. It would be much better to go all-out for service to the serious reader than to compete with the Corner Drugstore in providing love stories, westerns, and crash diets for the bored and insomniacs. To serve its serious readers as diligently as an investment firm serves its serious customers, to have phone orders, deliveries and pickups, to provide photocopying, to maintain carrells for uninterrupted study, to keep portfolios on the serious reader and to cater to his inclinations, is the objective as seen from this point of view.[5]

In one way or another, most public libraries make gestures in all of these directions. Few, if any, have the temerity to limit their publics exclusively to certain segments of the population or to limit their offerings to "serious" rather than "light" materials. Few if any become information centers at the price of foregoing their cultural and humanistic roots. The latitude of public library goals is shown below, based on the returns from a combination of sixty-three library leaders, ninety-two libraries identified as "exemplary," all fifty state libraries, forty non-librarians able to relate the public to broad societal factors, and selected others, comprising 306 in all.[6]

[3] Glazer, "The Library," p. 80.

[4] Dan Lacy, "The Dissemination of Print" in Conant, *The Public Library,* pp. 114ff.

[5] Edward C. Banfield, "Needed: A Public Purpose" in Conant, *The Public Library,* pp. 102ff.

[6] Public Library Association, *A Strategy for Public Library Change: Proposed*

1. Free service to all, with stress on reaching the unserved.
2. To provide information services.
3. To provide adult and continuing education.
4. To collect and disseminate all kinds of informational, educational and cultural materials, including non-print resources.
5. To support education—formal and informal.
6. To serve as a cultural center.

Most of these objectives should have high priority for small town and rural libraries. To what extent public libraries are achieving these objectives, and by what standards they are judged will be examined in the following section.

Norms. Each governing unit determines to a large extent the standards by which the performance of the public library will be judged. When comparative standards are invoked they are likely to be drawn from public libraries of similar size in the same geographic area. For example, a library board of a public library in a suburb of Chicago would use a rule of thumb standard of performance by taking a look at a nearby suburb of roughly the same size and socio-economic make-up. The Chicago library board, however, would use a rule of thumb standard by seeing what Detroit, St. Louis, and Cleveland were doing in their public libraries.

In addition to the application of these local comparisons, there is a carefully prepared statement of minimum standards usually arrived at about every ten years by committees of librarians under the general direction of the national professional organization, the American Library Association. Standards are adopted, rejected, or amended by the members of the Public Library Association, which is a membership division of the national organization. The standards so adopted are not uniformly representative of most libraries' practices. Any given library may find itself moderately close to the standard on a few items, well above the standard on a few, and far below the standard on others. "In substance, the standards are the essential elements found in those libraries that have achieved a reasonable degree of adequacy. It should be possible for librarians, library boards, or interested citizens to go through the document, standard by standard, and measure their own library service by answering

Public Library Goals Feasibility Study (Chicago: American Library Association, 1972), p. ix.

'yes' to this standard, 'no' to that, 'maybe' or 'partially' to others. When honest answers are affirmative for the majority of the standards, libraries are well on the way to giving quality service."[7] It is clear from this statement that such standards, while normative, also are heavily reflective of goals, met and unmet. It is unnecessary for present purposes to elaborate much on the minimum standards except to indicate that among the items applicable are the following. They should:

1. Be freely accessible by everyone.

2. Be systematized so that the small library can have access to materials available at larger libraries within its system.

3. Be easy to reach and to use.

4. Be explicit in the state law that public libraries must be established and maintained.

5. Be under jurisdiction of an appropriate official public authority (such as board) which is responsible to the government of the locality.

6. Coordinate its services with that of academic and school libraries.

7. Respond to a leadership role furnished by the state library.

8. Be a national program which supplements and stimulates library services throughout the states.

9. Provide materials, services, and activities commensurate with community needs.

10. Contain opposing views on controversial topics.

11. Follow approved personnel practices.

12. Provide physical facilities commensurate with programs of library services.

Status-role. The status-role of the librarian is not clear-cut. Several factors contribute to this blurred picture. The size of the community is an important one. The librarian in the large city might be required to have a higher level of education, of social attributes, of political awareness, and of executive ability than would be necessary for a librarian in a small village to possess. The jobs specified by the status-role for the incumbent in the large city and for his counterpart in the small village would vary greatly. The librarian of the large city would have to have much

---

[7] American Library Association, *Minimum Standards for Public Library Systems, 1966* (Chicago: American Library Association, 1967), p. 13.

of his orientation outward, away from the internal workings of his organization. The city hall, the tax allocation committee, prestigious industries and organizations on the local scene and the administrative personnel of other large libraries on the professional scene would be among his important day-to-day contacts. While generally informed about the inner workings of the organization, the librarian typically would have delegated the running of all of its parts to high ranking staff members. The small town librarian would also try to maintain the outside contacts but much more of the time would be absorbed by the inner workings of the library than would be true of the librarian in the big city. The small library would also lack the high level of work specialization typical of the large library so that to the public eye there might be very little difference in the tasks of the librarian and the desk assistant. In addition to these differences in the requirements for the status-role and the actual performance of its tasks, the occupation is at a state of semi-professionalization that allows a tremendous latitude in the degree of training and education seen necessary for a librarian. A thorough inquiry into the state of the public library made in the 1950's has this to say of the status-role of librarian:

> The findings established a solid factual base for correcting the caricatures of the profession that have arisen from the almost universal human tendency to assume the existence of general occupational characteristics from a few exceptional cases. Librarians have been pictured frequently as acidulous old maids, timid, retiring bookworms, or sweet impractical idealists, as masculine women and feminine men. The inquiry findings lead to the conclusion that as a group librarians have backgrounds, interests, and temperaments normal for persons engaged in the intellectual occupations.[8]

Power, authority, and influence. The public librarian is a government official whose office is established by the state under permissive legislation and whose institution is generally initiated by the local unit of government, the village, city, township, or county. The librarian is given authority to run the library in a manner compatible with the policies determined in

[8] Robert D. Leigh, *The Public Library in the United States: The General Report of the Public Library Inquiry* (New York: Columbia University Press, 1950), p. 193.

conjunction with the local library board. As in the case of the county agricultural agent, there is little power inherent in the position as such. To the extent that the librarian can involve himself with the power forces of the community, he can influence public opinion concerning the library. Such an alignment with power groups can be fully as important on the state as on the local level. In all the states where library progress, in terms of state aid, library demonstrations, or favorable legislation has been made, the state library associations with the backing of strategic local power groups and with an active state library have invariably been necessary.

Territoriality. While public libraries are similar in function and basic services, they differ greatly in size, support and specialization. Differences in them derive largely from the size of the community or area served. There were 8,200 public libraries in 1962, for example, but only 5,770 had budgets of more than $2,000 per year.[9] Many of the small town and village public libraries operate on extraordinarily small budgets indeed.

Public libraries are an urban phenomenon in that they require fairly heavy concentrations of wealth to afford the necessary expenditures for materials, staff, and physical plant, and fairly heavy concentrations of people so that dissemination of materials can take place effectively. Not too many years ago librarians intent upon maximum geographic coverage sought to determine how many people were required for a practical administrative unit, and how many dollars such a unit would have to raise. Striving after such geographic spread did not turn out to be particularly productive of a well distributed library service. The emphasis has turned to a service in the most rural, the most remote spot, not so much by the banding together of a great number of governmental units, as by systematizing the relation of the smaller, to the larger, to the still larger unit, in such a way that inter-library loans could provide as specialized requests for the rural as for the urban resident. To claim that such a system actually gives a service to the rural resident as readily accessible as to the urban resident would be overstating the case. Clearly the resident of New York City has much more choice of the superb collections than does the person who lives in the isolated Adirondack region. It is equally clear that the Adirondack dwell-

---

[9] "Library" in *Encyclopaedia Britannica*, Vol. 13, p. 1038, (1966).

er has a lot more than he might otherwise have by being able to request through a library of extremely limited holdings a specialized title which will be borrowed from the smallest library in the network, even though the request may have to go to the New York Public Library.

Urban residents make greater use of library services than rural residents, in part because of a higher educational level, but also simply because the city residents are closer. The use, even for city dwellers, dwindles as the distance from the public library increases. ". . . One study revealed that about 20 percent of the people living less than three miles from the library used it, as against 12 percent of those living from three to five miles and only 8 percent of those living over five miles away."[10] The size of the city itself is a determining factor. The smaller the city, down to 25,000 the larger the relative use of library service. Although living in a large city does not assure access to a superior library service, and living in a sparsely settled area does not deny one a service, the public library must work harder to maintain the service in the sparsely settled region and the patron must put forth more effort to see that he gets what he needs.

Facilities. The facilities of the very small public library are visible from the front door. On the other hand, no single person probably ever sees all the facilities of a large library, and probably only a portion of the library staff has any realization of the scope of the facilities. Few of the patrons have such extensive interests that they come to know about more than a part of the facilities. The music patron who listens to a recording of a composition, the score for which is before him, and who borrows books that analyze the composition, for instance, may not necessarily know about the map collection. The historical researcher using the periodical and newspaper holdings through the microfilm viewer may not know of the businessman's use of current aerial survey maps and market analyses.

A cumulative system of comprehensive bibliography and periodic lists of books in print put out for the book trade are the backbone of book ordering. More selective bibliographies compiled within the profession and without are among the facilities. Library buildings—the main library and its system of

[10] Bernard Berelson, *The Library's Public: A Report of the Public Library Inquiry* (New York: Columbia University Press, 1949), pp. 40-42.

branches—constitute a basic facility. In rural areas, housing facilities are often arranged in a part of some local government building and branch quarters are often rented.

Social rank.   In a study involving some 6,700 high school students and their attitudes toward work and selected occupations, the occupation of librarian was found to be rated rather low. By the boys, the occupation was rated equal with the recreational director, the cashier in a bank, and the real estate agent, but below the teacher, the electrician who owned his own business, the manager of a five-and-ten-cent store, and the registered nurse. The girls rated the occupation even lower.[11] Based upon the earnings of females 25-64 years old in the experienced labor force in 1969, librarians have average earnings similar to elementary and secondary school teachers. The median for female librarians was $7,080 in 1969 as compared with $7,029 for female elementary school teachers and $7,310 for female secondary school teachers.[12] Small town and rural librarians usually earn less than city librarians.

Whereas the social rank of the librarian must be inferred because of lack of research on the subject, the social rank of the library's public has received considerable attention. Although people of all walks of life use the library, the proportion of children and young adults using the library is greater than for other age groups. Relatively more middle-income groups use the library than the rich or the poor, relatively more single than married people use it, slightly more women than men, and more skilled workers than unskilled. Berelson suggests that most if not all of these personal characteristics of the library user are attributable to another factor—that formal education retains its role as a major determinant of library use. Larger proportions of college trained people are found in urban areas than on farms. The significance of this should be obvious when we consider that from 10 to 15 percent of adults having only a grade-school education are library users, as compared with about four times as many of the college-educated. Berelson says:

> ... the library clientele is remarkable for its wide interest in all media of communication. As a group, the library users

[11] *Youth and the World of Work* (East Lansing: Social Research Service, Michigan State College, 1949), p. 67A.

[12] 1970 Census of Population, Subject Reports, *Earnings by Occupation and Education,* PC(2)-8B, Table 7.

read more magazines than do their fellows, and they tend to read and see and hear more 'serious' communication content.

Thus, they constitute a 'communication elite.' This interest in the sources of ideas and information suggests another characteristic of library users. There is a tendency for them to be 'opinion leaders' in their community, that is, persons who influence other people. As a group, they are more curious about the world than their fellows; they know more; they have more ideas and opinions; their word is respected more.[13]

Boundary maintenance.   One type of boundary maintenance springs from the library's educational objectives. Since the nation's school systems also have education as an objective, the suggestion is continually appearing that the public library system be incorporated into the public school and/or public college and university system. Without treating the cogent reasons that librarians advance to attack this proposal, almost universally librarians rally to the support of the separation of school and library system, thereby maintaining boundaries. Another occasional threat is the appointment of a non-professional librarian to a high library position. Such appointments are sometimes understandable, as when a state library agency whose main objective is library extension is headed by a political scientist conversant with local politics in the state. Some jobs are summed up by the appointing boards as most needing culture, broad knowledge, administrative ability, and "connections." When an appointee who met these qualifications but was not library-trained was made head of the biggest government library in the land, numerous articles in library periodicals criticized the appointment, and the new "head" made graceful references in his maiden speech to his anomalous position in addressing the national convention. A program of state aid to local libraries requiring the local maintenance of personnel standards has been known to be jeopardized because the community wished to observe boundary maintenance by the hiring of local people, rather than "imported" people with the specified qualifications.

Systemic linkage.   Many evidences of the social processes just treated are found in the local public library's attempt to maintain linkage with its constituency. The annual report, the

[13] Berelson, *The Library's Public,* p. 127.

work with and through community groups, the public relations program, and the calendar of local events, all seek to maintain and strengthen this linkage. Where linkage has not been achieved, it is the librarians through their association or through their state extension agency who probably are the vigorous change agents seeking to effect the linkage. In other words, it generally is the library seeking to establish itself in the community, rather than the community seeking the library. This statement ought to be modified by a reference to the diverse goals previously mentioned. If the overriding objective is to reach those not yet served, the disadvantaged, the illiterate, the hard to reach, naturally the linkage will be achieved with much more effort than if the objective is to serve serious readers better.

According to Leigh, the library "may also be thought of as a constituent part of public [or mass] communication: the machinery by which words, sounds, and images flow from points of origin through an impersonal medium to hosts of unseen readers and audiences."[14]

While the library may be viewed in this way, mass media channels of communication most frequently call to mind such sources as radio, television, film, newspapers, and magazines. As suggested by Bogart, the rise of such media has been closely linked to the growth of national cultures, to increased literacy, and to "key events in the technological revolution—from movable type to the transistor."[15] Apart from interpersonal communication, the media play a large role in the communication of innovations and change in all societies.[16] We will examine briefly some of the mass media with respect to their utilization by rural people.

COUNTRY WEEKLIES AND FARM MAGAZINES

While many rural people in America are not without the influence of urban and metropolitan newspapers, the country weekly retains a unique position among the mass media. According to one writer, "The position of the country weekly news-

[14] Leigh, *The Public Library*, p. 25.
[15] Leo Bogart, "Audiences" in *International Encyclopedia of the Social Sciences*, Vol. 3, p. 70.
[16] See Everett M. Rogers and F. Floyd Shoemaker, *Communication of Innovations* (New York: The Free Press, 1971).

paper is that of a pulsing, throbbing institution which reaches to the grass roots of the community social structure, reflecting its life, customs, and civilization."[17] Unquestionably, the unpretentious country weekly does exercise an important educational, political, and social force in rural communities.

The function of country weeklies. In 1972, there were 8,682 weeklies and 398 semiweeklies, a large number of which were published in small towns and villages in the Nation.[18] With the rise of metropolitan dailies and the decline in the farm population, it is not surprising that the number of weeklies has declined from approximately 16,000 in 1900. Country weeklies tend to be numerous in the middle west and plains states.

Despite the obvious inefficiencies and economic shortcomings besetting the small country weekly, its survival is remarkable. The explanation rests, at least in part, in the intimacy or the Gemeinschaft-like nature of the country weekly. "It is this close association with the affairs of intimate interest, with the moments of anguish and happiness in life," Barnhart thinks, "that has earned for the weekly newspaper a traditional place in the homes of small-town and rural America."[19]

One of the most important functions of the country weekly, in contrast to larger newspapers, is the detailed reporting of "community news." Local interest stories represent "good" journalism everywhere, but in no other instance are local events so completely covered. Reporting of births, weddings, deaths, group meetings of community organizations, and visiting of neighbors are the stock in trade of the country editor. The personal knowledge of such an event only increases the necessity to read about it in the newspaper.

A second function of the country weekly is the role of leadership that can be and often is utilized by virtue of the strategic position in regard to communication. This function may be exercised through the editorial, through projects for community betterment, or through both. Through the editorial, the country editor may easily play the role of a public opinion leader for the

---

[17] Thomas F. Barnhart, "Weekly Newspaper Management" in George L. Bird and Frederic E. Merwin, *The Newspaper and Society* (New York: Prentice-Hall, Inc., 1942), pp. 355-356.

[18] *Statistical Abstract of the United States, 1972,* p. 500, from *Ayer Directory of Newspapers, Magazines, and Trade Publications.*

[19] Barnhart, "Weekly Newspaper Management," p. 353.

community. Certainly countless community projects have been initiated and carried out through the efforts of the country weekly editor. It would be an unbalanced discussion, however, if some of the difficulties facing country editors were not considered. In a study of adult education, one Pennsylvania editor writes this about the problems he faces:

> It is our opinion that every newspaper in the country could use one more "writing man" but even the most financially able papers now find it nearly impossible to add another "unproductive" man to their staff and payroll. Only those who earn their keep with money-making work can any longer be justified . . . My business could very well use one more extra man—if I could pay him, but I can't. He could either do some of the business "work" and allow me time for writing or be editor and allow me some time to run the business. I now do both in 80 to 90 hours per week. . . . Not more than 40 man hours go into the writing and editing of the news content of my paper, approximately half of which I do myself.[20]

Another editor reports the difficulties of avoiding numerous factions in promoting community projects. A Florida editor writes: "I organized a Community Forum backed by churches, bringing in speakers and preparing groundwork for a study group this winter. Speakers represented Florida universities, patriotic groups, various religions. International understanding was the main theme I tried to promote, but patriotic groups caused dissension."[21]

Farm magazines. Like the country weeklies, the farm magazines are important in educating rural people. With the growing commercialization and specialization, there has been a proliferation of special interest, farm-oriented periodicals. However, the specialized clientele cannot be very large, and the circulation of farm periodicals has been declining. While the circulation of all farm periodicals was about 12 million in 1967, less than ten years earlier (1958) circulation amounted to approximately 19 million.[22]

[20] Written communication from the study of adult education in rural areas by J. Allan Beegle, "Mass Media of Communication," in C.P. Loomis, et al., *Rural Social Systems and Adult Education* (East Lansing: Michigan State College Press, 1953), p. 304.

[21] Ibid, p. 303.

[22] *Statistical Abstract, 1972,* p. 500.

In his survey of the magazine reading public, Smith[23] shows that urban residents read magazines much more than farm or village residents and that farmers and farm managers are similar to semi-skilled urban workers in the proportion of readers. In a sample of urban and farm people, it has been shown that magazine reading is closely related to use of library. Among those who use the library frequently, almost half read from four to six or more magazines regularly.[24]

On the basis of research evidence, farm papers and magazines play an important role in changing farm practices. Wilkening[25] found that Wisconsin farmers most frequently said farm magazines were the most important source of information about new things in farming. A repeated pattern revealed by the farmers studied was that they first read about new things and then talked about them with other farmers. Newspapers were considered of minor importance as sources of new information by Wisconsin farmers.

RADIO AND TELEVISION

The radio and television are educational and entertainment media having an important impact upon farm people. With few exceptions, radio and television are urban creations and are important media in the urbanization of rural life. Numerous studies show the influence of the radio on farm families to be important.

Radio and television in rural areas. A very large percentage of homes with electricity in the United States have one or more radios. This has been true for at least 20 years, although rural areas have always lagged behind urban areas in level of living measures. In 1971, 65.4 million homes wired with electricity had a radio—or 99.8 percent of all such homes. On the other hand, the proportion of homes with a black and white television set increased from 46.7 percent (of all homes in 1952) to 99.8 percent (of wired homes) in 1971.[26]

[23] Joel Smith, *The Characteristics of Magazine Audiences—A Survey of the Literature* (New York: Columbia University master's thesis, 1950), Chapter 5.

[24] Angus Campbell and Charles A. Metzner, *Public Use of the Library and Other Sources of Information* (Ann Arbor: Institute for Social Research, 1950), p. 9.

[25] Eugene A. Wilkening, *Adoption of Improved Farm Practices* (Madison: Wisconsin AES Research Bulletin 183, 1953).

[26] *Statistical Abstract of the United States, 1972*, p. 691, from Billboard Publications, Inc., *Merchandising Week*.

While broadcast stations, both radio and TV, are usually urban-centered, few rural areas are without adequate coverage. Commercial broadcast stations on the air in January 1971 numbered 7,149. Of this total there were 700 TV stations. The following states reported having less than four TV stations: New Hampshire, Rhode Island, Utah, Vermont, Wyoming, and Delaware. California had 49 and Texas had 56.[27]

As shown in Table 1, virtually all segments of the nation have access to information and entertainment from this medium.

TABLE 1
Percent of Households with Television Sets, 1955 to 1970

Areas	Percent of Households with TV				Percent of TV Households having Color Sets, January 1969
	June 1955	May 1960	August 1965	April 1970	
All Households	67	88	92	96	—
Inside SMSA's	78	91	94	96	34
Outside SMSA's	50	82	89	94	28
Region					
Northeast	80	92	94	96	29
North Central	72	89	94	96	34
South	53	82	90	95	29
West	62	87	92	94	40

Source: *Statistical Abstract of the United States, 1972,* p. 497.

While much of the programming clearly is designed for a mass audience, some programs are explicitly intended for an agricultural clientele.

THE ROLE OF THE MEDIA IN THE DIFFUSION AND ADOPTION PROCESS

Research on the diffusion and adoption of agricultural innovations has served to delineate five stages in this process: awareness, information, evaluation, trial, and adoption. Individuals tend to use different sources of information at the different

[27] Ibid, p. 496.

stages. In the first two stages—awareness and information—mass media, including magazines, newspapers, radio, and TV rank as the most important information sources. In the last three stages, however, neighbors and friends rank first as the most important sources. Bohlen summarizes the role of information sources as follows: "At the awareness stage, mass media are mentioned more frequently than all other sources combined . . . At the evaluation stage friends and neighbors become the most frequently mentioned source . . . Mass media drop to fourth in order of importance at this stage and continue there for the remaining stages."[28]

Rogers and Burdge[29] point out that "adopter categories," a classification of members of a social system based upon innovativeness, may be characterized by patterns of media usage. The adopter categories, a brief description, and characteristic media usage, follow:

1. *Innovators.* This group comprises the first 2.5 percent to adopt a new idea. Innovators are venturesome and participate in cosmopolitan social relationships. Typical sources of information are from scientists, other innovators, and research bulletins.

2. *Early adopters.* This group is made up of the next 13.5 percent to adopt an innovation. It is composed of progressive localites who have the greatest contact with the local change agent. Other characteristic media sources include farm magazines and Extension bulletins.

3. *Early majority.* This adoption category includes the next 34 percent to adopt an innovation. As a group, they are deliberate in coming to a decision and are more conservative than the previous group. Early majority members use farm magazines, and friends and neighbors as their primary sources of information.

4. *Late majority.* The next 34 percent to adopt form the "late majority." Individuals in this group are skeptical of new ideas. Friends and neighbors are the most frequent sources of new information.

[28] Joe M. Bohlen, "The Adoption and Diffusion of Ideas in Agriculture," in James H. Copp, ed., *Our Changing Rural Society* (Ames: Iowa State University Press, 1964), pp. 281-282.

[29] Everett M. Rogers and Rabel J. Burdge, *Social Change in Rural Societies* (New York: Appleton-Century-Croft, 1972), pp. 356-360.

5. *Laggards.*   The last 16 percent to adopt a new idea or practice comprise this group. Members hold traditional values and
exercise little opinion leadership. Information sources include
mainly friends and neighbors but also radio farm shows.

A LIBRARY ASSOCIATION AND
A STATE LEGISLATURE

To illustrate the elements and processes of the rural library
and mass media as social systems, we present a case which describes how the Wisconsin Library Association managed to secure legislation to establish a regional library demonstration
project. The action, now considered among professional librarians as a model in its effectiveness, obviously involves systemic
linkage between the association (the change agent) and the state
legislature (the target system). In reality any effective program
of adult education, whether carried on by an association, a library, or any of the other social systems, involves many of the
considerations presented here.

THE LEGISLATIVE CAMPAIGN[30]

The principles observed in developing the legislative program
that made possible the Door-Kewaunee Regional Library Demonstration are basic to any program requesting funds or authority, whether on a local, county, state or national level.

Although considerable care was exercised in framing the
bill—a skilled bill drafter sat in with us—we found out later,
partly through the Attorney General's Office, that the bill had
several loopholes. It would have been wiser to have consulted
more than one legal advisor and to have had the opinion of education and health people with similar experiences and problems.
We thought our bill was explicit but we found our later that it
was not clear in all details. Had we submitted the draft to more
people with varied experiences we would have avoided some am-
biguities. [*Note that status-roles (bill drafter, legal advisor, etc.)
must be involved to put proposed action in proper form to meet
universalistic standards of specificity.*] These difficulties accen-

[30] Margie Sornson Malmberg, "The Legislative Campaign" in *The Idea in Action* (Madison: Wisconsin Free Library Commission, 1953), pp. 8-10.

tuate the wisdom of proceeding slowly and avoiding pressure operations.

Once the bill had been approved by librarians and other interested groups, [*supporting social systems*] over-all strategy [*or plan for systemic linkage*] was agreed upon by the board of the library association and the Joint Extension Committee. It was decided that one person should be selected to work directly with the members of the legislature, to call the signals for group action, and to make quick decisions of strategy based upon "on the spot" information. [*Authority was vested in one person to co-ordinate or "quarter back" action, thus taking advantage of situations requiring quick decisions.*] Chosen as executive secretary, it was my task sometimes to initiate and always to coordinate the activities of librarians, trustees, organizations and friends so that our joint efforts would produce the greatest impact. President Jane Billings and I consulted constantly to avoid any action that might not have the wholehearted support of the library association membership. Having someone on the scene all the time has its advantages; however, no one planning such a program should think that such an arrangement removes the need for concerted action by others. The full responsibility can never be shifted to one person; no program should ever be built on the strength of one personality. No program should be won unless people want it and support it.

Since we knew that people must know, need, want and understand a program before they will work for it or support it, we attempted to help them know and understand our goals and how we hoped to achieve them. [*Systemic linkage requires an understanding of the intentions and objectives of the change agent.*] We prepared brief, colorful, and attractive brochures, we spoke at meetings, used the newspapers and radio, in addition to the word of mouth campaign. [*Mass media were used.*] While certain persons were responsible for enlisting the support of specific organizations, we sought to have everyone feel a responsibility for selling the campaign to friends and legislators. It would have been wise to have selected one person from each library district to be responsible for coordinating the activities of the district instead of working directly with individuals. [*More local "quarter-backing" with constituents was needed.*] Although we might have found more brochures helpful, we couldn't finance more than we did. Of course, too much material, not sufficiently condensed, can cause more harm than good. Brevity and sincerity were stressed in everything we did. [*These are ideal standards for all mass media. Brevity includes implications of instrumental action of a Gesellschaft nature; sincerity, the affectual and particularistic aspects of the Gemeinschaft.*]

In telling people about our program we reminded them of the legislative procedures, the crises that might arise, the hearings to be held, the votes to be taken, and what would be expected of them on sudden notice. We cautioned them that, in their enthusiasm, they should not oversell the program, promising things we would be unable to deliver. People need to be kept informed if one expects them to respond intelligently. They need to be informed of the results of their activities if they are to continue their interest.

Great care went into the selection of sponsors for our bills in both the Senate and the Assembly. Assembly and Senate sessions were observed for some time to ascertain who would be best. [*Selection of the sponsors is the initial step in systemic linkage between change agent and target system.*] We were fortunate in securing people with considerable personal prestige [*or social rank*] from both parties, and some held membership on important committees. Every section of the state was represented and all showed marked interested in the bill. While it turned out that we didn't actually need the Senate bill, having it had strategic advantages several times in keeping our opposition guessing, and, of course, the Senate sponsors were better informed than they might have been otherwise. Therefore they were more interested and helpful. While some states do not permit the introduction of a bill in both houses, it is advantageous in giving a second chance in the event one house turns the bill down. Some people insist it makes no difference who introduces the bill, but it has always seemed to me that a bill endorsed by people with prestige and enthusiasm has a better chance of passage.

During the period that Senate and Assembly sessions were being observed to evaluate possible sponsors, rules and procedures were observed closely. [*For effective systemic linkage the change agent must know the norms of the target system, in this case the legislature.*] This later proved helpful at several critical stages. It was important to read the newspapers daily to learn how others evaluated events of the day, to get copies of all calendar procedures, to learn all the rules and to acquire a general awareness of the total picture. In addition it was important to make friends with legislators, newspapermen, elevator operators, and others. Often it was the newspaperman who gave me vital help, and on more than one occasion it was the friendly elevator man who knew where someone was who had to be seen at once. [*Note how the status-roles which are strategic in the communication with different social ranks are used.*] A private card file was kept on every member of the legislature, filled with pertinent information that proved helpful in interviewing them. It is always easier to talk to someone when you have briefed yourself on his interests. [*While each legislator plays status-roles in the legislature, he is also a person and must be dealt with in terms of his other status-roles as an actor and his personal characteristics.*]

This card file of information proved particularly helpful when we were preparing for the hearings. Since hearings provide the opportunity for proponents and opponents to present their cases before the committee who will recommend or disapprove favorable action by the whole house, it was vital that they be well planned. The Assembly Education Committee came first, and for weeks all their hearings were attended to observe the members in action, to know the kinds of questions they asked, to observe the types of people who seemed to make the best impression, and generally to familiarize myself with things that would be helpful for our hearings. It was soon apparent that brief, clearly and enthusiastically presented talks made the best impression. [*The process of communication with its particular standards is illustrated.*] We were able to avoid the "selfish interest" charge that had been leveled at us in the past by securing speakers from such organizations as the PTA, Farm Bureau, CIO, County Boards Association, and the Council of Agricultural Cooperatives. We won a favorable report from the Education Committee. Before the Joint Finance Committee we emphasized those features most impressive to men concerned with budgetary problems, presented by people they respected and accepted. [*Communication must be keyed to the interest and competence of the immediate target.*] The Assembly had already passed the bill when the Joint Finance Committee reported it unfavorably by a very close vote. The action of this committee made it essential that we redouble our efforts to secure Senate passage.

While we had been encouraging people to inform their legislators about our goals and our bill, as soon as we knew when the Assembly would vote on the measure we arranged for concerted action. By phone, telegrams, letters, and personal contacts the Assemblymen felt the impact of our friends' opinions on the day the bill was to be voted on. People wrote what they believed rather than parroting phrases of ours, signing mimeographed cards or other such mass actions that do not reflect originality. It has been my experience that such communications quickly find their way into the wastebasket rather than to the attention of the person for whom they were intended. [*Processes of communication with legislators in a democracy have definite standards; sincerity and originality here are taken as indicative of potential power or the way votes may be cast in elections rather than as mimeographed or machine-like action of an organization.*] We developed a renewed healthy respect for the worth of every individual, for we never knew who would present the information, the friendship, or the influence that was needed to give us a majority vote. Similarly, Senate action was planned and in part executed. We had far more crises in the Senate, and it was here that a detailed knowledge of rules and procedures paid dividends. Having briefed Lieutenant Governor Smith in advance paid off when he broke a tie vote in our favor when our opponents sought to table the measure; it was a knowledge of pairing an absent proponent's vote with a negative vote that saved us twice, and we were saved another time by arranging for reconsideration of the bill the following day when more of our friends would be present after a first defeat. Had we not been aware of what to do at each time and had we not arranged for such eventualities in advance we could not have won, for at that time our floor leader was deeply embroiled in another matter and didn't have time to plan strategy. He welcomed our plan of action, executed it beautifully, and we won by one vote.

Each of these emergencies emphasized the importance of timing. [*Perhaps the most important decision-making process in the strategy of change is deciding when to act.*] Legislators are busy, harassed people who appreciate it when those wanting their support or advice display an understanding of procedures, present their case briefly, concisely, clearly, and with enthusiasm. They respect and admire effective, efficient, well-timed action. They welcome and appreciate such action on the part of many at the proper time as a reflection of peoples' thinking, but such pressure at any other time merely annoys or frustrates them. They are likewise appreciative when they are not approached while they are deeply embroiled in another problem. In brief, an understanding of proper timing for group or individual action is essential if one is to avoid being either a pest or an annoyance.

As each crisis arose we realized that something one might call good manners, for want of a better word, paid dividends. [*The importance of norms and social roles cannot be overemphasized.*] Legislators responded to an appreciation of their problems by a good listener. They welcomed someone who never knocked another program, posed as an authority on every measure or threatened retaliation if in opposition. They welcomed good sportsmanship and were grateful that everyone was thanked for courteousness and kindness if not for support in the event they had voted against us. It was the knowledge that everyone had been thanked that made it easier to approach them again in the special session when we had to pass the bill over the governor's veto. It was that display of thoughtfulness and sportsmanship that encouraged some of them to vote for us in that special session so that the veto was overridden.

Legislators do respond to the will of the constituents. The people back home know their legislators as neighbors, fellow businessmen, or fellow clubmen. They are the ones who can best influence the individual legislator. That is why it is so important that people know the goals, the plans, and the procedures and progress of the campaign. Then they can, in their own way, at the right time, let their friend and neighbor, the senator or the assemblyman know what they want. They have the vote! They are the ones to make their wants known!

SELECTED REFERENCES

American Library Association. *Minimum Standards for Public Library Systems, 1966.* Chicago: American Library Association, 1967.

Berelson, Bernard. *The Library's Public.* New York: Columbia University Press, 1949.

Bertrand, A. L., and Homer L. Hitt. *Radio Habits in Rural Louisiana.* Baton Rouge: Louisiana Agr. Expt. Sta. Bull. 440, September, 1949.

Bohlen, Joe M. "The Adoption and Diffusion of Ideas in Agriculture" in James Copp, ed. *Our Changing Rural Society.* Ames: Iowa State University Press, 1964.

Conant, Ralph W., ed. *The Public Library and the City.* Cambridge: MIT Press, 1965.

International Encyclopedia of the Social Sciences. "Mass Communication." Vol. 3, p. 40 ff.

Leigh, Robert D. *The Public Library in the United States.* New York: Columbia University Press, 1950.

Loomis, C. P., et al. *Rural Social Systems and Adult Education.* East Lansing: The Michigan State University Press, 1953. See Chap. 8, "Public Libraries," by Ruth Warncke and Chap. 13, "Mass Media of Communication," by J. Allan Beegle.

Public Library Association. *A Strategy for Public Library Change: Proposed Public Library Goals Feasibility Study.* Chicago: American Library Association, 1972.

Rogers, Everett M. and Rabel J. Burdge. *Social Change in Rural Societies.* New York: Appleton-Century-Crofts, 1972, Chapter 13.

Rogers, Everett M. and F. Floyd Shoemaker. *Communication of Innovations.* New York: The Free Press, 1971.

Smith, Joel. *Michigan Farmers' Use of Radio and Newspaper Market News.* East Lansing: Quarterly Bulletin of the Mich. Agr. Expt. Sta., May, 1956.

14

Behavioral Change—Strategies and Concepts

In the previous chapters we have concentrated upon the more important social systems composing rural society. Where feasible we have attempted to point out major changes and the direction of change for these systems. Especially for directed social action, the change agent-change target model is basic for the analysis of social organization and processes of change.[1] The earlier chapters have carried this theme. In this chapter, we present what we believe to be a model that complements and supplements the change agent model presented in Chapter 1 and used throughout the text. Such an analytical tool is needed for analyses of social systems in general, for expositions by observers of change, and in the training of change agents. One such analytical tool has been provided by the PAS model—the processually articulated structural model.

Change Agent-Change Target Systems and the PAS Model. Table 1 gives the essence of the PAS model that incorporates the elements and processes used in the previous chapters but it includes more. The model systematically incorporates both statics and dynamics, social structure and process or change. Wilbert Moore has this to say about the PAS model: It "made a notable advance by inviting in . . . the strangers [process and change] to put the house on rollers and permit it to move, while furnishing the interior with flexible and moveable partitions and occasionally discordant inhabitants."[2] The PAS

[1] See a presentation of the change agent-change target model in Charles P. Loomis "Toward a Theory of Systemic Social Change," in Irwin T. Sanders, ed., *Inter-Professional Training Goals for Technical Assistance Personnel Abroad* (New York: Council on Social Work Education, 1950). Also see citation in Footnote 4. For an earlier presentation of the PAS model see Charles P. Loomis, *Social Systems: Essays on Their Persistence and Change,* Princeton, N.J.: D. Van Nostrand, 1950).

[2] "Editorial Introduction" in Charles P. and Zona K. Loomis, *Modern Social Theories* (Cambridge: Schenkman Publishing Co., 1974), p. xxiii.

TABLE 1
Elements, Processes and Conditions of Action of Social Systems
The Processually Articulated Structural (PAS) Model*

Processes (Elemental)	Social Action Categories	Elements
1) Cognitive mapping and validation	Knowing	Belief (knowledge)
2) (a) Tension management and (b) Communication of sentiment	Feeling	Sentiment
3) (a) Goal attaining activity and (b) Concomitant "latent" activity process	Achieving	End, goal, or objective
4) Evaluation	Norming, Standardizing, Patterning	Norm
5) Status-role performance+	Dividing the functions	Status-role (position)
6) (a) Evaluation of actors and (b) Allocation of status-role	Ranking	Rank
7) (a) Decision making and (b) Initiation of action	Controlling	Power
8) Application of sanctions	Sanctioning	Sanction
9) Utilization of facilities	Facilitating	Facility
Comprehensive or Master Processes (1) Communication (2) Boundary maintenance	(3) Systemic linkage (4) Institutionalization	(5) Socialization (6) Social control
Conditions of Social action (1) Territoriality	(2) Size	(3) Time

*For a more detailed version of this figure see Figure 1 in Charles P. Loomis *Social Systems*, p. 8. For the relation of the above concepts to the Gemeinschaft-Gesellschaft continuum see Ibid., pp. 61 ff.
+Status-role, alone of the concepts, includes both element and process.

model will furnish the means of organization for most of this chapter. It will be relied upon to perform the same function as it has elsewhere: to furnish a basis for possible comparisons among activities involving socio-economic change in general.[3] Also it will be used to organize certain findings that are relevant for agricultural development from the MSU Five-Nation Study.[4] Some concepts, even though previously defined, are again defined in this chapter.

Because an example seems the best means to convey the abstractions of social change, we propose to deviate from the non-focused use of the term "system" and to treat social change in-

[3] This was first published as a chapter in a government bulletin in Spanish under the title "Variables Culturales en el Desarrollo Institucional," by Charles P. Loomis in *Desarrollo Institucional—Seminario Sobre Desarrollo Institucional* (Patrocinadores: Ministerio de Agricultura y Ganaderia de El Salvador y A.I.D., Washington, D.C., San Salvador, 1971). For an effort to relate the change agent-change target to the PAS model in the analysis of social change see, J. Paul Leagans and Charles P. Loomis, eds., *Behavioral Change in Agriculture—Concepts and Strategies for Influencing Transition* (Ithaca, New York: Cornell University Press, 1971). See especially Chapter 10. Also see Charles P. Loomis and Zona K. Loomis, *Socio-Economic Change and the Religious Factor in India* (New Delhi: Affiliated East West Press, 1969); Charles P. Loomis and Joan Huber, *Marxist Theory and Indian Communism* (East Lansing: Michigan State University Press, 1970); and *Modern Social Theories,* Ibid.

[4] The study was planned and/or carried through by Hideya Kumata, Charles P. Loomis, Robert Stewart, Frederick Waisanen and associates. The study is based upon modified probability samples drawn from among persons aged 21 and over in Costa Rica, Mexico, Japan, Finland, and the United States. (All figures as given in the text refer to the countries in this order.) It was financed by the Carnegie Corporation, the Ford Foundation, the National Institutes of Health and the Mich. Agri. Exp. Sta. The useable interviews were: 1,040 from Costa Rica, 1,414 from Mexico (1,126 from places 2,500 and over and 288 from rural areas), 990 from Japan, 893 from Finland and 1,528 from the United States.

Some writings based upon data from this study include the following: Charles P. Loomis, Zona K. Loomis, and Jeanne E. Gullahorn, *Linkages of Mexico and the United States,* Mich. Agri. Exp. Sta. Res. Bul. 14, (East Lansing: 1966). In this residents of rural and urban Mexico, the Spanish-speaking Chicanos of the U.S. Southwest, and the general public of U.S. are compared on various dimensions. Jeanne E. Gullahorn and Charles P. Loomis, "A Comparison of Social Distance Attitudes in the United States and Mexico," *Studies in Comparative International Development,* Vol. 11, No. 6 (1966). Charles P. Loomis, "In Praise of Conflict and Its Resolution," *American Sociological Review,* Vol. 32, No. 6 (Dec., 1967). Charles P. Loomis, "In Defense of Integration," *Centennial Review,* Vol. 14, No. 2 (Spring, 1970). In this publication U.S. blacks at varying levels of education are compared with categories mentioned in Loomis, Loomis, and Gullahorn.

volved in rural change and institution building by treating the social relationships studied in two farming villages near Turrialba, Costa Rica, not far from the Inter-American Institute of Agricultural Sciences. (See Figures 1 and 2).

AN EFFORT TO MODERNIZE AGRICULTURE: A CASE OF NEAR FAILURE

That Costa Rica's education system is one of the most effective and advanced in Latin America is the frequent claim of both

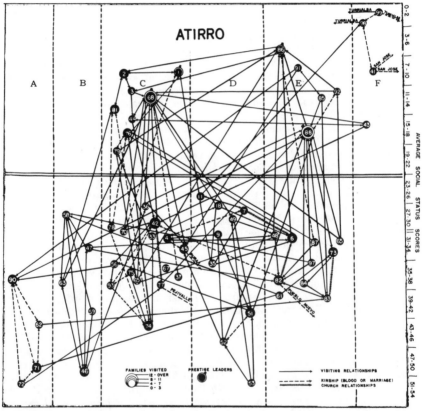

FIGURE 1. Informal social networks in Atirro, Costa Rica. Circles represent families, the size being determined by number of visits; arrows indicate direction of visits; broken lines depict kinship and those with crossbars indicate ritual kinship (godparent, etc.). Family-friendship groups are separated by vertical lines and identified by letters; rank of families is indicated by the vertical scale.

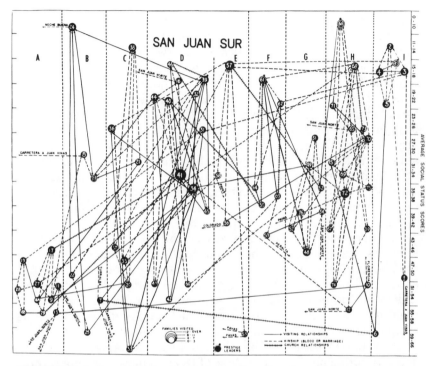

FIGURE 2. Informal social networks in San Juan Sur, Costa Rica. See explanatory legend for Figure 1.

the Costa Ricans and others who write about this country. "We have more teachers than soldiers" is a slogan not outmoded by war.[5] Less than 20 percent of the general population and less than 30 percent of the rural population are illiterate. In Latin America, only Argentina, Uruguay, and Chile have such small percentages of illiterates. In 1965, 20 percent of tax funds in Costa Rica went for education.[6]

The rural teacher as out-of-school change agent. The goal of

[5] John and Mavis Biesanz, *Costa Rican Life* (New York: Columbia University Press, 1946), p. 10. Also see Eduardo Arze Louriera and Roy A. Clifford, "Educational Systems," in Charles P. Loomis, et al., *Turrialba: Social Systems and the Introduction of Change* (Glencoe, Ill.: The Free Press, 1953), p. 172.

[6] F. B. Waisanen and J. T. Durlak, *The Impact of Communication on Rural Development: An Investigation in Costa Rica,* A Final Report submitted to UNESCO/NS/2516/65, Article 1.4, (Paris: December 1967), p. 13.

the proposed program was the improvement of agriculture and health in the area. Although fairly broad in its aims, the ends and activities were reasonably specific, two of which were to provide chlordane for the elimination of field ants that cause great damage to crops, and to build privies to cut down on the incidence of hookworms. The Inter-American Institute of Agricultural Sciences at Turrialba enlisted the help of the national ministry of education and the teachers of the thirty-two villages surrounding Turrialba to carry out the program. At about the same time that this program was launched, early in the 1950's, an all-out effort was being made to vitalize the national agricultural service. In order to avoid interference with that effort and to try another approach, the decision was made to use change agents other than the extension workers. The presence of a school in every village of any size and the services of one or more teachers in each of the schools made the rural school teacher a natural choice. During the school vacation period special workshops and courses in simple agricultural and health procedures that would improve life in the area were conducted for the elementary teachers. The program was begun with considerable enthusiasm and it was reasonably well financed.

At the outset it seemed that the teachers as change agents had some valuable advantages. Most of the teachers were men, their knowledgableness over that of the ordinary village dweller was recognized, and they were held in high esteem.[7] Careful studies based on probability samples of specific areas as well as the whole country demonstrated that few professionals, if known personally to the informant, were considered to be as reliable in the advice or information imparted as the teachers.[8] However,

[7] Ibid., p. 17. One report implies that in Costa Rica teachers are "natural" change agents who in an area comparable to that in Turrialba "by their high credibility, expertise, developmental concern and continued presence in the village . . . are the principal change agents of this [San Isidro del General] and other rural areas of Costa Rica."

[8] Waisanen and Durlak used the "self-anchoring" scale to study the reputed reliability and credibility of various professionals and mass media especially for change agents. After introducing the notion of the ten-step ladder the informant was told "Let's suppose at the *top* of the ladder stand all those things in which you have *complete confidence* and which you are *ready to believe* with little doubt. At the *bottom* of the ladder are those things which are unreliable, unbelievable, and in which you have no *confidence*. On which step would you place

when teacher were not known personally they were accorded relatively low reliability and credibility as compared with priests and medical doctors who were not known personally to the informant. Sociologists who specialize in the study of the professions have noted this phenomenon with respect to groups other than teachers. When incumbents of status-roles are evaluated as inferior in reliability and accorded low confidence because of not being known personally, we may assume that the professionalization of the status-role leaves something to be desired.

Let us turn to a discussion of this and other aspects of status-role as used in the PAS model (Table 1). We shall be watching for evidence that might throw light on reasons for the failure of the rural teachers as change agents.

DIVIDING THE FUNCTIONS:
STATUS-ROLE AS A UNIT INCORPORATING
BOTH ELEMENT AND PROCESS

The two-term entity, status-role, contains the concept of a status, a cultural element implying position, and the concept of role or functional process. Both are important determinants of what is to be expected from an incumbent. (Item 5, Table 1) Although in both industrialized and traditional societies the size of communities is correlated positively with the number and variety of status-roles available to members, it is well to remember that a high level of living has never been attained in a society without a considerable division of labor, i.e., differentiation of status roles. "A nation can be wealthy only if few of its resources

---

[the following; each presented with a separate discussion] 'School teachers whom you know personally,' 'School teachers whom you do not know personally,' 'Medical doctors whom you know personally'? [etc.]." Teachers "known personally" were more highly evaluated in reliability and credibility than medical doctors, priests, nurses, and midwives who were likewise "known personally." How important the condition "known personally" turns out to be is given in the text, above. F. B. Waisanen and J. T. Durlak, *A Survey of Attitudes Related to Costa Rican Population Dynamics* (San Jose, Costa Rica: American International Association for Economic and Social Development, 1966), pp. 132-139.

are required to produce food for subsistence,"[9] and if there are many status-roles for its citizens. As traditional societies are modernized and the proliferation of status-roles occurs, "economic development of various primitive and agrarian economies will produce greater similarity among world cultures."[10]

In modern cultures, societies are dynamic because high evaluation is placed upon the quest for knowledge. The scientists and philosophers, like Max Weber's ethical prophets, see to it that change is omnipresent. No successful scientist can differ much from his fellow scientist in the fulfillment of his status-role. This holds true whether he is in the "hard" sciences or in the social sciences, irrespective of other attributes such as his nationality. In peasant cultures there is considerably more room for an individualized interpretation of the status-role from society to society. In non-traditional societies the range of status-roles available to an individual is wide, but there is not much variation in playing a given role. A Norwegian physicist will do pretty much the same thing as an Italian or Japanese physicist. Whether we consider the scientist who is responsive to the world of science or the peasant of traditional society, culture through the status-role largely determines what is expected locally. The following oversimplified description may serve to illustrate how culture in a traditional society is important in the status-role of the farmer or herdsman.

> To draw an analogy . . . assume that a social scientist, upon returning from summer vacation, finds on his desk invitations to lecture before various women's clubs, to join an administrative committee of his university, and to run for political office in his community. These invitations draw him away from what he had been before—a research worker. In this situation the Yaqui Indian would accept every invitation but would also continue his research; each activity [or what a Yaqui farmer or herdsman actually does] would be well organized . . . The Pueblo would probably refuse all invitations so as to remain a pure scientist [i.e., farmer], but even if he did accept just one he would never lose his re-

[9] E. O. Heady and J. Ackerman, "Farm Adjustment Problems and Their Importance to Sociologists," *Rural Sociology*, 24, No. 4 (December, 1959), pp. 315ff.

[10] Wilbert E. Moore, "Creation of a Common Culture," *Confluence*, 4, No. 2, pp. 232-233.

search perspective . . . The Navaho would not understand the invitations and would leave at the first opportunity for another vacation.[11]

Presumably the Yaquis, Pueblos, and Navahos manifest consensus on expectancy patterns within their own societies. If a given Pueblo farmer would start behaving as a Navaho farmer in the above mentioned aspects, he would appear as a deviant and sanctions would be applied. In a sense this is what happened with the effort to use school teachers as change agents in the Turrialba area. Popular expectations of what could and should be done within the status-role of teacher were violated. This is what happened from the villagers' point of view.

The teachers had to be concerned with the installation of privies. The villagers who respected the teacher's knowledge in the classroom and who were willing to be influenced by the teacher's opinions about non-school matters, nevertheless found themselves uneasy when they talked about privies with the teacher. They felt it was not an easy subject to talk about with someone to whom one normally shows a certain amount of deference. Privies were not properly a concern of teachers. The school inspectors felt very uncomfortable about the new work of the teachers. Ordinarily it was their task to supervise the teachers and to rate them on their classroom activity. They had no standards for rating them on this new task, and so there was ambiguity in both status-roles, that of the supervisors and that of the supervised. Pressure was exerted within the village toward the end of pushing the teacher out of this new agricultural extension status-role and back into the familiar teaching status-role. Even though the teachers could ordinarily muster considerable influence, they could not resist this solidary and sustained pressure.

In sociological terms, the filling of the new status-roles by incumbents having had different roles had never been legitimized. Although the process of legitimation is not elaborated here since it is more clearly a part of norming which is treated later, suffice it to say that by this process change is made rightful in the eyes of the members of the change agent-change target systems.

[11] Edward M. Bruner, "Differential Cultural Changes: Report on the Inter-University Summer Research Seminar, 1956," *Social Science Research Council Items,* Vol. 11, No. 1 (March, 1957).

Even after legitimation has been achieved the change agents must "deliver the goods;" that is, they must act to achieve their objectives. This will be discussed later under achieving. Any concept—status-role, for example—represents a distillation of a number of interrelated thoughts. It says something to another scientist only if it stands for the same interrelated thoughts to both. It often happens that terms are used that convey somewhat different meanings to different readers.

In this discussion it is maintained that the field of psychology specializes in personality systems, that the fields of sociology and political science specialize in the phenomena studied through the use of the concept of the social system, and that the cultural anthropologist specializes in that field conceptualized in the cultural system. Each field has its own conceptual scheme, and not all of the concepts used in explanation and prediction in one specialty are applicable in another. This, of course, may seem obvious, but the frequency with which psychologists, for instance, describe social systems using psychological concepts often surprises sociologists. A number of social psychologists think they have overcome this difficulty. They believe that in articulating the relationships between the social system, the personality system, and the cultural system the one common term used by all is that of status-role.

In Figure 3, an attempt is made to indicate how the three systems may be interrelated with the status-role forming the interlinking triangle using the terms Toennies developed. "T" on the chart indicates a tentative location of the status-role of the traditional man of knowledge in a peasant village. As will be noted, he is heavily influenced by social and cultural factors that place him in the status of Gemeinschaft-like value orientation. The empirical scientist, of course, falls in the rational or Gesellschaft-like orientation and would, in Toennies' thinking be governed by the societal components of rationality derived from Gesellschaft.

The personality system is influenced of course by "energy" from the biological system. Beliefs, values, and expressive symbols contribute to the "actor" in role and these come from the cultural system. The status-role of the social system influences this "actor" in various ways, determining in part what is expected from him.

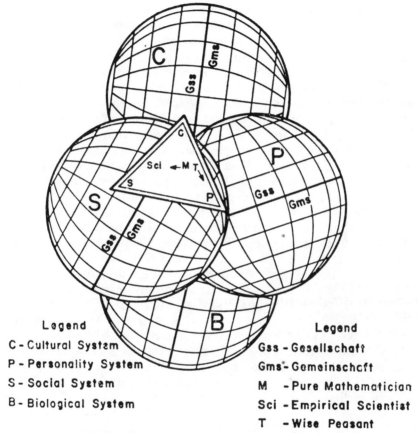

FIGURE 3. Linkage of systems by status-roles in cognitive mapping and validation—a tentative model.

In a conference on agricultural development Harry Triandis,[12] a social psychologist, in an effort to explain the presence of chaperones among family groups of mixed sex condones the practice and condemns societies which do not have this need to protect brothers and sisters from engaging in sex. Thus, he writes, "In cultures . . . in Western societies the needs of the parents 'have introduced internal controls (guilt) into the child's personality.'" He writes further, "The custom of chaperoning

[12] Leagans and Loomis, *Behavioral Change,* pp. 401-402.

[practiced in various cultures] with strong taboos prohibiting brothers and sisters to find themselves together unchaperoned, . . . seems to an American silly, wasteful, time-consuming, old-fashioned . . . but he does not realize that he may be paying a price in excessive sexual maladjustment for not having this custom." The sociologist might not be so prone to condemn guilt for violating the incest and other taboos. We would argue that the existence of a transcendental god in a given culture provides a built-in support for father figures who may help inculcate the superego. Probably the actors in such cultures have more internalized guilt than others. Max Weber might have observed that the honesty of the Puritan Boston and Quaker Philadelphia bankers was based upon the guilt they might feel if they filched funds. We believe it is important that this "social psychological consideration" be given attention in developing status-roles for change agents in developing societies. Business and trading might not be very profitable if it were necessary in every business transaction to have the equivalent of a chaperone stand by. One of Max Weber's important theses, often ignored, is that the Protestants, especially the Calvinists, Methodists, Baptists, and Pietists, internalized norms of brotherhood and honesty which were supposed to be applicable to *all mankind.* Thus they were effective far beyond the family and religious sect, and in this way different from those of the Jews, Parsees, Jains, and similar groups that have also amassed capital, but under less universalistic norms.

RANKING: RANK AS AN ELEMENT

Rank as used here is equivalent to "standing" and always has reference to a specific act, system, or subsystem. Rank, then, represents the value an actor has for a system in which the rank is accorded (Item 6, Table 1). The position of the spheres ranging from bottom to top of Figures 1 and 2 is determined by the ranking a family received when knowledgeable judges who were living in the villages evaluated the family in terms of its "importance for the community." It is not difficult to perceive that in the large estate community, Atirro (Figure 1), a type of "proletariat" or work group holds the positions at the bottom. Above this "proletariat" are the intermediary supervisors and professionals who form a sort of "middle class;" above them are the owners of the hacienda, the commissary, and the coffee mill noted in the upper right side of Figure 1. The location of the horizontal line shows at what point interaction decreases up and down the social class structure. If the figure represented a social system in which a very few members formed an "upper crust" who interacted almost exclusively with each other, and everyone else in the social system formed the hoi polloi among whom there was no significant difference in rank, the horizontal line would be very close to the top of the figure. The ranking system of Atirro (Figure 1) is a modified version of such a pattern. Statistical procedures determine the location of the line that figuratively separates the lower from the upper classes. By such a device one can "see" three classes in Figure 1.

The stratification structure in the family-sized farming community of San Juan Sur (Figure 2) is far less obvious. In fact, there is no point at which interaction from the bottom to the top is significantly less than that which prevails among the members at the top and among the members at the bottom. Although differential ranking is assigned to the members of this social system, the rate and frequency of interaction is apparently not a function of ranking. Figure 2 portrays a much more unitary social system than does Figure 1. It is not possible from charts such as Figure 2 to find points at which interaction was class or caste structured as was possible in Figure 1. In this respect description of the stratification structure in the relationships of the family-sized farming community presented in Figure 2 is not as simple as that in Figure 1.

It should be obvious that such ranking patterns in target systems are of great importance in plans for directed change and institutional building made by change agents. They should be taken into account in both tactics and strategy as developed by change agents interested in modernizing agriculture. In the large estate community of Atirro for instance it would be quite easy for the administrator to change the facilities and processes of some agricultural operations such as pruning the coffee trees. All he would have to do would be to provide the facilities and order the *jornaleros* through their supervisor to carry out the required instruction and to initiate the change. At most, simple demonstrations would be needed. It would be quite a different matter to accomplish this objective in the family-sized farming community, the relationships of which are depicted in Figure 2.

This will be discussed further in the treatment of the concepts, controlling and boundary maintenance.

Evaluation of actors and allocation of status-roles as process. In the communities depicted in Figures 1 and 2, rank is accorded as is usual in Costa Rica. Rank comes from various qualities such as (1) authority and power, the legitimized and nonlegitimized ability to influence others; (2) kinship relations; (3) personal attributes and achievements such as age, sex, beauty, skill, and ability; and (4) property holdings and wealth. The latter may function as symbols of social status or means of initiating action by which authority or power over others is established. However, rank does not necessarily derive alone from wealth and power. Each of the judges here who ranked the families gave reasons for the placements. Often they said the man they had placed high was *muy honorado,* very honorable. In a way this could be thought of as comparable to the Brahmin in India who might be without wealth and power and yet have high prestige. The owner of the hacienda, Atirro, derives his social rank mostly from the first and last criterion mentioned above. The principal leader in San Juan Sur (number 66, Figure 2) derives his social rank mostly from the third criterion. He is a very clever and effective speaker and although possessing only two years of education has many human relations skills.

CONTROLLING: POWER AS AN ELEMENT

Power as defined here is the capacity to control others (Item 7, Table 1). It has many components that may be classified as authoritative and nonauthoritative control. Authority is the right to control, determined and legitimized by the members of the social system and built into status-roles as discussed previously. Unlegitimized coercion and voluntary influence are nonauthoritative. Two somewhat different manifestations of the power structure in the villages (Figures 1 and 2) may be noted. On the one hand there are so called "grass-roots" or popular leaders with many visiting relationships; on the other, there are leaders called "prestige leaders," who are those individuals who would be chosen to make representations for the village to the governor of the state. Power as derived from social relationships described on the charts comes largely from clique groups or what some call congeniality groupings. These groupings are delineated by the vertical lines on the charts and are determined by the answers of all informants to the question, "In case of a death in the family, whom would you notify first?" The rank of the cliques descends from right to left on the charts. In each of the communities these systems of relationships are important for change agents who may wish to reach all members of a given clique through one or more leaders. As will be noted on the charts, most of the so-called prestige leaders are in the upper classes in the large estate communities and occupy higher positions of rank in both communities than most other members. It is obvious that grass-roots or congeniality leaders as well as the prestige leaders have power. Of course, the large estate community is so organized that the most powerful individual is the owner and usually he has made the administrator the second most important person. The owners of haciendas in the area do not all live on the haciendas. Some spend considerable time abroad or in San Jose. It is of interest to those change agents advancing improved agricultural practices and stocks that very often the ordinary worker manifests more antagonism toward the manager than toward the owner, who is generally called the *patron.* Not infrequently the *patron* and the administrator play a sort of game by which the *patron* retains both his power, prestige, and even esteem. Generally the manager cannot be both loved and in control. When he takes his position as administrator he may well know or even be informed that he will be hated. Workers frequently told the interviewers that some of the things about which they were most bitter and complained most would be corrected if only the *patron* knew about them. Often a large fiesta takes place when the *patron,* who has been away, visits the hacienda. At this time the *patron* plays the game of over-riding the administrator and granting certain small favors in order to retain prestige and esteem.

Decision-making and its initiation into action as process. Since charts such as Figures 1 and 2 were available for all thirty villages in the municipality of Turrialba, (all in the sphere of influence of the Inter-American Institute of Agricultural Sciences), some interesting consequences developed. As a sort of experiment the director of the Institute invited all of the prestige and popular leaders to a demonstration at which chlordane was used to eliminate ants that infested the area and greatly reduced crop production. The day after the demonstration hundreds of villagers appeared at the Institute requesting the chlordane. Another example of the power of influence and informal leadership occurred when interviewing began in the village represented in Figure 2. Villagers were hesitant to provide the data that the interviewers requested. Some refused to be interviewed. We noted that Maximino Torres, (number 66, at the top of the clique H) left in a hurry on foot to walk five miles to the trade center in Turrialba. We learned later that he went directly to the *Jefe Politico,* the most powerful representative of the government in the municipality, to find out what we were doing. Fortunately, we had previously visited the *Jefe Politico* and explained the purpose of the study and its connection with the Institute. After Maximino Torres returned to the village, in a matter of hours young and old, men and women, from all parts of the village began coming to the interviewers inviting them to come and interview them. Often refreshments were served. Two years after the interviewing the author had occasion to walk into the village again, the only way to get there during the rainy season. He was surprised to find a substantial new concrete bridge across the small river in place of the usual narrow wooden bridge. Upon inquiry he found another manifestation of how decisions are made an initiated into action in the village. On her way home from school during the rainy season a small girl fell in this river and was drowned. This created a crisis in the village. All who could walk gathered and marched behind Maximino Torres the five miles to the office of the *Jefe Politico* where they demanded a bridge. It was installed as soon as the dry season came and materials could be hauled in.

Those familiar with the village culture of Latin America will recognize that in the family-sized farming villages this type of action is very common. The informal leaders usually rise to prominence both because of personal characteristics and other qualities such as wealth and education. Maximino Torres does not own the largest farm in the community and his education is little more than two years. However, no one could talk with him long without noting that he has qualities of leadership, including some measure of charisma, that quality mentioned by Max Weber in connection with ethical prophets. When Maximino delivers an oration, his command of the language is superb. He is influential and nonauthoritarian. His power does not derive from formal office. Such informal leadership crops up in most social systems, and no doubt it exists on the large estate as well as in the community of small, family-owned farms. But its manifestations in the hacienda community are quite different. In a power-centered situation such as that on the hacienda, where the power is concentrated in the hands of the owner, the manager, and the various supervisors, it would be unthinkable that nonformal power such as that held by Maximino Torres could be articulated for community endeavors such as bridge-building. In neither type of community was the teacher mentioned as a prestige leader unless he or she was a member of a village farm family. Although the local priest has high prestige and, of course, considerable power, he likewise is not mentioned as a prestige leader. In the networks of relations designated on Figures 1 and 2, neither the teacher nor the priest appears as prominent in either the visiting patterns among the villagers or among those who would be chosen to represent the village before the governor, namely the prestige leaders.

Of course, the effort of the Institute to use the teacher as a change agent met with very different results in villages with family-sized farming units and in hacienda villages. In point of fact the project was designed more for the family-sized villages. On the large estates many changes such as disposal of refuse, for which privies were built on family-sized farms, could be handled as an expenditure of the hacienda. On large estates how ants are to be killed and waste disposed of can be determined by the *patron,* the administrator, and other similar power figures. Likewise if these actors were to oppose the changes advocated by the teacher as change agent, the teacher's position would be in jeopardy.

NORMING, STANDARDIZING, PATTERNING: NORM AS AN ELEMENT

The rules that prescribe what is acceptable or unacceptable are the norms of the social system (Item 4, Table 1). Among the most important norms for the change agent to understand are those by which the three most generalized values of society are allocated: power, wealth, and prestige and esteem. Force is often used to obtain wealth and power but prestige and esteem or general ranking accorded by an actor's fellows and peers is less often so achieved. Max Weber noted that the ethical prophet

might, because of his charisma, be highly evaluated by immediate followers but if he were to establish an organization meant
to bridge generations and fit himself and followers into status-
roles, the charisma must be routinized. The high evaluation formerly accorded the personal qualities of the individual must be
transferred to qualifications attached to position, the elemental
component of the status-role.

Norms for change agents. Karl Deutsch dramatized the restraints peasants in traditional societies place on innovative
behavior. He noted that "in traditional cultures that have moved
up to the very limit of subsistence, further innovations promise
very modest and marginal rewards, but swift and terrible risks
that are intensely salient. To this degree, a traditional agriculture that fills up its Malthusian process to the limits of subsistence becomes an engine for teaching its people to fear and
distrust innovations. It becomes a Pavlovian conditioning
mechanism against innovation." (Presented at a symposium
edited by Leagans and Loomis.) Thus, from experience, members of traditional society learn to fear innovators who, unless
they have charisma, will be negatively sanctioned as deviants.
As Durkheim observed, the traditional society is anchored in
stable consensus which he called "mechanical solidarity" supported by repressive norms.

George Foster, an anthropologist, presents a somewhat different explanation for the conservative nature of traditional society.[13] He maintains that the members of traditional society explain achieving in economic activities in accordance with "pure
conflict" conditions of the zero-sum type. This form of explanation is more generally used for political activities by conflict
theorists (Marx, Weber, and others). According to Foster, norms
for activity in peasant and traditional societies restrict individuals from achievement because, as in the zero-sum type game,
the total that all actors considered together can achieve is given.
Under these circumstances any achiever who adds to his original portion has done so in the view of himself and others only at
the expense of taking it away from others. (This basic way of
viewing the world would be more correctly treated later under

---

[13] George M. Foster, "Peasant Society and Image of Limited Good," *American
Anthropologist,* 67 (April, 1965), pp. 293-315 and 68 (Fall, 1966), pp. 210-214. See
also *Human Organization* (Winter, 1970) pp. 303-323.

"knowing," but here we are interested in the norms that result from this type of cognitive mapping.) In societies in which it is believed that all may gain from individual attainment of wealth, the norms or rules of the game do not prohibit competitive striving as much as in traditional societies.

In the case of the effort to make teachers into change agents in the Turrialba area the inspectors' norms did not lead them to approve the extra income the teachers might earn by engaging in the project. Likewise villagers were opposed if not indignant when teachers advised them on agricultural and sanitation matters. It was as if they might say: "Let them stick to doing what they know something about. Let them teach our children as best they can, but don't let them try to teach me what to do."

Evaluation as a process.   The process through which positive and negative priorities or values are assigned to concepts, objects, actors, or collectivities, or to events and activities, either past, present, or future is identified as evaluation in the PAS model. If the values of individuals and pluralities result from the process of evaluation defined in this manner, all of the nine elements in Table 1 can, under certain conditions, be values; likewise the social action categories can also be thought of as values. Activities such as birth control or family planning can be evaluated.

In the Michigan State University Five-Nation Study, informants from probability samples drawn from among those twenty-one years of age and older in Costa Rica, Mexico, Japan, Finland, and the United States were questioned to ascertain their evaluations of birth control as an activity.[14] It was considered wrong for married couples in Costa Rica, rural Mexico, urban Mexico, Japan, Finland, and the United States respectively by the following percentages of informants: 55.2, 49.1, 43.4, 24.5, 11.7, and 23.9. In few nations is population increasing so rapidly as in Costa Rica and Mexico, and obviously these figures indicate that birth control is evaluated much more negatively there

---

[14] See footnote 8. The manner in which questions are stated is, of course, important in such research. Our birth control question was stated as follows: "Family planning or birth control has been discussed by many people. What is your feeling about a married couple practicing birth control? If you had to decide, which one of these statements best expresses your point of view: It is always right; It is usually right; It is usually wrong; It is always wrong." Of course, provision was made for, No answer, Don't know, etc.

than in the United States, Japan, and Finland. Obvious also is the importance of this evaluation for change agents who are attempting to reduce the birth rate. If the teachers who were attempting to change health and agricultural practices in the Turrialba area of Costa Rica had attempted to advance birth control (which they did not), disapproval of their activities would have been greater than it was.

Evaluation and legitimation of change and change agents. Elsewhere we have attempted to specify the processes that are crucial for the change agent as he attempts to bring about directed change through institution building. Here only the crucial part evaluation plays will be mentioned. The processes of initiation, legitimation, and execution are important for institution building but it is the process of legitimation that is most akin to evaluation. Legitimation is the process whereby the proposed change is made "rightful" to the target system. Prestigeful sponsors, rituals, prayers, and other legitimizing procedures are used in this aspect of the strategy of change. Of course, those actors with legitimizing authority vary from culture to culture. In cultures such as that of the United States they may be prestigeful personalities from the scientific, literary, sports, entertainment, military, judiciary, and religious worlds. For some programs in India, Brahmins or other priests may be helpful. In Russia, outstanding Communist party members may be important.

In this connection it is pertinent to report a case of belated legitimation which the author had occasion to observe as he attended a workshop held at the Inter-American Institute of Agricultural Sciences in Costa Rica for agricultural workers. Monsignor L. G. Ligutti, the executive director of the National Catholic Rural Life Conference, in his formal address to the extension agents and other administrative personnel from all parts of Latin America, advised them to call upon local Catholic priests to help with important agricultural and health programs. His words came too late to save the efforts of the teachers in the Turrialba experiment, but having seen how this effective Catholic leader worked, the author believes that if Monsignor Ligutti had advised the village teachers of the area to have the local priests support the program and if he had himself helped with the legitimation in the local Catholic system, the program would not have failed. He told the extension agents from the

Latin American countries to let him know if a priest refused to help, and he would see that the reluctant priest changed his mind. He implied that the priest would hear from him or Rome.

ACHIEVING: END, GOAL, OR OBJECTIVE AS AN ELEMENT

The end, goal, or objective is the change (or in some cases the retention of the status quo) that members of a social system expect to accomplish through appropriate interaction (Item 3, Table 1). In Marxist thought, interests or what we call ends, are of central importance, but norms and evaluation, and beliefs and sentiments (and the relevant articulating processes) are considered to be epiphenomena. It is, of course, true that in acts actually executed or experienced, there is a merging of ends, norms, beliefs, and sentiments. Students of change and change agents, however, can achieve a precision of thought not otherwise possible if the various elements are separated for analytical purposes. There is a degree of actual separation in real life too, as societies become increasingly differentiated. For example, those agencies responsible for cognitive, cathectic and moral activities such as schools, cultural and recreational centers, law courts, and churches are differentiated.

One of the problems common to areas in the process of development is that of rising but unfulfillable expectations. In a probability sample drawn from Costa Rica, 1,500 informants twenty years of age or older were asked: "How many years of school would you like your son(s) to complete?" (or: "If you had sons of school age . . .?"). The percentages who wanted university, high school, and elementary schooling for their sons were as follows: 43.6, 23.3, and 20.2. Informants were then asked, "Do you consider this to be possible?" Percentages of those answering yes, no, don't know, or giving no information were respectively as follows: 65.1, 23.6, 10.1, and 1.1.[15] Of course, in Costa Rica and elsewhere outside of the Communist world, educational achievement of children is highly related to the income of parents. About the same proportion of informants want university training for their children as have family incomes of less than $1,000 per year. With only about 3 percent of the population having

[15] Waisanen and Durlak, *A Survey of Attitudes,* pp. 166-167.

family incomes of $4,000 and above there seems to be plenty of evidence here of rising unfulfillable aspirations.

In an effort to discover how people regard their conditions of life in relation to where they want to be, the so-called "self-anchoring" scale was used.[16] Informants in the Five-Nation Study were told: "Now here is a picture of a ladder. Suppose we say that at the *top* of the ladder stands a person who is living under the best possible conditions of life, and at the *bottom* stands a person who is living under the worst possible conditions of life. On what step would you say you are at present?" The percentages of informants who placed themselves on the bottom three steps of the ten-step ladder for the general public of Costa Rica, urban Mexico, rural Mexico, Japan, Finland, and the United States were respectively as follows: 20.2, 22.7, 26.4, 9.0, 6.1, and 2.6. Looked at another way, the average step placement on the ladder for Costa Rica, Mexico, Japan, Finland, and the United States was respectively as follows: 4.6, 4.4, 4.7, 5.5, and 6.8.

The pressures of rising expectations in Mexico, Japan, and Costa Rica may be noted from the manner in which the same informants responded when asked to place themselves on this hypothetical ladder as they thought they would stand in five years. The average step placement on the ladder respectively as above was: 6.0, 6.1, 6.0, 6.3, and 7.8. Only about half as many of the Costa Ricans, Mexicans, and Japanese placed themselves on the bottom three rungs when looking five years into the future. For the Americans and for the Finns those on the three bottom steps, although in the same direction, indicated an anticipated change which in absolute numbers was negligible. Obviously, relatively large proportions of Costa Ricans and Mexicans are not satisfied with life as it is. The belief that people in traditional societies are "happily poor" is nonsense. The programs the change agents initiate, legitimize, and execute must be those that offer improved conditions of life for the members of the change target system. Apparently the rural people in the thirty-two villages in the Turrialba area were not convinced that the agricultural and health programs advanced by the village teachers would make a better life for them.

---

[16] For a discussion of the scale see F. P. Kilpatrick and Hadley Cantrill, *Self-Anchoring Scaling: A Measure of Individuals' Unique Reality Worlds* (Washington, D. C.: The Brookings Institution, 1960).

Goal attaining and concomitant "latent" activity as process. There is frequent reference in discussions such as this to what is called rational action. Usually rational action is manifest and not latent. It is manifest because its relation to the goal is both recognized and intended by the actor. Of a different order is latent action; that is, action that produces results that either are not intended by the actor or that come about without his knowing it. As an example of manifest activity, the Inter-American Institute of Agricultural Sciences gave a demonstration on the use of chlordane in the control of ants to the leaders of the thirty-two villages in their immediate sphere of influence. The calculated objective was to induce the villagers to wish to adopt the use of chlordane for ant control. The objective was realized very much as anticipated. If the villagers had, as the result of the demonstration, pronounced the director of the Institute a God or even a prophet, it would have been latent activity because the result would not have been intended. Very often the unintended results do strengthen the target system by providing it integration. An example is the rain dance of the Hopi Indians, which unifies the society even though it does not bring rain. A latent result in the thinking of many change agents of various types of directed change in developing as well as developed countries is the flight of rural people to the ghettos of the cities as modernization and development shuffle and relocate them.

KNOWING: BELIEF (KNOWLEDGE) AS AN ELEMENT

A belief is any proposition about the universe that is thought to be true (Item 1, Table 1). The present section deals with the cognitive aspect of an actor's behavior.

In the Five-Nation Study, beliefs were probed using a Lickert-type question to find the extent of belief in the following proposition: "I believe the world would really be a better place if more people had the same religious beliefs I have." The percentages of informants for the general public of Costa Rica, urban Mexico, rural Mexico, Japan, Finland, and the United States who agreed with the statement are as follows: 73.4, 82.6, 93.4, 27.3, 52.4, and 48.5. Obviously the responses reported here did not come from scientists, who subscribe to the following norms as identified by Merton: universalism, communism (in the sense that the substantive findings of science are a product of social collaboration and are assigned to the community, constituting a common heritage from which the discoverer's equity is limited or removed), disinterestedness, and organized skepticism.[17] Skepticism, criticism, and disinterestedness, of course, cannot exist in the minds of those who know that only they are always right. Even for those who are not scientists the application of scientific norms to what one will and will not believe would appreciably change the task of the change agent and the nature of the change target. This brings us to the process of cognitive mapping and validation.

Cognitive mapping and validation as process. Cognitive mapping and validation may be defined as the activity by which knowledge, or what is considered true and what false, is developed. In the national probability samples from the Five-Nation Study, another difference in cognitive mapping emerges. Informants were asked to indicate whether they agreed or disagreed, and to what extent, with the following statement: "Everyone should think the same about what is right and what is wrong." The percentages agreeing for Costa Rica, Mexico, Japan, Finland, and the United States were respectively 90.0, 94.9, 65.5, 86.9, and 49.0

When the proportions agreeing to this proposition for different levels of education are studied, the part the teacher may play in developing the scientific attitude may be contemplated. In the United States, the higher the level of education the less likely the informant was to agree with the above dogmatic statement. However, the informants in urban Mexico who disagreed with the above statement were not better educated than those who agreed. We hypothesize that teachers and education in Costa Rica and in Mexico do not reduce dogmatism to the same extent that they appear to in the United States. We have no proof of a connection, but we speculate that this may be another reason for the failure of the effort of the teachers in the Turrialba area as change agents in health and agriculture. We are led further to speculate that open-mindedness, tolerance, and flexibility are not only functions of the number of years of exposure to the educational process, but are also functions of the content of the edu-

[17] Robert K. Merton, *Social Theory and Social Structure* (Glencoe, Ill.: The Free Press, 1957), p. 553.

cational program. An understanding of the many guises with which "truth" has been viewed through the ages by the peoples of the world is of special importance in this regard.

FEELING: SENTIMENT AS AN ELEMENT

Whereas beliefs embody thoughts, sentiments embody feelings about the world (Item 2, Table 1). Some change agents appeal to the patriotism of decision makers in the change target. In general, as traditional and new nations begin to modernize, nationalism and patriotism increase. In the Five-Nation Study, we obtained answers to the following "self-anchoring" question: "Imagine that you are on the middle step of a 10-step ladder. On the top steps of the ladder are things which, in your judgment, are more important than you as an individual. And on the bottom steps are things less important than you as an individual. On what step would you put your country?" The respective average step placement for Costa Rica, Mexico, Japan, Finland, and the United States was as follows: 9.00, 9.35, 5.84, 7.92, and 8.47. It is obvious that if this approach measures the loyalty people might have for their countries, both Costa Ricans and Mexicans are highly imbued with this sentiment.

In an effort to ascertain some measure of the attachment respondents have for their countries these same persons were asked, "Can you imagine that conditions could get to the point that you would consider moving to another country?" The percentage of informants answering this question in the negative for Costa Rica was 82.4, and for whites and blacks respectively in the United States, 85.4 and 77.5.[18] For Mexicans, Japanese, and Finns the percentages were 83.6, 88.3, and 74.4. These differences are not great and our hypothesis that the percentage for Costa Rica would be higher than for the United States was not validated.

In the study from which these data come, another hypothesis was not validated, namely, that "the family (as evaluated) in terms of the amount of interaction taking place among its members and in terms of its members' evaluation (of it in comparison with other organizations) is more important in both Costa Rica

---

[18] Loomis, "In Praise of Conflict," p. 890.

and Mexico than in the United States."[19] The directors of the study were surprised that these data indicate that appeals to family sentiments would be no stronger in Costa Rica and Mexico than in the United States.

To what extent could one use loyalty to his community for motivational purposes? To ascertain to what extent the community of residence was a true home base and not just a way station the respondents of the Five-Nation Study were asked, "Have you ever considered moving from this town or community?" The proportions answering, "No," were 69.0, 72.7, 67.7, 51.4, and 51.7. From this we may judge that if Turrialba is typical of Costa Rica, the sentiment of community loyalty may be used for motivation purposes by change agents.

Tension management as process. This process may be defined as action by which elements of the social system are articulated in such a manner as to (1) prevent sentiments from obstructing goal-directed activity, and (2) avail the system of their motivating force in achieving goals. Prayer is among the many tension-managing activities, and the only one to be discussed here. For the probability samples mentioned above drawn in the United States and Mexico informants were asked "When you have a decision to make in your everyday life do you ask yourself what God would want you to do?"[20] For urban Mexico, rural Mexico, and the United States the proportions answering in the affirmative were respectively 90.2, 89.2, and 70.4. The frequency with which this prayerful activity was engaged in is indicated by the percentages of informants who answered "Always" when questioned. For these same samples the percentages were respectively 56.4, 65.8, and 18.4. Assuming that the same proportions as reported for Mexico would hold for Costa Rica, for which we do not have comparable data, we could assume a high level of religiosity in Costa Rica. This impression is reinforced by the religiosity manifested in the Costa Rican villages in which the author worked. It reinforces the impression that had the church

---

[19] Loomis, Loomis, and Gullahorn, *Linkages of Mexico.* For the following frequency categories of relatives getting together outside the home, namely: never; few times a year; once a month; few times a month; once a week, for Costa Rica were: 13.9, 22.0, 12.6, 19.9 and 31.6; for Mexico 10.8, 18.7, 13.8, 14.4 and 42.2; for Japan 3.8, 37.1, 23.7, 17.7 and 17.7; for Finland .6, 24.6, 33.8, 14.8 and 26.2; for the United States 3.7, 10.2, 17.1, 11.7 and 57.4.

[20] Ibid., p. 57.

legitimized and supported the efforts of the teachers in the Turrialba area, the attempts to effect change might have been more successful.

Communication of sentiment as process. Through this process action is taken by the members of a social system which leads to motivation to achieve goals, conform to norms, and carry out systemic action through transfer of feeling by symbols. Elsewhere an attempt was made to demonstrate how the two processes, tension management and communication of sentiment, are utilized in the promotion of change by communists after social systems are torn by disruption, and how they may be used when communities are disabled by disasters.[21] There is no doubt that within the realm of sentiment communication, much dynamic force exists which, if understood more clearly, could be harnessed.

FACILITATING: FACILITY AS AN ELEMENT

A facility is a means that, except for slaves, is nonhuman and is used within the system to attain the members' ends (Item 9, Table 1). Mass media is one such facility that often is used effectively to help change agents attain goals. In the effort of the teachers in the Turrialba area to advance agricultural and health practices little use was made of mass media, and radio and television were not used at all. Radios, purchased by the Institute, and placed in each village, might have increased the chances for success, if pertinent radio programs and forums on the subject had been planned.

Another facility prominent in this particular attempt at change was the demonstration of the use of chlordane. Village leaders saw it and were enthusiastic. They communicated their enthusiasm to the villagers who came in unprecedented numbers to stock up. The quantity held by the Institute was insufficient, and many went away empty handed.

Utilization of facilities as process. From the point of view of the change target, how members use their facilities presupposes some surplus over subsistence and some choice among facilities. Concerning the first supposition of surplus, the informants in the Five-Nation Study provide some information. "Property is

---

[21] Loomis, "In Praise of Conflict."

something that should be shared" was the statement to which informants in Costa Rica, Mexico, Japan, Finland, and the United States agreed by the following percentages: 62.5, 63.5, 52.6, 18.0 and 40.2. It is tempting to speculate that the remarkably lower number agreeing with the statement in Finland is connected with Finland's proximity to Russia and its unhappy experiences with that country. A related statement: "Some people have too much property and others don't have enough" elicited the following percentages respectively: 84.3, 82.3, 56.8, 80.8, and 61.2. From these figures can we argue that countries in Latin America could easily go the route of Cuba insofar as the relation of facilities and private property is concerned?

We asked the informants in our Five-Nation Study, "Do you own stock or any other shares in any private enterprise?" The percentages responding "Yes," were as follows: 3.3, 12.4, 18.1, 15.9 and 24.1. The same informants were also asked: "Have you ever thought about buying stock or other shares in any private enterprise?" The percentages responding "Yes," were as follows: 13.9, 42.4, 26.1, 35.4, and 59.7. It is interesting to compare the Costa Rican and Mexican responses with those of the Finns on these questions in relation to the matter of "sharing property" and giving consideration to leaving the home land. One is tempted to speculate that Finland's proximity and experience with Russia conditions these answers. Will Cuba produce the same results for our neighbors?

An important question for the change agent is "How does the change target use its surplus?" In the Turrialba area, for example, would a farmer be more likely to buy a votive candle or a bag of chlordane? If the farmer is already attempting to exterminate ants by some means, the change agent's job (to switch him to a more effective ant control) is far different than if the farmer protects ants because they are the friends of the monkey-god as in India. Many times the utilization of facilities is not done as effectively as it might be simply because the members of the change target do not know what is available. They use the facilities with which they are familiar because they have not seen and do not know about improved means. It can be something as simple as substituting a fly swatter for a piece of paper, or something as complicated as installing electricity to replace candles. Media devoted to description and sale of facilities are of invaluable aid in extending the horizons of the change target. Mail-order catalogs and county fairs are examples of media that fill this function. Of course the availability of a facility does not insure that it will be extensively used. Credit offices offering loans at low rates of interest and easily understood methods of saving such as postal savings accounts are examples of facilities that require considerably more than availability to insure use.

THE MASTER PROCESSES

Of the six master processes of the PAS model, communication, boundary maintenance, systemic linkage, socialization, institutionalization, and social control, there is only space to discuss briefly the first four, which are, we believe, the most important in the analysis and discussion of institution building and the strategy of change.

Communication. Communication is the process by which information, decisions, and directives pass through the system and by which knowledge is transmitted and sentiment is formed or modified. In addition to the numerous ramifications of communication through personal means, other means such as mass media, mail service, telephone lines, highways, and advertising devices should be included.

In the efforts of the officials of the Inter-American Institute of Agricultural Sciences to reach the target population, sociograms depicting interrelationships were of assistance. How the complete network of personal communications was achieved by one demonstration to a few leaders substantiated to the Institute administrators the value of the sociogram. Likewise the teachers studied such charts in the courses they took on the strategy of change at the Institute. Since these teachers who were to become change agents lived in the villages the charts were of great interest to them.

As revealed by the Five-Nation Study, communication through the various mass media reaches the largest percentage of people in Finland and the United States and the least in Costa Rica and Mexico.[22] It has been hypothesized that certain adop-

---

[22] The percentages of informants respectively reporting not viewing television were as follows: 90.0, 63.9, 14.1, 43.3, and 11.5. The percentages not listening to radio as reported were: 36.3, 23.3, 53.5, 7.8, and 20.5; those reporting not reading newspapers were: 45.1, 64.7, 9.7, .7, and 18.2; and those reporting not reading magazines were: 76.3, 42.9, 48.2, 7.4, and 5.6.

tions (such as the plow, for example) are brought about, not so much by a man's change in receptiveness or by an increase in his psychological motivation, as by his seeing that the tool exists, is available and is used by others with whom he has a chance to interact. According to this hypothesis travel to a city might make people adopters of many things seen there. This observation recalls Ralph Beals who observes that in potential for producing change "one road is worth about three schools and about 50 administrators."[23] Various diffusion studies have found urban contact, urban pull, mass media contact, etc., very important in the adoption of agricultural and health practices. The available evidence indicates that any society which becomes isolated from the activities that take place in the world's major routes of transport, cities, and knowledge centers will be disadvantaged by a lower level of living than would otherwise be the case. Iron curtains, bamboo curtains, and high tariffs, exact their penalty in terms of an opportunity to develop.

Boundary maintenance. Through boundary maintenance the solidarity, identity, and interaction patterns within social systems are maintained. If a change agent is working on the problems of a small village, the boundaries that might prove difficult between him and the change target could be the resistance to change by a hacienda owner who sees no advantage to himself in improvements for his laborers as long as labor is cheap. It could also be the resistance to a poultry program if the change agent is a man and poultry is viewed as women's work.[24] Another type of boundary would be encountered if the proposed change espoused by the change agent were to be directly in conflict with cherished beliefs and sentiments of those who comprise the change target as might well be the case for ant extermination in parts of India or birth control in a traditional Catholic country.

On a larger front it might be fear of institutional innovation that provides the change target with a boundary that might be formidable for a change agent. While the local power structure might not be opposed *ipso facto* to more goods and services, only a little projection might reveal that such institutions as company stores or company credit would be drastically altered by

---

[23] "Notes on Acculturation," in Sol Tax et al., *Heritage of Conquest* (Glencoe, Ill.: The Free Press, 1952), p. 232.

[24] Thomas L. Norris, "Economic Systems: Large and Small Land Holdings," in Loomis et al., *Turrialba,* pp. 102-103.

modernization; that people could move about more freely and that the local reservoir of cheap labor might dry up; that extensive small land-holdings might change the relation of the big estate to the government. Many of the feared consequences are often vaguely visualized but are no less threatening because of it.

On a still larger front is the barrier posed by free or restricted trade, depending upon which side of the argument one finds himself. Of course, boundary maintenance affects the extent of international collaboration which is possible. Informants in the Five-Nation Study responded to the following statement indicating whether and to what extent they agreed with it: "It is a good thing for companies and business firms from other countries to do business and have factories in our country." For Costa Rica, Mexico, Japan, Finland, and the United States the percentages respectively agreeing were: 68.7, 68.1, 35.6, 41.0, and 57.2. It is interesting to speculate whether the Cubans, before Castro, would not have responded as did Costa Ricans and Mexicans. Although we tend to think of underdeveloped economies as exercising high boundary maintenance, here is an instance where the more modernized societies express a greater desire for boundaries than do the less developed ones.[25]

Systemic linkage.   This is the process whereby the elements of at least two social systems come to be articulated so that in some ways and on some occasions they may be viewed as a single system. Whereas the processes previously discussed deal chiefly with interaction within a system, systemic linkage relates members of at least two systems.

Several linking processes were involved in the Inter-American Institute of Agricultural Sciences' institution building activities, that used the local village teachers as agricultural and health change agents. First the Institute involved and obtained agreement on the part of the National Ministry of Education for the experiment, and in effect the two agencies became the change agent system. The change target systems to which the change agent system was to be linked, of course, were each of the thirty-two villages. This linkage, for reasons discussed above, was never finalized to a significant extent. The linkage that proved

[25] Henri Mendras, *Les Paysans et la modernisation de l'agriculture* (Paris: Centre National de la Recherche Scientifique, 1958).

most productive and of greatest duration was that between teacher and such groups as athletic clubs, especially soccer clubs.

Depending upon the objective, a few people may comprise the change target for the attempt to be successful or a very high percentage may have to be involved. A community's drinking water, for example, may be chlorinated with a relatively few people linking with the change agent before the decision. Karl Deutsch mentions an example of the opposite situation, where a great number have to be involved. Literacy and the birth rate are negatively correlated. It is, however, not enough that a few people become literate for the birth rate to show a change. Even when literacy is extended from 10 percent to 60 percent of the population, there is no correlation. But by the time literacy reaches 80 percent of the population the birth rate begins to drop. His idea of the "threshold" at which point changes can be observed because of a wider and wider linkage should be of interest to change agents involved in system building.

The so-called "package program" of Indian agriculture is an illustration of a systemic linkage designed to insure an input from all relevant facilities and services in such a way that there will be an optimal or "highest profit combination" output. Nations that are unabashedly planners, such as India and Russia, seem to encounter considerable difficulty in effectively linking many systems. Nonetheless, nations that are only occasionally planners and that then go about planning a bit furtively, as the United States, link a good many sub-systems not ordinarily thought of as compatible bedfellows (such as the private and public sector) when an otherwise unobtainable goal is important. Molders of public opinion who ordinarily denounce socialistic tendencies if there is any deviation from private enterprise were peculiarly silent about criticism and noticeably jubilant about results when the race for leadership in the space program led to the moon landings. If it is just as imperative in the eyes of the people of Guatemala and Pakistan to increase food supply and to modernize as it seemed to be in the eyes of Americans to maintain space leadership, perhaps their motives in systemically linking the government with the private and industrial sectors should appear no more threatening than our own motives in the space adventure. That we still view any such alliance with deep suspicion is shown by the Five-Nation Study. Informants were asked whether and to what extent they agreed with the following statement: "The only way to provide good medical care for all of the people is through some program of governmental health insurance." The percentages respectively agreeing for Costa Rica, Mexico, Japan, Finland, and the United States were as follows: 84.9, 84.1, 90.3, 83.9, and 57.2.

Socialization. Socialization is the process whereby the social and cultural heritage is transmitted. In primitive and developing societies the family is of crucial importance for socialization. In industrialized societies specialized institutions of various types carry on socialization in addition to that which the child receives in the family and from friends and neighbors. The high evaluation which Costa Ricans place on schools and education has been mentioned. In an effort to ascertain how people generally feel about socialization for agricultural development, informants included in the Five-Nation Study were asked the following question: "Some people believe that the government should play a bigger part in training rural youth in agricultural practices. What is your feeling on this statement: 'Rural youth who remain on the farm should be given more training to make them better farmers, even if we have to pay more taxes'?" Proportions of informants from the various countries who agreed with this statement are respectively as follows: 82.6, 93.3, 42.7, 78.1, and 59.4. If these figures are a valid indication there seems to be no question about the readiness of Costa Ricans and Mexicans for agricultural development. Such answers might indicate that the Costa Rican Ministry of Education and the Inter-American Institute of Agricultural Sciences might well have trained vocational agricultural teachers to give this type of training directly to Costa Rican rural youth.

Other findings from the Five-Nation Study indicate that both in Costa Rica and in Mexico the people have been socialized to accept thoroughly the society in which they were reared. The informants were asked to indicate whether and to what extent they agreed with the following statement from the well-known F-Scale used by Leo Srole to measure authoritarianism: "Children should be taught that there is only one correct way to do things." The percentages respectively agreeing are as follows: 78.3, 94.8, 58.8, 63.9, and 60.2. These data substantiate the contention that industrialization, urbanization, and other processes involved in modernization change people; such a milieu seems to exert a socializing process of its own.

CONDITIONS OF SOCIAL INTERACTION

The elements and processes constitute the working components, i.e., the parts and articulating processes, of the social system. Not all aspects of social action are encompassed in these concepts, but the remaining components are partly systemic, that is, partly structured and partly under the control of the actors of the system. Space, time, and size are such components.

Territoriality. The setting of the social system in space is called its territoriality, and it determines within limits how much space each person or group may have, the frequency and intensity of interaction within the group, and probabilities of systemic linkages between groups and between change agent and change target systems. In the Turrialba area a rather simple consideration involving the change agent-change target relation was studied. A study was made in one of the communities to ascertain a location where most people could see a poster display. On the large estate of Aquiares it was found that the greatest number of contacts are made at the butcher shop. Since no local refrigeration exists, a steer or hog is butchered almost every day and the people come to buy fresh meat as it is needed. It was recommended that certain posters developed by change agents be displayed in the butcher shop.

How services of farmers are related in space and the relation of prices to markets has been the concern of agricultural social scientists at least from von Thuenen's time to the time of Galpin, Christaller, Loesch, Berry and others.[26] Effective directed change and institution building require considerable knowledge

[26] Johann Heinrich von Thuenen, *Der isolierte Staat in Beziehung auf Landwirtschaft und Nationaloekonomie* (Jena: Fischer, 1930); Charles J. Galpin, *The Social Anatomy of an Agricultural Community,* Wisconsin Agricultural Experiment Station Research Bulletin No. 34, (Madison, Wisc., 1915); Walter Christaller, *Die zentralen Orte in Sueddeutschland* (Jena: Fischer, 1933); August Loesch, *Die raeumliche Ordnung der Wirtschaft* (Jena: Fischer, 1941); and Brian J. L. Berry, *Geography of Market Centers and Retail Distribution* (Englewood Cliffs, N. J.: Prentice-Hall, 1967).

of interrelations and linkages of locality groups. Unfortunately time and space will not permit further elaboration but the importance of understanding such linkages may be illustrated by the statement of the economist, Kenneth Boulding, to the effect that central place theory, the discipline and science devoted to these matters, may be the "queen of the sciences."

Time. Time as a condition is inexorable and cannot be completely controlled by man. Even though man is ths only animal that bridges the generations through the transmission of culture, he is nonetheless time-bound and this is reflected in all studies of the strategy of change. In the effort to use teachers as change agents in the Turrialba area, time often came into consideration. Training for the change agent role was carried on when school was not in session. In this area people are not as time conscious as they are in industrialized societies. *Hora española* and *mañana,* not *hora inglesa* and today, describe timing of events to which change agents must become accustomed.

In institution building and directed social change, when to act or start programs and when not to act is as important to change agents as it is to military strategists. Just as the successful military strategists are often said to have a superb sense of timing, so also must effective change agents have the ability to correctly time their actions.

Size. Insofar as size of social systems is not controlled by the actors, it may be discussed as a condition of social action. Although inventions that improve man's efficiency in the use of energy tend to increase the size of certain systems, various systems in different organizations, societies, and epochs are remarkably similar. It is interesting to note how frequently eight and twelve persons comprise the supervisory unit in various organizations. The original squad in armies is an example. Another aspect of size as a condition is the number of persons per unit of space. Some think this is a condition and uncontrolled because of man's inability to manage reproduction; others, such as many Catholics, consider it a moral issue. The extent to which beliefs in countries such as Costa Rica and Mexico affect the evaluation of birth control was discussed above. Ralph Cummings[27] of the Rockefeller Foundation thinks the present runaway growth of population will continue so that if famine is to

[27] Leagans and Loomis, *Behavioral Change,* p. 79.

be avoided food production per year must be doubled or tripled. At the present time, concern about famine and the rapid pollution of man's environment has made the problem of population size most important.

SUMMARY

Institution building and development are not simple processes to be achieved by the separate contributions of a society's economy, policy, or its research and educational establishments. Nor can one academic discipline alone claim success in predicting or explaining the course of social and economic development. In reality it depends on favorable conditions not only in rural institutions but in the sectors of "agri-climate," which supply, transport, market, finance, purchase, and provide the technical advantages and inventions as well as a stable governmental administration for agricultural production. The complexity and magnitude of the processes involved in effective institution building are so great that many scientific disciplines must be brought to bear on them if they are to be predicted, understood, and furthered. This being true, it is necessary to assist specialists in the various scientific disciplines involved in institution building to understand each others' frames of reference and concepts.

Often in the past, disproportionate efforts have been made to educate the agricultural producer. The enlightenment of the peasant is important, but too little attention has been given to institution building aimed at improving his incentives, technology, and facilities, which would encourage and enable him to respond as desired. Policy and strategy must deal with all sectors of the total system and its sub-systems that affect the producer. Most sectors of the whole society must change. The approach must be macroeconomic in order to permit and encourage microeconomic change.

As agriculture in developing societies becomes increasingly dependent upon the development of other sectors, the coordinating and service roles of government become increasingly complex and important. Moreover, the traditional agriculturist, exploited and neglected by representatives of the larger society for many generations, distrusts governmental and educational officials. Also governmental and other administrative officials may lack the required administrative capabilities for either institution building or operation. Their traditional origins may foster corruption and nepotism. Changes in incentives of government and organizational structure may be required to get results. Often a government's use of political power to attain development objectives involves political costs exceeding immediate political gains. Nevertheless, societies must develop governmental strategies for the economical and effective use of their power. Professionally trained, socially minded, and adequately supported and organized administrative personnel are the indispensible condition of system building and development.

If traditional agricultural societies are to modernize, hindrances must be removed that prevent freedom of effective human action and use of resources for human betterment. Land tenure systems, marketing arrangements, and human relations generally must not only permit but facilitate efficient action and economical use of both human and nonhuman resources. The concepts and tools developed in fields such as agricultural economics and rural sociology are applicable for system building and its evaluation. However, the optimum combinations of labor, capital, land, entrepreneurship, and other "inputs" will be different in developing countries than in industrialized societie. . Developing societies are universally burdened with underemployment of labor and heavy farm-family food requirements. The prescriptions carried over to developing societies by agricultural economists from industrial societies may be more pertinent to the commercial pockets of agriculture generally found in developing countries than to subsistence farming. Nevertheless, the potential rationality and desire for an improved life on the part of the traditional agriculturists should not be underestimated.

Science applied to the control of disease has resulted in such decreasing death rates and consequent rapid population growth rates that the world faces critical food and other shortages on a scale never before known. Unless agricultural science produces disease-resistant and otherwise regionally suitable plants and animal stocks and improves cultural practices and agricultural knowledge generally, famine appears to be inevitable. If famine is to be avoided through worldwide institution building and agricultural development, all scientific disciplines must team up on the problem. Control of environmental pollution requires a similar approach. This holds whether the sciences focus on nature in general, scarce resources in particular, the personality, human power, politics, culture, health, or education.

There is not sufficient stored knowledge available to save us, but much knowledge now available is ineffectively used. It is in the behavioral sciences that knowledge necessary for agricultural development is most lacking. While effective and economically feasible birth control measures are now available to slow the rate of population growth, the behavioral sciences do not possess sufficient knowledge concerning the organization and motivation of people to greatly increase the use of them. The potential contribution of the behavioral sciences should make it possible to speed up institution building for agricultural and societal development generally without undue application of force, violence, or cruelty.

SELECTED REFERENCES

Desai, A. R. *Essays on Modernization of Underdeveloped Societies.* Bombay: Thacker & Co. Ltd., 1971.

Eisenstadt, S. N. *Modernization: Protest and Change.* Englewood Cliffs, N. J.: Prentice-Hall, 1966.

Foster, George M., ed. *Traditional Cultures and the Impact of Technological Change.* New York: Harper and Row, 1962.

Hagen, Everett E. *On the Theory of Social Change: How Economic Growth Begins.* Homewood, Ill.: The Dorsey Press, 1962.

Horowitz, Irving. *Three Worlds of Development.* New York: Oxford University Press, 1966.

Lerner, Daniel. *The Passing of Traditional Society: Modernizing the Middle East.* Glencoe, Ill.: The Free Press, 1958.

Levy, Marion J. Jr. *Modernization and the Structure of Societies.* Princeton, N.J.: Princeton University Press, 1966.

Loomis, Charles P. *Social Systems—Essays on Their Persistence and Change.* Princeton, N.J.: D. Van Nostrand, 1960.

Loomis, Charles P. and Zona K. Loomis. "Social Change and its Conceptualization." Ch. 9. in *Modern Social Theories.* Cambridge, Mass.: Schenkman Publishing Co., 1975.

Loomis, Charles P. and Zona K. Loomis. *Socio-Economic Change and the Religious Factor—An Indian Symposium of Views on Max Weber.* New Delhi: Affiliated East-West Press, 1969.

McClelland, David C., ed. *The Achieving Society.* New York: The Free Press, 1967.

Moore, Wilbert E. *Social Change.* Englewood Cliffs, N.J.: Prentice-Hall, 1963.

Mosher, A. T., ed. *Creating a Progressive Rural Structure.* New York: Agricultural Development Council, 1969.

Rostow, W. W. *The Stages of Economic Growth: A Non-Communist Manifesto.* London: Cambridge University Press, 1960.

Smelser, Neil J. and Seymour M. Lipset, eds. *Social Structure and Mobility in Economic Development.* Chicago: Aldine, 1966.

Swanson, Guy E. *Social Change.* Glenview, Ill.: Scott, Foresman & Co., 1971.

Wharton, Clifton R., ed. *Subsistence Agriculture and Economic Development.* Chicago: Aldine, Atherton, Co., 1969.

Worsley, Peter. *The Third World.* Chicago: University of Chicago Press, 1964.

15

The Uses of Rural Sociology*

As the following section shows, no specialty in sociology has a stronger claim to having been applied for the betterment of human life than rural sociology. The work of rural sociologists on the diffusion of improved practices and facilities and health care and delivery systems in rural areas is especially noteworthy in this regard. The general "diffusion" of rural sociological literature on the very subject of *diffusion* in itself is a phenomenon worthy of attention. In the following pages facts about diffusion that may not have been sufficiently detailed in preceding chapters (See Chapter 13 where the mass media are a focus) are elaborated.

Beginning with Charles Galpin, rural sociologists have made substantial contributions to the fields of community and regional planning. These studies are basic to central place theory, and are important for developing economies and problems related to the control of pollution. While interest in central place theory appears to have declined on the part of sociologists, this condition is not so among the human geographers. The contributions of rural sociologists to these and other important areas are detailed in the following sections.

From the earliest days of their discipline, the demands of "pure" science have been distinguished from those of "applied" science by rural sociologists. For them, the world of the professional agriculturalist and farmer has been their arena of action at the same time that the world of the social scientist has continued to command their allegiance. A prominent sociologist, a specialist in diffusion of ideas and personal influence, notes in a lead article in the *American Journal of Sociology* that his own work bore a parallel to "the twenty-year-old tradition of research

* Paul F. Lazarsfeld, et al., eds., *The Uses of Sociology,* Chapter 24, "Rural Sociology," by Charles P. Loomis and Zona K. Loomis, (New York: Basic Books, Inc., 1967).

by rural sociologists on the acceptance of new farm practices . . . [while the two branches of inquiry] were hardly aware of each other's existence or of their possible relevance for each other."[1] The present chapter has been written in part to broaden the awareness of others to rural sociology—the first sociological specialty to be linked significantly to the practicing professions and occupations.

HISTORICAL BACKGROUND[2] OF THE LINKAGES OF RURAL SOCIOLOGY

The first of "annual informal gatherings, which eventually expanded into the rural section of the society and then into the Rural Sociological Society,"[3] was held in 1912. The occasion was the annual meeting of the American Sociological Society, whose theme that year was rural life. Just one year before this meeting, the Roosevelt Country Life Commission, which had questioned thousands of rural people about the shortcomings of rural life, had published its famous report. It is but one of 154 rural sociological studies mentioned by Brunner[4] as having preceded the Purnell Act of 1925 by which federal funds for rural sociological research in land-grant institutions were specified. Most of these early studies were done outside colleges of agriculture. The non-college-of-agriculture influence has continued to be strong, as have been the United States Department of Agriculture connections and experiment-station activities. The monumental *Systematic Source Book in Rural Sociology*,[5] published in the early thirties, came out of such a combination.

[1] Elihu Katz, "Communication Research and the Image of Society: Convergence of Two Traditions," *American Journal of Sociology,* LXV (1960), 435-441.

[2] Edmund deS. Brunner, *The Growth of a Science* (New York: Harper, 1957). Here (p. 144) see a listing of the presidential addresses before the Rural Sociological Society, many of which have dealt with the history of rural sociology. See also Charles J. Galpin, *My Drift into Rural Sociology* (Baton Rouge: Louisiana State University Press, 1938); and Walfred A. Anderson, *Bibliography of Researches in Rural Sociology* (Ithaca: New York Agricultural Experiment Station Rural Sociology Publication 52, 1957).

[3] Brunner, *op. cit.,* pp. 3, 4.

[4] *Ibid.,* p. 5.

[5] Pitirim A. Sorokin, Carle C. Zimmerman, and Charles J. Galpin, *Systematic Source Book in Rural Sociology* (Minneapolis: University of Minnesota Press, Vol. I, 1930; Vol. II, 1931; Vol. III, 1932).

The setting for *using* sociology—for putting it to work in a rap-idly changing rural society—is clearly indicated by these early linkages. The farmers' movement, the farmers' organizations, such organizations as the Roosevelt Country Life Commission, the American Country Life Association, the federal legislation concerning agriculture, and the federal bureaus and depart-ments devoted to agricultural affairs constituted or reflected a nationwide rural-life movement to which rural sociology has been functionally related from the first. No balder statement about its useful intent can be made than that of William H. Sew-ell: "Most research in rural sociology is for the purpose of help-ing in the solution of practical problems of rural people and rural society."[6]

In reviewing rural sociology from its beginnings a half-cen-tury or more ago, the idea of "uses" becomes blurred. What of a classic such as Galpin's *Social Anatomy of an Agricultural Community?*[7] Is its contribution to ecology generally, and to the University of Chicago group particularly, to be considered a "use"?[8] And should rural sociology be credited with useful tech-niques such as the sociogram which it has so profitably em-ployed, since a rural sociologist did not actually invent the tech-nique, and since other specialties within sociology have also put it to advantageous use, although by some decades later than the rural sociologists? To answer such questions, and to get infor-mation about how rural sociology has been used, we turned to the rural sociologists of the United States. Some responses were very helpful in appraising the relative importance of groups of studies, but not so helpful on how such studies have been used. Others were extremely helpful on reporting uses which were almost surely made, but were impossible to document. It cannot be stated too emphatically that the present chapter makes no claim to being exhaustive. Some excellent studies will not be mentioned here if their use is in question. Real but intangible uses will not be mentioned here if they are not documentable.

[6] William H. Sewell, "Some Observations on Theory Testing," *Rural So-ciology,* XXI (1956), 1.

[7] Charles J. Galpin, *The Social Anatomy of an Agricultural Community* (Madison: Wisconsin AES Bulletin 34, 1915).

[8] Bruce L. Melvin writes: "I heard [Robert E. Park] say at the meeting at Pur-due University in 1925 that [he] took his suggestions for city studies from C. J. Galpin." Personal correspondence.

Even the most solid of uses usually are documentable, however, only because the investigator has been in personal contact with the user. Therefore much of the documentation will be confined to personal letters which are on file with the senior author.

To give some order to the wide range of uses indicated by the letters, we have followed the rough and sometimes overlapping categories suggested by the most frequently cited and most numerous uses. Three streams of sociological thought and procedures can be singled out as being rich in ultimate application, influential in delineating problems, and of consequence in their solution. One of these is ecological, or the specifications of the space dimensions of pluralities: the delineation of locality groupings such as the neighborhood, community, and region and the diverse uses to which both the findings and the procedures have been put. The second is a mélange of communication, influence, and social change which most often is called diffusion. The third is that area of investigation which is a response to the needs of government, both in policy formation and in legislation.

LOCALITY GROUP DELINEATION

The spatial relations among and between social systems such as families, neighborhoods, communities, associations, and similar pluralities have changed radically in America during the last half-century and are similarly changing the world over, as rational organization, industrialization, and bureaucratization affect larger and larger portions of populations. Institutions rooted in a given historical territorial pattern are less than adequate when spatial relations change. To rural sociologists, Galpin's Wisconsin Experiment Station Bulletin *The Social Anatomy of an Agricultural Community,*[9] published in 1915, is the most important pioneering study of rural locality groupings. Galpin's basic observation was the "road turnings"; that is, the ruts vehicles wore into the ground as they turned from the farm

[9] Op. cit. Galpin's work was supplemented in time by many others who added refinements to delineation methods and adapted them to changing conditions. Among his early and best-known successors should be mentioned John H. Kolb, Dwight Sanderson, Carl C. Taylor, and Carle C. Zimmerman. For a more complete statement concerning both successors and forerunners, see Brunner, *op. cit.,* Chapter 2.

home. The well-worn rut in the direction of trade center A, as contrasted with the little-worn rut in the direction of trade center B, would identify the farm family with trade center A. Of course, as the trade-center dimensions changed from the "team haul" of the horse-drawn wagon to the "tin Lizzie spin" of the early farm automobile days to the fast transportation of the modern four-lane highway, the "road turnings" have been supplanted by other cues which have been found to be useful in demarcating an area. Nevertheless, so simple, explicit, and persuasive were the Galpin-Sanderson methods of determining trade-center community boundaries that in New York for many years the State Board of Education would not approve consolidation of school districts unless these procedures were used for reorganization on a "natural trade center" community basis.[10] What happened in New York was paralleled, with various methods of delineation of locality-groupings, all across the country as the small school districts of a basically neighborhood-oriented, agricultural society yielded to the larger trade-center pluralities of an increasingly urban society.

A number of innovations in method of delineation[11] were climaxed by a related search for "optimum" configurations to serve various social and economic purposes. In effect, these latter studies sought to determine how big and inclusive an administrative unit must become in terms of number of people, taxable

[10] Edmund deS. Brunner writes that "the Galpin-Sanderson methods of determining community boundaries were used at first by New York State. . . . The N.Y. State Board would not approve a consolidation unless these procedures had been followed in determining the social community. . . . [They] also were used in a number of states in laying out communities, areas of representation on county committees in the Agricultural Planning Program." Personal correspondence. See Dwight Sanderson, *Locating the Rural Community* (Ithaca: Cornell University Extension Bulletin 413, 1939); John H. Kolb, *Rural Primary Groups* (Madison: Wisconsin AES, 1921); Carle C. Zimmerman and Carl C. Taylor, *Rural Organization: A Study of Primary Groups in Wake County* (Raleigh: North Carolina AES Bulletin, 1922); and Donald G. Hay and Robert A. Polson, *Rural Organizations in Oneida County* (Ithaca: New York AES Bulletin 871, 1951).

[11] T. Lynn Smith was largely responsible for creating awareness of the importance of such factors as land division, settlement patterns, and the layout of roads. He did much of the basic research for this emphasis. See his article "The Social Effects of Land Division in Relationship to a Program of Land Utilization," *Journal of Farm Economics*, XVII (1935), 703-709. Sanders and Ensminger developed the "neighborhood cluster method" for delineation of communities and neighborhoods within communities. See Irwin T. Sanders and Douglas Ensminger, *Alabama Rural Communities: A Study of Chilton County* (Montevallo: Alabama College Bulletin 136, 1940).

wealth, and accessibility to other resources to insure a stipulated minimum service and how small it must remain to be responsive to the needs of its constituents. The legion uses to which these studies have been put should not obscure the solid impact of accomplishments: of communities prepared to accommodate to a highway relocation because social factors as well as engineering factors have been available and used;[12] of schools which spring from and belong to the communities which they serve because considerations other than population factors were known to be important;[13] of the reduction of marginal memberships in such organizations as county libraries and regional health units because integration is based on something more solid than geographic proximity;[14] of vitalized neighborhoods working together on problems significant to all.[15] It is impossible to specify how

[12] In response to the authors' request for examples of uses of rural sociology, Walter C. McKain, Jr., writes that rural sociological research in "Connecticut, Pennsylvania, and Texas, to mention only three [states] . . . has helped . . . communities anticipate the opportunities and changes that are occasioned by highway programs, and by demonstrating how highways can be used to stimulate economic areas." See Walter C. McKain, *The Connecticut Turn Pike* (Storrs: Connecticut AES Bulletin 387, 1965).

[13] C. Horace Hamilton writes that the work done by rural sociologists in North Carolina "on community, and especially medical ecology, . . . was of great use to the Governor's Commission on Education Beyond the High School." Personal correspondence. See C. Horace Hamilton, *Community Colleges for North Carolina, a Study of Need, Location, and Service Areas* (Raleigh: North Carolina AES Bulletin, 1962); and John F. Thaden, *Equalizing Educational Opportunities through Community School Districts* (East Lansing: Michigan AES Special Bulletin 410, 1957).

[14] Therel R. Black writes that in Utah Joseph A. Geddes' "Study on libraries . . . resulted directly in the passage of Utah legislation for the establishment of library districts and the providing of a state library system." Carl F. Kraenzel writes along the same line for the state of Montana, and Charles E. Lively notes that the Missouri State Library used sociological data on stratification and occupational subareas for the distribution of books. From personal correspondence.

[15] James W. Longest, Frank D. Alexander, and Jean L. Harshaw, "The Function of the Neighborhood in the Farm and Home Management Program: A Case Study," *Rural Sociology,* XXVI (1961), 186-191. Of course, rural sociologists have put to work groupings other than those featuring locality. "Work . . . done by James Longest and Frank Alexander in their Cornell AES Bulletin, *The Method Used for the Formation of Home Management Programs in a Town of Verona in Oneida County* resulted in letting leaders identified by local people in the community select their own members for . . . discussion groups," writes a Missouri informant. Allen Edwards writes along the same line for South Carolina. Personal correspondence.

many formulas for state aid have been based on sociologically determined "needy areas," but that pedestrian fact does not make less important the equalized opportunity resulting therefrom.

Various modifications of delineation method made it possible for laymen to devise fairly accurate approximations of area demarcations. For example, an "optimum efficiency index" was developed which was based on density of population, total population, economic base, and location of roads and highways. The governmental and administrative units of a southeastern state were modeled after this formula. In the same region a North Carolina rural sociologist devised a measure of the combination of graduated community ability and need on the one hand, and a graduated scale of hospital service on the other, which led to a probably unique system of hospitals, with one metropolitan county hospital and smaller rural hospital branches.[16] Two fundamental formulas and other planning devices, developed in Michigan and North Carolina by rural sociologists, have been used by many other states in determining the number and location of hospitals to be built under the Hill-Burton program. The two formulas are (1) bed-death ratio formula and (2) percentage formula as related to average daily requirements for hospitalization. The techniques developed there for delineating hospital service areas have also been widely used.[17] Sometimes it was discovered that a supposedly significant ecological factor was relatively minor. The location of health facilities in one state was altered when it was established by rural sociologists that age, education, level of living, and occupation contributed to the use of the health facility, but that distance from it played a relatively minor role.[18]

Nor have the uses been entirely governmental. On the one hand the churches limited the practice of "overchurching" as studies showed the affiliations of farm families with the larger centers.[19] A far-sweeping example may be found in the Rural

[16] Horace Hamilton, personal correspondence.

[17] Ibid. See C. Horace Hamilton (collaborator), *Hospital Care in the United States* (New York: Commonwealth Fund, 1947).

[18] John C. Belcher, *Medical Service Relationships in Harper County* (Stillwater: Oklahoma AES Bulletin, No. B-477, 1956). Belcher writes that "the principal finding [here] is that distance is not . . . . [but] age, education, level of living and occupation are significantly associated with both use and health levels." Personal correspondence.

[19] Edmund deS. Brunner, personal correspondence. C. Milton Coughenour in a

Life Division of the Methodist Church of Oklahoma which "re-mapped the parish organization of the entire state, using Hagood's level-of-living indexes and rural sociology population studies as base."[20] At the same time market-research organizations reshaped their advertising campaigns and retooled their sales programs. The old Dodge Motor Company required local agents to do a rough community delineation in the manner of the then prevalent locality delineation methods. For the first time salesmen *knew* the social boundaries of their sales territories.[21] Especially during World War II, the various personnel of the Agricultural Extension Service—the county agricultural agents, the home demonstration agents, and the 4-H Club agents—who were linked with rural sociologists through the Agricultural Experiment Stations and by USDA connections sought, on the sociologists' advice, to find meeting places which were consonant with "natural groupings."[22] The American Medical Association was stimulated toward making studies of physician distribution after rural sociologists showed a high incidence of sickness in counties with the fewest physicians.[23]

Large migrations provide a dual need for the application of sociological-population facts—an application in the areas of both out-migration and in-migration. Especially in the case of slow, steady out-migration, the projection of school enrollments, of relief loads, of employment opportunities, and of markets is more than a simple extrapolation. It requires the judgment of

---

letter broadens the concept of uses: "The most extensive use of information collected by rural sociologists in Kentucky has been made by welfare agencies, the Extension Service, churches, the community leaders in Eastern Kentucky and the Southern Appalachians. For years members of the Department have funneled information and provided counsel to groups of these kinds." In this work the following type of publication was much used: James Brown, *The Family Group in a Kentucky Farming Community* (Lexington, Ky.: AES Bulletin, 1952). See also Emory J. Brown, *Elements Associated with Activity and Inactivity in Rural Organizations* (State College, Penn.: AES Bulletin 574, 1954).

[20] Otis Durant Duncan, personal correspondence. See also Margaret Jarman Hagood, *Farm Operator Family Level of Living Indexes for Counties of the United States,* 1940 and 1945 (Washington: Bureau of Agricultural Economics, 1947). This work and earlier indices by Charles E. Lively, Robert L. McNamara, and Raymond A. Mangus have been invaluable both as bases for sampling in surveys and for planning regions for administration.

[21] Edmund deS. Brunner, personal correspondence.

[22] See especially headings under Ensminger in Anderson, *op. cit.*

[23] Charles E. Lively, personal correspondence.

rural sociologists on such factors as net migration, replacement ratios, and dependency ratios. If most of the out-migration is directed to a few common points, projection rates for the receiving communities is subject to the same judgmental decisions. Most enterprises in areas of out- and in-migration, both in the private and public sectors of the economy, are extremely reliant on the studies of sociologists for any realistic appraisal of the future. For example, the numerous migration studies on the Southern Appalachians have been utilized by schools, churches, and public agencies in northern cities such as Chicago, Detroit, and Cincinnati, as programs and policies are developed to deal with the adjustment problems of southern migrants.[24]

In the early 1940's the rural sociologists in the United States Department of Agriculture under the leadership of Carl C. Taylor were requested to assist in determining the "optimum" social and economic configuration for modern settlement, including arrangements of services, forms of holdings, and other variables. For years economists and sociologists had debated the advantages and disadvantages of Durkheimian mechanical vs. organic solidarity, or Toennies' Gemeinschaft vs. Gesellschaft, and had argued the efficacy and inefficacy of the "checkerboard system" of land division used generally in the United States since the passage of the bill establishing it in 1785. T. Lynn Smith calls it "one of the most vicious modes ever devised for dividing lands,"[25] especially because it imposed distances which impeded neighboring. Other writers argued against the small trade center with too few people to provide adequate services. The problem was subjected to empirical testing when Nathan L.

[24] See the sections, Migration and Mobility in Anderson, *op. cit.* B. H. Lubke writes: "Dr. Roscoe Giffin, sociologist at Berea . . . worked closely with some of these urban agencies in setting up programs and policies to deal with adjustment problems of southern migrants." Personal correspondence. A classic in rural sociology and important, as indicated below, in the development of Bureau of Census breakdowns is Edmund deS. Brunner, *et al., American Agricultural Villages* (New York: Doran, 1927). For an insightful analysis of the relation of small towns to large cities, see Arthur J. Vidich and Joseph Bensman, *Small Town in Mass Society* (Princeton: Princeton University Press, 1958). This and the following were cited by rural sociologists in response to requests for suggestions on uses: Otto G. Hoiberg, *Exploring the Small Community* (Lincoln: University of Nebraska Press, 1955); and Irwin T. Sanders, *Making Good Communities Better* (Lexington: University of Kentucky Press, 1950).

[25] T. Lynn Smith, *The Sociology of Rural Life* (New York: Harper, 1947), p. 267.

Whetten[26] studied settlement patterns in Saskatchewan, Canada. There the development of highways and modern communication had proceeded concomitantly with land settlement. He found a relatively large number of small centers developed to serve local families. Other studies by means of aerial photography[27] have been made of actual settlements in the western part of the United States where settlers were free to build homes where they wished, unimpeded by team-haul limitations. There, although the checkerboard system of land division had been imposed as in the Midwest, there was no evidence from the studies that people settled in the middle of their holdings, the place designated by many farm-management specialists as the most economically rational. Instead they typically built along the roads and within reasonable distance of neighbors. Also the studies revealed that even after the square units of the official surveys had been imposed, subsequent division tended to form longer rectangles (rather than squares) in the "string-along-the-road" or "line type" settlements. The application of such findings may be seen by visiting the Columbia River Basin settlement under the Grand Coulee Dam. The settlement pattern is the result of the Columbia Basin Joint Investigations contributed to by rural sociologists, accepted in large measure by action agencies and implemented on the basis of "140 years of westward movement and 40 years of reclamation settlement experience."[28]

Many rural sociologists and other professionals in the field of agriculture grew up on family-sized farms and tend to entertain a bias for that sized holding, as against the hacienda and the "factory farm." It is possible that many of the studies testing the relative merits of the two systems of settlement spring from a nostalgic commitment to the way of life nurtured by the family-

[26] Nathan L. Whetten, The Social and Economic Structure of the Trade Centers in the Canadian Prairie Provinces with Social Reference to Its Changes, 1910-1930 (Cambridge: Harvard University unpublished Ph.D. Thesis, 1932).

[27] Walter R. Goldschmidt, "Some Evidence on the Future Pattern of Rural Settlement," *Rural Sociology,* VIII (1943), 370-386. See also Irving A. Spaulding, "Perspective on Urbanization," *Rural Sociology,* XXVII (1962), 1-7.

[28] Carl C. Taylor, "The Sociologists' Part in Planning the Columbia Basin," *American Sociological Review,* XI (1946), 321-330. Columbia Joint Investigations (Washington: USDA and Cooperating Agencies, 1944). For documentation, see Charles P. Loomis and J. Allan Beegle, *Rural Social Systems* (New York: Prentice-Hall, 1950), pp. 237. ff. See also Murray A. Straus, *Matching Farms and Families in the Columbia Basin Project* (Washington AES Bulletin 588, 1958).

sized farm. The use of such studies in resettlement and relocation seems to be solidly based, however, on the virtually uniform
findings that the socioeconomic advantages accrue to the family-sized farm rather than to the larger holdings. Along with
these studies are others which demonstrate the great cost, in
terms of human suffering and maladjustment, of unplanned settlement.[29] Reclamation projects which occasioned the moving of
families were guided in their resettlement work by such
findings. Similarly, the settlement pattern used for the reservoir
families under TVA who had to be transplanted elsewhere was
under the direction of an action agency which gave prime consideration to the recommendations of rural sociologists such as
Frank Alexander, with whom they worked closely during the entire process.

A related use occurred with frequency during the war years,
when labor shortages on the farms and in industry were serious.
Such shortages were relieved by relocation and recruitment of
workers. Seasonal surplus farm labor was located largely by
rural sociological studies, notably those of the Division of Farm
Population and Rural Life. Their findings were used widely by
Ford, Kaiser, and others for recruiting large numbers of persons
to work in shipbuilding and in the automobile industry.[30]

The problems to which the rural ecologists turned their attention parallel very closely the problems which arose as fewer and
fewer people were required on the nation's farms. Today there is
a relatively new emphasis on nonagricultural development of
the rural economy, based squarely on "the fact that probably
only one farm boy out of every ten will have the opportunity to

[29] For bibliographical and substantive findings on this subject, see especially
Smith, *The Sociology of Rural Life*, Chapter 13. See also Walter R. Goldschmidt,
As You Sow (Glencoe, Ill.: The Free Press, 1947); and Charles P. Loomis *et al.*,
Turrialba: Social Systems and the Introduction of Change (Glencoe, Ill.: The
Free Press, 1953). For the results of misguided settlement on the Great Plains,
see Carl F. Kraenzel, *The Great Plains in Transition* (Norman: University of
Oklahoma Press, 1955).

[30] Paul J. Jehlik, personal correspondence. The opposite process also occurred,
as the Farm Security Administration used these studies for recruiting workers
"for dairy farms in such states as Ohio, Indiana and Illinois during the early
World War II period of a critical shortage of farm workers." There is some
evidence indicating that rural sociological studies influenced policy in the
United States treatment of large holdings in conquered countries after World
War II.

take over an adequate-sized commercial farm. . . . We have also made computations of the potential growth of the rural labor force in the 1960's in the absence of migration, which delimit the magnitude of the rural development problem."[31]

There could be no such exodus from farm to city, of course, without improved farm practices which enable one farmer now to produce the foods and fibers which twenty produced before. And technological knowledge in the hands of a few specialists is far from enough to motivate farmers to try new methods, to take risks in discarding the known ways, to learn to apply the up-to-date technique, and to make personal and family adjustments consequential to the new practice. A large body of rural sociological literature deals with adoption practices and the characteristics of those who adopt at differential rates.

DIFFUSION OF IMPROVED PRACTICES AND TECHNOLOGY[32]

Ecological considerations were given early attention by rural sociologists as they attempted to speed up the spread of improved practices, breeding stocks, and technology. Systems of influence and power were recognized as bearing a relation to the degree that social systems were Gemeinschaft-like, or neighborhood groupings, or Geselleschaft-like, or trade-center oriented. Influentials in these two situations were categorized as neighborhood, "grass roots," or popular leaders in contrast to county-wide or trade-center leaders.[33] These terms were gradually supplanted by those developed by Merton and Zimmerman:[34] the

[31] Louis Ducoff, personal correspondence.

[32] The two outstanding books on the subject are Herbert F. Lionberger, *Adoption of New Ideas and Practices* (Ames: Iowa State University Press, 1960); and Everett M. Rogers, *Diffusion of Innovations* (New York: The Free Press of Glencoe and Macmillan, 1962).

[33] Charles P. Loomis and Douglas Ensminger, "Studies in Social Organization, Administration, Attitudes, and Opinions," in Charles P. Loomis, *Studies of Rural Social Organization* (Ann Arbor: Edwards Brothers, 1945), Chapter 5. See also Charles P. Loomis, *Social Systems: Essays on Their Persistence and Change* (Princeton: Van Nostrand, 1962), Essay 2.

[34] Carle C. Zimmerman, *The Changing Community* (New York: Harper, 1938), pp. 5, 7. See also Robert K. Merton, *Social Theory and Social Structure* (Glencoe, Ill.: The Free Press, 1957), p. 393. Pitirim A. Sorokin was using the term *cosmopolitanism* in 1927. See his *Social Mobility* (New York: Harper, 1927), p. 541.

localites and cosmopolites. The various diffusion studies of such traits as the planting of hybrid corn and the use of weed killers, insecticides, and so on soon established that the localities tended more toward late adoption of practices than the cosmopolities, who tended to be the initiators. Also it was found that early adopters and innovators tended to rely on cosmopolite sources of information, such as mass media, coming in from outside the local neighborhoods, while late adopters relied more on local sources of information, especially friends and neighbors. One study demonstrated that each neighborhood may have its own "characteristic pace of diffusion" and that the "neighborhood educational level, and prevalence of favorable scientific farming attitudes generated a rank order of locality groups most closely approximating that of the average diffusion rate."[35] In the adoption process, cosmopolite influences are relatively great in the awareness stage, but in subsequent stages before adoption, localite influences are greater.[36] All these findings have been used by the Agricultural Extension Service both in planning and executing promotion campaigns. In fact, one of the most important changes which can be noted is the agricultural experts' knowledge of sociological and diffusion-study terminology. Thirty years ago few if any agriculturalists would have known the meaning of cosmopolite, localite, innovator, early and late adopter, and fewer still would have used these terms. Now the terms have fairly wide usage among nonsociological professional agricultural personnel throughout the United States. The terms are also diffusing in Europe and in developing countries where rural sociologists are working.

Perhaps for sociologists the most significant diffusion event in the history of the discipline is the spread of diffusion knowledge itself. By 1955, rural sociologists of the North Central states under assistance from the Farm Foundation had collected

---

[35] C. Milton Coughenour, "The Rate of Technological Diffusion among Locality Groups," *American Journal of Sociology,* LXIX (1964), 325-339. Quotations are from the manuscript of the paper before publication. Of course, pluralities other than neighborhoods are important in diffusion. See Eugene Wilkening, *Adoption of Improved Farm Practices as Related to Family Factors* (Madison: Wisconsin AES Research Bulletin 183, 1953).

[36] George M. Beal and Everett M. Rogers, "Informational Sources in the Adoption Process of New Fabrics," *Journal of Home Economics,* XLIX (1957); and Bert L. Ellenbogen and G. Love, *Age, Status and the Diffusion of Preventive Health Practices* (Ithaca, N.Y.: AES Bulletin 64, 1964).

and published a report derived from the various diffusion studies. This report, *How Farm People Accept New Ideas,*[37] immediately came under such heavy demand that in the first four years over 80,000 were distributed, and translations had been made into several languages. In 1961 the same Sub-Committee on Diffusion decided to bring together and publish those studies on diffusion which would give more emphasis than the first bulletin did to the process through which individual adopters accept new ideas. This bulletin, called *Adopters of New Farm Ideas—Characteristics and Communications Behavior,*[38] like its predecessor, has met world-wide demand. In 1955 Beal and Bohlen, rural sociologists at Iowa State University, popularized and extended a visual presentation developed by Neil Raudabaugh, illustrating the diffusion of farm innovations. Eight years later they had given their presentation to 180 meetings, conferences, and other gatherings, to all types of change agents such as salesmen and dealers, advertising-agency personnel, extension workers, and industrial managers. Although many of the presentations were to church, education, and agricultural extension groups which did not pay a fee, it may be noted, for those who judge the success of a service by how much people are willing to pay, that some private firms paid handsomely for the demonstration and for subsequent consultations with its initiators.

Among the earliest and most famous of the rural sociology diffusion studies was that by Ryan and Gross.[39] This study, which focuses on the adoption of hybrid seed corn, found that the modal frequency of being aware of the new trait came seven years after the first farm operator had heard of it. The modal frequency of adoption came ten years after the trait was first adopted. The length of time between first awareness and general awareness, on the one hand, and first adoption and general adoption constitutes the essential data which have been used in a variety of ways. Ryan and Gross noted that the rate of diffu-

[37] North Central Rural Sociology Subcommittee for the Study of Diffusion of Farm Practices, *How Farm People Accept New Ideas* (Ames: Iowa Agricultural Extension Service Special Report 15, 1955).

[38] North Central Rural Sociology Subcommittee for the Study of Diffusion of Farm Practices, *Adopters of New Farm Ideas: Characteristics and Communications Behavior* (East Lansing: Michigan AES Bulletin, 1961).

[39] Bryce Ryan and Neal C. Gross, "Acceptance and Diffusion of Hybrid Corn Seed in Two Iowa Communities," *Rural Sociology,* VIII (1943), 15-24.

sion approximated the S-shaped growth or learning curve, a form first recognized by Tarde and later applied by Chapin and Pemberton.[40] Of the two most widely distributed publications mentioned above on diffusion of farm practices, one states that "about 14 years elapsed between the introduction of hybrid seed corn and its adoption by most farmers. Soil testing, as a basis for fertilizer application, has been recommended for 20 years, yet the majority of farmers have not adopted it."[41] Policies and procedures for reducing this time lag are based on the diffusion studies.

One use related to the above-mentioned characteristics of diffusion may be illusted by Agricultural Extension practices involving the S-shaped rate-of-diffusion curve. The Director of Agricultural Extension in a Northern Plains state observed in his Ph.D. dissertation that the spread of artificial breeding of dairy cattle conformed to the S-shaped curve as expected. He went further and noted that after the success of the program was demonstrated and subsequent adoptions diminished in rate, there was an excessive wastage of time by the Extension staff who expended as much effort or more during the period of fall-off of adoptions as they had in the period of rapid rise of adoptions.[42] The surplus of effort after two or three years has been reduced considerably, at least in this investigator's own staff.

In the second of the two widely distributed diffusion reports,

[40] Gabriel Tarde, *The Laws of Imitation,* translated by Elsie C. Parsons (New York: Holt, Rinehart, and Winston, 1903); F. Stuart Chapin, *Cultural Change* (New York: Century, 1928); and H. Earl Pemberton, "The Curve of Culture Diffusion Rate," *American Journal of Sociology,* I (1936), 547-556. Sorokin has denied the validity of the S-shaped curve for cumulative distributions or the normal curve for noncumulative distributions in acceptance or spread of all ideas and traits. Rural sociologists have disagreed with him, but in the present authors' view Sorokin has the advantage of a broader vista than his critics. The interchange illustrates the importance of adequate conceptualization in explanation and prediction. It is necessary that the "givens" or "other things equal" be specified. To maintain that the diffusion of an order to a well-trained army or to actors in other authoritarian situations follows the same pattern as the spread of hybrid seed corn in Iowa is absurd. It may be compared to the claim that such behavior as learning and growth under "voluntary" conditions which may approximate the S-curve is the same as that of the "do or die" type which may more nearly fit the J-curve, so often used by sociologists to describe social phenomena.

[41] North Central Rural Sociology Subcommittee for the Study of Diffusion of Farm Practices, *Adopters of New Farm Ideas,* p. 3.

[42] John T. Stone, *How County Agricultural Agents Teach* (East Lansing: Michigan AES Service, Mimeo Bulletin).

Adopters of New Farm Ideas, the following stages are specified: (1) Awareness, (2) Interest-information, (3) Evaluation-Application-Decision (4) Trial, (5) Adoption. Although stages as employed by various investigators differ, stages comparable to these were validated by various investigators as the adoption of antibiotics was observed among farmers.[43] Likewise a set of stages which roughly parallels those specified above was validated for adoption of practices among Pennsylvania dairy farmers. Diffusion specialists themselves are dissatisfied with the conceptualization of stages and seek a reconceptualization which will show that "adoption of a farm practice is a bundle of related events flowing through time, not an instantaneous metamorphosis."[44] Nevertheless, the concept of stages has been generally diffused to change agents in agriculture and must be considered a use to which diffusion studies have been put.

A use of diffusion studies dependent on the specification of stages in the adoption of technology and ideas is the emphasis now placed on the trial or "dry-run" stage. Rogers observes that "most persons will not adopt an innovation without trying it first on a probationary basis."[45] Ryan and Gross found in their pioneering study that "however clearly the advantages of hybrid corn had been demonstrated by community experience, most farmers insisted upon personal experimentation before they would adopt the innovation completely."[46] The importance of the trial stage is further emphasized by the fact that innovators and early adopters move to it much faster than others, this being one of the chief features differentiating those who adopt early from those who adopt late. This, coupled with the research evidence suggesting that the adoption stage directly follows the trial, further increases the importance of the trial. For example, one study proves that a "free trial speeded up the adoption process for a weed spray as much as [an estimated] one year."[47] For

[43] George M. Beal, Everett M. Rogers, and Joe M. Bohlen, "Validity of the Concept of Stages in the Adoption Process," *Rural Sociology,* XXII (1957).

[44] James H. Copp, Maurice L. Sill, and Emory J. Brown, "The Function of Information Sources in the Farm Practice Adoption Process," *Rural Sociology,* XXIII (1958), 146-158.

[45] Rogers, *op. cit.,* pp. 85-85.

[46] As summarized in Rogers. *Ibid.,* p. 85.

[47] Gerald Klonglan *et al.,* "The Role of a Free Sample in the Adoption Process," paper presented at the Midwest Sociological Society, St. Louis, 1960. Of course it may be argued that the trial provides knowledge necessary for adoption. The cognitive aspect of adoption is crucial in adoption. See Leonard M.

a considerable time Agricultural Extension Services have
known the importance of the trial period, as have business concerns selling such items as milk separators and vacuum
cleaners.

In the last decades various sociological studies have shown
that the effort expended in extending the various services to
farmers and ranchers is disproportionately small toward the
"lower or disadvantaged third." Often administrators have ex-
cused this lapse because they are relying on the "trickle-down"
or "two-stage" models of diffusion. Two variations of these
models are dominant: (1) that if change agents spend most of
their time working with adoption leaders, these latter can be relied on to serve as models and disseminators of the new practice;
and (2) that mass-media messages flow from radio and print to
opinion leaders who in turn disseminate the ideas to those less
liable to mass-media influence. Diffusion studies based on empirical reality have posed a question about the efficacy of such
models and have belied the earlier belief that complete dissemination would occur by introducing the practice in question to the
strata which are typically the early adopters. One Ohio study[48]
found that only 2 per cent of the farmers were reached exclusively by indirect trickle-down effort expended by Agricultural Service workers, whereas 79 per cent had been reached by either
direct contact with the agent or a combination of direct and indirect contact. As have many diffusion studies, Missouri investigations[49] found that influentials in the diffusion process were
concentrated in the upper social ranks or strata, but their influence not only caused ideas and practices espoused by them to
trickle down to farmers of lower rank but also spread the items
to people of their own rank and upward to those of superior rank.
The efficacy of the trickle-down model depends, of course, on the
social structure and value orientation of the target system, and
diffusion studies have emphasized this vital consideration.

Sizer and Ward F. Porter, *The Relation of Knowledge to Adoption of Recommended Practices* (Morgantown: West Virginia AES Bulletin, 446, 1960).

[48] Everett M. Rogers and Harold R. Capener, *The Clientele of the County Extension Agent* (Wooster: Ohio AES Research Bulletin 858, 1960).

[49] Herbert F. Lionberger, "Community Prestige and the Choice of Sources of
Farm Information," *Public Opion Quarterly,* XXIII (1959), 110-118. See also Her-
bert F. Lionberger and C. Milton Coughenour, *Social Structure and Diffusion of
Farm Information* (Columbia: Missouri AES Bulletin 631, 1957).

A society with closed castes requires different strategy than an open-class society. In the latter, the innovators and early adopters may be higher in rank and class than others. Majority adopters, both those called "early" and "late," may constitute about 68 per cent of the population and have about average social rank. They may be influenced by the early adopters, but seldom by the innovators, as models. Laggards and late adopters have the lowest social rank. In terms of sources of information "laggards and the late majority are most likely to depend upon friends and neighbors in the immediate locality as a source of new farm information than upon other sources. Innovators . . . [who get their ideas from agricultural scientists and others] cannot depend upon . . . others in the locality. . . . On the other hand, by the time the late majority and laggards consider adopting an idea, they are surrounded by other farmers who have information and opinions about it."[50]

The terms *traditional vs. modern,* and other parallel "ideal types" such as Gemeinschaft-like and Gesellschaft-like have been used to order actors, neighborhoods, communities, and other units in diffusion analysis.[51] To rural sociologists working in both the countries of the industrialized West and developing societies, the importance of a quality which has been called "economic rationality" seems obvious. The differences in motivation of farmers in the State of Washington in which "Gaines wheat . . . seed was released to seed growers one year and the next to the general public and . . . adopted by *over half* the wheat growers"[52] stands in contrast to village peasants of a developing country such as India. Various scales have been developed which are designed to reveal the rigidity of attitudes toward a whole complex of ideas: caste, superstition, the causes of misfortunes, and the most efficacious remedies. The placement of the individual actor on these scales (which roughly measure traditionalism-modernity in specific cultural settings) has been found to correlate

[50] North Central Rural Sociology Subcommittee for the Study of Diffusion of Farm Practices, *Adopters of New Farm Ideas,* p. 8.

[51] Rogers, *op. cit.,* Chapter 3. For special consideration of the family in relation to diffusion, see Wilkening, *op. cit.*

[52] Ivan Nye, referring to a study in the state of Washington. Personal correspondence. See also Santi Priva Bose, "Characteristics of Farmers Who Adopt Agricultural Practices in Indian Villages," *Rural Sociology,* XXVI (1961), 138-146.

highly with other scales measuring length of time required for adoption. As would be expected, the more modern, rational, or secular the actor's score on the one scale, the earlier his adoption rate tends to be. Also the modern, rational, secular, and Gesellschaft-like actor is found to place a high value on science and education, while those at the other end of the continuum display attitudes in which economic rationality is not of importance. Other scales constructed to measure social-psychological attributes, applied to actors in the United States, find a general willingness to be inquiring and flexible to correlate highly with the actual behavior of innovation and adoption—an attribute called "management orientation" as opposed to "traditional work orientation" made up of the opposite of such traits.[53] The use of such studies in the short run may be found in the different strategy used by action agencies working in target systems of the two different types. In the long run the importance of developing rationality through educational systems and other training centers becomes obvious. Innovators and early adopters are generally better educated, younger, possessed of more accurate self-images, less rigid and dogmatic, more specialized as agriculturalists, and more cosmopolitan than laggards and other later adopters.

Considerable attention has been given to the spread of ideas in interpersonal networks. One study[54] reports that the need for person-to-person information varies at different stages in the adoption process, beginning with only 37 percent at the awareness stage and proceeding successively to 50, 63, and 50 percent in subsequent stages. Personal influence from peers seems to be most necessary "when uncertainty prevails, [and the actor] . . .

[53] Daryl J. Hobbes, Factors Related to the Use of Agricultural Chemicals on Iowa Farms (Ames: Iowa State University unpublished, M.S. Thesis, 1960). For a summary of various scales by the Italian rural sociologist, M. B. Benvenuti, Daniel Lerner, James H. Copp, and A. W. van den Ban see Rogers, *op. cit.*, pp. 62 ff. See also Denton E. Morrison, "Achievement Motivation of Farm Operators: A Measurement Study," *Rural Sociology*, XXIX (1964), 367-385.

[54] George M. Beal and Everett M. Rogers, *The Adoption of Two Farm Practices in a Central Iowa Community* (Ames: Iowa Agricultural and Home Economics Experiment Station Special Report 26, 1960). In reference to the previous discussion of the trial it should be noted that 95 percent of the respondents in this study stated that experience with the innovation gained then was reported as most important.

feels a need for reinforcement of his opinion through personal interaction."[55] In the early thirties rural sociologists began plotting social relations with sociometric techniques somewhat following the original work of Moreno. Always it was assumed that new traits and ideas would spread over the grapevine or network of relations.[56] The sociometric charts developed for neighborhoods and communities in various parts of the world were often used because they were relatively understandable. An administrator of a reclamation project or a resettlement colony, or a director of a state Agricultural Extension Service, who had little or no sociological training could understand the importance of interaction and relationships as symbolized on the charts and take these factors into account in his decisions. One such chart was used to explain why in two years 40 per cent of the colonists left the Dyess Colony in Arkansas.[57] Merely plotting relations of leavers compared with stayers proved that in the tension-fraught community whole sociometrically delineated groups left in defiance of the administration and later, after having made the break from the colony and separated from other defiant colleagues, evaluated the situation differently and asked to return. Such usage of sociometry has some aspects of the diffusion studies in which it has been employed recently by various diffusion specialists.[58] Sociometry then came to be used as a means of explaining adoption and diffusion. Models such as two-step communication and the trickle-down process could be studied and their limitations noted in relation to the stages of adoption, to the types of adopters, and to evaluative aspects of the social system in which the diffusion was taking place. Also such social factors as rank or stratification, extent of rationality or modernity in contrast to traditionalism, and cosmopolitanism vs. localism of actors in the network could be included. Many change agents, including Extension agents, made crude sociometric charts of the systems with which they worked. In their use many practices besides that of the spread of agricultural traits were studied by specialists in rural diffusion. Such qualities of inter-

[55] Rogers, *op. cit.,* p. 222.

[56] Loomis and Beegle, *op. cit.,* Chapter 5.

[57] *Ibid.,* pp. 140-142.

[58] For a summary of the application of sociometry, see Rogers, *op. cit.,* pp. 228 ff.

est to the community as leadership, group cleavage, and hidden power figures came under analysis.[59]

Nonagricultural traits of interest to rural sociologists have also been traced for their diffusion patterns. A pilot study which investigated the acceptance of Salk vaccine yielded enough information to be the basis for a state immunization campaign.[60] The relative effectiveness of the change agents has also been the subject of a diffusion study. For instance, one such study sought to determine the sources of information most used in new farmhouse construction in a particular county. So many farmers were building into their homes the suggestions which came from contractors and from lumber dealers that the Agricultural Extension Service, which had seen itself in the role of supplier of such information, decided to revamp its program. It shifted some of its work from the farmer to the lumber dealers and contractors in order to increase the diffusion of knowledge which needed imparting through these channels.

It has been found that some traits diffuse more rapidly than others. Dimensions which modify the adoption rate have been identified as: (1) cost, risk, and economic returns possible to the adopter, (2) complexity, (3) visibility, (4) divisibility, (5) compatibility with other social and cultural traits. Knowledge derived from research on these variables has been increasing.[61] One result in application of diffusion studies is the recognition that few traits can be adopted without occurrence of compensating changes in traits already in use. Action programs have occasionally planned for such modifications in the initial promotion of a diffusion program. The TVA, for example, promoted the "trial acre program"; that is, a "bundle" of improved practices developed by rural sociologists in Tennessee in order to help slow-to-adopt farmers to utilize available resources.[62] The "bundle" was constituted of interrelated items, so that given the

---

[59] Loomis et al., op. cit. In this publication see the work in applied sociology of Roy A. Clifford, Eduardo Arze Louriera, Antonio Arce, Norman W. Painter, Charles Proctor, Ralph H. Allee, Olen E. Leonard, and others.

[60] John C. Belcher, from personal correspondence. See his article "Acceptance of the Salk Polio Vaccine," Rural Sociology, XXIII (1958), 158-171.

[61] North Central Rural Sociology Subcommittee for the Study of Diffusion of Farm Practices, Adopters of New Farm Ideas, p. 4. See also F. C. Fliegel, "Differences among Improved Farm Practices as Related to Rates of Adoption," Pennsylvania AES Bulletin 691, 1962.

[62] Charles L. Cleland, personal correspondence.

initial change set in motion by the adoption of one item, the remainder of the bundle would complement the necessary adjustment. Such an approach had been previously stressed in the
intensive experimental development programs of the Farm Security Administration.[63]

Economic enterprises in the United States were quick to see
that commercial advertising and marketing could improve from
studies which revealed the motives for adoption or nonadoption.
Frequently mentioned uses of the diffusion studies are such activities as marketing, ad building, message formulation, and
corporate public-image creation. One team which did much pub-
licizing of diffusion studies reports presentations to at least
twenty major corporations and long-term consultation with one
of the largest petroleum companies in the nation on how to develop a working structure to market products from a new plant
built in the Midwest.[64]

Major policy decisions within commercial companies dealing
in such produce as fertilizer and agricultural chemicals have
been made and modified in the light of information from the diffusion studies about the adoption policies of farmers. How and
when a new product is introduced, what the selling and promotion strategy will be, the criteria by which dealers would be selected, and the methods by which they would be trained have
been influenced by the studies. A few commercial companies,
themselves caught up in the spirit of research, completed a three-
year experiment of their own in which they attempted to construct and implement an experimental dealer-training program
in which the objective was threefold: to improve the operation of

[63] For the "package" or "flexible felt needs" approach as used in the Farm
Security Administration, see Charles P. Loomis, *Studies of Rural Social Organization in the United States, Latin America and Germany op. cit.,* Chapter 19,
"The New Mexican Experiment in Village Rehabilitation." For the package approach in India, see Douglas Ensminger, "The Original Fifteen Pilot Extension
Projects," in Ministry of Community Development, Panchayati Raj and Cooperation, *Evolution of Community Development Programme in India* (Delhi: Government of India Press, 1963). See also Howard W. Beers and Douglas Ensminger, "The Development Block as a Social System?", *Indian Journal of Public
Administration,* V (1959), 1-18.

[64] Joe M. Bohlen and George M. Beal, personal correspondence. For a general
treatment of action research, see Walter L. Slocum, "Sociological Research for
Action Agencies—Some Guides and Hazards," *Rural Sociology,* XXI (1956), 196-
199.

local dealers, increase their profits, and secure more nearly optimum use of fertilizer and agricultural chemicals.[65]

A variable of the diffusion process has been found to reside in the recipient's evaluation of the communicator and the form and style of the communication. Consequently a related study of rural acceptance of radio and television caused what has been reported to be almost immediate change in the programing and the advertising rates of both media. An allied use of rural sociological work, although not central to diffusion studies, came about as marketing information for consumers' programs was altered to be more attuned to different audience preferences as a result of evaluative studies of Agricultural Extension Service.[66]

FUTURE NEEDS FOR DIFFUSION RESEARCH AND APPLICATION

Rural sociologists trained in the industrialized West, in discussing patterns of diffusion, talk about the S-curve and frequently do not specify all the system conditions that attend the process of diffusion. Whether the diffusion is of improved practices or of disease, the findings which permit description of adoption following the S-curve usually ignore the importance of the element of authority, force, and power as related to the process. (In footnote 40 reference is made to this). In Communist countries social change and diffusion have been speeded up through various means, including the application of force. Although Western studies have considered the "influential" and the "opinion-leader" types of actors who initiate, legitimize, and executive action in pluralities, not enough is known about the use of power and authoritarian procedures in speeding up change. Thus Lionberger found that once "influentials" had given their approval to an innovation, the rate of adoption increased markedly.[67] To

[65] *Ibid.*

[66] Alvin L. Bertrand, personal correspondence.

[67] Herbert Lionberger, "Some Characteristics of Farm Operators Sought as Sources of Farm Information in a Missouri Community," *Rural Sociology,* XVIII (1953), 327-338. For steps in the direction advocated here, see the following excellent studies: Christopher Sower, John Holland, Kenneth Tiedke, and Walter Freeman, *Patterns of Community Involvement* (Glencoe, Ill.: The Free Press, 1957); Paul A. Miller, *Community Health Action* (East Lansing: Michigan State College Press, 1953); Christopher Sower and Walter Freeman, "Community Involvement in Community Development Programs," *Rural Sociology,* XXIII

the present authors it seems strange that although the S-curve describing adoption patterns is mentioned, no article on diffusion known to them mentions the J-curve so common in many sociological analyses. It seems that in power-centered systems the diffusion of orders might follow the J-curve rather than the S-curve. In any case, the means used by totalitarian systems in achieving adoption should be better understood by rural sociologists. Leaders in many still "free" developing countries are impatient with progress along lines of S-curve adoption.[68]

The criticism above of diffusion studies particularly as applied in underdeveloped countries indicates future possibilities.[69] For

---

(1958), 25-33; George M. Beal, Paul Yarbrough, Gerald E. Klonglan, and Joe M. Bohlen, *Social Action in Civil Defense* (Ames: Iowa Agricultural and Home Economics Experiment Station, 1964); Joe M. Bohlen, George M. Beal, Gerald E. Klonglan, and John L. Tait, *Community Power Structure and Civil Defense* (Ames: Iowa Agricultural and Home Economics Experiment Station, 1964); Edmund deS. Brunner, Irwin S. Sanders, and Douglas Ensminger, *Farmers of the World* (New York: Columbia University Press, 1945); Wade H. Andrews, *A Case Study of Rural Community Development and Leadership* (Wooster: Ohio AES Research Bulletin 808); Linwood Hodgdon, "Psychological and Sociological Factors in Rural Change," *Journal of the Indian Medical Association,* XL (March 16, 1963), 289-292; David E. Lindstrom, "Influence of Rural Institutions on Economic Development," *Illinois Agricultural Economics,* IV (1964); Selz C. Mayo "An Analysis of the Organizational Role of the Teacher of Vocational Agriculture," *Rural Sociology,* XXV (1960), 334-345; C. Paul Marsh and A. Lee Coleman, "Farmers' Practice-Adoption Rates in Relation to Adoption Rates of 'Leaders,' " *Rural Sociology,* XIX (1954), 180-181. Slocum, *op. cit.;* Afif I. Tannous, "Social Change in an Arab Village," *American Sociological Review,* VI (1941); Frank and Ruth Young, "Toward a Theory of Community Development," in *Science, Technology and Development:* 7, Social Problems of Development and Urbanization, United States Papers prepared for the United Nations Conference on the Application of Science and Technology for the Benefit of the Less Developed Areas, 1963; and William V. D'Antonio, William H. Form, Charles P. Loomis, and Eugene C. Erickson, "Institutional and Occupational Representations in Eleven Community Influence Systems," *American Sociological Review,* XXVI (1961), 440-447.

[68] Howard W. Beers, "Application of Sociology in Development Programs," *Council on Economic and Cultural Affairs Paper* (January, 1963). See also Edward O. Moe, *New York Farmers' Opinions on Agricultural Programs* (Ithaca, N.Y.: AES Bulletin 498, 1952).

[69] For reference to ideas sketched below, see the following by Charles P. Loomis: "Social Change and Social Systems," in Edward A. Tiryakian, ed., *Sociological Theory, Values and Socio-Cultural Change* (New York: The Free Press and Macmillan, 1963); "Tentative Types of Directed Social Change Involving Systemic Linkage," *Rural Sociology,* XXIV (1959), 383-390; and "Systemic Linkage of El Cerrito," *Rural Sociology,* XXIV (1959), 54-57.

instance, from studies of social systems during time of disaster, it is entirely possible that we may apply much from the "halo effect" which is common at one phase of recovery from disasters brought on by bombardment, tornadoes, earthquakes, and panics. At this period of high emotive integration it might be possible to inculate into the reshaping social system some diffusion items which would be ignored during ordinary times, when actors are at a less receptive pitch. Indeed, this receptivity to a new order after the old has been badly shaken seems to be at the base of planned disruption by Communist revolutionaries. Specialists in diffusion and social organization should be given the opportunity of exploring this possibility as a means of increasing the pace of social change during the strategic moment in a natural disaster sequence. Although much remains to be known about diffusion in the industrialized West—for example, why chlorination of water was so much more easily diffused than fluoridation of water—all too little is known about means for bringing rapid change with a minimum of suffering. Diffusion methods as they exist in a totalitarian society should be better understood, even though they would not be practiced. The "leap-frog" change wrought by totalitarian governments in the developing nations has too much appeal to the masses of people anxious for national progress to afford ignorance on the subject by the great democratic powers of the world. And incidentally such knowledge might help to explain differences in spread of such similar processes as water chlorination and fluoridation.

LEGISLATIVE AND GOVERNMENTAL POLICY FORMATION USE OF RURAL SOCIOLOGY

Despite the lack of agreement among sociologists and others concerning what is rural and what is urban and what constitutes the difference, there is virtually no disagreement concerning the utility of the census tabulation which separates the rural farm and the rural nonfarm population. The availability of the two separate tabulations may be traced directly to early rural sociological work and should be documented as a use. Galpin's early analysis of the 1920 census schedule, which the Bureau of the Census had tabulated by units no smaller than states, was done on eight selected counties. This tabulation, along with Brunner's study of 140 agricultural villages, resulted in the rural farm, rural nonfarm distinction made thereafter by the Bureau of the Census. The uses of the farm, nonfarm breakdowns as well as the rural, nonrural are manifold, some of the more important from the point of view of rural sociologists being the allocation of funds in accordance with legislation to the land-grant institutions for extension services, research in agricultural experiment stations, and the support of vocational agricultural education.

It is probably unnecessary to elaborate here the general uses of population material such as the important one of legislative representation, such items as distribution of state and federal aid, and market-research agencies' dependency on the demographer's figures. There is considerable evidence that no other lines of investigation and reporting are so much in demand by both public and private sectors of the economy and society as are population figures. Public utilities such as power and telephone companies and governmental services such as state departments of education plan their expansions, contractions, buildings, and location of equipment and resources in accordance with population projections by counties and minor civil divisions. One response concerning uses of rural sociology sums up a commonly expressed observation: where rural sociology is having difficulty in becoming established, or where it is first established in experiment stations, "I have been interested in noting how often the first bulletin to appear is a study of the population of the state with its various breakdowns—studies which apparently action programs and administrators, and even politicians, find to be useful."[70]

The excitement generated by a region's demography is con-

[70] Carl C. Taylor, personal correspondence. Among the most important of these many analyses are J. Allan Beegle (with Dale Hathaway and Keith Bryant), *Rural America 1960,* Census Monograph (forthcoming), and Douglas G. Marshall, *The Story of Price County, Wisconsin: Population Research in a Rural Development County* (Madison: Wisconsin AES Research Bulletin 220, 1960). See also Clinton L. Folse, *Illinois Rural and Urban Population* (Urbana, Ill.: AES Bulletin, 1952); and Ray E. Wakeley and Paul J. Jehlik, "Regional Research in Population Dynamics," *Rural Sociology,* XVIII (1953). Many bulletins by these and such other rural sociological demographers as J. Allan Beegle, Otis D. Duncan, C. Horace Hamilton, Clinton Jesser, George W. Hill, Conrad Taeuber, Selz C. Mayo, Lowry Nelson, Robert L. Skrabanek, J. F. Thaden, T. J. Woofter, and Margaret J. Hagood have been widely used. See the 253-item list of publications under Population in Anderson, *op. cit.*

veyed in the following excerpts from an observer's account of the release of two population tables—nothing more—to local news media in a southern city. The demographer got amazing acclaim for telling people that what was happening was the opposite of what they wanted to happen. But he did it with figures, and that sounded so objective that they did not attack him. The newspapers soon realized that these population studies had news value. The newsmen started to study the tables on arrival and soon had the first of a series of feature stories ready for the next edition. Their analyses were not quite the kind that the demographer himself would have done, but they were not bad. Too many persons tended to forget the limitations of estimates. But the response! The letters fell into several categories:

1. "You cad! Our town has 10 percent more telephones, etc., and you say we are losing population."
2. "Wonderful. Now, please tell us how many veterans and dependents of deceased veterans there are in the state?" (There were several of these demands for impossible things—things which could not be pulled out of a hat as the agencies seemed to expect.)
3. "Tell us more." Realistic requests for more information than the local small-town paper had printed, from architects, school boards, regional offices of the post office, and others. Our favorite sequence of such letters started with a request from a district bottling company for data on all counties in their area. A few days later a request from the southern headquarters office of the bottling company in a nearby state asked for estimates for all counties in the demographer's state. We had a good time guessing that the first man had been getting chewed out for his declining sales, but had found his sales had slipped less than the population was estimated to have declined. We gathered that the headquarters office was impressed with the data when a few days later a manufacturer of glass bottles in a distant state wrote for the estimates.
4. "The United States senator from the district called for copies, before his own newspaper in Washington could have carried the items. He later borrowed the stencils so that he could distribute copies to all the banks in the area."[71]

[71] Edna S. Pedersen in personal correspondence, describing incident from demographic work of Harald A. Pedersen.

A uniquely specific use of demographic work by rural sociologists comes out of the State of Kentucky. The legislature of that state has designated that liquor licenses, granted on the basis of population, should be dispensed in intercensal years only in accordance with the intercensal population estimates as made by the Department of Rural Sociology at the University of Kentucky. Another southern state has through its rural sociology department provided nondemographers with a short method for rule-of-thumb projection of population by age from one decennial census to another.

In addition to the published census material, there are related unpublished materials and reports, emanating from rural sociologists and others in various divisions of the United States Department of Agriculture, which are significant for their utility. For example, the allocation of loan funds to the various states by the Farmers Home Administration has been based on such unpublished materials. Within the USDA itself, and within a number of other federal agencies, constant use is made of annual reports on the Hired Farm Working Force which are a source of information on earnings and employment of farm wage workers and occasional information on educational attainment, skill level, and occupational history of farm wage workers.[72]

There is general knowledge of the great movements represented in public policy whereby civil rights of a minority group are safeguarded, poverty is attacked in the Appalachians, or land is reclaimed through irrigation. And it is no surprise to anyone that basic research on the status of rural people in the affected areas has contributed to the formulation of the policy and the legislation concerning it. The work of rural sociologists on ethnic relations and integration has been sizable.[73] Its actual

[72] Louis J. Ducoff, Chief of the Farm Population Branch, Economic and Statistical Analysis Division of the USDA, writes: "Census data on the farm and rural population by States are used in the allocation of funds to extension services, to agricultural experiment stations for research, and for the support of vocational agricultural education. Unpublished materials prepared by our office are used by the Farmers Home Administration in the annual allocation of loan funds to the States.... Our annual reports on the Hired Farm Working Force ... are widely used within the Department and by other Federal agencies and also supply information in connection with proposed legislation affecting farm wage workers." Personal correspondence.

[73] See Robin M. Williams, Jr. "Concepts of Marginality in Rural Population

use is a bit difficult to document, although traditionalists often denounce the Supreme Court decision of 1951 which outlaws "separate but equal" educational facilities on the basis of its being a decision based on social science rather than on the law. There are other indications, somewhat negative, to be sure, which would indicate that rural sociological studies of race relations have been potent enough to be feared, and if possible suppressed, by supporters of the southern status quo. There is today restrictive legislation which prohibits "cultural studies" from being made with federal funds. In part this developed from an interracial study done in Mississippi by a rural sociologist some twenty years ago. Although the completed report was marked "confidential, for administrative use only," when it was submitted to its sponsoring agency, an administrative leakage to legislators (presumably to those most sensitive to any change in the status quo of the Negro) led to the legislation which ever since has been a barrier to free study of ethnic relations under the aegis of the government. Another important development, the so-called War on Poverty, has its genesis in the Southwestern Land Tenure Committee and other such committees composed largely of rural sociologists. These committees are often credited with being responsible for the Rural Development and Rural Areas Development programs[74] which were the forerunners of the War on Poverty in rural areas. For every one such Gargantuan project there are dozens and hundreds of others which depend for their inception or execution on the services of rural sociologists.

For example, rural sociological studies based on many kinds of investigations, besides the ecological type of study dealt with earlier in this chapter, are fundamental to changes in a wide

---

Studies," *Rural Sociology,* V (1941), and also his *Strangers Next Door* (Englewood Cliffs, N.J.: Prentice-Hall, 1964). See also Vernon J. Parenton and R. J. Pellegrin, "Social Structure and the Leadership Factor in a Negro Community in South Louisiana," *Phylon* (1956); and T. Lynn Smith, "An Analysis of Rural Social Organization among the French-Speaking People of Southern Louisiana," *Journal of Farm Economics,* XVI (1934), 680-688.

[74] Alvin L. Bertrand, personal correspondence. For a listing of sixty-one items on land tenure, including the well-known studies by Harold C. Hoffsommer, Edgar A. Schuler, Arthur F. Raper, Otis D. Duncan, Joseph Ackerman, and Robert T. McMillan, see Anderson, *op. cit.* See also Alvin L. Bertrand and Floyd L. Corty, eds., *Rural Land Tenure in the United States* (Baton Rouge: Louisiana State University Press, 1962).

array of educational institutions. Development of standards for school and university attainment,[75] curriculum planning at the state levels, realistic rural-area educational planning, and agricultural extension policy have shown a sensitivity to the findings of such studies as the correlation of the spread of curriculum changes and the cultural backgrounds of communities, the educational aspirations and the comparative educational achievement of rural youth, and the impact of mechanization on agricultural systems. Vocational education has been widely expanded to include manpower retraining. Rural industrialization studies have provided basic data for the planning of the content of retraining programs and for the location of retraining and development centers.[76] School dropouts constitute a general educational problem in both urban and rural communities. In one state the rural sociology department of the state university prepared an Experiment Station Bulletin devoted to the subject, which has become required reading for student teachers. The Extension Service in the same state has widely publicized the findings of the school dropout study, with the result that the author is engaged in a follow-up study specifically for rural youth dropouts.[77] An acceleration in research in a closely related field, *socialization and personality formation,* is evident among rural sociologists as it is among general sociologists. The importance of this work cannot be judged by the use to which it has been put. A few programs have been planned and initiated on state-wide bases, in which utilization is made of these studies of personality formation, socialization throughout life, and role taking. Initial work with the parent in order to reach the child is one such program. Specialities such as criminology, geriatrics, and the

[75] Otis Durant Duncan and C. Arnold Anderson in personal correspondence. See also William H. Sewell, "Community of Residence and College Plans," *American Sociological Review,* XXIX (1964), 24-38; and Lowry Nelson, *The Education of the Farm Population in Minnesota* (St. Paul: Minnesota AES Bulletin 1944). Concerning this study, Nelson notes that it showed the low attendance level of the state, "next to Kentucky which was on the bottom as regards white males 16-17 years of age. [It] was a 'shocker' for the state. [The Farm Bureau became interested and so did other county groups interested in youth, so that the state] came up to 24 in 1950 . . . now I could never . . . say that the rise in rank was due to my work but . . ." See also E. Grant Youmans, "Factors in Educational Attainment," *Rural Sociology,* XXIV (1959), 21-28.

[76] Alvin L. Bertrand, personal correspondence.

[77] E. Grant Youmans and C. Milton Coughenour, personal correspondence.

like take into account findings of researches on pertinent personality structures. Not essentially rural in nature, this work is being done by a group which includes many names identified with rural sociology.[78]

Policy formation in the field of conservation increasingly bears the mark of rural sociological studies. For example, after the broad policies of conservation were determined in the construction of Dalles Dam, there remained the unresolved financial settlement between the federal government and the Yakima Nation of Indians whose property had been used in the construction of the dam. At the request of the Indian Service of the United States Department of the Interior, an analysis of the socioeconomic status of the Yakimas was done by rural sociologists, and in large part on that basis the financial compensation was decided.[79]

Conservation of resources has been increasingly defined in terms of a man-land relationship, and for the "man" part of the duality, rural sociologists help to supply the information necessary for effective planning. Legislative programs and governmental policies on conservation of natural resources, leases, water rights, and subsurface minerals all reflect heavily the land-tenure studies of rural sociologists.[80] And who can say how important the many contributions of rural sociologists in the

[78] Lee G. Burchinal, Archibald O. Haller, and Marvin J. Taves, *Career Choices of Rural Youth in a Changing Society* (St. Paul: Minnesota AES Bulletin 458, 1962); William H. Sewell, "Infant Training and the Personality of the Child," *American Journal of Sociology,* LVIII (1952), 150-159; William H. Sewell and Archibald O. Haller, Jr., "Factors in the Relationship between Social Status and the Personality Adjustment of the Child," *American Sociological Review,* XXIV (1959), 511-520; James Cowhig, Jay Artis, J. Allan Beegle, and Harold Goldsmith, *Orientations toward Occupation and Residence: A Study of High School Seniors in Four Rural Counties of Michigan* (East Lansing: Michigan AES Special Bulletin 428, 1960). See these publications for a more complete listing of studies, including those of E. Grant Youmans and John R. Christiansen. A different kind of socialization is that of the Agricultural Extension agent. See Ivan F. Nye, *The Relationship of Certain Factors to County Agent Success* (Columbia: Missouri AES Research Bulletin 498, 1952). See also Eugene Wilkening, "Roles of Communicating Agents in Technological Change in Agriculture," *Social Forces,* XXXIV (1956), 361-367.

[79] Prodipto Roy, personal correspondence.

[80] For example, see George W. Hill, Walter Slocum, and Ruth O. Hill, *Man-Land Adjustment* (Madison: Wisconsin AES Bulletin 134, 1938); and George W. Hill, *Man in the "Cut-over"* (Madison: Wisconsin AES Bulletin 139, 1941).

health field were in the formation of the Hill-Burton legislation on hospitals? Many believe that it was fundamental. What is the demand for outdoor recreation, and, once filled, how much is it used? How accessible can farm woodlots be to satisfy the reasonable demands of the public and the equally reasonable demands of the farmer-owner? What human and controllable factors can be linked to forest fires, and how can the control be exerted? There are rural sociologists on the Forest Service Staffs of California, Ohio, Louisiana, and Colorado who help to interpret the human equation in federal and state practices for forest conservation and use.

Pennsylvania, Missouri, and Louisiana attempt to take into consideration the social factors and their implications as they assess accidents within the state. Rural sociologists contribute thus indirectly to the labor and traffic legislation as it is formulated in those states.

Various kinds of public welfare programs are based on research work originating among rural sociologists. A sizable amount of these concern problems of the aging. In one state rural sociologists undertook an interview study of a probability sample of persons sixty-five years of age and older, the study being financed by the State Department of Public Assistance. The information unearthed in the pilot county has, in the long run, been utilized for developing programs for older people in the state, especially by a state Council of Aging. Another state reports that its training programs in the Division of Public Health Education, as well as in the Regional Offices of the Department of Health, Education and Welfare, use as teaching materials the systematic data from older persons within the state collected by rural sociologists. Also the Midwest Council for Social Research on Aging has applied in its recommendations various sociological studies of the aging and aged. Interestingly enough, the school of medicine uses the same materials in its teaching program.[81]

Studies of the aged and retired and their level of living, done in Kentucky, Connecticut, and Wisconsin, were exhibited at a House of Representatives hearing prior to the passage of social-security legislation. Studies from these same three states and from Texas were similarly presented to the United States Senate

---

[81] A. H. Anderson and Walter L. Slocum, personal correspondence.

prior to the passage of social-security legislation in that chamber.[82]

Present-day uses of studies continue their day-to-day usefulness to government, but nothing in today's governmental scene equals in urgency the record set in the depression years of the 1930's for utilization of social science. A few studies stand out as signals which alerted a nation to the desperate plight of segments of the population. Carl Taylor and associates' *Disadvantaged Classes in American Agriculture*[83] and the monograph *Rich Land—Poor People*[84] might be cited. It can be claimed for the one that it provoked the top WPA administrators into a realization of the necessity for research in rural areas. It can be claimed for the other that it is typical of a host of such studies of the depression years which shocked, electrified, and moved to action the more complacent segments of the population. As the Franklin D. Roosevelt administration struggled with the depression, the major support for rural sociological research shifted to the Federal Emergency Relief Administration where Dwight Sanderson from Cornell, J. H. Kolb from the University of Wisconsin, and T. J. Woofter from the University of North Carolina served successively as Co-ordinators of Rural Research in the Rural Section of the Division of Research and Statistics. The documentation of the impact of the Great Depression on rural America stands as one of the monuments built by rural sociologists.[85] Since they are depression publications, they focus on welfare and economic needs. A sampling of the subject matter (usually published by the United States Government Printing Office and

[82] I. M. Baill, *The Farmers and Old Age Security* (Washington, D.C.: USDA AMS Bulletin 151, 1955). Here see references to the work by rural sociologists which went into a report by W. G. Adkins, Louis J. Ducoff, John R. Christiansen, Robert E. Galloway, Walter C. McKain, Jr., Roe R. Motheral, William H. Sewell, Robert L. Skrabanek, and others. See also *Hearings before the Committee on Ways and Means*, House of Representatives (83rd Congress, 2nd session), HR 7199 (Social Security Act Amendments of 1954), pp. 195-223.

[83] Carl C. Taylor, Helen W. Wheeler, and E. L. Kirkpatrick, *Disadvantaged Classes in American Agriculture* (Washington, D.C.: Farm Security Administration and Bureau of Agricultural Economics, Social Research Report No. VII, 1938).

[84] Max R. White, Douglas Ensminger, and Cecil L. Gregory, *Rich Land—Poor People* (Indianapolis: USDA, Farm Security Administration Research Report, 1, 1938).

[85] Many of these publications are listed in Anderson, *op. cit.,* under the heading Relief and related headings.

dated sometime in the thirties) is suggested from some of the works here enumerated. *Landlord and Tenant on the Cotton Plantation,* by Thomas J. Woofter with the collaboration of Gordon Blackwell, Harold Hoffsommer, James G. Maddox, Jean M. Massell, B. C. Williams, and Waller Wynne, Jr., is one of the classics on the subject. A. R. Mangus' work *Rural Regions of the United States* opens with the statement: "The need for public assistance in the open country, villages, and small towns during the depression has followed definite geographic patterns." Outstanding among the dozens of monographs coming out of the period are, *The People of the Drought States,* by Conrad Taeuber and Carl C. Taylor, *Five Years of Rural Relief* by Waller Wynne, Jr., *Rural Families on Relief,* by Carle C. Zimmerman and Nathan L. Whetten, *Rural Youth on Relief,* by Bruce L. Melvin, and *Six Rural Problem Areas, Relief—Resources—Rehabilitation* by P. G. Beck and M. C. Forster. Some important publications of the time in the bureaucratic tradition, although presenting work of rural sociologists, did not bear their names. Such a monograph was *The Future of the Great Plains,* published by the United States Department of Agriculture in 1936.

For a generation of sociologists to whom the Great Depression is dusty history, it is fitting to catch the sense of purpose with which the hunger, misery, and frustration of large areas were revealed to those who could do something about it. Perhaps only the urgency of the civil-rights movement now matches what many rural sociologists saw then as their mission. One respondent writes:

> I addressed a large crowd of Missouri Welfare persons at Rolla, in my first year at Missouri, giving facts about the way country people were living in the Missouri Bootheel area, especially as to food. I told them of children who were starving right in the middle of excellent farm land. Local persons were at the meeting. Some were angry; others were astonished. It was part of the movement which was the beginning of living improvement in the Missouri Bootheel. Eventually the Farm Security Administration took hold, physical examinations were given, and improvement was on its way.[86]

[86] Charles E. Lively, personal correspondence. See also the classical evaluation of the rural rehabilitation program: Olaf Larson, *Ten Years of Rural Rehabilitation in the United States* (Washington, D.C.: USDA, BAE, 1947).

The proliferation of monographs was paralleled by a proliferation of federal action agencies, and both were a response to economic and social emergency. The times called for action—swift, ubiquitous, incisive—and, understandably, not always prudent and coordinated. The federal agencies of the time have been depicted as "barging into almost every local community, administering action programs that strongly affected local affairs, and dealing with things which were far from being non-controversial."[87] Strong local opposition to some of the administrative policies was common, and the contradictory goals and procedures of the differing agencies, or even of the same agencies at different times, caused confusion and resentment. Administrative districts of the several agencies seldom coincided with each other, or with local subdivisions of the county, or with natural communities or neighborhoods. Local representation very frequently ignored local informal leadership.

In order to coordinate these various programs, the agencies were reorganized in 1938, and the Division of State and Local Planning in the United States Department of Agriculture was set up to assist in establishing a more satisfactory linkage between the Secretary of Agriculture and the farmer at the grass roots. At the same time, to coordinate all these agencies at the local level, land-use planning committees at all levels of government were formed. The basic local unit was at the neighborhood and community level. Community and neighborhood delineation seemed to be of paramount importance, and dozens of rural sociologists in the Division of Farm Population and Rural Life of the Department of Agriculture and other federal agencies had assisted in such delineation in thirty-two states by 1941. Never have so many rural sociologists been employed in the government service. The satirical-minded might observe that the resulting improved linkage of the USDA to the farm groups of the nation was too successful. In a few years subsequent to the establishment of this mechanism for grass-roots state and federal planning, politicians and farmers' organizations had it abolished. The politicians feared its potential as a political weapon, and the farmers' organizations perceived that their almost monopolistic right to represent the farmers was in jeopardy.

[87] Milton S. Eisenhower and Roy I. Kimmel, "Old and New in Agricultural Organization," *1940 Yearbook of Agriculture* (Washington, D.C.: U.S. Government Printing Office, 1940), p. 1130.

Yet in the relatively few years of heavy government employment of rural sociologists, models for future types of studies were set, and linkages between theory and practice were accomplished which were landmarks for the discipline. So many programs came into being during this time that it proves to be a particularly propitious moment to observe the process of institutionalization. Most of the programs started off in a blaze of enthusiasm, and the early personnel were dedicated to a cause, much in the manner noted by Weber many years before. As formulated also by Weber, the programs became adjusted to less idealistic standards as increasing bureaucratization of the agencies took place. This tendency was scarcely observed by the agency itself, but was patently clear from the continuing results of a series of evaluation studies. One such study, for example, showed that the Farm Security Administration, in its loan and rehabilitation program, kept raising the floor of the minimum-income levels of the farm families it was reaching. In its earliest days of operation the poorer classes were being reached, but a combination of load of work, poor responses to repayments, bureaucratic pressures on the field workers to get increased productivity, and other factors caused the aid to flow increasingly to the "more productive" families. The poorer classes became progressively less represented in the program. As soon as this trend became publicized through the release of the various rural sociological studies, renewed attempts were made by the agency to develop programs which would more effectively reach the lower-income groups. The final institutional structure of this agency and many others was in part shaped in this manner by rural sociologists.

The group of studies of neighborhoods, cliques, and informal groupings has been one of the most-used by agencies interested in extension or education, settlement, resettlement, and other action programs. For example, the Soil Conservation Service has based its program consistently on what are called "neighbor groups." From five to fifteen families who are friends and informal acquaintances are the basic unit of organization.[88] Methods developed by rural sociologists have been used in the training of soil conservationists in delineating these neighbor groupings.

[88] Selz C. Mayo and W. E. Barnett, "Neighbor Groups—An Informal System of Communication," *Rural Sociology*, XIX (1952), 271-273.

Within a few years after organization, 33,000 of these groups had been located, including 284,000 farmers, and most of the groups remained active.[89]

An imaginative application of the social sciences together with the use of appropriate techniques for the development of agriculture, management, health, education, and other facets of social organization may be found in some of the programs in developing countries. The "basic democracies" which are being cultivated in Pakistan[90] and the credit organizations in Korea[91] might be cited as programs which have made differences in the lives of considerable numbers of people. But for boldness of range and magnitude of undertaking, we must turn to the Indian story. To be sure, the attempt to remold that huge nation by means consistent with its democratic tradition far exceeds the application of rural sociological principles. For present purposes, only a small part of the whole story whose end, of course, is nowhere in sight, will be recounted: the social change generated by the virtual partnership between the government of India and the Ford Foundation's Indian program, the latter under the administration of an American rural sociologist.[92]

The method chosen to move the country forward was that of government-led development programs intended to raise per-capita income and set growth in motion through a series of five-year plans applied under free democratic conditions.[93] A realistic catalogue of agricultural needs characterized the first two five-year plans, but their implementation proved to be somewhat too fragmented to achieve the desired results. Some of the projects undertaken during the first two planning periods were:

[89] T. Wilson Longmore, "Special Agencies within the Department of Agriculture," in Charles P. Loomis et al., eds., Rural Social Systems and Adult Education (East Lansing: Michigan State College Press, 1953), Chapter 7.

[90] Harold A. Pedersen, personal correspondence. Edgar A. Schuler was also influential in this development. See his early contributions to the Journal of Pakistan Academy of Village Development.

[91] Linwood L. Hodgdon, personal correspondence.

[92] Douglas Ensminger has been the Ford Foundation's Representative in India since the inception of its program there in the early 1950's. The short presentation of its current agricultural program is based on The Ford Foundation and Agricultural Development in India (New Delhi: The Ford Foundation, March, 1965). See also Carl Taylor, Douglas Ensminger, Helen Wheeler Johnson, and Jean Joyce, India's Roots of Democracy (Bombay: Orient Longmans, 1965).

[93] Ibid., p. 9.

Training centers for village workers, aid to extension departments for agricultural colleges, training centers in village crafts, training women for village extension work in home economics, organization and leadership of village youth activities, in-service training for village development personnel, strengthening the role of village school teachers in rural development, rural health service, research and training centers for village planning and rural housing, and scholarships to superior Gram Sevaks (Village Level Workers).[94]

These measures had varying degrees of lasting success, but evaluations of the total program attributed the increased agricultural yield in considerable measure to expanded crop acreage. Since there was little more land which would come into production, and since the combined projects left the food problem far from solved, new alternatives were sought in the Third Plan. The Intensive Agricultural District Program, or what is more commonly called the "package program," was then undertaken.

Unlike the earlier programs, which, although mutually reinforcing, were undertaken separately, the package program stressed improved practices which were to be used in combination—such practices as selection of improved seed; treatment of seed to prevent plant disease; improved tillage and equipment, fertilizer, and plant protection; improved harvesting, storage, and marketing. Also, unlike the earlier programs, the package programs were pilot programs, strategically located in respect to visibility and success probability and constituted so that whatever progress they might accomplish would virtually be a showcase demonstration of improved agricultural practices.

The objectives for the Stage I part of the long-term project are considered to have been accomplished in view of the following: yields have increased by 20 to 25 per cent among the million or more farmers in the pilot projects who have recovered two to three times as much money as they have invested in such inputs as fertilizer and insecticides; supporting organizations have been developed, such as are represented by the ten thousand agricultural officers at various governmental levels; warehouse organizations are now capable of making accessible to the farmer fertilizer and other supplies; effectiveness of co-operative societies is claimed to have increased. Diffusion practices and

[94] *Ibid.,* p. 12.

standard-of-living studies are discernible in the workings of the package program presently nearing completion of a phase as the third five-year plan draws to a close. This phase has been characterized by an approach new to India, by which the staff, through a district extension operation, is learning to understand, educate, and work with rank-and-file farmers in large numbers both in groups and as individuals. Stage II is presently emerging, the social targets of which are joint program planning between extension workers and village leaders, full program participation by all farmers, more complete farm planning, the simultaneous development of all farming enterprises using simple practices, better use of village resources in production, and joint efforts to make the co-operatives and other institutions more effective.

The concerted attack on underproduction of sufficient food for the nation is coupled with a similar emphasis on control of the stupendous swelling of the Indian population, this latter drive being timed to make the most of a technological break-through in cheap, easily used contraceptive devices in those parts of India where there is the greatest readiness. Practically all that is known about social organization, social rank, the use of power, effective communication systems, the diffusion process, ecological methods, the ends for which men strive, and the norms they employ in their striving has been applied and modified in this ongoing story of a great nation's first steps toward agricultural self-sufficiency.

NON-USES OF RURAL SOCIOLOGY

Many eminent rural sociologists who have devoted major portions of their professional careers to particular lines of study will search in vain in these pages to find to what use their work has been put. This is regrettable, and it is excusable only in the light of the great difficulty which attends the documentation of use. It also probably reflects a society which does not use all of the available knowledge in its problem solving. Surely health investigations, in aspects other than the ecological, have unearthed information which should be useful to policy makers and administrators. Factors of health affected by or related to occupation, ethnicity, diet, sex, age, and the particular symptomatic conditions which might be clues to abnormalities are of importance equal to the ecological aspects of illness.[95] These are all under-represented here because of the difficulty in demonstrating exactly how the data have been used. Other areas of long and painstaking research which seem almost neglected in the foregoing pages are stratification;[96] the small town; family studies; the rural-urban fringe; the impact of technology on rural life, co-operatives, and farmers' organizations;[97] and the impressive body of information concerning aspirations and career choices of rural youth.

Let us repeat here that the main body of this chapter represents a compilation of rural-sociology uses which was garnered from three successive waves of inquiry directed by the authors to a large cross section of rural sociologists of the United States. The many omissions in the presentation cannot in the least be attributed to them, but a great many inclusions would not appear here were it not for their thoughtful help. Also, the points of emphasis brought out in this chapter were reinforced by the emphases which were apparent in their hundreds of letters. Finally, the documentation of works referred to in the text is to a degree compiled in accordance with their suggestions. Textbooks have purposely been avoided as source material, the only two

[95] Thus Anderson, *op. cit.*, lists 228 items classified under Health. See Richard A. Kurtz, Donald E. Saathoff, and John N. Edwards, *Hospital Social Systems and Differential Perceptions* (Lincoln: University of Nebraska, HRP Report 2, 1961). The item most frequently mentioned by respondents in the present chapter is Charles R. Hoffer *et al.*, *Health Needs and Health Care in Michigan* (East Lansing: Michigan AES Special Bulletin 365, 1950). The many rural sociological studies of farm accidents have been widely used. See William G. Mather and Prodipto Roy, *A Study of Accidents to Pennsylvania Farm People* (Harrisburg: Department of Public Instruction in Cooperation with Pennsylvania State University, 1957).

[96] Harold Kaufman, *Prestige Classes in a New York Rural Community* (Ithaca: New York AES 1944); Otis Dudley Duncan and Jay W. Artis, "Some Problems of Stratification Research," *Rural Sociology*, XVI (1951), 17-29; William H. Sewell, *The Construction and Standardization of a Scale for the Measurement of the Socio-Economic Status of Oklahoma Farm Families* (Stillwater: Oklahoma AES Technical Bulletin 9, 1940). Also see Anderson, *op. cit.*

[97] Carl C. Taylor, *The Farmers' Movement* (New York: American Book Co., 1953). See also Wayne C. Rohrer and Carl C. Taylor, "Adult Educational Programs or Activities of the General Farmers' Organizations and Cooperatives," in Loomis *et. al.*, *Rural Social System and Adult Education*, Chapter 5. In this latter publication see the writings in applied sociology of Sheldon G. Lowry, Wayne C. Rohrer, T. Wilson Longmore, Frank C. Nall, Jack Preiss, Olen E. Leonard, and others.

exceptions being two textbooks now out of print which were particularly rich in use documentation.

Almost half a century after the Purnell Act of 1924, which made federal funds available for rural-sociological research through the land-grant colleges and universities, only three out of four of the educational agencies entitled to the funds make use of them for their intended purposes. The truly strong rural sociology departments or sections of departments are relatively few; perhaps they could be counted on the fingers of one hand. Certainly such a count would not require both hands. Thus any discussion of the nonuses of rural sociology must make reference to the lack of universal appreciation of its utility. Rural sociologists in Wyoming, Idaho, Arizona, or South Carolina would perhaps have fewer colleagues of their discipline with whom to compare notes than would rural sociologists now in many developing countries. However, for readers who are nonrural sociologists it is pointed out that generally in those states in which rural sociology is underrepresented the other social sciences, including general sociology, are likewise underrepresented. Generally it may be assumed that nonuse of rural sociology, because of its unavailability, does not differ essentially from nonuse of general sociology and other sociological specialties. There is still a discernible tendency among some college presidents, deans of agriculture, and directors of agricultural experiment stations and extension services to reflect the old school of thought in much the same way as some biologically oriented deans of colleges of medicine once considered that all the important problems of their units lay outside the social sciences. A few college presidents who could by no standard be branded anti-intellectual often prided themselves on their humanistic and literary backgrounds and believed sociology, including rural sociology, had less to offer than literature.

Notwithstanding the fact that only three out of four of the States have rural sociology departments or sections, the discipline is stronger and more used here than in other countries. In recent years Holland, West Germany, France, and other European countries have been fostering the discipline and putting it to use in much the same manner as it has been used in the United States. In fact, the relative recent growth of the discipline is greater in these old industrialized countries than it is here.

A nonuse of rural sociology which is perhaps most irritating to the rural sociologist frequently occurs on the state and federal level in the United States, as recognized leaders in the field of agriculture attempt to give the broad view of where we are going and whence we came. The lack of impact and the sense of injustice because of it is well shown in this excerpt from one of the respondents contributing to the present chapter.

> Last night . . . I skimmed Stewart Udall's *The Quiet Crisis,* and I found material from Thoreau, Major Powell, Gifford Pinchot, F. L. Olmstead, Walt Whitman, and other poetic and journalistic social thinkers. And also Lewis Mumford, some of it good stuff . . . . But the academic rural sociologists had no more place in it than they have in the Security Council of the United Nations. This is a book showing the need for conservation throughout the country. . . . If we do not even make an impression upon the Honorable Secretary of the Interior . . . we have not broken even the surface of the "fiberglass curtain" which surrounds the National Capital.[98]

It is difficult to say which is the worse of two evils: being ignored or being misrepresented. Another sociologist[99] recalls reading a report of a committee of agricultural administrators employed by one of the great foundations, on which his own dean, now retired, served. Policies for collaboration in agriculture with Latin American countries were specified. Those implemented by the nonsocial-science disciplines were openly emphasized because "sociologists were often socialistic."

Often thought of by their colleagues in general sociology to be of quite a conservative stripe (probably as farmers are reputed to be conservative on the national and state political scenes), rural sociologists may have created a quite opposite impression by an incident at the American Association of Newspaper Editors in Washington, D.C., in April, 1959. Castro was addressing the group, and at one point he picked up a copy of *Rural Cuba* by rural sociologist Lowry Nelson. "We are getting many ideas from this book by Professor Nelson of the University of Minnesota," declared the Cuban dictator.[100]

[98] Otis Durant Duncan, personal correspondence.
[99] Charles P. Loomis.
[100] Lowry Nelson, personal correspondence. A use of rural sociology high-

In any event it seems clear that neither have rural sociologists marketed their wares so that policy makers invariably think of their work when they face decisions nor have they apparently created an accurate image of themselves among potential users of their investigations.

WHAT OF THE FUTURE?[101]

The reader of this chapter will have noted that many uses of rural sociology grow out of localized research bases. Often there is no way to avoid what one respondent called the "patchwork" approach to research and its application. Another writes, "When rural sociologists were called on to help guide and formulate policy for broad national policies, we weren't able to deliver. Our research had been spotty, spasmodic, and concentrated on small local areas."[102] Some integration for state studies and their application has been supplied by the unit which earlier had the title Division of Farm Population and Rural Life and now is known as the Farm Population Branch of the Economic Research Service of the United States Department of Agriculture. Strategically placed rural sociologists in the various federal

---

lighted here is the studies of Argentina, Bolivia, Cuba, Brazil, and Mexico done respectively by the rural sociologists Carl C. Taylor, Olen E. Leonard, Lowry Nelson, T. Lynn Smith, and Nathan L. Whetten. These books, produced during and shortly after World War II at the request of the United States Department of State and financed by that Department, furnish the best general available knowledge of rural life of the countries mentioned. See Carl C. Taylor, "Early Rural Sociological Research in Latin America," *Rural Sociology*, XXV (1960), 1-9. See *ibid.* for an excellent applied sociological contribution by Manuel Alers-Montalvo. For the rural sociologists' contribution in producing such strategic materials as cinchona bark (for quinine), rubber, rotenone, and fiber plants during World War II, see Loomis, *Studies in Rural Social Organization, op. cit.,* Chapter 14.

[101] James H. Copp, ed., *Our Changing Rural Society: Perspectives and Trends* (Ames: Iowa State University Press, 1964). Among the other fine contributions in this monograph, see Thomas R. Ford and Willis A. Sutton, Jr., "The Impact of Change on Rural Communities and Fringe Areas—Review of a Decade's Research." An admirable investigation which might serve as a model in integration of disciplines which are in large measure the responsibility of William B. Baker is the following: fourteen reports of the Saskatchewan Royal Commission, beginning with *The Scope and Character of the Investigation* and ending with a *Program of Improvement* (Regina, Saskatchewan: Province of Saskatchewan Royal Commission on Agriculture and Rural Life from 1955 to 1957).

[102] Walter C. McKain, personal correspondence.

agencies help to provide a degree of integration, such as the sociologists in the research units of the USDA, in the Agricultural Research Service in the Federal Extension Service, and in the Bureau of the Census.

Occasionally efforts from many parts of the country are somehow integrated, as was the case when the rural sociologists of the State Experiment Stations and the Farm Population Branch of the USDA joined forces to supply to Congress the data required for the 1954 amendment to the Social Security Act which extended coverage to farmers and farm operators. If rural sociology is to provide the knowledge and experience necessary to bring the so-called "human element" adequately into agricultural policy and planning, more emphasis must be given to over-all general considerations in the nation and the world. There should be a national base for this integration. Since the United States has no national university as many countries do, the location of such a base will not be easily determined. For the short run, at least, it seems advisable to strengthen the Farm Population Branch by supplying it with more research funds which may be used in state-federal collaboration.

Changes in training and in job opportunities are already at hand by which rural sociologists of the future may expect that their work will be expanded in breadth and in depth. The theoretical and methodological training of rural sociologists is increasingly indistinguishable from that of the less applied specialties. The claim that rural sociology suffers from poverty of theory, if ever true, certainly is unfounded now, and in the field of methodology rural sociology often leads the way. The professional opportunities available in the Extension Service, in rural-urban planning as rural-urban interests merge in the great metropolitan areas, in the national poverty program, and in the developing nations of the world give a working latitude quite unknown to rural sociologists a generation ago. The very persistence in the developing nations (as well as in a nation as sophisticated in social organization as the USSR) of a "farm problem"—a comparative unresponsiveness of the agricultural sector of the economy to vigor and growth at the same rate as that experienced by other economic sectors—belies the widely held notion that, with the blurring of the rural-urban difference, rural sociology is little different from general sociology in the problems with which it deals. The recent resurgence and growth of rural sociology in Europe and in the more developed countries contradicts the thought that industrialization decreases the importance of rural sociology. Already the perspective of a sizable group of rural sociologists is considerably broadened as support for their work has increasingly come from private foundations of national and world scope, as well as from the Office of Education, the National Institute of Health, and the Department of State. It is very likely that the rural sociologist of the future will continue occasionally to include among his research sites his immediately local and provincial surroundings. It is even more likely, however, that such parochial concerns will be given the advantage of comparative perspective by equally occasional inclusions of research sites of magnitude, "foreignness," and cultural complexity. All the omens are that "the best is yet to be."

Author Index

Subject Index